AS LONG
AS THIS LAND
SHALL LAST

AS LONG AS THIS LAND SHALL LAST

A History of Treaty 8 and Treaty 11 1870-1939

René Fumoleau, OMI

*"As long as this land shall last,
it will be exactly as I have said"*

–Chief Monfwi,
during treaty negotiations
at Fort Rae in 1921

McClelland and Stewart Limited

The Canadian Publishers
McClelland and Stewart Limited
25 Hollinger Road, Toronto

Printed and bound in Canada

To the youngest
Indian child in the
Northwest Territories

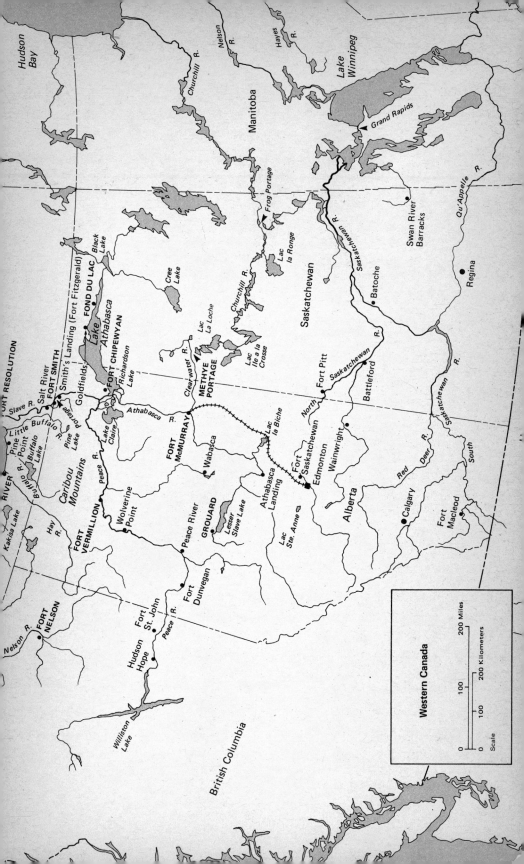

Contents

Chapter VI: A Decade of Desperation, 1928-1939

List of Abbreviations

RCMAFS	Roman Catholic Mission Archives Fort Smith
OMIAFS	Oblates of Mary Immaculate Archives Fort Smith
OMIAEd	Oblates of Mary Immaculate Archives Edmonton. (Have been transferred to the Provincial Archives of Alberta, Edmonton.)
OMIAWpg	Oblates of Mary Immaculate Archives Winnipeg
HBC	Hudson's Bay Company
ACAT	Anglican Church Archives Toronto
CMS	Church Missionary Society (Anglican)
ASGM	Archives des Soeurs Grises de Montreal (Grey Nuns Archives)
CSP	Canada Sessional Papers
IANDO	Department of Indian Affairs and Northern Development, Ottawa
PC	Privy Council
NWMP	North West Mounted Police
RNMP	Royal Northwest Mounted Police
RNWMP	Royal North West Mounted Police
RCMP	Royal Canadian Mounted Police
PAC	Public Archives of Canada
RG10, B.S.	Records Goup No. 10, Black Series. The public records section of the Public Archives of Canada is divided in Records Groups. Group No. 10 contains Indian Affairs material; it is divided in two series R.S., Red Series (Eastern Canada) and B.S., Black Series (Western Canada).
IBNWTA	Indian Brotherhood of the Northwest Territories Archives

List of Maps

Western Canada /6-7

Indian Treaties 1850-1889 /309

Early Transportation Routes to the Athabasca-Mackenzie District /310

Inception of the Contact-Traditional Stage by Temporal Intervals and Regional Zones /311

Proposed Treaty Boundaries /312

Transportation Routes and Stops of the Treaty 8 Commission /313

Game Preserves /314

Treaties 8 and 11 /315

Foreword

There are very few occasions when a book is written and published which can affect the lives of so many.

Never in the history of the Indian people of the north has there been a complete presentation of all the facts surrounding our struggle for recognition as a viable race of people and our legitimate claims to northern lands.

A great need has been met here in bringing together scattered documents which shed new light for many on the situation faced by our people. It has taken a keen mind and a northerner who cared to spend the countless hours to give birth to such a publication.

Our people's battle for the survival of their way of life in the face of invasion; their struggle to set the record straight as far as the treaties were concerned; their struggle to be heard, in the face of high odds, is set out here in readable form that is understandable and can touch the mind of the smallest child and the oldest man.

This book, and the September 6, 1973, decision of Justice Morrow in the Supreme Court of the Northwest Territories, together vindicate the interpretation of Treaties 8 and 11 which the Indian people have consistently maintained; that the treaties did not involve cession of Indian land, but were merely friendship or peace treaties implying a mutual respect for the rights and way of life of both parties involved. History has let us down sadly.

It is to be hoped that this book will help to clear away much of the ignorance that has blinded those charged with responsibilities toward the Indian people. If the book achieves the readership it deserves, it will engender a new respect for the Indian position and considerable sympathy for the recent historical experience of the Indians of the Territories.

Father Fumoleau's involvement grew out of a deep concern on the part of Roman Catholic Priests of the South Mackenzie District that the Indian people of the Northwest Territories in their struggle for justice faced the obstacle of ignorance of the facts within the general public. This group of committed priests decided to do something about it and Father Fumoleau took up the burden. Resources were few and scattered, yet mutual concern that this compilation had to be done was sufficient to spur on the study for the past two years, until we at last see the story of the Northwest Territories unfold and the experience of our people since contact with the white man revealed.

It is the deepest respect and appreciation that we have for the author who buried himself in interminable months of researching to come up with such a wealth of valuable material.

While the conclusions are those of the author and may not necessarily be those of the Indian people we feel that much of the material presented speaks eloquently for itself. The book is a major feat and can only serve to promote a re-evaluation of the past by both Governments and ourselves.

James J. Wah-Shee
President Indian Brotherhood of the
Northwest Territories
Yellowknife, Northwest Territories
October, 1973

Preface

On March 24, 1973, sixteen Indian chiefs of the Northwest Territories claimed an interest in an area comprising some 400,000 square miles of land located in the western portion of the Territories, and presented a caveat for registration under the Land Titles Act. After nearly six months of legal procedures in the Supreme Court of the Northwest Territories, the Honourable Mr. Justice William G. Morrow ordered and adjudged on September 6, 1973:

1.   I am satisfied that those who signed the Caveat are present-day descendants of those distinct Indian groups who, organized in societies and using the land as their fore-fathers had done for centuries, have since time immemorial used the land embraced by the caveat as theirs.

2.   I am satisfied that those same indigenous people as mentioned in (1) above are *prima facie* owners of the lands covered by the caveat – that they have what is known as aboriginal rights.

3.   That there exists a clear constitutional obligation on the part of the Canadian Government to protect the legal rights of the indigenous peoples in the area covered by the caveat.

4.   That notwithstanding the language of the two Treaties [8 and 11] there is sufficient doubt on the facts that aboriginal title was extinguished that such claim for title should be permitted to be put forward by the caveators.

5.   That the above purported claim for aboriginal rights constitutes an interest in land which can be protected by caveat under the *Land Titles Act.*[1]

The judgement provides some long-awaited answers. At the same time questions are being asked: What are these treaties? Why were they signed? What promises were made during the negotiations? Have the promises been kept? What has been the effect of the treaties? The reader will find in the pages of this book the historical information necessary for a better understanding of the two treaties and of Mr.

Justice Morrow's judgement.

Both treaties cover geographical areas with similar early political histories: Treaty 8 included Northern Alberta, Northwest Saskatchewan and a small part of the Northwest Territories; Treaty 11 comprised most of the Mackenzie District of the Northwest Territories. This study will focus in detail on all of the Northwest Territories area and on the northern Saskatchewan and Alberta posts of Fond du Lac and Fort Chipewyan in Treaty 8 country. Old water routes connected these posts with Fort Smith and Fort Resolution within the boundaries of the Northwest Territories, and the history of government policies as applied to these two treaty areas provides interesting contrasts and similarities.

Documents relating to Treaties 8 and 11 are scattered all across Canada, and consequently are not accessible to most people. This book is a result of extensive research for the purpose of collecting the documents relating to Treaties 8 and 11, and making them available to interested Canadians, both Indian and non-Indian. The documents are presented here neither to justify nor condemn, to moralize nor to philosophize, to apologize nor to plea; and still less to offer legal solutions. Quotations must stand on their own merit, without benefit of the author's analysis or comment, which could be influenced by personal feelings. It goes without saying that the best description of a painting can never equal viewing the painting itself. Similarly, commentaries and analyses of these old documents would never satisfy the demands of this historical study. The documents must speak for themselves to show exactly what was known, thought, said, or done at a given period in the past. No meaningful document was consciously selected or rejected in order to prove one point or another. All documents relating to one particular event are presented together, whether they agree or contradict each other. Some documents on Treaty 8 and on Treaty 11 certainly remain undiscovered. However, it is extremely doubtful if any would substantially contradict the documents now available.

There is a dimension to documentation which for the first time has been recognized by Mr. Justice Morrow's judgement. This is the Indians' side of the story, which is only available through oral history. While treaty commissioners wrote official reports based on their perception of events, it has now been established that the best source of information on the Indian treaties "seems to be among long-time residents and Indians in the N.W.T.".[2] The Honourable Mr. Justice Morrow, having listened throughout the summer of 1973 to testimonies from Indians and others who remembered the treaty-making negotiations, concluded. "There is no doubt in my mind that their testimony was the truth and represented their best memory of what to them at the time must have been an important event. It is fortunate indeed that their stories are now preserved."[3] In a history of the treaties, the discussions among Indian chiefs themselves, or between them and treaty commissioners or Indian agents, can supply more valuable information than the actual text of the treaties. Indian people, and they alone, can describe their understanding and their expectations of the treaties, their intentions when signing them, and the past and present significance of these treaties in their minds.

The memory of Indian people is remarkably vivid and faithful to detail. This can be related to cultural conditioning which makes accurate perception and memory of environmental features and changes an essential condition for survival. Just as details of a trail through the bush are imprinted on his memory, so will the details of an important event of his life be permanently fixed in the Indian's memory. Among the elders this memory of the past is most significant, since their lives in those early days were uneventful, relatively untouched by the barrage of information and change which marked the turn of the century and subsequent decades in modern history. Interviews with these older Indian people, residents of the Northwest Territories and participants in the events of Treaties 8 and 11, have been recorded since 1966. This important work was carried out by the Company of Young Canadians, by the Indian Brotherhood of the Northwest Territories, and by anthropologists from the University of Iowa. These recordings were made available for this study and constitute an essential element of its historical documentation.

The Indian people of the Northwest Territories, the Indian Brotherhood of the Northwest Territories, the Department of Indian Affairs and Northern Development, the Diocese of the Mackenzie, the Congregation of the Oblates of Mary Immaculate, the Public Archives of Canada, the RCMP Archives in Ottawa, the Glenbow Institute in Calgary, the Alberta Provincial Archives, the Hudson's Bay Company House in Winnipeg, the Anglican Church Archives in Toronto, the Government of the Northwest Territories, the Sisters of Charity (Grey Nuns of Montreal), and many other individuals and organizations have helped immensely to make this book possible. A grant from the Department of Indian Affairs and Northern Development eliminated financial difficulties. I would also like to express appreciation to Imperial Oil Limited for facilitating the distribution of this book.

This book owes most of its interest to its editor, Jacqueline Weitz, Ph.D. No one could have edited the manuscript with more competence and dedication.

My most sincere gratitude to all.

R. Fumoleau, OMI

Introduction

Every story has three sides,
yours, mine, and the facts.

When the explorers, adventurers, and settlers arrived in the new world, they mistakenly called the original inhabitants of the two Americas, "Indians". At first, wonder and delight prevailed in both groups. Some newcomers explored, led through the forests and along the rivers by Indian guides. Others built trading posts, depending on furs supplied by Indians. Most grouped in settlements, welcomed by Indians to share their land. Initial friendship and goodwill did not last long. As immigrants became more and more numerous, they needed more and more land. Sharing, never an intrinsic ingredient in European colonization, was replaced by practices of taking and keeping. The Indians were soon regarded as an embarrassment, since what was being taken belonged to them. Depending on time and place, different methods of handling the Indians were tried. Often they were treated benevolently, sometimes enslaved, frequently massacred, occasionally annihilated, or systematically assimilated as individuals or tribes. When all else failed they were banished into the hinterland to await the next advance of civilization.

After the American Revolution, marked differences soon emerged in the manner in which British colonies to the north and the new, independent nation to the south handled their Indian populations. Drastic measures were employed by the Americans, usually characterized by force and cruelty. In Canada, British tradition remained strong. The British practice of recognizing the title of original inhabitants to their ancestral lands was generally adopted by the Canadian Government. However, the term "title" had no common definition mutually understood by all concerned. Land ownership in the European sense was a concept foreign to Indian culture. While Indians recognized the private ownership of personal goods, they did not apply it to land. For the Indian, title was the right to use the land and its riches, to range freely through the country. This concept persists today in Indian thinking.

The treaties, adhesions to treaties, and land surrenders which were negotiated throughout Canada after 1781 were attempts at mutual agreement between white settlers and Indian people. Most treaties and land surrenders were signed after the Indians had lost control of their territory. Their only choice was to lose their land with a treaty, or to lose it without one. Usually they were guaranteed official use of a "reserve", which was held in trust by the Crown. This was a measure to protect the Indians from further encroachments, and to offer them security against the aggressiveness of their white neighbours. Other treaty gifts: free education, free medical care, cash annuities, groceries, etc., also helped to win the Indian people's good will. Protecting the Indian was not the main reason for treaties, however. Overriding all other considerations was the land: the Indians owned it and the white people wanted it. Even when the Indians posed no threat, treaties were still signed, as a moral or ethical gesture: a gentleman's way to take without grabbing. Indian treaties stand unique in political and judicial chronicles. Between 1781 and 1902, four hundred and eighty-three treaties, adhesions, and land surrenders were signed in Canada. Treaties signed after 1867 have been called the "numbered treaties", ranging from One to Eleven. Treaty No. 163, signed in 1877 is better known as Treaty 7; Treaty No. 428, signed in 1899, is Treaty 8.[4]

The move westward from the Atlantic to the Rocky Mountains in the early part of the 19th century was a search by Canadian settlers for lands to farm and to ranch. Indian hunters and the wildlife that sustained them were progressively replaced by farmers and domestic animals; bows, arrows, and guns became less useful than plows. North of the Canadian fertile belt lay the Mackenzie Basin. Today, the area encompasses the northeastern part of British Columbia, the northern portions of Alberta and Saskatchewan, the greatest portion of the District of Mackenzie in the Northwest Territories, the southeastern corner of the Yukon, and the basin of the Peel River in the northern Yukon. This was the area covered by Treaties 8 and 11, a land little suited to agriculture. The Indians who lived there were self-reliant and independent. In the north were the Loucheux (Kutchin) and Hares. Bear Lake Indians, Mountain Indians, Dogribs and Chipewyans (including the Yellowknife group) inhabited the central Mackenzie Basin. Kaskas and Sekanies were found to the west, with Slaveys, Chipewyans, Beavers and Crees in the Athabasca District.

These Indians lived their ancestral way of life until the end of the 19th century. Their social organization was simple, consisting of small groups for hunting and fishing, with few contacts between neighbours. The Hudson's Bay Company discouraged immigration to this vast fur reservoir, anxious to sustain the Indian as a strong, able-bodied trapper.

All of this was to change with the discovery of gold in the Yukon in 1896. Hundreds of prospectors travelling north to the gold fields passed through the Athabasca-Mackenzie District. Their presence, and the expectation of mineral wealth, hastened the signing of Treaty 8 in 1899-1900. The area included in the treaty extended as far north as the southern shore of Great Slave Lake. Between the years 1900 and 1920, the physical and economic condition of the northermost Indian tribes would have warranted any assistance which the Government could have given them. Pressure was brought to bear on Ottawa to sign a treaty with the tribes along the Mackenzie River, but the value of the land did not seem to warrant the expense of treaty making. In 1920, when oil gushed forth from Indian land at Fort Norman, there was no more hesitation. Terms of a treaty surrendering the district were quickly prepared for signing the following summer. Profit and economics had exerted their influence where philanthropy had failed.

Many words of the treaty text, their meaning and their consequences, were beyond the comprehension of the northern Indian. Even if the terms had been correctly translated and presented by the interpreters, the Indian was not prepared, culturally, economically or politically, to understand the complex economics and politics underlying the Government's solicitation of his signature. The Indian people did know that they could not stop the white people from moving into their territory, and in their minds the treaties primarily guaranteed their freedom to continue their traditional life style, and to exchange mutual assistance and friendship with the newcomers. By Treaties 8 and 11, the Canadian Government intended to extinguish the Indian title to the immense Athabasca-Mackenzie District. The Indian people intended to sign friendship treaties. The tomahawk and wigwam, the army officer and feather-bonneted Indian depicted on the commemorative medal, bore little resemblance to northern conditions, to Treaty Commissioners or to northern Indian chiefs. They are symbols of the anachronism of the treaty itself. In spite of the hands clasped in agreement as depicted on the treaty medal, it is very probable that the two parties neither understood each other nor agreed on what the treaty meant.

The Treaty Commissioners for both Treaties 8 and 11 acknowledged the assistance which they had received from Albert Lacombe, in 1899, and from Gabriel Breynat, in 1921. Both men belonged to the Congregation of the Oblates of Mary Immaculate (OMI), a Catholic missionary society which had worked with the Canadian Indians in the West and Northwest since 1845. This history has drawn extensively on the letters and documents belonging to Bishop Breynat. He was the only person to be present at the signing of both Treaty 8 and Treaty 11. He wrote more on these treaties than any other witness of either treaty. As a young priest he had come to Fond du Lac, Saskatchewan, in 1892. He was present there in 1899 when the treaty party arrived for the signing of Treaty 8. He was consecrated Bishop of the Mackenzie diocese in 1901. From then until 1943, he travelled the length and breadth of the diocese, which included northern Alberta and northern Saskatchewan, extended to the North Pole, and covered the whole Mackenzie District of the Northwest Territories. Few people knew the country as well as he did. Few people knew the Indians as well as he did. He worked with them and for them throughout his life and was rewarded by demonstrations of their trust and gratitude.

The second part of this history examines the years between 1922 and 1939, a period replete with discontent, broken promises, evasions, and deceptions. Prime Minister St. Laurent passed this judgement on Government performance during that time: "Apparently we have administered the vast Territories of the North in a continuous state of absence of mind."[5] The Federal Government transferred administration of the Mackenzie District to a territorial government, known as the Northwest Territories and Yukon Branch, established in 1921. Its policies were often contrary to the best interests of the Indian people. Treaty promises made by the Federal Government were ignored by both the territorial government and by the provincial governments of Saskatchewan and Alberta. Especially serious was the breach of promises to guarantee the Indian his freedom to trap and hunt, and to provide protection from the encroachment of white trappers. These promises were broken, forgotten, and finally disavowed. The game laws were often in direct violation of Indian rights, and caused hardships unequalled in Indian history. The Indians depended on trapping for 95 per cent of their income and on hunting and fishing for their food. When these activities were threatened and restricted, it meant economic disaster for the native people.

As development accelerated in the Mackenzie District, the Indians fell behind, unable without assistance to keep pace. Numerous appeals were made to Government, repeating the same theme: promises were made, they must be kept. In 1937, the Indians at Fort Resolution boycotted treaty payments in protest against the treatment they were receiving. It was a serious confrontation between government officials and Indians, and could have been one of the factors which influenced a change in game laws the following year.

The Indians were at a great disadvantage. They spent most of their time in the bush, without the opportunity to become familiar with the changes taking place around them. They were unable to react to these in any cohesive manner, leaving themselves vulnerable for exploitation and abuse. Many efforts were made to alert the Canadian public to the injustices which were being done to the northern Indians. But none of these efforts could halt the advance of prospectors and miners who were rolling back the northern frontier to the Arctic coast. Oil at Norman Wells, uranium at Port Radium, and gold at Yellowknife occupied the attention of government and business. For the first time in 1939 the value of mineral production exceeded the value of the fur catch. Significantly, not one Indian was yet employed in mining or prospecting at that date.

The year 1939 marked the end of an era. With the outbreak of World War II, the north would see further changes which would widen the gap between the Indian people and a mechanized society. It is not the purpose of this history to examine post-war and contemporary developments and their effects on Indian rights. Not only are many government documents unavailable for study before the expiration of thirty years, but historical perspective is considerably too shallow to do justice to the topic. Rather, the focus is on Treaty 8 and Treaty 11; on the events and conditions preceding and following the signing; on the people, on the government, on promises. Until 1967 very few people in the Northwest Territories, white or Indian, had ever read the texts of the two treaties. Now with the discovery of oil in the Arctic, old treaties, land claims, and broken promises become everybody's business. This history is intended to make available to all people information they otherwise would not have, and to notify the Canadian public that some debts might be long overdue.

Notes to the Preface and Introduction

1. In the Supreme Court of the Northwest Territories: In the matter of an Application by Chief François Paulette *et al.* to lodge a certain Caveat with the Registrar of Titles of the Land Titles Office for the Northwest Territories. 1973. Reasons for Judgement of the Honourable Mr. Justice W.G. Morrow, p. 56.
2. IANDO, file 1/1-11-20, A.R.K. Macdonald to Special Advisor Treaties, 4 October 1967.
3. In the Supreme Court of the Northwest Territories; In the matter of an Application by Chief François Paulette *et al.* to lodge a certain Caveat with the Registrar of Titles of the Land Titles Office for the Northwest Territories. 1973. Reasons for Judgement of the Honourable Mr. Justice W.G. Morrow, p. 7.
4. *Canada Indian Treaties and Surrenders From 1680 to 1890,* Ottawa, Queen's Printer, 1891. Reprint Toronto, Coles Publishing Co., 1971, Vol. II, p. 56.
Copy of Treaty and Supplementary Treaty No. 7, Ottawa, Queen's Printer. Reprint 1966.
Canada Indian Treaties and Surrenders From No. 281 to No. 483, Ottawa, King's Printer, 1912, Reprint Toronto, Coles Publishing Co. 1971, Vol. III, p. 290.
5. R.A.J. Philips, *Canada's North,* Toronto, Macmillan, 1967, pp. 161-162.

Chapter I

The Old Northwest Territories, 1870-1895

Government, 1870-1880

The year 1867 was the year of Confederation. New Brunswick, Nova Scotia, Ontario, and Quebec united to form the Dominion of Canada. Three years later, in 1870, the Hudson's Bay Company surrendered its rights to the Northwest in return for compensation in land and money. This brought under the control of the young Canadian Government a vast territory which comprised all of Alberta and Saskatchewan, most of Manitoba, two-thirds of the present-day Ontario and Quebec, including what is now mainland Newfoundland (Labrador), and the area which is known today as the Northwest Territories. To establish Canadian dominion over this western land, Parliament designated the Lieutenant Governor of the new Province of Manitoba to administer the Northwest Territories between the years 1870 and 1876. In 1876 David Laird was appointed the Lieutenant Governor of the Northwest Territories, with the territorial capital at Swan River Barracks. In 1877 the capital was changed to Battleford. Again in 1883 it was moved to Regina, where it stayed until 1905.

This immense area was in fact Indian territory. In order to "extinguish Indian title" to this land, Canada followed the same procedure used earlier in the eastern part of the country, i.e., signing treaties with Indian tribes. One hundred and twenty-three treaties and land surrenders had already been signed with eastern tribes by the time of Confederation. On August 4, 1870, Edmund Allen Meredith, Under Secretary of State for the Provinces, outlined for the Lieutenant Governor of the Northwest Territories the main thrust of his Indian policy for the new Canadian territories:

> You will also turn your attention promptly to the condition of the country outside of the Province of Manitoba, on the North and West; and while assuring the Indians of your desire to establish friendly relations with them, you will ascertain and report to His Excellency the course you may think the most advisable to pursue, whether by Treaty or otherwise, for the removal of any obstructions that might be presented to the flow of population into the fertile lands that lie between Manitoba and the Rocky Mountains.[1]

With this kind of impetus, treaty signing became an annual event. There was a rash of "numbered treaties" between Canada and the Indian people inhabiting the southern part of the Northwest Territories and the Province of Manitoba.

Treaties 1 and 2	1871	Southern Manitoba
Treaty 3	1873	Western Ontario
Treaty 4	1874	Southern Saskatchewan
Treaty 5	1875	Central and Western Manitoba
Treaty 6	1876	Central Saskatchewan and Alberta
Treaty 7	1877	Southern Alberta

These treaties covered the fertile Canadian prairies between Winnipeg and the Rockies north of the 49th parallel, and one after the other opened the West for settlement, fulfilling to the letter the Government's expansion policy.

In 1872 the Dominion Lands Act gave major impetus to immigration and settlement by providing 160 acres of free land to anyone who would build a homestead and settle the land. Immigrants from western European countries and eastern Canada began the trek westward.

In those early years Canada had difficulty establishing sovereignty over this vast region, to say nothing of fulfilling its obligation and responsibilities to the Indian inhabitants. The roles played by the Hudson's Bay Company factors, the North West Mounted Police and the missionaries were crucial to Canada in both of these endeavours. Through the decisive years both before and after Confederation the presence of these three groups influenced the peaceful development of the Canadian Northwest.

It was in the interest of the Hudson's Bay Company to promote friendly relations between the Indian tribes and itself, and between the Indians and the white settlers. For many decades it ruled the Unorganized Territories tactfully and held them for the British empire until the days of Confederation.

To re-establish the law and order which disappeared from the Canadian prairies after the removal of the Hudson's Bay Company rule, Canada, in 1873, formed the North West Mounted Police. It was renamed the Royal North West Mounted Police in 1904, and in 1920 the Royal Canadian Mounted Police. It was also needed in the early days to maintain Canadian sovereignty over western Canada. The larger population of the American West was already spilling over the border and was becoming too influential. There was need for a railway between eastern Canada and British Columbia and it could only be built through a peaceful and indisputably Canadian territory.

In Alberta, the Fort MacLeod detachment was established in 1874. Almost immediately this police force became highly respected by both whites and Indians, and it prevented the Canadian West from becoming as wild and as lawless as its American counterpart.

> The Indians of the district were amongst the most warlike and powerful of the tribes of the West, and the country was infested by outlaw whisky traders, horse thieves and cut-throats who, heavily armed and well established, resented the coming of the Mounted Police with their law and order programme. Yet, inside 6 weeks, Colonel MacLeod and his men had cleaned up the whole region, driven out the lawless whisky traders, and had the Indians living in peace and quietness.[2]

In 1871 the United States ceased making treaties with the Indians and the subsequent Indian Wars are infamous. Through their hard work, understanding, and fairness, the North West Mounted Police prevented the kind of battles and massacres which took place south of the border, e.g., the battle of the Little Big Horn, 1876; and the massacre at Wounded Knee, 1890. Crowfoot, chief of the Blackfoot nation, acknowledged the value of the Police presence:

> If the Police had not come to the country, where would we all be now? Bad men and whisky were killing us so fast that very few, indeed, of us would have been left today. The police have protected us as feathers of the bird protect it from the frosts of the winter.[3]

Other Indian chiefs who signed Treaty 7 have clearly stated that it was their faith in the Police which led them to trust the Canadian Government for which it stood. Chief Red Crow said he signed the treaty for one reason: "because Stamixotokon [NWMP Colonel MacLeod] has made me many promises. He kept them all – not one of them was ever broken."[4]

Among the Christian missionaries the name of Father Albert Lacombe, OMI stands out. He was a Metis Catholic priest who had lived with the prairie Indians since 1852. He knew conditions before the opening of the West and witnessed the rapid deterioration of Indian tribes in contact with civilization. By 1875 the living conditions of the Indians had reached such a deplorable state that he wrote to the Lieutenant Governor of the Northwest Territories, the Honourable Alexander Morris:

> Another cause of the demoralization of the Indians . . . and not the least, seems to be in some districts a lack of honesty on the part of Government employees in their dealings with the Indians. The Indian's ignorance and lack of competence is used to fool him and to lie to him either through the Treaties or in other Indian agency matters.

25

Later on, the Indians realize they have been fooled and then their discontentment knows no bound . . . The Canadian Government must consider itself as the father and the *guardian* of all the Indian tribes living now within the Canadian Confederation. If it considers itself a true protector of these people who are living in a harsh environment it goes without saying that the Government should treat them accordingly.

The first and the foremost thing to do with the Indians . . . must be to make meaningful treaties and to take all possible means to gain their confidence before the coming of immigrants. As for myself, I think that too little is offered to the Indians in return for the ownership of their lands. By signing treaties with them we deprive them of their lands, of their hunting, of their rivers, of their lakes and leave to them only reserves which very soon will be surrounded by White settlements and consequently be devoid of game.[5]*

On July 27, 1877, the Minister of the Interior invited Father Lacombe to accompany the Commissioners of Treaty 7, due to "your familiarity with the language of the Blackfeet . . . and your intimate knowledge of the Blackfeet and other Indians".[6]

Fifteen years after the signing of Treaty 7, Vital Grandin, OMI, Catholic Bishop of Saint Albert (Edmonton), made this comment which is probably valid for all previous and subsequent treaties:

Although they were afraid of the Treaty, the Indians desired it. They were always after us for information . . . They understood the necessity of accepting the Treaty, but even with all the explanations made to them, before as well as during the Treaty negotiations, I doubt if they ever understood the consequences of their signing. I even doubt if they understand them today.[7]

The role of the Christian missionaries in the development of the Canadian West is controversial. Did the Christian message and religious teaching serve to diminish the aggressive spirit of the Indian, preventing him from recognizing the threat, and effectively disarming and discouraging him from fighting for his rights and homeland? Or did the missionary teachings provide the bridge between the two conflicting cultures, assisting the Indian through the inevitable process

*This and other documents used in this book were originally written in French and have been translated into English. Whenever the word "sauvages" appeared in a French text, it has been translated as "Indians" for the following reasons: the word "sauvage" derives from the Latin word "silva", meaning forest, and originally meant someone able to manage his economic life in a forest or in a wilderness, alone. This original meaning persisted until recently when "sauvage" came to mean cruel and brutal. Sir Alexander Mackenzie explained that savageness refers to a very high degree of the virtue of tolerance. Until 1920, "Department of Indian Affairs" was officially translated: "Departement des Affaires des Sauvages" (Canada, Sessional Paper, 1921, No. 1). In the N.W.T. the French-speaking Metis still talk of "les Sauvages" when referring to the Indian people.

Similarly, the word "half-breed" was commonly used in the past, and appears in many quotations of this book. Most people now seem to prefer the word "Metis". Today some people prefer the word "Inuit" to "Eskimo".

of change which neither the missionaries nor the Indian people could avoid or slow down, whether by peaceful or violent means? The final judgement of history has yet to be made.

Once the Canadian prairies were pacified, traders and settlers established themselves securely on the rich farming land. But the pioneer spirit was not dead and unsettled lands still beckoned. The way west was blocked by the Rocky Mountains, causing some traders to move north along the rivers into the Athabasca and Mackenzie basins. The smallpox epidemics which decimated the Indian tribes of the prairies in 1875, 1876, and 1881, made the promise of northern furs and the allegiance of the northern Indians even more attractive. Continuous improvements in the transportation systems also fostered immigration of more people into the northern districts at the end of the 19th century.

The history of the prairies was repeated for the Indians of the Athabasca-Mackenzie District, with fur traders, missionaries, and the Mounted Police playing similar roles to those they had played on the prairies.

New Transportation Routes, 1868-1885, and a New Economy, 1885-1895

Until 1856 all freight and travellers destined for the trading posts in the Athabasca-Mackenzie District followed the "Fur Trade Routes", or "HBC Routes" from southern and eastern Canada. One route led from York Factory, on Hudson Bay, up the Hayes and Nelson Rivers to Lake Winnipeg. The other water route was from Montreal to Thunder Bay (Fort William), across rivers and lakes to Lake Winnipeg. From Lake Winnipeg the way west was up the Saskatchewan River, then northward through a maze of lakes and rivers to the Frog Portage. After crossing the 400-yard Frog Portage, traffic moved up the Churchill River, reaching Lac Ile à la Crosse and finally Lac la Loche, the limit of the land which drains into Hudson Bay. Between Lac la Loche and the Mackenzie River system, the twelve-mile-long Methye Portage (Portage la Loche) was the corridor for all travel from the south to the Athabasca-Mackenzie District. On the northern side of the height of land, the Clearwater River flows to the Athabasca River, eventually leading to the Mackenzie River and the Arctic Ocean. The round trip from the Northwest to Lake Superior required one summer season. Upon reaching Lake Superior the traveller was still only halfway to Montreal. Long-distance travel along these routes was halted in the winter months, with the only means of transportation in the Northwest itself being by dog team. This was a slow and expensive way to travel or to transport freight.

On the south side of the Methye Portage, water transportation depended on canoes and on flat-bottomed vessels about 35 feet long, known as York boats. Each boat was manned by a crew of eight or ten, and could carry about five tons of cargo. Oars were used on the downstream journey, but to travel upstream the crew had to walk on the river bank and "track" the boats with a long tow line. Scows were used instead of York boats on the Athabaska and Mackenzie rivers. They were flat-bottomed boats, approximately 50 feet long, 10 feet wide, rowed with 20-foot-long oars and steered with a 35-foot-long sweep balanced at the stern. Usually scows made but one trip down the rivers, and were broken up for lumber when they reached their destination. In the late 1880's, up to one hundred scows were built in a year at Athabasca Landing.[8]

Some Indian and Metis people found employment on the rivers manning the boats, canoes, and scows. A few of them became great voyagers and acquired a certain level of social and economic importance. Their work took them away from their people for entire summers, bringing them in contact with traders, travellers, and native people from other parts of the country. They exchanged information and ideas and learned about the size and conditions of the land which they and their neighbours inhabited. For the most part, however, the northern Indians did not travel very widely, and were much more isolated than the Indians of eastern Canada or the prairies. They were self-reliant on their own land, and Inspector Jarvis noted in 1897, after returning from the first NWMP patrol north of the 60th parallel:

> I may mention that the Indians in the vicinity of Fort Smith hardly ever move from their homes, excepting to visit their lines of traps. I understand that this has been the custom for generations and there are many old Indians hereabouts who have not been even to Chipewyan, which might be styled the metropolis of the district. I found this to be the custom of many of the northern Indians up to and along the Peace River. They have no ambition and little knowledge of the outer world, and as long as they have enough to fill themselves with they are happy.[9]

These Indians did not experience the effects of Western civilization until the end of the 19th century and the need for treaties was still many years in the future.

Since the time of its amalgamation with the North West Company in 1821, the Hudson's Bay Company had continuously improved and increased its transportation equipment on the Methye Portage. It completely controlled all traffic crossing the twelve-mile divide and it was determined to maintain its monopoly. This memorandum in 1876 reflects the policy of the Company:

> Should any boats arrive at Portage la Loche not employed by the Company, but carrying passengers, priests, missionaries or freight intended for Mackenzie's Rivers, you will decline furnishing transportation for them beyond that point or assistance in any way whatsoever.[10]

This situation could not last forever and some years earlier the Hudson's Bay Company itself had unwittingly given the signal for a transportation revolution which would shatter its own monopoly and change transportation in the North. In 1868 when the Company was negotiating the transfer of control of Rupert's Land and the Northwest Territories to the Government of Canada, a major change was made in the Company's transportation policy. Accordingly, the Company advised Alexandre Taché, OMI, Bishop of St. Boniface (Winnipeg), that in the future he would have to make his own arrangements for the transportation of supplies to the small Catholic missions down north. Nothing daunted, Bishop Taché studied his maps and found that he could move his freight on the North Saskatchewan River as far as Fort Pitt, then overland to Lac La Biche which drains into the Athabasca River. The Methye Portage had been by-passed for the first time. Bishop Taché had pioneered a new gateway to the Athabasca country. Free traders seized the opportunity to use the new route and to compete with the Company in the Athabasca District.[11] With its transportation monopoly ended, the Hudson's Bay Company finally abandoned the Methye Portage route in 1886.

Transportation in the North was further changed by the appearance in 1882 of the steamboat *Grahame*. Built by the Hudson's Bay Company at Fort Chipewyan, the *Grahame* was a 135-foot vessel capable of carrying 150 tons of freight. It travelled the Athabasca and Slave rivers between Fort McMurray and Smith's Landing (Fort Fitzgerald). The *Wrigley*, built by the Company at Fort Smith in 1885, carried freight and passengers from the northern end of the sixteen-mile portage between Smith's Landing and Fort Smith, down the Slave River, across the Great Slave Lake and down the Mackenzie River. These large boats, capable of heavy loads, required only small crews. The days of the York boats, canoes, scows, and native voyageurs were over.

Towards the end of the century, overland travel began to emerge as an alternative to the waterways. The railway linking Montreal to Calgary was completed in 1880 and reached Edmonton in 1891. In the late 1880's the trail from Edmonton to Athabasca Landing, the new gateway to the Mackenzie River system, was improved enough to permit the passage of wagonloads of freight for the entire region north of Edmonton. Edmonton, with a population of 1,165 persons in 1895, depended entirely on the fur trade. The improved and less expensive transportation system linking it with the Mackenzie District allowed free traders to move North and start new businesses. In 1887 they established trading posts in competition with the Hudson's Bay Company at Fort Rae, Fort Providence and Fort Good Hope. Some fur buyers did not settle permanently. They covered the territory as far north as Fort Resolution and returned to Edmonton as soon as they had bartered their trade goods for fur. In 1887 a newly-formed trading company, Hyslop and Nagle, opened its doors at Fort Rae, offering the Hudson's Bay Company its strongest competition. A few years later another Hyslop and Nagle post was opened at Fort Resolution

(1893-1894). The resulting competition brought higher fur prices, which in turned lured white trappers northward with the promise of fortunes in fur. By 1894 Carr and Duncan, the first white trappers north of the 60th parallel, had settled in Fort Resolution.

During the 25-year period from 1869 to 1894 significant changes in transportation decisively affected the economy of the Northwest. After the successful challenge to the Hudson's Bay Company monopoly and the improvements in travel, white trappers and settlers slowly moved in from the south. Some of these changes benefited the native people, some created serious problems. In many cases the Indians and Metis were bypassed entirely. But one fact was certain: these events would influence the timing of Treaty 8.

No Treaty – No Help, 1870-1889

In 1876 the Government of Canada signed Treaty 6 with the Indians of central Alberta and Saskatchewan. North of this area the Northwest Territories and the northern half of both Provinces formed what was called "unceded portions of the Territories".[12] Until 1897 it was thought that if ever another treaty were necessary it would include this entire area. History shows, however, that the vast Unceded Territories were eventually dealt with by the Government under separate treaties: Treaty 8 (1899-1900),[13] Treaty 10 (1906-1907), Treaty 11 (1921). In these pages, facts of general interest on life and conditions which affected these treaties will be studied, since geography and history link all of these districts. Details on local statistics and conditions, however, are given only for the area covered by the present-day Northwest Territories, for Fort Chipewyan (Alberta), and for Fond du Lac (Saskatchewan).

Life for the Indians of the Athabasca-Mackenzie District has always been a struggle. Until the end of the 18th century when the fur trade was introduced to the territory, the existence of these tribes, their sufferings and hardships, were known only to their immediate neighbours. Nor was life much easier with the transition to a trapping economy. The once self-sufficient hunter became more and more dependent on the trading post for essential and non-essential goods. But this transition from a hunting to a trapping economy has never been completed. There still remain, after a century of change, strong indications that whatever their occupation, Indians have never relinquished the characteristics and values of their hunting life and hunting economy. These values must surely have deeply influenced their thinking and attitude about the treaties.

The extreme physical hardship which the Indians of the Athabasca-Mackenzie District endured was reported, along with fur and business reports, by the traders at the Hudson's Bay Company posts. One of these reports, dated July 15, 1873, was written by Roderick Macfarlane, Factor of the Fort Chipewyan post:

Fond du Lac: Owing to an unprecedented scarcity of reindeer . . . the quantity of meat and grease furnished this summer is not a fourth of the amount yielded in ordinary years, while the fur hunt scarcely averaged $30.00 for each male adult . . . 2 Indians perished by starvation and some 23 men, women, and children were also carried off by the epidemic.

Fort Chipewyan: The epidemic first broke out at this place . . . the deaths were more numerous at Chipewyan in proportion to the population than was the case elsewhere . . . .[14]

The Hudson's Bay Company had always helped the Indians in time of famine. However, after 1870 it argued that the Canadian Government must assume responsibility for the Northwest Territories and its native people. Macfarlane complained to Lieutenant Governor Laird in 1880.

. . . owing to the scarcity of food animals, and the comparative failure of the fisheries, numbers of Indians will doubtless suffer many privations betwixt [now] and Spring. We have already expended a lot of fish and potatoes on them; in short, but for the assistance thus annually rendered to starving Indians, throughout the North, many of them would assuredly perish. Even as it is, now and again, cases occur beyond our reach, which from a scarcity of food, result in death! It strikes me very forcibly that *something* must be done and that speedily to help these poor people.

Confirming my remarks as applicable to the District of Peace River, Athabasca, English River and the Mackenzie, I am really unaware of anything that has yet been accomplished by our rulers . . . since the territory was transferred to Canada . . . .[15]

The Canadian Government did not feel it had any obligation toward a people with whom it did not have a formal agreement. Nor did the Government see any purpose in making a treaty with Indians whose land was apparently of such little value.

Anglican and Catholic missionaries were also concerned with the hardships of the northern Indians. During the years between 1870 and 1890, the Bishop of St. Albert, Vital Grandin, OMI, wrote many times to the Prime Minister of Canada and to the Lieutenant Governor of the Northwest Territories "respecting the poor Indians . . . not yet looked after by the Government".[16] To Grandin's requests on behalf of the Indian people, Mr. Thomas Wadsworth of the Indian Department replied that "as they [the Indians] were not then under the Treaty he could not do anything for them".[17] Undaunted by repeated negative replies, the Bishop asked Sir John A. Macdonald:

. . . to find the means for delaying and at the same time preventing the destruction of these poor Indians . . . [and] the Government to interest itself on behalf of these Indians and not to abandon them because the country they inhabit cannot be made use of.[18]

. . . it seems to me that at Ottawa no one has a just conception of the extreme misery of our Indians in the N.W.T., especially in winter. In summer they receive their pay, find ducks and wild fruits and can live after a fashion, but in the month of December . . . At our own establishment of Saint

Albert, since the beginning of the month, we have not given less than 60 meals a day . . . [19]

On July 28, 1883, two Chipewyan chiefs of the eastern Athabasca District, Samuel Egon and Michel Deneyou, wrote an appeal for help to the Prime Minister in the syllabic characters of their language. One page of this letter is reproduced on page 33. In translation, "People who can trap furs and work are not too badly off, but many cannot work and really suffer. For such people we have to plead with you. You have previously supplied us with twine to make fishnets, with gunpowder and leadballs, and we are very thankful to you.

"However it would be good if you could help them out also with some clothing material. Old women, old men, orphans, widows and their children have no clothes."[20]

From 1881 to 1885 two factors of the Hudson's Bay Company, Macfarlane from Fort Chipewyan and the Chief Factor Lawrence Clarke, supplied the Indian Department with information and statistics on the Unceded Territories north of Treaty 6. Edgar Dewdney, Indian Commissioner for the Northwest Territories, also provided information. This was all forwarded to the Prime Minister. Following severe epidemics between the years 1873 and 1881, Macfarlane reported that "the present tendency is toward an increase of the population at one and all of our trading stations".[21] His census of 1884 gave the Indian population for four of the trading posts. The "Census of Whites" for the Mackenzie District included Indian and Metis wives and children. Macfarlane also established the "List of Native population entitled to Government Land Grants." This included the Metis people south of Great Slave Lake. Metis were not permitted to sign Indian treaties, but were entitled to a grant of land whenever an Indian treaty was signed in their area.

With his census report Macfarlane included some advice to the Government on treaty boundaries:

> Looking as we do to an early settlement of the Peace River Country and its future connection with Europe via Lake Athabasca and Churchill, I believe it would be advisable to make a Treaty with all of the Indian inhabitants of the huge tract of territory extending north of the existing treaties to the southern shore of Great Slave Lake. But should these not be speedily done the Government had better be prepared to assist many of these Indians, as well as these of the Mackenzie River District, with liberal supplies of twine for nets, ammunition and other necessaries to aid them in eking out a living when the usual years of scarcity come shortly round.[23]

He was probably the first person to advocate that the treaty boundary be drawn as far north as Great Slave Lake, or even to include part of the Mackenzie River District. While Macfarlane saw possible commercial links with Europe as a reason for speedy treaty negotiations, Chief Factor Clarke had another approach. He advised the Government that as time went on the northern Indians "may be taught by the

nous manquent : du plu (belleteries) ceux qui s'occupent , et aussi

ceux qui travaillent , ceux là seuls pour eux bien

c'est encore ; mais ceux qui ne peuvent travailler, ceux là ils sont nombreux

pour eux ils souffrent , nous vous demandons ce sera ; assurément c'est nécessaire (nous vous ferons une demande)

Déjà du fil à rêt, de la poudre,

du plomb , vous nous avez accordé ; pour cela de très grands

remerciements nous vous offrons

Maintenant si avec des habillements vous leur venez en aide à la bonne heure

ce sera bien. Les femmes âgées . celles là qui sont , les vieillards

ceux là qui sont , les veuves leurs enfant

avec vivant , les orphelins . sans mère

ni père , sur eux des vêtements ne paraissent

la vie est dure pour eux . Daignez les prendre en pitié

Macfarlane's 1884 Census[22]

Indian Population (Lake Athabasca-Great Slave Lake District)
Fort Chipewyan   414
Fond du Lac   233
Fort Smith   115
Fort Resolution 230

List of Native Population Entitled to Government Land Grants (Lake Athabasca-Great Slave Lake District)

	Adults		Children	
	Male	Female	Male	Female
Fort Chipewyan	23	24	46	45
Fond du Lac	5	2	11	3
Fort Smith	9	11	10	16
Fort Resolution	11	12	18	18

Census of Whites (Mackenzie District)

	Adults		Children		Total
	Male	Female	Male	Female	
Rampart House	2	1	1	2	6
Peel's River and La Pierre's House	11	6	12	9	38
Fort Good Hope	8	4	6	8	26
Fort Norman	2	2	1	4	9
Fort Liard	7	4	4	5	20
Fort Nelson	5	3	5	3	16
Fort Simpson	14	6	9	10	39
Fort Providence	13	14	8	7	42
Fort Rae	8	4	8	6	26
Big Island	5	4	9	8	26
TOTAL	75	48	63	62	248

Plains Indians to put a greater value on their country and will be more reluctant about ceding it".[24]

Lawrence Vankoughnet, Deputy Superintendent General of Indian Affairs in 1883, did not recognize the Government's responsibility to help the Indians at this time, as their territory was "situated some fifty miles north of the boundaries of Treaty No. 6, and is therefore *outside* of Treaty limits", but he explained to Prime Minister John A. Macdonald that a treaty with the northern tribes could be a worthwhile investment in terms of the Prime Minister's interest in railway construction:

> The undersigned was informed from several quarters while in the Northwest that very much uneasiness exists among the Indians in the unceded part of the Territories at parties making explorations into their country in

connection with railroads, etc., without any Treaty being made with them; and it was reported to him by persons who were well acquainted with these Indians that they are most anxious to enter into Treaty relations with the Government and that it is in the interest of humanity very desirable that the Government should render them assistance, as their condition at many points is very wretched. The Indians in the unceded portions of the Territories are not numerous; but at the same time they could of course do great injury to any railway or any public work which might be constructed in their country, unless the Government had a previous understanding with them relative to the same.[25]

This did not move the Prime Minister to alter his opposition to a treaty with the Athabasca-Mackenzie District Indians. In the margin of a letter dated 1884, he noted: "the making of a treaty may be postponed for some years, or until there is a likelihood of the country being requested for settlement purposes."[26]

This policy of no-treaty-no-help was opposed by the missionaries. In 1886 Grandin appealed to the Prime Minister on behalf of the Indians, brushing aside the idea of a treaty as a prerequisite for help:

... although the Montagnais, or Chipewyans, have made no treaty with the Government, they are no less the subjects of His Majesty, and as such, it appears to me that your Government cannot fail to take their case into consideration.[27]

Bishop Isidore Clut, OMI, advised the Prime Minister that "twenty-seven out of a band of thirty Indians died of starvation on the shore of Peace River".[28] Reverend Gough Brick, of the Church Missionary Society, reported that Indians of the Peace River District "have already killed their horses for food" and they "were reduced last winter even to eating old shoes and cowhides, boiled, it is assumed, as much as possible into pulp".[29] He was told by the Superintendent General of Indian Affairs:

The Indians of the Peace River Country ... were outside of Treaty limits and ... the Government had never interfered in any way with their hunting grounds, and, as the Government had not treaty with those Indians, it had not felt it incumbent upon it to assist them, as it had Indians with whom it had Treaty relations.[30]

In July, 1888, the Church of England Synod reported to the Minister of the Interior on the deplorable conditions in the Athabasca Diocese. This report, with additional details supplied by Archdeacon William D. Reeve of Fort Chipewyan and by Reverend Edward H. Black of Fort Wrigley, was reprinted in the *Manitoba Free Press,* the *Toronto Mail,* and the *Ottawa Citizen* some fourteen months later. Several cases of death by starvation and a few of cannibalism were reported. At Fort Chipewyan,

... thirty Indians died about two months ago from starvation ... ten persons succumbed at Fort Wrigley ... One fine young man, named Bond, came into the Mission after having for three weeks lived on roots, which he dug out of the frozen snow ... [A few days later] the young man was again obliged to go out and dig for roots; and while away he fainted and was frozen to death before he was found. At Fort Laird [Liard?] ten deaths occured last winter.[31]

A policy statement was forthcoming from the Government in 1887. Beset by appeals from every side, the Superintendent General of Indian Affairs, Thomas White, left little doubt that the Government intended to maintain its hard line on Indians and treaties in the north:

Repeated applications have been made by Indians inhabiting the regions situated North of the Northern boundary of Treaty No. 6, which Treaty embraces the District of Saskatchewan, and North, East, and West of the boundaries of Treaty No. 3, which Treaty comprehends a portion of the District of Keewatin, for Treaties to be made with them by the Government; also applications have been received from time to time from the Hudson's Bay Company for relief to be given by the Government to the sick and destitute Indians of these regions; and quite recently the Hudson's Bay Company has renewed its solicitations in the same behalf, alleging that serious sickness is now prevalent among the Indians of the Peace River District, and that there is an apprehension of there being an insufficiency of food during the Winter in consequence of a prevailing scarcity of rabbits and lynxes on which these Indians are in the habit of depending for a subsistence. The diseases from which they are suffering are stated to be measles and croup.

The grounds upon which the Indians claim that a Treaty should be made with them are, that explorations with a view to the construction of Railways and public works have been made in their country, and they claim that as it is evident that land within the territory inhabited by them is to be used for these purposes, it is only fair that before such appropriations of land are made Treaty stipulations should be concluded with them as the owners of the soil. They also urge that owing to the diminution in the number of fur-bearing animals and of game they require the annuities and other emoluments that would be secured to them under Treaty to enable them to subsist.

The Hudson's Bay Company alleges that, as the Crown has purchased the Company's interest in these regions as well as in the North West generally, the expense of providing and caring for sick and destitute Indians should devolve upon the Government as their natural protectors, and that the Hudson's Bay Company should not charge itself with the same.

Considerable correspondence has been had with various parties in respect to this matter. The Government has hitherto declined to make Treaties with the Indians referred to, on the ground that the lands within the regions inhabited by them were not required for settlement, and with the exception of occasionally gifts of twine for fishing nets and ammunition furnished to some of the Indians in the Western part of the region, especially to those living directly North of the boundary line of Treaty No. 6 in the vicinity of Isle la Crosse no other relief has been afforded by the Government to the Indians of those regions.

The 60th degree of North Latitude would appear to be the furthest Northern limit to which the Indians of the regions referred to interested in Treaties being made with them extend, and the shores of James or Hudson Bay would be the Eastern boundary of those regions, and the East side of the Rocky Mountains the Western boundary.

Within this vast region the Indians are not very numerous. So far as ascertained, those whose hunting grounds lie in the Eastern section of the territory number 4016. The Indians who claim the country in the central part of the said territory are said to number 1441 souls; and those in the Peace River District are said to number 2038.

The Indians inhabiting these regions are known as the Beaver Tribe, Slaves, Yellow Knives, Cariboo Eaters, Dog Ribs, Chippewayans, Crees, and a few Half-breeds.

A vast portion of these regions remains unexplored, and the parts that have been explored are reported to be for the most part unsuitable for agriculture with the exception of the Peace River District, wherein cereals of some descriptions and root crops are said to grow successfully.[32]

White's Deputy, Lawrence Vankoughnet, echoed this statement in January, 1887. He maintained that the transfer of the Hudson's Bay Company's interest in the country to the Dominion of Canada in 1870 did in no way relieve the Company of its responsibility to assist the sick, aged, and destitute Indians. This position rested on the fact that no white settlement had followed the transfer, and consequently, there had been no disruption of the hunting and trapping economy of the Indians. Therefore the Company had suffered no loss; in fact it had profited on the cash and land compensation it received. Treaties would be made only when they were necessary to prevent trouble with the Indians over land that was needed for development.[33]

The Government's policy did not escape public criticism. In the *Calgary Tribune* of February 5, 1887, an article entitled "Starving Indians" disclosed that the Indians of the Peace River region were suffering from pestilence and famine but could not receive Government help because they had no treaty.

If the matter is looked at squarely, it is surely a fearful thing that any community under Canadian rule should perish for lack of assistance that it is possible to render. It is not a duty that we owe to the Indians as much as one that we owe to ourselves and to humanity in general. Not only is the Country under a moral obligation to render assistance to these people but it would be good policy to do so. Sometime soon a treaty will have to be made with them as a preliminary to the opening of their splendid country and were timely assistance to be rendered them now in their time of need it would pave the way for a good feeling when the treaty came to be made that would not be to the disadvantage of the Country.[34]

The hardships experienced by the Indians were shared to some degree by other northerners. During the winter of 1887-88 the servants of the Hudson's Bay Company at Fort Simpson, N.W.T., did not have full rations for months and "have been reduced sometimes to eat the

furs in store – 24 large bears, 40 beaver skins, and 7 wolverines . . . .
Considerable number of furs have also been eaten by the Indians
when starving."[35] Bishop Breynat in his autobiography remarked that
once when he was a young priest at Lake Athabasca, "we each had a
bear-toe for supper". To celebrate Sundays and feast days, "everyone
at the Fort Chipewyan mission had two sugar cubes".[36] The Sisters of
Charity, who had arrived at Fort Chipewyan in 1874, were happy with
a daily diet of fish and potatoes, supplemented on great feast days by
a "little rice, dried apples or wild berries."[37] Harsh as they may seem,
there is no reason to doubt that accounts of suffering and deprivation
among the inhabitants of the North, both Indian and non-Indian,
were faithfully recorded.

After the extremely hard winter of 1887-1888, Bishop Clut peti-
tioned the Indian Department to make an annual grant of $500 to en-
able the Roman Catholic Bishop of the Mackenzie to buy fish hooks
and twine for nets, to be distributed amongst the Indians and perhaps
"prevent the recurrence of such fearful calamities as occurred last
winter."[38] Cautiously, Superintendent General White advised the
Prime Minister that the Government could afford such an expenditure, as "it has not been unusual . . . to authorize the purchase of
fishing tackle and ammunition to a moderate amount for Indians outside of Treaty limit."[39] One year later, in May, 1889, Parliament voted
the $500. Records of the transactions required for the purchase and
distribution of the twine and fish hooks cover 60 pages of documents
retained by the Public Archives of Canada. For example, expenditures
are recorded for Fort Resolution and Fort Rae ($38.84 each), and for
Fort Smith ($23.80).[40] The gratitude of the Indians for the Govern-
ment's generosity is recorded at length.

At about this time the Government began using the Hudson's Bay
Company as an intermediary for distributing some scanty relief. In
1888, "an Order in Council was passed authorizing an expenditure of
$7000 to relieve the pressing needs . . . throughout the unorganized
territory."[41] In case of actual starvation the distribution of relief was
left to the judgement of the factor at each trading post. One invoice
dated November 30, 1889, probably covering a one-year period,
showed an expenditure of $4900.62 for supplies furnished to sick and
destitute Non-Treaty Indians in the North.[42] In later years the Chief
Accountant of the Department of Indian Affairs often complained
that the Hudson's Bay Company made too liberal use of this relief
fund. In 1897 the $20,000 provided in relief for the Indians in the
Unorganized Territories proved to be inadequate. The economic implications of this arrangement of the Dominion Government with the
Hudson's Bay Company were duly noted by the Chief Accountant:

> As these items of relief are undoubtedly used to maintain the allegiance of
> the Indians it follows that to a certain extent we are discriminating in the
> field of free trade in favour of the Hudson's Bay Company. We do not

recognize accounts from other traders. The true source of the supplies is concealed from the Indians, and the Hudson's Bay Company gets the benefit of the generosity of the Government.[43]

The Indians of the Unceded Territories must have realized that they could not get as much assistance from the Government as the Indians who had made treaties. "Very few of them were against the treaty, and a large majority were in favour of it",[44] but their reasons of starvation, privation, sickness, and physical hardship were not enough to convince Government officials. It was in 1890, when news came that the North was floating on oil, that the Government finally initiated treaty negotiations. The history of this period leaves little doubt that the food rations and money which accompanied the offer of treaty had an inordinate influence on these people who had suffered so much.

The North is Floating on Oil, 1888-1891

The Geological and Natural History Survey of Canada began sending its surveyors to the Northwest in the early 1880's. They were the first government representatives to venture north and rapidly discovered that it was much more than a wasteland. After his tour of part of the Athabasca River basin in 1882-1883, Robert Bell mentioned repeatedly in his report the presence of "petroleum bearing sandstone", "petroleum-impregnated marl", "flowing asphalt", "petroleum strata", "petroleum bearing strata", "tar", "petroleum bearing rocks", "petroleum producing strata" and "free petroleum".[45]

A few years later, Robert G. McConnell, another member of the Geological Survey staff, travelled through the district of Athabasca, between the Peace River and the Athabasca River, north of Lesser Slave Lake. He reported the presence of enormous quantities of tar, bitumen, natural gas, oil, and pitch. He estimated the amount of tar at 4,700 million tons.[46]

In 1887-1888, McConnel explored the Mackenzie, Rat, Porcupine, Liard, Slave, and Hay rivers, and also the area around Great Slave Lake. His report disclosed, among other interesting details:

> Petroleum – The Devonian rocks throughout the Mackenzie Valley are nearly everywhere more or less petroliferous and over large areas afford promising indications of the presence of oil in workable quantities. The rocks in several places around the western arm of Great Slave Lake are highly charged with bituminous matter, and on the north shore tar exudes from the surface and forms springs and pools at several points. The tar from these springs is used by fur traders and others in the country for pitching boats and canoes, and they report that a pool when exhausted quickly renews itself. In descending the Mackenzie, bituminous limestones were noticed at the "Rock by the River Side", [close to Fort Wrigley], at Bear Rock [Fort Norman], at the Ramparts [Fort Good Hope], and at numerous other places. Near Fort Good Hope several tar springs exist, and it is from these that the Hudson's Bay Company now obtain their princi-

pal supply of pitch. The springs are situated at some distance from the river and were not examined. Still farther down, in the vicinity of Old Fort Good Hope [approximately 140 miles North of present Fort Good Hope] the river is bordered for several miles by evenly bedded dark shales of Devonian age which are completely saturated with oil. The shales here have been reddened in many places by the burning of oil which they contain.

The possible oil country along the Mackenzie valley is thus seen to be almost co-extensive with that of the valley itself. Its remoteness from the present centres of population, and its situation north of the still unworked Athabasca and Peace River oil field will probably delay its development for some years to come, but this is only a question of time. The oil fields of Pennsylvania and at Baku already show signs of exhaustion, and as they decline the oil field of northern Canada will have a corresponding rise in value.[47]

This news startled the Canadian Government. Senator John C. Schultz of Manitoba quickly realized that the North was one of the richest parts of Canada, or "Canada's Great Reserve" as he called it. He became one of the main promoters of northern exploration and development. His enthusiasm triggered ambitious plans for developing the area into a prosperous oasis of natural resources to supply the needs of the rest of the country.[48] At a Senate meeting in March, 1888, he moved "that a Select Committee be appointed to inquire as to the value of that part of the Dominion, lying north of the Saskatchewan watershed, east of the Rocky Mountains, and west of Hudson's Bay, comprising the Great Mackenzie Basin".[49] The motion was carried, and action was taken immediately.

The third report of the Select Committee, headed by Schultz himself, mentioned the presence in the Mackenzie Basin of auriferous deposits, of silver, copper, iron, asphaltum, and other minerals.

. . . While the petroleum area is so extensive as to justify the belief that eventually it will supply the larger part of this continent and be shipped from Churchill or some more northern Hudson's Bay port to England.[50]

The evidence submitted to your committee points to the existence in the Athabasca and Mackenzie Valleys of the most extensive petroleum field in America, if not in the World. The uses of petroleum and consequently the demand for it by all Nations are increasing at such a rapid ratio, that it is probable this great petroleum field will assume an enormous value in the near future and will rank among the chief assets comprised in the Crown Domain of the Dominion.[51]

The map which accompanied the Report of the Senate Select Committee on Resources of the Great Mackenzie Basin, showed the area west of the Mackenzie River to be "auriferous territory". It is reproduced (p.312) and also shows the "Petroleum Territory", which included the Mackenzie River delta area as far east as Baillie Island and Franklin Bay, the Mackenzie River valley, the area northwest and southwest of Great Slave Lake, the lower Peace River valley, the Athabasca

River valley, and the area north of Lesser Slave Lake.[52]

The *Edmonton Bulletin* caught up with the enthusiasm of the politicians. In the issue of April 27, 1889, the petroleum situation of the world was examined, with attention to the producing and undeveloped oil fields, world oil requirements, and the problems of oil transportation:

> . . . but special attention is given to the oil fields of the Athabasca and Mackenzie which are estimated to cover a greater area than those of all the rest of the world combined, and are quite as accessible, in the matter of distance, to the markets of the world as either the United States or Russian oil fields. Railway communication alone is lacking to their development. Indeed with railway communication they would be better situated for supplying the west coast of America and China and Japan than either Russian or United States fields. The completion of the Alberta and Northwestern railway will assure the development of the oil industry in the vast field described of such proportions as can only be imagined. With that road completed there is no reason why within ten years the Mackenzie basin should not export more oil than either Russia or the United States. The financial effect on Canada in general and on this part of the Northwest in particular would be more than marvellous.[53]

As has been shown, from 1870 to 1888 the Canadian Government had no interest in the poor Athabasca-Mackenzie District. It refused repeatedly to acknowledge any responsibility for the Indians inhabiting that desolate country. Suddenly, with the discovery of "immense quantities of petroleum", the expense and obligation of a treaty with the Indians began to look minimal when compared to the enormous wealth to be acquired from them. The Privy Council Report of 1891 set forth clearly the intentions and expectations of the Government:

> On a report dated 7th of January, 1891, from the Superintendent-General of Indian Affairs, stating that the discovery in the District of Athabaska and in the MacKenzie River Country, that immense quantities of petroleum exist within certain areas of those regions, as well as the belief that other minerals and substances of economic value, such as Sulphur, on the south coast of Great Slave Lake, and Salt, on the MacKenzie and Slave Rivers, are to be found therein, the development of which may add materially to the public wealth, and the further consideration that several Railway projects, in connection with this portion of the Dominion, may be given effect to at no such remote date as might be supposed, appear to render it advisable that a treaty or treaties should be made with the Indians who claim those regions as their hunting grounds, with a view to the extinguishment of the Indian title in such portions of the same, as it may be considered in the interest of the public to open up for settlement.
>
> The Minister, after fully considering the matter, recommends that negotiations for a treaty be opened up during the ensuing season with the Indians interested in those portions of the MacKenzie River Country, and in the District of Athabaska, including the Peace River Country, as well as in that portion of country which lies south of the District of Athabaska, and north and west of the Northern boundary of Treaty No. 6, embraced

within the following limits as shown in pink upon the map of the Dominion of Canada hereto annexed: . . . The whole Indian population in the Peace River, Athabaska and the MacKenzie River Districts would (if the above figures are correct) be 15,900.

As regards the Indians of the MacKenzie River Country, it will not be necessary to treat with all of them, but merely with those whose hunting grounds lie within the territory, a surrender of which it is proposed to ask the Indians interested therein to make. . . [54]

At one time the idea of a treaty extending north to the 60th parallel was dismissed as extravagant, but in the frenzy of discovery, the 63rd parallel soon became the northern boundary proposed for a future treaty with the Indians. This would include the Fort Simpson, Lac la Martre, and Fort Rae areas, for a total of 319,000 square miles.[55] An additional 59,597 square miles were considered at the suggestion of Hayter Reed, Indian Commissioner for the Northwest Territories.[56] This covered the districts of Ile à la Crosse and Lac la Ronge.

On December 15, 1890, McConnell had prepared for the Minister of the Interior a new census of the Indian population, as well as a list of the trading posts where the treaty could be signed, and an estimate of the provisions required for distribution to the signatories.

Government Census of 1890

	Men	Women	Children
Fort Chipewyan	90		
Fond du Lac	60		
Fort Smith	56		
Fort Resolution	86		
Fort Simpson	130	136	234
Fort Providence	92	106	258
Fort Rae	128	147	340

Fort Wrigley with about 50 hunters is outside of the proposed boundary, but the Indians all belong to the Fort Simpson Band and traded there until a few years ago, and should therefore be included with Fort Simpson.

The posts of Nelson and Liard are both outside of the boundary and in British Columbia, but should be included . . .

The Indians of Liard and Nelson, if treated with, should be met at the former point. At one time they all traded at Liard along with a number of others who have lately been drawn to Cassiar District.[57]

The total Indian population to be treated with was 4,500. The provisions required were: 190 sacks of flour; 9,600 pounds of bacon; 1,125 pounds of tobacco; 1,125 pounds of tea; and 3,500 pounds of sugar.[58] Other estimates were drawn up and more correspondence exchanged. However, on July 3, 1891, the Superintendent-General of Indian Affairs wrote, "before going any further in this matter, we had better wait to see whether the money will be voted for this year or not".[59] This caution was prompted by the political confusion which followed the death of Prime Minister John A. Macdonald on June 6, 1891. The money was not voted.

The next five years saw a succession of four Prime Ministers. Stability returned to Government with the election in July, 1896, of Sir Wilfrid Laurier, who was to continue in office for fifteen years. The politicians had been disappointed with the rate of oil exploration and exploitation in the north, and soon lost interest in treaty negotiations. It was not until the Klondike gold rush that public attention was once more focused on the wealth and opportunities hidden in the north, and treaty negotiations began.

Notes to Chapter I

1. Canada, *Sessional Papers,* 1871, No. 20, p. 8.
2. R.G. MacBeth. "The Jubilee of the Mounted", *The Beaver,* Vol. IV, No. XI. August 1924, pp. 406-407.
3. The Hon. Alexander Morris, P.C., *The Treaties of Canada with the Indians,* Toronto, Belfords, Clarke & Co., 1880. Reprint Toronto, Coles Publishing Co. 1971, p. 272.
4. J.K. Howard, *Strange Empire,* New York, William Morrow and Co. 1952, p. 271.
5. PAC, RG10, BS, file 3518, Lacombe to Morris, 13 February 1875.
6. *Ibid.,* file 8506, Mills to Lacombe, 27 July 1877.
7. OMIAEd,B-VIII-100d, *Mémoire de l'Evêque de Saint Albert sur ses difficultés avec le Départment Indien,* Chap.II, p. 10.
8. F.J. Alcock "Past and Present Trade Routes to the Canadian Northwest." *The Geographical Review,* Vol.X, No.2, August 1920, pp.68, 69, 80.
9. A.M. Jarvis, Inspector NWMP, "Northern Patrol", *Annual Report of the Commissioners of the NWMP,* 1897, pp.162-163.
10. H.A. Innis, *The Fur Trade in Canada,* Toronto, University of Toronto Press, 1970, p. 371.
11. G.R. Rae, *The Settlement of the Great Slave Lake Frontier, Northwest Territories, Canada: From the eighteenth to the twentieth century,* University of Michigan, Ph.D. 1963. Published on demand by University Microfilm, A Xerox Co. Ann Harbor, Michigan, USA., 1971, pp. 158, 218.
P. Duchaussois, OMI. *Mid Snow and Ice,* London, Burns Oates & Washbourne, 1923, pp. 55-59.
12. PAC, RG10, BS, file 241,209-1, Vankoughnet to John A. Macdonald, 5 November 1883.
13. The Fort Nelson Indian Band gave its adhesion to Treaty 8 in 1910.
14. PAC. *McFarlane Papers,* MG29, D9, vol. 1, pp 332-333. Macfarlane was his own orthography. Now, many people write his name MacFarlane or McFarlane.
15. *Ibid.,* pp. 808-809, Fort Chipewyan, 24 December 1880.
16. PAC, RG10, BS, file 19502-1. Grandin to His Hon. the Lieutenant Governor of the North-West Territories, 1 August 1880.
17. *Ibid.,* Grandin to John A. Macdonald, 27 September 1880.
18. *Ibid.*
19. *Ibid.,* 24 January 1881.
20. PAC, RG10, BS, file 241, 209-1.
21. *Ibid.,* Macfarlane to Clarke, 28 May 1884.

22. PAC, RG10, BS, file 241,209-1.
23. *Ibid.* Macfarlane to Lawrence Clarke, 28 May 1884.
24. *Ibid.,* Clarke to Dewdney, Indian Commissioner, 28 December 1883.
25. *Ibid.,* Vankoughnet to John A. Macdonald, 5 November 1883.
26. *Ibid.,* Dewdney to Superintendent General of Indian Affairs, 25 April 1884. Macdonald's note is dated 27 May 1884.
27. *Ibid.,* Grandin to John A. Macdonald, 13 February 1886.
28. *Ibid.,* file 19,502-1. Clut to John A. Macdonald, 18 May 1888.
29. *Ibid.,* Vankoughnet to John A. Macdonald, 19 May 1888.
30. *Ibid.*
31. *Manitoba Free Press,* 10 & 28 September 1889. *Toronto Mail,* 30 September 1889. *Ottawa Citizen,* 19 September 1889.
32. PAC, RG10, BS, file 241,209-1, Superintendent General of Indian Affairs to the Hon. the Privy Council of Canada, 19 January 1887.
33. *Ibid.,* Vankoughnet to John A. Macdonald, 19 January 1887. See Appendix VII
34. *Calgary Tribune,* 5 February 1889.
35. PAC, RG10, BS, file 19,502-1, Indian Commissioner to Secretary [of Indian Affairs ?], 30 September 1889.
36. G. Breynat, OMI., *Cinquante Ans au Pays des Neiges,* Montreal, Fides, 1945, Vol. 1, pp. 92, 159.
37. P. Duchaussois, OMI. *The Grey Nuns in the Far North, 1867-1917,* Toronto, McClelland & Stewart, 1919, p. 131.
38. PAC, RG10, BS, file 19,502-1, Vankoughnet to John A. Macdonald, 30 May 1888.
39. *Ibid.*
40. *Ibid.,* J.W. Shore, Accountant, to Deputy Minister of Indian Affairs, 19 February 1891.
41. *Ibid.,* file 19, 502-3, Scott to Pedley, 29 May 1905.
42. *Ibid.,* file 19,502-1, HBC. to the Dominion Government, 30 November 1889.
43. *Ibid.,* file 19,502-3, Scott to Deputy Superintendent General of Indian Affairs, 7 March 1910.
44. *Ibid.,* file 19,502-1, Exchange of correspondence during the first three months of 1890 between one Indian Agent, the Indian Commissioner for the Northwest Territories, the Minister of the Interior, Dieudonné Desjarlais (trader at Lesser Slave Lake), the Superintendent General of Indian Affairs, and the Deputy Minister of Indian Affairs.
45. R. Bell. *Report on Part of the Basin of the Athabasca River, N.W.T.,* Geological & Natural History Survey of Canada, Published by authority of Parliament, Montreal, Dawson Brothers, 1884.
46. R.G. McConnell. *Report on a Portion of the District of Athabasca Comprising the Country between Peace River and the Athabasca River North of Lesser Slave Lake,* Ottawa, Queen's Printer, 1893.
47. R.G. McConnell. *Report on an Exploration in the Yukon and the Mackenzie Basins, N.W.T.,* Geological & Natural History Survey of Canada. Annual report 1888-1889, Published by authority of Parliament, Montreal, William Foster Brown and Co. 1890. pp. 31D, 32D.
48. Schultz had previously greatly influenced the development of the Red River area (Winnipeg) and had also advocated the Red River Surveys, one of the factors causing the Metis rebellion led by Louis Riel in 1870.
49. Canada Senate, *Journals,* 27 March 1888, pp. 65-66.
50. *Ibid.,* 1888, Appendix 1, p. 11.
51. *Ibid.,* 2 May 1888, p. 163.
52. *Ibid.,* 1888, Appendix 1, map follows page 310.
53. *Edmonton Bulletin,* 27 April 1889.
54. Canada Privy Council, O.C. 52, 26 January 1891.
55. PAC, RG10, BS, file 19502-1. Map 26 January 1891.
56. *Ibid.,* file 75,236-1, Reed, Indian Commissioner to Deputy Superin-

tendent General of Indian Affairs, 2 April 1891.

57. *Ibid.*, Memorandum of Proposed Treaty with Northern Indians, 15 December 1890.

58. *Ibid.*, Scott to Deputy Minister of Indian Affairs, 11 April 1891.

59. *Ibid.*, Dewdney, Superintendent General of Indian Affairs to Vankoughnet, 3 July 1891.

Chapter II

Treaty 8, 1897-1900

Introduction

The signing of Treaty 8 must be viewed in relation to political and economic developments which were shaping the future of a young nation. The North West Mounted Police had succeeded in bringing law and order to the prairies, thus establishing Canadian political sovereignty over the southern portion of the land which had come under the Dominion flag in 1870. Development was going ahead steadily, insured by Indian treaties and facilitated by improved transportation systems.

But opportunity in the Unceded Territories lying north of the prairies soon began to attract adventurers and settlers. Between 1896-1898 the move north was to the gold fields of the Klondike. The effect which this had on the country and on the native population was far-reaching, encompassing the responsibilities of the North West Mounted Police in patrolling and administering the Athabasca-Mackenzie District, as well as the decision to make treaty with the Indians.

Sovereignty, economics, and development were key factors in this decision taken by the politicians in Ottawa. Yet limited knowledge of the country and of the people would militate against the treaty being of long-term benefit to either the Government or the Indians.

Treaty 8 covers a large area. It took the Treaty Commission two summers to obtain the adhesion of all of the Indians concerned. At the same time, the Half-Breed Commission was settling accounts with the Metis, thus effectively dividing the native people into two groups, Treaty and Non-Treaty Indians. What happened in the North in

1899-1900 is crucial for understanding the present-day claims of the Indian people and the judgement of Mr. Justice Morrow.

The reader may be momentarily confused by apparent contradictions in the accounts of events surrounding the signing of Treaty 8. The documents which have been used to reconstruct this period reflect the bias or interest of individuals and will necessarily differ on points of detail or interpretation. This is not to say that these differing versions do not converge at a point just beyond historical vision.

The Glitter of Gold Behind the Treaty, 1897-1899

The Klondike Gold Rush

By the spring of 1897 the Klondike gold rush was on. Train-loads of gold-seekers poured into Edmonton and Vancouver from around the world. Predictions were made that 50,000 people would travel the Athabasca and Mackenzie rivers enroute to the gold field,[1] outnumbering by far the resident population of the area. This figure was highly exaggerated, but the several hundreds who did travel these rivers did not pass by without being noticed:

> When McMurray was reached, a happier lot of men it would be hard to find, laughing, shaking hands and congratulating each other on their safe arrival. And to see the natives stare when the fleet of boats arrived and the rush of men trooped up to the Hudson's Bay Company's store to post letters and make a few purchases. It's hard to tell what they thought, but they were certainly too dumbfounded to speak, merely standing at a safe distance to view the advancing crowd. It was enough to make others besides the natives stare. Fancy a little hum-drum hamlet three hundred miles from civilization, so to speak, dead to the world for half the year and in the other half they perhaps see or hear of a single boat passing down the river. Then of a sudden to have their solitude disturbed and the even tenor of their daily existence outraged by the advent of sixty-three boats and a crowd of men, hilarious with joy at getting safely over the rapids, yelling and dancing in the exhuberance of their animal spirits. It would keep a white man guessing to hold his own with his head piece, let alone an Indian. This will be an event for the Indians of Fort McMurray to hand down to posterity and tell of round the fire place while the wind howls down the chimney. This is probably the most peculiar and impressive sight that has ever taken place, or even will take place, in the history of McMurray.[2]

By the end of 1898, 860 prospectors reached Fort Smith. Of this number about 70 returned to Edmonton or remained in the vicinity of Great Slave Lake. About 790 reached Fort Simpson.[3] Most of these wintered near the trading posts or in shacks along the Mackenzie River. By the end of August, 1899, "529 miners and 186 boats had gone by Fort Wrigley".[4]

Many halted their rush to the Klondike when news spread that rich gold mines existed at the eastern end of Great Slave Lake. Companies were formed and a few hundred explorers, experts, and miners visited the area.[5] Rumours of their success reached Fort Resolution in January, 1899. With the temperature at 45° below zero, "all the men there, mainly defeated Klondikers who were waiting to go back to Edmonton, set out for a point 150 miles away to the northeast of the frigid and inhospitable shores of the Lake. There many staked claims and came back, wondering perhaps, what had possessed them to go at all . . . "[6] Prospecting flourished also on the north shore of the Lake.[7] There was talk of a colony of miners and agriculturists from the American Midwest. On the south shore, one party prospecting the vicinity of Buffalo River (where Pine Point mine has since been developed), sent out excellent samples of galena in the spring of 1899. Lead-zinc deposits had been explored earlier by government surveyors, and local Indians were familiar with the location of deposits of quartz and various ores. Ed Nagle, a Fort Resolution trader, tells how prospectors examined samples of ore shown to them by an Indian and then "ridiculed the native and told him it was valueless, but made certain to find out where he had found it. They then sneaked off to stake the area".[8]

All contemporary records indicate that this increased mining activity on the shores of Great Slave Lake was an important reason for including the area within the boundary of Treaty 8. Father Breynat noted in his diary of 1899.

> Worrying about the news of rich gold mines having been discovered on Great Slave Lake, and desiring to assure its rights to the greatest part of the loot, the Government prudently hurried to send a treaty commission to deal with the Indians and to purchase from them a complete surrender of their land rights in exchange for a perpetual yearly rent and other gifts.[9]

"Loot" may have been the best word to use, considering the grievances which the Indians had against the prospectors. Charles Mair, a member of the Half-Breed Commission of 1899, related this social problem to the Government's decision to make a treaty:

> The gold-seekers plunged into the wilderness of Athabasca without hesitation, and without as much as "by your leave" to the native. Some of these marauders, as was to be expected, exhibited on the way a congenital contempt for the Indian's rights. At various places his horses were killed, his dogs shot, his bear-traps broken up. An outcry arose in consequence, which inevitably would have led to reprisals and bloodshed had not the Government stepped in and forestalled further trouble by a prompt recognition of the native's title . . . The gold seeker was viewed with great distrust by the Indians, the outrages referred to showing, like straws in the wind, the inevitable drift of things had the treaties been delayed. For, as a matter of fact, those now peaceable tribes, soured by lawless aggression, and sheltered by their vast forests, might easily have taken an Indian revenge, and hampered, if not hindered, the safe settlement of the country

for years to come. The Government, therefore, decided to treat with them at once on equitable terms.[10]

Newspaper reports of similar incidents elsewhere gave substance to the Indians' indignation. The Government could not ignore this situation in the North for much longer:

There are 500 Indians camped at Fort St. John who refuse to let police and miners go further north until a treaty has been signed with them. They claim that some of their horses have been taken by miners and are also afraid that the advent of so many men into their country will drive away the fur; hence their desire to stop the travel north.[11]

Inspector Routledge duly recorded the Indians' complaints.[12] Missionaries, for their part, deplored the corruption which accompanied the arrival of the prospectors. Thus far the Athabasca Indians "had been shielded from the corrupting influences that too often accompany the advance of European civilization."[13] According to Anglican Church writings of the time, protection for the Indians was urgently needed:

The influence of the class of people now rushing into the country in search of gold, is worse than I can describe.[14]

I have always dreaded the incoming of a mining population, on account of the effect it would have upon the morals of our people, but did not think it would touch us so closely . . . [15].

. . . the Klondyke "Rush", while it had produced some good results, such as the increased eagerness of the Indians to have their children educated, at the same time had brought several evils in its train.

The arrival of so many traders, and consequently the keen competition in the fur trade, has not tended to improve matters. Drunkenness, immorality, and every other accompanying vice peculiar to modern civilization, is daily on the increase . . . The Canadian Government proposes to make treaty with our Indians next summer and we are hoping that one result will be to place more effectual restrictions upon the liquor trade.[16]

If the protection and welfare of the Indians were important considerations in the Government's decision, it is not evident in this official statement by the Deputy Minister of Indian Affairs:

Although there was no immediate prospect of any such invasion by settlement as threatened the fertile belt in Manitoba and the Northwest Territories and dictated the formation of treaties with the original owners of the soil, none the less occasional squatters had found their way at any rate into the Peace River district.

While under ordinary circumstances the prospect of any considerable influx might have remained indefinitely remote, the discovery of gold in the Klondike region quickly changed the aspect of the situation. Parties of white men in quest of a road to the gold fields began to traverse the country, and there was not only the possibility ahead of such travel being greatly increased, but that the district itself would soon become the field of prospectors who might at any time make some discovery which would be followed by a rush of miners to the spot. In any case the knowledge of the country obtained and diffused, if only by people passing through it, could hardly fail to attract attention to it as a field for settlement.

For the successful pursuance of that humane and generous policy which has always characterized the Dominion in its dealings with the aboriginal inhabitants, it is of vital importance to gain their confidence at the outset, for the Indian character is such that, if suspicion or distrust once be aroused, the task of eradication is extremely difficult.

For these reasons it was considered that the time was ripe for entering into treaty relations with the Indians of the district, and so setting at rest the feeling of uneasiness which was beginning to take hold of them, and laying the foundation for permanent friendly and profitable relations between the races.[17]*

In addition to extinguishing Indian title to the land, the Government was looking for tighter control over both Indians and whites, to insure peaceful settlement and development of the land, and to promote the harmonious co-existence of Indians and whites. In the North, as everywhere else, economic considerations far out-weighed all others in the formulation of Indian policy.

A new political entity, the Yukon Territory, was created at that time. Given the economic implications of gold in the Yukon, there is some wonder that the Government did not initiate treaty negotiations with the Yukon Indians at the time of the gold rush. No document has

*Modern historians agree on the motives behind the negotiations of Treaty 8:

"There were talks of railway from Edmonton to the Nelson River or to the Liard River, and thence to the Yukon. All these reasons compelled the Government to organize some kind of administration and to deal by treaty with the Northern Indians as had been done with the Prairie Indians." – Bishop Grouard, *Soixante Ans d'Apostolat* p. 358

"Since a find of minerals was liable at any time to send a rush of other and more permanent settlers there, it became necessary for the Government to get some control of the Crees, Chipewyans and Beavers in the Athabasca and Peace River countries. It was consequently decided to send a party of Commissioners in to bring these tribes into treaty relations with the Government." – K. Hughes, *Father Lacombe, The Black Robe Voyageur,* 1911, p. 377

"It was not so much to preserve order as to protect them [the Indians] from the Whites, who, now that the country south was fast settling, would surely encroach on their domain, that this treaty [Treaty 8] was made." – Sir C.E. Denny, *The Law Marches West*, 1931, p. 300.

"Large crowds of gold-seekers were then moving to the Yukon, (1898). To prevent any trouble between these foreigners and the Indian tribes whose territories they were crossing, a Treaty commission was sent to the Great North in 1899." – A.G. Morice, OMI, *Histoire Abrégée de l'Ouest Canadien,* 1914, p. 130

"Reacting first to the advent of prospectors and settlers during and after the Klondike gold rush, the department [of Indian Affairs] made preparations to bring under treaty the Indians of the Athabasca and Peace River districts north of Treaty 6 and south of Great Slave Lake." – M. Zaslow, *The Opening of the Canadian North,* 1971, p. 224-225.

yet been found to indicate that a treaty was ever considered. Perhaps Ottawa was afraid that the Indians would put too high a price on their rich land and decided to avoid the formality of a treaty.

As for the Athabasca-Mackenzie District, it was the Klondike gold rush with all of its attendant political, economic, and social implications, which finally forced the Government to come to terms with its responsibilities in that part of the North covered by Treaty 8.

North West Mounted Police Patrols, 1897-1899

On January 4, 1897, a North West Mounted Police patrol left divisional headquarters at Fort Saskatchewan, Alberta, by dog-team. It was the first of annual patrols which would penetrate the Peace River country and the north beyond. Led by Inspector Arthur Murray Jarvis, the first patrol reached Fort Resolution on February 13, and was back at Fort Saskatchewan on April 14, having travelled more than 2,-000 miles. Ostensibly the patrol was in the Athabasca District "to look into various matters such as the prevalence of destructive fires, traffic in liquor, and the allegedly wholesale setting out of poison by white trappers in the area".[18] As the first official Government presence in the north, other than the Dominion land surveyors who had travelled the country since 1882, the police patrol would also serve to secure Canadian sovereignty over the vast land. Complete reports of all northern patrols from 1897 until the First World War are published in Canada Sessional Papers for the edification, no doubt, of interested foreign powers.

These reports constitute the earliest and only official records of the northern districts. For the purpose of evaluating conditions affecting the signing of Treaty 8, these reports are invaluable. They describe the Indian's way of life, his complaints as increasing numbers of traders, trappers, and prospectors invade his ancestral hunting grounds, and his reactions when confronted for the first time with the enforcement of Canadian laws.

The next two patrols were led by Inspector W. R. Routledge. In the winter of 1897-1898 he reached Fort Simpson, covering 2,172 miles in 80 days. The following winter the patrol went as far as Fort Resolution, proceeding on the way back into the Peace River country which was to be included in Treaty 8. Throughout the journey the patrols were vigilant for evidence of violations of fire, liquor, poison, and game laws, faithfully recording details of irregularities.

Liquor Traffic

Although relatively minuscule in volume, the illegal traffic of liquor in the North was one of the first targets of the police patrols. Jarvis reported that,

   . . . considerable quantities of spirits and extracts are smuggled in and given and traded to the Indians . . . Some of the Indians are said to journey all the way to Edmonton in the Spring to trade their furs, and return with whisky which they smuggle through for themselves and other Indians who intrust them with furs to take out for the same purpose.[19]

Routledge noted that this liquor traffic "is confined to the lower class of White hunters and Half-breeds employed on the River".[20] During the time of the patrols the prohibitory clauses of the Northwest Territories Act were strictly enforced, e.g., "Thomas McClelland [was] trading liquor and causing drunkenness in the Indian camps. I tried him, found him guilty and fined him $300 and costs."[21] The news of the Klondike gold rush led Routledge to fear an increase in liquor problems:

> In view of the number of strangers who will now pass through those districts en route to the northern gold fields, many of whom will remain for prospecting purposes, and the fact that the Indians have had, so far, little dealings with Whites outside of the Hudson's Bay Company's officials, missionaries and a few White hunters, I would respectfully suggest that the prohibitory law be strictly enforced."[22]

The Use of Poison Baits

The use of poison to kill fur-bearing animals was unknown in Indian territory until the arrival of white hunters and trappers in the Athabasca and Mackenzie Districts.[23] Frank Russell, an American naturalist, spent three winters in the Mackenzie District and noted that at Fort Rae during the month of February, 1894:

> Mr. Hodgson and I maintained a "trapping track," or rather, a line of poisoned baits, thirty miles in length. The Dog Ribs were so afraid of strychnine that they would not even touch an animal killed by it . . . The Loucheux of the Lower Mackenzie are not so timid, they use strychnine for baits without fear. Nearly every clerk [trader] sets a few baits each winter, which usually succeed in killing the favorite dog of the post, a red or cross fox, or very rarely a silver fox.[24]

Everywhere along his route, Inspector Jarvis found evidence that poison was being used:

> Some damage [by poison] has been done, principally by the destruction of Indian hunting dogs, which are valuable to their owners, and also a great loss of fur takes place by poisoned animals wandering off when poisoned, and are also dangerous to hungry Indians who may discover and eat the poisoned carcasses.
>   Indians complained bitterly of the use of this poison put out by White men and Half-breed trappers with whom they are unable to compete, and think it hard that people who are not owners of the country are allowed to rob them of their living.[25]

A few whites and half-breeds were taken to court by Jarvis, convicted of using poison, and fined $25 or $50. Small wonder that "the Indians were much pleased at the visit of the Police and their action towards the suppression of laying out poison".[26] Inspector Routledge's report of 1898 indicated that "the use of poison in the North country seems to have been pretty well stamped out".[27] It was the white trappers "who were the greatest offenders",[28] and the departure of some for the Klondike gold fields reduced the use of poison. However, it still remained an occasional means of getting furs and a source of complaint to the Indians until late in the 1930's.

Game Laws

On July 23, 1894, royal assent was given to "An Act for the Preservation of Game in the Unorganized Portions of the Northwest Territories of Canada".[29] Men like Macfarlane had questioned the validity of game laws in a country not yet surrendered to the Crown. Could such regulations be imposed on Indians without injustice? Day Hort Mac-Dowell, Member of Parliament, had this to say on April 30, 1894:

> As to the legal right of the Government in prohibiting the Indians and Half-breeds catching fish out of season, or killing game out of season, I believe that by a recent decision of the Imperial Privy Council, which was given about 14 months ago, they have every legal right to do this: that there is no necessity for the Government to make a Treaty with Indians, or anybody else; that the treaties made have merely been to bring about a peaceful, happy and speedy conclusion of the entry of whites into lands formerly occupied by Indians, but that the Privy Council have decided once and for all that the whole North West of Canada belongs to Her Majesty, that it is her property, and that she has absolute rights to do whatever she wishes. And in consequence if Her responsible advisors recommend Her to prohibit fishing and shooting out of season, even though Treaty has [not?] been made with the Indians, it is a perfectly justifiable and legal act.[30]

The Game Act came into force on January 1, 1896. Section 4 of the Act stated that: "except as hereinafter provided, buffalo and bison shall not be hunted, taken, killed, shot at, wounded, injured, or molested in any way, at any time of the year until the first day of January, A.D. 1900".[31] Other sections of the act concerned musk-oxen, moose, deer, mink, otter, beaver, muskrat, swan, wild ducks, geese, etc., but apparently only the regulations concerning buffalo were seriously enforced by the police patrols of 1897, 1898, and 1899. Accounts of the Indians' reaction to these laws are not without humour and pathos. At Smith Landing (Fort Fitzgerald), the centre of buffalo country, Inspector Jarvis reported:

> . . . on my arrival I found a party of hunters who had already made their long hunting snowshoes and were ready to start in search of buffalo . . . These people had never heard of a Game Law and were much surprised on hearing of it, but willingly gave up their hunt when I explained to them the necessity of complying with this law.[32]

A party who had prepared their outfit for a buffalo hunt, when told by me of the necessity of complying with the law, cheerfully desisted and postponed their hunt, at any rate, during my stay in the country.[33]

But not everyone was so cheerful and obliging. Inspector Routledge had this to report:

One François Byskie, a Chipewyan Indian, was brought before me charged with the killing of 2 buffalo near "Lying Wood" Mountain on the 14th of December 1897. The man pleaded guilty to the charge and gave as his reason that he was starving. If he had contented himself with killing one, which would have satisfied his wants sufficiently long to have enabled him to kill other game, I probably would have believed his story, but having killed 2, all that were in sight at the time, I came to the conclusion that it was the spirit of mischief that prompted his action . . . I fined the man in the sum of $10, or in default 10 days imprisonment with hard labour.[34]

Routledge emphasized protection of the buffalo as a future source of food and was satisfied that, "provided white men with evil intentions do not encourage the Indians to break the law, I think they will not trouble the buffalo".[35] The Inspector's faith was rewarded one year later, when the same François Byskie while on a hunting trip, reportedly "came up to some fresh buffalo tracks, the temptation to follow was strong, but, after consideration, he concluded not to do so, and fired his rifle in the air several times to scare them away, and continued his journey in an opposite direction."[36] The Indians must have experienced some bewilderment, nevertheless, when they saw buffalo and musk oxen being killed by sportsmen in search of trophies and not food. * Caspar Witney, a sportsman who passed through in 1895, expressed this opinion on the threat to buffalo:

Bison are not being killed in large numbers nor shot frequently as individuals. They range over a country too large and too difficult to reach, and require more skillful hunting than the average Indian is capable of. When I was in the country in the winter of 1894-1895 not even a bison track had been seen up to the time of our hunt . . . The extermination of wood bison through their hunting by Indians is not to be apprehended . . . [37]

Building Trust

In the face of the frequent misery and starvation of the Indian people, the Government's concern for preserving game seemed misplaced. Constant H. Giroux, OMI, Catholic missionary at Arctic Red River, wrote to Inspector Jarvis on July 1, 1897, and contrasted the Government's prompt action and efforts to preserve valuable animals and its

*Sportsmen of some renown came into Indian territory in seach of trophies: Frank Russell, 1894; Caspar Witney and Henry Toke Munn, 1895; David T. Hanbury, 1896.

apparent unconcern for the Indians. "I, at the same time, would beg of you to endeavour to get the same Government to show as much zeal in preserving the lives of human beings who are to be found therein."[38] The police patrols of 1897, 1898, and 1899 witnessed and recorded these conditions:

> . . . a large number of Indians, both Crees and Chipewyan, living near Fort Chipewyan, are suffering from hunger on account of the small supply of furs . . . The Hudson's Bay Company and Mr. Colin Fraser, before my arrival had advanced a certain amount of assistance to these starving people, some of whom died during my stay at Chipewyan. I [Inspector Jarvis] also gave a small amount of relief . . . [39]
>
> During my [Inspector Routledge] stay at Resolution a party of starving Indians from Fond du Lac, Great Slave Lake [Snowdrift] visited me. They were in a wretched state, having travelled some 150 miles on a scanty allowance of fish, to make known the condition of their people.[40] . . . in the winter of 1898-1899, the Indians at Fond du Lac [Sask.] were in very destitute circumstances . . . [41]

From Fond du Lac Father Breynat gave this account of that terrible winter:

> Dogs died of hunger, and people had no more transportation. Some people walked to the village for three days without food . . . Some arrived with hands and nose frozen . . . An old man who came to the Mission, had left his camp 4 days ago with his nephew. As the young man couldn't walk any more, he was left 30 miles behind, alone. I went with another man, and rescued him . . . Influenza followed famine . . . The old man, "a Man's Shadow," was found dead, outside, and half eaten by dogs.[42]

These words echo descriptions of similar misery written ten and twenty years earlier. Previous appeals to Ottawa had taken months to be heard and years to be answered. Now with the presence of the North West Mounted Police, government did not seem so remote nor assistance so far away. By means of the annual patrol, the Police had gained the respect of the people, giving as it did the semblance of protection against intruders and security in troubled times. Some people at Fort Chipewyan firmly believe that their forefathers signed Treaty 8 because they were told that "the Queen will never let your children die from hunger".[43] This might well be true.

Ottawa Prepares For the Treaty, 1897-1899

In November, 1897, the Honourable Clifford Sifton, Minister of the Interior and Superintendent-General of Indian Affairs, and James Walker, a retired officer of the Royal Northwest Mounted Police and former Indian Agent, met in Calgary to discuss the necessity of treaties with the Indians of the Athabaska and the Yukon. In a letter of November 30, 1897, Walker put in writing his thoughts on the subject:

From all appearances there will be a rush of miners and others to the Yukon and the mineral regions of the Peace, Liard, and other rivers in Athabasca during the next year . . . In the face of this influx of settlers into that country, no time should be lost by the Government in making a treaty with these Indians for their rights over this territory. They will be more easily dealt with now than they would be when their country is overrun with prospectors and valuable mines be discovered. They would then place a higher value on their rights than they would before these discoveries are made and if they are like some of the Indians of Saskatchewan, they may object to prospectors going into that country until their rights are settled.[44]

The Commissioner of the North West Mounted Police acting on reports from his officers in the field, wrote to Ottawa pointing out,

. . . the advisability of Government taking some immediate steps towards arranging with the Indians not under treaty, occupying the proposed line of route from Edmonton to Pelly River. These Indians, although few in number, are said to be very turbulent, and are liable to give very serious trouble when isolated parties of miners and travellers interfere with what they consider their vested rights.[45]

Both these letters circulated among the various Ottawa offices. Copies were also sent to Amédée Emmanuel Forget, the Indian Commissioner of the Northwest Territories, who commented on January 12th, 1898:

I am convinced that the time has now come when the Indian and Half-breed title to at least a portion of the territory to the north of that ceded to the Crown under Treaty No. 6, should be acquired, i.e., those tracts which are already partially occupied by Whites as miners or traders, and over which the Government has for some years past exercised some measure of authority.

I am aware that for some time past, the extension of Governmental authority into the Lesser Slave Lake and Upper Peace River Districts in advance of the acquisition of title to the territory has been regarded more or less jealously by the Native population therein more particularly by the large halfbreed population of the Lesser Slave Lake District.[46]

The Privy Council report of June 27, 1898 (No. 1703), described at length all previous discussions and reasons for a treaty. Sifton prepared a similar summary with the conclusion that "the time has come when the Indian and Half-breed population of [these] tracts of territory . . . should be treated with for the relinquishment of their claims to territorial ownership . . . ."[47] However, the necessary arrangements could not be completed in time to sign the treaty that year. Officials of the Department of Indian Affairs fearing that the Indian people would be deeply disappointed by the delay, agreed that "no time should be lost in notifying the Indians of the intention of the Government to treat with them next spring",[48] and that "it will be necessary to take immediate steps to assure the Indians that the Government has no intention of ignoring their rights".[49] Treaty plans would have to go forward quickly before the Indians of the North could learn too much about treaty-making from their southern brothers. These latter would have had much to say about the difference between written and oral promises:

> . . . the Wood Crees and Halfbreeds about Lesser Slave Lake who are closely connected with some of the Edmonton Indians may be found imbued with an intention to demand all those things the Crees from the South always claim they were promised, and blame the Government for not embodying in the written treaty, asserting that they were amongst the terms. These were, in the main: Full rations for all time; White men to work for them – making farms, building houses, etc.; all sorts of stock and implements; in short, sustenance without exertion on their part. And if such an intention grows before you treat, you may meet with much unreasonableness. . . [50]

Whether made to be honoured or broken, promises could never remove all suspicion and anxiety from the minds of the Indian people.

Who Will Sign the Treaty?

"A treaty cannot be successfully negotiated with the Indians unless the Half-breed claims are also considered".[51] This declaration by the Indian Commissioner, Forget, could not be ignored by Ottawa officials preparing the treaty. It would have been convenient to consider all Metis as white people, who had no rights to special consideration or protection. But such was not the reality.

Canadian Metis do not have official status and the word itself, "Metis", can be used with different meanings. An official definition reads: "A person of mixed white and Indian blood, having not less than one-quarter Indian blood, but does not include either an Indian or a non-Treaty Indian as defined by the Indian Act".[52]

The significance of the Metis' role in the history of the Canadian West has not been sufficiently appreciated. Lord Dufferin, Governor General, proclaimed during an official visit to Manitoba in 1877:

> . . . the Halfbreeds were the ambassadors between East and West. The absence of really savage struggles between Whites and Indians was due in great part to their influence. They were indispensable at treaty negotiations.[53]

Nonetheless, the Metis "Rebellion" of 1885 which culminated in the battle of Batoche, left bitter memories in the minds of the Metis. They had suffered in their bodies and in their souls. At the end of the 19th century they still resented the cruel manner in which Canada had treated them.

Metis have been part of northern history from the beginning of the fur trade. Many families had moved westward from Rupert's Land in quest of land, fur, adventure, or seeking employment with the Hudson's Bay Company. By the late 1890's a number of Metis had settled in the Athabasca-Mackenzie District. Laurence William Herchmer, NWMP Commissioner in Regina, remarked on December 2, 1897, that "the Half-breeds of Lesser Slave Lake [were] dissatisfied with the presence of the Police in that district."[54] He feared they could influence the Indians during treaty negotiations. Indian commissioner Forget supported the suggestion, "stongly impressed" upon him "by Grouard and persons who had full knowledge of the situation," that the government "be prepared to deal with the Half-breeds simultaneously with the Indians as, otherwise . . . the influence which the Half-breeds might exercise over the Indians might be detrimental to our treating with the latter."[55] He also recommended that as many Half-breeds as possible should be taken into treaty "with the same privileges as the pure-blooded Indians" rather than be given "scrips"[56] or scripts, i.e., certificates enabling them to select for themselves 240 acres of land.

In the past, many Metis had been permitted to join Treaties 1 to 6. What offer was to be made to the Metis of the Athabasca-Mackenzie District? Of prime importance was that "their acquiescence in the relinquishment of the aboriginal title should be secured." Finally, it was considered more conducive to their welfare and more in the public interest to take them into treaty than to give them scrip. Metis would be allowed to take treaty, if they so desired, on the judgement of the Commissioners who would determine which Metis would be dealt with as Indians.[57] Those who were unwilling or not allowed would receive a scrip[58] to either $240 or 240 acres of land.[59] One of the Indian treaty commissioners, James A. J. McKenna, was not entirely satisfied with these terms. He wrote to Sifton on April 17, 1899:

> I fear that the Commissioner who will be charged with effecting a settlement with the Halfbreeds will find it very difficult to do so under the scope given him by the Act, and that the consequent dissatisfaction among the halfbreeds may lead to their using their influence with the Indians in such a way as to make it difficult to negotiate a treaty.[60]

Those fears were not unfounded as the history of the Half-breed Commission of 1899 will show.

Treaty Boundaries

Since 1896, most of the traffic to the Yukon progressed via the Pacific Coast. A few overland routes from Edmonton to the gold fields were attempted but proved to be difficult. Communities and businessmen of Western Canada, desiring to profit in the trade for supplies, and strongly supported by the Northwest Territories Government, pressured the Dominion Government to establish a safe overland road from Edmonton northward. By 1899 a passable road had been built between Fort St. John and Peace River Crossing. The presence of many gold miners and/or prospectors, the expectation of an intense traffic on this overland route to the Klondike, and the necessity to establish peaceful relations between Indians and newcomers were deciding factors in determining boundaries for the Treaty. On a map dated January 12, 1898, Indian Commissioner Forget outlined an area where there was "considerable activity in mining matters". It covered the valleys of the Athabasca and Peace Rivers north of the Treaty 6 area, and the valleys of the Nelson, upper Peace, and upper Liard Rivers in British Columbia.

> Beyond these points, however, I do not consider that the Government would be justified in undertaking the negotiation of treaties which would involve very heavy outlay for comparatively inadequate returns insofar as the value of the territory to be ceded, or the rights of the Indian owners, are concerned . . . . I would not be in favor of undertaking the cession of territory beyond the latitude of Fort Simpson on the Mackenzie River and then only if absolutely necessary, and would confine the treaty entirely to the valley of that river excluding the Great Slave Lake District . . . . The Mackenzie Basin is at present only affected to a limited extent by the Gold Movement. . . .[61]

Three months later, Forget repeated that the treaty should not include the area inhabited by, "the Indians about Great Slave and Great Bear Lakes and along the Mackenzie River . . . their territory so far as is at present known is of no particular value and they very rarely come into contact with Whites. . . ."[62] Officials discussed at length whether or not the northeastern part of British Columbia should be included in the treaty. This would include the districts of Fort St. John, Fort Nelson, Fort Halkett, and Hudson's Hope, bringing the boundary to the Rocky Mountains. A natural boundary would have much more appeal to the Indians than an artificial one. Moreover, this area was the route taken by many miners and prospectors headed for gold fields in the Yukon. ". . . the lives and property of those who may enter therein [would be] safeguarded by the making of provision which will remove all hostile feeling from the minds of the Indians and lead them to peacefully acquiesce in the changing conditions".[63] On the other hand, an agreement between the Federal Government and the Province of British Columbia in 1876 had stipulated that the Province itself would be responsible for negotiating with the Indians for their land and for setting up Indian reserves.[64]

The name "Treaty 8" was used for the first time on January 7, 1899, by David Laird who had been named Indian Commissioner for the Northwest Territories the year before. In his memorandum he noted certain practical considerations for determining the itinerary of the treaty party:

> The Treaty Commissioners would not have time to go north beyond Fort

Smith. It may perhaps be possible to drop [the treaty boundary] down the
Great Slave River as far as Fort Resolution. If this could be done, the
whole territory to the Southern shore of Great Slave Lake might be included in the surrender . . . I, however, do not deem it advisable to attempt going to Fort Resolution this year unless the Government, on account of applications for permits to mining prospectors, consider[s] highly
important that the surrendered territory should extend to Great Slave
Lake.[65]

Sifton felt that due to the "many claims now staked at Great Slave
Lake", the area was indeed desirable for a treaty.[66] His final recommendation to the Treaty Commissioners stated:

In view of the reported mining development in the Great Slave Lake Region it is important that a treaty should be extended to embrace that
country if at all possible.[67]

The best description of the boundaries of Treaty 8 was provided by
Laird when some years later he was asked to explain these boundary
decisions:

The scope of the Commissioners' instructions was to obtain the relinquishment of the Indian and Halfbreed title in that tract of territory north
of Treaty 6 to which Governmental authority had to some extent been extended by sending Northwest Mounted Police there to protect and control
whites who were going into the country as traders, travellers to the Klondike, explorers, and miners. The territory watered by the Lesser Slave
Lake, the Peace and Athabasca Rivers, the Athabasca Lake, the South of
Great Slave Lake and their tributaries, was where these whites were
finding their way, and the Commissioners did not deem it necessary to extend Treaty 8 farther than they did . . . .[68]

Two factors which could have influenced the boundaries and the timing of Treaty 8 should be mentioned here. Agitation by the Metis people of the Lesser Slave Lake and Peace River areas for recognition of
their land claims could well have accelerated treaty plans since traditionally, settlement with the Metis had never preceded an Indian
treaty.

This theory is more credible when comparison is made with the Yukon where, at the time of Treaty 8, political, economic, and social factors were similar to those in the Athabasca-Mackenzie area, but where
there was no Metis population to be pacified.

In a similar vein, the influence of a powerful Edmonton politician,
in the person of Frank Oliver, could well have been a determining factor in setting boundary lines. In promoting an all-Canada route to the
Klondike, with Edmonton as the gateway, Oliver would try to draw
Ottawa's attention to northern Alberta.

Reserves or Land in Severalty?

Under all previous treaties, lands had been set aside for Indians signing the treaties. These lands have been called "reserves" and are "held
by Her Majesty for the use and benefit of the respective bands."[69] The
area to be covered by Treaty 8 was unlike the western prairies or the
fertile belt. Also the social organization of northern Indian bands
differed from that of the Plains Indians. For these reasons, Forget
doubted that a reserve system could be applied in the north. He proposed, instead, that a certain amount of land would be allocated to
each Indian family.[70] The question was discussed by a Privy Council
Committee which decided on June 27, 1898, that "the Treaty Commissioners should be given discretionary powers both as to the annuities to be paid to and the reservations of land to be set apart for the
Indians."[71] McKenna expressed his views on the reserve system in a
letter to Sifton dated April 17, 1899:

> . . . it might be desirable to give the Commissioners a freer hand. We can
> scarcely rely on the experience of the past in dealing with the Indians now
> to be treated with. When the Government negotiated for the surrender of
> the Indian title to the land in the organized territories, it had to deal with
> Indian nations which had distinct tribal organizations. The communal
> idea was strong and made necessary the setting apart of reserves for the
> continuance of the common life until the Indians could be gradually
> weaned from it.
>
> The most that can be said in favour of the reserve system, however, is
> that reserves made is easier for the Government to control and feed the
> Indians in a country where it was necessary to do so. Experience does not
> favour the view that the system makes for the advancement of the Indi-
> ans. We should not be anxious to extend it for its own sake; and the con-
> ditions of the country to be treated for are not such as to make its exten-
> sion necessary. From information which has come to hand it would
> appear that the Indians whom we are to meet fear that the making of a
> treaty will lead to their being grouped on reserves. Of course, grouping is
> not now contemplated; but there is the view that reserves for future use
> should be provided for in the treaty. I do not think this is necessary.
>
> From what I have been able to learn of the North country, it would ap-
> pear that the Indians there act rather as individuals than as a nation, and
> that any tribal organization which may exist is very slight. They live by
> hunting, and by individual effort, very much as the halfbreeds in that
> country live. They are averse to living on reserves; and as that country is
> not one that will ever be settled extensively for agricultural purposes it is
> questionable whether it would be good policy to even suggest grouping
> them in the future. The reserve idea is inconsistent with the life of a
> hunter, and is only applicable to an agricultural country. The most the In-
> dians are likely to require in the way of reserves are small fishing stations
> at certain points which they might desire to have secured to them. I do
> not think the Commissioners should go further in the way of general res-
> ervations, unless they should find that circumstances compel them. But

they should have authority to guarantee to every Indian settled upon, or in occupation of land, an individual title thereto. The limit might be put at 160 acres as the Indians are likely to require very small holdings.[72]

Sifton gave the Treaty Commissioners their final instructions on the matter, on May 12, 1899. Indian people could either select reserves for their bands or hold land "in severalty". This meant that any Indian family could have its own small reserve, apart from those of other families or bands:

> As to reserves, it has been thought that the conditions of the North Country may make it more desirable to depart from the old system and, if the Indians are agreeable, to provide land in severalty of 160 acres to each, the land to be conveyed with proviso as to non alienation without the consent of the Governor General in Council. Of course, if the Indians prefer reserves, you are at liberty to undertake to set them aside.
>
> The terms of the treaty are left to your discretion with this stipulation that obligations to be assumed under it shall not be in excess of those assumed in the treaties covering the North West Territories.[73]

For all practical purposes these discretionary powers would assure the best possible bargain for the Government.

Land Payment: Cash or Credit?

Most previous Indian treaties had promised a perpetual annuity of five dollars for each Indian. From December, 1898, until April, 1899, Indian Affairs officials discussed the pros and cons of perpetual annuities as opposed to a single cash payment at the signing of the treaty. James Ansdell Macrae, Secretary of the Department of Indian Affairs, believed that a single payment "say, for the sake of argument, $100.00 per head" would appeal to the Indians more than remote advantages. He argued that the situation had altered since the first treaties, and,

> . . . what might have been deemed advantageous in granting such annuities when the Indians were looked upon as a disappearing race should be regarded as disadvantageous now that their ability to continue to exist, and increase, under changed conditions is established.[74]

Indian Commissioner Forget favoured instead the annuity plan, introducing a kind of slide-rule arrangement for greater economy:

> . . . basing the amount of annuity to be offered on the comparative value of the country to be ceded . . . for instance, while the Lesser Slave Lake and Peace River Indians might be tendered an annuity of $5.00 per head, those at Fort MacMurray and Fort Chipewyan might be offered $4.00, and those further north, if treated with, $3.00 per head. . . [75]

He furnished the Department with an estimate of the Indian population of the area in 1898:

Fort Chipewyan and Fond du Lac	841
Fort Smith	280
Fort Liard	205
Fort Simpson, Rampart House and vicinity	599
Fort Good Hope and vicinity	1,255
Fort Norman and vicinity	604
Fort Resolution and vicinity	533
Fort Providence and vicinity	1,382

Laird objected to doing away with annuity payments and offered several financial arguments to support his case:

> In the first place, even though only $100 were paid to each Indian accepting the treaty, it would, estimating the number at 3700, involve a vote of $370,000 for payment to Indians alone this year, a sum which Parliament would probably hesitate to grant. Again, the proposal, though it might be welcomed by the Indians of today would be unjust to their children and descendants. The money, in some cases, $800 or $1000 to a family, would be to a great extent squandered forthwith, and future generations of Indians would reap no benefit from it whatever. All the same, if they became destitute the Government would have to come to their assistance and the expense of employing agents to look after them would not be obviated. The question of commuting with the Indians for their annuities is, in my opinion, one that will have to be deferred until they have made some progress in civilization.[76]

For his part, the accountant in the Department of Indian Affairs did an in-depth study of alternative methods of payment. His memorandum dated March 27, 1899, listed the following plans:

1. $25.00 per head every 10 years.
2. $50.00 per head every 10 years.
3. A single payment of $50.00 per head.
4. A single payment of $100.00 per head.
5. $5.00 annuity per head.
6. $2.50 annuity per head.

His calculations "for a period of 30 years" showed the cash saving or expense for the Government for each of the six plans.[77] An important memo from McKenna to Sifton on April 17, 1899, summarized the arguments for and against annuities. It also exposed the philosophy behind the policies of the Department:

> As to the payment of annuity, although Mr. Laird is favorable to it I am rather disposed to the contrary view, and Mr. Ross with whom I discussed the matter questions its benefit and is of the opinion that the Indians themselves will not place much value on it. I do not know that we have any reason to be desirous of extending the system if it can be avoided. As to the North country there is the objection that the yearly payment would cost a large sum.
>
> Since Treaty 3, the Dominion in all treaties with the Indians has under-

taken to pay $5 a year to each Indian in perpetuity, and $15 to headmen and $25 to Chiefs. Now the question arises: – if this was considered a fair money compensation for the land in Manitoba and the organized territories, what would be a fair compensation for the land in the territory now to be treated for. The former land was admirably suited for agriculture. Its settlement was necessary for the real making of the Dominion. The building of the transcontinental railway made the wiping out of the Indian title urgent; and the changing condition interfered with the Indians' means of livelihood and mode of life. There were, therefore, good reasons for giving them the maximum of compensation. The latter land is not of appreciable value agriculturally. There is no urgent public need of its acquirement. There may be mineral development and some consequent settlement in spots; but this will not bring sudden or great changes likely to interfere to any marked degree with the Indian mode of life and means of livelihood. I think it would not be illiberal to answer the question by saying that half the amount which we agreed to pay under former treaties would be ample compensation for the Indians who are to be parties to the proposed one. And as the making of the treaty will not be the forerunner of changes that will to any great extent alter existing conditions in the country, and as the Indians will continue to have the same means of livelihood as they have at present, it may fairly be laid down that the object of the Commissioners should simply be to secure the relinquishment of the Indian title at as small a cost as possible.

The difficulty is that if we start to negotiate on the perpetual annuity principle the Indians will hold out for the same terms as were given their neighbours to the immediate south; and the cost of paying a yearly annuity in that country added to the amount of the annuity, would make the price paid for it altogether out of proportion to its value.

But how shall we proceed if not in the old way? We could hardly give the Indians Halfbreed scrip. That would practically amount to paying them once for all in paper money subject to a heavy discount. It would be fairer to pay them a reasonable sum in cash. It has been objected that if this be done the Indians will squander what they receive. There is truth in this. But annuity is also squandered; and it is – generally speaking – only a question of squandering a little each year in perpetuity or a large sum at once. It has been held that such a procedure would be unjust to future generations in that it would fail to provide compensation to them for the alienation of their title; and would necessitate the Government's coming to their assistance in the event of the Indians becoming destitute in the future. But the fact is that the annuity amounts to very little, either as respects the compensation of future generations, or in the way of providing against destitution. As compensation for territorial title it is more fanciful than real. And it may safely be stated that the extent of relief to Indians has never been appreciably lessened by any annuity paid them. Indeed, for years provision has quietly been made for extending through the Hudson's Bay Company relief to Indians outside of treaty; and whether annuity be given or not, we must always be prepared to grant aid in the years when the hunt is a failure. If in the future the country should be depleted of its fur bearing animals, permanent provision would have to be made to assist the Indians; and in that event I fear that the payment of an annuity would be found to be simply an additional burden.[78]

After two long pages of financial alternatives which rivaled those of the accountant in complexity, McKenna still favoured one large payment over small annuities. His final and most sensible reason was that "The adoption of this course might possibly result in some of the Halfbreeds, who are estimated at 1,700, preferring to enter such a treaty to taking Halfbreed scrip".[79]

Sifton disregarded the advice of Macrae and McKenna. He informed the Treaty Commissioners on May 12, 1899, that "the Government . . . has concluded that it is best to proceed upon the usual lines of providing for the payments of annuities to the Indians."[80]

Protection of Game

Officials in Ottawa who had drafted the terms of Treaty 8 failed to make adequate provisions for the protection of what was essential to the Indians, i.e., game and forest. Many of the treaty promises which had taken months to discuss and prepare were of secondary importance to the Indians. Their main concern was for the protection of their freedom to hunt, trap, and fish. McKenna had foreseen the necessity of some mention of protection and conservation of the environment, and had offered this advice:

> The Commissioners should, I think, be authorized to add that the Government will cause notice to be given to white men that the forests and game are to be protected and will be ready should occasion call for such action to send Mounted Police to secure such protection.
>
> I am convinced that the forest fires caused by prospectors last year have so angered the Indians that some specific undertaking as to protection will have to be given. It may be necessary to go further and say that the ear of the Government will always be open to well grounded complaints from the Indians, and that when aid is asked and really required it will be forthcoming. Assistance will have to be given when needed.[81]

Only when the Treaty Commissioners promised them that they would be free to hunt and trap and fish for a living, and that their rights would be protected against the abuses of white hunters and trappers, did the Indians at each trading post of the Treaty 8 area consent to sign the Treaty.

Father Lacombe Invited

From the very beginning of treaty preparations, Indian Commissioner Forget realized that "the Northern native population is not any too well disposed to view favourably any proposition involving the cession of their rights to their country".[82] Inspector Routledge reported that the Indians and Metis showed considerable interest in the treaty question and held meetings at Lesser Slave Lake; an Anglican Missionary wrote:

> The Indians, all thro[ugh] the Peace River District, are considerably ex-

cited over the proposed Treaty. As far as I can gather they are determined to refuse either Treaty or "Scrips" and to oppose the settlement of their country by Europeans. So, until the gov't comes and the result is known, we shall have a rather anxious time.[83]

The Government became alarmed by these rumours of unrest. On May 3, 1899, the Privy Council Committee assessed the situation and recommended that the Government enlist the help of Father Lacombe:

> . . . the Commissioners appointed to negotiate a treaty with the Indians of the Athabasca District and adjoining country, and to deal with the claims of the Halfbreeds, will meet with great difficulty in their mission for the reason that the Halfbreeds are dissatisfied with the measure of recognition which by law is accorded to their claims, and because the Indians are suspicious of Governmental interference and are hostile to the incoming of White men whose advent they fear will destroy their hunting grounds. Moreover, the Commissioners will be handicapped at the very beginning of their negotiations by the fact that the Department of the Indian Affairs cannot furnish them with any reliable information as to the manners, customs and characteristics of the Indians of the North country.
>
> The Minister submits that these considerations have led him to the conclusion that it would be very desirable if the Commissioners could have the assistance and council of the Very Reverend Father Lacombe. Father Lacombe has been so long in the country as a missionary, knows the Indians and the Halfbreeds so intimately, and possesses their confidence in so marked a degree that he would be able to render most valuable and effective assistance to the Commissioners in their difficult mission.
>
> The Minister being convinced that it is in the public interest that everything possible should be done to assure the success of the Indian Treaty negotiations, and to satisfy the reasonable claims of the Halfbreeds, recommends that the Very Reverend Albert Lacombe, OMI, be attached to the Commission appointed to negotiate a treaty with the Indians of the District of Athabasca and adjoining country.[84]

The decision apparently pleased all Government officials. When the proposed treaty was under discussion in the House of Commons in June of that year, Sifton declared:

> Along with this Commission we have asked the Reverend Father Lacombe to go, not as a member of the Commission, but in an advisory capacity. Everyone who has lived in the northwest for the last fifteen or twenty years, Protestant and Catholic, knows well that there is no man in the northwest looked upon by the Indians with the same reverence and affection as Father Lacombe.[85]

Lacombe was then 72 years old. He argued that he was too old, but when the Prime Minister added his persuasion, Lacombe advised Sifton on May 14, 1899:

> My religious Superiors of Edmonton and St. Albert approving of my appointment by your department, I am glad to inform you that I accept the

position to be a member of the Commission going this summer to make treaties with the Cree-Indians and Halfbreeds of Lesser Slave Lake, Peace River, Athabaskaw, etc. . . .

I hope my health will stand to the fatigues and difficulties of such a trip.

It is for your sake and the sake of the Country that I am willing to accept such a position.

Wishing you good health and success in your undertaking for these treaties.[86]

Lacombe accepted this role of advisor more out of a sense of duty than of personal inclination. The difficulties of the trip worried him but he could not refuse to help achieve better understanding and friendship between the Indians and Canada. He wrote in his diary on May 27, 1899: "My health is holding out. I foresee that I can make this journey. Anyway, may the will of God be done. I am ready for anything so as to do some good for all."[87] Other missionaries also helped to establish friendly relations between the Indians and the Government at the time of Treaty 8. Their motives were probably similar to those of Father Lacombe. Certainly they were not naive enough to believe that the treaty would solve all of the Indians' problems, but they could hope that things would not get worse. In later years many felt that they had been used by the Government, and were greatly disappointed to see that the Indians were not treated as well as had been promised. This deception is expressed by Constant Falher, OMI, in a letter to Bishop Breynat:

If in 1899 we had not prepared the Lesser Slave Lake people to accept a treaty with the Government; if Bishop Grouard had not advised the chiefs to sign the treaty, telling them there was nothing which was not to their advantage; the treaty would still be waiting to be signed today. When Bishop Grouard sent me to Wabasca (at the request of Mr. Laird) to prepare the people and calm them, (it was then said that they were more or less in a state of revolt) I carried with me the Government promises, and I was very surprised when later on I was shown the document supposedly signed by the Indian Chiefs at Grouard [a village at the west end of Lesser Slave Lake] and thereabouts. So many important things are missing . . . but we do remember these things, and we suffer.[88]

Although they encouraged the Indians to take advantage of the treaty, the missionaries recognized that it was the end of an era, the end of "Fur and Mission" days. Bishop Grouard revealed to Lacombe that the changes necessitating or resulting from the signing of a treaty worried him. "You know that the Government will make a Treaty with the Indians. This makes me extremely worried. Alas, our good days are over!"[89]* Father Lacombe was more optimistic. One week before the first signing of Treaty 8, he wrote Grouard:

*In his autobiography, *Soixante Ans d'Apostolat*, Grouard included an entire chapter on Treaty 8. Clearly mentioned is his concern, at the time of Treaty 8, about how much the government would interfere, "help or hinder our missionary work."

Are not the Church and the Government going to work together, and open officially this great Northern district to civilization and to brotherly relations and harmony between the White man and the Indian? Does not the Government seem to acknowledge what the Church has done so far for the good of the poor Indians?[90]

Father Lacombe accompanied the Treaty party to four of the nine posts where Treaty 8 was signed in 1899. He was present for the signing at Lesser Slave Lake, Peace River Landing, Fort Vermillion and Fort McMurray. He did not return with the Treaty party the following year, when treaty negotiations were completed.

In the Eyes of the Law

In 1899 the Minister of Justice of the Government of Canada was asked to commute the death sentence passed on an Indian from Great Slave Lake. Although unrelated to Treaty 8 or its signing, this incident is significant in establishing the accepted legal opinion of the day regarding Indians. The Deputy Superintendent of Indian Affairs, James A. Smart, based his plea for mercy on the legal responsibility of the convicted Indian:

> I have the honour to draw attention to the fact that the accused was from Great Slave Lake, a section of the country inhabited by Indians with whom no Treaty has as yet been made and which is not yet in touch with civilization, and that he can therefore hardly be regarded otherwise than as an untutored savage. . . .
>
> I submit for your consideration the impossibility of judging only by the white man's methods, the conduct of a savage governed by superstitions and whose habits are entirely opposed to those of civilization . . . the enforcement of the extreme penalty might create an impression, amongst the Indians with whom the accused is connected, that contact with civilization imperilled their existence. Such an impression would defeat the object, recognized by the Indian Act and the provision made by Parliament from time to time for the Indians, namely gradually to inculcate in them habits of thought similar to those of the white population in this country. As a first step in this direction it may be necessary in the not remote future to negotiate a Treaty with the Indians of Great Slave Lake; and it would be unfortunate if these people were found then to hold the view that the white man's justice was without mercy and without consideration of their ignorance and general condition. . . .
>
> . . . I have the honour to ask your consideration of the question whether the interests of justice would not be best served by treatment of an Indian unacquainted with civilization in a manner no more severe than would be accorded a child below the age of fourteen years, concerning whom there is a prima facie presumption that he does not understand the nature and consequences of his act. Even the most highly educated Indian until enfranchised is subject to civil disabilities though capable of crime. Whatever his actual age he is still an infant in the eyes of the law; and in view of the wide distinction between him and an Indian of the class of the ac-

cused it appears to be a matter fairly open to question whether the latter should be considered more responsible for his actions than a child of the age mentioned.[91]

In the eyes of the law an Indian was treated as a child, not able to understand the nature and consequences of his act. If Smart's argument would be applied to the signing of Treaty 8, it seems hardly likely that the "untutored savages" of the north would be able to legally bind themselves by a treaty in the first place, much less be responsible for its legal consequences on future generations of Indians.

Treaty 8 – Summers of 1899 and 1900

Final Approach – Text of the Treaty

A few months before its signing, the importance of Treaty 8 for the Canadian public was discussed in an article appearing in the *Ottawa Citizen* of February 28, 1899:

> In an immense tract of land north of the Athabasca River, extending from the Rocky Mountains to Hudson's Bay, there are about 2700 Indians and 1700 half-breeds with whom treaty arrangements have not yet been entered into. With the march of civilization northward, necessity has arisen for negotiating treaties with the scattered inhabitants of this territory. Mining operations are being carried on as far north as Great Slave Lake, and the Indians and half-breeds have objected to the White man's invasion. The gov't promised a year ago to appoint a commission to negotiate a treaty, and in pursuance of this promise, Mr. Jas. Ross, of the Northwest Territorial gov't, Regina; Mr. David Laird, Indian Commissioner at Winnipeg, and J. A. J. McKenna, will leave Edmt. [Edmonton] about May 24 next. They will confer with Indians and half-breeds at different points on the way to Great Slave Lake and there come to terms.
>
> Little is known of the northern Indians and half-breeds as they have never been subject to gov't control and have remained practically without the pale of civilization. The Indians are Wood Crees, Chipewyans, and Beavers, and like the half-breeds, are engaged in hunting fur-bearing animals for the Hudson's Bay Company. It is probable that some have drifted from the south with the pressure of civilization upon their hunting ground, but the majority are natives of the country they now inhabit. The policy of the gov't in dealing with the Indians in other parts of Canada has been to pay them a gratuity at the making of the treaty and to provide for the payment in perpetuity of an annuity, in consideration of the surrender of their territorial rights.
>
> The conditions of the country to be treated for differ considerably from those existing in the territories formerly ceded, and the commissioners who are given discretionary powers, will have to be guided by circumstances. The commissioners will devote the whole of next summer to the work, and it is expected that they will bring back not only a satisfactory treaty, but much information about this part of Canada.[92]

During the summer of 1899, the *Edmonton Bulletin* printed detailed accounts of the progress of both the Treaty 8 Commission and the Half-breed Commission. Charles Mair, a member of the Half-breed Commission, also published long articles in the *Toronto Globe*. These were later collected in his "Narrative of the Athabasca and Peace River Treaty Expedition of 1899",[93] which is the most comprehensive document available on the subject. The trip was neither a fast nor a pleasant one. Although steamboats had been in service on the Athabasca River for nearly fifteen years, the members of the Treaty party travelled with two scows and one York boat, which were pulled upstream by thirteen trackers. The party left Athabasca Landing on June 2, 1899, but due to lack of manpower, travelled only 8 miles during the first two days. The ten members of the NWMP escort were enlisted to track one of the scows:

> Nothing indeed can be imagined more arduous than this tracking up a swift river, against constant head winds in bad weather. Much of it is in the water, wading up "snies"*, or tortuous shallow channels, plunging into numberless creeks, clambering up slimy banks, creeping under or passing the line over fallen trees, wading out in the stream to round long spits of sand or boulders, floundering in gumbo slides, tripping, crawling, plunging, and, finally, tottering to the camping-place sweating like horses, and mud to the eyes – but never grumbling.[94]

After nineteen days the Treaty party finally reached Lesser Slave Lake. It was time for the Indians to hear "the just and generous terms proffered by Government to an isolated but highly interesting and deserving people".[95] As found in the official Government version, Treaty 8 read as follows:[96]

TREATY No. 8.

ARTICLES OF A TREATY made and concluded at the several dates mentioned therein, in the year of Our Lord one thousand eight hundred and ninety-nine, between Her most Gracious Majesty the Queen of Great Britain and Ireland, by Her Commissioners the Honourable David Laird, of Winnipeg, Manitoba, Indian Commissioner for the said Province and the Northwest Territories; James Andrew Joseph McKenna, of Ottawa, Ontario, Esquire, and the Honourable James Hamilton Ross, of Regina, in the Northwest Territories, of the one part; and the Cree, Beaver, Chipewyan and other Indians, inhabitants of the territory within the limits hereinafter defined and described, by their Chiefs and Headmen, hereunto subscribed, of the other part:

WHEREAS, the Indians inhabiting the territory hereinafter defined have, pursuant to notice given by the Honourable Superintendant General of Indian Affairs in the year 1898, been convened to meet a Commission representing Her Majesty's Government of the Dominion of Canada at cer-

---

*A snye is a narrow channel of a river. This word, commonly used in the North, is the way English speaking people write the French word *chenal*, according to the way it sounds.

tain places in the said territory in this present year 1899, to deliberate upon certain matters of interest to Her Most Gracious Majesty, of the one part, and the said Indians of the other.

AND WHEREAS., the said Indians have been notified and informed by Her Majesty's said Commission that it is Her desire to open for settlement, immigration, trade, travel, mining, lumbering, and such other purposes as to Her Majesty may seem meet, a tract of country bounded and described as hereinafter mentioned, and to obtain the consent thereto of Her Indian subjects inhabiting the said tract, and to make a treaty, and arrange with them, so that there may be peace and good will between them and Her Majesty's other subjects, and that Her Indian people may know and be assured of what allowances they are to count upon and receive from Her Majesty's bounty and benevolence.

AND WHEREAS, the Indians of the said tract, duly convened in council at the respective points named hereunder, and being requested by Her Majesty's Commissioners to name certain Chiefs and Headmen who should be authorized on their behalf to conduct such negotiations and sign any treaty to be founded thereon, and to become responsible to Her Majesty for the faithful performance by their respective bands of such obligations as shall be assumed by them, the said Indians have therefore acknowledged for that purpose the several Chiefs and Headmen who have subscribed hereto.

AND WHEREAS, the said Commissioners have proceeded to negotiate a treaty with the Cree, Beaver, Chipewyan and other Indians, inhabiting the district hereinafter defined and described, and the same has been agreed upon and concluded by the respective bands at the dates mentioned hereunder, the said Indians DO HEREBY CEDE, RELEASE, SURRENDER AND YIELD UP to the Government of the Dominion of Canada, for Her Majesty the Queen and Her successors for ever, all their rights, titles and privileges whatsover, to the lands included within the following limits, that is to say:

Commencing at the source of the main branch of the Red Deer River in Alberta, thence due west to the central range of the Rocky Mountains, thence northwesterly along the said range to the point where it intersects the 60th parallel of north latitude, thence east along said parallel to the point where it intersects Hay River, thence northeasterly down said river to the south shore of Great Slave Lake, thence along the said shore northeasterly (and including such rights to the islands in said lakes as the Indians mentioned in the treaty may possess), and thence easterly and northeasterly along the south shores of Christie's Bay and McLeod's Bay to old Fort Reliance near the mouth of Lockhart's River, thence southeasterly in a straight line to and including Black Lake, thence southwesterly up the stream from Cree Lake, thence including said lake southwesterly along the height of land between the Athabasca and Churchill Rivers to where it intersects the northern boundary of Treaty Six, and along the said boundary easterly, northerly and southwesterly, to the place of commencement.

AND ALSO the said Indian rights, titles and privileges whatsoever to all other lands wherever situated in the Northwest Territories, British Columbia, or in any other portion of the Dominion of Canada.

TO HAVE AND TO HOLD the same to Her Majesty the Queen and Her successors for ever.

And Her Majesty the Queen HEREBY AGREES with the said Indians that they shall have right to pursue their usual vocations of hunting, trapping and fishing throughout the tract surrendered as heretofore described, subject to such regulations as may from time to time be made by the Government of the country, acting under the authority of Her Majesty, and saving and excepting such tracts as may be required or taken up from time to time for settlement, mining, lumbering, trading or other purposes.

And Her Majesty the Queen hereby agrees and undertakes to lay aside reserves for such bands as desire reserves, the same not to exceed in all one square mile for each family of five for such number of families as may elect to reside on reserves, or in that proportion for larger or smaller families; and for such families or individual Indians as may prefer to live apart from band reserves, Her Majesty undertakes to provide land in severalty to the extent of 160 acres to each Indian, the land to be conveyed with a proviso as to non-alienation without the consent of the Governor General in Council of Canada, the selection of such reserves, and lands in severalty, to be made in the manner following, namely, the Superintendent General of Indian Affairs shall depute and send a suitable person to determine and set apart such reserves and lands, after consulting with the Indians concerned as to the locality which may be found suitable and open for selection.

Provided, however, that Her Majesty reserves the right to deal with any settlers within the bounds of any lands reserved for any band as She may see fit; and also that the aforesaid reserves of land, or any interest therein, may be sold or otherwise disposed of by Her Majesty's Government for the use and benefit of the said Indians entitled thereto, with their consent first had and obtained.

It is further agreed between Her Majesty and Her said Indian subjects that such portions of the reserves and lands above indicated as may at any time be required for public works, buildings, railways, or roads of whatsoever nature may be appropriated for that purpose by Her Majesty's Government of the Dominion of Canada, due compensation being made to the Indians for the value of any improvements thereon, and an equivalent in land, money or other consideration for the area of the reserve so appropriated.

And with a view to show the satisfaction of Her Majesty with the behaviour and good conduct of Her Indians, and in extinguishment of all their past claims, She hereby, through Her Commissioners, agrees to make each Chief a present of thirty-two dollars in cash, to each Headman twenty-two dollars, and to every other Indian of whatever age, of the families represented at the time and place of payment, twelve dollars.

Her Majesty also agrees that next year, and annually afterwards for ever, She will cause to be paid to the said Indians in cash, at suitable places and dates, of which the said Indians shall be duly notified, to each Chief twenty-five dollars, each Headman, not to exceed four to a large Band and two to a small Band, fifteen dollars, and to every other Indian, of whatever age, five dollars, the same, unless there be some exceptional reason, to be paid only to heads of families for those belonging thereto.

FURTHER, HER Majesty agrees that each Chief, after signing the treaty, shall receive a silver medal and a suitable flag, and next year, and every third year thereafter, each Chief and Headman shall receive a suitable suit of clothing.

FURTHER, Her Majesty agrees to pay the salaries of such teachers to instruct the children of said Indians as to Her Majesty's Government of Canada may seem advisable.

FURTHER, Her Majesty agrees to supply each Chief of a Band that selects a reserve, for the use of that Band, ten axes, five hand-saws, five augers, one grindstone, and the necessary files and whetstones.

FURTHER, Her Majesty agrees that each Band that elects to take a reserve and cultivate the soil, shall, as soon as convenient after such reserve is set aside and settled upon, and the Band has signified its choice and is prepared to break up the soil, receive two hoes, one spade, one scythe and two hay forks for every family so settled, and for every three families one plough and one harrow, and to the Chief, for the use of his Band, two horses or a yoke of oxen, and for each Band potatoes, barley, oats and wheat (if such seed be suited to the locality of the reserve), to plant the land actually broken up, and provisions for one month in the spring for several years while planting such seeds; and to every family one cow, and every Chief one bull, and one mowing-machine and one reaper for the use of his Band when it is ready for them; for such families as prefer to raise stock instead of cultivating the soil, every family of five persons, two cows, and every Chief two bulls and two mowing-machines when ready for their use, and a like proportion for smaller or larger families. The aforesaid articles, machines and cattle to be given one for all for the encouragement of agriculture and stock raising; and for such Bands as prefer to continue hunting and fishing, as much ammunition and twine for making nets annually as will amount in value to one dollar per head of the families so engaged in hunting and fishing.

And the undersigned Cree, Beaver, Chipewyan and other Indian Chiefs and Headmen, on their own behalf and on behalf of all the Indians whom they represent, DO HEREBY SOLEMNLY PROMISE and engage to strictly observe this Treaty, and also to conduct and behave themselves as good and loyal subjects of Her Majesty the Queen.

THEY PROMISE AND ENGAGE that they will, in all respects, obey and abide by the law; that they will maintain peace between each other, and between themselves and other tribes of Indians, and between themselves and others of Her Majesty's subjects, whether Indians, half-breeds or whites, this year inhabiting and hereafter to inhabit any part of the said ceded territory; and that they will not molest the person or property of any inhabitant of such ceded tract, or of any other district or country, or interfere with or trouble any person passing or travelling through the said tract or any part thereof, and that they will assist the officers of Her Majesty in bringing to justice and punishment any Indian offending against the stipulations of this Treaty or infringing the law in force in the country so ceded.

Treaty 8 Negotiations

Lesser Slave Lake

The Treaty party arrived at Lesser Slave Lake on June 20, 1899, and Treaty 8 was signed first by the Indians at that post on June 21, 1899. The adhesion of this band was considered of great importance, because once the Treaty was signed there, other bands would easily follow. It is not clear from the reports of the Treaty negotiations how well the terms of the Treaty were explained to the Indians, nor how much they understood. Treaty Commissioner Laird gave as one reason for the Treaty that, "the Queen wants all the whites, half-breeds and Indians to be at peace with one another, and to shake hands when they meet."[97] Many prominent Indians took part in negotiations, among them Chief Keenooshayo and Councillor Moostoos. Father Lacombe was called upon to talk to the Indians:

> Father Lacombe spoke at some length in Cree and advised them to take treaty . . . After the Father sat down Commissioner Laird asked them, if they were satisfied, to stand up. A native named Jerou jumped to his feet before the interpreter had finished speaking and threatened to club any man who failed to stand up. They all arose amid much laughter.[98]

James K. Cornwall,* otherwise known as Peace River Jim, left a signed affidavit of his recollections of treaty negotiations at Lesser Slave Lake:

> 1. I was present when Treaty 8 was made at Lesser Slave Lake and Peace River Crossing.
> 2. The treaty, as presented by the Commissioners to the Indians for their approval and signatures, was apparently prepared elsewhere, as it did not contain many things that they held to be of vital importance to their future existence as hunters and trappers and fishermen, free from the competition of white man. They refused to sign the Treaty as read to them by the Chief Commissioner.
> 3. Long discussions took place between the Commissioners and the Indian Chiefs and headmen, with many prominent men of the various bands taking part. The discussion went on for days, the Commissioners had unfavorably impressed the Indians, due to their lack of knowledge of the bush Indians' mode of life, by quoting Indian conditions on the Prairie.
>   Chief Moostoos (the Buffalo) disposed of the argument by telling the Chief Commissioner that "a Plains Indian turned loose in the bush would get lost and starve to death".
> 4. As the Commissioner's instructions from Ottawa required the Treaty to be signed first at Lesser Slave Lake before proceeding North, and as the white population living in the Indian Territory had been requested by the Government, prior to the coming of the Commission, to be prepared to deal with them as such, the whites had done everything in their power to assist the Commissioners, by using every honorable influence that was possible.
> 5. The Commissioners finally decided, after going into the whole matter, that what the Indians suggested was only fair and right but that they had no authority to write it into the Treaty. They felt sure the Government on

---

*Cornwall has been characterized as "the greatest steamboat man," successfully promoting the development of northern Alberta and the Peace River country. He was involved in all aspects of transportation, from building steamships and pioneering new routes, to promoting railway companies.

behalf of the Crown and the Great White Mother would include their request and they made the following promises to the Indians: – –

 a– Nothing would be allowed to interfere with their way of making a living, as they were accustomed to and as their forefathers had done.

 b– The old and destitute would always be taken care of, their future existence would be carefully studied and provided for, and every effort would be made to improve their living conditions.

 c– They were guaranteed protection in their way of living as hunters and trappers, from white competition; they would not be prevented from hunting and fishing as they had always done, so as to enable them to earn their living and maintain their existence.

6. Much stress was laid on one point by the Indians, as follows: They would not sign under any circumstances, unless their right to hunt, trap and fish was guaranteed and it must be understood that these rights they would never surrender.

7. It was only after the Royal Commission had recognized that the demands of the Indians were legitimate, and had solemnly promised that such demands would be granted by the Crown, also, after the Hudson's Bay Company Officials and Free Traders, and the Missionaries, with their Bishops, who had the full confidence of the Indians, had given their word that they could rely fully on the promises made in the name of QUEEN VICTORIA, that the Indians accepted and signed the Treaty, which was to last as long as the grass grew, the river ran, and the sun shone – to an Indian this means FOREVER.[99]

Cornwall did not limit his comments on Treaty 8 to this affidavit. He wrote many memos and letters to the Department of Indian Affairs and to other officials. He became one of the most valiant fighters in support of the specific promises made by the Commissioners to the Indians at the time of the Treaty. His efforts, along with those of other witnesses to the signing, will be discussed in later chapters.

Half-breed Commission

The half-breeds at Lesser Slave Lake made the task of the scrip Commission a difficult one. They objected to the kind of scrip that was offered: non-transferable for themselves and non-negotiable for their children until they reach legal age. In previous land settlements on the prairies, speculators had bought half-breed scrip at unbelievably low prices. To protect the Metis against such abuse, the Government had issued non-transferable scrip for the 1899 negotiations. At Lesser Slave Lake, Lacombe eloquently urged the Metis to safeguard their own and their children's interests by accepting this scrip. But the Metis were adamant and demanded scrip made out to the bearer. If the Commissioners could not agree to their demand, they refused any further negotiations. This decision was undoubtedly influenced by unprecedented amounts of cash brought into the country by itinerant traders and scrip "hunters" who followed the Government Commission. Already some resentful Metis and unscrupulous traders, not fancying tighter Government control in the District, had spread false rumours and set some Indians against the Treaty.

The members of both Commissions held a meeting among themselves and agreed they would have to meet the Metis' demands for transferable scrip. This move was upheld by Lacombe who explained why he had changed his position:

> Referring to the meeting of the Half-Breeds today at which I acted as intermediary and advisor, after careful consideration of what was urged as to the form of scrip, I have come to the conclusion that very much trouble will arise if the parents be not able to make use of their children's scrip for their benefit during their minority. As you have no doubt observed, the Half-Breeds here have evinced more intelligence and industry than did the Half-Breeds to whom scrip was issued in 1870 and 1885, and although I came here strongly impressed with the desirability of doing everything possible to prevent the parents from using the scrip of their children and from freely disposing of their own, the conditions here have led me to the conclusion that action in that direction will not result in any benefit to the Half-Breeds here but to their disadvantage, for they are determined to make prompt use of their scrip and that of their children. I find that the Half-Breeds here, when they heard that scrip was to be issued, counted upon turning it into money for investment in cattle for themselves and their children. Very, very few if any of them will take land scrip, and I am convinced that none of those who take money scrip will use it in direct payment for land, and the result of the impediment to free disposition will therefore be the depreciation of the scrip. They are bound to dispose of it and it is in their interest that they should be in a position to get the best return possible for it. The dissatisfaction with the form of certificate is so great and so widespread that I fear if the Commissioners have to persist in using it the dissatisfaction will spread in advance of the Indian Commission and make it very difficult if not impossible to further extend the treaty which I am so anxious to have all the Indians enter into. In the interest of the Half-Breeds and in the public interest, I would therefore advise that if it be in the power of the Commissioners, they should take upon themselves to amend the scrips as to meet the wishes of the Half-Breeds.[100]

Printed scrips were corrected and made payable to the bearer. The three Anglican ministers in Lesser Slave Lake at the time, congratulated the Half-Breed Commission for having "adopted the wisest course open to you".[101] Whether the Half-Breed Commission had reluctantly yielded to pressure, or really believed its own arguments, the decision cost the Metis dearly. Scrip buyers made an easy fortune. A total of 1,195 money scrips at $240 each, and 48 land scrips for 240 acres of land were issued throughout the Treaty 8 area. Over half went to Metis at Lesser Slave Lake. The Metis at Fort Smith could not be reached by the Commission and received their scrips only in November. Perhaps they were spared the gouging which went on at all the other posts that summer. For $75 cash, two Winnipeg bankers, Alloway and Champion bought the first scrip issued to the Metis at Lesser Slave Lake.[102]

The highest price paid for scrip was at the Landing [Peace River

Landing]. There the competition was very keen and up to $130 was paid for a $240 scrip. The lowest price was at Vermilion and Wolverine Point, on Peace River. There the price was as low as $70. C. Alloway of Winnipeg followed the Commission throughout, buying scrip. R. Secord also bought on Upper Peace River, the Athabasca and Wapiscow. But on the Lower Peace Alloway had the market to himself.[103]

The Government had dealt with the Metis. Their account was settled and the books closed.

Fort Chipewyan

The Treaty Commission had suffered such a delay that its members wondered if they could complete their work that summer. Once the Treaty had been signed at Lesser Slave Lake, "not having had any trouble or controversy with the Indians, the Commissioners were able to divide sometimes into three parties and pay treaty at three different places at once".[104] McKenna's party arrived at Fort Chipewyan on July 13, 1899. An account of the event is found in the diary of the Catholic mission:

July 13 – Two members of the Commission . . . landed here at noon and called a meeting of all the Indians for 3 P.M. The meeting took place in the Fort's [Hudson's Bay Company's] yard. All the heads of families were present. Noticing that the missionaries were absent from the gathering, Mr. McKenna wrote and invited them to be present at the discussions, and all the Fathers went there.

The Commissioner explained the Government's views and the advantages it offered to the people. The Chief of the Crees spoke up and expressed the conditions on which he would accept the Government's proposals:

    1. Complete freedom to fish.
    2. Complete freedom to hunt.
    3. Complete freedom to trap.
    4. As himself and his people are Catholics, he wants their children to be educated in Catholic schools.

In his turn, the Chipewyan spokesman set the same conditions as the first speaker. The Commissioner acknowledged all the requests which both had voiced.

Mr. Driver, in charge of the Fort, interpreted for the Crees, and Mr. Pierre Mercredi, his assistant, interpreted for the Chipewyans.

Then the Treaty was read and signed by both Government representatives, and witnessed by the Fathers, and by the most important people of the locality.

The Treaty Commissioners nominated a chief for the Chipewyans who had no chief until then. The Treaty Commissioners also officially acknowledged the Cree Chief previously chosen by the band. Two councillors were given to each of the Chiefs, to replace them if need be.

The Chief of the Crees was named Justin Marten (Mekitin), and the Chief of the Chipewyans is Alexandre Laviolette . . . As it was already 9 P.M. and everybody was feeling tired due to this day's excessive temperature, treaty money was paid to the Chiefs only. All the other people would be paid the following day . . . . At noon, the next day (July 14) everything was over and both Commissioners left for Fort Smith.[105]

The journal of the Hudson's Bay Company related the event with very similar details:

(1899) 13 July: The Indian Commissioners J. H. Ross and James McKinnal [McKenna] arrived to treat with the Chipewyans and Cree Indians and they all assembled at 4 o'clock P.M. and the Treaty was concluded and signed by the Indian Chief Alexandre Laviolette and Headmen Julien Ratfat and Sept Heezell and by the Commissioners and 3 Priests and some Coys [Company's] clerks and Colin Fraser [a free trader].
14 July: . . . The Commissioners are dealing out the Money to the Treaty people in the forenoon and left after dinner.[106]

McKenna recalls that the Chipewyans had a long list of demands including a railway link with the south. They were skeptical about the Treaty and wanted answers for many questions:

These Chipewyans lost no time in flowery oratory, but came at once to business, and kept us, myself in particular, on tenter hooks for two hours. I never felt so relieved as when the rain of questions ended, and, satisfied by our answers, they acquiesced in the cession.[107]

Father Breynat's recollection of the occasion reflects the main concern of the Indians:

Discussions were long enough but sincere; Crees and Chipewyans refused to be treated like Prairie Indians, and to be parked on reserves. . . . It was essential to them to retain complete freedom to move around.[108]

By noon the next day, the distribution of treaty money was over and the Treaty Commissioners left for Fort Smith. In the evening Laird, Grouard and Lacombe, all members of the second Treaty group, sailed into Fort Chipewyan, accompanied by Brother Jean Marie le Creff. The appearance of this second group was cause for special celebration. A correspondent from the *Edmonton Bulletin,* who was on board the scow, recounts that he was quite startled when they received the customary welcome and were,

. . . greeted by a general firing of guns by the Indians and Half-breeds as well as the Free traders on shore, and it looked from the boats in the dark as if a battle were raging, judging by the flashes seen in all directions. The shore for about a mile was literally ablaze.[109]

During his stay, Lacombe was to note in his diary that "The Treaty was made amiably. All the Indians are contented".[110] In the chronicle of the Grey Nuns no mention is made of the Treaty, other than details of the reception given by the school children for the visitors.[111]

It would seem that few people were concerned with the land ownership question, the real reason for the coming of these visitors. The Indians themselves were satisfied with the Treaty, believing that it would protect their freedom to hunt, trap, fish, and move freely through the country. For them, these were the real issues. Pierre Mercredi, interpreter for the Chipewyan, indicated in a later statement what had become of that precious freedom to hunt:

> I interpreted the words of Queen Victoria to Alexandre Laviolette, Chief of the Chipewyans and his band . . . I know, because I read the Treaty to them, that there was no clause in it which said they might have to obey regulations about hunting. They left us no copy of the Treaty we signed, saying that they would have it printed and send a copy to us. When the copy came back, that second clause (that they shall promise to obey whatever hunting regulations the Dominion Government shall set) was in it. It was not there before. I never read it to the Chipewyans or explained it to them. I have no doubt that the new regulation breaks that old treaty. It makes me feel bad altogether because it makes lies of the words I spoke then for Queen Victoria.
>
> Just after the treaty was signed, and the new copy came here, the Indian Agent said that the Chipewyan people could not kill beaver because of a new law. The old Chief came to me and told me that I had spoken the words for Queen Victoria and they were lies. He said that if she had come and said those words herself, then, and broken them, she would have been an awful liar.[112]

This was only the beginning of a gradual, but steady erosion of the Treaty promises made in 1899.

Fond du Lac

Father Breynat travelled back to his mission at Fond du Lac with the second Treaty group, leaving Fort Chipewyan on July 18, 1899. He explained to Laird that his duties would prevent him from taking part in Treaty meetings and negotiations. The Indians would certainly be leaving for the caribou hunt right after Treaty day, and he would have much to do. Events drew him into the Treaty discussions, however, according to his own account:

> The Indians were wearied from already waiting so long after the scheduled date for the treaty and they eagerly went to the meeting. Chief and councillors were elected and accepted without any difficulty.
>
> The meeting took place a few steps from the mission. Right after the text of the proposed treaty had been read, translated and explained, the Honorable Laird knocked at my door.
>
> "Complete failure!" he said. "We must fold down our tents, pack our baggage and leave."
>
> He explained that as soon as the discussion started, Chief Moberley . . . nearly got into a fight with the interpreter, good-natured Robillard. They had already taken off their vests, and the police had intervened. The chief had jumped into his canoe and left to the other side of the bay.
>
> "Evidently there is nothing we can do," added Laird pitifully, with tears

in his eyes. He was a good old man with a sensitive heart. I offered him my sympathy:

"Let me try," I said, "everything might turn out all right."

Chief Moberley was the very best hunter of the entire tribe. How many times his gun had saved indigent people who without him would have died of starvation. He was also very conscious of his superiority and his pride would not tolerate any opposition. He feared that the treaty might restrain his freedom. His pride could only despise the yearly five-dollar bait offered to each of his tribesmen in return for the surrender of their rights, until then undisputed, and which, one must admit, rightly so – he held as incontestable.

Robillard tried to placate him by explaining this and that – he only made him angrier. Thus the fight!

I called for one of the elected councillors, Dzieddin ("The Deaf"), known for his good character, his great heart and his good judgement. I explained to him: "If Chief Moberley, a great hunter and a very proud man, can despise and reject the help offered by the government, many old people without any income and many orphans, will appreciate receiving a five dollar annuity along with free powder, bullets, fishnets etc." I added, "Accept and sign the treaty on behalf of all those poor people. Anyway, even all of you together, all the Caribou Eaters, you cannot help it. You may accept the Treaty or not, but in either way the Queen's Government will come, and set up its own organization in your country. The compensation offered by the Government may be quite small, but to refuse it would only deprive the poor people of much-needed help."

Dzieddin was convinced by this argument and he signed the treaty. Many Indians had previously always been needy. Now they started to leave the Hudson's Bay store and those of the free traders who had followed the treaty party, looking like wealthy people with supplies of tea, flour, sugar, gunpowder etc. Some families had received as much as $150 or more. The better off people who had sided with Chief Moberley were gradually drawn by the lure of an easy gain and came to receive their allowance.

One of the Chief's best friends came to me for advice – "So many people have already accepted Treaty. Don't you think it would also be good for me to accept it?"

At last Chief Moberley himself came, with two or three of the last objectors. They went back, with happy hearts and a canoe loaded with goods. The first day's quarrel was completely forgotten. Good old Robillard, the interpreter, was laughing within himself when he shook hands with them in farewell.[114]

The treaty document for the Fond du Lac band bears two sets of signatures. Laurent Dzieddin and another councillor, Toussaint, signed first. Moberley, also known as Maurice Piché, signed two days later as "Chief of Band". A note above his signature reads:

The number accepting Treaty being larger than at first expected, a Chief was allowed, who signed the Treaty on the 27th of July before the same witnesses to signatures of the Commissioner and Headmen on the 25th.[115]

The Treaty 8 Indian Annuities Book shows that Moberley's band, 383 members, received their treaty money on July 25, 1899. The first person paid was Laurent Tzaddie, headman, [Dzieddin], and the second was Toussaint, headman. Maurice Piché (Moberley) was 84th. He received $12 as everyone else, and then, "after treaty, was elected Chief and paid $20 more". A final entry in the Annuities Book repeats: "Paid No. 84 as Chief".[117] Articles appearing in the *Edmonton Bulletin* gave this optimistic report of events at Fond du Lac:

> Commissioner Laird, who had gone to Fond du Lac at the easterly end of Lake Athabasca, had been successful there.[118]

> The Treaty negotiations have been very successful. At Fond du Lac, on Lake Athabasca, where it was expected that no more than 200 Indians would be found, 380 were paid. These were the most removed from civilization of any of the Indians treated with. They are Chipewyans and live on the Caribou of the barren grounds. They made some difficulty about the Treaty at first, fearing that their acceptance of money would bind them personally in some way. Their little acquaintance with the Whites had made it possible to circulate silly stories amongst them with some success. But in the end all came in.[119]

In his diary of 1899, Breynat recorded the Indians' reluctance to sign a treaty and his own feelings that a treaty was unavoidable:

> Whether we like it or not, the Government steps into the country and it has absolute power. Instead of risking the loss of everything, it was wiser for the Indians to accept, as a lesser evil, the Government's proposals which anyway are relatively liberal.
>
> Right away, the distrust of the Indians, so often deceived in their trading, was obvious. Having also been excited by some troublesome Metis whispering all kinds of stories into their ears, they firmly refused to accept offers which seemed to be too good to be sincere.
>
> Although the good Mr. Laird declared again and again that he was totally unconcerned, he could hardly hide the deep frustration caused by his failure. He would have had to pack (which he had already started to do), and go somewhere else for better luck, without the intervention of the priest.[120]

Although his mediation had "alienated for a while some people whose pride he had wounded", Breynat never regretted his role in the Fond du Lac negotiations. He considered the Treaty to be primarily a friendship treaty, as did most people in the North. For a newspaper interview many years later, Breynat was able to look back and assess the significance of what he had done:

> In 1899 and 1900 a royal commission, headed by Hon. David Laird, travelled through the north negotiating treaties with the Indians. At Fort Smith, Fort Chipewyan and other northern points, their overtures were met with haughty refusals from the natives.

Content with their lives as hunters and fishermen, these children of the woods were suspicious of the white men for they had heard stories from the south.

Bishop Breynat was acting as interpreter for the commission at many of the points* and, at the request of the commissioner, undertook to persuade the Indians to sign the Treaty.

The natives had great faith in their bishop, and explained their objections to him. He in turn explained them to the commissioner, and when a satisfactory arrangement had been reached, the Natives signed the Treaty, with Bishop Breynat's personal assurance that all the promises would be kept.†

"That is why I am so interested in seeing that the Indians of the north receive fair treatment. I gave them my word. And I have always been taught, and taught others, that promises should be kept. So I must see that the promises I made to those Natives on behalf of the commissioners are respected," Bishop Breynat explains today.[121]

Smith's Landing – Fort Smith

Travelling down the Slave River from Fort Chipewyan, the Treaty party reached Smith's Landing on July 15, 1899, and treated with 270 Chipewyans on July 17.[122] "There was no difficulty in making the treaty at Fort Smith".[123] Few documents are available to verify this, and the recollections of Antoine Beaulieu, a 16 year old boy at the time, add only a few details. He speaks of what impressed him most:

What I understood then was that they won't stop us from killing anything and there won't be no law against anything, game and so on. . . . They said if you take this money you will never be in trouble or hard up or anything if you take this money . . . all they done was had some talk then paid out the treaty . . . In one day it was all over.[124]

The Treaty party left Smith's Landing on July 18th by the Hudson's Bay Company's steamer Grahame, on their southbound trip to Fort McMurray.[125]

Journey Completed

On August 4, 1899, Lacombe wrote in his diary: "everything goes as everywhere else . . . everybody satisfied".[126] The Treaty had just been signed at Fort McMurray and the Treaty trip was nearing its completion. Upon returning to Edmonton, Lacombe sent this report to Sifton on September 10, 1899:

The Honourable Mr. Laird, our leader . . . His kindness, his politeness, his patience and his ability toward the Indians as well as the Halfbreeds and Whites have been of great help for the success of our mission. So in the same way the other members of the two commissions have acquired the

*Evidence shows that young Father Breynat did not take part in Treaty 8 negotiations other than at Fond du Lac.

†Obviously, this paragraph refers only to Breynat's role in 1921.

esteem and consideration of the different tribes, among whom the treaties have been made. Everywhere we passed the Halfbreeds and Indians have received the commissions with great satisfaction and happiness. Everywhere the treaties and issuing of scrips have been performed to the satisfaction of all concerned.

As advisor of the commissions, I hope that I have done all in my power to help the Government in interpreting and explaining to the Halfbreeds and the Indians the intentions and good will of the Government toward the good of their future . . . . Another thing very important and of a great help to us in our work was the presence of Doctor West with the commissions. His kindness and good work to attend so carefully the sick we met on our way, gained for our party a great sympathy and sincere gratitude toward your Government. Doctor West knows well the way of dealing best with the Indians and sick Halfbreeds . . . So I am happy in stating that the commissions you have appointed to proceed with the Indian Treaties in the Athabaskan District have been successful to the satisfaction of all, and this enterprise so well accomplished is a great credit to your Government. Of course the country has been put to great expense to fulfill such an undertaking, but that money has not been wasted; the result shows that it has been properly used . . . . I am happy to have done some good for the Indians and Halfbreeds and have proved once more in this country my good will toward the ruling powers of the Dominion . . . [127]

In a final article on the Treaty party, the *Edmonton Bulletin* commented that the only difficulty in dealing with the Indians had arisen "from the fact that they had very loose initial organization". With some perspicacity the reporter concluded: "all now hinges on the manner in which promises made are fulfilled in the future."[128]

The official report of the Treaty 8 Commission was presented to the Minister of the Interior, the Honourable Sifton, on September 22, 1899.[129]

Sir, – We have the honour to transmit herewith the treaty which, under the Commission issued to us on the 5th day of April last, we have made with the Indians of the provisional district of Athabasca and parts of the country adjacent thereto, as described in the treaty and shown on the map attached.

The date fixed for meeting the Indians at Lesser Slave Lake was the 8th of June, 1899. Owing, however, to unfavourable weather and lack of boatmen, we did not reach the point until the 19th. But one of the Commissioners – Mr. Ross – who went overland from Edmonton to the Lake, was fortunately present when the Indians first gathered. He was thus able to counteract the consequences of the delay and to expedite the work of the Commission by preliminary explanations of its objects.

We met the Indians on the 20th, and on the 21st the treaty was signed.

As the discussions at the different points followed on much the same lines, we shall confine ourselves to a general statement of their import. There was a marked absence of the old Indian style of oratory. Only among the Wood Crees were any formal speeches made, and these were brief. The Beaver Indians are taciturn. The Chipewyans confined themselves to asking questions and making brief arguments. They appeared to be more adept at cross-examination than at speech-making, and the Chief at Fort Chipewyan displayed considerable keenness of intellect and much practical sense in pressing the claims of his band. They all wanted as liberal, if not more liberal terms, than were granted to the Indians of the plains. Some expected to be fed by the Government after the making of treaty, and all asked for assistance in seasons of distress and urged that the old and indigent who were no longer able to hunt and trap and were consequently often in distress should be cared for by the Government. They requested that medicines be furnished. At Vermilion, Chipewyan and Smith's Landing, an earnest appeal was made for the services of a medical man. There was expressed at every point the fear that the making of the treaty would be followed by the curtailment of the hunting and fishing privileges, and many were impressed with the notion that the treaty would lead to taxation and enforced military service. They seemed desirous of securing educational advantages for their children, but stipulated that in the matter of schools there should be no interference with their religious beliefs.

We pointed out that the Government could not undertake to maintain Indians in idleness; that the same means of earning a livelihood would continue after the treaty as existed before it, and that the Indians would be expected to make use of them. We told them that the Government was always ready to give relief in cases of actual destitution, and that in seasons of distress they would without any special stipulation in the treaty receive such assistance as it was usual to give in order to prevent starvation among Indians in any part of Canada; and we stated that the attention of the Government would be called to the need of some special provision being made for assisting the old and indigent who were unable to work and dependent on charity for the means of sustaining life. We promised that supplies of medicines would be put in the charge of persons selected by the Government at different points, and would be distributed free to those of the Indians who might require them. We explained that it would be practically impossible for the Government to arrange for regular medical attendance upon Indians so widely scattered over such an extensive territory. We assured them, however, that the Government would always be ready to avail itself of any opportunity of affording medical service just as it provided that the the physician attached to the Commission should give free attendance to all Indians whom he might find in need of treatment as he passed through the country.

Our chief difficulty was the apprehension that the hunting and fishing privileges were to be curtailed. The provision in the treaty under which ammunition and twine is to be furnished went far in the direction of quieting the fears of the Indians, for they admitted that it would be unreasonable to furnish the means of hunting and fishing if laws were to be enacted which would make hunting and fishing so restricted as to render it impossible to make a livelihood by such pursuits. But over and above the provision, we had to solemnly assure them that only such laws as to hunting and fishing as were in the interest of the Indians and were found necessary in order to protect the fish and fur-bearing animals would be made, and that they would be as free to hunt and fish after the treaty as they would be if they never entered into it.

We assured them that the treaty would not lead to any forced interference with their mode of life, that it did not open the way to the imposition of any tax, and that there was no fear of enforced military service. We showed them that, whether treaty was made or not, they were subject to the law, bound to obey it, and liable to punishment for any infringements of it. We pointed out that the law was designed for the protection of all, and must be respected by all the inhabitants of the country, irrespective of colour or origin; and that, in requiring them to live at peace with white men who came into the country, and not to molest them in person or in property, it only required them to do what white men were required to do as to the Indians.

As to education, the Indians were assured that there was no need of any special stipulation, as it was the policy of the Government to provide in every part of the country, as far as circumstances would permit, for the education of Indian children, and that the law, which was as strong as a treaty, provided for non-interference with the religion of the Indians in schools maintained or assisted by the Government.

We should add that the chief of the Chipewyans of Fort Chipewyan asked that the Government should undertake to have a railway built into the country, as the cost of goods which the Indians require would be thereby cheapened and the prosperity of the country enhanced. He was told that the Commissioners had no authority to make any statement in the matter further than to say that his desire would be made known to the Government.

When we conferred, after the first meeting with the Indians at Lesser Slave Lake, we came to the conclusion that it would be best to make one treaty covering the whole of the territory ceded, and to take adhesions thereto from the Indians to be met at the other points rather than to make several separate treaties. The treaty was therefore so drawn as to provide three ways in which assistance is to be given to the Indians, in order to accord with the conditions of the country and to meet the requirements of the Indians in the different parts of the territory.

In addition to the annuity, which we found it necessary to fix at the figures of Treaty Six, which covers adjacent territory, the treaty stipulates that assistance in the form of seed and implements and cattle will be given to those of the Indians who may take to farming, in the way of cattle and mowers to those who may devote themselves to cattle-raising, and that ammunition and twine will be given to those who continue to fish and hunt. The assistance in farming and ranching is only to be given when the Indians actually take to these pursuits, and it is not likely that for many years there will be a call for any considerable expenditure under these heads. The only Indians of the territory ceded who are likely to take to cattle-raising are those about Lesser Slave Lake and along the Peace River, where there is quite an extent of ranching country; and although there are stretches of cultivable land in those parts of the country, it is not probable that the Indians will, while present conditions obtain, engage in farming further than the raising of roots in a small way, as is now done to some extent. In the main the demand will be for ammunition and twine, as the great majority of the Indians will continue to hunt and fish for a livelihood. It does not appear likely that the conditions of the country on either side of the Athabasca and Slave Rivers or about Athabasca Lake will be so changed as to affect hunting or trapping, and it is safe to say that so long as the fur-bearing animals remain, the great bulk of the Indians will continue to hunt and to trap.

The Indians are given the option of taking reserves or land in severalty. As the extent of the country treated for made it impossible to define reserves or holdings, and as the Indians were not prepared to make selections, we confined ourselves to an undertaking to have reserves and holdings set apart in the future, and the Indians were satisfied with the promise that this would be done when required. There is no immediate necessity for the general laying out of reserves or the allotting of land. It will be quite time enough to do this as advancing settlement makes necessary the surveying of the land. Indeed, the Indians were generally averse to being placed on reserves. It would have been impossible to have made a treaty if we had not assured them that there was no intention of confining them to reserves. We had to very clearly explain to them that the provision for reserves and allotments of land were made for their protection, and to secure to them in perpetuity a fair portion of the land ceded, in the event of settlement advancing.

After making the treaty at Lesser Slave Lake it was decided that, in order to offset the delay already referred to, it would be necessary for the Commission to divide. Mr. Ross and Mr. McKenna accordingly set out for Fort St. John on the 22nd of June. The date appointed for meeting the Indians there was the 21st. When the decision to divide was come to, a special messenger was despatched to the Fort with a message to the Indians explaining the delay, advising them that Commissioners were travelling to meet them, and requesting them to wait at the Fort. Unfortunately the Indians had dispersed and gone to their hunting grounds before the messenger arrived and weeks before the date originally fixed for the meeting, and when the Commissioners got within some miles of St. John the messenger met them with a letter from the Hudson's Bay Company's officer there advising them that the Indians after consuming all their provisions, set off on the 1st June in four different bands and in as many different directions for the regular hunt; that there was not a man at St. John who knew the country and could carry word of the Commissioners' coming, and even if there were it would take three weeks or a month to get the Indians in. Of course there was nothing to do but return. It may be stated, however, that what happened was not altogether unforeseen. We had grave doubts of being able to get to St. John in time to meet the Indians, but as they were reported to be rather disturbed and ill-disposed on account of the actions of miners passing through their country, it was thought that it would be well to show them that the Commissioners were prepared to go into their country, and that they had put forth every possible effort to keep the engagement made by the Government.

The Commissioners on their return from St. John met the Beaver Indians of Dunvegan on the 21st day of June and secured their adhesion to the treaty. They then proceeded to Fort Chipewyan and to Smith's Landing on the Slave River and secured the adhesion of the Cree and Chipewyan Indians at these points on the 13th and 17th days of July respectively.

In the meantime, Mr. Laird met the Cree and Beaver Indians at Peace River Landing and Vermilion, and secured their adhesion on the 1st and 8th days of July respectively. He then proceeded to Fond du Lac on Lake Athabasca, and obtained the adhesion of the Chipewyan Indians there on the 25th and 27th days of July.

After treating with the Indians at Smith, Mr. Ross and Mr. McKenna found it necessary to separate in order to make sure of meeting the Indians at Wabiscow on the date fixed. Mr. McKenna accordingly went to Fort McMurray, where he secured the adhesion of the Chipewyan and Cree Indians on the 4th day of August, and Mr. Ross proceeded to Wabiscow, where he obtained the adhesion of the Cree Indians on the 14th day of August.

The Indians with whom we treated differ in many respects from the Indians of the organized territories. They indulge in neither paint nor feathers, and never clothe themselves in blankets. Their dress is of the ordinary style and many of them were well clothed. In the summer they live in teepees, but many of them have log houses in which they live in winter. The Cree language is the chief language of trade, and some of the Beavers and Chipewyans speak it in addition to their own tongues. All the Indians we met were with rare exceptions professing Christians, and showed evidences of the work which missionaries have carried on among them for many years. A few of them have had their children avail themselves of the advantages afforded by boarding schools established at different missions. None of the tribes appear to have any very definite organization. They are held together mainly by the language bond. The chiefs and headmen are simply the most efficient hunters and trappers. They are not law-makers and leaders in the sense that the chiefs and headmen of the plains and of old Canada were. The tribes have no very distinctive characteristics, and as far as we could learn no traditions of any import. The Wood Crees are an off-shoot of the Crees of the South. The Beaver Indians bear some resemblance to the Indians west of the mountains. The Chipewyans are physically the superior tribe. The Beavers have apparently suffered most from scrofula and phthisis, and there are marks of these diseases more or less among all the tribes.

Although in manners and dress the Indians of the North are much further advanced in civilization than other Indians were when treaties were made with them, they stand as much in need of the protection afforded by the law to aborigines as do any other Indians of the country, and are as fit subjects for the paternal care of the Government.

It may be pointed out that hunting in the North differs from hunting as it was on the plains in that the Indians hunt in a wooded country and instead of moving in bands go individually or in family groups.

Our journey from point to point was so hurried that we are not in a position to give any description of the country ceded which would be of value. But we may say that about Lesser Slave Lake there are stretches of country which appear well suited for ranching and mixed farming; that on both sides of the Peace River there are extensive prairies and some well wooded country; that at Vermilion, on the Peace, two settlers have successfully carried on mixed farming on a pretty extensive scale for several years, and that the appearance of the cultivated fields of the Mission there in July showed that cereals and roots were as well advanced as in any portion of the organized territories. The country along the Athabasca River is well wooded and there are miles of tar-saturated banks. But as far as our restricted view of the Lake Athabasca and Slave River country enabled us to judge, its wealth, apart from possible mineral development, consists exclusively in its fisheries and furs.

In going from Peace River Crossing to St. John, the trail which is being constructed under the supervision of the Territorial Government from moneys provided by Parliament was passed over. It was found to be well located. The grading and bridge work is of a permanent character, and the road is sure to be an important factor in the development of the country.

We desire to express our high appreciation of the valuable and most willing service rendered by Inspector Snyder and the corps of police under him, and at the same time to testify to the efficient manner in which the members of our staff performed their several duties. The presence of a medical man was much appreciated by the Indians, and Dr. West, the physician to the Commission, was most assiduous in attending to the great number of Indians who sought his services. We would add that the Very Reverend Father Lacombe, who was attached to the Commission, zealously assisted us in treating with the Crees.

The actual number of Indians paid was: –

7 Chiefs at $32	$ 224	00
23 Headmen at $22	506	00
2,187 Indians at $12	26,244	00
	$26,974	00

A detailed statement of the Indians treated with and of the money paid is appended.

We have the honour to be, sir,
Your obedient servants,
DAVID LAIRD,
J. H. ROSS,
J. A. J. McKENNA,
Indian Treaty Commissioners.

The Treaty party of 1899 had successfully accomplished its assignment. No untoward incidents had disrupted the official plan to extend Canadian jurisdiction further to the North and West,

> . . . the whole population of Indians and Half-breeds throughout the district of Athabasca are perfectly satisfied with the liberal manner in which they have been dealt with by the Government of Canada, and in consequence no trouble or friction whatever need be apprehended in bringing the country under Government control.[130]

Most of the Indians and Metis of the country had been visited by the Treaty party. A few bands had not been reached, however, and Treaty would be offered to them the following year.

Fort Resolution, Summer, 1900

The following summer a new commissioner, Macrae, visited four posts and secured the adhesion of 1,200 Indians to the Treaty. Two Indian bands, apparently still unknown to the government, seemed to have asked for Treaty with such insistence in 1900 that Macrae could not rebuff them.

There came to meet me . . . two bands of Indians, undoubted inhabitants of the tract covered by Treaty No. 8, with whom I was not empowered to deal, one of Crees from Sturgeon Lake and one of Slaves from the Upper Hay River. Both of these desired to enter into treaty, and it became necessary to decide whether they, after having come from distant points to meet one whom they looked upon as a representative of the government, were to be dismissed nonplussed and dissatisfied, or be allowed to give in their adhesions. It being impossible to communicate with the department, and as the title of these people to the benefits of the treaty was beyond question, the conclusion was unhesitatingly adopted that it was my duty to assume responsibility and concede those benefits to them.[131]

The Dogrib, Yellowknife, Slavey and Chipewyan bands, inhabiting the shores of the Great Slave Lake, met with the Treaty party at Fort Resolution. There is no written account of what happened there, other than the official text of the Treaty. But the events of those days can be reconstructed, by the recollections of Indian people who were present at the time. One of them, Johnny Jean Beaulieu, born in 1888, remembered:

I was a young boy at the time . . . Some white men had come to Fort Resolution . . . There was talk that they were going to make a treaty in Fort Resolution. This started the people discussing it among themselves; some said that it wasn't worthwhile at all because the future was unknown and a treaty signed would be no good. Others felt that treaty simply meant that they would be given a sum of money. So they left it all up to the Chief. If the Chief agreed that they could accept the money, they would.[132]

Susie* (Joseph) Abel, Dogrib, was present at Treaty negotiations with his family and band. Seventy years later he gave this interesting testimony:

Finally the Agent showed up. They came up the sny, crossing the bay. We had never seen a scow before – It was just like a little rocky island, it was so big. And when it got closer we saw a red cloth – we know now that it was a flag, but did not know it then. They were getting closer, closer. Now we saw the big oars, splashing water once in a while, one oar for one man. The boat had no head, that is, it was not pointed in the bow. We had never before seen a boat with no head. The sun was just about setting. After sundown they landed.

We all went to meet the boat. We had never seen a scow before. It hit the shore with its flat head. It was just like a wharf. We all looked at how it was made.

The Agent walked up to meet us. He said, "I'm pleased to see all this bunch. It is late in the season. I was afraid everyone had left for the bush. On the Queen's word I have come with money. I'm going to issue the money to all the Indians. I am pleased that lots of people are still here." And one of the Indian leaders told the Agent, "You are glad to meet us. But everyone is pretty near starving. We were supposed to leave the fort.

*In most northern Indian languages, there is no "J" sound. "Susie" is the common way to pronounce the English "Joseph."

But we heard you were coming, so we've been waiting without food." The Agent said, "I haven't got much food, but I brought some flour and bacon. I can give you some flour and bacon for the kids and old people. It is late now, so we won't talk more. But I will give you 700 pounds of flour and 300 pounds of bacon. You can divide it among yourselves."

So the Indians took the flour. One of the leaders gave it out to all the people. They opened the sacks and gave a cup to every person. In those days we didn't have many dishes. So some guys took their shirts off and they took the flour in their shirts. But some, even in their camp had nothing to put the flour in. Some women – in those days they wore aprons – they picked up their aprons to put the flour in. Someone cut the bacon. They threw it in the apron on top of the flour. When they had given out all the flour and bacon, everyone was so happy, they were frying bacon and cooking bannock. You could hardly see all night from the smoke of the frying bacon.

The Agent said, "Tomorrow, I am going to put up a tent. We will have a meeting before I give money. Everyone – old, young – has got to come and hear what is said." So the Indians went back to their tents, and the Agent went back to the scow. In the scow there was a place to sleep. We saw all the mosquito bars rigged inside the scow. In those days there were no White men except the trader, the Mission, and the interpreter. So there was no place for a white stranger to sleep.

In the morning, the Agent put up a tent. We had never seen a one-pole tent before. It was a great big one. Everyone went over to listen. When we got to the tent there was a table and chairs for the Agent and the interpreter. We sat on the ground on one side. The Treaty Commissioner said, "We don't come to make trouble. We come for peace and to talk about money. We come for peace. From now on, there will be lots of White men. So if the White men come you will treat them just like your own brothers. And the White men, if they see a poor Indian in trouble, they will help, just like he was their own brother. That is why we came here. There will be lots of Métis (of Whites and Indians) later on. From now on White men and Indians are going to be like one family. That is why I tell you this. We have never talked about this before, and you will remember it. That is why I brought this money."

An Indian by the name of N'doah said, "Funny, this is the first time we have gotten free money." None of the Indians liked the way N'doah sounded (they were afraid he would make trouble). So they said that they were going to take another man to speak. So they took Old Drygeese for the Indians. The old people said, "Andare Wetah (Old Drygeese) is the man to talk for us." And Andare Wetah said, "All right, I will talk for you."

Drygeese said, "This money never happened before, so we want to know if something will be changed later. If it is going to change, if you want to change our lives, then it is no use taking treaty, because without treaty we are making a living for ourselves and our families."

The Agent said, "We are not looking for trouble. It will not change your life. We are just making peace between Whites and Indians – for them to treat each other well. And we do not want to change your hunting. If Whites should prospect, stake claims, that will not harm anyone. I have come here to issue this money, that is all."

So Drygeese said, "All right, if you're going to give us money. But before you issue money I want you to sign what you said and let me have one copy of what you sign."

Big Michel, Michel Mandeville, was interpreter. He was a good interpreter.

Drygeese said, "We won't stop you from giving us treaty, but we are going to have a meeting amongst ourselves, especially the old people, today. So if you want to give treaty, it will have to be tomorrow."

So everyone went home. The old people were talking amongst themselves. I [Susie Abel] didn't follow the old people, because I was just a young man, so I didn't know what they talked about.

The next day they came back to the tent for treaty. When they had all gathered, Drygeese spoke to the Agent, "Don't hide anything that I don't hear. Maybe later on you are going to stop us from hunting or trapping or chopping trees down or something. So tell me the truth. I want to know before we take treaty." The Agent said, "I do what I am told – give you fellows money. There will be no trouble for anybody. We will not stop anything."

Drygeese said, "If that's the way it is, I want to tell you something. As you have said, 'As long as the world does not change, the sun does not change, the river does not change, we will like to have peace – if it is that way, we will take the money and I want you the Agent to sign that that is the way it is going to be." . . . "I would like a written promise from you to prove you are not taking our land away from us." . . . Then Chief Drygeese said, "There will be no closed season on our land. There will be nothing said about the land. I may be the Chief, but I would like to hear what my people have to say." All the people agreed.

The Agent said, "OK." So he signed the paper. So they gave us the money now.

The Agent gave Drygeese one sheet, and there was a sheet for the Agent, and one for the Hudson's Bay man to keep. The Agent signed four sheets.

That was the first time we saw money. Every person got $12.00, even the kids. ([I] was a young man then, and in those days, if your dad was alive you were not the boss and your Dad did all the trading – that is, collected the money in this case).

In those days, we never saw cash before, we just traded. We didn't know how to use it. So the trader told the Indians, "If you want to spend money in here, the money you got for your whole family, if you spend it here (in my store), I'm going to give you extra goods, maybe $10 or $15 extra."

There were two stores, Northern Traders, and the Hudson's Bay Company. So the Indians didn't know how to handle the money. They just took $1 to buy this, another $1 to buy that. So that's why the trader offered us maybe $25 or so in extra goods, if we spent it all in his store.

So they gave us treaty. And they picked up all the Chiefs and Councillors from all over. They put Drygeese as head Chief [that is, for the Dogrib Band], and next is Benaiyah, and the next is Sek'eglinan. These were the three Chiefs for Wuledeh [Yellowknife River Dogrib Band].[133]

The role of Drygeese, Dogrib Chief, remained vivid in the memory of

Joseph Abel. Chipewyan Indians, on the other hand, would remember the part played by their own Chief. Details clearly remembered by one person may have been forgotten by others. In order to present events in chronological order, several transcripts have been combined. Obvious repetitions indicate that the testimonies agree on important issues.*

Angus Beaulieu: The Indians thought Pierre Beaulieu would be the right guy for Chief so they got him to sit as Chief there with the Treaty Party . . . .

Johnny Beaulieu: They made [him] the spokesman, and he asked for a lot of things as long as the earth stands . . . .

Angus Beaulieu: The Treaty party promised a lot of things. There would be no changes, there would be rations, many things like this, but Pierre said, "We have to have something signed saying we could have all this and there would be no changes, before we can take treaty" . . . They talked for about a day and the Treaty party didn't agree at all . . . .

Johnny Beaulieu: Chief Drygeese said, "If you don't want to take our words, if you don't take our words, we might as well go away, leave the Treaty." So they walked out, all walked out . . . They never reached an agreement and the meeting was adjourned for the day.
The next day Pierre Beaulieu kept stalling them because he didn't quite understand them and they asked what kind of person he was.

Angus Beaulieu: They asked the priest [Father Dupire], "What is that guy anyway, (Pierre Beaulieu), an Indian or a Half-breed?" The

*The following interviews are quoted:

  Angus Beaulieu, Metis, born 1934. Great-grandson of Pierre Beaulieu, who was presented as chief in 1900, but not accepted because he was a Metis. Interviewed by Roy Daniels, then of the Company of Young Canadians, February 1969.

  Johnny Beaulieu, Chipewyan, 1882-1969. Son of Pierre Beaulieu. Interviewed by Marilyn Asheton-Smith, then of the Company of Young Canadians, 1969. Translated by Elsie Zoe, Dogrib.

  John Jean Marie Beaulieu, Chipewyan, born 1888. Grandson of Pierre Beaulieu. Interviewed by Dora Unka, Chipewyan, 1969; by Dave Smith of the Department of Anthropology, University on Minnesota, Minneapolis, June 1969; and by Robert Sayine, Chipewyan, April 1972. John Jean Marie Beaulieu is the most important witness.

  Johnny Tassie, born 1895. Interviewed by Robert Sayine, 1972.

  Pierre Smallnose Drygeese, born 1888. Interviewed by Beryl C. Gillespie, of the Department of Anthropology, University of Iowa, 1968.

  Pierre Frisé (Freezie), born 1887. Interviewed by Tom Unka, Chipewyan, 1972.

  Frank Norn, Metis, born 1903. His father was one of the official interpreters at all treaty meetings from 1900 until 1927.

  Henry (Honoré) Drygeese, Chipewyan, born 1896. Son of the first *Chief Drygeese*. Interviewed by Antoine Liske, Dogrib, February 1972.

  Pierre Michel, Chipewyan, born 1902. Interviewed in October 19, 1971, by Elizabeth Petrovitch, then of the Indian Brotherhood of the N.W.T.

priest said, "He is a Half-breed." So the Treaty party didn't want a Half-breed to be Chief, so they picked another guy, Louison Dosnoir, who was an Indian guy. No one could tell yet who was Treaty or who wasn't, because there was no treaty yet. But the priest could tell who was a Half-breed and who wasn't. So this is how it started.

Johnny Jean Marie Beaulieu: A large tent was pitched up . . . All of the older people went into the tent. The Chiefs wanted everyone to hear what was said so they asked everyone to come. The women were to come too if they wished. The younger children were kept away from the tent . . . .

Johnny Beaulieu: So they got Louison Dosnoir to take Pierre's place.

Johnny Jean Marie Beaulieu: The Chiefs agreed, Louison would speak for them all; they had previously discussed it amongst themselves and had chosen him to speak for them. Louison accepted to speak. He said that if nothing would change and the Indians would live as they had in the past, he'd agree to take the Treaty money . . . .

Angus Beaulieu: Louison said the same thing as Pierre said, that they have to have something signed to show that there will be no changes . . . .

Johnny Jean Marie Beaulieu: He emphasized that he did not want the buffalo to be closed from the hunters as it had been done at Fort Smith.[134] The people had told him to talk for the buffalo: Why the law against killing the buffalo? . . . He asked the Indian Agent why the closed season on the buffalo, for three years now, and why they had never asked the people. He said that there had to be an open season on the buffalo . . . the people are not taking that many buffalo; only about 10 families really hunting them much. Louison said that maybe we won't take the treaty if we cannot hunt the buffalo . . . .

The Whiteman said, "I'm going to give you some money." We asked him if it was because he was putting the buffalo in a park that he was giving us the money. We had all we needed and the money would not replace the value of the buffalo they were locking up. We don't want the buffalo locked up. We told him that if he put the buffalo in a park, we would not take the money. He told us he had nothing to do with a park and that he was sent here only to give out the treaty money. He also told us we did not live on only the buffalo and we would do without. But we insisted that we would not take the treaty money if he locked up the buffalo. So then he said they would not put the buffalo in a park and we could live on whatever we wanted to . . . The ducks could not keep us alive for they come in the spring and leave in the fall and we would have to go hungry in the winter. We were told we would be given enough money to live on during the winter. And he told us we had no say on our lands and not to complain. He also said it is the Whiteman's land now. Before, he told us we could always live off our land and hunt and fish. Now he was telling us we could do neither . . . .

Already it was bad, lots more was said, and there were arguments . . . The White man kept saying that he was not the boss so he could not promise much. The Chief asked why the boss would not come to Fort Resolution to speak with them. They wanted to talk to him . . . Louison said that if we could not get a definite answer on what was talked about it was of no use. He told the Commissioner, "I know this country, and the way you are talking, you talk like you know it better than me . . . Take your money in your suitcase and go if you are not going to listen to the people."

They had put the Treaty medal on him, but they wouldn't listen to his talking for the buffalo, and he threw it down and quit . . . .

Frank Norn: While the Chief was talking he took his cap off and put his cap on the table and he took the medal that they put on his neck, put it on his cap, took his uniform coat off and he said, "My underwear has got some holes in it and there are women and everything here, so give me a chance to go back to my place and I will change my pants and I will come back." They didn't know what the heck he was doing. He went over there and soon after that he was bringing his uniform pants back into the tent. He put his pants down on the table and he said, "That's enough. I don't want to be your Chief; that sun is just about the same place as it was when you made that promise to me, and if you are going to break it now, it's only yesterday you made this promise to me and already you are breaking it, what about the years to come?"

Johnny Jean Marie Beaulieu: He turned to Snuff and said, "If they are going to give you money for the land, don't take it; if for nothing, then take it."

Frank Norn: He never even got his treaty, he walked out of the tent and he sat amongst the people . . . .

Johnny Jean Marie Beaulieu: Then they gave the medal to Snuff, we called him Copenhagen . . . .

Johnny Beaulieu: He was chosen as Chief, but he started to talk foolishly . . . .

Angus Beaulieu: He started talking about the cold and the dogs and everything else. And the Treaty party said, "There, that's the guy we want as Chief." So that's how they got nothing. This is how they got to agree with everything without anything being signed or anything solid.

Snuff was chief of the band on the east arm of Great Slave Lake. The above comments are by a person from another band. All other accounts of Snuff's behaviour indicate that he spoke for the same things as the other two chiefs:

Johnny Jean Marie Beaulieu: Snuff said that he would agree with the treaty as long as nothing changed for the Indians, and all that was said was not changed either. Concerning the land he said that the White man was not to say that he had bought the land from the Indians with Treaty money. "I tell you the same as Louison," he said.

Concerning wildlife, Snuff said that it would not be closed to the Indians as long as the earth lasts. And if the White man agreed, the treaty would be made, otherwise there would be no money given out. We did not ask for the money.

In the Indian language, treaty is translated "giving money out". When Snuff said there would be no money given out, he meant there would be no treaty.

Johnny Jean Marie Beaulieu: Snuff said, "You all heard him [Treaty Commissioner] we will stay on this land like we always did and as long as there is still Indians alive, our land will not be taken from us. All that we need for our livelihood, our hunting, fishing, and trapping, concerns this land." He addressed everyone and explained it again. They all agreed that the treaty was fine because it did not concern the land.

The whiteman said, "This money is for you to use for whatever you choose. As long as any of you live you will receive this money." He said again that as long as the sun shines and river flows you will have this treaty. Old man Snuff told the people then to sign the treaty, so the whiteman could not go back on his word. Only then, old man Snuff said to the whiteman that because of the paper they had written on, by which the whiteman was bonded, they would accept the treaty money.

The Slavey Indians from Hay River went to Fort Resolution for Treaty. Sunrise was their leader, and he was chosen as chief. Old Lamalice was elected councillor. Indians of the Hay River trading post and vicinity numbered about 140, and were reported to be "peacefully inclined and mild in their disposition".[135] But they certainly approached the negotiations and bargaining with the same determination as the other bands.

Johnny Jean Marie Beaulieu: After the discussions the Indian Agent said, "I got rations now down at the bay. You think that it is alright? Rations are going to come every time! . . . After treaty is paid, the Head Chief is going to give rations to everybody."

Pierre Frisé: They brought it in and said that, "If you take Treaty you will be getting this every year." That was our biggest mistake, because after that, they did not do it . . . .

Frank Norn: The treaty meeting was about 3 days and a half, I think, before they ever resolved the treaty . . . but even after all these discussions, when the treaty was first signed, it was never explained to the people, they thought they would just give them the money and they would be satisfied . . . Treaty rights were not much explained to the people . . . .

Johnny Tassie: We didn't know the Whiteman's papers and they used long words we couldn't understand . . . .

Johnny Jean Marie Beaulieu: They talked nice to us in them days but nobody understood their language . . . .

Pierre Michel: The interpreter had tried very hard for us not to sign treaty, but we have lost. The final decision came and all the priests and the RCMP gathered to witness the signing of the treaty. But to be honest, we have no idea what was written on the paper, since we do not speak English nor write it . . . .

Undoubtedly most people took the Treaty Commissioner at his word, when he explained to them why the Treaty party had come:

Johnny Jean Marie Beaulieu: "We heard you were poor down here, we heard this and we want to give you some money to live with and some rations too . . . We are just trying to help you," the Indian Agent boss said . . . .

Pierre Smallnose Drygeese: The agent said, "I think you don't know about this Treaty but this Treaty means to make friends, Indians and whitemen, because later on there will be lots of people, white-men, coming to your country and then you will be friends with them; be no enemies. This does not mean to talk about anything forbidden, or anything like that; we won't stop you from hunting or nothing. As long as the sun rises and the river does not turn back, this talk will be forever; there will be no fighting and nothing forbidden." – that's what they told them. They gave money just to make friends, just like one; that's all they mentioned in the first place.

During the discussions the chiefs had asked the Commissioner for a written document and according to Johnny Jean Marie Beaulieu, "they made a paper".

With or without official papers, it is clear that the Indians signed the Treaty to create a spirit of friendship with the newcomers. It was, as Susie Abel recalls, "for future relationship with the White people."

Frank Norn: Reserves were not mentioned . . . No land transaction was made . . . They did a lot of talking about buffalo but nothing much about land . . . That's when the closed season started on the buffalo, previously the Indians did not know about a closed season on the buffalo . . . It was promised that it was only going to be two or three years, that' all . . . but the buffalo season was never opened.

There is evidence that land and medical care were discussed, but the Indians were concerned above all else, with protection of their hunting, trapping, and fishing rights. If this had not been guaranteed there would have been no Treaty. All of the chiefs stressed this during the negotiations:

Henri (Honoré) Drygeese: Chief Drygeese said that, my people will continue to hunt, trap and fish as it was before, there will be no regulations for my people. If you take my word, only then I will accept the treaty . . . "

Pierre Michel: Chief Drygeese said "My people have lived here many years without you coming to bother us. We have lived without your money to this day. My people will continue to live as they were before and no White man will change that . . . You will in the future want us to live like White man does and we do not want that . . . The people are happy as they are. If you try to change their ways of life by treaty, you will destroy their happiness. There will be bitter struggle between your people and my people . . . .

"We will not be around when our young children grow up, they will never remember this, but you people will, and the promises that have been made here will not break. Our people in the future will continue to receive Treaty money, and you people will help my people when they are in need of assistance. The Great Slave Lake belongs to my people as well as to any Native who stays on this land. I speak not for myself but for all the people here and also for those who are Natives of this land. In the future you will not put any regulations against Wildlife. These things belong to my people. They depend on them for food and clothing; you will not take it away from my people. What I say now will remain as it is. There will be no changes in what I say even if I will not be around the next ten years or so."

Johnny Jean Marie Beaulieu: And the Indian Agent said, "As long as the sun shines and the river flows this is your land to hunt on forever . . . This land is yours. As long as we pay the treaty, nothing is going to change" . . . "If this is so, we will take the treaty," the Chiefs said.

Johnny Beaulieu: So they tricked and lied to the Indian people, and that is how treaty came about.

The original text of Treaty 8 is kept in the Public Archives of Canada.[136] The adhesions of 1899 were written on very cheap paper, while those of 1900 were on parchment. Examination of these documents reveals a curious discrepancy in the signatures. The majority of chiefs could not write their names, either in English letters or syllabic characters. The use of a cross mark has been an accepted practice in these cases. Over the years thousands of Indian people have signed their names with this simple mark, which in most cases is as unique and personal as handwriting. Yet, on the Treaty 8 documents nearly all of the marks next to the chiefs' names are identical, perfectly regular with a similar slant, evidently made by the practised hand of one person. The confusion surrounding the Chipewyan signatures at Fort Resolution illustrates the seriousness of this matter. The Treaty document shows two sets of two signatures, though the 113 Chipewyans were entitled to only one chief and one councillor. First the names of Louison Ah Thay (Dosnoir) and Oliver Ajjericon appear, followed by marks which are patently forged. Then in another place there are the signatures in syllabic letters of Vital Lamoelle and Paulette Chandelle. These last two are written with different ink, at a different time, and seem to be the only ones written by Indians. It can be assumed that the name of Louison Dosnoir had been written on the prepared document before he resigned as chief. After his resignation, Lamoelle was selected as chief of the Chipewyans. He was absent during the discussions which were led by Snuff and Drygeese on behalf of all four bands, but returned when negotiations were completed and the treaty already signed. When he arrived he was asked to add his signature to the document, along with that of Chandelle, as councillor. After the signing, Treaty annuities were distributed. The records show Louison Ah Thay (Dosnoir) listed first of the thirty-four heads of families.[137] The title "Chief" was written next to his name, but then crossed out. He received $12. Paulette Chandelle, listed second, was paid $22 as Headman. Far down on the list, in the 28th position, appears the name of Vital Lamoelle, designated "Chief", receiving the chief's allotment of $32. In the light of these records, it is difficult to know which, if any, of these signatures on the Treaty are valid, or if those who did sign had the authority to do so.

The role of the missionaries in the negotiation of 1900 is mentioned by very few witnesses. Only two mission diaries have survived. Thomas Jabez Marsh, an Anglican minister, accompanied the Hay River Indians to Fort Resolution. He noted in his diary:

> About midnight of the 24th [July, 1900], the Commissioner arrived at Resolution and at 1:00 P.M. of the 25th the Treaty was read to the Indians and signed by them, and then the payment was made forthwith. The R.C. priest made himself very conspicuous before the Indians and seemed to succeed in making himself very popular with the Commissioner A.J. Macrae, somewhat at the cost of absolute justice and fairness, although in the end I think the impression was that the Englishmen are universally Protestants, which was encouraging to us, and inclined the Indian to listen more readily to us.[138]

The Hay River Catholic mission diary also related the events of this Treaty day:

> Mr. Marsh (Anglican minister) showed to the government officials all the Indians gathered around him as being Protestants, and boasted about having civilized them. The officials, being themselves Protestants, were quite happy to meet at last a minister who seemed to have succeeded in his work. He received everything he asked for on behalf of the Indians. This governmental help was a new obstacle for us.[139]

It appears that the missionaries were less concerned about the Treaty negotiations than their own religious rivalries.

Marsh's entry is significant because it fixes the time when the Treaty party arrived and when actual negotiations began, 1:00 P.M., July 25. On the same day, the Treaty was signed and annuities distributed. It would appear that negotiations lasted only during the afternoon, hardly time enough to explain the legal and social implications of such an agreement. It is probable that further discussions took place during the days that followed, since the Treaty party did not leave Fort Resolution until July 27th. But the Treaty had already been signed.

Metis at Fort Resolution

At Fort Resolution as everywhere else, the Treaty drove an official wedge between Indian and Metis. The payment in full of $240 was made in the form of scrip, and profited the Metis very little.

Johnny Beaulieu: [The Treaty Officials] told us that the Treaty Indians and the Metis were on different terms as far as Treaty was concerned – They said that the Metis will get a scrip . . . After the treaty was signed, they passed out all the money and my father got a scrip. We did not know what it was or how much it was worth. There was a trader here, and he kept after my father to sell the scrip to him, so my father did, for seventy-five dollars . . . .[140]

Angus Beaulieu: They gave scrip paper to half-breeds. We didn't know what those were about either, but we took it. There was a trader, Hislop and Nagle, who gave the scrip money, $75.00, to the half-breeds.[141]

After 1900, some Metis in the Treaty 8 area were again asked to join the Treaty. Government officials and missionaries encouraged them to do so. Grouard also wrote to the Minister of the Interior protesting the enfranchisement of Metis who had accepted treaty:

. . . we have there a certain class of people whom we have always considered as Indians although it may be that long ago some drops of White blood have been infused into their veins. For all purposes, they are pure Indians, having the same language, the same mode of living, shifting camps, hunting, fishing; in fact no difference at all can be made and they form an homogenous population. When the Treaty was offered last year, they took it and were pleased. For their best interest, their own welfare and the welfare of their families, it is perfectly clear that they must be obliged to keep faithfully to the treaty. But at the instigation of some Scrip-hunters and traders, some of the aforesaid people are tempted to call themselves Half Breeds and repudiate their treaty agreement in order to ask for scrip. Now, I venture to state that if such whims of these people were carried through great troubles would soon follow all over this country. The money they would get for their scrips, (if granted to them) would be expended in a few months, and then these men, their families and their children in future would find themselves deprived of all the benefits they might have drawn from the treaty, their condition would become much worse than it was before, and compared to their relatives, the other Indians faithful to the treaty, they would be in a greatly inferior condition . . . So I venture to hope . . . that wise steps may at once be taken and discrimination be exercised in granting scrips to real halfbreeds only and treaty rights to all who are really Indians.[142]

As had been foreseen and feared, the Metis people were left in an unenviable position. Any claim they had on the Government for protection and support was extinguished with the scrip settlement. Some managed to survive as trappers, fishermen, or hunters. A few became farmers or labourers. The majority, however, drifted aimlessly between the white and Indian world, not belonging to either.

Summary

The haste of the Treaty Commissioner in securing Indian signatures on a piece of paper removes any illusions that the Treaty was a contract signed by equal partners. How to characterize it remains a question, but the fact remains that Government officials in Ottawa, who drafted the terms of the Treaty, had little knowledge or comprehension of Indians, or their way of life in the Northwest. Given the extreme physical hardships which the Indians had experienced through many winters, it is no wonder that the prospect of supplies and cash was a deciding factor for them in accepting the Treaty. The Commissioners could afford some self-satisfaction since they had overcome resistance and dispelled suspicion wherever they encountered it. They could report to Ottawa:

> . . . it was possible to eradicate any little misunderstanding that had arisen in the minds of the more intelligent, and great pains were taken to give such explanations as seemed most likely to prevent any possibility of misunderstandings in future.[143]

Without doubt, the support of the missionaries and the presence of the North West Mounted Police encouraged the Indians to put faith in the Government representatives. The Treaty was seen by the Indians as a friendship pact, which would permit peaceful settlement of the country; land surrender or relinquishment of title were not issues for them. However, there were certain basic assurances which they wanted from the Government: freedom to hunt, trap, fish, and move freely. When promises were given that these would be protected, the Indians accepted government assistance, satisfied that their livelihood and that of their children would not be endangered. Expedient answers and facile promises were the substance of these Treaty negotiations.

1. PAC, CMS microfilm A-120. Books and letters of the Church Missionary Society, London, G.1 series, C 1/0, 1898, document 75, W.D. [Reeve, Bishop of] Mackenzie River to Baring-Gould, 8 February 1898.
2. J.G. MacGregor, *The Klondike Rush Through Edmonton,* Toronto, McClelland & Stewart, 1970, p. 107.
3. *Ibid.,* p. 235.
4. PAC, CMS microfilm A-120, cited above, 1899, unidentified newspaper clipping quoting Mrs. Spendlove.
5. OMIAFS, 091-C12, folio 176, Grouard OMI. to Clut OMI., 14 December 1899.
6. J.G. MacGregor, *The Klondike Rush Through Edmonton,* p. 249.
7. C. Mair, *Through the Mackenzie Basin,* Toronto, William Briggs, 1908, pp. 107-110.
8. J.G. MacGregor, *The Klondike Rush Through Edmonton,* p. 249.
9. OMIAFS, 091 MB, p. 40.
10. C. Mair, *Through the Mackenzie Basin,* pp. 23-24.
11. *Ottawa Citizen,* 30 June 1898. *Winnipeg Free Press,* 28 June 1898.
12. Canada, *Sessional Papers,* 1900, No. 15, p. 12.
13. PAC, CMS microfilm A-121, Books and Letters . . . , 1900, document 103, Lofthouse to Baring-Gould, 5 April.
14. *Ibid.,* microfilm A-120, 1898, document 86, George Holmes to Fox, 15 April.
15. *Ibid.,* document 146, Reeve to Baring-Gould, 29 July 1898.
16. *Report of the Missionary Society of the Church of England,* 1899, p. 430.
17. Canada, *Sessional Papers,* 1900, No. 14, pp. xviii,xix.
18. RCMP, Archives, Ottawa. *History of the Force in the Athabasca and Great Slave Lake Area,* Typed manuscript, p. 12.
19. A.M. Jarvis, Inspector NWMP. "Northern Patrol", *Annual Report of the Commissioners of the NWMP,* 1897, pp. 162,169.
20. W.H. Routledge, Inspector NWMP. *Annual Report of the Commissioners of the NWMP,* 1898, p. 94.
21. A.M. Jarvis, *Annual Report of the Commissioners of the NWMP,* 1897, p. 160.
22. W.H. Routledge. *Annual Report of the Commissioners of the NWMP,* 1898, pp. 94-95.
23. *Ibid.,* p. 96.
24. F. Russell, *Explorations in the Far North,* Iowa City, University of Iowa, 1898, p. 105.
25. A.M. Jarvis, *Annual Report of the Commissioners of the NWMP,* 1897, p. 170. *cf.* pp. 160, 162-169, 171.
26. *Ibid.,* p. 158.
27. W.M. Routledge, *Annual Report of the Commissioners of the NWMP,* 1898, p. 96.
28. *Ibid.,* 1899, p. 12.
29. Canada *Statutes,* 57-58 Victoria, 1894, Chapter 31.
30. PAC, *MacFarlane Papers,* MG 29- D9, Vol. 1, pp. 1829-1830.
31. Canada *Statutes,* 57-58 Victoria, 1894, Chapter 31.
32. A.M. Jarvis, *Annual Report of the Commissioners of the NWMP,* 1897, p. 162.
33. *Ibid.,* p. 171.
34. W.M. Routledge, *Annual Report of the Commissioners of the NWMP,* 1898, pp. 88, 95, 96.
35. *Ibid.,* p. 96.
36. *Ibid.,* 1899, p. 11.
37. C. Whitney, *On Snowshoes to the Barren Grounds,* New York, Harper and Brothers, 1896, pp. 116-117.
38. PAC, RG10, BS, file 19,502-3, Giroux OMI. to Jarvis Inspector NWMP, 1 July 1897.
39. A.M. Jarvis, *Annual Report of the Commissioners of the NWMP,* 1897, p. 160.
40. W.M. Routledge, *Annual Report of the Commissioners of the NWMP,* 1899, p. 12.
41. Canada, *Sessional Papers,* 1900,

No. 15, p. 12.

42. G. Breynat, OMI., *Cinquante Ans au Pays des Neiges,* Montreal, Fides, 1945, Vol. 1, pp. 172-180.

43. F. Cueff, OMI., Letter to the author, 11 October 1971.

44. PAC, RG10, BS, file 75,236-1, James Walker to Clifford Sifton, 30 November 1897.

45. *Ibid.,* L.W. Herchmer to the Comptroller NWMP, 2 December 1897.

46. *Ibid.,* Forget to Secretary of Department of Indian Affairs, 12 January 1898.

47. *Ibid.,* Clifford Sifton to the Governor General in Council, 18 June 1898.

48. *Ibid.,* Forget to McKenna, 28 June 1898.

49. *Ibid.,* McKenna to Forget, 6 July 1898.

50. *Ibid.,* Macrae to McKenna, 3 December 1898.

51. *Ibid.,* Forget to Secretary Indian Affairs, 1 June 1898.

52. Alberta, *Revised Statutes,* 1942, c. 329.

53. P.B. Waite, *Arduous Destiny: Canada 1874-1896,* Toronto, McClelland and Stewart, 1971, p. 66.

54. PAC, RG10, BS, file 75,236-1, Herchmer to Comptroller NWMP, 2 December 1897.

55. *Ibid.,* Forget to McKenna, 16 April 1898.

56. *Ibid.,* Forget to Secretary Indian Affairs, 12 January 1898.

57. Canada, *Privy Council,* OC No. 1703, 27 June 1898.

58. PAC, RG10, BS, file 75,236-1, Memorandum respecting Indian Treaty, 28 December 1898.

59. Canada, *Privy Council,* OC No. 918, 6 May 1899.

60. PAC, RG15, B-la, Vol. 329, file 518,158. McKenna to Sifton, 17 April 1899.

61. PAC, RG10, BS, file 75,236-1, Forget to Secretary Indian Affairs, 12 January 1898.

62. *Ibid.,* 25 April 1898.

63. *Ibid.,* Sifton to His Excellency the Governor General in Council, 30 November 1898.

64. Canada, *Privy Council,* OC No. 2749, 6 December 1898.

65. PAC, RG10, BS, file 75,236-1, Laird, Memorandum Respecting Proposed Treaty No. 8 and Halfbreed Claims, 7 January 1899.

66. *Ibid.*

67. *Ibid.,* Sifton to Laird, McKenna and Ross, 12 May 1899.

68. *Ibid.,* file 241,209-1, Laird to Secretary Indian Affairs, 29 April 1904.

69. Canada, *Office Consolidation of the Indian Act,* Ottawa, Queen's Printer, 1969, Section 18 (1), p. 8.

70. PAC, RG10, BS, file 75,236-1, Forget to Secretary Indian Affairs, 12 January 1898.

71. Canada, *Privy Council,* OC No. 1703, 27 June 1898.

72. PAC, RG10, BS, file 75,236-1, McKenna to Sifton, 17 April 1899.

73. *Ibid.,* Sifton to Laird, McKenna and Ross, 12 May 1899.

74. *Ibid.,* Macrae to McKenna, 3 December 1898.

75. *Ibid.,* Forget to Secretary Indian Affairs, 12 January 1898.

76. *Ibid.,* Laird, Memorandum Respecting Proposed Treaty No. 8 and Halfbreed Claims, 7 January 1899.

77. *Ibid.,* Accountant Department of Indian Affairs, Memorandum showing the amounts to be voted in addition to the sum already available following the adoption of any of the alternative schemes proposed in McKenna's memorandum of the 3rd. instant, 27 March 1899.

78. *Ibid.,* McKenna to Sifton, 17 April 1899.

79. *Ibid.*

80. *Ibid.,* Sifton to Laird, McKenna and Ross, 12 May 1899.

81. *Ibid.,* McKenna to Sifton, 17 April 1899.

82. *Ibid.,* Forget to Secretary Indian Affairs, 25 April 1898.

83. PAC, CMS microfilm A-120 (*op. cit.* note 1), 1899, document 68, George Holmes to the Committee, 3 April.

84. Canada, *Privy Council,* OC No. 892, 3 May 1899.

85. Canada, Commons, *Debates,* 1899, col. 5694.

86. PAC, RG10, BS, file 75,236-1, Lacombe, OMI. to Sifton, 14 May 1899.

87. OMIAEd, D-1-105. Lacombe's Diary; *En Route pour le Nord avec une Commission Royale,* 27 May 1899.

88. RCMAFS, file: Indiens-Traité avec eux, Falher, OMI. to Breynat, 13 August 1937.

89. OMIAEd, B II-801, Grouard, OMI. to Lacombe, 31 March 1899.

90. *Ibid.,* B VII-22, Envelope 1880-1912, Lacombe to Grouard, 14 June 1899.

91. PAC, RG10, BS, file 190,194, Smart to Minister of Justice, 15 November 1899.

92. *Ottawa Citizen,* 28 February 1899.

93. C. Mair, *Through the Mackenzie Basin.*

94. *Ibid.,* p. 40.

95. *Ibid.,* p. 51.

96. PAC, RG10, Vol. 1851, Treaty No. 428.

97. C. Mair, *Through the Mackenzie Basin,* p. 56.

98. *Edmonton Bulletin,* 10 July 1899.

99. This affidavit was signed in duplicate and sworn in the presence of S.A. Dickson, Commissioner for oaths, in Edmonton, on November 1, 1937. One copy was sent to Ottawa, the other copy is retained at RCMAFS, file: Indiens-Traité avec eux.

100. PAC, RG15, B-la, vol. 329, file 518,158, Lacombe to Laird, 22 June 1899.

101. *Ibid.,* Holmes, White and Robinson to Laird, 26 June 1899.

102. *Edmonton Bulletin,* 6 July 1899.

103. *Ibid.,* 25 September 1899.

104. *Ibid.,* 17 August 1899.

105. OMIAFS, 091-MC *Codex,* and *Chronique de la Mission de la Nativité,* Vol. 1, pp. 56-58.

106. HBC Archives, B 39/a/60. Published by permission of the HBC.

107. C. Mair, *Through the Mackenzie Basin,* pp. 65-66.

108. G. Breynat, *Cinquante Ans au Pays des Neiges,* Vol. 1, pp. 186-187.

109. *Edmonton Bulletin,* 17 August 1899.

110. OMIAEd, D-1-105, Lacombe's Diary, 15 July 1899.

111. ASGM, *Chroniques de Fort Chipewyan,* 1899, p. 90.

112. *Winnipeg Tribune,* 19 July 1939.

113. PAC, RG10, Vol. 1851, Treaty No. 428.

114. G. Breynat, *Cinquante Ans au Pays des Neiges,* Vol. 1, pp. 188-190.

115. PAC, RG10, Vol. 1851, Treaty No. 428.

116. *Ibid.*

117. IANDO, Library Archives, *Indian Annuities Book,* Treaty 8, 1899.

118. *Edmonton Bulletin,* 31 August 1899.

119. *Ibid.,* 11 September 1899.

120. OMIAFS, *Codex* 091-MB, 1899, p. 40.

121. *Toronto Star Weekly,* 24 June 1939.

122. *Edmonton Bulletin,* 31 August 1899.

123. *Ibid.,* 28 August 1899.

124. In the Supreme Court of the N.W.T. Transcript of evidence in the action in the matter of an application by Chief François Paulette, *et, al.,* to lodge a certain caveat, 1973, pp. 313, 317.

125. *Edmonton Bulletin,* 28 August 1899.

126. OMIAEd, D-1-105, Lacombe's Diary, 4 August 1899.

127. *Ibid.,* B-VII-22, Envelope 1880-1912, Lacombe to Sifton, 10 September 1899.

128. *Edmonton Bulletin,* 11 September 1899.

129. *Treaty No. 8,* Ottawa, Queen's Printer, Reprint 1969, pp. 5-9.

130. PAC, RG 15, B-1a, Vol. 329, file 518,158, Walker and Coté to Sifton, 30 September 1899.

131. Canada, *Sessional Papers,* 1901, No. 27, p. xxxix.

132. IBNWTA, Transcript of Johnny Jean Marie Beaulieu's interview, 1969.

133. IBNWTA, Transcript of Susie Abel's interview by Dr. June Helm, professor of Anthropology, Univer-

sity of Iowa, Iowa City, 5 July 1971.

134. "An act for the preservation of Game in the unorganized portions of the Northwest Territories of Canada" came into effect on 1 January 1896. Among other provisions, it established a closed season on buffalo until 1 January 1900. The closed season was extended to 1 January 1912.

135. W.H. Routledge, *Annual Report of the Commissioners of the NWMP,* 1898, p. 90.

136. PAC, RG10, Vol. 1851, Treaty No. 428.

137. IANDO, Library Archives, *Indian Annuities Book,* Fort Resolution, 1900.

138 Alberta Provincial Archives, *Hay River St. Peter's Mission Diary,* ACC 70-387-MR 4/3.

139. OMIAFS, 091-CH,H424, Vol. 1, p. 25.

140. Johnny Beaulieu, Interview, 1969.

141. Angus Beaulieu, Interview, 1969.

142. PAC, RG10, BS, file 590,185, Grouard to Sifton, 10 September 1900.

143. Canada, *Sessional Papers,* 1901, No. 27, p. XL.

Chapter III

The Years Between The Treaties, 1900-1920

Introduction

Difficulties arising from Treaty 8 were soon experienced by both the Indians and the Government. Although these were not acute in the early years, the limitations of the Treaty were soon evident, as economic, social and political changes reached the North. These same changes would, in turn, determine the time and terms of Treaty 11.

After the gold rush had passed through the Athabasca-Mackenzie District, some white trappers and free traders moved into the country. This new breed broke the monopoly of the Hudson's Bay Company and altered the nature of the fur trade. Fierce competition for furs caused intensive and reckless trapping in some areas. Speculation and high prices encouraged unscrupulous trading practices. Northern game and fur became increasingly scarce as the Government was unable or unwilling to protect the Indian people and their economy.

A few Canadians looking for farm land headed north to the Peace River District, after reading Government pamphlets extolling *Canada's Fertile Northland* (1907), *The Great Mackenzie Basin* (1910), and the *Unexploited West* (1914). The direct result of this influx of settlers seeking land title was the curtailment of the Indian's right to move freely. The Government survey of Treaty and Non-Treaty land forebode little benefit for the Indians and by 1912 the boundaries of the North West Territories were permanently fixed.

Some adventurers, trappers, prospectors, traders, and scientists penetrated the more remote country north and east of Great Bear Lake. Among these D'Arcy Arden, John Hornby, George Douglas, Vilhjamjur Steffansson, William Boland are still remembered.

With the creation of the Province of Alberta in 1905, new impetus was given to developing "Edmonton's hinterland". A former Edmonton politician, Frank Oliver, was named Federal Minister of the Interior and Superintendent General of Indian Affairs. Railway companies were encouraged to extend their operations from Edmonton to the North and Northwest.

With this increase of population and commercial operations, the North West Mounted Police extended its activity. This served to augment Government authority in the Treaty 8 area, leading gradually to tighter control and administration. Over the years, proposals were made to Ottawa to extend Treaty 8 to the Indians north of Great Slave Lake, who could also benefit from Government relief. Many officials opposed this on the grounds that no profitable use could be made of the land. Delay followed delay. Later, when the discovery of oil outside of the Treaty 8 area made it highly desirable to "extinguish the Indian title", a new treaty was needed: Treaty 11.

Following Treaty 8

Views by Indians

> Treaty day used to be a big day for the people . . . A long time ago in every settlement where the Treaty was paid it was a big day and everyone used to have lots of fun, good dance that night, or next night. When you think about the Treaty now, it's like putting a plug of chewing tobacco in your mouth and chewing it, and spitting it, that's just the way the Treaty is today.[1]

Every summer, representatives of the Department of Indian Affairs visited all the main trading posts for the distribution of annuities, groceries, ammunition, and fishnets. They listened to complaints, and advised the Indians that their problems would be referred to the Government in Ottawa. Usually, a doctor and a few members of the NWMP accompanied the Treaty party and helped the Indians in any way they could. Treaty meetings became the highlight of summer gatherings, before the Indians left for winter hunting grounds.

Treaty Commissioner Macrae did not return after the trip in 1900. Henry Anthony Conroy replaced him as Pay Officer in 1901. As a young clerk, he had accompanied the original Treaty party in 1899. He was appointed Inspector for Treaty 8 on April 1, 1902,[2] and made the annual visit until his death in 1922. He was named Treaty Commissioner for Treaty 11 in 1921. Johnny Jean Marie Beaulieu recalls that during the first years payments were quite uneventful:

> The second year [1901] they paid treaty it was like the first, the same guy, nothing was changed. He [Conroy] asked the Indians: "How you making out last winter? That's the law . . . You can hunt anywhere, and we won't tell you anything what to do!" It wasn't until later that anything came [Game Laws]. The way the Indian Agent told the people, it wasn't a prob-

lem until the fifth time the treaty is coming in."[3]

Frank Norn remembers that the only new discussions in 1901 were about home brew.[4] Susie Abel went again to Fort Resolution in 1901 and noticed that the annuity had been reduced:

> The Agent told us: "Everyone gets $5 from now on. The $7 [remaining from the original $12 given at the first treaty] we are going to put aside as treaty rations . . . for fishnets, flour, all kinds of ammunition, groceries, whatever you need . . . Every summer we're going to pay treaty and at the same time we're going to bring all this stuff for you to issue among yourselves."[5]

Initial excitement and novelty soon gave way to disillusionment when it became clear that rations and money were the only return the Indians could expect on Government promises.

Views by Missionaries

Missionaries began to see the effects of Treaty 8 on their work as well as on the Indians. Richard Young, Bishop of the Anglican Athabasca Diocese made this analysis:

> It will be followed by an increase of traders and other white men in the country. In the first instance, this will be attended with a good deal of concurrent evil. It will also tend to draw the Indians from their occupation as hunters and trappers, and unavoidably cause a considerable amount of unsettlement. On the other hand, it is a necessary step in the opening-out and development of the country. It anticipates the certain occupation of the country by miners, settlers, etc., with some amount of order and government. It will restrain the Indians from superstitious panics and bloodshed, . . . It will preserve them from the periodical starvations that have again and again decimated, if not worse, whole camps. It will eventuate in more settled habits of life, in their taking up farming, and receiving educational advantages for their children. The future of the Indian, under a just and kind Government, is not extinction; rather is it by degrees absorption – the addition of one element in the mixture of races that is going to make up the future population of Western Canada.[6]

Serious consequences for mission schools followed Treaty 8. The Department of Indian Affairs granted $72 annually for each Indian child whose parents had signed the Treaty. For Metis children, whose parents had chosen scrip, there was no payment. Rev. George Holmes, Anglican minister at Lesser Slave Lake, assessed the situation thus:

> I am sorry to say that the result of the Treaty here does not brighten our future prospects . . . The Commissioners were empowered to treat all as Indians who were willing to accept Treaty; but to our great disappointment, and the severe loss of the Schools, only a small minority accepted it, the rest all choosing "Scrip" instead. They regarded the term "Indian Treaty" as much below their dignity, though they saw that the Treaty would be of the most practical and lasting benefit, both to themselves and

their children. Pride of origin and not the future welfare of their families, decided their choice . . . After selling their scrip they [the Metis] are responsible for the support and education of their children, and can claim nothing more from Government than white settlers . . . .[7]

Bishop Grouard wrote to the Mother General of the Grey Nuns on September 1, 1899:

> The Government made treaty with the Indians of the Athabasca [District] and promised them schools of their own denominations. I asked that the Holy Angels Residence [Fort Chipewyan] be officially recognized as a Boarding School for 100 Indian children. At least some assistance will be given, I hope, and the scope of the good work will increase . . . [8]

The Fort Providence school could not receive Government assistance as it was "out of the country united to Canada by the last Treaty," and Grouard considered, at one point, transferring half of its staff to Hay River, within the Treaty boundary, where a new school would be built.[9] On September 24, 1901, a disillusioned Bishop wrote to the Prime Minister: "Treaty promises are far from being fulfilled . . . The Indians, as well as myself, have some right to be treated with a little more generosity".[10]

Views by Outsiders

A few white travellers to the North in the early 1900's, wrote accounts of their visits to several posts during Treaty days. Their passing glance at an unfamiliar ceremony left some of them puzzled by its significance. David T. Hanbury arrived at Fort Resolution on July 7, 1901:

> There we found a large encampment of Indians – Dog Ribs, Yellow Knives, and Slave Indians. They assemble here annually at this season to await the arrival of the Indian Commissioner and receive their treaty money and allowance. The Yellow Knives and Dog Ribs have only recently "accepted treaty", i.e., have renounced all claim to exclusive ownership of the district, and placed themselves on the same footing as white men with respect to land and game, receiving in return five dollars per head and allowances of flour, bacon, tea, tobacco, and ammunition. What advantage the Government expects from this convention is not clear, for it is unlikely that white men will ever settle in this region.[11]

Elihu Stewart visited Fort Resolution in 1906. He was quite impressed by the "hundred or more Indian lodges" of the Chipewyan and Slavey Indians assembled there "for the payment of 'treaty', as they call it, that is to say, the Federal Government's grant to Indian tribes".[12] Ernest Thompson Seton travelled through Fort Smith and Fort Resolution in 1907. His impression was that the Indians had "surrendered their lands to the Government", but were not confined to reserves, having the freedom "to hunt as their fathers did". However, he was deeply touched by this complaint of Pierre Squirrel, chief at Fort Smith:

> You see how unhappy we are, how miserable and sick. When I made this treaty with your government, I stipulated that we should have here a policeman and a doctor; instead of that you have sent nothing but missionaries . . . [13]

Agnes Cameron, a newspaper journalist, was in Fond du Lac and Fort Resolution during the Treaty days of 1908. Although titillating and amusing, this narrative would contribute little to the public's understanding and appreciation of northern Indians:

> The Canadian Government has sedulously kept faith with its Indians and has refrained from pauperizing them by pap-feeding or ration-folly; very largely today the Canadian Indian plays the game off his own bat.
>
> The raison d'etre of these annual "Treaty payment parties" is merely the acknowledgement on one side and recognition on the other that the Northern Indian is a British subject protected by and amenable to British law. In addition to the present five dollars per head each year, the Canadian Government sends in by the Indian Agent presents of fishing twine and ammunition, with eleemosynary bacon for the indigent and old. The Chiefs strut around in official coats enriched with yellow braid, wearing medals as big as dinner-plates . . . .
>
> Down at the Treaty tent, Dog-Rib and Yellow-Knife are being handed the five one dollar bills which remind each that he is a loyal subject of His Majesty Edward the Seventh . . . Each head of a family is issued an identification ticket which he presents and has punched from year to year. A father "draws treaty" for his olive-skinned branches until each marries and erects a tepee for himself. Government Agent Conroy, big bodied and big hearted, sits on a nail-keg, represents the King, and gives out largesse; and Mr. Laird presides over the Doomsday book . . . .
>
> Birth, dowry [marriage?], divorce, death, each must be noted on the treaty ticket, with a corresponding adjustment of the number of dollar bills to be drawn from the coffer. If a man between treaty-paying and treaty-paying marries a widow with a family, he draws five dollars each for the new people he had annexed. If there is an exchange of wives (a not infrequent thing), the babies have to be newly parcelled out. Through all the family intricacies Mr. Conroy follows the interpreter with infinite patience and bonhomie. To the listener it sounds startling as the interpreter, presenting two tickets says, "He married these three people – this fellow." "O, he give dat baby away to Charles." We hear in a dazed way that "Mary Catholic's son married his dead woman's sister who was the widow of Anton Larucom and the mother of two boys." A young couple, looking neither of them more than sixteen or seventeen, return with a shake of the head five of the fifteen dollars proffered them, and the interpreter explains, "Their little boy dies – there's only two of them."
>
> Gregory Daniels in a Scottish voice, which cannot quite hide its triumphant ring, pushes back his five dollars and demands forty-five. "I got a wife and siven since last year, she's a Cree wumman." Another Half-breed asks anxiously if he would be allowed to send for a [liquor] "permit" like a

White man if he refused to take treaty.

One man with long black hair and a cheese-cutter cap creates consternation at the tent-door by claiming treaty for two wives and seventeen children. Mr. Conroy, scenting an attempt to stuff the ballot-box, produces seventeen matches, lays them at my feet on the tent-floor and asks The-Lean-Man to name them. He starts in all right. We hear, "Long Lodge, Little Pine, Blue Fish, Birdtail, Little Bone, Sweet Grass, Ermine Skin," and then in a monotone he begins over again, "Long Lodge, Little Pine, Blue Fish," and finally gives it up, eagerly asking the interpreter to wait "a-little-sun". The drama of paying and recording has gone on for half an hour and we have quite forgotten The-Lean-Man, when back he comes with Mrs. Lean-Man, Sr. and Mrs. Lean-Man, Jr. Each spouse leads her own progeny. Seeing is believing, and off Lean-Man goes with a fat wallet. We wander into the stores to see what purchases the Indians will make. One young blade is looking at a box of stogies, and the clerk says, "He can afford to blow in his wad on perfumes and cigars, that chap, he got a silver fox last winter." They tell the story of how Old Maurice, Chief of the Chipewyans, put his first Treaty money in a cassette [small storage box] and kept it there all the year because he had heard one White man tell another that money grows, and he wanted to see if a White man lies when he talks to another White man.[14]

With these few, cleverly chosen words, the image of the Northern Indian as a primitive simpleton was vividly sketched for an undiscerning and unsuspecting Canadian public.

Views by Officials

North West Mounted Police and Indian Affairs officials reported few major problems within the Treaty 8 area:

> . . . in the northern country in 1901 there have been a few cases where relief was absolutely necessary, but it has been among very old Indians, who are unable to work for themselves . . . or a few who were too ill to work for themselves and with no one to work for them. These are all cases that would probably have perished of starvation had not relief been given. . . . One hears occasionally of cases of extreme hardship, where Indians and their families have gone on hunting expeditions, been unsuccessful and reduced almost to starvation, but their cases are rare.[15]

> . . . The Indians generally are well behaved in this part, and are prospering. I may say that since Treaty payments a few isolated cases have arisen necessitating the issue of temporary relief.[16]

Inspector Christopher H. West, NWMP, was also a medical doctor. He attended the annuity payments of 1903 and expressed satisfaction with the situation:

> Fort Chipewyan, Fort Smith, Fond du Lac, Resolution and Hay River, where everything went off in a quiet and orderly manner . . . There were several cases of sickness among the Indians at different places visited, but nothing of a serious nature. The Indians seem to be prosperous in their

way, fur plentiful everywhere and the prices high. The provisions left by
the government at each point for the sick and destitute, go a long way to
aid those who are too old to hunt or rustle for themselves. As far as I have
been able to find out the Indians are satisfied with the way they are
treated by the Government.[17]

In the summer of 1908, Inspector Ephrem A. Pelletier, NWMP, met 125
men, women, and children of the Yellowknife and Dogrib bands
crossing Great Slave Lake in their York boats. They were hurrying to
Fort Resolution to await the Treaty Commissioner: "They were a
passable looking lot, fairly well dressed, reported a poor fur year, but
seemed fairly well provided with the necessaries of life."[18] The Fort
Resolution Indians were also reported to be "satisfied and
contented".[19]

Problems

Only four or five years after the signing of the Treaty, William Norn,
the interpreter at Fort Resolution, expressed what was in everyone's
mind:

> I wonder what the treaty is going to look like another 20 or 25 years from
> now. Even now, you start thinking about when the first treaty was paid
> and now everything seems to be going backwards. Maybe the whole treaty
> will just go downhill, because even now, compared to what is used to be,
> things are going downhill, so we may as well just roll it right down the
> hill.[20]

During the years 1913-1920, treaty parties and Indian people experienced problems with delays, sickness, land surveys, and game regulations. Finally, in 1920, frustration reached a climax and erupted in the
boycott at Fort Resolution.

Delays

Improvement in the northern transportation system did not seem to
benefit the Treaty party making its way into the Athabasca-
Mackenzie District each year. Accidents and delays often meant that
rations were lost or damaged, or that the Indians missed the party
altogether.

The Treaty party of 1913, led by Conroy, was expected in Fond du
Lac on June 19. Crossing Lake Athabasca, navigation became impos-
sible due to heavy ice, and the party turned back to Fort
Chipewyan.[21] The delay was disappointing, and the Chief at Fond du
Lac wrote to the Minister of the Interior, William J. Roche:

> The necessities of life in this country are very limited and when the Treaty
> party fails us we feel it keenly. As it is, we must now hurry away to find
> something to eat . . . It may surprise you to know that the caribou failed
> to pass this winter and as a result many men, women and children are

hungry for food. The food we counted upon on June 21st [Treaty day] would have been very timely.[22]

This same year, Conroy disregarded their request for building tools, as they "show no inclination to build dwelling places at Fond du Lac, preferring to lead a more or less nomadic existence". He added: "Sufficient assistance is rendered them each year in the shape of supplies and twine and shot to enable them to live without hardship, and any considerable additional assistance rendered at the present time would merely serve to promote laziness and thriftlessness.[23] In 1914 there was "an unfortunate accident in the Stony Rapids on the Athabasca River. The scow was smashed by an enormous wave, and sank immediately. The treaty money was saved, but the rest of the outfit, including the treaty records, was a total loss. Fortunately there was no loss of life."[24] The disrupting consequences of World War I reached as far north as Fort Resolution, and nearly caused the cancellation of Treaty days in 1915. An incident the previous winter was the reason:

> . . . there were some German trappers hunting in the Great Slave Lake district. They greatly upset our Indians by telling them that Germany would send some Zeppelins to Fort Resolution during the spring to throw bombs on the fur traders' posts; then the Indians would be taken up in the dirigibles to be thrown down to earth from a great height. These Germans have now left the north and are outside. The Indians at first sent word to the Fort Resolution post that they would not attend treaty this year for fear of the Germans. When in June they saw that the Germans had failed to come they knew that they had been fooled, and came to Fort Resolution as in previous years.[25]

In 1918 the Treaty trip started badly in Fort McMurray. It continued on, plagued by boat trouble and the elements:

> On account of the general confusion at the . . . scene of the April flood, we could not find out the exact condition of the treaty supplies. We were told the flour had all been underwater, also the bacon, but the latter was not much injured.
> Then a leaky scow, towed by the Nu-Tra-Co., was to be our quarters . . . The second day it's raining and cold. As there is no protection from the rain in the scow, it is very uncomfortable . . . .
> The wind put our gas boat, which refused to start, and the scow containing the treaty supplies, out of control; the scow promptly filled with water and the contents of the scow began to drift about at the mercy of the wind and waves, but fortunately, all was rescued, although some of it in a somewhat worse condition than when it left the wrecked warehouse at Fort McMurray.
> Then the scow began to leak so badly that it showed symptoms of sinking and again wetting the goods [Treaty supplies] . . . We continued the trip riding on wet flour sacks and gasoline barrels . . . The wind began to blow and the scow began to ship water . . . During our sleep an occasional wave breaking over us, dampened our blankets . . . Heavy rain all through

the night . . . The wind increased in violence, blowing the launch and scow on shore . . . The scow promptly filled with water . . . We carried the contents of the scow ashore and spread it out to dry in the sun . . . Above Smith landing and the rapids, the engine again refused to go, and we proceeded to drift past our objective, in the direction of the [Fort Smith] rapids. [Only the scow could be paddled ashore] – No more Nu-Tra-Co. It is a memory!

Otherwise the trip was uneventful.[26]

By 1919 Treaty money was due to many Indians who had missed payments over the years. Some had not received their Treaty money for "2, 4, 10, 12, even 18 years". *The statement of Arrears in Annuities in Treaty 8* shows the following numbers who had not received all of their payments:

at Fort Chipewyan	127 Indians
at Fond du Lac	183 Indians
at Fort Smith	96 Indians
at Fort Resolution	95 Indians
at Hay River	19 Indians[27]

When John McLean, Assistant Deputy and Secretary of Indian Affairs became aware that the Government owed so much money to the Indians, he instructed Agent Card in Fort Smith:

It is not intended that you should show this list to the Indians or traders and lead them to understand that all these arrears are due and will be paid, but the list should be treated as a confidential official document . . . When you have satisfied yourself of the correctness of the claim, you should pay 2 years' arrears in addition to the current year's annuity, paying first the arrears for the latest years of absence. For example, a family absent 1914 to 1918 should be paid this year: annuity for 1919 and arrears for 1917 and 1918. You should also show in the remarks column "arrears still due for . . . persons for 1914, 1915, and 1916".[28]

All Indian Annuities Books are retained by the Archives of the Department of Indian Affairs and Northern Development.

Health

Although no article of Treaty 8 made any reference to medical assistance, the Treaty Commissioners had promised medicines and care to the Indians, and "assured them that the Government would always be ready to avail itself of any opportunity of affording medical service."[29]

In 1900 a doctor accompanied the Treaty party: "Dr. Edwards . . . gave advice and dispensed medicines to large numbers of Indians and vaccinated many";[30] in 1901, "Dr. Edwards vaccinated some Indians".[31] Inspector W.H. West, RNWMP, was a qualified doctor and accompanied the Treaty parties the following years, but his visit once a year could not improve health conditions very much. The Indian Agent at Fort Smith advised his department on February 3, 1912: "A permanent medical officer at this point would be a great benefit to the Indians: nothing has a more civilizing effect upon them than a display of the white man's skill in healing, nothing convinces them more readily of the white man's interest in them".[32] Dr. MacDonald arrived the next year and remained permanently when the Catholic Church opened St. Ann's Hospital in 1914, under the direction of the Grey Nuns. Other Indians were not as fortunate as those at Fort Smith. Conroy reported frankly: "It is a physical impossibility for Dr. MacDonald stationed at Fort Smith, to visit with any degree of frequency such posts as Fort McMurray, Fort Chipewyan, Fond du Lac, Fort Resolution, Hay River, Fort Providence, Fort Simpson, Fort Wrigley, Fort Norman and Fort Good Hope".[33] The distance between Fort McMurray and Fort Good Hope is 1330 miles by water.

Traditional Indian medicines were no defence against diseases unknown before the white man's arrival. The native people dropped before the epidemics, and in the absence of doctors, the Indian Agents could only count the dead. Thirty-three Indians died of Spanish influenza in northern Alberta in 1919.[34] Two years later, a smallpox epidemic swept over the Treaty 8 area from Fort Chipewyan to Fort Resolution. The doctor accompanying the Treaty party that year was kept busy:

> Doctor Inge made his rounds of the various camps reporting some 35 cases of smallpox . . . At Fort Resolution we found that a very considerable number of the Indians had left, fearing the smallpox . . . . Doctor Inge reported 6 cases of smallpox. Ordered the police to have them removed to a nearby island and rationed . . . There have been some 89 cases reported with 6 deaths . . .
>
> Doctor Inge has made several hasty visits, but almost the entire responsibility has fallen on the Sisters of Charity, who have as usual done heroic service. Noticeably at the Smith hospital. The epidemic would appear to have passed its worst stage, and I hope will be over before the cold weather begins.[35]

The Indians had asked for medical care before signing the Treaty. It had been promised to them. Pitifully little was provided in the years that followed. How much more could have been done and was not, is a question that history does not answer.

Land Surveys

In 1910 Breynat and Frank Oliver, Minister of the Interior, travelled together down the Mackenzie River. Breynat took the occasion to inform the Minister of the necessity for a land survey in all small villages, and for the allowance of lots large enough for everyone to have a garden. In the summer of 1913 a land survey of the Mackenzie District trading posts was begun by Chief Surveyor Fawcett. When Breynat heard of it, he wrote to Ottawa, asking that the Indians' holdings would be respected:

A few Indians have erected, at different times, rather convenient houses from which it would be hard to eject them when the survey of these posts is made.

There are no reserves, and there will not be any for a long time.

Would it not be possible to reserve indefinitely for the use of these Indians the lands upon which they have squatted?[36]

The Deputy Superintendent General of Indian Affairs, Pedley, wrote back on May 9, 1913, inquiring about the amount of land occupied by Indians:

I shall be obliged if you will at any convenient time or from time to time inform me of the different points along the Mackenzie River at which you state some Indians have erected houses and where you recommend that lands should be reserved for them. Will you kindly state at the same time the approximate number of Indians at the various points.

It may be some time before this Department can take up the question of sending a surveyor down the Mackenzie River for the express purpose of laying out lands as reserves for Indians at the different points where they reside. It is, however, desired to keep this matter in view and I shall be obliged if you will be good enough to inform me in case this matter should at some time become urgent.[37]

By that time the land survey was already planned, and Pedley instructed the surveyors to reserve for the Indians as much land as they needed:

At each of these settlements there will undoubtedly be one or more lots or blocks of land which are used by the Indians either permanently or for camping purposes or considered to be necessary for their use and consequently should be secured for them . . . I may explain that the region referred to, that is to say, between Great Slave Lake down the Mackenzie to Fort Good Hope, has not been covered by any treaty, but it is considered to be very desirable in order to secure the good will of the Indians and to avoid friction that at least all the lands near the settlements to which the Indians are entitled or are necessary for their reasonable wants, should be secured to them by having them regularly surveyed in the same manner as the remainder of the settlements.[38]

I shall be much obliged if Mr. Fawcett, is instructed . . . to lay out lands which he finds used or occupied by Indians in the same manner as he does for White men.

The Surveyor-General suggests that each individual Indian should not be provided with a separate lot; it is suggested that the surveyor should use judgement in this matter to the extent of laying out a block of land for a number of Indians who are settled together; but should an individual Indian or others be at some other points, that these should have their separate lots surveyed as occupied and not be expected to remove in order to be all together at one point in a settlement unless they are quite willing to be all together.[39]

The Indians along the Mackenzie River had not signed any Treaty, yet neither the Government nor the surveyors distinguished between Treaty and Non-Treaty land. To the puzzlement of the Indians, trading posts in both areas were surveyed during the years 1913-1915. Lands reserved for Indians were allocated, with or without benefit of Treaty. Fawcett reported on August 7, 1913, that sixty-four Indians were living or trading at Fort Wrigley and that they owned twelve small shacks there:

> These Indians are non treaty and . . . as mostly all Indians, of a roving disposition . . . only two of them have gardens and I have laid out separate lots for them as they desired. The remainder are grouped at intervals along the water front and have their houses all in a small space. For these I laid out lots for each group as suggested.[40]

The total Indian population in the Fort Simpson area was 360, of which 47 lived near the trading post. Determining their land needs was quite simple for Fawcett:

> . . . as they were Non-treaty Indians and there was no reserve for them, they were entitled to the land on which their houses were built. Therefore I laid out lots for them where I thought it necessary . . . There is also quite an Indian settlement about 4 miles up the Liard River from Fort Simpson and on its left bank, where the Indians wish a reserve laid out and Mr. Harris asked me to survey it for them.

> . . . this Indian reserve lot for the Indians about Fort Simpson contained 495 acres and was surveyed during February and March, 1914.[41]

According to Fawcett's report, five to six hundred Indians traded at Fort Good Hope and owned twenty-four log shacks. Fort Providence Indians owned only two log houses. Four hundred Indians traded at Fort Resolution, and owned four log houses. Fawcett, as well as most of his contemporaries, believed that areas unfit for cultivation were of little value:

> There is a settlement at Fort Rae, which is situated at the end of the northernmost arm of Great Slave Lake, and another, Fond du Lac, [now Snowdrift]. Neither of these needs to be surveyed as they are both situated on barren rocky points and owe their very existence to the fur industry.[42]

The Surveyor General, Henry J. Bury, planned an official inspection of the surveyed lots during the summer of 1914. This was cancelled when his equipment was lost in a boat accident, and he was forced to return to Ottawa.[43] Fawcett furnished information and sketches on the survey of northern posts, which were studied to determine if the Indian's rights had been respected. Some officials tried to rationalize the amount of land reserved for Indian use:

> The lots of land are small in every case. If the country should be settled these would not be sufficient for the ordinary wants of the Indians. There is, however, very little prospect of settlement taking place to any extent at any of the points above mentioned. I think for the present the lands laid

out by Mr. Fawcett are sufficient. The Indians will be secured in the little plots in which they have erected houses, besides the additional lands which have been laid out for them for gardening purposes. The surveys of any additional land may be put off for an indefinite period or until we have obtained a report from one of our own officers on the necessity of making such surveys.[44]

For the Indians who had signed Treaty 8, the survey seemed to be a threat to their right to move freely through their ancestral land. John Piché, a northern prospector, advised the Department of Indian Affairs on March 28, 1914:

. . . the Indians around Fort Smith, Smith Landing [Fort Fitzgerald], Fort Chipewyan and Fond du Lac are being told that the Government is about to put them onto reserves and deprive them absolutely of their right to hunt . . . The Half-breeds are agitating the Indians by telling then that . . . the Police will herd them like cattle and will not let them go to hunt.[45]

Among the Indians living along the Mackenzie River outside of the Treaty area, there was a general distrust of the Government's intentions in surveying their land. The Indian Agent at Fort Simpson urged Ottawa to deal with the Indians before dividing up their land further:

There is considerable curiosity evinced by the Indians as to why a survey is being made of the various settlements in this district, and I have several times been asked by them for an explanation of the Government's intentions in having the said survey made. I have answered that so far as I know it is to protect the rights of the settlers who may come in at a future date. This does not seem to satisfy them and all sorts of absurd rumours are current, and a certain amount of dissatisfaction is expressed . . . [There] is a general dislike of seeing an influx of strangers into the country. I would respectfully suggest to your department that the time has come to give treaty throughout this northern country and that by so doing all trouble and annoyance would be obviated.[46]

Pedley was not satisfied with the land survey. He thought that the plots were too small. On February 24, 1915, he requested Conroy to "ascertain as accurately as you can, the locations and extent of other plots of land near the settlements that, in your opinion, should be obtained for the Indians".[47] Bury returned to inspect the "Indian reserves" in the summer of 1915. In October he issued his report which was sharply critical of the survey conducted by Fawcett:

In every instance where Mr. Fawcett had laid off a reserve for the Indians the area thus set aside was not calculated on the number of families or members of the band, and consequently the size of each reserve varies to a considerable degree. For instance, at Fort Resolution a rocky promontory of Great Slave Lake had been set aside as a reserve and the area was only 63 acres . . . .

While I was at Resolution the Chiefs of the Chipewyan, Yellowknife, and Dogrib tribes were very emphatic in their refusal to accept the reserve as laid down by Mr. Fawcett. I myself am of the opinion, after cruising this location, that it is quite unsuitable for the needs of the Indians. Besides being rocky and exposed there is also no timber growth, agricultural land or good fishing in the vicinity, so that I would beg leave to suggest that this reserve be cancelled.

The Chief of the Chipewyan tribe had already expressed a wish that his band be located in the neighbourhood of the Little Buffalo River, where I am credibly informed there is a large area of good agricultural land, together with some merchantable stands of timber.

At Hay River a similar state of affairs was in evidence. Chief Sunrise, of the Slave Band, expressed his disapproval in no uncertain manner.

After cruising this particular plot, I am inclined to agree with him that it is entirely unsuitable for the needs of his band looking to future requirements. The land itself is for the most part rocky and towards the Hay River is inclined to be of a low and marshy character.

Chief Sunrise, himself, informed me that he and several of the members of his band were desirous of locating at a point up the Hay River, distant approximately twelve miles from the mouth. In consequence, therefore, I beg leave to suggest that the reserve as laid out by Mr. Fawcett at this post be also cancelled.

At Fort Providence, I had an opportunity of travelling over the reserve laid out there and found that . . . probably sixty percent of the whole area consists of a spruce swamp, which is absolutely useless.

This year, I unfortunately did not have the opportunity of looking over the reservations at Fort Wrigley, Fort Simpson and Fort Good Hope . . . .

As far as the reserves surveyed are concerned, I do not think that he [Fawcett] consulted with the Indians in any manner whatever except possibly at Fort Good Hope and Fort Simpson.

It would seem, therefore, desirable to refrain from having the present reserves confirmed by Order in Council, pending a proper selection made by the local Indians and approved of by the Department.[48]

Dissatisfaction with the land survey was one of the causes of the trouble at Fort Resolution during the Treaty days of 1916. It was the first year that Indian Agent Card came to pay annuities and the third year after Susie Drygeese had succeeded Old Drygeese as chief of the Dogribs. Pierre Smallnose Drygeese was there and recalls what happened:

Susie, they put him into chief and they had Treaty twice with him and then Agent – his name Gus, Giel, or something – this Gas [Card] started to talk about land but didn't mention this at first when they start (to take Treaty). So Chief Susie Drygeese and Gas talk about land. Susie says, "not mentioned when we start, not worth talking about now. We have to have the land to live off the wild life."

They started to talk back and forth with Gas but Gas won't listen to what Susie tell him and Susie says, "If you don't want to listen to what I said, no use arguing around like this, might as well go home," and then the old man rushed out.

He (Susie) says to the [Indian] people, "No use talking; everyone go home." Gas got so excited, scared, don't know what they will do to him. Indians mad and left before taking Treaty. And Gas there alone with interpreter, scared, He told his interpreter the Indians are mad; told interpreter to be a guard all night while he sleeps. Afraid Indians will kill him. Interpreter refused to guard him so he says, "I'll give you $5 if you will watch me all night." Next morning interpreter tells the Indians, "Good thing you left, he was scared and gave me $5 to watch over him."[49]

Bury had advised earlier that the land reserved for Indians at Fort Resolution was not suitable,[50] and the Indians, for their part, would continue to resist any proposal to limit their freedom.

The land allocation resulting from the survey of 1913-1915 cannot be called a "reserve" as the term is defined in the Indian Act, i.e., land "held by Her Majesty for the use and benefit of the respective bands for which they were set apart."[51] Rather, it is "land reserved for Indians"; specifically, land where Indian people only may build houses. The legal status of this land is not clear, since the Government did at times transfer the right to this land without band consent. Evidently, this is not the kind of land settlement called for by Treaty 8. Yet allocation of land to Northern Indians proceeded on a piecemeal basis, compounding the confusion caused by Fawcett's survey. The case of the Fort Smith Reserve illustrates the ineptitude of bureaucracy to isolate issues or identify priorities.

Fort Smith Reserve

As early as 1911 an Indian Agent was stationed at Fort Smith. In 1915 he was asked by Ottawa to provide information on desirable reserve land for the Chipewyans. Not only was the land near the post being discussed, but also more extensive tracts, "that may be required as Indian Reserves under the terms of the Treaty."[52] The reason behind the Government's interest in the Fort Smith Indians was clear. A Wood Buffalo Preserve was planned for the area, a move which would deprive the Indians of their traditional hunting grounds. The task of selling the idea fell to Treaty Pay Officer Bury in 1916.

At first the Chief and principal men of the band showed great hostility to the proposal, claiming that from time immemorial they had been accustomed to hunt and trap over the area which was created as a sanctuary and that they had hunting lodges and shacks on this land, which they would have to relinquish. The Chief pointed out to me, that the mere fact of the Indians having to look around for new trapping grounds meant that it would take them a long time to become conversant with the haunts and habits of the game, and that it would be a matter of many years before they could expect to achieve the degree of success they had hithertofore enjoyed when they trapped over lands of which they had an intimate knowledge . . . .

After considerable discussion they decided to acquiesce in the proposal but intimated that they should receive some compensation for being deprived of their hunting and trapping privileges.

I was not then authorized to state whether or not the Government as represented by the Animal Parks Branch of the Department of the Interior would consent to the payment of compensation and managed after much discussion to persuade the Indians that their interests would be well looked after in the matter by our Department and assured them that when they were ready to take up Reserves, such lands would be set aside for them provided, of course, that they were not within the Buffalo Sanctuary.[53]

Before the Treaty Party left, the band had agreed on the locations for three reserves. One was near the Salt River, one at Pine Lake, and one on either side of the Slave River at Pointe de Gravois. The latter was agricultural land, while at Pine Lake there was good fishing. The third, at Salt River, eventually the most contentious, covered valuable salt deposits and rich grazing land. Bury noted that white settlers were entering the district to stake the Salt Spring country and to squat on the agricultural land. He recommended an early survey and confirmation of the Indians' claims.[54]

Two years later, Indian Agent Card advised Ottawa that "white men of a very poor type" have hunted and trapped in the buffalo country. They, rather than Indians, were responsible for the shooting of some buffalos. In the same memorandum Card proposed, and he was probably the first man to do so, that the whole country north of the 60th parallel should be declared a national game reserve for the benefit of Indians.[55] In 1920, Card recommended to the Dominion Park Branch the selection of the Salt River site as the location of the main Indian reserve. He touched on the real issue behind the delay:

. . . these reserves would not be a menace to the wood buffalo. I have not found the Indians otherwise than inclined to respect the law when the purposes of the law was duly explained to them by a competent authority.[56]

A resolution of the Advisory Board on Wildlife Protection sought, nevertheless, to exclude the Indians from the Salt Plains.

What the Board was afraid of was that the Salt Springs would be corralled by the Indians to the detriment of settlers, and that the location would be a strategic point for the Indians to kill the buffalo which go to the Springs not only for food, but for salt.[57]

Bury reiterated the priority of the treaty promises and the necessity for the Indians to make a living in their own country:

Recently they [the Indians] have intimated they desire to secure as a reserve some 11,000 acres near the Salt river, but outside of the Buffalo park, and I believe that we should not be carrying out our promises to the Indians unless we used every effort to have such a reserve set aside. . . .

If it is the intention of the Animal Parks Branch to take measures to commandeer large areas of the country and thereby prevent or hinder the Indians from earning their usual livelihood, then I think the responsibility of assisting the Indians to earn their living should devolve on them. I am confident that such action will result in our department being called upon to materially increase relief to these Indians unless, of course, they are able to setlle down on some good hay lands of the nature which it is proposed to set aside . . . .

In the large project of preservation of game, I am certain that if we antagonize the Indians it will cause endless trouble in the future, whereas if we approach this question in a proper manner and seek the Indians' co-operation and not their hostility, much useful work can be done.

The most effective way of winning their co-operation is to accord them their reasonable requests with respect to Reserves.[58]

The Department of Indian Affairs, on being instructed to select an Indian reserve far from the Salt Springs and from the wood buffalo range, suggested that the interests of the buffalo should not outweigh those of the Indians:

The rights of the Indians under their Treaty should receive some consideration, especially when it is remembered that these Indians were practically debarred from occupation of a large area of land which from time immemorial has been the scene of their hunting and trapping . . . . These Indians . . . showed an inclination to cooperate with the Government in the preservation of the Wood Buffalo, and I feel that they should in return be given sympathetic consideration in the matter of selecting their reserve.[59]

Conroy himself explained that the Indians had signed their treaty and asked for their reserve many years before the setting aside of the buffalo sanctuary. He also dismissed the idea that the buffalo sanctuary would be endangered by the creation of a reserve at Salt Plains.[60] The Dominion Land Surveyor, for his part, urged the creation of reserves:

The Treaty Indians are very anxious that their reserves should be selected and surveyed without further delay. As yet no Indian reserves have been surveyed in the Mackenzie District. With the influx of prospectors it is urgent that the Indians should be located on reserves with as little delay as possible. It is also necessary to have such reserves determined before proceeding with the creation of buffalo game reserves.[61]

The Advisory Board on Wildlife Protection was forced to reconsider. At an interdepartmental meeting a compromise was proposed:

. . . Could we establish a reserve at the mouth of the river, where the Indians could live, and then allow the plains to be used for hay purposes without actually giving them the area where the hay is, without giving the hay land the same standing as an ordinary Indian Reserve? . . . . We would want our patrol men to be able to shoo off any Indians who might take the notion to reside there . . . . I think that Indians . . . certainly should not have the means, or opportunity of poaching on the buffalo.[62]

The following year, 1921, the Indians were told that the proposed reserve locations were only part of all the land to which they were entitled by the Treaty: "the area remaining will be located . . . at a later date."[63] The prospect of being confined to the proposed reserve alarmed the band at Fort Smith. Chief Squirrel and headman Michel Mandeville informed the Indian Agent on July 4, 1922, that the Indians "had no wish nor intention of living on a reserve."[64] They were assured that this was not the Government's intention. Whatever that intention was, the Indians' right to the land was still at issue in 1930, according to Parker, Inspector for Indian Affairs:

> There appears to be some doubt as to the standing of certain lands at Salt River, about twenty miles below Fort Smith. I understand that these lands were surveyed some years ago for Indian occupation. The Fort Smith Indians are inclined to live there more than at Fort Smith. At Salt River they are able to get fish and their residence there should be encouraged. Already, however, some undesirable whites are building there and this should be stopped by declaring the land an Indian reserve.[65]

It was not until 1941 that an Order in Council established Salt Plains Indian Reserve No. 195, for the use of the Fort Smith Indians, with a total area of 110.4 acres.[66] The remaining lands to which they would be entitled under Treaty 8 were never allocated.

Game Laws

The problems arising from unaccustomed game laws and from the competition of white trappers were the subject of annual complaints at treaty time. At the signing of Treaty 8, Indians had established protective game laws to safeguard the wild-life of the country from over-trapping. This had been promised to them by the Commissioners. These measures were not enforced, however, allowing white trappers and free traders to plunder the territory's game and fur resources. The game restrictions which necessarily followed were imposed on white and native trappers alike, causing consternation and much hardship for many Indians.

Four years after the signing of Treaty 8, Conroy reported that "the Indians at Fond du Lac were very much worked up over the close season for beaver and other game, but after hearing an explanation were satisfied."[67] In 1911 the Province of Alberta closed beaver hunting for two years. When Conroy and Sergeant Mellor arrived at Fort Chipewyan in 1913, "the Indians were . . . full of complaints about the closed season for beaver."[68] The Chief, Laviolette, had been fined and was understandably angry.[69] In 1916 the Department of Indian Affairs heard directly from Chief Vital of Fort Resolution:

> The games here are getting scarce right now. It is hard sometimes to make a living. Please gvt [government] can give free grant to kill some buffalo, when we are hard up for grub, when we come in contact with it. Rabbits are scarce and small games besides that also . . . .
>
> I will be please leave us the way we are in getting our little wants that is to say, Moose, rabbits, fish, and other games. This is a very hard country of months of cold weather. . . .[70]

The Convention for the Protection of Migratory Birds in Canada and the United States, signed in 1916, provided for a closed season on migratory birds. Later on, it was submitted in Canadian courts that the signatories to the Convention "could never have intended the provisions of the convention to transcend the very purpose for which the convention was intended, namely to prevent the natives in the areas concerned from living in their normal way."[71] The convention only intended to preserve migratory birds from wanton slaughter, but not to deprive the native people of their customary sustenance. In the first few years, the Migratory Birds Act was not always enforced against Indians and Eskimos.

In 1917 the "Act respecting Game in the Northwest Territories of Canada" was passed by Parliament. Section 4 of the Game Act established closed seasons on moose, caribou, mink, muskrat, ptarmigan, wild geese, wild ducks, and other like animals. This proviso was added:

> The game therein mentioned may be lawfully hunted, taken or killed, and the eggs of birds therein mentioned may be lawfully taken, by Indians or Eskimos who are bona fide inhabitants of the Northwest Territories, or by other bona fide inhabitants of the said Territories, and by explorers or surveyors who are engaged in any exploration, survey or other examination of the country, but only when such persons are actually in need of such game or eggs to prevent starvation."[72]

The problem was to know to which level of starvation one must be reduced before being allowed to take protected game. Application and interpretation of this clause caused Indian Agent Harris at Fort Simpson some difficulties. He advised Scott, by now Deputy Superintendent, that the Game Laws were neither enforceable nor justified:

> Between Fort Simpson and Fort McPherson, a distance of approximately eight hundred miles, there is no executive officer of the law, so that, if the law is to apply to Indians, in this section just referred to, the law will be more or less a dead letter, and I believe this has a bad moral influence on the Indians . . . It has been my endeavour to show that Indian Agents are placed among them especially to protect their interests, and to see that they are not imposed on by strangers who come into the country.[73]

Harris' position was that "the Act was directed against whites coming into the country, and placed no restrictions on the Aborigines." He was supported in this interpretation by Conroy and a somewhat cautious Deputy Minister of Justice:

> It is perhaps arguable that no prohibition is imposed on Indians, Eskimos, and bona fide inhabitants of the N.W.T. . . . I would suggest that you should . . . endeavour to have the Act so amended that it will not affect them [Indians] in any way. The Indians of this Northern country, instead of being restricted in their hunting, have much greater need of being induced more than they do . . . I do not think it would be altogether just to the In-

dians of the North, where Treaty has not yet been made, to place any restrictions on them as far as the game in the country is concerned.[74]

At Fort Chipewyan in 1919, "the Indians talked extensively on the open seasons for fur, advocating the extension of the open season for all fur-bearing animals."[75] In 1921 the closed season was still an issue, to which was added a tax grievance according to the Indian Agent's report:

> [The Indians] complained of the short open season for beaver . . . and that due notice should be given to the band . . . last year many did not hear that there was an open season until it was too late to trap them. They also complained of the Provincial Government's fur tax, and demanded that it should be removed.
>
> Instead of this tax being paid by the traders, as I imagine was the intention, the trader deducts it from each pelt he buys. He may deduct the exact amount or what his cupidity suggests. The Indians maintain that in many cases the tax amounts to more than their annuity.[76]

Game laws and their application to Indian people came up in the House of Commons on June 6, 1920, when Oliver Robert Gould asked if Indians were permitted to hunt "all the wild game that comes there." The Solicitor General, the Honourable Arthur Meighen, gave this reply:

> The Indian outside his reserve must comply with any provincial restrictions with respect to hunting or the preservation of game. The Indians have sometimes resisted the imposition of these restrictions by the provinces, but the policy of the department has been to get them to comply. I do not want to give that as a final opinion, but that is my impression.[77]

That policy was to be tested the same year, during the Treaty boycott at Fort Resolution.

Treaty Boycott at Fort Resolution, 1920

Old Drygeese, chief of the Dogrib Band and signatory of Treaty 8 in 1900, died on July 18, 1913.[78] Susie (Joseph) Drygeese took his place, and at Treaty time, 1914, was officially recognized as chief. During the trouble at Fort Resolution in 1916, it was Susie who had angrily rebuffed the Indian Agent when the subject of land ownership was raised. Angry as they were then, Dogribs, Chipewyans, Slaveys and Yellowknifes openly rebelled when game regulations were imposed on them in violation of Treaty promises, and they boycotted the Treaty days of 1920. An eye-witness account describes the scene that greeted Indian Agent Card when he arrived to make Treaty payments:

> . . . [A] large encampment of Dog-Rib and Yellow Knife Indians on the Flat before the fort. They had come in to trade their spring hunts and meet Mr. Card, the Indian Agent.

Pierre Mercredi, the factor [store manager], told us that the Indians, of whom there were about a thousand camped around, were in a most rebellious mood, determined not to take their treaty money on account of one of their number having been fined at Fort Smith that spring for killing a duck. This, they said, was entirely contrary to their treaty and if such was the White man's way of observing treaties they would have nothing to do with it.

I learned afterwards that Indian Agent Card had a pretty hot three days with these disgruntled Dog-Ribs and Yellow Knives. It was only the good offices of Pierre and his influence with the motley tribesmen that caused them to accept King George's Treaty money once again . . . .[79]

The Indians were protesting the game laws found in the North West Game Act of 1917[80] and the Regulations for the Protection of Game in the Northwest Territories, 1918.[81] Police Inspector George Frederick Fletcher, as guardian of these laws, was directly concerned with the protest:

The Roman Catholic Bishop, Breynat, informed Mr. Kitto* and myself that the Indians were very much exercised over the provisions of the Game Act, so Mr. Kitto held a meeting of the Indians at which I was present. On being asked to state their grievance the Indians said that they depended on the game for meat and that they never had more than a day's feed in hand at once, and that if they were stopped from shooting game they would starve, and that they only wanted to be allowed to shoot enough to keep themselves alive. They also said that fish were very scarce in the Great Slave Lake this year and on many days they got no fish in their nets. All these statements were substantiated by the traders and missionaries. Mr. Kitto pointed out to the Indians that if they were in need of the game for food and could get no other food the Game Act allowed them to shoot game to prevent starvation. These Indians are always in a more or less starving condition. They shoot very little game in any case as ammunition is very dear and hard to get. The Indians interpreted Mr. Kitto's words as permission to shoot what game they wanted for their own use when they needed it, which is always. I have instructed my detachments to see that the Indians do not waste or sell any game.[82]

At that time and until this day, the events at Fort Resolution in 1920 are as significant to the Indians as the signing of the original Treaty in 1900. In order to reconstruct what took place, the diaries of the Grey Nuns,[83] the Catholic mission[84] and the RCMP[85] have been used to establish the sequence of events:

Sunday, July 11: The Indians arrived for Treaty.

Thursday, July 15: Treaty party arrived in P.M. The Doctor and Mr. Card arrived from Fort Smith with Bryan's schooner. The Indians refuse to take treaty – they are unhappy.

*F. H. Kitto, Dominion Land Surveyor, who was making an inquiry on the resources of the Mackenzie basin, during the summer of 1920.

Friday, July 16: Bishop Breynat arrived at Fort Resolution from Fort Providence. Sergeant Conway on duty with Treaty party.

Sunday, July 18: Bishop Breynat left in P.M. on Hudson's Bay Company schooner. All Indians and whites are present on the lake shore, the former ones fire volleys. Treaty was paid but the Indian Agent had to draw in his claws, due to the steadfastedness of the Indian people claiming their rights to hunt and to fish without restriction.

Monday, July 19: Sergeant on duty with Treaty party . . . Treaty party [left] for Hay River in P.M. The Agent Card . . . leaves today to Hay River.

Tuesday, July 27: Indians leaving [for the bush] . . . When discussing hunting matters with the Government Agent, their firm determination compelled him to draw in his claws . . .

The testimonies of Johnny Jean Marie Beaulieu, Henri (Honoré) Drygeese, Susie Abel (brother-in-law of the Chief), and Alexis Charlo are combined to provide a coherent account of what happened as these witnesses remember it.[86]

Johnny Jean Marie Beaulieu: The government decided to close season regulations for game. Since the Natives depended upon game for their livelihood, it was decided that the matter be first discussed before accepting the treaty . . . .

Alex Charlo: At Fort Resolution, Pierre Mercredi, Hudson's Bay Company manager, told them that treaty is a good thing, but they are going to try to close caribou, so don't take it at all . . . .

Henri (Honoré) Drygeese: The Chief disagreed very much about this change . . . They can't change their word so fast about what was said at the first treaty . . . The sun and the river have not changed a bit yet, but you have changed your words around again, so we will not accept treaty . . . .

Johnny Jean Marie Beaulieu: Our spokesman told the whiteman, "Do you remember what you promised us before?" The white man said, "No". We told him, "Why is it then, you did not read the paper we signed?" . . . The time they began the treaty, they kissed the Bible and everything. Why do you lie to us? Why do you do this? Why do you change now? Drygeese told them, "You gave us money and paper, now you want to change the law. We will give you back all the money. We can do without the money, we did without it long before. You can't pay to be the boss of us." Susie Drygeese told the Indian Agent, "If you say there is a caribou season, we are not going to take that treaty . . . Why do you tell us how to run our land? We did not give it to you . . . "

Susie Abel: If you want to talk about land, go back to where you came from. We did not ask you to come here in the first place.

Johnny Jean Marie Beaulieu: The chiefs concluded that the White man was trying to take our land for the treaty money that was given to

126

the people . . . The [Treaty] party lied and it is never nice to lie. We Indians do not bother people that way. White men are always coming here, but we do not bother them. We mind our own business. But they keep bothering us about our land. Card was the Indian Agent then, a different guy than the first one. Drygeese told the people to go home. Everybody so damn happy that everybody not taking treaty, all yelling, even the women . . . Everybody got up. They were cheering . . . The noise was like thunder . . . Some of the men went for tea. Packages and parcels were brought to Chief Vital's tent for a feast . . . .

Henry (Honoré) Drygeese: The Indian Agent knew that he lost by what the Chief said, so he tried so many times to convince the Chief to take the Treaty money. He sent the message to the Chief, but the Chief would not budge on what he had said to the Indian Agent. Again the Chief told him that if he doesn't listen to what his people want, he can begin by buying back his treaty, because his people didn't want the treaty. "It will be finished if you do not take my word," said the Chief.

Johnny Jean Marie Beaulieu: The Chiefs and the people were all standing together for a little while at Vital's tent . . . Alphonse Mandeville came there to say that Bishop Breynat wanted to see Chief Drygeese. Drygeese said he would go to see that Bishop for sure. The Chiefs and the older people followed to see what the Bishop wanted. There were so many people inside the father's house that I couldn't pass the door . . . .

Susie Abel: The Bishop said, "You don't know the White man, but the White men are so strong. When they talk about something, they never forget. There is no use arguing, so you might as well take treaty. I'm going to tell you what to say first."

Johnny Jean Marie Beaulieu: Drygeese said: "You are here to teach the people to pray to God. You can not talk for them and tell us about treaty. That is not your business."

The Bishop said: "That is right, but I must tell you, it is the best thing for you to do."

Drygeese said: "Us Tatsonottine (Yellowknife Indians) we are not going to take that treaty. We must have the caribou. But those people, this side, can do as they want, that is their business". He told the Bishop that the buffalo business [closed season] is not going to happen with the caribou, because that is how the people live.

The Chief came back and told the people the (same) thing. Everybody was happy that they are not going to take the treaty, then, they started the Hand Game, and nothing happened until the next day.

Nobody said nothing until noon the next day, and then Bishop Breynat asked to see the Chiefs again, and they went to see him. The Head Chief told the Bishop: "why do you want us to take the Treaty? If you write paper for us, and give it to all the Chiefs, that says we can hunt the caribou any time and anywhere, we will take that treaty . . . Now what I'm going to tell you, you are a bishop and not to help the White man, but to help the Indian; we have to live on the meat. If you don't write the paper, we will leave and not take that money." The Bishop said: "OK."

"You must make papers for what we say; some chiefs are still in the bush. One paper go to the doctors, and one to the Mission house (the priest). Whatever we say will be the law. You are a bishop and you can not lie. Nothing must change, now, forever."

The Bishop added . . . that the White man will not close off any hunting from the Indians as long as the earth lasted. Not one animal would be closed to hunting from the Indians as long as the earth lasted.

Henry (Honoré) Drygeese: The Bishop continued to tell the people that . . . they will continue to go hunting and things they have done in the past. So the Chief finally said that the Bishop will be the witness when they fix the paper [treaty] again . . . .

Alexis Charlo: So the Chiefs laid down the conditions for the treaty. The conditions were: That a land boundary be given for the Dogribs which will consist of from Snowdrift to Artillery Lake, up to Seymour [Aylmer] River to Contwoyto Lake to Great Bear Lake, [to Mackenzie River, back to Slave Lake.] Also, that there will be no closed season for game for the Dogrib Nation so long as the sun rises and the Great River flows. Only when these conditions are accepted by the government, only then will we accept the treaty money. This was the agreement made.

Susie Abel: Susie Drygreese says: "If you want to talk about land, draw a map for us, special for Indian Reserve, for everybody that holds treaty, for hunting groups. Give me one copy to keep. And if you sign it, and I find someone who will explain it to me right, then I will take treaty, but not before then. We will take treaty, but the way I tell you about this land. You give me a map and I'll draw it."

The Agent says: "OK, what is it?" And Susie Drygeese says, "From Reliance, following the Coppermine River to Great Bear Lake, around the Horn Mountains and the West side of Great Slave Lake between here and Providence to Birch Lake – all that land is what we need. Not only the Wuledeh people but the Rae people too so we can hunt and be just like one. So as long as the world runs and the Indian is still alive, this land will remain and no one is going to talk [further] about it."

The Agent says: "OK". So he starts to write and he draws a map and was writing at the same time. And he wrote down everything the Chief said. Susie wants an interpreter who can read what the Agent says [that is, translated into Dogrib] to see if he's writing good.

Johnny Jean Marie Beaulieu: Chief Drygeese told the Bishop: "Maybe you didn't make it right, maybe you're trying to help Card." Pierre Mercredi read it. We wanted to hear it. It said, "No law for nothing

J.A. Coté, Scrip Commissioner and Father Albert Lacombe, Athabasca Landing, 1899.
(Glenbow – Alberta Institute)

Treaty 8 Commission leaving Edmonton for the North, under a Mounted Police escort, May 29, 1899

1899 Half-Breed Commission leaving Fort McMurray to ascend the Athabasca River.
(Glenbow – Alberta Institute)

(Public Archives of Canada)

Chipewyan Chief and headmen who accepted Treaty 8 at Fond du Lac, 1899. Left to right: Laurent Dzieddin, Chief Moberley, and Toussaint. *(Glenbow – Alberta Institute)*

Tracking Treaty Commission boats on the Athabasca River, 1899. *(Glenbow – Alberta Institute)*

Fort Chipewyan, 1899. Left to right: residential school, Roman Catholic Church, and Oblate Mission. *(Glenbow – Alberta Institute)*

Facing page: Dogrib Indians and Yellowknife Indians arriving at Fort Resolution to sign treaty, 1900. *(Provincial Museum and Archives of Alberta, E. Brown Collection)*

Pierre Beaulieu. In 1900, Fort Resolution Indians wanted him to be their Chief, but the Treaty Commission did not accept his election because he was a Metis. *(RCM Fort Resolution)*

Dogrib children near Great Slave Lake, 1900. *(Provincial Museum and Archives of Alberta, E. Brown Collection)*

Dogrib Indians receiving Treaty payment at Fort Resolution, July 1915. *(Public Archives of Canada)*

Chief Vital and Bishop Breynat, Fort Resolution, 1912. *(Hudson's Bay Company)*

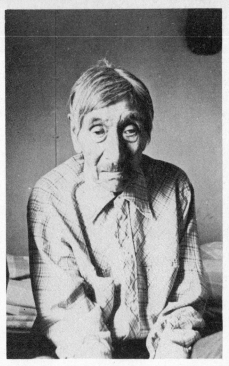 

Johnny Jean Marie Beaulieu. *(IBNWTA)*   Chief Pierre Squirrel of Fort Smith, 1920. *(IANDO)*

Indian Commissioner Conroy making treaty at Fort Providence, 1921. *(Public Archives of Canada)*

Official party in camp at Fort Providence, 1921. Others are probably members of the judicial party which was there at the same time.

The *Hubaco* pulled the 1921 Treaty party houseboat from Fort Providence to Fort McPherson and back. *(Hudson's Bay Company)*

Fort Norman, 1921. *(Glenbow – Alberta Institute)*

Inspector Bruce, RCMP; Treaty Commissioner Conroy; and Hugh Pearson, Dominion Lands Surveyor, at Fort Providence, 1921. *(Public Archives of Canada)*

Chief Tseleie, Fort Good Hope. This photo was probably taken in the summer of 1922, when the chiefs received their treaty medal, one year after the signing of Treaty 11. *(Roman Catholic Mission, Fort Good Hope)*

Indians at Fort Providence, 1921. *(Public Archives of Canada)*

Imperial Oil well, Number One, at Norman Wells, 1921. *(Glenbow – Alberta Institute)*

Townspeople welcoming arrival of steamboat, Fort Good Hope, 1921. *(IANDO)*

Group of Indians outside Hudson's Bay Company post at Fort Good Hope, 1921. *(Hudson's Bay Company)*

Payment of Treaty at Hay River, 1924. Second from left, back row, is Rev. Stoddart. Front row, left to right: J.F. Moran, two chiefs, Dr. Bourget, and Indians. *(Dept. of Indian Affairs, Ottawa)*

Treaty payments, Fort Rae, 1939. *(Richard Sterling Finnie)*

Julien Yendo, last survivor of the chiefs who signed Treaty 11 in 1921. Photo taken at Fort Wrigley. *(IBNWTA)*

Victor Lafferty *(IBNWTA)*

Indian Agent T.W. Harris at right, with his assistant, Fort Simpson, 1921. *(IANDO)*

when you are out of town for killing anything. If there is anything coming up in the White man's law, it won't bother you."

Pierre Mercredi read it to us. He said the paper was good for all time. There were many witnesses. Everyone was there . . . .

Henry (Honoré) Drygeese: The interpreter started to read it to the people and the Chiefs. And it sounded so good the way it was written down, Susie Drygeese's words about reserves and land and everything. So Susie Drygeese says, "I am pleased now. No more arguing about land, as long as we got a map, so we will take treaty now."

So the Agent wrote down on four sheets, and signed four copies of the paper of what Susie Drygeese said . . . Susie Drygeese took one copy, and they gave one copy to the Bishop, and one they were going to leave at the Hudson Bay Company, and one went to the Agent. Susie says, "So if one copy is lost, we will still have it." So there were four copies.

They wrote down all what is being said during the treaty. They made a new treaty again, this time they made it legalized so it would not happen like the first time.

Susie Abel: So Susie Drygeese is pleased now, because everything is written down the way he said it. And the interpreter read it in front of everyone and they were all pleased and it was signed, what Susie Drygeese said.

So then Susie says, "We might as well take treaty now," so they started giving treaty.

Susie Drygeese talked right and everyone was pleased, because this "treaty" was signed [this 1920 document].

So the Chief's terms were met. Then the government officials agreed. The people can go hunting and trapping any time they want to. The Bishop read the written promise to the people and then all the people agreed it was alright to accept the treaty money. So it took a couple of days to have everything settled.

Henry (Honoré) Drygeese: The Chief said that as long as he lives he will continue to do what he pleases on his land. There will be no regulation against hunting and the people. The Indian Agent agreed: "What the Chief said here will be as he said. There will be no change in what you said now. You will do what you please, and the land is yours, and it will not be taken away from you." And Drygeese said, "All my people will claim this land as their own and it will not be taken away from them." The Indian Agent also agreed to this.

Johnny Jean Marie Beaulieu: Card and Bishop Breynat made that paper, no law for nothing, given to all the Chiefs . . . Susie Drygeese told the Bishop and Card, "If you break this, the treaty is broken, no more treaty forever."

Even the White man and the Half-breeds got to sign [this paper.] Indian Agent got to take one outside to show his boss what the people in the Northwest Territories say. Everybody, Non-Treaty and Treaty, bosses, signed on the paper. Nothing will change. No talk of land, no game closed season. And then the Chief Susie Drygeese kneeled to the Bishop and kissed his ring.

But at the time of the flu, 1928, they had to burn everything, even paper [Treaty document] and that is when we lost what they promised to us . . . so, the two full days' talk of this . . . treaty day went for nothing.

Efforts to locate the other three copies of the Treaty of 1920 and the map have been of no avail.

Preparing Treaty 11

Living Conditions: Destitution and sickness

Conditions similar to those which had prepared the Indians to sign Treaty 8 were experienced by their brothers living north of Great Slave Lake along the Mackenzie River. Official attention was called to these by Conroy, when in 1907 he went into the Mackenzie River District, beyond the boundaries of Treaty 8.[87] Everywhere he went he found destitution, starvation, and sickness. At Fort Providence:

> About 300 Indians. They have not been very prosperous for some time owing to the scarcity of fur-bearing animals – last year being the worst they have experienced for years. They have therefore been very hard up, and have had to receive help from the H. B. Co. to quite a large extent."[88]

Forts Simpson, Wrigley, Norman, Good Hope, Arctic Red River, McPherson, and Fort Rae were also reported to be in the same pitiful conditions. The same year the Anglican Minister at Fort McPherson, C. E. Whittaker, reported "on account of the scarcity of both rabbits and reindeer, considerable privation was experienced by some of the Indians, and some deaths from starvation were reported."[89] Two years later a Police patrol went north from Fort Chipewyan to Fort Simpson. Sergeant Richard Field gave this account of the trip:

> At Fort Providence, great scarcity of fur is reported also, game and fish were also stated to be very scarce. The Indians were in a very destitute condition, this state being made worse by the traders having closed down upon them, giving no credit whatever, because of no fur, consequently the Indians are unable either to obtain ammunition whereby they could kill game, nor yet can they get nets wherewith to fish.
>
> The Indians spoke to me regarding treaty, wondering when they would be taken into treaty. I think the time has now arrived when something will have to be done as they are in a deplorable condition. . . .
>
> We left Providence at 6 A.M. January 30 for Fort Simpson and camped the first night at "Little Lake", about 30 miles from Providence. Here were several Indian families living. I visited all their camps and found them in a shocking state of destitution; they were subsisting totally on fish and very few of these; one man informed me that he had only four small jackfish

for his family of five for a week, having no other food of any description, not even tea. We left the following morning at 5 A.M. and called in at some more Indian houses and found them all in the same starving state; one of the Indians asked me to go with him a little way into the bush and see his grandparents. This I did and found them living in a brush teepee; they had eaten nothing then for five days, and were in such a weak condition that they could not move; they simply looked like skeletons. Around here there was such an awful state of starvation that I sent a man back to Fort Providence to get provisions for these old people; he returned the following day with the food I had requisitioned for. On my return from Fort Simpson I learned that the old woman died the following day after the provisions arrived; undoubtedly the cause of death was over-eating after so long a fast. We proceeded on our journey and visited the various Indian houses along the route and found the same state of starvation everywhere. We gave a little food from our supplies where most needed, the consequence being that we were out of provisions for a day and a half ourselves before arriving at Simpson, February 4.[90]

The following year, 1910, Corporal Arthur Mellor made a patrol from Smith's Landing to Fort Rae. Conditions at Fort Providence had not improved over the previous year and were equally bad further north:

Things were in a most lamentable state at [Fort] Rae; the Indians were practically all starving, owing to the entire absence of caribou. Father Roure, the priest there, informed me that this is the only time the deer have failed to arrive, during his 42 years stay at the place.

To add to the horrors of starvation, a mysterious epidemic has also attacked them, with the result that 70 out of an entire population of about 600 are dead, and many more are sick.[91]

The consequences of privation were noted by Bury during his tour of the Mackenzie District in 1913. He had this to say about the health of the Indians:

Disease and sickness still claim an unnecessarily large percentage of the population due largely to inter-marriages, mode of living, neglect, and ignorance. The most common diseases are consumption, dysentry and scrofula . . . It would seem very desirable to increase the staff of medical men in the north.[92]

In 1918, Spanish influenza spread to the Mackenzie District. "Several Indians died [from it] during the winter between Fort Norman and Great Bear Lake."[93] Kitto, Dominion Land Surveyor, was moved by the deterioration he witnessed during this trip in 1920:

The Indian population has lost its vitality and the race in consequence is gradually dying out . . . the Eskimo population on the other hand appears to be quite vigorous and healthy.

Information supplied me indicated that Indians suffer from various causes, including lack of proper nourishment, unsanitary and inadequate living quarters, hardships and exposures increased by the conditions just mentioned, tuberculosis, scrofula, whooping-cough, measles, venereal diseases, and inter-marriage.

The lot of the Indians in this district is not an easy or a happy one. Living conditions are getting harder every year and the Indians eke out an existence under anything but cheerful conditions.

Their own habits do not tend to mitigate such circumstances. With very few exceptions they are exceedingly lazy, dirty, improvident and immoral. On the other hand, when taken in charge by those who understand them and have their welfare at heart, they respond very readily. This is exceptionally true of the children as can be observed at any of the Roman Catholic or Anglican schools:

Old Chief Pierre Squirrel of Fort Smith, in addition to a number of white men whom I interviewed, maintains that venereal diseases were introduced to the district, and the native population contaminated by them during the time of the Klondike rush. Since that time it would appear that the natives allowed it to spread among themselves . . . .

Whooping cough and measles annually carry off large numbers of children as well as some adults. Last winter some 22 or 23 school children died at Providence from these causes. . . .

The Roman Catholic hospitals and the Roman Catholic and Anglican missions are doing most excellent work for the Indian Welfare, but they are sadly in need of medical assistance . . . . .

The Fort Smith hospital has the benefit of the services of a medical officer of the Department of Indian Affairs, Doctor MacDonald. The Saint Marguerite's hospital [at Fort Simpson] has no such advantage and the need of a medical man here is most apparent . . . These hospitals were both visited by me and I cannot speak too highly in their praise. They are a great boon to both whites and natives.[94]

Years earlier, Bury had also commented on the medical help offered by northern missionaries:

Taken in conjunction with their work of an elementary medical character, they have succeeded in arresting the scourge of consumption and other diseases that are so inseparable from the Indian and due for the most part to ignorance and wrong mode of life. In achieving this they have demonstrated their useful influence on the Indian.[95]

The hospital at Fort Smith was opened in 1914. The Government contributed $1500 toward the cost of furniture and paid the hospital an allowance of one dollar per day for each patient. A hospital was opened at Fort Simpson in 1916. These were the only two in the Mackenzie District. Built and owned by the Catholic Church, both were operated by the Grey Nuns.[96] At Fort McPherson and Herschel Island, the people were cared for by Doctor Doyle, without benefit of hospital facilities. Under these circumstances, the Government's promises of medical care, made during negotiations for Treaty 11, would undoubtedly dispose the Indian people to consider the Treaty seriously.

While the Mackenzie District was a harsh country where even the most skillful hunters and trappers could experience hard times, there were also many periods of ample food and good health among the Mackenzie River Indians.

Trapping Economy

The Indians of the Mackenzie District depended totally on fur for their income. Between 1915 and 1920 the fur market peaked, reaching its highest point during the winter of 1919-1920. At Fort Simpson the Hudson's Bay Company paid $1000 for 154 muskrat skins. White fox averaged $40 per pelt, from a previous $2.50. The price for marten jumped from $2.50 to $31; for mink from $1.00 to $14.00.[97] The fur boom attracted many white trappers. In 1921 there were 140 trapping licences issued to non-Indians in the Mackenzie District. Approximately 100 fur buyers followed the white trappers northward. Furs were plentiful and the prices were high, but the price of goods also increased.[98] By Christmas, 1919, the stores were sold out of supplies which were expected to last until the supply boat arrived in the summer. Nothing could be bought for less than a dollar, whether a pound of flour, a piece of candy or a stick of wood. This was for the Indians a deplorable experience with paper money. Previously they had handled Hudson's Bay Company tokens and "Made Beavers" in a time honoured system of barter. Learning the rules and penalties of the new money game was a luxury the Indians could not afford. Their trapping returns soon dropped with the competition of white trappers. The transient buyers lured them with worthless merchandise to squander their ready cash. The established companies retaliated by cutting off credit to the Indians. When the fur market crashed in April 1920, an uncertain future lay ahead for the Northern Indian who depended on the fur trade for his income.

Pressure on Ottawa

In November 1900, Duncan C. Scott, Chief Accountant of the Department of Indian Affairs, predicted, "in all likelihood there will be numerous adhesions to Treaty 8 during the next few years."[99] The first proposal came from Conroy after his trip through the Mackenzie River District in 1907. He reported the miserable conditions he had seen and advised: "In conclusion, I would say that my present experience leads me to strongly recommend that these Indians be taken into treaty. Their adhesion could be taken to Treaty No. 8."[100]

In 1909, Conroy wrote again to Pedley,[101] including a rough sketch of the Indian territory suitable for Treaty. [102] But Ottawa was digging in for a long resistance. The same Scott advised his superior that, "there are no funds available, and it is a question of doubtful utility whether treaties should be made in this far northern district."[103] The Government had recently signed Treaty 10 with the Indians of northern Saskatchewan, and did not welcome proposals for another one. As had happened before, the Department's accountant would dictate Government Indian policy.

Predictably, Northern missionaries also directed their solicitations to Ottawa. "Bishop Bompass [of the Anglican Mackenzie Diocese] . . . during the early 1900's . . . on a number of occasions suggested that a Treaty be made with the Indians to extinguish their claim to the land."[104] On December 27, 1909, Bishop Breynat wrote to the Minister of the Interior, Frank Oliver. He had evidently discussed the matter with Conroy the previous summer, and employed here the arguments most likely to influence the Government:*

> Upon a demand manifested by several, I take the liberty to write you in favour of the Indians of the Mackenzie District with confidence that the Government will do something to help this poor miserable crowd, the most disinherited in the Dominion, and practically the only who have not yet benefitted by the solicitude justly boasted with which the Government of Canada has always watched with conservation the Indian races so interesting in its territory.
>
> Has not the time arrived to stretch the Treaty to the Arctic Ocean on the same conditions already concluded with the tribes of Peace River, Athabasca and Great Slave Lake?
>
> The following are the reasons that seem to me sufficient to initiate the affirmative:
>
> 1/ The Goverment definitely and exclusively would acquire not only all the rights, but all the appearances of right to the immense soil which extends to the Arctic Ocean and let it not be said that they are waiting until the Country is a new Klondike, or until the Indians have been extinguished little by little with misery before commencing to pay the expenses.
>
> 2/ They will have more power to patrol the country, and protect the White men in the discovering of mines, more or less impending; also make the Indian more respectful toward the police, several of whom do not fear to claim the country as appertaining to them, and refuse the Government the right to carry laws against them who never by any contract acknowledged its authority.
>
> The country is very quiet, and our Indians naturally submissive, but their cunning pride could occasion them to commit actions of which they would be the first to regret them, but it would be more prudent to warn them beforehand.
>
> 3/ The expenses of the Treaty would relatively be small, considering the small number of Indians, about three thousand five hundred (3,500) and it would be a great help to them who are absolutely in need of it.
>
> If the Government deems it necessary to help the petition of the Indians – a petition which I myself strongly support – might I suggest the name of Mr. H. Conroy, Inspector of Treaty No. 8 to regulate with the Indians in the name of the Government the conditions of the Treaty. He knows the country and thoroughly understands the Indians. They will appreciate his devotedness and patience in occuping himself in their interest. I never heard a complaint uttered against him, far from that! In a word he has gained the confidence of all the Indians.

*It would appear that Breynat wrote this letter in French and asked someone else to translate it into English.

If there is a possibility, the Treaty should be given next spring. The winter announces very severe, and rabbits and fur have been so scarce for several years, that our poor Indians are indeed reduced to great misery, that when a slight epidemic passes, like the two preceding years, many of them fall victims for want of nourishment and care. All help from the Government would come in good time. If it is absolutely impossible, in waiting for better times, would the Government allow a certain amount of money to purchase thread for nets and ammunition which Mr. Conroy could distribute to whom he judged suitable.[105]

He sent a copy of this letter to Conroy, to whom he could express the underlying reason for all of his arguments:

You will find herewith enclosed a copy of my application to the Government in behalf of the Indians of Mackenzie River. I am sure you will recommend it whenever you have an opportunity. You know, as well as I do, how great and urgent are the needs of those poor tribes. The Government should do something for them . . . . The Indians are all anxious how they will make their living this winter. No deer! No rabbit![106]

On February 7, 1910, Conroy sent his copy of Breynat's letter to Pedley and again pleaded for a treaty:

Treaty should be made with those Indians as soon as convenient . . . . I think that the Bishop is right in advising the Department to make treaty with those Indians of the Mackenzie Valley as I observed last summer two large parties of miners and prospectors going into that district for the purpose of mining. There is some talk by the Indians south of that district that the reason for making treaty with them was on account of minerals being discovered on the shores of the Great Slave Lake. They think that when they see men and mining machinery arriving, that they have as good a right to receive treaty as those south of them.

The support of the sick and destitute Indians by the H.B.C. and traders has cost the Department quite large sums in the past and I think that the proper way to deal with them is to give them treaty.[107]

Both Conroy and Breynat knew the value of using expediency as an argument in convincing the Government to make a treaty. They knew from experience that the mere absence of a formal surrender would not delay appropriation of Indian land if it were for the economic advantage of the country. They both wanted to insure some benefit and recognition for the Indians before this would happen. Again, as in the previous year, the Chief Accountant disagreed:

I have read the memorandum from Inspector Conroy, and the communication addressed to the Minister by Bishop Breynat . . . I have elsewhere stated as my opinion that the northern limit of these Treaties should be the 60th parallel of latitude.

The Department at present relieves destitution and endeavours to prevent suffering by the issue of supplies through the H.B.C. and this entails considerable expenses from year to year . . . Our Indian policy in the Mackenzie River district should be to extend to these Indians certain privileges of education and medical attendance . . . relieve destitution wherever possible and provide for occasional visits by our Inspectors.

I may remark incidentally that there are no funds available for the expenses of making treaty.[108]

Deputy Superintendent Pedley accepted the opinion of his Chief Accountant and so advised the Minister, Frank Oliver, on February 23, 1910:

> With reference to the attached letter from Bishop Breynat in which he asks that Treaty should be made with the Indians of the Mackenzie River . . . no provision has been made for this expenditure . . . Although I would not postulate that the territory of the Mackenzie River Indians should never be ceded to the Crown, it seems to me that at present there is no necessity for taking that action. The influx of miners and prospectors into that country is very small, and at present there is no settlers. The Department relieves cases of pressing necessity through the H.B.C. and I think we should be prepared to meet the request made by the Bishop for twine for nets and snares, and that we should request Dr. Rymer to go down the River on the Hudson Bay Co. Steamer when she makes her annual trip. By taking these steps and by keeping in touch with the needs of the Indians, I think we will be discharging all present obligation.[109]

Conroy persisted, however, being more convinced each year of the necessity for a treaty. In his report of 1913, he stressed that the Indian people themselves were requesting a treaty:

> During my occasional visits to the posts in the territory north of Great Slave Lake extending all the way to the mouth of the Mackenzie River, I have been petitioned and earnestly requested by the various chiefs of the different tribes inhabiting this north country to endeavour, if possible, to arrange for their entry into treaty so that they might be on the same footing as the tribes to the south of them.
>
> They seem to be very despondent at the present time, continually hoping that the department will see its way clear to influencing the government to accede to the above request.
>
> I would strongly suggest that this question be immediately considered with a view in the near future of bringing each of these tribes within the scope of treaty administration. The following are the tribes, approximate population, headquarters that I have reference to:

Tribe	Population	Headquarters
Slave band	300	Fort Providence
Slave band	350	Fort Simpson
Slave band	150	Fort Wrigley
Loucheux and Mountain	300	Fort Norman
Hare	500	Fort Good Hope
Loucheux	150	Arctic Red River
Takudah	300	Fort McPherson
Dogrib	1,000	Fort Rae
Slave	350	Fort Liard

My reasons for making this suggestion are as follows:

1. From the point of view of economy in administration I have no hesitation in saying that it would require considerable less appropriation to support these Indians than at present under the existing system of grants from the sick and destitute funds.

2. When once these Indians come under treaty, the department will be in a position to know without any doubt whether cases of destitution and sickness are deserving or not, whereas at the present time there is no system by which this grant can be effectively gauged or controlled.

3. The Indians themselves are extremely anxious to come into treaty, and in such circumstances I am of the opinion that, if their wishes are acceded to, it will be both to their advantage and in the interests of the department.[110]

He repeated these arguments in 1914[111] and again in 1915, insisting that the northern Indians,

be allowed to tender their adhesions to Treaty No. 8. They have from year to year expressed a great desire to do this, and . . . I am of the opinion that it would be a beneficial matter both to the Indians and the department.[112]

The unreality of the Government's policy was reflected in this short passage on the North taken from a twenty-three volume study published in 1914, *Canada and Its Provinces:* "The only land to which the Indians have not ceded their title to the Crown is situated in the far northern parts of Canada, and it is doubtful whether it will at any time in the future be necessary to extinguish the Indian title over these territories."[113]

The Indians Are Heard From

Expressing themselves to Government officials who visited them, Indians outside of Treaty 8 looked to the Government for assistance and relief during hard times. They must also have recognized a need for Government protection as settlers began to move into their land. In the past they had given evidence of their co-operation, good will, and friendship, and were willing to pledge it for the future. A number of official reports disclosed the feelings of the Indians about a possible future Treaty:

1902, Conroy: The Indians on the north side of Great Slave Lake are anxious to come into treaty, as are those of [Fort] Providence on the Mackenzie River. They claim that the Slaveys and Yellowknives, who were taken into treaty in 1900, have hunting-grounds outside of treaty and are akin to them.[114]

1903, N.W.M.P. Inspector West: Bands outside the treaty limit at Mackenzie River and Great Slave Lake are anxious to become Treaty Indians.[115]

1909, Sergeant Field: At Fort Providence . . . The Indians spoke to me regarding Treaty, wondering when they would be taken into treaty.. . . at [Fort] Simpson . . . there is considerable destitution also owing to the great scarcity of fur throughout the country . . . I learned that the Indians at this place are also very anxious to be taken into treaty . . . .[116]

1909, Corporal Mellor: The [Fort] Liard Indians are certainly the most squalid impoverished lot I have yet met. They are at present starving, the fish lakes being seemingly exhausted, moose very scarce and no rabbits. I personally saw several very pitiful cases of starvation among them. They are very anxious to obtain treaty . . . Most of them had never seen a policeman before and my arrival caused considerable excitement amongst them . . . .

The chief of the [Fort] Simpson Indians, rejoicing in the name of "Norwegians" asked me to tell the government that his Indians did not want treaty . . . .

There is nothing new at [Fort] Providence. The Indians there are clamouring for treaty.[117]

1912, Corporal Charles LaNauze: At Providence . . . Indians are asking for treaty here, and from what I saw it would be a Godsend for them . . . .

The Fort Liard Indians sent down a message to the government that they want treaty there . . . .[118]

1912, Fort Simpson Indian Agent Gerald Card: The Indians of the latter place [Fort Liard] sent word for me to write to the Government and say that they were unanimous in their desire to be admitted to Treaty. Bishop Breynat also informs me that the Indians of Fort Providence are also anxious to accept Treaty. And while I have no commission to speak for them, I think the [Fort] Simpson Indians would not wish to be left out were a Treaty with the Indians of the above places to be effected . . . .[119]

1913, Corporal C.D. LaNauze: The chief of the [Fort] Providence Indians came to me and wanted me to tell the Government of their need for treaty. They cannot understand why the [Fort] Resolution and Hay River Indians get treaty and they not.[120]

1914, Conroy: . . . At all the northern posts, the Indians applied to me to be allowed to take treaty, and I would suggest that measures be taken to include them as soon as possible. They take the stand that they wish to be treated in the same manner as the other Indians . . . .[121]

1914, Chief Surveyor S.D. Fawcett: I understand that the Indians here [Fort Norman] would be quite willing to accept treaty and from all appearances it would be of great benefit to them.[122]

1914, Fort Simpson Indian Agent Thomas W. (Flynn) Harris: There is no doubt that each succeeding year will bring a greater number of people into the North especially now that a railroad is being built to Fort MacMurray, and it will be necessary for the Indian question to be regulated . . . .

From the Indians' point of view, I believe the making of Treaty will be the best thing for them.

I am not prepared to say that all the Indians are ready to take treaty, but if it is offered, and given to those who will take it, I feel assured that the others will fall into line . . . .[123]

> 1915, Inspector Charles Rheault [arrived at Fort Rae on December 22 . . .
> and stayed till December 26th]: All the Indians who came in paid
> me a special visit . . . They are again asking for Treaty. I hope that
> the Government will grant it to these Indians, as it will better them
> considerably . . . .[124]

A treaty was not forthcoming, since, in the words of Scott, "It has not been the desire of the Government to make a treaty with the Indians, too far in advance of settlement by white people."[125]

Fort Simpson Indian Agency 1911

Canada's sovereignty over the Mackenzie District was not demonstrated by government presence during the early years of this century. The Royal North West Mounted Police established detachments at Fort McPherson in 1903, at Fort Resolution and Fort Simpson in 1913. The Commissioner of the Northwest Territories was virtually unknown to most northerners. His accomplishments between 1905 and 1921 were undistinguished:

> Lieutenant Colonel F. White, appointed Commissioner in 1905, remained
> in office until his death in 1918, when he was succeeded by W.W. Cory.
> Through his period of tenure, Commissioner White governed the North-
> west Territories from Ottawa without the aid of a Council, on annual
> budgets that never exceeded 6,000 dollars . . . No ordinances were passed,
> none of the old ordinances of the Northwest Territories were repealed and
> no new policies were enunciated.[126]

Periodically, a few officials passed through the country. Conroy made regular trips on the Mackenzie every summer after 1907. The Minister of the Interior visited in 1910. A list compiled by Kitto of Government officials stationed in the District in 1920 included:

1. At Fort Smith: Gerald Card, who is:

> Indian Agent
> Agent of the Canadian National Parks Branch
> Mining Recorder (Mining, Lands and Yukon Branch)
> Recorder of Vital Statistics
> Coroner
> Justice of the Peace
> Issuer of marriage licences

2. At Simpson: Thomas W. Harris, who is:

> Indian Agent
> Mining Recorder (Mining, Lands and Yukon Branch)[127]

Indian agencies were opened at Fort Smith and at Fort Simpson in 1911, "to distribute relief and carry out experiments in farming." Fort Smith was within the boundaries of Treaty 8, but Fort Simpson was not, which made the move an unusual one.[128] It was Indian Agent

139

Card who arrived at Fort Simpson with 2 horses, 4 oxen, and 10 tons of implements and supplies,[129] on July 2, 1911. Apparently, the Indians did not immediately recognize the benefits of an agency, an agent and his equipment. They refused to shake hands with him "as they thought he had come to take their country away from them".[130]

> A considerable number seemed to be suspicious of the good intentions of the government in placing the demonstration farm in what they termed their country. They seemed to regard the coming of farm stock and implements as the beginning of a movement towards settlement, with the result of the gradual extinction of large game and all fur-bearing animals, the hunting and trapping of which is their sole means of subsistance. But, while suspicious and more or less unfriendly, being apparently of a gentle and timid disposition, they were not aggressively hostile.[131]

Six months after his arrival, Card had become "quite friendly"[132] with the Indians. In this report of March 1912 he congratulated himself:

> the initiation and carrying on of the work of the agency in a country in which the Indian title has not been extinguished by treaty, and in which both Indians and half-breeds are jealous of their rights, has been a delicate task.[133]

The Fort Simpson agency was quite successful in its first year due to the "helpful co-operation of the Hudson's Bay Company officials" and of "Bishop Breynat and his clergy . . . [who have been] of great service in establishing cordial relations between the government and the Indians." Nevertheless, Card recognized the doubtful legitimacy of his presence there:

> Those who were formerly unfriendly are beginning to change their disposition and are coming to understand the beneficient objects of the government in establishing an Indian agency and farm at this point. But, in my opinion, the situation will continue to be delicate, and any indiscretion may provoke trouble until the Indian title is extinguished by treaty.[134]

Conroy visiting Fort Simpson in 1912 was impressed with the work that had been done: farming experiments had been successful, oxen and horses were healthy and the sawmill had cut 60,000 feet of lumber.[135] The agricultural possibilities of the Mackenzie District had been tried and tested. Remotely, reluctantly, but nevertheless surely, the Government was preparing for the next treaty.

The Missionaries

In 1862 the Catholic Diocese of Athabasca-Mackenzie was formed, extending over the geographical area of the two Districts. The two were separated in 1902, with Bishop Grouard remaining in charge of the Diocese of Athabasca. After his consecration as Bishop on April

6, 1902, Breynat was assigned to the Diocese of the Mackenzie, where he remained until his resignation in 1943. His name has become synonymous with the Catholic Church in the North, embodying the influence and prestige of missionary tradition:

> . . . cassocked priests and self-abnegating nuns in their log missions had become the pivot around which nearly all aboriginal life revolved . . . From Athabasca to the Arctic the influence of the Holy Roman Church was almost paramount. And, from his wooden mission at Fort Resolution, beside the storm-tossed waters of Great Slave Lake, Monseigneur Breynat – a man of vast foresight, tireless energy and remarkable business acumen – ruled his swarthy flock with consummate tact and rare ability . . . [136]

Breynat was known outside of the Northwest Territories, as well. *Canadian Men and Women of the Time*, 1912, speaks of him as a "fine specimen of those who have spent their lives on behalf of the Indians of the North."[137] By 1920 there were Catholic missions at every main trading post in the Mackenzie, with the exception of Fort McPherson.

The Anglican Diocese of Mackenzie River was established in 1884, with William Carpenter Bompas as first Bishop residing at Fort Simpson. William Day Reeve succeeded him in 1891, and remained until 1907. No appointment was made until 1913, when James R. Lucas was consecrated Bishop of the Diocese, a charge he exercised until 1926. One of his first decisions was to transfer the Bishop's residence from Fort Simpson to Fort Chipewyan in northern Alberta. At that time the valley of the Slave River and a small area around Fort Chipewyan were transferred from the Diocese of Athabasca to that of Mackenzie River, which was nearly coextensive with the Mackenzie District. Edward Sittichinli, Loucheux, was ordained a minister of the Anglican Church in 1903, and worked as a missionary until 1928. He made Fort McPherson his headquarters and was the only resident Anglican minister there between 1918 and 1924. By 1920, in addition to schools in Hay River, Fort Simpson and Herschel Island, the Anglican Church had missions at Bernard Harbour, and Aklavik.

In the first decade of this century, the Canadian Government did not acknowledge or accept much responsibility for the education and health care, or for the social and political life of the Indian people of the Mackenzie District. When Breynat asked the Department of Indian Affairs for financial assistance for the northern schools, he received this reply: "The Mackenzie, being a missionary field, is the Church's responsibility."[138] The Churches did not take the responsibility lightly. Whatever was needed was done, in the measure of the means at hand:

> The activities of the Roman Catholic and Anglican Missions in these far north lands are most praiseworthy . . . Schools, hospitals and convents form part of the general scheme . . . Various industrial and agricultural operations are also pursued in connection with this work and the Natives

benefit by the results obtained and the example set.

These missions . . . are constantly ministering to the sick and destitute and without their friendly services the natives, and at times even the whites, would find it difficult to exist.[139]

In 1913, Bury recorded his impressions of the missionary effort. While praising its achievements, he pointed out its limitations:

In spite of the efforts of the missionaries in the north for the past 70 years, the Indian has remained an Indian to this day.

In his general characteristics, habits, customs, and mode of life he is practically unchanged . . . where a church is located, the missionary Indians attend with a fair amount of regularity, and take an interest in religious matters which is commendable . . .

It cannot be said that missionary effort in the north has been successful in causing the Indian to realize in any way his position as a civilized Canadian citizen. The missionaries have done good, hard, creditable work among the tribes, and the influence of the missions on the northern Indians is both far-reaching and important . . . but circumstances reveal the fact that, today, the Indian from a wordly point of view is no better off than he was before the advent of the missionary . . .

In their efforts to impress upon the savage the habits of cleanliness, sobriety, truthfulness and good living, the missionary has met with a great deal of success . . .

In conclusion it may be stated that the work of the missionary in the north will always bear the imprint of sincerity, devotion and self-abnegation, and their influence with the Indians is very real and effective and exercised at all times in a thoroughly just and disinterested manner.[140]

With the accumulation of years, the missionary's involvement in the lives of the people deepened in direct relation to the sincerity of his concern for their well-being. In good conscience he could not withhold his advice if circumstances were such that some advantage for them might result. The Indian people respected and trusted the missionary. They saw him infrequently, perhaps for one month out of twelve, yet his words and his actions made lasting impressions on them. To what extent this influence bordered on control, or remained in the realm of guidance and advice is a question that could only be answered by the Indians who were present for the signing of the Treaty.

Schools

The Indian negotiators for Treaty 11 were unschooled, unlettered men. They had no background or training for understanding the language of the Treaty, much less the concepts it embodied. Terms such as "Crown land", "federal jurisdiction", or "His Gracious Majesty" were unfamiliar and unrelated to their previous experiences. To understand the formal language of the Treaty and to relate it to the political, social and economic scene in Canada would have required much more schooling than was available in the Mackenzie District school system during the first two decades of this century.

Two day schools operated in the Northwest Territories. Attendance was not compulsory, and since few parents and children could see the benefit, enrollments were consistently low. The residential schools were first opened as orphanages and for a long time were "essentially hostels for unwanted, orphaned and diseased children."[141]* Proportionately few children attended these schools. A residential school was opened by the Grey Nuns in 1867 at Fort Providence, and one at Fort Resolution in 1909. The government supplied beds and mattresses for this latter residence, and gave a yearly allowance of $72 per student. It was raised to $125 in 1911, following a visit to the Mackenzie District of the Minister of the Interior and Superintendent General of Indian Affairs, the Honourable Frank Oliver. Until then he had not favoured the boarding school system. But after seeing the hard living conditions of the people and having inspected the schools, he concluded that if Indian children were to receive any schooling it could only be provided by the boarding schools.[142]

Kitto provided this listing of schools in the Mackenzie District in 1920:

Fort Smith Day School	Catholic
Fort Resolution Boarding School	Catholic (72 children)
Hay River Boarding School	Anglican (47 children)
Providence Boarding School	Catholic (80 children)
Simpson Boarding Schools	Catholic and Anglican
McPherson Boarding School	Anglican
Herschel Island Day School	Anglican

The progress being made by the children is remarkable, and too much praise cannot be given to those in authority . . . The children are given valuable instruction in various manual arts. The girls receive training in sewing, fancy-work, cooking and general housework. The boys are instructed in building, agriculture, and various other subjects. All children are taught the English language. In the senior grades of the R.C. Schools, French is also taught. Their religious instructions are supplemented by valuable lessons in health, cleanliness, sanitation, nursing, and first aid to the sick and wounded. It is remarkable the way in which these children respond. Coming into the schools at tender ages without being able to speak a word of English, they frequently surpass in a few years the average corresponding classes of white children.[143]

Enrollment figures from the Fort Providence school demonstrate that this education reached very few children:

*Following the epidemic of scarlet fever in 1865, the Hudson's Bay Company built a school for the orphans in Fort Norman and engaged a school master, Mr. Murdo McLeod, under the direction of Reverend Bompas. The school was closed in 1868. (H. A Cody, *An Apostle of the North*, p. 385). In 1871, twenty-six children attended the Fort Providence residential school, of whom twelve were orphans. (OMIAW, Letter from Sister Ward, March 28, 1871, Mackenzie File.)

Year	Grade 1	2	3	4	5
1919-1920	42	16	10	11	
1920-1921	28	9	9	12	1
1921-1922	29	10	4	4	1
1922-1923	23	8	11	5	2[144]

Transportation and Communications

In the years preceding Treaty 11, the Indians of the Mackenzie District had little opportunity to learn about the rest of Canada. Some improvements had been made in transportation and communication but these did not have a direct effect on Indian life.

The trading companies operated a few steamboats during the short summer months. The *Liard River* and the *Lady Mackworth* travelled the Liard and Nelson rivers. The *Fort Rae* crossed the Great Slave Lake. The *Mackenzie River* and the *Northland Trader* took the Mackenzie River run, including 200 miles on the lower Slave River. Eight days were needed to make the trip from Fort Smith to Fort McPherson, but it took seventeen days for the return trip. Few tourists ventured into the District and those who did had to be ready to fend for themselves. Following the oil strike at Norman Wells in 1920, the Police had the authority to refuse entry to those who were not properly equipped, as well as to those who were unfit or undesirable.[145]

Steamboats in summer and dog teams in winter were the means of transporting the mail. By 1920 mail service was established for all posts along the Mackenzie River:

> The Post Office Department maintains a mail service throughout the Mackenzie District . . . Every post receives all classes of mail at least once a year by steamboat and at more frequent intervals when similar opportunities arise. Fort Smith and Resolution receive 5 winter mails; Hay River, Providence and Simpson receive 3 winter mails. Wrigley, Norman, Good Hope, Arctic Red River, and McPherson receive 2 winter mails.[146]

Deliveries were often weeks behind schedule, as was duly noted by the manager of the Hudson's Bay Company at Fort Simpson: "February 19: Mail arrived from the South today, 20 days behind schedule time . . . March 18: Mail arrived from Providence today, 18 days behind time."[147] When a new schedule was introduced in 1921, providing "11 mails during the season from McMurray to Fort Smith", the Commissioner of the Northwest Territories praised it as "excellent service".[148]

By 1920 neither the telegraph nor the wireless had reached into the Mackenzie District. The nearest stations were at Fort McMurray and Peace River. This isolation from the rest of Canada might well explain the public's lack of interest in the Mackenzie District prior to the discovery of oil. It can certainly explain the handicap which the Indians brought with them to the Treaty negotiations.

Summary

The political, social and economic events which followed Treaty 8 to a large degree shaped Treaty 11. As the effects of Treaty 8 were gradually becoming apparent to those who had to live with them, other forces were at work overshadowing the past and precipitating change. Nothing in their culture, history or experience had prepared the Indians for the role of treaty partner which was thrust upon them. No apprenticeship was encouraged, no recourse was allowed. The drama which had been acted out in 1899 was to be repeated again in 1921, with new actors, in a new setting. Only the dialogue would remain the same. It had been tried, tested, and proven to withstand the vicissitudes of time.

Notes to Chapter III

1. IBNWTA, Transcript of Frank Norn's interview by Gerald Sutton of Yellowknife, 29 June 1972.
2. *The Civil Service List of Canada, 1903,* Ottawa, S. E. Dawson, Printer to the King's Most Excellent Majesty, 1904, p. 184.
3. IBNWTA, Transcript of Johnny Jean Marie Beaulieu's interview by David Smith, 25 June 1969.
4. IBNWTA, Transcript of Frank Norn's interview by Gerald Sutton of Yellowknife, 29 June 1972.
5. IBNWTA, Transcript of Susie Abel's interview by Dr. June Helm of the University of Iowa, 5 July 1971.
6. ACAT, *Annual Report of the Church Missionary Society,* 1899-1900, p. 473.
7. ACAT, *Letter Leaflet,* Vol. X, No. 11. September 1899, Rev. George Holmes' letter, p. 364-365; Vol. XI, No. 2, December 1899, Rev. George Holmes' letter, p. 44.
8. ASGM, Chipewyan, Historique, Document 53, Grouard to Mother General, 1 September 1899.
9. *Ibid.,* Document 55, Grouard to Mother General, 19 March 1900.
10. RCMAFS, file: Fort Chipewyan, Grouard to Prime Minister, 24 September 1901.
11. D. Hanbury *Sport and Travel in the Northland of Canada,* New York, Macmillan, 1904, pp. 24-25.
12. E. Stewart, *Down the Mackenzie and Up the Yukon in 1906,* London, John Lane, 1913; New York, John Lane; Toronto, Bell and Cockburn, p. 75.
13. E. T. Seton, *The Arctic Prairies,* New York, International University Press, 1911, pp. 94, 148.
14. A. Cameron, *The New North,* New York and London, D. Appleton and Co., 1910, pp. 131, 132, 163-167.
15. Canada, *Sessional Papers,* 1902, No. 28, Report of Inspector C. H. West, Commanding Peace River Sub-district, pp. 58-59.
16. *Ibid.,* Annual report of Superintendent C. Constantine, commanding 'G' Division, p. 56.
17. *Ibid.,* 1904, No. 28, Report of Inspector C. W. West, Peace River sub-district, p. 40.
18. *Ibid.,* 1910, No. 28, Report of Inspector Pelletier, p. 143.
19. *Ibid.,* 1912, No. 28, Report of Sergeant Field, p. 170.
20. IBNWTA, Transcript of Frank Norn's interview by Gerald Sutton of Yellowknife, 29 June 1972.
21. IANDO, file 777/28-3, Vol. 1, H. A. Conroy to D. McLean, Assistant Deputy and Secretary of Indian

Affairs, 24 September 1913.

22. *Ibid.*, Chief William Baptiste to Minister of the Interior, 1 July 1913.

23. *Ibid.*, Conroy to McLean, 24 September 1913.

24. *Ibid.*, Conroy to Scott, 13 June 1914.

25. Canada, *Sessional Papers,* 1916, No. 28, Inspector C. A. Rheault's patrol report, p. 199.

26. IANDO, file 779/28-3, Vol. 2, Extract from report of Sergeant A. H. Roy, dated Fort Fitzgerald, July 25th. 1918; and Fort Smith Indian Agent's Diary during annuity payments, July 28th, 1918.

27. IANDO, file 779/28-3, Vol. 2, Statement of Arrears of Annuity in Treaty 8.

28. *Ibid,* McLean to G. Card, 5 May 1919.

29. *Treaty No. 8,* Ottawa, Queen's Printer, Reprint 1969, p. 6.

30. Canada, *Sessional Papers,* 1901, No. 27, Report of Commissioner for Treaty No. 8, p. xl.

31. *Ibid.*, 1902, No. 27, Report of H. A. Conroy, p. 201.

32. *Ibid.*, 1913, No. 27, Report of Fort-Smith Indian Agent, p. 130.

33. *Ibid.*, 1915, No. 27, Report of H. A. Conroy, Inspector for Treaty No. 8, pp. 82-83.

34. IANDO, file 779/28-3, Vol. 2, Card to Assistant Deputy and Secretary of Indian Affairs, 17 September 1919.

35. *Ibid.*, Indian Agent Card's diary, Annuity Payments, 1921.

36. *Ibid.*, file 191/30-1, Vol. 1, G. Breynat to A. Coté, Assistant Deputy Minister of the Interior, 25 April 1913.

37. *Ibid.*, Frank Pedley, Deputy Superintendent General of Indian Affairs to Breynat, 9 May 1913.

38. *Ibid.*, Frank Pedley to W.W. Cory, Deputy Minister of the Interior, 27 May 1913.

39. *Ibid.*, file 191/30-3, Pedley to Cory, 19 June 1913.

40. *Ibid.*, file 191/30-1, Vol. 1, S. D. Fawcett to Deville, Surveyor General, 7 August 1913.

41. *Ibid.*, file 191/30-3, Fawcett to Surveyor General, 20 April 1914.

42. *Ibid.*, 11 February 1914.

43. IANDO, file 777/28-3, Vol. 1, Conroy to Scott, 13 June 1914.

44. IANDO, file 191/30-1, Vol. 1, S. Bray, Chief Surveyor to Scott, 11 September 1914.

45. *Ibid.*, A. G. MacKay to Frank Pedley, 28 March 1914, and Extract from a letter of the 24th. February 1914 from John Piché.

46. PAC, RG10, BS, file 336877, Thomas W. Harris to Assistant Deputy and Secretary of Indian Affairs, 12 February 1914.

47. IANDO, file 191/30-4, Scott to Conroy, 24 February 1915.

48. *Ibid.*, file 191/30-1, Vol. 1, Henry J. Bury to Scott, 4 October 1915.

49. IBNWTA, Transcript of Pierre Smallnose Drygeese's interview by Beryl C. Gillespie, anthropologist from the University of Iowa, 31 July 1968.

50. IANDO, file 191/30-1, Vol. 1, Bury to Scott, 4 October 1915.

51. Canada, *Office Consolidation of the Indian Act,* Ottawa, Queen's Printer, 1969, Section 18 (1), p. 8.

52. IANDO, file 191/30-11-1, Assistant Deputy and Secretary of Indian Affairs to A. J. Bell, 25 January 1915.

53. *Ibid.*, Bury to McLean, 5 July 1920.

54. *Ibid.*, Bury to Scott, 9 November 1916.

55. PAC, RG85, Vol. 661, Memorandum of Card, 4 September 1918.

56. PAC, RG85, Vol. 611, file 2742, Card to Harkin, 10 June 1920.

57. IANDO, file 191/30-11-1, McLean's Memorandum, 18 June 1920.

58. *Ibid.*, Bury to McLean, 5 July 1920.

59. *Ibid.*, Deputy Superintendent General of Indian Affairs to Harkin, 22 July 1920.

60. *Ibid.*, Conroy to Scott, 29 November 1920.

61. PAC, RG10, BS file 336877, F. H. Kitto, D.L.S. *Report of a Prelimi-*

nary *Investigation of the Natural Resources of Mackenzie District and their Economic Development, made during the summer of 1920,* Ottawa, Department of the Interior, Natural Resources Intelligence Branch, Section XXI.

62. IANDO, file 191/30-11-1, Hoyes Lloyd, Secretary Canadian National Parks to McLean, 9 June 1921.

63. *Ibid.,* A. F. MacKenzie, Acting Assistant Deputy & Secretary of Indian Affairs to Card, 9 May 1922.

64. *Ibid.,* file 779/28-3, Vol. ? Indian Agent Card's Diary, Annuity Payments, 1922.

65. N.W.T., Territorial Council, *Minutes of the Sessions,* 21st. Session, 10 December 1930, p. 143.

66. Canada, *Privy Council,* OC 8761, 11 November 1941.

67. Canada, *Sessional Papers,* 1905, No. 27, Conroy's report, p. 201.

68. *Ibid.,* 1915, No. 28, Report of Sergeant A. H. L. Mellor attending treaty payments, p. 197.

69. *Ibid.,* No. 27. Conroy's report, p. 79.

70. IANDO, file 777/28-3, Vol. 1, Chief Vital to Department of Indian Affairs, 28 June 1916.

71. In the Supreme Court of Canada, on Appeal from the Supreme Court of Alberta Appelate Division, between Michael Sikyea, Appellant, And Her Majesty the Queen, Respondent, 1964, *Appelant's Factum,* p. 9.

72. Canada, *Statutes,* 7-8 George V, 1917, Chapter 36, An Act Respecting Game in the Northwest Territories of Canada, Section 4 (3).

73. RCMAFS, file 13-7, Harris to Scott, 27 February 1919.

74. *Ibid.*

75. PAC, RG18, Fl, Vol. 12, file G-1316-21, Sergeant Joy's report to Officer Commanding Great Slave Lake Sub-district, 29 July 1919.

76. IANDO, file 779/28-3, Indian Agent's Diary, Annuity Payments, 1921. Report to Assistant Deputy & Secretary of Indian Affairs, 16 August, 1921.

77. Canada, Commons, *Debates,* 1920, Col. 3280.

78. Old Drygeese died of quinsy (suppurative tonsillitis). He was buried on 20 July 1913.
Edmonton Bulletin, 27 August 1913.
ASGM, *Chroniques de Fort Resolution.*
Fort Resolution, Catholic Mission, Vital Statistics Records.

79. P. H. Godspell, *Arctic Trader,* New York, G. P. Putnam's Sons, 1934, pp. 193-194.

80. Canada, *Statutes,* 7-8- George V, 1917, Chapter 36, An Act Respecting Game in the Northwest Territories of Canada.

81. Canada, *Privy Council,* OC 1053, 1 May 1918.

82. PAC, RG18, Fl, Vol. 12, G-1316. Inspector Fletcher's report to Officer Commanding 'G' Division, August 1920.

83. ASGM, *Chroniques de Fort Resolution,* p. 74.

84. Fort Resolution, RCM, *Codex Historicus..*

85. PAC, RG18, Vol. 3068, RCMP Diary.

86. IBNWTA, Transcript of Alexis Charlo's interview by Roy Daniels and James Wah-shee, December 1968. Alexis Charlo, born in 1890, is a Dogrib Indian from Fort Rae.

87. Canada, *Sessional Papers,* 1909, No. 27, Report of the Deputy Superintendent General of Indian Affairs, p. xxii.

88. PAC, RG10, BS, file 336,877, H. A. Conroy, memorandum, 18 December 1907.

89. ACAT, *Annual report of the Missionary Society of the Church of England,* 1907, p. 47.

90. Canada, *Sessional Papers,* 1910, No. 28, Report of Sergeant Field, pp. 182-183.

91. *Ibid.,* 1911, No. 28, Report of Corporal A. H. L. Mellor, p. 189.

92. PAC, RG10, BS, file 336, 877, H. J. Bury, *Report of the Territory covered by Treaty No. 8 and the District North of Fort Simpson along the val-*

ley of the Mackenzie R., 1913.

93. PAC, RG18, Fl, Vol. 12, file G-1316, Report of Constable Smyth, 22 July 1919.

94. F. H. Kitto, 1920 report, Section XXII.

95. H. J. Bury, 1913 report.

96. G. Breynat, *Cinquante Ans au Pays des Neiges*, Vol. II, pp. 238, 246, 268, 340; Vol. III, p. 329.

97. Information Canada, Production of Raw Furs in Canada by Provinces and by Years, season 1919-1920.

98. PAC, RG18, Fl, Vol. 12, file G-1316, Report of Inspector Anderson, 3 February 1920.

99. PAC, RG10, BS, file 55340, Scott to the Secretary of Indian Affairs, 29 November 1900.

100. *Ibid.,* file 336,877, Conroy, Memorandum, 18 December 1907.

101. *Ibid.,* Conroy to Pedley, 5 February 1909.

102. *Ibid.,* Map, 5 February 1909.

103. *Ibid.,* Scott to Deputy Superintendent General, 18 February 1909.

104. IANDO, file 1/1-11-22, Position paper with respect to land in the N.W.T. concerning the fulfillment of treaty, by Frank Carter and A. D. Hunt, 2 May 1968. No other document has been located to support this opinion, although research was made by both Canon T. R. Millman, Archivist, Anglican Church of Canada, (letter to the author, 22 June 1973) and A. D. Hunt, himself now Assistant Deputy Minister, Department of Indian Affairs and Northern Development, (letter to the author, 6 July, 1973).

105. PAC, RG10, BS, file 336,877, Breynat to Frank Oliver, Minister of the Interior, 27 December 1909.

106. *Ibid.,* Breynat to Conroy, 29 December 1909.

107. *Ibid.,* Conroy to Deputy Superintendent General of Indian Affairs, 7 February 1910.

108. *Ibid.,* Scott to Deputy Superintendent General, 17 February, 1910.

109. *Ibid.,* Pedley to Oliver, 23 February 1910.

110. Canada, *Sessional Papers,* 1915, No. 27, Report of Inspector Conroy, pp. 83-84.

111. *Ibid.,* 1916, No. 27, Report of Inspector Conroy, p. 86.

112. *Ibid.,* 1917, No. 27, Report of Inspector Conroy, p. 81.

113. A. Shortt and A. G. Doughty, eds. *Canada and its Provinces: a history of the Canadian People and their Institutions,* 23 Vols., Toronto, 1913-1917, Vol. 7, p. 598.

114. Canada, *Sessional Papers,* 1903, No. 27, Report of Inspector Conroy, p. 178.

115. *Ibid.,* 1904, No. 28, Report of Inspector C. H. West, p. 40.

116. *Ibid.,* 1910, No. 28, Report of Sergeant R. Field, p. 183.

117. *Ibid.,* Report of Corporal A. H. L. Mellor, pp. 185-186.

118. *Ibid.,* 1913, No. 28, Report of Corporal La Nauze, p. 211.

119. PAC RG10, BS, file 336,877, Card to Secretary of Indian Affairs, 9 February 1912. Fort Liard Indians were in close contact with the Fort Nelson Indians who adhered to Treaty 8 in 1910, and no doubt influenced their requesting a treaty in 1912.

120. Canada, *Sessional Papers,* 1914, No. 28, Report of Corporal C. D. La Nauze, p. 240.

121. *Ibid.,* 1916, No. 27, Report of Inspector Conroy,p. 86.

122. IANDO, file 191/30-2-1, Report of surveyor Fawcett, 7 February 1914.

123. PAC, RG10, BS, file 336,877, Harris to Assistant Deputy and Secretary of Indian Affairs, 12 February 1914.

124. Canada, *Sessional Papers,* 1917, No. 28, Report of Inspector Charles Rheault, p. 255.

125. PAC, RG10, BS, file 336,877, Scott to Conroy, 7 May 1914.

126. Robert Carney, *Relations in Education between the Federal and Territorial Governments and the Roman Catholic Church in the Mackenzie District, N.W.T., 1867-1961,* Unpublished M. A. Thesis, University of Alberta, 1971, pp. 33-34.

127. F. H. Kitto, 1920 report, Section X.
128. Canada, *Sessional Papers,* 1912, No. 27, Report of the Deputy Superintendent General of Indian Affairs, p. XX.
129. *Ibid.,* 1913, No. 28, Report of Inspector Field, p. 193.
130. *Ibid.,* Report of Corporal La Nauze, p. 211.
131. *Ibid.,* No. 27, Report of Indian Agent Card, p. 125.
132. *Ibid.,* No. 28, Report of Corporal La Nauze, p. 211.
133. *Ibid.,* No. 27, Report of Card, p. 127.
134. *Ibid.,* p. 126.
135. *Edmonton Bulletin,* 29 August 1912.
136. P. H. Godsell, *The Vanishing Frontier,* Toronto, Ryerson Press, 1939, p. 20.
137. H. J. Morgan, ed., *The Canadian Men and Women of the Time,* Toronto, William Briggs, 1912, p. 138.
138. G. Breynat, *The Flying Bishop,* London, Burns and Oates, 1955, p. 132.
139. F. H. Kitto, 1920 report, Section VI.
140. H. J. Bury, 1913 report,
141. R. Carney, *Relations in Education,* pp. 165-168.
142. G. Breynat, *Cinquante Ans au Pays des Neiges,* Vol. II, pp. 188-192.
143. F. H. Kitto, 1920 report, Section VII.
144. RCMAFS, file: Statistiques Diverses.
145. F. H. Kitto, 1920 report, Section XXIV.
146. *Ibid.,* Section V.
147. A. F. Camsell, "What Happened at Fort Simpson N.W.T., During Winter 1921?", *The Beaver,* July 1921, p. 19.
148. N.W.T., Territorial Council, *Minutes of the Sessions,* Memorandum of the Commissioner to the Council, 12 May 1921, p. 10.

Chapter IV

Treaty 11

Introduction

> You know that 50 or 60 years ago, many people believed that the Indian problem would solve itself out.
> — Thomas A. Crerar, Superintendent of
> Indian Affairs, June 7, 1944

The expected solution of the Indian problem was the gradual disappearance of the Indians themselves. This was indeed the situation in the Northwest Territories by the turn of the century. As late as 1940 eminent anthropologists and historians questioned the survival of the race:

> Through economic and social changes both the outward and the inward lives of the [N.W.T.] Indians have altered. Over a long period – most of the 19th century – these changes threatened to bring about the extinction of the Indian race. Alcoholic excesses and diseases previously unknown, particularly smallpox, tuberculosis, and influenza, decimated their ranks and reduced their number from what was estimated by some authorities to be 13,000 to one-third of that total.[1]
>
> Nearing their end also, it would seem, are the Athapaskan tribes of the Mackenzie Valley . . . The Athapaskans lacked vigour to react to the stimulus and are slowly fading away in despair.[2]

These opinions seemed to be substantiated by census figures of the Northwest Territories Indians published by the Department of Indian Affairs.

1913:	5,262
1914:	4,928[3]
1915:	4,003
1916:	3,769[4]
1919:	3,764[5]

Kitto released a count of the total population of the Mackenzie District in 1920. His estimate of the Indian population, however, does not agree with other figures of the period.

Whites, permanent residents	150
Half-Breeds	200
Esquimos (scattered roving bands)	250
Treaty Indians (Ft. Smith, Ft. Resolution, Hay River)	900
Non-Treaty Indians (along Mackenzie River)	3,500[6]

This decline in their numbers hardly put the Indians in a position of strength for negotiating a Treaty with the Government. How much consequence could be attached to demands on the future made by a vanishing race?

Any judgment on Treaty 11 must be rooted in an understanding of the concept of leadership which the Indians brought to the negotiations. Traditionally the Mackenzie River Indians lived under the guidance of men who had earned respect by reason of their superiority in medicine, wisdom or hunting. Official leadership was almost non-existent. The power of decision was vested in the total membership of the group or band, and unanimous consent was required before action was taken; the chief was but a spokesman for his fellows.[7] An early demonstration of this was observed by Samuel Hearne about 1770. During bartering sessions at the trading post, those who appeared to be leaders were, in fact, only spokesmen, selected to give the group solidarity and prestige in the bargaining:

> Indeed, the generality of Europeans who reside in those parts, being utterly unacquainted with the manners and customs of the Indians, have conceived so high an opinion of those leaders, and their authority, as to imagine that all who accompany them on those occasions are entirely devoted to their service and command all the year; but this is so far from being the case, that the authority of those great men, when absent from the Company's Factory, never extends beyond their own family; and the trifling respect shown them by their countrymen, during their residence at the factory, proceeds from motives of interest.[8]

Any semblance of political organization among the Mackenzie Indians was superimposed by a system other than their own. Accounts of how this was done emphasize the basic limitations inherent in this surrogate leadership:

> Whatever authority is possessed at present by the chief is generally vested in him by the fur traders and the Canadian Government, who find it advisable to deal with an established representative. Thus the chief is given a uniform and insignia of office and is issued special rations by the traders and the Government treaty officer. He is more or less chosen by agreement between the members of the band and the traders but his authority hardly extends beyond representing his band with the Government and the fur companies . . . .[9]

Frank Norn, a native of Hay River and the Treaty party's official interpreter for many years, described one method of selecting a chief:

> And in them days when they were going to get a new chief for the council, they don't vote. Well, the [Anglican] minister was here and the R.C. was down here, and the R.C. ask two people what they think about the man because they are going to choose him as a councillor and a chief, and the Bay Manager they all get together and talk about it and the Hudson's Bay Manager, the Minister and the Priest and all these White people know that he's a good guy, and that's all and they tell the people that they choose this man as a councillor and chief and it's satisfactory, everyone says he's a good man and a good chief. And that's the way they used to do it.[10]

As they approached Treaty negotiations, the Indians brought with them quite different views on government than did the Treaty Commissioners. Both parties had been brought to the Treaty by an accumulation of events which had affected each differently, influencing their reasons for negotiating a Treaty. How much either one understood the other would be crucial to the success of their agreement.

Oil is King

From the time of the Klondike Gold Rush prospectors penetrated the Mackenzie District. Placer gold was known to exist on the Liard, Nahanni, and Gravel Rivers; silver and lead on the south shore of Great Slave Lake; copper on the Coppermine River; iron in the Richardson Mountains; salt at the Fort Smith Salt Springs; and considerable quartz deposits in the easterly section. Northern mineral resources were still unexploited. It was only a matter of time before the big strike.

And when it came, it was oil, forty-five miles north of Fort Norman, at the site of present day Norman Wells. Alexander Mackenzie had seen it oozing from the ground there in 1789, as he passed by enroute to the Arctic Ocean; geological surveys had established the existence of an immense oil field within the Mackenzie Basin in the late 1880s; and amid considerable excitement, red-brown crude had been collected from the surface near Fort Norman and brought to Athabasca Landing in 1912.[11] The location of the first test well was chosen in 1914, "as a site where a hole of moderate depth could not fail to penetrate the petroliferous formations which had been discovered".[12] In 1918-1919, the Imperial Oil Company began drilling in four locations: near Fort McMurray, at the west end of Great Slave Lake, close to Peace River and at Norman Wells. This activity did not escape public attention, and cautious predictions were offered by the Minister of the Interior, Arthur Meighen:

> I am not sure when these discoveries will be made, or whether they ever will be made, but the prospects are indeed bright. I have no doubt that

those engaged in the work anticipate that it will not be long before discoveries are made.[13]

There is every reason to hope, if not to believe, that we may see a very considerable oil discovery in this country.[14]

It was on Indian territory, still unsurrendered by any treaty, that the first gusher at Norman Wells came in on August 25, 1920, revealing the underground treasure of the Northwest Territories:

At 783 feet a strong flow of oil was struck. For ten minutes a column of oil spouted from the 6-inch casing to a height of 75 feet above the derrick floor, after which the well was capped. The flow on that occasion probably exceeded 600 barrels of oil. On two subsequent occasions the valve was opened, with similar results.[15]

The oil strike caused much excitement among speculators and prospectors across the country. Canadian newspapers described the event with superlatives: "Biggest Oil Field in the World":

It stretches all the way from Fort Norman to the Arctic Coast, and the explorer Stefansson was camped on the far end of the same oil vein when he was on Victoria Island. The season's experimentation has absolutely proven the existence of an enormous body of oil-bearing rock in the Mackenzie River territory, compared to which Mexico and Peru are in the miniature class.[16]

First well sunk yields 1,000 barrels an hour.[17]

Northern oil wells prove successful. One thousand gallons an hour is the production of the first well brought in the Fort Norman district and the Imperial Oil Co. is preparing to punch a district 200 miles in width and nobody knows how long, full of holes for wells. That these will all be producers is the word brought down from that district by Alf Patrick who drilled the first well.[18]

According to the *Calgary Gazette,* the "district to be punched full of producing wells" was not merely 200 miles wide, but rather 600 miles wide, and "nobody knows how long . . . ".[19] The *Montreal Star* and the *Vancouver Province,* both reported "colossal activity at Fort Norman."[20]

RCMP Inspector Fletcher was not as optimistic. As early as August 1920, he warned that "any attempt to start an oil boom in Fort Norman oil shares or leases should be, if possible, discouraged.[21] Mr. M.B. Green, Calgary manager for the Imperial Oil Co., also tried to cool the excitement. He was quoted in the *Calgary Herald:*

As for Fort Norman, the oil there is not and will not be worth one red cent, for it is doubtful if a railroad, the only means by which the oil could be transported upon a commercial basis, would ever be built to that far northern outpost; certainly not unless oil should be found there in overwhelming quantities. . . .

The only value of the oil discovery at the present time, said Mr. Green, is purely scientific. It was now known that oil is there; further than that stood a stone wall. Whether it is there in sufficient quantity to warrant the spending of millions of dollars to attempt to get it out is not known yet by any means.[22]

But Green's admonitions were of little avail. No longer was transportation a major problem in the development of the North. Heavy equipment could be hauled on the larger steamboats and barges travelling the Athabasca, Slave, and Mackenzie Rivers. A railway had replaced the old ox-cart road from Edmonton to Fort McMurray on the Athabasca River. The construction cost of a pipe-line to carry the oil to southern markets was estimated at fifty-five million dollars.[23] In a letter dated November 1, 1920, the RCMP Superintendent of the Force's "G" division, advised his superior in Ottawa of the situation:

> I am of the opinion that if oil, gold, etc. are found in paying quantities in the McKenzie and Great Slave districts, it will not be long before a railroad is pushed North from Peace River to Vermilion, thence to a point near Providence on Great Slave Lake.
>
> In conversation with Mr. Taylor, Manager of the Imperial Oil Company for this district, I was informed that before they can commercialize this oil they must receive it in greater quantities. Should this occur they propose to build oil barges to convey the oil to Fort Smith, thence by pipe line to end of steel at Fort MacMurray, thence tank cars to their refinery at Regina. He informed me that even with this tremendously long haul from Fort Norman, he was of the opinion that it could be laid down at Regina cheaper than at the present time, and would be a great saving to their company.[24]

Kitto reported that:

> One of the last suggestions is that the oil should be taken downstream in river tankers to the [Mackenzie River] delta, piped across the [Rocky] Mountains through MacDougall's Pass, and taken down the Yukon waterways by other river tankers to tide water on Behring Sea . . . .[25]

To profit from the oil boom, prospectors and speculators had to reach the Norman Wells area as soon as possible. With winter coming, plans were made to go by plane, on foot, or by dog team. The *Edmonton Journal* of January 18, 1921 carried this story:

> "Fast Dirigible Service to Oil Fields of North"
> An aeroplane factory for Edmonton and the operating of a thirty-six hour dirigible passenger service between this city and Fort Norman are main proposals in a scheme which will be explained to the city council this evening. . . .
>
> In March the aviators expect their first dirigible to arrive here, when plans will be made for the first flight to the new oil centre of the far north. It is proposed that the ship on its maiden trip to Fort Norman will carry twenty-five newspapermen and government officials who will be the guests of the aeroplane concern. . . .

In April, the firm will bring a large dirigible here for service between Edmonton and Fort Norman. This machine will be capable of carrying at least 25 passengers with an allowance of 200 pounds of baggage for each passenger.

It is proposed that the charge for the trip will be $1,500. This would no doubt include the return trip for those wishing to merely stake claims and return at once to the capital city.[26]

After the dog derby in Le Pas, Manitoba, prospectors vied for the services of competing teams: "Fort McMurray to Fort Norman can be made in 15 days . . . Want dog sleigh racers to dash to Fort Norman . . . mushers holding out for $5000 before attempting the long run".[27]

The annual report of the Royal Canadian Mounted Police gave this account of the winter traffic:

Owing to the reports of oil having been found in the Fort Norman district, it was anticipated that a considerable rush into that territory would take place, and during the winter some 24 parties made the trip from here [Edmonton], by dogtrain to Fort Norman to stake claims.

In addition, other parties went from places in the North, and also came overland from Dawson and Whitehorse. Owing, however to the regulations governing oil leases having been changed, the actual number going into the district to stake claims was not considerable.[28]

In summer the easiest, fastest, and most pleasant way to Fort Norman was by river. The newly formed Alberta and Arctic Transportation Company quoted these prices for its service:

New Steamer Service to Fort Norman Oil Fields from Peace River and from Fort MacMurray. . . . Return tickets from MacMurray to Oil Fields, $200.00. Meals at $1.00 each when navigating, [but] across the portages, passengers will have to be in a position to feed themselves.
Upper berths at $1.00
Lower berths at $1.50[29]

A transportation boom had hit the Mackenzie River. That summer of 1921, before the first steamer reached Fort Providence, 92 boats of every description had already passed this village on their way north.[30]

The Territorial Government Emerges

Unaccustomed importance and responsibility fell abruptly on the Government of the Northwest Territories. Commissioner William Wallace Cory had recently succeeded the first man to hold the office, Lt. Col. Frederick White. So little governing had taken place between 1905 and 1920 that councillors had never been named, nor a territorial administration established. Cory wasted no time. On October 27,

155

1920, he enacted his first ordinance:

AN ORDINANCE RESPECTING ENTRY INTO THE N.W.T.

> The Commissioner of the N.W.T. enacts as follows:
> 1 – This ordinance may be cited as the "Entry Ordinance".
> 2 – No person shall enter, or attempt to enter the provisional District of Mackenzie, N.W.T., unless he has satisfied the Officer in Charge of the R.C.M.P. at Edmonton, Alberta; Fitzgerald, Alberta; Peace River, Alberta, or Dawson, Yukon Territory, that such person is not, in the opinion of the Officer, likely to become a Public charge while he is in the Territory.[31]

Each person entering the Territories was issued a "Clearance Certificate", certifying that he was "mentally and physically able, and properly equipped and outfitted". He was required to present his certificate for endorsement at each police post along his route. Those who did not comply were promptly dealt with:

> On June 24, 1921, at Fort Smith, W. R. James . . . entered the N.W.T. without a Clearance Certificate . . . ordered him out of the Territories, he left that day.[32]

The Ordinance was shortlived. One year later it was cancelled, being declared beyond the Commissioner's power.

The Territorial Government began to take shape. With four newly named councillors, the first session of the Northwest Territories Council was held on April 28, 1921. Oil and gas were the main items on the agenda. Further progress in organizing the administration of the Mackenzie District was reported by the Commissioner on May 9, 1921:

> The strike of oil by the Imperial Oil Company at Fort Norman in August 1920, had a stimulating effect on the staking and recording of oil claims and made it evident that it would be necessary . . . to open a Mining Recorder's Office . . .
> We have organized a complete staff, both for service in Ottawa and for service in the Mackenzie District.[33]

Two additional councillors were soon named. Major Lachlan Burwash, appointed as the Mining Recorder, was assigned to open the first territorial administration headquarters at Fort Smith. He and Major David L. McKeand left Peace River on May 5, 1921, with a party of twenty-two men. Travelling in two scows with thirty tons of supplies they arrived without mishap on May 26, 1921.[34] They wasted no time. By the end of the summer, the territorial staff "had accomplished wonders . . . Cellars were dug for two buildings, the lot partly fenced and a half acre broken and planted with vegetables".[35] The territorial administration had special duties to perform. These included a general inspection of lots in all villages between Fort Chipewyan and

Fort Good Hope, "... for the purpose of ascertaining who are in possession of the lots and who are entitled to same, ... a general inspection of the oil wells and the suitability of the country for the installation of a pipeline ... "[36]

Another memorandum from the Commissioner's office on May 12, 1921, dealt with matter concerning the well-being of the 150 white residents of the Northwest Territories and future settlers: logs, buoys, and beacons, future radio telegraph posts, census, claim recording procedures, timber regulations, registrars, Notaries Public, geological surveys, water power branch, ordinances, liquor permits, one territorial gasoline boat, rations and supplies, and oil regulations. Not one word of the memo made any reference to the 3500 Indian people of the District, although these regulations, plans, and administrative details affected an area which was still Indian Territory. Neither the necessity for a treaty, nor the possibility that the Indians would refuse one, was ever considered by the Territorial administration. It was as though the Indians had ceased to exist in the Mackenzie District, with no rights in the past, nor claims on the future. The fact that the Federal Government signed a treaty with the Indians a few months later did not affect territorial plans for development. The administration persisted in its convenient illusion.

Ottawa Prepares the Treaty, 1920-1921

> The Treaty was signed when it was discovered that our land was more valuable than our friendship.
>
> —James Wah-Shee

Politicians in Ottawa viewed the oil discovery as an event of national significance.[37] The economic implications for Canada were staggering:

> It would be a splendid thing if we had a territory as well populated and as far developed as Alaska from which we could draw great natural products that could be exchanged for our manufactured goods ...
>
> The first great wealth of that country to be developed will be its mineral wealth ... If the oil discovery which was made last summer at Fort Norman is half as good as we are led to believe, it is quite possible that that immense wealth which I have mentioned may be tripled or quadrupled in oil ... The potentialities of mineral wealth of this great north country are almost beyond belief ...
>
> The eyes of the mineral operators are upon us today. Oil is King. We have struck oil in the North and we want all the reliable information we can get for the people who are turning their attention to these northern oil fields ... [38]

With prosperity would come problems, not the least of which would be the influence of oil companies on the national economy:

> We have our oil wells up in the Mackenzie River district and we need a railway there to enable private enterprise to develop them. Of course the

great Imperial Oil Company will put in their plant, but that will be another monopoly. If the Imperial Oil Company, the big child of the Standard Oil Company, puts in a pipe line, you will not see cheaper oil. A railway must be built or some method of transportation provided.[39]

Obviously, the Canadian Government could no longer remain indifferent to the North; the stakes were too great. The first step was to secure ownership of this "vast domain of country, rich in natural resources and favourable for development."[40] Some representation was made for a treaty in the summer of 1920, but the Government was not yet prepared. From Fort Simpson, Indian Agent Harris wrote to the Department on January 25, 1920:

> I have the honour to report that on the occasion of my last visit to Fort Providence, the Indians of that place waited on me, and requested me to make application to the Department to have Treaty made with them, and thus place them on the same footing as the Indians of the neighbouring points of Hay River and Fort Resolution on Great Slave Lake. I am of the opinion that it would be beneficial to the Indians of the Mackenzie River to make treaty at all the posts where Treaty has not yet been made, and to bring them all under the control of the Department.[41]

The Commissioner of the Hudson's Bay Company inquired if treaty was to be paid to the Indians of Fort Providence during the summer of 1920, ". . . in connection with the extinguishment of the Indians' rights to the Oil Lands lying to the North of Great Slave Lake".[42] The Department replied:

> The Indians' rights to lands lying north of the Great Slave Lake have not been extinguished and therefore this Department does not propose to pay treaty to the Providence band of Indians next summer.[43]

The question of jurisdiction was raised by Conroy. On February 6, 1920, he wrote to Duncan C. Scott, former Chief Accountant promoted to Deputy-Superintendent-General of Indian Affairs:

> I am credibly informed that oil leases have been granted covering lands in the vicinity of Fort Norman and Pointe Aux Esclaves on Great Slave Lake.
>
> I would point out that the Indian title has not yet been extinguished with respect to the entire country north of Great Slave Lake and in my opinion it would be desirable to take a surrender of this territory from the Northern Chiefs as soon as possible in order to avoid complications with respect to the exploitation of the country for oil. This can best be done by taking their adhesion to Treaty number Eight. I have in past years recommended this line of action, but as there was no great influx of Whites in the district the matter has been held in abeyance.[44]

Kitto advised the Government to legalize its activities in the Mackenzie District:

The non-treaty Indians north of Slave lake and on Liard river number about 3,500. The recent discoveries of oil at Norman have been made on lands virtually belonging to those tribes. Until treaty has been made with them, the right of the Mining Lands and Yukon Branch to dispose of these oil resources is open to debate. Chiefs of these tribes are aware of their position and claim that until the government makes treaty with them they should not be expected to observe our game laws or to part with their oil lands. The extension of Treaty No. 8 to include all Indians to the Arctic Coast should be proceeded with immediately.[45]

The persistent Conroy followed with another memorandum dated October 13, 1920. This is a masterpiece of logic, persuasion and timing, and undoubtedly had great impact in Ottawa:

I beg to recommend that immediate action be taken to extend Treaty to the Indians along the Mackenzie.

I have advocated this step for some years and conditions are changing so rapidly in that country that it has become imperative to take action immediately. For your information I am summarizing the more important reasons for this step. I cannot impress upon the Department too strongly the seriousness of the situation and the urgent necessity of dealing with these Indians immediately if endless disputes and disagreements with the Dominion Government are to be avoided.

1st. The rapid and unexpected exploitation of the country.

2nd. The establishment of oil industries throughout the district.

3rd. The ordinary and gradual, but of late much augmented, immigration of prospectors, trappers, traders and others employed by the various oil companies – immigration is bound to increase rapidly, as oil has actually been found and the question of transportation will add both to the difficulties and to the influx of white settlers. Already lands which might, with great advantage, have been claimed by Indians have been secured by whites. During the past, year by year, little by little, the rights of the Indians have been encroached upon. It has now come to the time where this is being, and will be increased a hundredfold, and the rights of the Indians will have to be protected.

A statement of the case is as follows: –

1st. Justice of Treaty: At every post which I visited this year, and this includes every one from Edmonton to the Arctic Ocean, the Indians desired to be included in the Treaty. This feeling is universal. They see their neighbours to the South with certain definite rights and privileges and there is no reason why the same justice should not be accorded to them.

2nd. As previously stated, and to my mind, the most important point of all is the fact that the rapid and unprecedented encroachment of white people means that the Indians, unless protected, will be robbed of their fair share of the best land. It must be taken into consideration that the aboriginal owners are entitled to their shares of oil bearing lands as well as agricultural lands but to obtain this it is necessary to make Treaty, otherwise great injustices will be done them.

3rd. Definite jurisdiction will be obtained over these people who are now outside of all authority, barring the Mounted Police, whose only posts from McMurray to MacPherson, near to the mouth of the Mackenzie, a distance of probably 2500 miles, are at Great Slave Lake and Chipewyan. A certain amount of oversight may be exercised which considering the influx of white settlers is more than desirable. At present, our Agent at Simpson has absolutely no jurisdiction over them. Prices for fur have been abnormally high and an absolute collapse is expected. Treaty will be of immense benefit to these people.

4th. The fact that these people accept Treaty will tend to stability, law and order.

5th. Unless treaty is made the Dominion Government will be involved in endless disputes and disagreements with squatters and others. The making of treaty and the segregation of reserves will eliminate a very large portion of this trouble.

6th. The making of this Treaty can be done conveniently and economically as an adhesion to Treaty 8, and will include practically all the Indians in the North West Territories still outside of the jurisdiction of the Dominion Government; there may be some in the barren lands who will not be included but as these lands will not be wanted for many generations I think this is the last charge that will be asked from the Dominion Government and it will give title to all the land which will be needed for probably a century.

The Cost

The population of this country, and in this I have included the Indians of Fort Liard convenient to our Agency at Simpson, and the Indians at Fort Rae who may be visited either on the way down the MacKenzie or on the way back, as the steamer must stop there on one occasion, is as follows: –

	No. in Band
Arctic Red River (Loucheux)	125
Fort Good Hope (Hare Skins)	368
Fort Liard (Slaves)	217
Fort Macpherson (Loucheux)	120
Fort Norman (Hare Skins)	343
Fort Providence (Slaves)	197
Fort Rae	759
Fort Simpson (Slaves)	364
Fort Wrigley (Slaves)	71
Mackenzie Delta and coast line	170
Trout Lake (Slaves) (Providence)	70
Nomads	550
Total	3,364

It is probable that when treaty is made 2,500 Indians will join. It will be understood that I am making a maximum estimate in all cases. Granting them the same privileges which were accorded the Indians of Treaty 8, which were a gratuity of $12 and after that an annuity of $5, the first year's expenditure would be as follows: –

2500 Indians at $12.00 .... $30,000
(This safely includes Chiefs and Head men)

```
Incidental expenses............................................................1,000
Treaty Supplies [Flour, Bacon, tea, tobacco] ....................5,000
Expenses of Commission ......................................................3,000

2nd year
2500 Indians at $5.00............................................................12,500
300 Indians admitted to treaty for the first time at $12.....3,600
Incidental Expenses.............................................................1,000
Treaty supplies ....................................................................5,000
Paying officers' expenses......................................................1,500

3rd year
2800 Indians at $5.00.........................................................12,400[14,000]
Incidental expenses............................................................. 1,000
Treaty supplies ....................................................................5,000
Paying officers' expenses...................................... •...........1,500
```
                      Total $82,500

As the Department gradually centralizes its authority in that country by the establishment of Agencies its expenditure will undoubtedly be reduced and the country will be called upon to pay not more than $18,000 per annum at the maximum, and a large part of the travelling expenses will be eliminated. In return for this will be ceded the rights to the enormous territory of 150,000 square miles,* comprising all the district north of Great Slave Lake from the barren grounds to the Western extremity of the hunting grounds in the Rocky Mountains.

Conclusion. I cannot recommend too strongly that immediate action be taken to have this treaty made. It is difficult for people in civilization to realize the rapidity with which conditions are changing and the danger with which these changing conditions are fraught. To my mind this is one of the most important questions with which the Department is faced and I have heard on all sides that delay will be attended with serious consequences. I most earnestly commend it to your attention.[46]

It was proposed to extend the Treaty boundaries beyond those which were proposed in 1909. (cf. pp. 133, 312). The new map added the Eskimo territory along the Arctic coast and the south-east corner of the Yukon Territory to the Treaty area.[47]

Since 1907, Conroy had been thwarted in his attempts to promote a treaty for the Mackenzie District. However, after the discovery of oil, his views were diligently quoted in Ottawa. The Superintendent General of Indian Affairs wrote to the Minister of the Interior on November 23, 1920:

For some time we have been considering and postponing the question of taking a cession of the Indian title to lands in the Mackenzie River District . . . Our inspector Mr. H. A. Conroy, has recently returned from this

*The actual area ceded measures 372,000 sq. mi.

district, and has reported that immediate action should be taken to provide for the entrance of the Mackenzie River Indians into Treaty.

It is pointed out in this report that the question has become a very urgent one, owing to the rapid and unexpected exploitation of the country, the establishment of oil industries and the increasing immigration of prospectors, trappers, traders and white settlers. The Indians themselves are very anxious to be taken into treaty, as they are desirous that reserves should be set aside for them as soon as possible.

I think the proposed treaty should follow the main lines of Treaty No. 8, except that I do not think that it would be wise to allow the Indians the privilege of taking land in severalty, as provided by that treaty.[48]

The Department included treaty costs in its budgetary estimates for the year 1921. The Governor General was informed of the decision and the reasons behind it:

The early development of this territory is anticipated and it is advisable to follow the usual policy and obtain from the Indians cession of their aboriginal title and thereby bring them into closer relation with the Government and establish securely their legal position.[49]

A few details remained to be worked out, such as the transportation of the treaty party. Scott asked Breynat on February 16, 1921, "Whether the Mission Motor boat will be available and if so what price would be charged for the trip."[50] It was not available, and the Treaty party travelled down the Mackenzie River on a barge, towed by the *Hubaco,* an H.B.C. boat.

Breynat was in Ottawa in the spring of 1921. He had not expressed his views on a treaty since his unsuccessful efforts in 1910. The same Scott, who in 1910 as Chief Accountant had opposed Breynat's arguments, would now solicit his assistance:

When I arrived at Ottawa, Doctor Scott, Superintendent of Indian Affairs, advised me that, following the discovery of oil at Fort Norman, and to avoid any conflict between Indians and whites, the Government had decided to negotiate by treaty with the Indians the surrender of their aboriginal rights. "We would be very thankful to you", he added, "if you would accept to join the Royal Commission which will negotiate this treaty with the Indigenous people this summer. Your influence with these people will be greatly helpful to insure the success . . . ."[51]

Breynat expressed his reaction to the invitation and his reasons for accepting it in a personal letter written soon after:

When in Ottawa, I was pressingly invited to join the Royal Commission established to negotiate a treaty with the Indians and to purchase from them their remaining rights on the land and mineral wealth of the Mackenzie district. How could I have refused? This was an uncommon sign of esteem and a public recognition of the influence the Catholic Missionaries have on these people whose friendship the Government desires to win.

There was also a very practical side to my acceptation, i.e. travelling at the King's expense . . . So, my signature will be seen forever, together with those of our great chiefs of the Slavey, Hare and Loucheux tribes, and that of the Royal Commissioner, to bear witness, for future generations, to the good faith of the contracting parties.[52]

By this time Conroy had been named "a Commissioner to negotiate a treaty with the Indians occupying the territory north of the sixtieth parallel and along the Mackenzie River to the Arctic Ocean".[53] He and Breynat joined forces in Ottawa to insure that the hunting and fishing rights of the Indian people would be respected and protected. The Fisheries Department advised Indian Affairs on May 15, 1921:

> . . . the Bishop of Fort Resolution and your Inspector for that District called at this Department and explained why they are anxious that a clause should be inserted in a treaty that is now being concluded with the Northern Indians, granting them certain fishing rights in areas being reserved for them.
>
> It was pointed out to these gentlemen that not only has the policy of this Department always been to make it as easy as possible for the Indians in remote districts to obtain supplies of food, and in fact their fishing operations (where they are not entering into competition with commercial fishermen) were not being interfered with, but for years our regulations have definitely provided that any Indian or half-breed in that portion of the country is eligible for a free permit authorizing fishing by him, and that this permit even allows fishing for current need during the usual closed seasons. The Bishop was satisfied that this regulation is all that is required, but he wished that it should be put in the treaty so that its permanence would be assured . . . This Department does not consider it wise to insert such fishery clause in the Treaty as the Bishop and your Inspector desired.[54]

Conroy's initiative was further curbed when he was handed "an engrossed copy of the proposed treaty" and reminded of his limited authority:

> You shoud be guided by the terms set forth therein and . . . no outside promises should be made by you to the Indians.[55]

Ottawa selected the right man for the job, and then tied his hands. Conroy had known and visited the Indians of the Mackenzie since 1907. He was an honest, "big-bodied, big-hearted"[56] man, who had persistently promoted the Treaty for the benefit it would bring to the Indians. Now he was bringing them an ultimatum which was beyond negotiation. Years later Breynat recorded the indignation he himself had felt upon recognizing the Treaty for what it was:

> The Royal Commission arrived from Ottawa to negotiate with them [the Indians] the terms of a treaty, which terms were prepared in advance to be imposed upon them rather than freely discussed in a spirit of reconciliation and mutual concessions as often happens in the negotiation of treaties.[57]

Once Ottawa had decreed the time, terms, and conditions of Treaty 11, only one thing remained for Conroy to do: obtain the consent and signatures of the Indian people of the Mackenzie District.

"Conspiracy of Silence"

News coverage of Treaty 11 was confined to a few lines in the *Edmonton Journal* shortly before the signing:

> May 25, 1921: To get the Indian treaty expedition under way for its summer's program in the far north, H. A. Conroy, of the Department of Indian Affairs, has reached the city [Edmonton] and is now completing his arrangements for the unique trip down the Mackenzie [River] by which the hearts of the natives are to be gladdened and their purses enriched . . . [58]

> June 15, 1921: The Indian treaty party that is to distribute government money to the Mackenzie river natives got away from Fort McMurray on Tuesday . . . [59]

> June 25, 1921: Mr. Conroy and party . . . are going to visit the Indians in the extreme north and are visiting some tribes that have not been paid treaty up this time . . . [60]

Although during the months just preceding the Treaty, both the *Edmonton Journal* and the *Edmonton Bulletin* had featured many stories on oil and mineral discoveries in the Mackenzie District, neither had assigned reporters to cover the journey of the Treaty party, as the *Bulletin* had done in 1899. By 1921 an Indian treaty was no longer news. Equally hard to find are written accounts of the events of that summer by witnesses or participants. Treaty Commissioner Conroy wrote one letter which has been preserved and a short report printed with the official text of the Treaty.[61] However, his official report as Commissioner cannot be located, though files in the Public Archives of Canada[62] and at the Department of Indian Affairs[63] were thoroughly searched. Also missing from the files are the notes and personal diary of RCMP Inspector Wyndhan Valentine Bruce, who accompanied the Treaty party as official escort.

The log books of the H.B.C. schooner *Fort Rae,* and of the tug *Hubaco,* on which the Treaty party travelled, have not survived, nor have any records of the Hudson's Bay Company posts operating in the Mackenzie District at the time.[64] The Anglican Church records contain no mention of the Treaty. Very few details were noted in the diaries of the Catholic missions and of the Grey Nuns. White residents of the country wrote very little, or their accounts of Treaty 11 have been lost.

Whatever the explanation for this "conspiracy of silence," there is sufficient information provided by eye-witness accounts to reconstruct what took place along the Mackenzie River in the summer of 1921.

Among the oral testimonies which have been given, is that of Inspector Bruce,[65] whose memory replaces his notes and diary. The Indian people themselves, leading figures in the negotiations, have strong recollections of the signing of Treaty 11. How could it be otherwise when they have lived each day since, in its shadow?

Treaty 11

"Made in Ottawa"

Well in advance of the Treaty Commission's arrival in the Mackenzie, a public notice was posted to announce its purpose.[66]

NOTICE is hereby given that a Commissioner representing His Majesty's Government of the Dominion of Canada will hold meetings at the places and on the dates indicated hereunder for the purpose of making a treaty between His Majesty and the various chiefs of the Indian bands inhabiting the Mackenzie River district and such other adjacent lands as is seemed advisable to include within the provisions of such treaty.

The Commissioner will deal with the Indians and half-breeds of such district and adjacent lands with a view to the extinguishment of the aboriginal title to the said territory and lands.

All such Indians and half-breeds, except those half-breeds who have already been dealt with are invited to be present at the said meetings, to be held at the points and on the dates hereafter mentioned.

Providence	Tuesday	July 5th. 1921.
Simpson	Monday	July 11th. 1921.
Wrigley	Friday	July 15th. 1921.
Norman	Tuesday	July 19th. 1921.
Good Hope	Saturday	July 23rd. 1921
Arctic Red River	Wednesday	July 27th. 1921.
Macpherson	Monday	Aug. 1st. 1921.
Liard	Monday	Aug. 15th. 1921.
Rae	Tuesday	Aug. 23rd. 1921.

DUNCAN C. SCOTT

Ottawa.   Deputy Superintendent General
Mar. 23rd. 1921   of Indian Affairs.

Treaty Commissioner Conroy had received instructions to adhere strictly to the terms of the Treaty made in Ottawa. The text of the Treaty[67] was completely unfamiliar to the Indian people, who saw the paper it was written on for the first time on the day the Commissioner arrived. Very few could read it then; most have not read it yet.

TREATY NUMBER ELEVEN

ARTICLES OF A TREATY made and concluded on the several dates mentioned therein in the year of Our Lord One thousand Nine hundred and Twenty-One, between His Most Gracious Majesty George V, King of Great Britain and Ireland and of the British Dominions beyond the Seas, by His Commissioner, Henry Anthony Conroy, Esquire, of the City of Ottawa, of the One Part, and the Slave, Dogrib, Loucheux, Hare and other Indians, inhabitants of the territory within the limits hereinafter defined and described, by their Chiefs and Headmen, hereunto subscribed, of the other part: –

WHEREAS, the Indians inhabiting the territory hereinafter defined have been convened to meet a commissioner representing His Majesty's Government of the Dominion of Canada at certain places in the said territory in this present year of 1921, to deliberate upon certain matters of interest to His Most Gracious Majesty, of the one part, and the said Indians of the other.

AND WHEREAS, the said Indians have been notified and informed by His Majesty's said commissioner that it is His desire to open for settlement, immigration, trade, travel, mining, lumbering and such other purposes as to His Majesty may seem meet, a tract of country bounded and described as hereinafter set forth, and to obtain the consent thereto of His Indian subjects inhabiting the said tract, and to make a treaty, so that there may be peace and goodwill between them and His Majesty's other subjects, and that His Indian people may know and be assured of what allowances they are to expect and receive from His Majesty's bounty and benevolence.

AND WHEREAS, the Indians of the said tract, duly convened in council at the respective points named hereunder, and being requested by His Majesty's Commissioner, to name certain Chiefs and Headmen, who should be authorized on their behalf to conduct such negotiations and sign any treaty to be founded thereon, and to become responsible to His Majesty for the faithful performance by their respective bands of such obligations as shall be assumed by them, the said Indians have therefore acknowledged for that purpose the several chiefs and Headmen who have subscribed thereto.

AND WHEREAS the said Commissioner has proceeded to negotiate a treaty with the Slave, Dogrib, Loucheux, Hare and other Indians inhabiting the district hereinafter defined and described, which has been agreed upon and concluded by the respective bands at the dates mentioned hereunder, the said Indians do hereby cede, release, surrender and yield up to the Government of the Dominion of Canada, for His Majesty the King and His Successors forever, all their rights, titles, and privileges whatsoever to the lands included within the following limits, that is to say:

Commencing at the northwesterly corner of the territory ceded under the provisions of Treaty Number Eight; thence northeasterly along the height-of-land to the point where it intersects the boundary between the Yukon Territory and the Northwest Territories; thence northwesterly along the said boundary to the shore of the Arctic ocean; thence easterly along the said shore to the mouth of the Coppermine river; thence southerly and southeasterly along the left bank of the said river to Lake Gras by way of Point lake; thence along the southern shore of Lake Gras to a point situated northwest of the most western extremity of Aylmer lake; thence along the southern shore of Aylmer lake and following the right bank of the Lockhart river to Artillery lake; thence along the western shore of Artillery lake and following the right bank of the Lockhart river to the site of Old Fort Reliance where the said river enters Great Slave lake, this being the northeastern corner of the territory ceded under the provisions of Treaty Number Eight; thence westerly along the northern boundary of the said territory so ceded to the point of commencement; comprising an area of approximately three hundred and seventy-two thousand square miles.

AND ALSO, the said Indian rights, titles and privileges whatsoever to all other lands wherever situated in the Yukon Territory, the Northwest Territories or in any other portion of the Dominion of Canada.

To have and to hold the same to His Majesty the King and His Successors forever.

AND His Majesty the King hereby agrees with the said Indians that they shall have the right to pursue their usual vocations of hunting, trapping and fishing throughout the tract surrendered as heretofore described, subject to such regulations as may from time to time be made by the Government of the Country acting under the authority of His Majesty, and saving and excepting such tracts as may be required or taken up from time to time for settlement, mining, lumbering, trading or other purposes.

AND His Majesty the King hereby agrees and undertakes to lay aside reserves for each band, the same not to exceed in all one square mile for each family of five, or in that proportion for larger or smaller families.

PROVIDED, however, that His Majesty reserves the right to deal with any settlers within the boundaries of any lands reserved for any band as He may see fit; and also that the aforesaid reserves of land, or any interest therein, may be sold or otherwise disposed of by His Majesty's Government for the use and benefit of the said Indians entitled thereto, with their consent first had and obtained; but in no wise shall the said Indians, or any of them, be entitled to sell or otherwise alienate any of the lands allotted to them as reserves.

It is further agreed between His Majesty and His Indian subjects that such portions of the reserves and lands above indicated as may at any time be required for public works, buildings, railways, or roads of whatsoever nature may be appropriated for that purpose by His Majesty's Government of the Dominion of Canada, due compensation being made to the Indians for the value of any improvements thereon, and an equivalent in land, money or other consideration for the area of the reserve so appropriated.

And in order to show the satisfaction of His Majesty with the behaviour and good conduct of His Indian subjects, and in extinguishment of all their past claims hereinabove mentioned, He hereby, through his Commissioner, agrees to give to each Chief a present of thirty-two dollars in cash, to each Headman, twenty-two dollars, and to every other Indian of whatever age of the families represented, at the time and place of payment, twelve dollars.

HIS MAJESTY, also agrees that during the coming year, and annually thereafter, He will cause to be paid to the said Indians in cash, at suitable places and dates, of which the said Indians shall be duly notified, to each Chief twenty-five dollars, to each Headman fifteen dollars, and to every other Indian of whatever age five dollars, to be paid only to heads of families for the members thereof, it being provided for the purposes of this Treaty that each band having at least thirty members may have a Chief, and that in addition to a Chief, each band may have Councillors or Headmen in the proportion of two to each two hundred members of the band.

FURTHER, His Majesty agrees that each Chief shall receive once and for all a silver medal, a suitable flag and a copy of this Treaty for the use of his band; and during the coming year, and every third year thereafter, each Chief and Headman shall receive a suitable suit of clothing.

FURTHER, His Majesty agrees to pay the salaries of teachers to instruct the children of said Indians in such manner as His Majesty's Government may deem advisable.

FURTHER, His Majesty agrees to supply once and for all to each Chief of a band that selects a reserve, ten axes, five hand-saws, five augers, one grindstone, and the necessary files and whetstones for the use of the band.

FURTHER, His Majesty agrees that, each band shall receive once and for all equipment for hunting, fishing and trapping to the value of fifty dollars for each family of such band, and that there shall be distributed annually among the Indians equipment, such as twine for nets, ammunition and trapping to the value of three dollars per head for each Indian who continues to follow the vocation of hunting, fishing and trapping.

FURTHER, His Majesty agrees that, in the event of any of the Indians aforesaid being desirous of following agricultural pursuits, such Indians shall receive such assistance as is deemed necessary for that purpose.

AND the undersigned Slave, Dogrib, Loucheux, Hare and other Chiefs and Headmen, on their own behalf and on behalf of all the Indians whom they represent, do hereby solemnly promise and engage to strictly observe this Treaty, and also to conduct and behave themselves as good loyal subjects of His Majesty the King.

THEY promise and engage that they will, in all respects, obey and abide by the law; that they will maintain peace between themselves and others of His Majesty's subjects, whether Indians, half-breeds or whites, now inhabiting and hereafter to inhabit any part of the said ceded territory; that they will not molest the person or property of any inhabitant of such ceded tract, or of any other district or country, or interfere with, or trouble any person passing or travelling through the said tract or any part thereof, and that they will assist the officers of His Majesty in bringing to justice and punishment any Indian offending against the stipulations of this Treaty, or infringing the law in force in the country so ceded.

Fort Providence

Treaty Commissioner Conroy arrived at Fort Providence aboard the *S.S. Mackenzie River*, on Friday, June 24, 1921. He was joined there on the same day by Breynat, who had sailed from Fort Smith on June 9.[68] Although Fort Providence was the first place where the Treaty was to be presented to the Indians, and therefore of special significance, Conroy gave it only a brief mention in a letter to Scott:

On my arrival at Fort Providence . . . I found nearly all the Indians already at the Fort, awaiting our coming. On the following day, [Saturday June 25th] we discussed the terms of the Treaty with the Indians, and I explained to them why the Government had decided to make a Treaty with them, and answered their questions, in which I was greatly assisted by the Rt. Rev. Bishop Breynat. On the 27th, Monday, the Indians all came together and after some more talk, elected a chief, and received their money. In the election of this chief, they were unanimous, and elected the best one of their number, as was conceded by all those who live at Fort Providence ... Two days later, the Trout Lake band * arrived at the Fort, and on finding that those at the Fort had already come into treaty, made no difficulty in giving their adhesion.[69]

Some Indian people who were there in 1921 are still living at Fort Providence, and remember what happened during Treaty negotiations. Their combined testimonies describe the events and discussions which took place:†

William Squirrel: There were more Indian people for the treaty gathering than there are Indians living in Fort Providence right now ...

Victor Lafferty: Paul Lefoin, that's the only man they wanted for Chief because he was a good hunter. He was a good hunter and he never kept anything for himself. He'd kill a good fat moose, he'd tell them "go down and get it", he'd send them to get that meat ... also send some fellows for wood and make a big fire and boil up all that moose.

Jean Marie Sabourin: We did not know much about the white men ... the Commissioner ... stated he was here to make treaty. He said that any Indian who wants to take money is free to do so. This treaty is only for full-blooded Indians. But the chief said not to take money right away, for the white man might lie to us ... We sat around and talked. The first day we did not know what was going on, so the Commissioner talked to the people ...

William Squirrel: There was also a Bishop, witness to the Treaty. He [Breynat] was good in Slavey language, and translating to the Indians, he said that the government was offering good care to the Indians in return for the treaty and that the white man and the Indians were to live side by side on this land till the end of the world, and that from hereafter things would be good for the Indians ...

John Farcy: "How much money are you offering us for treaty?" the chief asked the Commissioner. "Five dollars", was the reply. So the chief laughed at this answer. "What good is five dollars to us, being ragged as we are" ... The chief wanted to know why the commissioner was offering five dollars to everyone. The commissioner replied that the government sent him to make treaty with the Indians and to shake hands with everyone ...

Victor Lafferty: When Conroy asked him [Lefoin] if he wanted to take Treaty, "Well, Lefoin says, well, if we do, what I say about my

---

*This band later moved to Kakisa Lake.

†Jean Marie Sabourin, born 1902, interviewed in 1969; Victor Lafferty, who was interpreter during the 1921 treaty negotiations, interviewed by Liz Petrovitch of Yellowknife on October 22, 1972; John Farcy, born 1887; William Squirrel, born 1897; Michel Landry, born 1892; and his wife Angelique Landry, born 1902; Joseph Minoza, born January 1, 1886. These latter were all interviewed by Joachim Bonnetrouge, also of Fort Providence, in 1972.

country? This is my country, he says, 'I'd like to hunt all over as far as I can go, he says, there's forts all around us. Fort Rae, Simpson, Liard, Upper Hay, in fact nearly everywhere I go down, he says, that's my country." He says, "If you don't stop us from hunting . . . We want to hunt just the same as before, the way we are making a living. Hunt big game, and fur and fish, birds, everything and we don't want you to put us on a reserve". He says, "I'm an Indian. I don't read, I don't write, he said, but still, I know what you've done outside [in the other provinces]. You put the Crees on reserves and the country's so small, it didn't last long, they didn't have nothing to hunt. And we don't want to be like that here. Do all that, Lefoin says, then I'll take Treaty."

William Squirrel: There was nothing said about setting lands aside for the Indians. You could live and do your things anywhere you felt like it . . .

Jean Marie Sabourin: The only thing talked about was hunting rights . . ."You will not take away our hunting rights," that is what the chief said . . . The hunting, fishing, and migratory rights were the topic discussion . . . . The Commissioner said "Your hunting rights will not be taken away from you . . . ."

John Farcy: The Commissioner said, "This land shall be as it is, you shall keep on living on it as before . . . ".

Michel Landry: The commissioner went on to say: "As long as the earth is still here there shall be no more restrictions placed on the Indians in regard to hunting, fishing, etc." The chief said: "You people say things like that but you lie, so you better put it down on paper." The commissioner returned to mention the sun and the river and said that the government will not run back on their word. The Treaty was interpreted again and it was at the time satisfactory to the chief so he accepted the treaty . . .

All the witnesses stress the fact that it was only after complete freedom to hunt, to trap, and to fish had been promised to the Indians, that they accepted the treaty:

John Farcy: There was nothing said about the land and the chief accepted the treaty when the commissioner said there would be no restrictions on hunting, fishing and trapping . . .

William Squirrel: The chief was not fully satisfied till when the commissioner said that things would not change according to the treaty . . .

Joseph Minoza: Chief Paul Lefoin said . . . that there would be peace between the Whites and the Indians as long as the land was still here and that the White man has to abide by the Indian's word and by what he has to say.

Michel Landry: On the last day, at the handing out of the money . . . the commissioner said: This money you are accepting will be a to-ken of peace between us and we shall be friends . . . The treaty as accepted was mainly for keeping peace between the white man and the Indian people . . . .

Angelique Landry: What was said at the first treaty was really good according to what was promised and the Chief Lefoin was quite a man in his own right and his demands were listened and adhered to . . . .

Victor Lafferty: Then Conroy took the pencil and said "Touch the pencil." Lefoin said: "I wouldn't touch the pencil unless you bring Bishop Breynat here, and what I say, and what you say will be all on the paper and Bishop Breynat will keep one and you take a copy". Conroy took the pencil again and he said "Touch the pencil and sign," and he said "no." So then Conroy took the pencil and he said, "While the sun rises on the east and sets in the west, and the Mackenzie River flows, nothing will be changed, it will be comfortable here, it will make you happy."

But the witnesses do not agree on whether a copy of the treaty was given to the chief or not.

Jean Marie Sabourin: No paper or manuscript was given to us, just straight talk . . . . The chief never got a copy. The treaty commissioner must have it. Even if the Chief got a copy he would not know what to do with it, we did not even know how to read. The chief only got a medal . . . [in 1922].

Michel Landry: The treaty papers which were signed were placed at the disposal of the missionaries in the name of Bishop Breynat. So when the restrictions [game laws] came up, the papers were asked for by the Indians and there were no papers to speak of. So to this day there are no original treaty papers to go by . . .

In testimony given on July 17, 1973, before the Honourable Mr. Justice William G. Morrow of the Supreme Court of the Northwest Territories, Victor Lafferty, William Squirrel, Michel Landry and John Farcy were more specific about a few details: Victor Lafferty, the interpreter, was not asked in 1921 "to read and translate any piece of paper or writing during the negotiations." The discussions took place in, and in front of, the Treaty tent. When these were finished, Conroy, the Chief, "and a whole bunch of us" went to the mission building for the signing of the Treaty, because the Bishop and a priest were there. The Chief wanted them to be witnesses, but Breynat "did not persuade" the people to take treaty.[70]

The Treaty was signed at Fort Providence on June 27, 1921 by:

> H. A. Conroy, Commissioner
> Paul Lefouin, Chief
> Harry Francis, headman
> Baptiste Sabourin, headman:

and witnessed by: W. V. Bruce, Inspector RCMP
                       F. H. Kitto
                       A. H. Miller
                       Bishop Breynat
                       J. A. R. Balsillie[71]

The words "signatories" and "signed" do not imply that all the Indian chiefs affixed their signature to the official version of Treaty 11. As in the case of Treaty 8, there is some question as to whether some chiefs did sign or not. A total of 258 Indians accepted the Treaty that day.

A great feast was prepared for the evening. Victor Lafferty recalls the excitement:

> They were cooking all day and when the sun was just about setting, all at once we hear 3 shots with a shot gun. My God, the two police, they were asleep in their tent, they run out . . . and we called them and said, "That's just for the feast. The feast is ready. That's why they're shooting".[72]

According to the Grey Nuns' diary, there were many distractions during the days before and after the signing. On the first day of Treaty negotiations, Saturday, June 25, Breynat organized a picnic at Ile-au-Veau. All the personnel attended.[73] On Sunday June 26th, the school children gave a concert. Conroy, and Kitto and many government officials attended and seemed to be pleased.[74] During the celebration and feasting on Monday evening, June 27, the *s.s. Distributor* arrived. On board were some Grey Nuns, Judge Dubuc and members of his judicial party.[75] These latter had arrived for the trial of a local resident accused of murder. The court was held on June 29, the first trial by jury in the Northwest Territories. On July 2, there was a banquet for all Government officials, followed by another concert. On July 5, the Treaty party tug, *Hubaco* arrived, and on July 6, "Mr. Conroy gave rides to all the school children, on his beautiful gas boat . . . Great amount of candies given by the generous Mr. Conroy."[76] Neither the Treaty signing itself, on June 27, nor the adhesion of the Trout Lake Band two days later were recorded in the diary.

That these were exciting and unusual times is further documented by articles in the *Edmonton Bulletin* of July 19 and July 26. These describe the trial in great detail, as well as the movement down the river of ninety-two ships, launches, scows and canoes, headed for the oil fields at Fort Norman. Heavy machinery was moved across the portage at Fort Smith, and an airplane flew over Providence for the first time on July 1. The Edmonton newspaper devoted only seven lines to the Treaty.

Fort Simpson

The Treaty party travelled 175 miles down the River, and landed at Fort Simpson on the evening of July 8. Here was one of the oldest trading posts in the Mackenzie. It was also the site of the first Anglican mission, opened in 1859, and had been the residence of the Anglican Bishop until 1913.

Conroy's report to the Department on July 11, gave very few details of the Treaty negotiations:

> . . . we found nearly all the Indians awaiting our arrival. At first the Indians at this point were nearly unanimous in their decision to let "well enough" alone and to remain in the condition in which they had been heretofore, but after several talks and explanations, they all entered into Treaty, and elected their chief and headmen entirely to the satisfaction of myself, the Agent and all the white inhabitants, whose opinion counts for anything. Here again I was greatly assisted by Bishop Breynat, who had accompanied me, and by the Father in charge of the Mission. I cannot dwell too strongly on the assistance rendered by the missionaries of the Roman Catholic Church to the Government officials on this and on all other occasions, in the Northwest Territories. I regret to say that at the time of writing, the supplies for the treaty have not yet arrived and some fears are entertained that they may have met with a mishap on Great Slave Lake . . . .
>
> In concluding this short synopsis of what has been accomplished to date, I may say that everything has been eminently satisfactory, without one discordant note. The members of the RCMP who have been detailed to escort your Commissioner have given every satisfaction, and our party has been a most pleasant one.
>
> Doctor MacDonald accompanies us, and is very devoted to the interest of the people among whom he has spent the last few years, and seems to have absolutely won their confidence. Agent Harris has rendered me every assistance since I have been in contact with him and undoubtedly has the confidence of both Indians and Whites in the country.[77]

In the Catholic Mission Diary three entries mention Treaty Days:

> Friday July 8, 1921: The Treaty Party arrived in the morning, and brought the Bishop. The Indians have no desire to accept the treaty.
> Monday July 11, 1921: The last of the Indians has accepted the treaty. By this evening, 301 have been paid. [in fact 347.]
> Tuesday July 12, 1921: The Bishop left with the Commission.[78]

In their diary the Grey Nuns gave details on Bishop Breynat's activities between July 8 and July 12, but gave the Treaty only passing mention: "Treaty Day at Fort Simpson for the first time, [the Indians] came in great number, and 300 received $12 each. They elected one chief (Antoine)."[79] Breynat wrote of himself in 1937, "I may say that I am responsible for the treaty having been signed at several places, especially at Fort Simpson . . . ."[80] But there is no information in the available testimonies and documents which show the extent of his involvement at Fort Simpson. In recalling the Treaty at Fort Simpson, Inspector Bruce did not remember "anything unusual . . . at all . . . and I think if there had been, I would have."[81]

There are old Indians living at Fort Simpson who recall that the

Treaty took them all by surprise. They did not know what was happening. Although quite a few could speak both Slavey and English, any kind of explanation was very difficult. Baptiste Norwegian (Mustard), born in 1876, is the oldest witness to the Treaty at Fort Simpson. He remembers how the Indians were confused, and influenced by promises and gifts:

> The Indians were trying to get more information about the treaty off the commissioner, but he would not give it to them and so without the Indians agreeing all together to the treaty, the commissioner gave out the money .... There was no answer of YES to the commissioner's promises, yet the treaty money was handed out ....
>
> One thing that he said good, was that if he [the commissioner] gave out the treaty money to the Indian, the Indian would never be in need of material things again ... A great many things were promised to the Indian if they signed the treaty and accepted the treaty. Whoever was chief was to order a barge full of goods and in return the Indian was not to give a cent... the Indians requested that the commissioner give them a paper saying all the things that the commissioner promised them. But the commissioner told them that the following summer when he gives out the treaty again, he would bring along a paper with the treaty on it.[82]

Testimony on the Treaty was given to Mr. Justice Morrow by four residents of Fort Simpson. Philip Lafferty, born 1906, Charlie Cholo, 1907, Ted Trindel, 1901, and Louis Norwegian, 1908,* all agreed that the treaty negotiations lasted for three days. However there was probably little discussed on Sunday, July 10. The chief who had been chosen for Treaty negotiations was Joseph Norwegian, but he "wouldn't agree because he wasn't too sure what would be the outcome of the treaty." When Joseph went away for lunch, Old Antoine was designated as chief, signed the Treaty and received his Treaty money.[83]

At Fort Simpson, 347 Indians gave their adhesion to Treaty 11. It was signed on July 11, 1921 by the following:[84]

	H. A. Conroy
	Antoine, [Nakekon]
	Korwergen, [Norwegian]
	Bedsedia, [Betsedia]

and witnessed by:	G. Breynat OMI.
	John G. Corry
	W. V. Bruce, Inspector RCMP
	A. F. Camsell
	T. W. Harris

James Lafferty, a Metis, was 21 years old at the time. He recalls both serious and humourous incidents.

*cf. Appendix VIII for the text of Louis Norwegian's testimony.

The Interpreter was Joe Villeneuve. He was a good interpreter. Jimmy Sibbeston was here. Archie Gardner also, Ted, Henry's wife and the old Pierre. I don't remember if Bishop Breynat was there when they gave the Treaty.

It was laborious. It took 3 days before they accepted the Treaty. I wasn't there all the time. Off and on I was there, two or three hours at a time. I found it to be quite long. First, the Indians didn't want to. One of them [Joe Villeneuve] said: If they want to give us treaty, the first thing they should give us is a machine to make money – to make dollar bills. They didn't want to take treaty. They were afraid of future restrictions, like now in spring-time we may not shoot ducks. They were afraid of such things. The old Antoine, he signed the treaty. That's the first chief. The old Norwegian also signed the Treaty.

They finally accepted because the white men were going to give things when people are in need, things to work with – axes, fish nets, and so on. That's the way they made treaty. They also gave rations – tea, sugar, bacon . . . After they signed the Treaty the people never kicked about it later on.[85]

Psychological factors impressed another young Metis. Ted Trindel, twenty years old at the time, describes the state of mind and of emotion which prevailed among the Indians of the Mackenzie in 1921:

In those days, if you promise an Indian something for nothing, he'll jump at it. He doesn't think of tomorrow as Today. The Treaty had been going on in the South already, with all the laws and acts and everything was already marked which they didn't show to these Indians. All they wanted was to give them five dollars to protect them against the White man when the White man comes into the country like what is happening now. And I don't see any protection yet . . . .

They [the Indians] didn't know what the White man was or anything else. So I don't see how you can judge those days with all the laws and stuff today. It was just like taking candy from a baby.

And old Norwegian [then 68 years old] they wanted him to be the Chief to take the Treaty, but he said no because he didn't understand what it was all about.

There was . . . old [Antoine] Nakekon [he was 63] . . . when they promised him an outfit or that they would take good care of him, that was just in line with him.

The Indians didn't know what treaty was. In fact, I swear they didn't know what it was all about. All they knew was, sort of peace way, so that there would be no more fighting. Finally they took the Treaty and the Treaty party told them that they could carry on hunting as they wished. But then again in the Treaty book it says that you'll be subject to the Law, and it says that after the Treaty you had to abide by whatever rules come along, but at Treaty time the Treaty party didn't tell them that. It was still your country. The Treaty was more or less to keep peace in the family. In fact the Indians didn't realize that they were signing their rights over. In other words, can you make a deal with a five year old baby? The Indian was smart in the bush, but as far as civilization was concerned, he had no more idea than a two year old baby. At the time of the Treaty in the

North I would swear that the Indian didn't know what he was doing. But the White man knew what he was doing.

The Treaty meeting lasted about a week. Fort Providence was the same. Like old Squirrel told me, the Indians asked the Treaty party why they gave them treaty but Conroy wouldn't tell them why. They got treaty but they wouldn't tell them why. How can an Indian accept anything when he knows nothing about the White man. The Indian is just a bush man.

Archie Gardner was the interpreter. And Bishop Breynat was there. Archie was a good interpreter. Naturally the Indians had his influence. I don't know what Bishop Breynat said or did, but there were a lot of Catholics so when the Bishop told them it was O.K. I guess they agreed that it was O.K.*

All the people knew was that they got treaty and that they would be helped. That's all there was to it. They weren't convinced one way or the other . . . .

I'm just saying what I think. I'm not for and I'm not against it. Even if I was Treaty what could I do?

To a White man, yes, the deal is there. But for an Indian, what did he know about that? Because he had no idea of what was going on, he didn't know what law was, he didn't know what a deal was, he didn't know what a contract was.

It's a big thing as far as I'm concerned. We were told about the Treaty to protect us against the invasion. And that's all it was – to protect the Indians and to keep them. That was the deal. But over all, as far as land, they didn't know that they were signing their rights over, they didn't know anything about minerals, oil or gold. If they'd seen gold they wouldn't know what it was.

At the time, people like me didn't realize what was going on. They had been paying in the South. All the rules, acts and laws were already ready. And they go by that, come down here – what did Mr. Indian in the Mackenzie know about law or treaty or anything else?

In fact I remember when there was no policeman here, no law. You just lived as you were. So the people who took the Treaty pretty well didn't know anything about the White man's way, law, or anything else.[86]

Fort Wrigley

The Treaty party left Fort Simpson on July 12, and travelled 160 miles down river to Fort Wrigley. The navigation time for this trip is approximately sixteen hours. Records show that the Treaty was signed at Fort Wrigley on July 13. Although a short time was allowed for discussions and negotiation, the seventy-eight Slavey Indians present for the Treaty, were not entirely reassured:†

*In 1921 there were 293 Catholics and 125 Anglicans at Fort Simpson.

†The following Indians testified about the Fort Wrigley Treaty: Julian Yendo, the 1921 chief, in interviews with C. Gerald Sutton of Yellowknife, on July 2, 1971, and with Henri Posset, OMI, of Fort Simpson, on November 20, 1971, and before Mr. Justice Morrow on July 18, 1973; Paul Moses, born in 1911, in an interview with Sutton, on July 2, 1971; Francis Tanché, in interviews with Posset, on January 5, 1973, and with Joachim Bonnetrouge on March 23, 1972; Philip Moses, in interviews with Sutton on July 2, 1971, and with Posset on November 19, and 21, 1971, and before Mr. Justice Morrow on July 16, 1973.

176

Francis Tanché: You should not refuse, said the Whites . . . Because this fall one barge will arrive: horse, cows, guns, all that is necessary for the band will come to the chief. Whatever you need to survive in the bush will be given to you. We will take care of you . . . But they [the Indian people] didn't agree very much. It didn't seem right to them . . . They were wondering if the Whites were saying the truth. So, the Whites added that as long as the Mackenzie River flows and as long as the sun rises, they will keep their promise truthfully.

There was some difficulty in getting a chief. Moses, who was the spokesman, wanted nothing to do with signing the Treaty, according to an eye-witness account:

Philip Moses: The old man [Moses] was quite aware that something in the future was going to happen; . . . The commissioner of the Treaty party told the people when he was paying out the Treaty money that as long as the sun rises and sets, and the river flows, there would be no changes in the lives of the people . . . The people of Fort Wrigley were promised by the Commissioner and the Bishop that there would be no laws for taking wild game . . . Nothing will be put into law for the game . . . .

Moses wanted Julian Yendo to be chief. Yendo was not in the village when the Treaty party arrived, and he attended the negotiations only "after most of the talking had been done . . . Just before the money was being paid out". He recalls: "[I] had three uncles. The three started talking together and they were pointing at me that is how I got to be Chief and other people were kind of scared . . . so they made me chief." The signing of the Treaty is described by Philip Moses, the only surviving witness:

I remember very well the signing of the treaty. White people came here to make us sign something. But we did not know what it was all about. Now we are told that the Government has taken over our country . . . and only now do we understand what was signed. But then, we did not understand anything. White people fooled us. It is unjust, and everything should be fixed up again. Bishop Breynat came with the Whites. The Bishop did not talk. Only the White people talked. But the Bishop was with them. His role was to keep God's words, and so we trusted him. The Bishop was with the Whites, that is why we thought it was a good thing to sign the treaty . . . .[87]

The Treaty document bears these signatures:

	H. A. Conroy
	Yendo
witnessed by:	Bishop Breynat
	W. V. Bruce, Inspector RCMP
	A. L. McDonald
	F. H. Bacon[88]

Born in October, 1885, Yendo was thirty-six years old in 1921. Although the original Treaty document shows his signature in syllabic characters, Yendo stated he did not sign it: "I do not remember having signed anything. Someone might have signed my name. A white man, or the Bishop might have done it."[89] This confusion is further complicated by other testimonies. In one interview, Philip Moses, the sole surviving witness said he "didn't see anybody signing any paper or making a cross or alphabets on any paper at all". On another occasion he declared: "It is Julian Yendo who signed the treaty. I saw him sign." Some Indians who knew Yendo stated that he was never able to read or write Indian syllabic characters. But according to Francis Tanché, Yendo and he exchanged correspondence in syllabics.[90] However, when Yendo resigned as chief on January 4, 1941, he signed his resignation with a simple "X" mark. These apparent contradictions cannot be satisfactorily explained. More knowledge is needed before a reliable interpretation can be given. Whether Yendo signed the Treaty or not, the Annuities book shows that Yendo, "Headman of the Slave Band No. 3 at Fort Wrigley" received $22, the customary annuity given to headmen.[91] Thus, the Fort Wrigley negotiations were within the pattern of the other communities in the Mackenzie District.

Nor were these the only incongruities related to the Treaty signing. Inherent in the concept itself, is an anomaly not often understood. Inspector Bruce sensed it when the Indians asked for a printing press to print dollar bills: "No joke was made about it; it was simply explained to them. But how the hell could a lot of them know that they could not do it?"[92] Edward Hardisty grasped the full impact of it. He had been a child of four years in 1921; he had become chief in later life. When reflecting on the Treaty at Fort Wrigley, he was describing all other Indian Treaties:

> To my mind, I think this treaty should have been signed when some people had a little bit know of writing and reading, not when they just come out of the bush, and did not know nothing, and did not know what they were signing. . . .[93]

Fort Norman

In travelling the 160 miles between Fort Wrigley and Fort Norman, the northbound *Hubaco* met the southbound *S.S. Northland Trader*. Some exchange of news must have taken place, for a passenger on the *Trader* was later quoted by the *Edmonton Bulletin:*

> . . . the Indian Treaty party under H. A. Conroy [travelling downstream] was met with near Fort Norman, and it is understood that some trouble had been experienced in getting the Indians to accept the Treaty money . . . .[94]

Fort Norman was the first settlement where the Treaty Commission met Indians of the Hare tribe. The discovery of oil just forty-five miles north of the trading post affected them very directly. There at "Discovery Well" was the location of an all white community, unique in the Mackenzie, which had its origin in the oil industry, rather than the fur trade. It was a microcosm of the Northwest Territories of the future, which had no place for the Indians. Entries in the Catholic Missions' diary for the spring of 1921, indicate the rapidity with which the change was taking place:

> April 2, 1921: Mail arrived. We learn that Norman is selected as capital of the North West Province.
> April 18, 1921: Nine white people arrive from Vancouver over the mountains. They say the Government will let people take 4-square mile claims (cost $1,240).
> April 25, 1921: Two white prospectors arrive from Edmonton via Athabasca. They forecast a great rush to here this summer. 5,000 persons.
> June 2, 1921: Imperial Oil Company plane flew from Simpson to Norman in 3 hours and 10 minutes.[95]

This was the first plane to fly North along the Mackenzie River. After so much excitement, neither the arrival of the Treaty Party nor the signing of the Treaty was recorded in the Mission diary.*

About one-third of the Indians were absent from Fort Norman. They had been at the post in the spring but returned to their hunting grounds for the summer. Conroy reported to Ottawa that these had left word that they were willing to take Treaty.[96] These Indians, numbering 136, received their gratuities and annuities the following year. Albert Wright was the first chief at Fort Norman. He could speak English, having been to school in Edmonton, and he was a good interpreter. Among those who were present for the signing of the Treaty at Fort Norman were Indians from Great Bear Lake, who regularly came to the post for trading. On July 15, 1921, 208 Indians adhered to Treaty 11. It was signed by the following:

> H. A. Conroy
> Albert Wright
> Saul Blondin

and witnessed by:

> Bishop Breynat
> W. V. Bruce, Inspector RCMP
> Geo. P. Johnston
> G. H. M. Campbell, Constable RCMP.[97]

---

*Pierre Fallaize OMI, was also present at Fort Norman on this first Treaty day, but he does not mention the event in his "Great Bear Lake Diary" (1920-1926) (OMIAFS – Manuscript B – 091 MB-B2). He noted instead some news which was of far more concern to him: "Alas! Bishop Breynat favors closing down for one year the "Mission du Rosaire", at Great Bear Lake.

An account of Treaty negotiations has been pieced together from the testimonies of Indian witnesses to the event.*

Saul Blondin was the second chief and Jim was the Chief of Bear Lake.

John Blondin was fifteen years old at that time. He talked fairly good French and English and he understood what went on at that time . . . .

The Treaty party came down. They said "You people are very poor, so we are going to give you a treaty. We will pay treaty money. It will be different from now on. Everything will change. There will be no more poor people . . . ". They asked the people if they wanted them to pay a treaty, but then the people did not want treaty at all at the time. Commissioner Conroy said that this was a sort of a gift from the Government . . . "The Government will give you relief or rations when you are sick." All these things were promised to the people.

At first the Indians didn't believe that they weren't going to be poor from then on. They figured the Treaty party was lying.

The people were scared to take the treaty because they didn't know what was coming. The Treaty party couldn't just come to the town and say, "Here, we'll give you the money for nothing". The Indians had feelings that the White people were going to take over something, that the White people were not giving the money away for nothing. They must be buying something, either the land or the people. That's how the Indians felt. So they just kept asking the White people what the money was for. They said "You just can't give us the money for nothing. It must mean something . . . ". The White people kept bugging the people for treaty. They said "You've got to take treaty". The people said no. So everyone went home. The next day, it was the same thing again. They talked about taking the Treaty all day. They tried to force the people to take the Treaty. The people didn't want it . . . .

Commissioner Conroy promised the people that this was their land. "You can do whatever you want," he said. "We are not going to stop you, just do what you were doing before. And also the birds and ducks and things like that, just continue on hunting as you used to before." This was the promise he made to the people . . . that we could go hunting and fishing, do whatever we wanted, that's the promise they gave. They talked about hunting moose and caribou, birds, anything. "Nothing will change," they said, "everything will be free to you people as it has been in the past. And you people can hunt all you want, do what you want to do and have free lands like you used to. Do whatever you want." The people just kept asking about hunting things, like birds and moose and also trapping. Conroy promised the people that they could do as they had done, nothing would change. Chief Wright kept asking them about a dozen times about the hunting and trapping. They said nothing would change. The Indians could keep on hunting like they used to. Nobody would bother them at all. That was the promise they gave to the people when they took the treaty. The people asked them about land and game, moose, trapping and stuff . They all said "Yes, yes." They never turned

* Joe Kenny, born 1903 and Albert Menacho, born 1893, were interviewed by Isadore Yukon of Fort Franklin in May, 1972; John Blondin, born 1906 and Johnny Yekaleya, born 1905, were interviewed by Bernard Masuzumi of Fort Good Hope, in April, 1972; Undated notes written by John Blondin, have also been used.

the people down at the time. That's why they took the Treaty – because they promised free land, freedom of hunting and everything . . . "You can keep on hunting and fishing and trapping. It will be just as you did before. Nothing will change." But yet the people didn't agree with what the Government said. "All we want", said the Commissioner, "is just that you take the Treaty money." But the people said no.

So on the third day the Bishop said that the White people were not lying. "They would keep their promise. They are telling you the truth." So the bishop started helping the Treaty party. In them days people were a hundred percent Catholic [80%to 90%]. So they began to talk amongst themselves. The Bishop was just like a God man, "so he must be telling the truth", they said. The Bishop said that the people in the Government don't lie. He said that they would be honest about the promises they gave the people. He said that they should take it. So they decided that God was not lying. He told the people that they should take the Treaty, so they figured that he was God and that God wouldn't lie.

Even though the Bishop said that they should take the Treaty, the people themselves did not want to take it yet. They talked amongst themselves until they got everything settled. That's when they finally got a treaty. They decided to take the Treaty on the third day. They talked amongst themselves and then they signed the Treaty. The White people were not talking about any lands, so they all made an agreement, and they all signed their names, the Commissioner and Albert Wright and all the others.

Then the Treaty party, Commissioner Conroy or whoever it was, said "as long as the Mackenzie River flows, and as long as the sun always comes around the same direction every day, we will never break our promise." The people and the Bishop said the same thing, so the people thought that it was impossible that this would happen – the river would never reverse and go back up-river, and the sun would never go reverse. This was impossible, so they must be true. That's why we took the Treaty.

The narrators would have the negotiations last 3 days. This seems unlikely since the Treaty was signed on July 15, just two days after it was signed at Fort Wrigley. There is no record of arrival time at Fort Norman, but it could not have been earlier than the 14th.

Fort Good Hope

After leaving Fort Norman the Treaty party would pass Discovery Well on the journey downstream. There is no record of a sfop-over there, but it is very likely that the *Hubaco* put into shore. The oil strike on this spot in 1920 had set into motion the forces which culminated in this voyage of the Treaty Commission down the Mackenzie. The arrival at Fort Good Hope, 130 miles downstream from the oil field was recorded in the Catholic Mission Diary by Alexis Robin, OMI: July 19, 1921:"Bishop Breynat, Father Trocellier, and the Treaty Party arrive.[98]"

There was no further entry to describe the negotiations, but fifty years later Father Robin could remember what had happened. He had been with the Indians since 1912 and knew them well:

Quite a few people were out in the bush, mostly the Eastern and Colville Lake bands. Before leaving the village they gave me their names and said: "If all the other people accept the treaty, we'll accept it also". Prior to Treaty day, some people said they did not want to receive Treaty. I told them: "You might just as well accept it, and bargain hard to obtain more than what is offered".

Before 1921, there was no chief; the H.B.C. manager told the Treaty Commissioner that Tseleie would be a good chief. I also think he was the best man for chief.

I did not attend the discussions, which lasted only 2 or 3 hours. Bishop Breynat did not do much about the Treaty. He was at the Mission building with Father Trocellier who arrived at Fort Good Hope that day. We were talking together when someone came and told Bishop Breynat to come and witness the treaty signatures.

The policeman did not know how to write the Indians' names and he spelled them all wrong. Some Indians signed the Treaty only the following year.

In the following years, all the people accepted the treaty money and they always had a big feast.[99]

Testimony by Indian people brings out many of the same details and adds others.*

Louis Caesar: During the first treaty we heard that we were supposed to pick a chief, so we picked Tseleie.

Louis Boucane: The chief did not want treaty but they kept talking to him until he got tired of it and said yes. There were only two of them but they kept bugging the people ... They asked the chief for two weeks ....

Louis Caesar: The Government party [was] in Good Hope ... about half a day, not very long.

Gregory Shae: The whites asked us if we wanted reserves ... But we told them that it would be kind of crazy to own little pieces of land. Because if the animals and furs disappear from that little piece of land what would the owner eat. We told them that we would rather hunt and trap all together ....

Louis Caesar: If the people were to own small pieces of land and if the animals never come there, they would have to move onto someone else's territory and there would be fighting and arguing. The chief said: No. The people wanted to go where they wished when they wished ... The treaty party continued to make promises to the people that the government would help them if they needed it ... They said that they will give us $10 each for the first year and then they will keep adding on $5 for each person every year. Like the second

* Louis Boucane, born in 1905, was interviewed by Gerald Sutton of Yellowknife in July, 1971; Louis Caesar, born in 1902, Gabriel Kakfwi, born in 1885, and Gregory Shae, born in 1896, were all interviewed by Bernard Masuzumi of Fort Good Hope in January, 1972. Louis Caesar testified also in front of Mr. Justice William G. Morrow, at Fort Good Hope on July 18, 1973.

year we will each get $15 . . . Then the third year $20. Then the fourth year $25, and so on . . . We agreed to the treaty because of these promises, and in those days nobody lies . . . .

Gabriel Kakfwi: The old Bishop was there too. He talked to the people about how good the treaty was . . . You see, the people believed everything the Bishop said because bishops and priests are not supposed to lie. So they believed him . . . .

Louis Caesar: Bishop Breynat wasn't present. After the treaty, the government built a two storey log house for the chief. They said that they were going to send food and rations for the upstairs part. They said that they were going to do this whenever it was empty. The chief moved in the house with his family and waited for the food and rations that were for his people. He waited until he died . . . .

The Treaty was signed on July 21, two days after the arrival of the Treaty Commission. One hundred and thirty-four Indians adhered to the Treaty, which was signed by the following:

> H.A. Conroy
> Simeon [Tseleie]
> Francois Nategal

and witnessed by:

> Bishop Breynat
> W.V. Bruce, Inspector RCMP
> F.H. Bacon
> J.H. Brashar, Corporal RCMP[100]

Louis Caesar recalls the celebration which followed Treaty Days:

> On treaty day, long ago, the government gave us the food for the feast after giving out the treaty money. They gave us rice, bacon and dried fruit for the feast. And after the feast there was drum dancing, square dancing and hand games. Everybody was there. We had fun.

The Treaty Party did not leave until three days later. Father Robin made this brief entry in his diary:

> July 24, 1921: The Bishop and the Treaty Party departed for Arctic Red River. All the people present in the village accepted the treaty, and are quite happy, although all said they would not accept it.[101]

Arctic Red River

The Treaty party crossed the Arctic Circle about twenty miles below Fort Good Hope. Two hundred and ten miles further downstream it landed at Arctic Red River, "on July 26, 1921, at 1:00 P.M.",[102] after a journey of twenty-four hours. This was Kutchin, or Loucheux territory, and 171 Indians were on hand for the negotiations. Other than the day and time of arrival no further information on the Treaty is found in the Catholic Mission diary. What is known about events at Arctic Red River comes from the recollections of Native people who were there:*

Amos Niditche: I remember when I was young everybody was talking about the treaty money . . . But everybody in our country at that time had lots of money because we had lots of furs and hunting was good and nobody was in need of money and about then this white-man came in and he was a big shot of some sort. He came and said: "I'm here to give you some money. But nobody knew what he was talking about . . . and the people asked lots of questions . . . He sounded very truthful. He said "I am giving you this money because in the future there will be lots of white people in your country and you will be here, and you will be remembered as the treaty people," and he put on the table $1000 and they got one man who was named as a treaty man.

After, he said this: "For the future even if there are lots of white-men, remember you are all Treaty Indians, you make your living here, you will have someone to look after you always; and remem-ber the whiteman will never be your boss." The Indian then took the money because they thought it was explained. All people then agreed and said "Yes." and they made two bosses [Indian chiefs] because if there are lots of whitemen in the future these bosses will be speaking for you.

Julienne André: They [the Indians] said, "This is our land, we were born here, it is our land and no one will take it from us". This white man [Conroy] and a Hudson Bay Clerk [Parsons ?] told us . . . this land is your land as long as you live and no one will take it from you. The people said, "Are you sure no one will take this land?" and the white people said, "Yes, we will not take your land".

William Norman: [Conroy] said to pass this Treaty, Treaty is not for the white people to bother you for anything, they won't bother your fishing wherever you fish, and things like that: and another thing, everything what you kill in the summer, whatever or wherever you hunt and you kill anything, it is free . . . all the Indians agreed to it and said it is O.K., and now we are going to pass a Treaty, he says. Then each person got twelve dollars.

William Firth: After three days of negotiations the people of Arctic Red River were still not willing to sign the treaty and it was only af-ter the arrival of Bishop Breynat that they finally consented. The Bishop spoke to them in French, which was translated by the resi-

*Julienne Andrew born 1887, and Amos Niditche born 1907, interviewed by Ed-ward Nazon of Arctic Red River on April 23, 1973; William Firth of Fort McPher-son was interpreter for the 1921 Treaty party at Arctic Red River, he was inter-viewed in 1966 by Les A. Wilderspin, assistant Indian Agent at Fort McPherson; William Norman, born 1900, testified in front of Mr. Justice William Morrow, at Arctic Red River on July 25, 1973.

dent priest, advising them to accept the terms offered, as the Government could take the land anyway and was only trying to help them by promising schools, medical aid and assistance in times of emergency.[103]

Treaty negotiations did not take three days. They were finished in half a day, and the Treaty was signed on July 26, the day of arrival. The following persons attached their signatures to the Treaty:

H.A. Conroy
Paul [Niditche]
Nide Aphi
Fabien-Loloo

and witnessed by:

Bishop Breynat
W.V. Bruce, Inspector RCMP
J. Lecuyer, Priest, OMI
J. Parsons.[104]

Years later, William Norman had original Treaty documents for a period of time:

> . . . several years ago, William Norman, one of the Arctic Red River Band Councillors, came to him [Mr. Firth] with some papers and asked him if they were of any importance. Mr. Firth said that examination proved that they were original papers relating to the signing of Treaty No. 11 . . . .[105]

This account is given by Wilderspin, who interviewed Firth in 1966. No trace has been found since of those papers.

Fort McPherson

Fort McPherson was the northernmost location where Treaty 11 was signed. To reach it from Arctic Red River, the Treaty Party travelled down the Mackenzie to Pointe Separation, then up the Peel River, a distance of seventy-five miles. Since the Indians at Fort McPherson were Anglican, Breynat did not accompany the Treaty Party, but waited at Arctic Red River for the return trip up the Mackenzie.

There is a brief entry in the semi-annual report of RCMP Inspector Stuart Taylor Wood: "The Treaty party visited [Fort] McPherson in July and paid treaty for the first time. Many of the Indians and Half-breeds had gone to their fishing camps at that time."[106] Other witnesses to the Treaty have recalled important information in their oral testimonies.*

---

*Andrew Stewart, born in 1907, was interviewed by Francis Blackduck of Fort Rae in 1970; Jimmy Thompson, born in 1895, was interviewed by Antoine Mountain in December, 1971; Johnny Kickovitch (or Kay), born in 1900, was in 1921 the police interpreter, the Indian band's first councillor, and the official interpreter during the treaty negotiations. He was interviewed by Francis Blackduck in April 1970 and by Gerry Sutton of Yellowknife on July 1, 1971; Jack Parsons, a white man, was man-

Jack Parsons: Conroy, that Indian Agent, he was a very good man. He explained to the people this way, and that way. He talked one, two days.

Johnny Kay: The first time, the man named Mr. Conroy came by gas boat, and nobody knew anything about a gas boat, that was the first gas boat they seen . . . Mr. Conroy said he came here to pay Treaty, but no one knows what he was talking about, and they set up a big tent on the sand bar right at the beach and they brought chairs and tables around that tent. He puts lots and lots of money on the table and the Chief asked him "What is this money for?" So Conroy told him "You are wearing the medal with the King's head on it and you see us shaking hands and the King, and you are doing the same thing with this money."*

Chief Julius asked him questions again. "After you give us this money, do we still have to do our living off the country, continue with our living off the country?" He said "Yes, you can do your living off the country as you always have done, and no one is going to boss you around after you have the Treaty". He also told him, "You are going to have land set aside": and the Chief asked him "What is this land for?" and he said "Just to keep it on hand", and he said they don't understand, no one knows what they are talking about, and the Chief asked him again, "Maybe you want to chase us into it someday," but he said, "No one will chase you around, we will keep this land and keep you there and someday there are going to be lots of white men come around and if they happen to find anything on your land, you will be taken care of". He asked him how big a land they were going to give him and he told him down to the mouth of the Peel River, to the Snake River, and then down Red River on this side of the shore, and then down to the Peel. This will be your land. Once this land is set aside for you, there will be no white man cut even one tree down on that land, and he also told him that it is just going to be kept aside and no white man would trap in it or do anything in it.

Johnny Thompson: We don't know about treaty, what it means. We never know that we get five dollars to give out land. They say that we gave out land that time, and that they told us that; they should have told us too what's going to happen . . . This man gave out land, his name is Conroy. A good friend first time. He talks nice, he told the chief: You are going to have all this land, all around this land. The chief told him nothing. The chief asked him why he is giving them all this land. [Conroy said]: You can go hunting, fishing, and

---

ager of the Hudson's Bay Co. store at McPherson from 1920 to 1925 and again in 1931-1932. He was interviewed in Halifax by Stuart Killon in July, 1972; Johnny Kay gave testimony also in front of Mr. Justice William Morrow at Fort McPherson on July 25, 1973.

*Medals were given to commemorate Treaty 11 in 1922.

trapping, it belongs to you.

Andrew Stewart: The chief was told . . . that there was supposed to be a reserve . . . that ground was given to him as a reserve . . . The old chief asked Conroy why he asked them to take this Crown land, and Conroy said that in the future there is going to be all kinds of people down there, Whites, that it would be better for the people.

Johnny Kay: [Conroy] promised them they would own Peel Reserve, he told us to put up posts . . . and put I.T. on it (Indian Territory) and Conroy said: . . . the time some white people come around . . . and they come to a post with I.T. on it, this white man will stop . . . so the first time we had all this land around, up to the river, and the tree line and way up, he gave us all this land. And after that, the government says I lost that Territory . . . .

The Indians were afraid that if they took this reserve, they would then have to stay on it. The chief made sure that this would not happen:

Johnny Kay: "They [the Indians] got to go all over, the way they do before", the chief said. [Conroy said]: "Nobody is going to make you stuck . . . Conroy explained that once they sign the Treaty they are going to continue to live on, the way they were at that time forever . . . The people could still go around to hunt and trap, sure, he said.

Jack Parsons: Well, I can remember Conroy when he was agent at the time of the Treaty, and he said it doesn't matter what other people tell you, what I tell you is right. The hunting and fishing will never be changed as long as the grass grows and the river flows. I remember that distinctly.

Johnny Kay: Conroy said: I will give you rations and traps . . . Anything you want, the government will give it to you. So, that year we get ration, flour, and bacon and sugar, tea, nets, all kinds of twine . . . What he [Conroy] said . . . and what the chief said, he wrote it down with the chief, and gave the chief a copy, and one for himself. The chief lost that, and the government tells us, that paper is lost too. I do not believe that . . . .

Two hundred and nineteen Loucheux Indians accepted Treaty money at Fort McPherson when Treaty 11 was signed there on July 28. The document bears these signatures:

> H.A. Conroy
> Jaby Lalo [Julius Saloo]
> Johnnie Kikawchik [Johnny Kay]

and witnessed by:

> W.V. Bruce, Inspector RCMP
> J. Parsons
> F.H. Bacon
> James Firth[107]

The confusion which surrounds the issues of land use, land owner-ship, use of natural resources, Indian reserves, and game preserves is nowhere more apparent than in the history of the Treaty at Fort McPherson. The Indians seemed to understand that the Crown land designated as the Peel River Preserve in 1923 had already been given to them as a reserve by Conroy in 1921. Government officials had quite a different view. A "Preserve" or "Game Preserve" does not mean an Indian reserve; rather it is an area on which only Indian peo-ple are allowed to hunt and trap. Non-Indian people are allowed on "preserves" only for purposes other than hunting and trapping. In many documents only the context can clarify the meaning of these terms. Small wonder that the Indians were indignant with explana-tions that their "reserve" was, in effect, not theirs. The Department of Indian Affairs was forced to investigate the grievance. In 1966, the tes-timonies of several Loucheux people were recorded in an exchange of correspondence between Department officials. Charles E. Callas, Su-perintendent of the Aklavik Indian Agency:

A . . . point worthy of consideration is the date the actual game preserve was discussed and if it was part of the preamble to the Treaty. I have nothing on file to answer this.

Knowing how involved and delicate the situation is I was able through interest in the older families to bring out in private conversations ques-tions into the history of the original Treaty meeting with Mr. Conroy. Through these questions directed to men who were present I learned that there is reason to believe that Mr. Conroy's interpreter outlined the prom-ised game preserve as a reserve for sole use of the Fort McPherson people present and their children's children, etc. Among those I talked with in the Aklavik Band were Chief Andre Stewart, Edward Sittichinly, the An-glican Minister, Alfred Semple, and Simon Modeste.

The old people of Fort McPherson firmly believe the game preserve was established as a reserve and insist this is what they were promised.

When Mr. Rheaume visited McPherson as a Member of Parliament talking of the land settlement it is reported the older people figured out what was coming to them for their "reserve" at twenty dollars per acre . . . .

I would say that if the Game Preserve was established by or through Mr. H.A. Conroy when discussing the signing of Treaty Number 11 that there is strong ground to believe that a misunderstanding occurred and the Indians of the McPherson Band may have a justifiable claim.

The reference of "preserve" could easily have been translated as "re-serve" and this error would normally be compounded by continued refer-ence to reserves by Agents, Government officials, and Indians from re-serves in the Provinces meeting at hospitals, seminars, etc.[108]

Les A. Wilderspin, Assistant to the Aklavik Indian Agent:

Peter Thompson . . . of Fort McPherson . . . is a lay reader in the Angli-can Church and is extremely well thought of by everybody. He told me that Mr. Conroy promised the people a tract of land for their sole use for hunting and trapping. He said that former Chief Johnny Kay had a map showing the boundaries of this preserve. However, Johnny Kay told me later that Chief Julius, chief at the time the Treaty was signed, had had all the papers relating to the treaty but had lost them. Peter Thompson also told me that the year following signing of the treaty a man named Craik, who, I gather, was a trader living near the mouth of the Peel River, had told him that the Government would pay money to the Indians if any oil or minerals were discovered on the preserve. By this I take it that he was told that the people owned the mineral rights . . . .

Fred Firth . . . remembered that an area was promised to the Indians for their sole use as a hunting and trapping ground . . . .

Johnny Kay was chief of the Loucheux 7 Band for a number of years and was one of the signatories of Treaty No. 11. – Johnny Kikawchik. He told me that Mr. Conroy said that the land from the Mackenzie River between the mouths of the Peel and Arctic Red Rivers extending back between these two rivers as far as the Snake River, would be set aside for the sole use of the Indians of Arctic Red River and Fort McPherson, and that money would be paid for any mineral discoveries on this tract of land.

I also talked with John Pascal, who is a member of the Indian Advisory Council for the Northwest Territories and was in Fort McPherson last week. He said that several of the old people at Arctic Red River had told him that a tract of land had been promised for their use and that mineral rights were granted with this land.

William Firth . . . told me . . . during the course of the negotiations, Chief Julius Salu [Jaby Lalo] asked Commissioner Conroy that a tract of land be set aside for the sole use of the Indians of Fort McPherson and Arctic Red River. Mr. Conroy said that the land between the Peel and Arctic Red Rivers from the Mackenzie back to the Snake River would be set aside. Mr. Firth told me that signs marked I.T. were given to the Chief and he was told that no white man could use this land without permission. Mr. Conroy was reported to have said that if gold or any other minerals were discovered in the tract the people would receive a share of the money from these. When the Commissioner's party left Fort McPherson they stopped in at Arctic Red River on the return journey and this same information was conveyed to the people there; Mr. Firth was present at the time this happened.

This information is pretty well the same as that given to me by Johnny Kay and I would say that both of these men are reliable people.[109]

Norm K. Ogden, Regional Director, District of Mackenzie:

Considerable publicity has been given to a claim by the Fort McPherson band that in accordance with the terms of Treaty Number 11 and a commitment made to that band by the Treaty Commissioner in 1921, a block of land referred to locally as the Peel River preserve was in effect set aside by the Government as a reserve, or hunting reserve, for the exclusive use of the Fort McPherson band of Indians.

Quite recently, when the Regional Advisory Council met in Fort Smith, Mr. John Pascal, a delegate from the Aklavik Agency, brought this to the Council's attention, and indicated that amongst the Indian people it is firmly believed that the reserve or preserve belongs exclusively to the Indians . . . .

As I mentioned earlier, our records are completely void of any material on which we can base answers to the band as regards their contention that they do have exclusive rights to the Peel River Game Preserve. In addition, we can find nothing here indicating whether or not the Treaty Commissioner, Mr. Conroy, ever committed the Government to setting apart the Peel River preserve for the Indians.[110]

Albert R.K. Macdonald, Head Natural Resources Section, Ottawa:

When you consider that solemn promises were given to the Indians, when they accepted Treaty, that they would be free to hunt, fish, and trap as before, you will realize that the Indians might misunderstand the intent of the Preserve. We have no way of knowing what explanation was given to the Indians or whether in fact, anyone even bothered to explain the purpose of the Preserve to them.[111]

Fort Rae

After signing the Treaty at Fort McPherson on July 28, the Treaty Party began its return journey. Travelling down the Peel River, then up the Mackenzie to Fort Providence, the Commission arrived at Hay River, on Great Slave Lake, August 12, 1921.[112] There were no Treaty negotiations here, as the Indians had signed Treaty 8 in 1900. The Treaty Party remained for five days, however, delayed by a storm which made the waters of Great Slave Lake unnavigable. When the wheather finally cleared, The Treaty Party departed for Fort Rae on board the HBC Schooner *Fort Rae,* leaving behind the little tug *Hubaco.*

Fort Rae was and still is the largest Indian settlement in the Northwest Territories. In 1921 it had a population of approximately 800 people. The Dogrib Chief who signed Treaty 11 was Monfwi, born on May 21, 1886. Called Ewaro'A (the Small Mouth), he was the son of Ewarotcho (the Big Mouth). According to the testimonies of eyewitnesses, he was the dominant figure in the negotiations with Conroy.

The witnesses' recollections of these events have been assembled to give as complete an account as possible. At Fort Rae more testimonies were collected than in any other place.*

*At the time of Monfwi's death in 1936, Jimmy Bruneau, born in 1881, became chief, and remained in that capacity until 1969, when he resigned his position. Jimmy Bruneau, still a resident of Fort Rae was interviewed on October 7, 1968, by Alphonse Eronchi of Fort Rae and on December 16, 1968, by James Wah-shee.

Other testimonies, include those of: Jonas Lafferty, a Métis, 1896-1973, and Harry (Lazare) Zoe, born in 1891, interviewed by J. Pochat, OMI, in October, 1971; Vital Thomas, born in 1904, interviewed by the author, on November 13,1972; Elise Murphy, daughter of Chief Monfwi, born in 1909, interviewed in 1968 by Joe Drybones. The interview was translated and transcribed by James Wah-shee; Harry Black, born in 1888. Interviewed by James Wah-shee in January, 1969; Noel Sotchia (Tsatchia), born in 1899, interviewed by James Wah-shee on January 12, 1969; Adele Lafferty, born 1899, interviewed by Violet Camsell, 1971.

Other Fort Rae residents also recorded their testimonies: Henri Lafferty, 1879-1970; Ned Heron, an employee of the Hudson's Bay Co.; Sammy Football, born in 1906 and his wife Adele, born 1912; David Sangris, born in 1879; Pierre Wedzin, born in

Vital Thomas: In 1921, Michel Bouvier, Louis Lafferty and myself were the only people who could speak English in Fort Rae.

Jonas Lafferty: Conroy, and his party arrived in Fort Rae. Well, that day, Chief Monfwi walked around and he shouted: "Why have these Englishmen come? Why do they come to bother me? They probably come for nothing. As for myself, it's no good to see Englishmen here. Us, the people, we live here, we are all right."

Then Conroy told Monfwi: "You look so pitiful, you and your people, we'll give five dollars to everyone, to help them a little bit." Monfwi said: "No, I won't take the money. At Fort Smith they signed treaty and it's no good. They said this. I hear it".

The same day Bishop Breynat told him: "My son, what the White man said, it's good for you and for all the people".

Chief Jimmy Bruneau: The next day, they put up a tent, outside the Catholic church, and started the meeting. Mr. Conroy told the Indian people that they have to choose one man for their Chief and some others for headmen.

Noel Sotchia: With Chief Monfwi were the councillors: the old Germain, First Councillor and leader of the Detchilaotti (Barren land band, Snare Lake Band), Pierre Liske, leader of the Southern band; Old Tatsi and Lacorde (Etto), both from Faber Lake; Josue Beaulieu and Jeremie [or Germain] Keha, both from Lac la Martre; also Raphael Rabasca; Slim Tongue's son; Councillor Louie's father, Susie (Old Prophet); Old man Edward, from Yellowknife; Big Knife's father (Bietcho Wetra).

Chief Jimmy Bruneau: Mr. Conroy informed the people that he came to Fort Rae from Ottawa, on the order of His Majesty the King, to give the Peace Treaty . . . The treaty was designed for the White man and the Indians to live together peacefully. It was to bring the White man and the Natives together, so that they could enjoy peaceful life in this country and share whatever wealth is in the land.

Harry Black: Monfwi sat with the Government official beside a table full with papers. The Indian Agent said: "Before many White people come this way it will be better to have a treaty now because in later years there will be many White people on your land and you may lose some of your rights. Before this happens, you should now consider the size of land and boundary that you want, to protect your hunting ground . . . In the future there will be many White people in this country and they might use up most of the game and the things by which you make your livelihood so by then your people will not be well off, so before this happens we want to make a treaty to prevent this from happening.

1907; Bruno Gaudet, born in 1887.

Their interviews, although not presented here, confirm the truthfulness of the other witnesses.

Noel Sotchia: While the White man is within our land, we expect help from him in times of need and vice versa. We are to live with the White man peacefully side by side as brothers, and either one is not to start trouble for the other since we are to be brothers . . . When the Indian is in troubled time, they are to help us and vice versa and if White people are in trouble they are to be helped. There is to be no trouble to exist in between.

The Dogrib Indians who had signed Treaty 8 at Fort Resolution in 1900, remembered that promises made then had not been kept. In 1920 they boycotted Treaty days, using the only means they had to protest the violation of their rights. Now, other Dogrib Indians were banding together, and they would not sign the new Treaty unless their hunting and trapping rights were guaranteed. They would allow white people on Indian land but not as hunters, trappers, or fishermen. These rights belonged exclusively to Indian people on Indian land.

Noel Sotchia: We would allow the White people to come to our land and since we do not know anything about oil and precious minerals on our land, we will not stop the White man from taking these natural resources from our land since we do not know how to make use of them. The treaty [was to] preserve our way of life.

Harry Black: Chief Monfwi stated that if his terms were met and agreed upon, then there will be a treaty, but if his terms were not met, then "there will be no treaty since you [Treaty Officials] are on my land. If it seems that you disagree with me, even slightly, then there will be no treaty."

The conditions laid down be the Chief were the same as those made by old Drygeese in 1900, and by Susie Drygeese in 1920, at Fort Resolution. Chief Monfwi wanted the "land boundary" to be drawn on a map. This would show Dogrib Territory, where Indian people could enjoy their rights forever.

Harry Black: The Indian Agent asked Chief Monfwi . . . what size of land he wanted for the band. Monfwi stated that "Many of my people are scattered across this country, some at Lac la Martre, Snare Lake, Contwoyto Lake, many of whom are still in the bush yet. The size of land has to be large enough for all of my people . . . Chief Monfwi asked for a land boundary starting from Fort Providence, all along the Mackenzie River, right up to Great Bear Lake, then across to Contwoyto Lake, Seymour [Aylmer] River, Snowdrift, along the Great Slave Lake, back to Fort Providence. The Indian Agent said that this was a fair sized piece of land and that he was in doubt. Chief Monfwi again told the Government official that if his terms were not accepted, there will be no treaty since he did not ask the Government officials to come to his country. They had a big discussion about the land boundary and they went toward evening

192

so they decided to end the meeting for the day to continue the next day. No agreement reached that day.

Jonas Lafferty: That same evening, Monfwi told the same thing to the Bishop: "Father, today I have said no. Tomorrow we'll see. I have to think more about it. But if there are any restrictions, then I won't take the money."

*Harry Black:*The next day we crowded into the meeting tent again and began the big discussion about the land boundary again. Finally they came to an agreement and a land boundary was drawn up. Chief Monfwi said that within this land boundary there will be no close season on game so long as the sun rises and the great river flows and only upon these terms I will accept the treaty money. Again more discussion took place.

Elise Monfwi: An RCMP [Inspector Bruce?] told Monfwi that his wishes were going to be met and that he was not going to lose any of his rights . . . It would be better to accept the treaty since there will be no close season for the Dogrib band as they can hunt, as they wish. On this land there will be no White man hunting and trapping.

Adele Lafferty: Some people were afraid that now everything will be closed, when the money is given to us . . . "We depend on living animals for food. We will be poor if the season will be closed for us," they said.

But Chief Monfwi told the Indian Agent, "If the season will be closed for my people I will not take treaty money. Not one of my people will take the money." The RCMP, the Bishop and the Indian Agent were all seated. The Indian Agent said "They will not be closed for you. As long as the river flows and the sun rises from east to west in this land of yours, nothing will be closed. You can continue on hunting, fishing, and trapping the way you have always done, like for ducks, caribou and fur-bearing animals of all types, for the reason that you have depended on them. Your children after you will also continue on living your ways of life. It will not be closed for you nor for your children. The old people said it would be good then, if their children were taken care of by treaty.

The protection of hunting and trapping rights occupied the attention of everyone. Land ownership was not considered an issue.

Jimmy Bruneau: We made an agreement, but land was never mentioned . . . a person must be crazy to accept five dollars to give up his land . . . It was never mentioned that there will be such things as reserves in the future, nor that the treaty was against the land.

Noel Sotchia: Land was never mentioned and we did not take the treaty to give our land to the Crown. If such was the case we would not have accepted the treaty money.

Gifts of fishnets, ammunition, tools, flour, tea, bacon, and matches, were discussed. The promise was made that the Government would provide care for the sick people. But Chief Monfwi was not to be diverted from his primary concern; securing land where his people's freedom would be insured. Bishop Breynat was present during these discussions and encouraged the Chief to trust the Commissioner.

Elise Monfwi: My son, he said, take the treaty, what the White man said is true. The Bishop told him that even if he Chief Monfwi accepted the treaty, they would not lose their rights but rather it would be as he asked.

Jimmy Bruneau: He said to the Chiefs that if they did not sign a treaty, the White people coming here would not know the Indian rights. No hardship would come out of accepting the treaty now.

Adele Lafferty: The Bishop said to Monfwi: "The Indian Agent is telling the truth. He is not lying. As long as the river doesn't flow backwards and the sun doesn't rise from west to east they will continue helping you. They don't mean to cause you any problem or troubles."

Jonas Lafferty: Monfwi said: "Father, if you weren't a man of God, if you didn't work in His name, I wouldn't say yes. But God sent you to us. I cannot say no. But there will be no restrictions on our land".

Jimmy Bruneau: The previous day, Monfwi had asked for a map and had asked that the Commissioner himself draw up on a map the boundary of the Dogrib territory. But the Commissioner had refused to give the paper to the Chief.

But Chief Monfwi maintained his position.

Jimmy Bruneau: "I will not accept the Treaty until I have a copy in my hand. I will accept the Treaty only when this area of land is given to the Dogrib band." The Chief again asked the Commissioner for the paper and the map, before he signed the treaty. This time, the Commissioner handed the paper [Treaty documents] to the Chief Monfwi and showed the marks on the map and said: "You sign the paper you keep a copy of it and I will keep a copy of it too".

Harry Black: After the land boundary map was drawn up, to ensure that the map was valid, the R.C. Bishop was called in to have a look at the map. He told Chief Murphy [Monfwi] that he was thankful to him, since he made a good agreement on the land boundary, and that no one had made such a good deal before. I was present when the Bishop made that statement.

Noel Sotchia: Before accepting the paper [the map], Monfwi asked the Bishop and the storekeepers along with the elders of the tribe to also sign their signatures on the treaty to make it valid.

Vital Thomas: Conroy asked Monfwi to pick up his witnesses and Monfwi picked up Bishop Breynat, the HBC man, Jim MacDonald

194

of the Northern Traders Company and Ned Heron.

Jonas Lafferty: Bishop Breynat said: "That's understood. I will write my name on the paper and there will be no restrictions. I will read the paper to you". Louis Lafferty interprets: "No restrictions as long as the sun rises, and as long as the river flows downstream. Monfwi said: "Because of your word, I will take the treaty".

Everywhere it was full of tents, right up to the Mission, and far away as far as can be seen it's full of the Indians' tents. Then, Monfwi comes out. He stands, and he shouts: "Because of the Bishop's word, I will write my name on the paper. The Bishop has only one word, not two. Hear me. My name is written on the paper. You too, you can take the treaty".

Then everybody shouted: "Yes, yes, that's good". All the Indians took the Treaty. There was plenty of money in the village . . . .

Vital Thomas: Conroy gave a paper to each of the seven chiefs.

Most witnesses recall the story in almost the same words. Some have forgotten a few details, but as Lazare (Henri) Zoe said: "I was still a young man, and there were more interesting things to do than listen to the old people talking".[113]

Noel Sotchia: Everybody was feeling happy because Chief Monfwi made it possible through the treaty to protect our way of life, which is trapping, hunting, and fishing. And it was agreed that no wording, paragraphs or phrases was to be changed by either party involved in the treaty. No one was supposed to break it, even the other White people who may come around. No one.

Elise Monfwi: My father (Chief Monfwi) said: "Nde Gohon Gotson . . . " as long as this land shall last, it will be exactly as I have said.[114]

After these lengthy discussions, when agreement had been reached, the Treaty was signed on August 22, 1921. Those who signed are the following:

> H.A. Conroy
> Morphy [Monfwi]
> Jermain [Germain]
> Josue Beaulieu

and witnessed by:

> Bishop Breynat
> W. J. O'Donnell
> W.V. Bruce, Inspector RCMP
> Ed. Heron, HBC
> Claude Wm. La Fountain

There were 443 Dogrib Indians who received gratuities at Fort Rae.

A few days after the Treaty signing Nicolas Laperrière, OMI, resident priest at Fort Rae commented in his diary:

> Mr. Conroy, representing His Majesty the King, came to conclude a treaty with the Indians. These had previously agreed not to accept anything, but as soon as they saw the dollars and the bacon, they eagerly held out their hands and forgot their resolutions and nice speeches . . . Most of the Indians went back to the bush; and I hope that the transient Whites, a travelling Great Plague, will not show up again.[115]

Copies of the Treaty and of the map had been given to Chief Monfwi. He reportedly kept these until his death in 1936. No trace of them has been found since. His daughter, Elise testified:

> When Chief Monfwi died, they put his little packsack on top of the coffin. The medal he had received and the papers [Treaty Documents] were in this little sack. The Fathers and everybody were there. They had the coffin there, and they were taking pictures.
> The house was full of people. When they were taking pictures, the Father took the papers, the medal, everything.
> In the summer time [1937] the Indian Agent came around and asked where were the papers signed for the area [Treaty]. We just got the medal back. They didn't ever get back the papers . . . my mother only had a medal casing, with the map inside, which she gave to the Indian agent.

The two priests at Fort Rae when Chief Monfwi died were Father Marcel Trassard, OMI, and Father Nicolas Laperrière, OMI. Neither made any mention of the incident in his diary. Nowhere among the mission records is there any mention or trace of the Treaty documents and maps. Nor is there any evidence that they were given to Breynat when he next visited Fort Rae.

Johnny Jean Marie Beaulieu explained the fate of the Treaty document:

> [In 1937] Lafferty was interpreting for the police, and he told [Chief] Bruneau that the priest had given it [the treaty paper] to them [police], he had seen it . . . Emyat [Indian Agent Amyot] and the police then talked . . . then Bruneau went to the police barracks with them and they got the paper back.[116]

Some believe that the documents were burned, along with those of Treaty 8, during the influenza epidemics of 1928. Others think that they are still with the Chief at Fort Rae, or a priest, or the Indian Brotherhood. Bruno Gaudet's opinion is probably the most realistic: "Nobody knows what happened to the documents."[117]

Journey Completed

Leaving Fort Rae, the Treaty party crossed Great Slave Lake to Fort Resolution. There the *Hubaco* and its houseboat took them up the Slave River to Fort Smith, where they landed on August 30, 1921.

They reached Edmonton on September 11, having travelled 4,228 miles.[118]

With the journey completed, the Department of Indian Affairs would have to pay a transportation bill of $11,617.93 to the Hudson's Bay Company, for services rendered.[119]

If an official report of the Treaty Commission was sent to the Government, it has not been located. It is assumed that the summary report reprinted with the text of Treaty 11, formed only a part of an original, more lengthy one. This summary dated October 12, 1921, was written by Conroy and addressed to the Department of Indian Affairs:[120]

SIR, – I have the honour to submit herewith the report on treaty made by me on authority granted by Order in Council, dated March 14, last, as Commissioner to negotiate a treaty with the Indians occupying the territory north of the 60th parallel and along the Mackenzie river and the Arctic ocean.

I left Edmonton on June 8, 1921, accompanied by Inspector W. B. Bruce, Constable Wood and Constable Campbell, of the Royal Canadian Mounted Police. Constable Campbell acted as my clerk for the summer.

Arriving at Fort McMurray on June 11, we left there on the 14th in a houseboat, the property of the Hudson's Bay Company, which company had made all arrangements for the transportation of the treaty party during the summer in the North.

We arrived at Fort Fitzgerald on June 18, crossed the portage to Fort Smith, and boarded the ss. *Mackenzie River* on June 20 for Fort Providence, at which place the first adhesion to Treaty 11 was to be taken. July 5 was the date set for the meeting of the Indians and myself to take place at Fort Providence, and, in order to arrive in good time, I thought it better for me and my party to proceed there by the ss. *Mackenzie River,* and let the houseboat take us up again at this point. The transportation of the houseboat across the portage at Fort Smith took several days.

On our arrival at Fort Providence, on June 20, I found the Indians were not at the post, as we were there before the date set for the meeting, so word was sent of my arrival, and the majority of the Providence Indians living at Willow Lake arrived on June 25, those at Trout Lake not till July 2. I had several meetings with them, and explained the terms of the treaty. They were very apt in asking questions, and here, as in all the other posts where the treaty was signed, the questions asked and the difficulties encountered were much the same. The Indians seemed afraid, for one thing, that their liberty to hunt, trap and fish would be taken away or curtailed, but were assured by me that this would not be the case, and the Government will expect them to support themselves in their own way, and, in fact, that more twine for nets and more ammunition were given under the terms of this treaty than under any of the preceding ones; this went a long way to calm their fears. I also pointed out that any game laws made were to their advantage, and, whether they took treaty or not, they were subject to the laws of the Dominion. They also seemed afraid that they would be liable for military service if the treaty was signed, that they would be confined on the reserves, but, when told that they were exempt from military service, and that the reserves mentioned in the treaty would be of their own choosing, for their own use, and not for the white people, and that they would be free to come and go as they pleased, they were satisfied.

Practically all the bands dealt with wanted more provision for medical attendance at each post, schools for their children, and supplies for their old and destitute.

I pointed out that they were still able to make their own living, and that Dr. A. L. McDonald, of the Indian Department, was then with me, and that they could see him, and that he would attend them free if they wished, but that it was impossible for the Government to furnish regular medical attention, when they were occupying such a vast tract of territory. Schools were already established, and their children receiving free education, and supplies were left at each point for the sick and destitute.

The treaty was signed at Fort Providence on June 27, and the following were paid: –

    1 Chief,
    2 Headmen, and
    255 others.

Our houseboat arrived on July 5, and we left Providence for Fort Simpson on the 7th, securing adhesion to the treaty there on July 11.

    1 Chief,
    2 Headmen, and
    344 other Indians were paid.

Adhesions to the treaty were obtained at Fort Wrigley on July 13.

    1 Headman, and
    77 others were paid.

At Fort Norman on July 15, –

    1 Chief,
    2 Headmen, and
    205 others were paid.

At Good Hope, July 21, –

    1 Chief,
    1 Headman, and
    208 others were paid.

At Arctic Red River on July 26, –

    1 Chief,
    1 Headman, and
    169 others were paid.

At Fort McPherson on July 28, –

    1 Chief,
    1 Headman, and
    217 others were paid.

At Fort Rae on August 22, –

    1 Chief,
    2 Headmen, and
    440 others were paid.

Practically all the Indians were dealt with at Fort Providence, Simpson, Wrigley, Arctic Red River and McPherson, and about 65 per cent at Fort Norman, Fort Good Hope and Rae, the remainder of these Indians having been at these posts in the spring and left word that they were willing to take treaty, but had to return to their hunting grounds for their summer's work.

At Fort Rae is the largest band of Indians, about 800, and this is the most inaccessible, being on the arm of Great Slave lake, difficulty in crossing this lake being experienced, more especially in the late summer and fall on account of storms, our party being stormbound at Hay River for five days prior to crossing. These Indians hunt in every direction from the fort, some as far as 200 miles, and only come to the post in spring to trade their furs, so that, in future, I would suggest that this be the first post visited when making payments.

We crossed the lake from Hay River to Rae in the Hudson Bay schooner *Fort Rae,* leaving our houseboat to take us up at Resolution, from which place we went on August 25, arriving at Fort Smith on August 30, Fort McMurray and Edmonton in September.

I much regret that I was unable, owing to the lack of time, to visit Fort Liard, and secure adhesion to the treaty by the Indians at that point, although they had sent word to Fort Simpson of their willingness to accept the same. I considered it advisable to proceed to Great Slave Lake, and cross to Fort Rae at the first opportunity, as the season was getting late.

Dr. A.L. McDonald joined the party at Fort Providence, and accompanied it to Good Hope, at that place having to return to Fort Resolution on account of smallpox having been reported, which report, fortunately, proved untrue. He joined the party again at Hay River, and remained with it until arrival at his headquarters at Fort Smith.

I was very glad to be accompanied by His Lordship Bishop Breynat, O.M.I., who has considerable influence with the Indians in the North, and would like here to express my appreciation of the help and hospitality accorded to me and my party in his missions, and I desire also to express my appreciation of the services rendered by Inspector Bruce, of the Royal Canadian Mounted Police, and by his party. Constables Woods and Campbell performed their duties in the most creditable manner.

The actual number of Indians paid was: –

> 7 Chiefs at $32 each $488
> 12 Headmen at $22 each

and

> 1,915 Indians at $12 each $22,980

H. A. CONROY,
Commissioner, Treaty No. 11.

In his annual report, the RCMP Commissioner gave this account of the role played by his men:

> One interesting duty performed was in connection with the making of treaty No. 11 with the Indians along the Mackenzie river and Great Slave Lake. This treaty was negotiated by H.A. Conroy, the Indian Commissioner, who was provided with an escort composed of Inspector W. V. Bruce and two constables, the constables rendering clerical assistance as well as serving as escort . . . .[121]

RCMP Inspector Fletcher was not especially eloquent about the treaty:

Mr. Conroy, Indian Treaty Commissioner, made treaty with the Indians
. . . I understand he had no difficulty in making treaty as the majority of
the Indians were anxious to take it.[122]

Years later, Breynat commented briefly on Treaty 11 in his
autobiography:

The same formalities, the same objections, the same promises were repeated in all the villages down to McPherson. But everywhere the treaty
was cheerfully accepted by the Indians, allured as they were, by the $12.00
offered to each, as a first compensation for surrendering their rights to the
Crown.

Most of them had never seen a dollar bill. At least a great number of
them had never fingered any of these little green papers which opened the
doors to all the stores and never failed to bring a smile in exchange for
more useful goods, tea, and tobacco, then flour, lard, sugar etc. . . . Never
previously had there been such an affluence in the Indian tents . . . Consequently, feasts and dances multiplied, to manifest the general joy . . . .[123]

The annual report of the Department of Indian Affairs offered a uto-
pian prediction for the future of Treaty 11:

This year the Department is establishing treaty relations with the Indians
of the Mackenzie River basin. New obligations and sources of expenditure arise as civilization forces its way into the wilderness. The compensation, if compensation is to be sought, for this drain upon the public funds
is both ideal and practical – ideal in the enviable position which this country occupies, as the guardian of its native race, practical in the growing
power of the Indian as a producer of wealth. There is no doubt that the
Indian is capable of graduating into useful and responsible citizenship.[124]

The Canadian Annual Review of Public Affairs, 1921 edition, printed
one thousand pages containing the most important news in Canada
during that year, without a single word about Treaty 11. The
Edmonton Bulletin published a naive account of the Treaty Commission in its issue of September 13:

As a result of the work of the government treaty party, which has been in
the northland during the summer, 372,000 square miles of territory has
been ceded by the various Indian tribes to the crown, and about 1,900 Indians who hitherto had not been reached have signified their willingness
to accept the government bounty.

. . . The Indian bonus consisted of $7 down and a lifetime gratuity of $5
per annum. In addition to this, the government supplies a certain amount
of food for the sick and destitute as well as ammunition and fishing tackle,
in return for which the Indians cede to the crown all their rights to the
land of forefathers, for "As long as the sun shines and the grass
grows". . . .

When all the Indians are on the books of the treaty party the roll will
carry about 3,000 names, Mr. Conroy thinks, and in all about 70 per cent
of the northern natives have now accepted the grant.

There is nothing spectacular about the payment of the treaty Mr. Conroy states, and long-winded speeches by the Indians, tom-tom concerts, and tea-dances are strictly taboo. Nothing but straight business goes, and the natives have been made to understand this clearly. The first procedure on the arrival of the treaty party is to pick a chief, who signs the documents for the whole tribe and who is personally responsible. The choosing of the chief is a democratic procedure and the commissioner states that desirable persons were chosen in practically every instance.

After the chief is chosen, the next matter on the program is a heart-to-heart talk in which the whole scheme of the treaty payment is explained to the chief, who then returns to his tribe and transmits the details to the natives. Next a meeting is called, at which questions are invited, and anything which perplexes the native mind is cleared up by the commissioners, following which the papers are signed by the chief and the money payments made.[125]

The *Edmonton Journal* printed a serious story on September 26, explaining for its readers the purpose of the Treaty and the meaning of its conditions. The article recognized the Indians' rights to the land and the Government's responsibility to secure title to it. Several paragraphs are devoted to the fine points of land ownership. There is no mention that the Indians retained their right to hunt, trap, fish, and move freely on the land. The story reflects the Government's intention and interpretation of the Treaty.[126]*

Treaty 11 was ratified by the Governor General on October 22, 1921.[127] Each adhesion of Treaty 11 was numbered by the Indian Affairs Branch in the consecutive numbered series of Indian Treaties and surrenders as follows:

Fort Providence	No. 2398
Fort Simpson	2399
Fort Norman	2400
Fort Good Hope	2401
Fort McPherson	2402
Fort Rae	2403
Artic Red River	2404
Fort Wrigley	2405[128]

Fort Liard: 1922

The waters of the Liard River between Fort Simpson and Fort Liard are among the most difficult to navigate. The Treaty party of 1921 had no time to make the trip. Inspector Fletcher reported in August: "The Indians there expressed themselves as anxious to take treaty; and are expecting the treaty to be made with them next year."[129] When Treaty Commissioner Conroy died on April 27, 1922, the Department of Indian Affairs hurriedly obtained an Order-in-Council which authorized Harris, the Indian Agent at Fort Simpson, to negotiate with the Indi-

*See Appendix IX for text of the article.

ans at Fort Liard and to complete the Treaty.[130] He described the negotiations which took place:

> . . . Arriving at Liard in the early morning of the seventeenth [July 1922]. The Indians of this place were all awaiting us, except the band from Trout Lake, which band is composed of about ninety persons, who are the most uncivilized of the district, and who have come into contact with the Whites less frequently than the others. I proceeded to make Treaty with them in the name of His Majesty King George V, according to my instructions. I was greatly assisted by Bishop Breynat and by Father Moisan, in making the Indians understand the terms of the Treaty, and in showing them that by treating with His Majesty, they were doing the very best thing they could for themselves and for their descendents. Here again, I was hampered by the fact that the supplies had not yet arrived, but Father Moisan had by judicious management, been able to save a portion of last year's rations, and I used these in giving a ration for the Treaty. The election of Chief and Headman proceeded in a very satisfactory way, and I had finished the payment before evening.[131]

Discussions, elections, payment, all took less than a day. The Treaty was signed before evening on the day of arrival, July 17. One hundred and fifty Indian people of the Slavey nation, gave their adhesion to the Treaty. The following signatures appear on it:

> Thomas William Harris, Commissioner
> Thomas E. Kinla, chief [Ekinla]
> Joseph Fantasque, headman
> David Celibeta, headman

witnessed by:

> Bishop Breynat
> F. Moisan, OMI, priest.
> A. Borbin, Constable RCMP
> Joseph Berrault, interpreter.[132]

The Treaty was ratified by an Order-in-Council on March 29, 1923.

The Catholic Mission diary mentions only that Mr. Harris came to pay the Treaty for the first time.[133] At a later date, two residents of Fort Liard recalled their bewilderment during Harris' visit. Baptiste Dudan (Dontra) 1885-1972, declared that Harris "did not explain what the Treaty was all about . . . They did not make any promise or nothing, just give money to the people". Even in 1971, Dudan did not know what the Treaty was. He received $5.00 every year; for him that was the Treaty. He believed he received it because he was poor.* Ned (Philip) Seya explained that he never knew why the money was given, nor what it was for.[134]

Harris suggested to the Department that the Indians at Fort Liard were entitled to receive an additional $5.00, in payment for the year 1921:

*Interviewed in Fort Liard, by Gerald Sutton of Yellowknife and Chief Baptiste Gazon of Fort Simpson, November 2, 1971.

I was authorized to pay these Indians a gratuity of $7.00 with their annuity of $5.00, but had not authority to pay them for 1921, when Mr. Conroy was unable to meet them at Ford Liard. The Indians of Liard brought to my notice the fact that it was not their fault that the treaty had not been made in 1921, as they were there awaiting your representative who failed to put in an appearance. I think it is only just that these Indians should receive arrears for 1921 . . . .[135]

Harris was Indian Agent at Fort Simpson from 1913 until 1930, and at Fort Good Hope from 1930 to 1933. He was well known for his understanding of the native people and he always remembered the spirit of friendship in which Treaty 11 was signed. The Territorial Administration complained continuously about "the leniency with which Mr. Harris . . . has dealt with Indians and Half-breeds coming before him for contraventions of the Game Act." In his capacity as Justice of the Peace, "Flynn" Harris based his judgements not only on the letter of the white man's law, but also on the special promises made to the Indian people at Treaty time.[136]

RCMP Inspector Bruce: Recollection of the Treaty Commission, 1921

The report filed by Inspector Bruce on his duties as escort for the Treaty Commission in 1921 has never been found. He witnessed the signing of the Treaty at every stop along the Mackenzie River, and by his own statement, "If there was anything unusual happening, according to my training, I would remember it." From his retirement in Sidney, British Columbia, Inspector Bruce recorded his recollections for C. Gerald Sutton, on June 13, 1972. The impressions which remained with him over the years are evidently of those events and issues which seemed of greatest importance at the time.

The whole idea of going there on that treaty thing, I was literally informed by Conroy and the others, was that oil had been struck at Norman and they figured that there was an enormous oil basin down the Mackenzie and that it might be developed then. So in the Council it was: "Alright, we've never made treaty with the Indians, let's make it."

The Government was afraid the whole country was going to be taken up with oil or one thing or another, and they wanted to get the Indian thing settled . . . I am quite sure that that was the idea, at least that's what I got from Conroy.

There was a good congregation of Indians at every place that a treaty was made. There was a lot of preliminary discussions and questions . . . asked and answered before there was any attempt to try and rush anybody into making a decision before they needed to, and I have an idea that in some cases the discussions would take place, . . . and [they would] adjourn till the next day or . . . the afternoon, or the Indians would discuss amongst themselves, and then reassemble. No, I am quite definite there was no coercion or anything like that used, they were quite free. I'm quite certain there was never any argument or controversy. There were a lot of questions asked by the Indian councillors or chiefs . . . Well, Conroy was quite patient and quite definite in his explanations and sometimes if there was anything at all that didn't seem to be quite understood . . . old Bishop Breynat would turn to both Conroy and the Indians who were speaking.

I understood all that was going on and I'm quite sure that the Indians did. Y'see. And if they hadn't have, I'm quite sure that old Bishop Breynat would have known that they did. I don't think that there was any, could have been, any misinterpretation or misunderstanding of what was said. Now, whether the Indian mind might have taken a different interpretation to what was said or meant, I, naturally enough, I can't say that. But personally I'd say no.

Well, the Indians always used to more or less retire . . . And discuss it among themselves. I think, as a rule there were about three Councillors who were more or less spokesmen and usually one, I presume, the Chief would be the one that they would refer to when they would discuss it themselves, and then they'd go back and you'd hear them talking on one thing or another, and then sometimes they'd come forward and ask a question, y'see.

Question: Would Bishop Breynat be in the company of the Indians when they would retire, or would he remain with Conroy?

Sometimes they would ask him, and sometimes they wouldn't. But mind you, those things were more or less formal, but they were also informal, y'know what I mean? Not like a court of law where you couldn't go up to the judge and say, 'Hey Judge, what about so and so?. If the Chief or anything was puzzled he'd come up and ask, which was perfectly right, that's the way it should be, to my way of thinking.

Question: Did Conroy go through it paragraph by paragraph or did he just express generally?

I think so. Yes, I know it took quite a long time. And there is no suggestion of trying to push anything through, or to gloss anything over. And, as I say, I know Breynat certainly wouldn't have stood for it. I remember Breynat at Providence, they had an Indian school there, and Bishop Breynat appeared. They were crawling all over him, he could hardly move. Now, they loved him. And when you take a man like that, he is going to see fair play.

They [the Indians] usually used to have the interpreters amongst themselves. Y'see, there were so many of them interpreters. Well, good night, I mean, dealing with the Hudson Bay all the time; and those were the ones that would tell the others. Now, as I say, we must have had a formal interpreter with us at each place. That I am quite sure of. But frankly I can't remember, but if they had been, they would have been sworn in, although it wasn't a court of law.

I know he [Conroy] was very patient with them. I suppose he had been dealing with them for years in different parts. But, of course, down the Mackenzie the dialects and languages were not all the same. I know the Hare Indians at Arctic Red River were different from the ones at Norman, but if I remember correctly, most of the Chiefs certainly understood English. Some of them were quite well spoken, but, of course, they had to be, they were dealing with the Hudson Bay all the damn time!*

What I remember mainly was Bishop Breynat because he accompanied us, and I think one of the main reasons why he was asked to come or volunteered to come was that his contact with the Indians and his knowledge of them and the trust that the Indians had in him made it very much easier for the Treaty Commissioner. I do know that he was loved by the Indians, and I can quite understand it, I loved him myself, and I'm not Catholic . . . He seemed to be known all over . . . He was pretty well known throughout the whole territory.

Bishop Breynat . . . was not a member of the Treaty party. He was present at all of them negotiations. He accompanied us all the way† and was present . . . as a witness, yes, I do know that they certainly trusted him and liked him, and not only that, he liked them.

Conroy would sign as Commissioner, I, as a rule, signed as a witness. I mean, Conroy would sign, the Chiefs would sign and I'd witness. And I am quite sure that in most cases Bishop Breynat signed as a witness too. Now, whether a copy of all that was left with the Indians or not, I do not know.

All the discussions, it seemed to be perfectly along with procedure, there was no coercion in any way, shape, or form.

Question: Do you recall whether in any given community the people did select the reserve?

No, I don't think so. I can't recall it and I don't think they did. My idea is that it was left for future discussion as to what reserves would be, and what land would be picked out. That, I think is absolutely correct. I think it was to be determined. I am quite positive of that.

Question: Do you recall how Conroy tried to give the people an idea of the size of reserves?

No, I can't. Actually speaking, I don't think it was mentioned . . . there wasn't any size mentioned. Now whether Conroy was empowered to give any idea of what the size would be, of course, it would have to depend on the number of the band, and the productivity of the fishing grounds or trapping grounds or whatever it was on that place . . . .

Well, my thinking at the time was that the reserves would be allocated within at least [at the most] three years . . . .

I can't understand . . . why reserves have not been allocated a long time ago. Because there isn't any question that it was certainly implied then.

Question: Do you remember if any particular emphasis was put on hunting and fishing rights or trapping rights, or things like that?

I certainly thought it was implied . . . I more or less always thought that it was understood, and I know I took it to be understood as in the Yukon. Because I know someone was trying to raise hell and I said, "Nothing doing, those Indians are entitled to this as long as they do it for themselves".

*Hare Indians were at Fort Norman and Fort Good Hope; Loucheux at Arctic Red River.

†He did not go to Fort McPherson.

So I certainly thought it was implied. Now whether there was any real actual mention of it I really can't say. And, as I say, it is so long ago, I can't really say what the provisions of the treaty were.

Question: Were you able to judge whether the making of Treaty was a great occasion to the Indians or a very significant event? Did they seem to regard it as that?

I think they seemed to think that they had recognition. I mean they were recognized by someone other than the Hudson Bay Company. Now that's a personal opinion . . .
  Well, you know, like all these Indians do, come in, they have a pow wow, they would gamble amongst themselves . . . Yes, I would really think they thought it was an event. Whether they figured it would change their lives, I don't know. But ninety-nine percent wouldn't want their lives changed.

Eskimos, 1921

When he visited the Mackenzie District in 1913, Bury made this assessment of the inhabitants of the country:

> The Eskimo seems more susceptible to the manners and customs of the white man, than the Indian . . . Their attitude to the white man is both cordial and dignified, being in great contrast to some of the northern tribes of Indians, especially those of the Dog-Rib band dwelling at Fort Rae on the north shore of Great Slave Lake. This band almost resents the intrusion of the white man, and does not welcome him at all.[137]

When Kitto made his tour in 1920, he rejected the validity of any land claims by the Eskimos:

> There are numbers of Eskimos living in the Mackenzie Delta, along the Arctic Coast, in Coronation Gulf and on the Coppermine River. No treaty has been made with these people, but as they are a purely non-resident people, they are not in the same position as the non-treaty Indians.[138]

The first boundary map for Treaty 11 was drawn in 1909 by Conroy. It did not include any Eskimo territory. When Conroy reopened the matter in 1920, after oil had been discovered on Indian territory, he proposed that Treaty 11 would include most of the Indians of the Northwest Territories. He explained:

> There may be some in the barren lands who will not be included, but as these lands will not be wanted for many generations . . . . . . it [the Treaty] will give title to all the land which will be needed for probably a century.[139]

Conroy must have known that there were Eskimos, not Indians, living "in the barren lands". The Eskimo territory from the Mackenzie River delta to the Coppermine River was shown as part of the Treaty area for the first time in 1920. The Eskimos were not asked to sign Treaty

11 in 1921; however, when they were invited in 1929, they refused. The Government might well have pondered this advice given by Major Burwash in 1923, and derived a lesson from it: "The eskimo will not be developed to the best advantage by the adoption of the methods that have been used in dealing with the Indians".[140]

Metis, 1921 – 1924

When scrip was given out in the Athabasca District in 1899, the Metis who received it often fell victims to disreputable traders and speculators. Conroy was determined that the same mistake would not be repeated in the Mackenzie District in 1921.

Kitto estimated that the Metis formed about 5 per cent of the total population of the Mackenzie. Many held permanent positions with the trading or transportation companies. Some worked for the missions. The majority, however, followed the Indian way of life. Since there was apparently very little future for farming in the Mackenzie, land scrip would be useless. Conroy had all this in mind, when he formulated his Metis policy in 1920:

> In making treaty with the Indians along the Mackenzie River, it will be necessary to treat with the Half-breeds . . . . I do not propose to extend the difficulties and the abuses which were practised when scrip was given out before. In Treaty 8, two kinds of scrip were given; first, land; second, money. It is in the former that most of the abuses occurred. I would now propose to treat with the families enumerated above, in money scrip only, as there is no land in that part of the country which is valuable for immediate settlement for agricultural purposes. I estimate that there will be 15 families to be dealt with in this manner. The other half-breeds in this country are mostly living the Indian mode of life, and I feel confident that I shall be able to take them into Treaty, as it is in their own interests to have this done. I do not think that there will be more than 75 families of half-breeds whom it will be necessary to take into Treaty . . . I shall, of course, use my best efforts to induce all people of Indian blood living the Indian mode of life to accept Treaty.[141]

When Conroy was appointed Treaty Commissioner, four months later, he was also given the authority to investigate the claims of half-breeds. His responsibility and terms of reference were spelled out by the Committee of the Privy Council on April 12, 1921:

> . . . concurrently with the treaty to be made during the coming season with the Indians of the Mackenzie River District . . . it will be necessary . . . to deal with the claims arising out of the extinguishment of the Indian title of the Half-breeds resident within the territory covered by the proposed treaty . . . .
>
> The Minister recommends that Mr. H. A. Conroy . . . who has had considerable experience in dealing with the claims of the Half-breeds resident within the limits of Treaty No. 8, be appointed a Commissioner to deal with the claims of the proposed treaty . . . .
>
> Half-breeds, whose right arising out of the extinguishment of the Indian

title has not been otherwise extinguished, found to be permanently residing within the territory covered by the proposed treaty on the date of the signing of the treaty at Fort Providence, shall be entitled to a grant of Two Hundred and Forty Dollars in satisfaction of their claims arising out of the extinguishment of the Indian title . . . .

The right of a Half-breed to share in the grant to the Half-breeds resident within the territory covered by the proposed treaty shall be considered to have been extinguished if such Half-breed has at any time joined a Band of Indians under treaty, although subsequently discharged therefrom, or if scrip has been issued to him or to his parents or guardian for him in settlement of his right, and the issue of scrip to any Half-breed shall be deemed to have extinguished the right of the child of such half-breed if the child was born after the date which fixed the right of the parents, but if the right of one parent has not been extinguished the fact that the right of the other has been, shall not affect the right of compensation of the child of such parents . . . .

The compensation in satisfaction of such claims as may be approved, amounting to $240 in each case, shall be paid to the claimants when the next annual treaty payments are made to the Indians of the said Mackenzie River District. The compensation to be paid the Half-breeds under eighteen years of age, unless they are married, in which case the compensation may be paid to the claimants themselves, shall be paid to the father, if living, or to the mother if the father be dead, and in the case of orphans under the age of eighteen years to the guardian on evidence of guardianship satisfacory to the Commissioner. The Minister of the Interior or his Deputy may, in special cases, authorize the delivery of such compensation to any person he may designate.

The minister observes that it is proposed during the present session of Parliament to amend the provision of Section 76, paragraph (b), of the Dominion Lands Act, which reads as follows: –

76. The Governor-in-Council may – (b) grant "lands in satisfaction of claims of half-breeds, arising out of the extinguishment of the Indian title;"

so as to provide for the settlement of these Half-breeds claims in the manner above set forth.[142]

Conroy could not distribute cash grants to the Metis in 1921, as the necessary legislation had not been passed by Parliament. He could only take evidence in reference to 176 such claims.[143] Again in 1922[144] and 1923 Parliamentary approval was delayed, and Metis claims were left unpaid. Indian Agent Harris reported in 1923, after his annual trip down the Mackenzie:

At every post . . . which I visited the Métis made inquiries as to when the Script promised them when Treaty was made with the Indians, would be given them; I had no information on this point, but told them that I presumed the Government would not delay in fulfilling their promise in this matter.[145]

The Dominion Lands Act was amended in 1923 to allow "grants not exceeding in any case the sum of $240.00 in cash in satisfaction of claims of Half-breeds arising out of the extinguishment of the Indian title."[146] On March 26, 1924, the Governor-in-Council authorized payment of $240 per person, for each Metis, adult or child, in the Mackenzie District.[147] During the summer the Metis claims were paid. Those south of Fort Simpson were paid by John F. Moran, Inspector for the Northwest Territories and Yukon Branch. Those to the North were paid by John A. McDougall, District Agent at Fort Smith. The number of Metis who received this grant was 138. McDougal reported that "in many cases the money was not expected, in most cases they did not know why they were getting it." He did not attempt to describe the state of mind of Tim Gaudet from Wrigley, "the prize package winner . . . He and the members of his family drew $2680. [$2640]".[148] Inspector Moran recalled that at Fort Resolution one Susie (Joseph) King Beaulieu presented himself to receive half-breed scrip, $240.:

> A large crowd gathered around my tent as my interpreter George Norn carried on our conversation . . . He [Beaulieu]said to me, "Many years ago Mr. McCrea [Macrae] of the Indian Department told me that later on someone else would finish his work" and now he wanted his money. I replied that his name was not on my list. He was getting excited so I told him I'd give him an answer the next day at 7 P.M.. . . .

When Macrae had paid scrip at Fort Resolution in 1900, he had told Susie King Beaulieu that he was not eligible to receive it. How could Moran convey this message again, without causing trouble? He acquainted himself with details of Beaulieu's life, and when Susie came to his tent the next day, he said:

> I had a dream last night . . . Mr. McCrea had appeared to me. I then described Mr. McCrea . . . and Susie began smiling, nodding his head in agreement . . . Mr. McCrea spoke to me saying, "Mr. Moran you are in trouble with my old friend, Susie, but Susie forgets what I told him. Tell Susie he misunderstood me when I last saw and spoke to him. Tell him his father and mother received script a long time ago at St. Boniface when he was a young boy and that, for this reason, there is nothing for him now". To make a long story short, I told Susie that Mr. McCrae asked me to give Susie a present from him – a plug of tobacco and a package of cigarettes – which I handed to Susie. I then shook hands with him and his beaming countenance told me how happy and pleased he was. He was the happiest person in all the North for had Mr. McCrea not only remembered him, but had sent him a present . . . .[149]

Conroy was true to his word and had encouraged many Metis to join Treaty. Bishop Breynat was active in the same cause, as Adele Lafferty of Fort Rae recalled:

> . . . when the people were signing for the treaty, the Bishop came to your [Violet Camsell's] grandfather, and said: "Take treaty money. It will be better for you and you will benefit from it. If you do not take treaty

money, you will be like the whiteman, you will not get anything out of it. You will live like the wind. But if you take treaty money like the Indians, the government will help you".*

When some Metis at Fort Resolution wanted to be included in Treaty 11, Breynat took their case to Ottawa:

> You are aware that Commissioner McCrea had refused to accept in the treaty the halfbreeds living the Indian way. His motives had their foundation in the rather bad reputation of some members of the – family, and consequently, the Commissioner saw trouble ahead for the Government if such people were accepted as treaty members. Since, I have heard very often expressions of regret for the non-acceptance into treaty of this type of halfbreeds. They are identified with the country as well as the Indians, they inter-marry with the latter, live their kind of life and should get the same protection.
>
> I would consider it a good policy on the part of the Department to offer treaty to those halfbreeds. Those who would accept it would enjoy the privileges of the Indians.[150]

Summary

Interpretation of the Treaty

The events leading up to and surrounding the signing of Treaty 11 will be subject to various interpretations, depending on the cultural context in which they are viewed. The intent and purposes of Goverment officials in making Treaty with the Indians would be readily understood by their country-men, both then and now. This would not necessarily be the case for the Indian people. An official opinion on this was given by Mr. Justice W. A. MacDonald of the Supreme Court of Alberta in 1944:

> An Indian Treaty, or for that matter any formal arrangement entered into with a primitive and unlettered people, should not be construed according to strict or technical rules of construction. So far as it is reasonably possible, it should be read in the sense in which it is understood by the Indians themselves . . . .[151]

The Indians could agree only to what they understood at the time, and their signatures can mean only that. Inspector Bruce himself clearly understood the terms and implications of Treaty 11, but conceded:

> . . . whether the Indian mind might have taken a different interpretation to what was said or meant, I, naturally enough, I can't say that.[152]

A few basic facts emerge from the evidence of documents and testimonies. These are: Treaty negotiations were brief, initial opposition

*Adele Lafferty, interviewed by Violet Camsell, of Fort Rae, September, 1971.

was overcome, specific demands were made by the Indians, promises were given, and agreement was reached.

For previous Treaties, "the supplies of food, clothing, money (usually in uncut sheets of one-dollar bills) were enormous . . . the logistics of Treaty-making were monumental."[153] In comparison, procedures for Treaty 11 were short and unimpressive. Discussions on the Treaty lasted but a few hours. How much explanation could be given by Conroy or understood by the Indians? This was the same Treaty that would keep hundreds of lawyers discussing for fifty years, leaving them in disagreement on the meaning of some of its clauses. Nor did the Indians get all of Conroy's attention. He was also Half-breed Commissioner and responsible for taking evidence from the Metis regarding their claims to scrip. Conroy left more written documents on transactions with the Metis than he did on Treaty negotiations with the Indians.[154]

Suspicion, apprehension, and reluctance characterized the manner in which most Indians approached the Treaty negotiations. Some had sworn that they would never accept Treaty money. Many sensed that they were on the threshold of an unknown future, and they were afraid. But in the end they all took the money. They understood from Conroy that whether they took treaty or not, they were subject to the laws of the Dominion. In fact, the Government had already imposed Canadian laws on the Mackenzie District. They had nothing to gain by refusing. Nevertheless, the Indians did not accept the Treaty *in toto,* as it was offered. They tried to secure for themselves some benefits which were not included in the original text prepared in Ottawa. They tried to bargain within the narrow limits allowed them. Later, when Government promises were not kept, some attempted to refuse their Treaty money, but learned that the Treaty was not renegotiable. Whether they accepted or refused the annuity, Treaty regulations were still valid; they could never turn back.

When the Indians agreed to sign Treaty 11, they were promising their friendship. For over 100 years the Northern Indians had been able to help newcomers to their country. They welcomed and assisted the white man and trained him to survive and adjust to northern conditions. By 1920 neither the Indians nor their assistance were needed. Rather, the Indians had to depend on the white man for some of their needs. They saw the white man's treaty as his way of offering them his help and friendship. They were willing to share their land with him in the manner prescribed by their tradition and culture. The two races would live side by side in the North, embarking on a common future. This concept of a Treaty was not unique to the Indian people. It had been expressed in 1880 by Alexander Morris, who represented the Government of Canada on early Treaty Commissions:

> I see the Queen's Councillors taking the Indian by the hand saying we are brothers, we will lift you up, we will teach you, if you will learn, the cunning of the white man. All along that road I see Indians gathering. I see

211

gardens growing and houses building; I see them receiving money from the Queen's Commissioners to purchase clothing for their children; at the same time I see them enjoying their hunting and fishing as before, I see them retaining their own mode of living with the Queen's gift in addition.[155]

The ear of the Queen's Government will always be open to hear the complaints of the Indian people.[156]

Let us have a wise and paternal Government faithfully carrying out the provisions of our treaties, and doing its utmost to help and elevate the Indian population, who have been cast upon our care, and we will have peace, progress, and concord among them in the North West; and instead of the Indian melting away, as one of them in older Canada tersely puts it, "as snow before the sun," we will see our Indian population loyal subjects of the Crown, happy, prosperous and self-sustaining, and Canada will be enable to feel, that in a truly patriotic spirit, our country had done its duty by the red man of the North West and thereby to herself. So may it be.[157]

In spite of these noble sentiments, official documents show that the Government in 1921 viewed Treaty 11 as a mere formality. Nor is there evidence that the Government ever developed a clear policy of fulfilling its obligations to the Indian people. For their part, the Indians never fully realized the extent of their participation in the Treaty: what they were expected to give and what they were entitled to receive.

Land Title

Most official documents indicate that Treaty 11 was a cession of land. The Indians of the Mackenzie District contest this interpretation. They do not believe that their fathers ever intended to surrender the land to the Goverment. They have never understood that Indian title to the land was extinguished by Treaty 11.

If Conroy asked the Indians to surrender their rights to the land, it is possible and probable that they did not understand him. Historians and anthropologists agree that the European concept of "land ownership" was unknown to the Indians of the Mackenzie District in 1921. This is still the case today, as was evident among the witnesses appearing before Mr. Justice Morrow in 1973. During the court hearing the terms "land", "land ownership", "land use", and "use of natural resources" were frequently used interchangeably. None of these had any relation to what the Indian people understood by the term "Treaty". In giving testimony, some witnesses spoke in their own Indian languages: Chipewyan, Slavey, Dogrib, and Hares. These all have a common origin, though spoken by tribes living a thousand miles apart. Over the years words have been coined to describe the new tools, foods, political and social practices introduced by the white man. Although there is a large collection of words used for "trade", "exchange", "agreement", "negotiations", not one tribe selected any of these to express its understanding of "treaty", or concepts related to it.

	"Treaty"	and	"Indian Agent"
Chipewyan	Tsamba Nalye		Tsamba Nale
Slavey	Samba Naye		Samba Nale
Hare	{ Sampa Naye		Sampa Nalle
	{ Sampa Raye		Sampa Ralle
Dogrib	Samba Nazja		Samba Nalle

"Treaty" is literally translated by "money is distributed"; "Indian Agent" by "the one distributing money". July is "the month when money is given", and the "first Treaty" is "the first time money was given". People express their thoughts with language. They communicate their interpretation of life in words which describe their understanding of it. "Money is distributed" clearly shows what significance the "Treaty" had for the Mackenzie Indians.

> In order that the white people won't overcrowd your land, we are going to give you some money.[158]

> You really mean it, by giving us this money, the white people will not crowd our land?[159]

> The chief said: "Why give me this money?" and the government man said: "We are giving you this to protect you. . . ."[160]

> If they [the Indians] took the money, they [the Government] would help the Indian people.[161]

> Now we are going to pass a Treaty, he [Conroy] says. Then each person got twelve dollars.[162]

It is evident that in 1921 no clear and definite statement was made of the purpose and consequences of Treaty 11, either by the Treaty Commission or by the Indians. This fact must detract from the value of documents which claim to extinguish Indian title. Clermont Bourget, M.D., Indian Agent at Fort Resolution from 1923 to 1935, describes the Mackenzie "land surrender":

> Treaties between Government and Indians, on the prairies and later on in the northwest, aimed at preventing troubles and wars between whites and Indians.
> The Government could have simply taken the proper land for settlement but it would have angered the Indians to see the Whites come and colonize these lands. They preferred to sign "treaty" with the Indian bands it acknowledged to be owners, but without a legal title, and first inhabitants of these regions.
> By this treaty, the Government asked the Indians to accept the White people as their neighbours and not to bother them. Through this bargain,

the Government, so to say, bought the country.[163]

In 1959 the Canadian Government established the Nelson Commission to investigate the unfulfilled provisions of Treaties 8 and 11. The five members of the Commission were evidently surprised to discover that the Indian people's ideas on land ownership had not evolved since 1921.

> It should be noted that although the Treaties 8 and 11 were signed sixty and thirty-eight years ago respectively, very little change has been effected in the traditional mode of life of the Indians in the Mackenzie District. Very few of the adults had received an elementary education and consequently were not able to appreciate the legal implications of the treaties. Indeed, some bands expressed the view that since they had the right to hunt, fish, and trap over all of the land in the Northwest Territories, the land belonged to the Indians. The Commission found it impossible to make the Indians understand that it is possible to separate mineral rights from actual ownership of land . . . .[164]

Most of the Indian witnesses in Mr. Justice Morrow's court were asked this question: In your opinion what did you or your forefathers give or surrender to the Government in return for the $5 annuity and other treaty gifts?

> We thought the Government was going to keep us like his sons, that is why he is passing the five dollars to us, like to his sons or children.[165]

> What we heard was that the exchange was to be peace prevailing among each other.[166]

No one mentioned land or title.

Treaty Promises

> The Language used in Treaties with the Indians should never be construed to their prejudice. If words be made use of which are susceptible of a more extended meaning than their plain import, as connected with the tenor of the treaty, they should be considered as used only in the latter sense . . . How the words of the treaty were understood by these unlettered people, rather than their critical meaning, should form the rule of construction.[167]

Shorn of its legalese, Treaty 11 has little of substance to offer the Indian people. There are a few specifics: an annuity, yearly rations, "once and for all, one grindstone, necessary files, and whetstones to each band." Were these latter expected to last as long as the sun shines and the river flows? Clauses dealing with reserves, education and medical care were cautiously vague. Any benefit from these would not come without a struggle.

Item: While it is a fact that the Indian people resisted a reserve system fearing they would be confined to a small piece of land, nevertheless, they would welcome settlement of their land claims. To date, there has been no land reserved for the Indian people of the Treaty 11 area. In sharp contrast are the Government's concessions in two famous land settlements. In 1867, the Hudson's Bay Company surrendered its trading monopoly over Rupert's Land and the Unorganized Territories for £300,000. It was permited to claim and select 1/20th part of the land, anywhere within the fertile belt, retaining all rights to that land. The Canadian Pacific Railways Company received land grants of approximately 25,000,000 acres, as well as generous tax exemptions.

Item: Education will be offered "in such manner as the Government may deem advisable," reads the Treaty text. The school system operating in the Mackenzie had been organized by the Catholic and Anglican clergies more than fifty years before the Treaty. It continued for more than twenty years after, without any noticeable benefit to the Indians resulting from the Treaty promise. The Federal Government had accepted responsibility for education and it was not meeting it. During the year 1936, the total expenditures of the Department of Indian Affairs for the education of adults and children in the Northwest Territories, (3,854 persons) was $37,865.16. In 1944, the budget had slipped to $37,566.00.[168]

Item: The Indians had asked for "more provision for medical attendance at each post," for they understood the need for medicines to combat the unfamiliar diseases which were invading their territory. Commissioner Conroy explained: "It was impossible for the Government to furnish regular medical attention . . . supplies were left at each point for the sick and destitute".[169] Until 1950, the missions carried the full burden of providing medical care to the Northern Indians, receiving only minimal assistance from the Government. The failure of the Government over so many years, to take every means possible to alleviate the sickness and suffering resulting from disease and epidemics, remains a national dishonour. In 1936 the expenditures of the Department of Indian Affairs for medical services to the 3,854 Indians of the Northwest Territories, in an area of half a million square miles, was $43,819. In 1944, it was reduced to $36,838.[170]

Upon hearing that ". . . as long as the sun shines and the rivers flow the Government will do this and that for you", an old Indian answered: "Wait and see 'as long as the rivers flow', you are more like little creeks which will dry up in a few years."[171]

Oral Promises: Hunting, Trapping and Fishing Rights

At first, when the first treaty, the chief didn't talk about things like we are having now. They were only concerned with wildlife, etc. . . . but for minerals these were the things they didn't understand that would bring in money. True, wildlife was the essential thing, then it was worth twice as much as today . . . .[172]

Contrary to the order from Ottawa that he "should make no outside promises", but strictly follow the Treaty text,[173] Conroy did promise the Indian people that they would be guaranteed full freedom to hunt, trap, and fish in the Northwest Territories if they would sign the Treaty. He made this oral commitment when it became clear that there would be no Treaty if this right was not recognized, and assurance given that it would be respected forever. Only when the Indians were satisfied that they would be exempt from any game laws and protected from the encroachment of white trappers and hunters did they agree to sign. Conroy's word was not enough however. It was Bishop Breynat who had to assure the people that the Treaty Commissioner was honest and sincere, and that the Government would honour his promises.

> I gave my word of honour that the promises made by the Royal Commissioner, "although they were not actually included in the Treaty" would be kept by the Crown . . . As the text of Treaty No. 8 and 11, which had been brought from Ottawa was not explicit enough to give satisfaction to the Indians, who were afraid to be treated as the Indians of the Prairies had been treated, (the conditions of the North being altogether different), the following promises were made to the Indians by the Royal Commissioner, in the name of the Crown:
> (a) They were promised that nothing would be done or allowed to interfere with their way of living, as they were accustomed to and as their antecedents had done.
> (b) The old and destitute would always be taken care of, their future existence would be carefully studied and provided for, every effort would be made to improve their living conditions.
> (c) They were guaranteed that they would be protected, especially in their way of living as hunters and trappers, from white competition, they would not be prevented from hunting and fishing, as they had always done, so as to enable them to earn their own living and maintain their existence.
> It was only after the Royal Commissioner had recognized that the demands of the Indians were legitimate, and had solemnly promised that such demands would be granted by the Crown, and also, after I had given my word of honour, with the Hudson's Bay Officials and the Free Traders and the Missionaries, who had the full confidence of the Indians, that they could fully rely on the promises made in the name of the Crown, that the Indians accepted and signed the Treaty.[174]

Breynat believed this himself, and fully expected that the oral promises made by Conroy would be added to the Treaty text. What actually happened was quite different:

> In 1921 a commission signed treaties with the Indians living in the valley of the lower Mackenzie, and here again the natives signed only after supplementary promises made by the commission had been guaranteed by Bishop Breynat.
> Unfortunately, due probably to oversight, no mention was made by the commissioners on their return to Ottawa of the supplementary promises

which had been necessary to get the Indians to sign the treaties. These promises have not been kept and the Indians protested. They asked Bishop Breynat to make good his word that he would see that the promises were respected by the government.

Imagine his surprise when officials at Ottawa said they had no knowledge of the promises which had been made to induce the natives to sign the treaties.[175]

Breynat had nothing in writing from Conroy to substantiate the validity of the oral promises. His case would be made to the Minister responsible for Indian Affairs, on his word alone:

I have given them [the Indians] my word that the Government would be true to their promises and this is the reason why I feel I must insist that the promises made at the time of the treaty be not overlooked any longer.[176]

Carelessness rather than dishonesty may have prevented these promises from being recorded in the first place. But it is difficult to understand why this situation has been allowed to continue.

The rights given by Treaties stand inviolate and above all other relationships between the Crown and the Indian people . . . Their precedency over any other enactment was understood between the parties when the Treaties were signed.[177]

At the time of Treaty 11, there were two laws in existence, which in principle, threatened the freedom of Indians to hunt and trap. These were the Migratory Birds Convention Act of 1916, and the Northwest Territories Game Act of 1917. This Act allowed Indians and Eskimos to take any game "but only . . . to prevent starvation." The precedence of the Treaty over other laws, in the subsequent course of events, has not been respected. In 1948, the "Act to amend the Northwest Territories Act" disregarded altogether the Indians' freedom to hunt and trap.[178] Ever since, the validity of territorial game laws as applied to Treaty Indians has been the subject of court cases before every tribunal in Canada.

The Role of the Chiefs

Traditional Indian power structure depended on the absolute support of the community. Power came up from the people, and the chief would consult them for every decision. This system contrasted sharply with the organization which was imposed by the Indian Act and confirmed by the Treaties. The selection of chief and headmen was then determined by forces outside of the Indian community:

Jean Baptiste Dontra, Fort Liard: . . . the time they signed the Treaty, the person who paid the Treaty, that's the one who made the chief and the councillor.[179]

Johnny Kay, Fort McPherson: Yes, he [Conroy] was standing right beside him [the chief]. Conroy told him to sign this piece of paper and he asked Conroy why he's going to sign it. And Conroy told him because after he signs it, from there on, he is a chief.[180]

A. Robin OMI, *Fort Good Hope:* Before 1921 there was no chief: the HBC manager told the Treaty Commissioner that Tseleie would be a good chief."[181]

The extent of this practice was indicated by the Assistant Secretary of the Department of Indian Affairs in 1910:

> I beg to say that, with one or two exceptions, the elective system of chiefs and councillors, under section 93 of the Indian Act, has not been applied to any band in the western provinces . . . Manitoba, Saskatchewan, Alberta, and British Columbia . . . and some years ago the Department adopted the practice of making appointments of chiefs and councillors for an indefinite term.[182]

The position in which these chiefs found themselves became untenable:

> During treaty negotiations, Indian Chiefs and Councillors were recognized as capable of handling the affairs of the tribes . . . . Once the Treaties were concluded . . . the Indian Chiefs and Councillors . . . no longer were regarded as capable of dealing with their own affairs or of meeting with representatives of the Crown for the settlement of differences which might exist between them.[183]

Created at treaty time, given the authority to sign some of the most important documents in Canadian history, the Indian Chiefs were then forgotten. Their authority was continuously challenged and their decisions repeatedly revoked by both the Federal and Territorial Governments.

The Role of Bishop Breynat

The influence of Bishop Breynat during Treaty negotiations has best been described by Philip Moses of Fort Wrigley:

> The Bishop did not talk. Only the white people talked. But the Bishop was with them . . . that is why we thought it was a good thing to sign the treaty.[184]

Breynat had been invited by the Government to accompany the Treaty Commission down the Mackenzie in 1921. Ottawa realized that his presence alone would serve to lessen any suspicion or hostility which the Treaty Party might meet along the way. He had lived with the Indians since 1892 and knew the situation in the North as well as any man. He knew that the Government considered the Northwest

Territories as part of Canada and that federal jurisdiction would inevitably apply, whether a Treaty was signed or not. With a Treaty the rights and status of the original inhabitants of the country would be officially recognized. They would receive compensation and protection in return for opening the country to settlement. Breynat conveyed to the Indians the idea that the Government was seeking their friendship and goodwill towards the settlers coming into the country. To accomplish this had been a deciding factor in his agreeing to travel with the Treaty Party. Further, a Treaty would serve to awaken the Government to its responsibilities for the welfare of the Northern Indians. Until then, the Roman Catholic and Anglican churches had been providing medical and educational services to the Indians, but the need was far greater than the limited resources which were available. Until his resignation in 1943, Breynat constantly reminded Ottawa of its responsibilities towards the Indians. The Indians have been faithful to their Treaty promises: can the Government of Canada boast the same? His arguments were based solely on the Treaty promises which he had witnessed in 1921: those that were written in the Treaty text and those that had been given orally by the Treaty Commissioner. He never regretted the role he had played as ambassador of goodwill between the Indian people and the people of Canada. But he was determined that the goodwill should produce the promised benefits to the Indians.

Conclusion

In the years 1920-1921 certain events occured which had a deciding effect on the transportation, economy, and politics of the Northwest Territories:

- discovery of oil at Norman Wells
- collapse of the fur market
- first bank in the Northwest Territories
- large steamers, gas boats and oil burning vessels on the Mackenzie River
- first trucks and tractors in the Northwest Territories
- railway from Edmonton to Fort McMurray
- first airplane flight
- first trial by jury
- establishment of a Territorial Administration
- naming of the first members of Council
- first ordinance by the Commissioner
- Commissioner's first visit to the Northwest Territories

It was these events, more than the signing of Treaty 11, which had far reaching significance for the Indian people. Their situation was much affected by these changes. Not only were their economic and political structures drastically altered, but their social and cultural foundations were critically shaken.

The Indians for their part were not opposing an enemy of flesh and blood; it was a culture conflict they had lost. Theirs was not a unique fate: many other tribal societies in other lands had crumbled before the irresistible European technology and the fruits of written empirical learning.[185]

Notes to Chapter IV

1. *Canada's Western Northland,* Canada, Department of Mines & Resources, 1937, p. 60. Quoted from Diamond Jenness.

2. Diamond Jenness, *Indians of Canada,* Ottawa, Queen's Printer, 1932, 6th. edition, p. 263.

3. Canada, Department of Indian Affairs, *Census of Indians,* page 1563, The census of 1913 indicated a total of 8,030 Indians in the Northwest Territories. Such a difference between the 1913 and the 1914 census resulted from the 1912 changes in the area of the N.W.T.

4. *Ibid.,* pp. 1564-1565.

5. Canada, *Sessional Papers,* 1920, No. 27. p. 58. All the census of the Department of Indian Affairs for the years 1917 to 1923 indicate the same number: 3,764.

6. PAC, RG10, BS, file 336,877, F.H. Kitto, D.L.S. *Report of a Preliminary Investigation of the Natural Resources of Mackenzie District and their Economic Development, made during the summer of 1920,* Ottawa, Department of the Interior, Natural Resources Intelligence Branch.

7. Dr. June Helm, "The Dynamics of a Northern Athapaskan Band", National Museum of Canada, *Bulletin,* No. 176, 1961, pp. 166-176. Dr. June Helm, "Leadership among Northeastern Athabascans", *Anthropologica,* No. 2, 1956. In the Supreme Court of the N.W.T., Transcript of evidence in the action, in the matter of an application by Chief François Paulette *et al.,* to lodge a certain caveat, 1973. Dr. June Helm's Testimony, 20 August 1973, pp. 28-31, 82-84.

8. Samuel Hearne, *A Journey from Prince of Wales Fort on Hudson's Bay, to the Northern Ocean, Undertaken by Order of the Hudson's Bay Company, for the Discovery of Copper Mines, & North West Passage, &c, in the years 1769, 1770, 1771 & 1772.* Toronto, Champlain Society, 1911, p. 289.

9. J.A. Mason, *Notes on the Indians of the Great Slave Lake Area,* New Haven, Yale University Publications in Anthropology, 1946, p. 33.

10. IBNWTA, Transcript of Frank Norn's interview by Gerald Sutton of Yellowknife, 29 June 1972.

11. *Edmonton Bulletin,* 30 August 1912, 5 September 1912.

12. Canada, Department of Mines, *Summary Report,* 1920, part B, p. 56B.

13. Canada, Commons, *Debates,* 8 June 1920, p. 3281.

14. *Ibid.,* 10 March 1920, p. 331.

15. Canada, Department of Mines, *Summary Report,* 1920, Part B, p. 58B.

16. *Edmonton Journal,* 19 October 1920.

17. *Calgary Gazette,* 30 October 1920.

18. *Sydney Post,* 30 October 1920.

19. *Calgary Gazette,* 30 October 1920.

20. *Montreal Star,* 19 March 1921; *Vancouver Province,* 19 March 1921.

21. PAC, RG18, Fl, Vol. 12, G-1316, Report of Inspector Fletcher, August 1920.

22. *Calgary Herald,* 29 October 1920.

23. Canada, Commons, *Debates,* 14 March 1921, p. 896.

24. PAC, RG18, Fl, Vol. 8, G-800-1-21, Officer Commanding 'G' Division to the Commissioner RCMP, November 1920.

25. F.H. Kitto, 1920 report, Section

XIV.

26. *Edmonton Journal,* 18 January 1921.
27. *Calgary Herald,* 25 February 1921.
28. Canada, *Sessional Papers,* 1922, No. 28, Commissioner's report, p. 45.
29. PAC, RG85, vol. 577, file 402, Folder Navigating Season 1921.
30. *Morning Bulletin,* 19 July 1921.
31. PAC, RG10, BS, file 336,877, An Ordinance respecting Entry into the N.W.T., 27 October 1920.
32. PAC, RG18, F1, Vol. 9, file 846-8-21. Inspector Fletcher to Officer Commanding 'G' Division, 19 September 1921.
33. NWT, Territorial Council, *Minutes of the Sessions,* p. 10.
34. *Ibid.,* O.S. Finnie, Acting Secretary NWT. Branch, Report to the 2nd. session, 14 June 1922. p. 28.
35. PAC, RG85, Vol. 581, file 501, Finnie to Cory, 8 June 1921.
36. NWT, Territorial Council, *Minutes of the Sessions,* Memorandum of Cory, 12 May 1921, p. 9.
37. Canada, Commons, *Debates,* James Alexander Caulder, 1921, p. 565.
38. *Ibid.,* Alfred Meighen, 14 March 1921, pp. 852-856.
39. *Ibid.,* Willis Keith Baldwin, 1921, p. 3206.
40. *Ibid.,* Alfred Thompson, 14 March 1921, p. 852.
41. PAC, RG10, BS, file 336,877, Harris to Secretary of Indian Affairs, 25 January 1920.
42. *Ibid.,* HBC Fur Trade Commissioner to Secretary of Indian Affairs, 3 February 1920.
43. *Ibid.,* McLean to HBC Commissioner, 7 February 1920.
44. *Ibid.,* Conroy to Scott, 6 February 1920.
45. F.H. Kitto, 1920 report, Section XXI.
46. PAC, RG10, BS, file 336,877, Conroy to Scott, 13 October 1920.
47. *Ibid.,* 1920 map of proposed treaty.
48. *Ibid.,* Scott to Lougheed, 23 November 1920.
49. *Ibid.,* Superintendent General of Indian Affairs to Governor General in Council, 9 February 1921.
50. *Ibid.,* Scott to Breynat, 16 February 1921.
51. G. Breynat, *Cinquante Ans au Pays des Neiges,* Vol. III, p. 16.
52. RCMAFS, file: Vicariat du Mackenzie, Faits Divers sur les Missions. Breynat to Abbé Guinet, 29 July 1921.
53. PAC, RG10, BS, file 336,877, McLean to Conroy, 13 May 1921.
54. *Ibid.,* Assistant Deputy Minister of Fisheries to McLean, 19 May 1921.
55. *Ibid.,* McLean to Conroy, 13 May 1921.
56. Agnes Cameron, *The New North,* NY. & London, D. Appleton & Company, 1910, p. 163.
57. NWT, Territorial Council, *Minutes of the Sessions,* Breynat to Commissioner of the NWT, 15 June 1938, pp. 1362, 1371.
58. *Edmonton Journal,* 25 May 1921.
59. *Ibid.,* 15 June 1921.
60. *Ibid.,* 25 June 1921.
61. *Treaty No. 11,* Ottawa, Queen's Printer, reprint 1957, pp. 3-5.
62. PAC, RG10, BS, file 336,877, and many other files of RG10 Section.
63. IANDO, Series 191/28-3.
64. HBC Archives, London, letters to the author, 2 December 1971, 1 June 1972.
65. IBNWTA, Transcript of Inspector Bruce's interview by Gerald Sutton, 13 June 1972.
66. PAC, RG10, BS, file 336,877, Public Notice, 23 March 1921.
67. PAC, RG10, vol. 1853.
68. OMIAFS, RCM Fort Smith *Diary.*
69. PAC, RG10, BS, file 336,877, Conroy to Scott, 11 July 1921.
70. In the Supreme Court of the NWT., Transcript of Evidence in the action, in the matter of an application by Chief François Paulette, *et al.,* 17 July 1973, pp. 330-364.
71. PAC, RG10, vol. 1853.
72. IBNWTA, Transcript of Victor Lafferty's interview, cf. footnote p.

169.

73. ASGM, *Chroniques de Fort Providence.*
74. *Ibid.*
75. *Ibid.*
76. *Ibid.*
77. PAC, RG10, BS, file 336,877, Conroy to Scott, 11 July 1921.
78. OMIAFS, 091-CH, FS.
79. ASGM, *Chroniques de Fort Simpson.*
80. RCMAFS, file: Indiens-Traité avec eux, Affidavit, 26 November 1937.
81. IBNWTA, Transcript of Inspector Bruce's interview by Gerald Sutton, 13 June 1972.
82. *Ibid.,* Transcript of Baptiste Norwegian's interview by Joachim Bonnetrouge, 1972.
83. In the Supreme Court of the NWT, Transcript of evidence in the action in the matter of an application by Chief François Paulette, *et al.,* to lodge a certain caveat, 1973, p. 237.
84. PAC, RG10, Vol. 1853.
85. IBNWTA, Transcript of James Lafferty's interview by Henri Posset, OMI, of Fort Simpson, January 1973.
86. *Ibid.,* Transcript of Ted Trindell's narrative, 3 January 1973.
87. *Ibid.,* Transcript of Philip Moses' interview by Henri Posset, OMI., 19 November 1971.
88. PAC, RG10, vol. 1853.
89. IBNWTA, Transcript of Julien Yendo's interview by Henri Posset, OMI, 20 November 1971.
90. *Ibid.,* Transcript of Francis Tanché's interview by Henri Posset, OMI, 5 January 1973.
91. IANDO, Library Archives, *Indian Annuities,* 1921, Vol. 2.
92. IBNWTA, Transcript of Inspector Bruce's interview by Gerald Sutton, 13 June 1972.
93. IBNWTA, Transcript of Edward Hardisty's interview by Gerald Sutton, 2 July 1971.
94. *Edmonton Bulletin,* 12 August 1921.
95. OMIAFS, 091-CH, FN, Vol. 2.
96. *Treaty No. 11,* Ottawa, Queen's Printer, reprint 1957, p. 4.
97. PAC, RG10, vol. 1853.
98. OMIAFS, 091-CH, FGH, Vol. 3.
99. Author's files, Yellowknife, Transcript of Alexis Robin OMI's interview by the author, 12 October 1971.
100. PAC, RG10, Vol. 1853.
101. OMIAFS, 091-CH, FGH, Vol. 3.
102. Arctic Red River, RCM, *Diary.*
103. IANDO, file 1/1-11-20, L.A. Wilderspin to Superintendent Aklavik Indian Agency, 26 April 1966.
104. PAC, RG10, Vol. 1853.
105. IANDO, file 1/1-11-20, L.A. Wilderspin to Superintendent Aklavik Indian Agency, 26 April 1966.
106. PAC, RG18, Vol. 12, file G-1316-11-21. Report of Inspector S.T. Wood, 1 January 1922.
107. PAC, RG10, Vol. 1853.
108. IANDO, file 871/3-8, C.E. Callas to Officer in charge, District of Mackenzie, 5 April 1966.
109. IANDO, file 1/1-11-20, L.A. Wilderspin to Superintendent Aklavik Indian Agency, 26 April 1966.
110. *Ibid.,* N.K. Ogden to Indian Affairs Branch, Ottawa, 14 June 1966.
111. *Ibid.,* A.R.K. Macdonald to Special Advisor Treaties, 4 October 1967.
112. Provincial Archives of Alberta, Accession 70.387, MR 415, Hay River Anglican Mission, *Journal of Events.*
113. IBNWTA, Transcript of Lazare (Henri) Zoe's interview by Jean Pochat OMI, of Fort Rae, 20 October 1971.
114. *Ibid.,* Transcript of Elise Monfwi's interview by Jean Amourous OMI, of Fort Rae, 1 August 1973.
115. OMIAFS, 091-CH, FR, Vol. 2, p. 232.
116. IBNWTA, Transcript of Johnny Jean Marie Beaulieu's interview by David Smith, 26 June 1969.
117. *Ibid.,* Transcript of Bruno Gaudet's interview by Marie Adele

Martin of Fort Rae, 1 February 1972.

118. *Treaty No. 11,* Ottawa, Queen's Printer, reprint 1957, p. 5. Canada, *Sessional Papers,* 1922, No. 28, p. 18.

119. PAC, RG10, BS, Vol. 4372, document 560,657, p. 160.

120. *Treaty No. 11,* Ottawa, Queen's Printer, reprint 1957, pp. 3-5.

121. Canada, *Sessional Papers,* 1922, No. 28, Report of the Commissioner, p. 18.

122. PAC, RG18, F1, Vol. 9, G-846-8-21. Inspector Fletcher to the Officer Commanding 'G' Division, 19 September 1921.

123. G. Breynat, *Cinquante Ans au Pays des Neiges,* Vol. III, p. 18. Chapter XII of Vol. I of Bishop Breynat's autobiography is devoted to and entitled: Relations between Indians, Metis and Government.

124. Canada, Department of Indian Affairs, *Annual Report for the Year ended March 1921.* Ottawa, King's Printer, 1921, p. 7.

125. *Edmonton Bulletin,* 13 September 1921.

126. *Edmonton Journal,* 26 September 1921.

127. Canada, *Privy Council,* OC 3985, 22 October 1921.

128. PAC. RG10, BS, Vol. 1853.

129. PAC, RG18, F1, Vol. 9, G-846-8-21, Inspector Fletcher to the Officer Commanding 'G' Division, 19 September 1921.

130. PAC, RG10, BS, file 567,205, McLean to Coté, 29 May 1922; McLean to Harris, 2 May 1922.

131. IANDO, file 191/28-3, Vol. 1, Report on Annuity Payments in Simpson Agency, 1922.

132. PAC, RG10, BS, file 336,877.

133. OMIAFS, 091-CH, FL, Vol. 1.

134. In the Supreme Court of the NWT. Transcript of Evidence in the action; in the matter of an application by Chief François Paulette, *et al.,* 31 July 1973, p. 536.

135. PAC, RG10, BS, file 336,877, Harris to McLean, 31 August 1922.

136. PAC, RG85, Accession 64/128, file 5809, Finnie to Richards, 7 October 1927; Richards to Finnie, 22 September 1927.

137. H.J. Bury, 1913 report.

138. F.H. Kitto, 1920 report, Section XXI.

139. PAC, RG10, BS, file 336,877, Conroy to Scott, 13 October 1920.

140. PAC, RG85, file 4017, Burwash to Finnie, 12 May 1923.

141. PAC, RG10, BS, file 336,877, Memorandum of Conroy, 13 December 1920.

142. Canada, *Privy Council,* 1921, OC 1172.

143. IANDO, file 1003-2-5, Vol. 1, Côté to Finnie, 8 June 1922.

144. *Ibid.,* Côté to Harris, 5 June 1922.

145. *Ibid.,* file 191/28-3, Vol. 1, Report of Harris on Annuity Payments, 1923.

146. Canada, *Statutes,* 13-14 George V, 1923, Chapter 44-8.

147. Canada, *Privy Council,* 1924, OC 471.

148. PAC, RG85, Vol. 340, file 800-16, John A. McDougal, District Agent in Fort Smith, Report on his trip down the Mackenzie River, 9 August 1924.

149. RCMAFS, John F. Moran, *Confidential Notes,* Vol. 1, p. 44.

150. IANDO, file 1003-2-5, Vol. 1, Breynat to Scott, 6 October 1923.

151. Special Joint Committee of the Senate and the House of Commons, appointed to examine and consider the Indian Act, *Minutes of Proceeding and Evidence,* Quoted from Justice W.A. Macdonald to T.A. Crerar, 21 April 1947, p. 559.

152. IBNWTA, Transcript of Inspector Bruce's interview by Gerald Sutton, 13 June 1972.

153. P.B. Waite, *Arduous Destiny: Canada 1874-1896,* p. 66.

154. PAC, Half Breed Commission, Accession 556,321.

155. The Hon. Alexander Morris, P.C. *The Treaties of Canada with the Indians,* Toronto, Belfords, Clarke & Co. 1880, Reprint Toronto, Coles Publishing Co. 1971, p. 231.

156. *Ibid.,* p. 72.

157. *Ibid.,* pp. 296-297.

158. In the Supreme Court of the NWT., Transcript of Evidence in the action; in the matter of an application by Chief François Paulette, *et al.,* 1973, p. 403.

159. *Ibid.,* p. 404.

160. *Ibid.,* p. 410.

161. *Ibid.,* p. 304.

162. *Ibid.,* p. 417.

163. Clermont Bourget, *Douze Ans chez les Sauvages,* Sainte Anne de Beaupré, P.Q., 1938, pp. 101-102.

164. Canada, *Report of the Commission appointed to investigate the unfulfilled provisions of Treaties 8 and 11 as they apply to the Indians of the Mackenzie District, 1959.*

165. In the Supreme Court of the NWT., Transcript of Evidence in the action; in the matter of an application by Chief François Paulette *et al.,* 1973, p. 460.

166. *Ibid.,* p. 351.

167. Indian Eskimo Association of Canada, *Native Rights in Canada,* 1st. edition, 1970, Quote from Chief Justice Marshall in *Worcester v. Georgia,* p. 170.

168. Canada, Indian Affairs Branch, *Annual Report for the Year ended March 31, 1937, Annual Report for the Year ended March 31, 1944.*

169. *Treaty No. 11,* Ottawa, Queen's Printer, reprint 1957, p. 4.

170. Canada, Indian Affairs Branch, *Annual Report for the Year ended March 31, 1937, Annual Report for the Year ended March 31, 1944.*

171. Clermont Bourget, *Douze Ans chez les Sauvages,* p. 59.

172. IBNWTA, Transcript of Antoine Liske's interview, no date.

173. PAC, RG10, BS, file 336,877, McLean to Conroy, 13 May 1921.

174. RCMAFS, file: Indiens-Traité avec eux, 27 November 1937.

175. *Toronto Star Weekly,* 24 June 1939.

176. RCMAFS, file: Tuberculose 1910-1946, Breynat to Crerar, 23 February 1937.

177. Special Joint Committee of the Senate and the House of Commons appointed to examine and consider the Indian Act, *Minutes of Proceeding and Evidence,* Submission of the Indian Association of Alberta, 21 April 1947, p. 575.

178. Canada, Statutes, *An Act to Amend the Northwest Territories Act,* 11-12 George VI, Ch. 20, 1948, section 3 (1).

179. IBNWTA, Transcript of Jean Baptiste Dontra's interview by Gerald Sutton, 2 November 1971.

180. *Ibid.,* Transcript of Johnny Kay's interview by Gerald Sutton, 1 July 1971.

181. Author's files, Yellowknife, Transcript of Alexis Robin OMI's interview by the author, 12 October 1971.

182. PAC. RG10, BS, Vol. 3944, file 121,698-31. Assistant Secretary of Indian Affairs to W.B.L. Donald.

183. Special Joint Committee of the Senate and the House of Commons appointed to examine and consider the Indian Act, *Minutes of Proceeding and Evidence,* Submission of the Indian Association of Alberta, 21 April 1947, p. 576.

184. IBNWTA, Transcript of Philip Moses' interview by H. Posset, 24 November 1971.

185. Fraser Symington, *The Canadian Indian,* Toronto, McClelland & Stewart, 1969, p. 240.

Chapter V

The Years After Treaty 11, 1922-1927

Introduction

It was on the North itself that the effects of Treaty 11 were most evident. Development could now accelerate in the climate of goodwill promised by the Indians. Transportation systems improved, making freight and passengers big business on the Mackenzie River and its tributaries. The Hudson's Bay Company regained its dominance of Northern waterways with its fleet of large steamers and small gas boats. By 1927, it could advertise a service from Edmonton to the Arctic and back in thirty-five days. The need for improved communications increased. Radio stations were opened by the Royal Canadian Corps of Signals (RCCS): Fort Simpson, 1924; Aklavik and Fort Smith, 1925; Herschel Island, 1926; and Fort Resolution, 1927.

The regular rhythm of the Indians' quiet life was only slightly altered by the signing of Treaty 11. Although remarkable developments were opening the North to communication with the rest of Canada, the majority of Indians still passed eleven months of the year in the bush, and depended on trapping and hunting for 90 per cent of their livelihood. The annual visit of the Indian Agent with money and rations brought the Indians together for a few days, and gradually became the focus of the summer social life. It did little, however, to improve the health, commerce, or economy of the Northern tribes. Disease and epidemics were not eliminated because a doctor passed by each year. Material well-being was not augmented because a few dollars changed hands on Treaty day.

The Government's reason for signing Treaty 11 was being served. That of the Indian was being overlooked in the distribution of rations and annuities. As time went on it became apparent that the two signatories of Treaty 11 had been at cross purposes.

The prospect of wealth in oil, minerals or fur lured adventurers North to explore this virgin country. These prospectors-cum-trappers offered the single greatest threat to the economy of the Indians. Contrary to Treaty promises that the rights of the Indians to hunt and trap would be protected against the encroachment and competition of white trappers, these latter were permitted to exploit the game resources almost at will. In addition to the eighty-six trading posts operated by the Hudson's Bay Company in the N.W.T., 130 more posts were opened by free traders to handle the increased volume of pelts. It was only a matter of time before strict laws were necessary to save Northern game animals from extinction. Enforcement of these laws against Indians caused severe hardship to a people who depended on game for existence. The injustice of the situation and the inequities it fostered drew protests from many sides. But the subtleties were lost on Ottawa. The Indians were given some game preserves, but their exclusion from government wildlife sanctuaries established on traditional hunting grounds was also carefully planned. Protection of animals took precedence over the protection of the Indian or his hunting rights. The Government sent more rangers, game wardens and veterinarians to the Wood Buffalo Park after 1923 than there were Indian agents or doctors in the entire Northwest Territories.

Treaty 11, 1922

In the summer of 1922, Indian Agent Harris made the trip down the Mackenzie to pay the first Treaty annuities to the Indians who had signed Treaty 11. Conroy had died a few months earlier and was replaced for that summer by Harris and RCMP Inspector Fletcher. This incident provided the classic dialogue for similar encounters between Indian Agent and Indian Chief in the years to come.

> How come it is you, not the first commissioner [Conroy] who is giving out money now? He answered saying that the first commissioner who talked about the treaty to you has died, so just for this summer it will be me giving money to you. The whiteman also said that he does not know anything about the first treaty that was signed so he cannot answer any questions about the treaty as was signed the previous year . . . [1]

Harris and Fletcher brought with them silver medals showing the portrait of the king and bearing the inscription: "Georgius V Dei Gra. Rex et Ind. Imp."* Each chief who signed Treaty 11 was entitled to receive one in commemoration of the event.[2] The fifteen medals costing $466.25,[3] had not been received in time for distribution the previous year. Now, one year later the chiefs could admire the image on the

---

*George V, King and Emperor of India

226

verso: a staff officer clasping the hand of an Indian, with a partly buried tomahawk at their feet; behind them are wigwams and the setting sun, with the inscription: Indian Treaty No. 11, 1921.

The other Indians were not forgotten. The head of each family had received a small piece of cardboard with his Treaty number, his name, and the number of persons in his family. This ticket would be checked by the Indian Agent as he made payment each year. It was a busy summer for Harris. He visited Fort Liard in July to take the Indians there into the Treaty for the first time. He also paid annuities at Fort Simpson, Fort Wrigley, Fort Norman, Fort Good Hope, Arctic Red River, and Fort McPherson. He made the trip in Breynat's gas boat, for which the Department of Indian Affairs paid the cost of the gasoline and the wages of the crew. According to Harris, the only sign of dissatisfaction among the Indians was found at Fort Simpson:

> There was some difficulty at first with the Chief, who said that he had been promised by the Commissioner, that whatever he asked for would be given him, and that this promise had not been kept. I replied that I had been present when the Treaty was made, and that I had heard no such promise, and that further, anyone making such a promise had gone beyond his powers and beyond his ability to fulfill such promise . . . the Indians appeared satisfied with this and the payments proceeded with no further trouble.[4]

When he reached Fort Wrigley the eighty-one Indians who had taken Treaty were waiting for him and received their payment immediately. At Fort Norman the two headmen replaced the chief who was away hunting. After paying the annuities to all the Treaty Indians, Harris "accepted the adherence" of 136 Indians who had not been present in 1921. At Fort Good Hope an additional 134 persons received their first Treaty money. Many of these Indians were sick and required treatment from Doctor Richardson. At Arctic Red River three persons were paid for the first time. At Fort McPherson, no time was wasted. "Immediately after midnight, I began the payments, and had finished and was ready to start the return trip at three A.M. . . . I paid thirty-six new adherents to the Treaty."[5]

Before setting out to visit the posts along the Mackenzie, Harris had examined the settlement plans based on the land survey of 1913-1914, for Fort Wrigley, Fort Norman, and Fort Good Hope. Ottawa had directed him to investigate certain lots "temporarily reserved to safeguard the Indians during their occupation thereof," and "to report whether you consider the Department should make an effort to obtain these different lots as permanent reserves."[6] There is no record that Harris ever carried out that mission, or reported on it.

Fletcher paid Treaty to the Indians at Fort Rae and Fort Providence:

> [At Fort Rae] 762 being paid altogether. These Indians were in good health, prosperous, and satisfied with having taken Treaty . . . There were

328 Indians of this band who did not take treaty last year; I therefore . . .
admitted them to treaty.

[At Fort Providence]: These Indians were in good health, and had no
complaints to make. Eighteen Indians were admitted to treaty here . . . .
This makes a total of 280 for this band.[7]

Fletcher's report is a lengthy one, with innumerable details. There
might have been some unpleasant incident at Fort Rae. His report
furnished no information, but an entry in the mission diary related
that, as soon as the Treaty payments had been made, Inspector
Fletcher "hoisted up the anchor to evade the Indian people's
recrimination".[8]

Viewed by Outsiders

The sights and sounds of Treaty days caused some outsiders who experienced them to reflect on their significance. Two tourists of the period saw the Indians as naive dupes:

> There are not more than half a hundred Indians "taking treaty" at Fort
> Smith . . . At Fort Resolution the numbers of Indians is much larger, and
> the treaty transaction is more animated and complicated . . . It would
> seem extraordinary that the Indians should come so far and take so much
> trouble to appear, for so small an amount of money, were it not for the
> fact that the occasion is regarded very much as an old home week festival
> is looked upon in the United States. There is glad reunion and
> jollification, endless pow-wow and pipe-smoking and feasting. Of course
> the treaty money scarcely ever leaves the post where it is paid out. The
> storekeepers – displaying their wares enticingly, outdoors as well as in
> their shops, before the eyes of the spendthrift redskins – get most of it.
> But the Indians seem to think the fun was worth the price they paid for
> their one grand annual jamboree.[9]

> The occasion for this meeting of the tribes is the paying off of treaty
> money. Each Indian who decides to co-operate with the Government re-
> ceives annually the imposing sum of five dollars. Once each year, on
> Treaty Day, the Indians assemble to receive this Government dole. It is
> not the money, however, that attracts them from far and near; it is the
> fact that later they can go back and say they have been to Resolution,
> where they appeared before the Whiteman as persons of consequence, em-
> broidered moccasins on their feet, and red silk kerchiefs about their
> necks.[10]

Residents of the country looked a little deeper and were able to sense
the tragedy inherent in the scene. Louise Rourke, wife of the manager
of the Hudson's Bay Company, lived in Fort Chipewyan from 1924-
1926. She made these notes on the events of 1926:

> The Treaty is a gift of money and goods to the natives, and seems to be in
> exchange for tribal rights which they have signed away. The money they
> receive amounts to five dollars for each child; it must cost some of them

more than this amount to get into the Settlement from a long distance, for they are sometimes travelling days, and even weeks, to the place where Treaty is to be paid. Rations of flour, sugar, bacon and tea, are part of the annual present to the Indian.

This is also the time for airing all the grievances of the past year, and the Indian Agent does his best to smooth out tangles and to patch up quarrels. Rations are then distributed and Treaty money paid. Also the Chief of a tribe gets a new suit of clothes from the Government. The Cree Chief whom I saw one year had a sort of naval uniform issued to him, with a peaked hat to match, and much gold braid. He was tremendously proud of himself in his Government suit, and strutted around the Settlement feeling a very fine fellow indeed. Everywhere he walked he was followed by an admiring crowd. The Chief is invited to discuss the affairs of his tribe with the Government party, and, if he has any grievance, efforts are made to set matters aright.

When the half-breeds begin to acquire racial self-consciousness they are usually anxious to give up accepting the yearly Treaty. This is a good sign, because it shows a spirit of independence, and a wish to establish themselves as responsible citizens, instead of continuing as "Wards of the Government". By accepting a lump sum from the Government in full payment of such liability as exists the native person immediately becomes "free of the Treaty". Sometimes a peculiar position occurs where one or two brothers in a family take Treaty and the rest do not.

Whatever the merits or defects of the Treaty may be, there is little doubt that a vast section of the native people would be sorry to see its payment discontinued, not so much for any possible advantage accruing to themselves, but because the payment of the Treaty is made an occasion for one of the most celebrated festivities in the Indian calendar. There are dancing and singing and the gathering of friends; sometimes the celebrations are continued for a fortnight . . . .

The Treaty party consists of the Indian Agent representing the district – which may be an area of some hundreds of miles – the "Indian" doctor, an interpreter, and possibly an official from the RCMP. The doctor usually made two visits a year at Fort Chipewyan, and perhaps the same number of visits were made by the Indian Agent. How it is possible for these gentlemen to be of any practical value to their territory is beyond the comprehension of anyone who has lived in the North . . . .

The bi-yearly visit of the doctor is, of course, a farce. Over and over again there are deaths amongst the people which might have been prevented had there been a doctor within reasonable distance: over and over again the cry goes out: "Send us medical men." But nothing happens . . . .

The Indians have a great respect for the members of the Treaty party; except amongst a few rare tribes, there is left to them little of that spirit of pride and independence which marked their race; therefore they look to the white man to shoulder their burdens and responsibilities, and the Treaty party represents the Power to which they can appeal for help or support. The most simple Indian still looks upon the "King in England" as a sort of "Great Chief", though in all probability he would not, to-day, express the idea in precisely that term; those who represent the King such as the Governor-General, he considers to be slightly lesser chiefs, and so on, all down the scale.[11]

Chick Ferguson, a white trapper, provides this superficial, but colourful account of Treaty days at Fort Providence:

As more canoes arrived and more tents and tepees appear like white mushrooms on the flat, the drums are seldom silent.

As usual, the Indian Agent is late getting here, and the Indians are grumbling. But at last his splendid gas boat rounds the point and is tied up at the tiny Mission dock. In front of the Mission a large tent is set up. Treaty will be paid at ten o'clock the next morning.

A few minutes before the hour, a Mountie, resplendent in flaming tunic, boots, spurs, and sidearm, saunters by. His broadbrimmed Stetson is set at the exact slight angle that does most for his features. Many Indians are already gathered around the Agent's tent; others are coming. Now the Agent appears with the Father Superior, who has his record book under his arm. They are joined inside the tent by the Mountie and a half-breed who is to act as interpreter. The Indian chief and sub-chiefs follow and, bursting with importance, take their places of distinction on kitchen chairs. All the others crowd around the tent's open end.

For a long while the Agent listens to the Indian big-shots as each in turn unfolds his laments, accusations, complaints and his demands. But at last the little table is piled high with stacks of dollar bills and Indians are coming forward to get their money – five dollars for each member of the family. By four or five o'clock the last one has collected his allotment of crisp new dollar bills and departed.

This is the time when the traders forget about closing hours . . . So imperative is their haste to lay hands on that flood of dollar bills that they post notices telling local people to keep out. That no merchandise will be sold except for cash over the counter. The stores are heaped with gaudy trinkets, home-brew ingredients, and flashy long-profit articles specially brought out for the occasion. Within a day or two almost every dollar of the treaty money will be in the traders' tills.

With treaty paid, the Agent gives out rations; flour, bacon, tea, blankets, nets, shotgun shells, and rifle cartridges; and a special "feast" allotment of flour, bacon and tea, taking the place of the "feast" that the traders used to give the Indians.

There is great activity as the Indians hurry to get the flour converted into great loaf bannock. When the baking is done and the bacon (salt pork) is broiled, someone fires three shots signalling that the feast is ready. Before the echoes have died away, Indians and half-breeds alike are rushing towards the designated place, each carrying his own plate, knife, and cup and soon all are sitting cross-legged in a huge circle. Men, women, and children eating . . . drinking cup after cup of steaming tea. There is much laughter and joking and fighting of mosquitoes. When the last crumb of bannock has been eaten and the last drop of tea swallowed, they start drifting away in little groups. The feast is over.

But not the evening's entertainment. At nine or ten o'clock there are more rifle shots – the signal to gather for the tea dance, again the drums sound, but with a different beat and rythm . . . .[12]

Indian Agencies

The reorganization of Indian Agencies in the Treaty 8 and Treaty 11 areas followed the extension of Government jurisdiction into the Mackenzie District.

The Agency at Fort Simpson had been opened in 1911 by Card, many years before Treaty 11. Since 1913 it was the headquarters for Harris who now would be responsible for the Indians of Treaty 11 at posts along the Mackenzie River and at Fort Liard.

In 1923 the Great Slave Lake Agency was established at Fort Resolution. It included Fort Resolution, Snowdrift, and Hay River under Treaty 8, Yellowknife River, Fort Rae, and Fort Providence under Treaty 11.[13] Dr. Clermont Bourget was given the responsibility of the agency as well as the medical care of the Indians.

In 1924 an Agency was opened at Fort McMurray. This replaced the Agency which had been operating at Fort Smith since 1911.[14] The new Agency would be responsible for the Indian bands of Treaty 8 in northern Alberta, Fond du Lac, Saskatchewan, and Fort Smith in the Northwest Territories. Indian Agent Card was in charge.

It was the duty of the Indian Agent to pay Treaty, settle disputes, record complaints, collect statistics, file reports, and in the case of Dr. Bourget, care for the sick. All this was accomplished in one yearly visit at each post. The records of those brief encounters between Indian Agent and Indian people can be used in piecing together a description of conditions at that time.

Bourget's Reports

Fort Resolution was headquarters for Bourget. When he first arrived in 1923, he was totally unprepared by anything in his past for that first experience of paying Treaty. In later years he recalled that day with humour and poignancy. (See Appendix X.) At all other posts that year, he encountered only minor problems:

> The Chipewyan and Yellow Knives bands . . . had a fair season in furs and caribou meat . . . quite a few equipped themselves with Evinrude engines for their canoes. But gasoline is paid three and a half dollars a gallon . . . Treaty goods were given, and sick and destitutes rations stored
> . . . .
> At Hay River . . . all the Slave Band of that post was present, they numbering only 114 . . . .
> At Fort Rae, a good season in furs, very little sickness . . . Their supply of nets is not sufficient . . . They asked for snaring twine . . . Chief Murphy also asked for some carpenter tools . . .
> At the Yellowknife River entrance . . . they would rather have more shots and less balls . . .
> At Fort Providence, the chief died and the choice of the band was unanimous for Martel Canadien who was appointed.[15]

In 1924 he made these observations on the conditions he encountered during his annual visit:

> At Resolution, the morals are at low tide at present . . . At the Yellow Knife River . . . my impression of this band was very bad . . . They seem

to have lost all ambition and courage and pride of themselves . . . Their credit is very bad and they give a very poor impression to anybody as they are in rags . . . [16]

The chief suggested the police and myself should rest in his house. The house was clean and so were the canvas sheets, the window drapes . . . The chief had moved his family under a large tent so they would not disturb our sleep. He advised me that a few Indians would probably come to see me but that he would keep them away. After a refreshing sleep we returned to our boat where the chief had sent two beautiful fresh fish.[17]

The general health of this [Hay River] band is fair . . . this band does not seem to thrive very much, and lacks the ambition of the Yellow Knives and Dog Ribs; and the sanitary conditions of their dwellings etc. are also very poor . . .

 At Providence . . . the whole population in that band is of poor stock, and lacks very much, as all these Bands, in the care of persons and houses. The sanitary and hygiene measures are altogether ignored by them . . . .[18]

At Fort Rae the problem was alcohol. One Indian asked to be enfranchised, so that he could have the same privilege to drink as the white man had. Bourget complained of "intemperate celebrations organized by the white Traders . . . This calamity . . . had taken proportions beyond description". This was especially disastrous since the Indians at Fort Rae had always been considered as "the best species of these races". The RCMP Corporal stationed at Fort Rae was of the same opinion: "The Indians here are a remarkably healthy aggregation . . . This is undoubtedly attributable to their being off the regular routes and practically isolated from contact with the white man."[19]

By 1925 Bourget could report that the bands were satisfied with the way the Department was treating them. He felt that he had gained their confidence. Fishing and hunting were good, but nevertheless, there were cases of malnutrition and tuberculosis at Yellowknife River and Fort Rae. He planned "to give the Indians lectures on hygiene with the help of a small moving machine, camera size, put on the market by the Eastman Kodak Co. . . . At present, they [the Indians] are a source of danger to the white people coming in contact with them."[20] Among the requests received that year was one from the chiefs:

The chiefs asked me to procure them a copy, for each, of the Treaty passed, as was given them by Mr. Conroy in the passing of the Treaty. They seem to attach much importance to having a copy of that document if at all possible.[21]

Treaty days in 1926 were without incident. Bourget mentioned his concern for the economic situation of the Indians and suggested "the possibility in time to raise on a small scale minks and martens if not the white fox, and I would like this industry to get established in the

North, believing they could benefit from it".

After visiting Yellowknife River in 1927, Bourget decided that in the future these Indians would go to Fort Resolution for Treaty, "so that they would not lose the little spirit learned by frequenting other people and the Forts". He had found them lacking in ambition, and reverting to their "savage" ways. He came away from Fort Providence with similar misgivings:

> The Indians of Providence and Trout Lake make the poorest impression of the whole Agency . . . they even lack the high pretension of our Yellow Knives or the hustling spirit of the real Dogribs of Rae and I really wonder if these people are able to support themselves . . . Many died last winter after a period of half famine along the river between Providence and Simpson.[22]

Bourget recognized that the future held little promise for the Indians: "We seem to be in a period of readjustment which will show seriously on the Indians."[23]

Harris Report

Harris depended on freighters stopping at Fort Simpson to take him on his yearly trip down the Mackenzie River. With this arrangement he was at each post only long enough for the crew to unload the cargo. A typical sailing schedule shows that the ship lost no time in port.

Fort Wrigley	June 19 from 11:00 A.M.	to 1:30 P.M.
Fort Norman	June 20 from 2:00 A.M.	to 8:00 A.M.
Fort Good Hope	June 20 from 10:30 P.M.	to 6:00 A.M. (June 21)
Arctic Red River	June 22 from 4:00 A.M.	to 7:00 A.M.
Fort McPherson	June 22 from 11:45 A.M.	to 9:00 P.M.[24]

Not surprisingly, the trip of 1923 was uneventful. One hundred and sixty-two Indians of the Fort Simpson agency adhered to the Treaty[25] and, "the whole payment was entirely successful and all the Indians whom I met seem to be well disposed towards the Government." Only at Fort Simpson did he encounter some resistance, but this was easily dismissed:

> Three families here, though present at the Fort, did not come to the Agency, nor take treaty. I inquired the cause, but could learn nothing except that they had decided not to take the money this year. I have never had any difficulty with any of those who refused so I am sure their refusal is for no personal grievance they have against me or the Department, but just for a whim.[26]

Throughout the Agency in 1924, again the "Indians were glad to accept the gifts of the Government without any quibbling". Only at Fort Good Hope were they less than happy, but Harris was able to placate them:

233

The chief told me that the Indians had decided not to take Treaty any more, as the man in charge of the Hudson's Bay Company's post had told them that in former times the Company always helped the Indians who were unable to help themselves, but that since they had taken this money, the Company had withdrawn their support. The post manager was unfortunately absent, so I was not able to confront him, but I told the Indians that the Government had been paying the Company each year for the support of their sick and destitute at least ever since I had been Agent, and for several years previously. All took Treaty, and everything passed off satisfactorily.[27]

When he visited Fort McPherson in 1925, the Anglican Bishop was waiting to discuss an unusual problem with him:

Rt. Rev. J.R. Lucas was present, and he told me that, on his advice, No. 4, John Martin, had decided to abandon the Treaty as the said John Martin had been ordained a Deacon of the Church of England, and would probably be ordained priest next summer, and that he considered it rather infra dignitatem for a priest to remain a Treaty Indian. I told Bishop Lucas that the fact of this man's refusal of the money could not in any way change his status, but that I should advise that Bishop to apply to the Department for John Martin's franchise, which I presumed would be granted, as anyone who was qualified for the priesthood should be qualified for Canadian citizenship. I would suggest that if the franchise is granted, John Martin's family remain in Treaty. John Martin took his Treaty for this year, and I presume the Bishop will communicate with you regarding his future.[28]

That same year the Indians at Fort Simpson complained that the promises which Conroy had made to them were not being kept:

On July 16th, all the Indians came down to the Agency, and Antoine began proceedings by saying that the promises which the Government had made them had not been fulfilled. I asked what these promises were, and he replied that they had been promised that they would receive from the Government everything they wanted, and would all be prosperous, if they accepted the Treaty. I replied that the Government had never made such a promise but that if they had been told this, that there was a misunderstanding somewhere . . . Antoine then said that the Late Mr. Insp. Conroy had told him that the supplies for the Sick and Destitute were to be put into his hands and to be issued as he thought proper, but that actually he did not know what became of said supplies. I replied that I would be very glad to give him these supplies, and thus relieve myself of the trouble attendent on their issue, but that such a course would not be approved by your Department [of Indian Affairs].[29]

Harris had registered this same complaint from these same Indians one year after the Treaty had been signed. (See page 227.) However, all he could do was to advise his department.

I believe it to be my duty to inform you that I know that certain promises were made these Indians at the first treaty which in my opinion never should have been made. The Indians at Fort Simpson did not wish to accept the Treaty at first, and I think the wisest course would have been to let them alone till they asked for it themselves, though I do not in any way wish to criticize the action of my superiors in the Department.[30]

When Harris paid Treaty there in 1926, the Indians of Fort Simpson had nothing to say: "the payments passed off very quietly and without the usual amount of talk".[31]

Cornwall – 1925

The northern Indians had a staunch supporter in "Peace River Jim", James K. Cornwall. He had been present for the signing of Treaty 8 at Lesser Slave Lake in 1899, and over the years had pressured the Government to honour the promises made to the Indians at Treaty time. An influential promoter of Northern development, Cornwall was one of the few who believed that "the commercial prosperity of the country is in the hands of the Indians". He understood better than most, that the Government of Canada had a responsibility towards the Indians of the North. In 1925 he sent this statement to the Department of Indian Affairs:

> The Physical condition of the Northern Indian is of such a nature that unless the Federal Authorities take notice of same a most serious situation will arise, and it will reflect on the Government, and will tend to show the violation of one of the important principles as laid down in the Treaty.
>
> At the time of the treaty a solemn compact was entered into whereby the Government undertook to take care of the Indians, both physically and materially, so long as the grass grew and the waters ran. This may not have been specifically stated in the Articles of Treaty, but was incorporated in the remarks of promises made. Twenty-five years have elapsed since first Treaty No. 8 was made . . . the physical condition of the Indian is much lower today than it was at that time. Tuberculosis, Scrofula, and numerous venereal and blood diseases are prevalent among several Tribes in the North . . . producing a race very inferior to the type that the Government made Treaty with. It is physically impossible for two Medical Men, which is all that is provided by the Government, to take care of six or eight thousand Indians, scattered between McMurray and the Arctic Ocean, with no other means of ministering to them other than a brief period at the time the Treaty is being paid . . . .
>
> All of the foregoing is common knowledge in the north country and is nothing short of a national disgrace: no treaty in the World's history is more justified in being characterized as a "Scrap of paper", as the lack of intelligent interest displayed by the Government in their treatment of the Indians in the north on the one hand, by the Dominion of Canada representing the King on the other.[32]

Trapping and Hunting, 1922-1929

Northern Indians signed Treaty 8 and Treaty 11 believing that the Government guaranteed them freedom to hunt and trap, and would protect them from the competition of white trappers. One year after the signing of Treaty 11, there was no indication that this would happen:

There has been a great influx of White trappers to this district this fall . . . There are approximately 40 White trappers between Fort Smith and Great Slave Lake . . . They very often crowd the Indians from their old districts. This will make it very difficult for the Indians to make a living. If it keeps on, some system of protecting the Indians and their hunting grounds will have to be adopted, or the Government will be obliged to feed the Indians . . . I have heard of one Indian being ordered off an old line by a White trapper who crossed his line.[33]

White trappers had moved northward in successive waves. Their presence in Indian territory was reported in 1897, 1898, and 1899 by the North West Mounted Police patrols in the Athabasca-Mackenzie District. The gold field of the Klondike and the oil strike at Fort Norman had lured many prospectors into the country. Many of these turned to trapping in the winter months and prospected in the summer for a few years while others remained in the country permanently to make a living at various jobs. In 1919-1920 the price for fur was the best it had been in years. With the improved methods of transportation white trappers and traders poured into the North to take advantage.

The railway from Edmonton to MacMurray had opened wide this great hinterland with its wealth of fur-bearing animals, its musk-oxen, its moose and its caribou. Hordes of white trappers and traders of a dozen nationalities had swept northward aboard every conceivable form of craft. Hardly a stream or tributary of the Mackenzie-Athabasca region but had its sprinkling of pioneer trappers, in their diminutive log cabins . . . .[34]

There were 110 trading stores in 1920 in the Northwest Territories: the number doubled by 1927. In Fort Rae alone forty-one trading licences were issued in 1926. Some traders were honest, but some used unfair practices to secure their harvest of furs and to lure the trade away from their competitors. Some peddled poor quality goods, tawdry trinkets, silk hosiery, alcoholic extracts, and yeast cakes, to speed up the manufacturing of home brew. An article appeared in the *Edmonton Bulletin* of August 2, 1924, exposing these unscrupulous operators:

Every year a host of free traders from the city go North to buy furs. These men merely pay a trading licence, they have no expensive establishments to maintain all through the North. They swoop down, take all they can get and disappear. "When the improvident Indian has 'blown in' his money the trading companies do not let him starve – naturally it is to their business interest – but what do you suppose the native gets from the fly-by night merchants? Nothing."

This spring, one trader from Edmonton floated down with a scow load of goods valued at about $10,000. He took out no licence because he was not "trading in fur with the Indians" but he got around it nicely. He tied his scow up, the Indians flocked down and he informed them that it was a cash proposition, so the natives withdrew their cash credit from the established companies and bought to the limit. The floating trader "made a clean-up", the Indians have no credit with the companies and where they

236

are going to get next winter's supplies of groceries, clothing and ammunition no one knows . . . .[35]

The effects of this invasion by trappers and traders on the Indian, on his economy and on his own honesty were soon apparent. When the fur trade became unsettled, the Indian was caught in the middle and his inaptitude for competition and his inexperience in cash transactions put him at a disadvantage.

Indignation and Inaction

In the face of this threat, Cornwall and Breynat renewed their pressure in defence of the rights of the Indians. They directed their efforts to the public, to the Territorial Government, and to Ottawa. The *Edmonton Bulletin* of November 14, 1922, printed an article by Cornwall, as head of the Northern Trading Co.:

> Indians And Whites In The North May Clash This Winter Over Disputes Regarding Trap Lines.
>
> White Trappers In The Search Of Fur Are Going Further Afield, Penetrating Territories Which The Indians Regard As Their Own, And Trouble Is Possible.
>
> This year an unusually large number of white trappers have gone down stream . . . This terrain is regarded by the natives as their special hunting area . . . The Indians being the weaker people are gradually being forced to the wall. They should have large hunting reserves made for them unless the Dominion wishes to see them exterminated, and furthermore they should be adequately protected. At the same time it should be distinctly understood that the White trappers are desirable . . . There is unlimited territory for both the White men and the Indians but it is not fair to either, to allow them to encroach on one another.[36]

The *Montreal Star* of December 9, 1922, ran a similar story entitled, "White Man Crowding in on Red Skin in Athabasca Country. Trappers' lines being laid in what is regarded as Indian Territory".[37] Breynat expressed his concern for the welfare of the Indians and the inadequacy of the Police protection that was provided in a letter to Cornwall with a copy to the Director of the Northwest Territories and Yukon Branch, Oswald Sterling Finnie:

> I do agree with you on the urgent necessity to do something to protect the native population amidst, if not against, the white men, who are flooding their trapping and hunting ground, but my experience of thirty-one years of *actual* residence in the North enforces in me a divergence of opinion on several points . . . Flynn Harris, whose experience among the Indians and his knowledge of the conditions of the North certainly cannot be challenged, is strongly against the opinion that "the White trappers are desirable" in our district. I must add that the general opinion of people down here is also against it. This winter, we have some thirty-six White trappers among our native population. They have their camps in an area of about sixty miles from the delta up the Slave River [from Fort Resolution up the

237

Slave River] . . . The RCMP . . . have here only one team of dogs for three men . . . Most unwillingly they have to wait to undertake an already too much delayed patrol amongst the white trappers . . . [The Police] should be directed to take very strong action against peddlers or any white man abusing the Indians, deceiving them in their trade, or appropriating to themselves anything left in cache by Indians in their camps or in the bush.[38]

Breynat wrote to the Deputy Superintendent General of Indian Affairs "with reference to the invasion of the hunting grounds of the Indians in the far North by White trappers". The reply he received read: "I beg to say that I have noted the contents of your communication."[39] An associate of Cornwall advised Finnie to exclude the white trappers:

Any white trapper invading this country is taking away the means of these Indians remaining self-supporting . . . Last year, the influx of trappers was so great . . . that there is very grave danger that the animals will become extinct in a very short time. Between Resolution and Smith we have no less than 55 white trappers . . . The country will soon be trapped out, and the Indians destitute.[40]

Cornwall himself had lost patience with Ottawa. In letters to the Minister of the Interior and to his Deputy, he accused the Government of being derelict in its obligations to the Indians. He stressed the need for,

an immediate regulation to protect the Indians from the inroads of unscrupulous white adventurers . . . I am seriously impressed by the necessity of the Indian department taking a more serious view of the necessity of immediately taking steps to protect the wards of the Government in the north . . . You should take up the question of giving the Indians more serious and intelligent attention than they have received in the past . . . Unless you are prepared to take a serious view of this situation, you will have a first-class bill of complaint . . . . The north country is about fed-up with side-stepping . . . What we want in the north is action, and some sort of intelligent and sympathetic understanding of our requirements . . . .[41]

Finnie received hard facts and hard advice from RCMP Inspector Stuart Taylor Wood. Statistics compiled in 1923 by the Police showed: 118 white trappers in the areas around Fort Smith and Fort Resolution; 46 in Fort Simpson, and 39 in the Fort Norman area:[42]

White men are infringing on the trapping ground of both Indians and Eskimo and will without doubt, in time, clean out this district of all fur . . . I would therefore urgently impress upon you the necessity of putting a stop to this influx of White men at once . . . If present conditions continue, it will not be long before the country is cleaned out as bad as Alaska and the Indians and Eskimo will become dependent on the Government for food and clothing.[43]

Incompatible Interests

White trappers argued that a few hundred of them could never exhaust the fur resources of an area of a million and a quarter square miles. The fact was that the few hundred were not spread over the country but were operating in traditional Indian hunting grounds around Forth Smith, Fort Resolution, Fort Providence, Fort Simpson, and Fort Rae. The Indian and the white trapper approached the hunting ground with different attitudes and goals. These were well explained by Ralph Parsons, Fur Trade Commissioner for the Hudson's Bay Company, in an article written for the Canadian Press:

> Very few white people, taking up trapping as an occupation, give any thought to conservation. The great majority take up trapping in the same way as they would take up any other occupation – to obtain the largest possible return in the shortest possible time . . . .
>
> The Indian may be lazy, improvident and shiftless, but, insofar as the conservation of the wild life is concerned, these failings may be almost regarded as virtues. Hunting is the only occupation for which the majority of Indians are adapted, but, whereas the "White" trapper will go into a territory and not be satisfied until he has cleaned it out, the Indian will only take what he requires to see him through from day to day. He has no incentive to make large hunts. He traps to fill his immediate needs only. It is only when the Indian comes up against the intensive competition of the "White" trapper that he goes to excess in trapping and in killing out wild life. With few exceptions, it will be found that where Indians have been left alone, there is no undue scarcity of animal life in their vicinity. The Indian is unwittingly a good conservationist. When fur is plentiful, he will probably take all he needs to buy his requirements. When they are scarce, he very soon becomes discouraged and does not consider it worthwhile to trap. Thus in years of plenty he is taking animals which, in all probability, would die from epidemic later anyway, and in years of scarcity, he leaves breeders which presumably are immune from the disease.
>
> The great difference between the "White" and the Indian trapper is that the White trapper goes into the country with the fixed idea of doing nothing else but trapping and of getting every possible skin he can. The Indian, on the other hand, is settled pemanently in the country and all he does is to make a bare living hunting for food and trapping to get the wherewithal to pay for his other few necessities.
>
> The majority of the White trappers are itinerants moving from one place to another and a great number of them are foreigners whose object is to take as much as possible out of the country and to put as little as possible back. The Indian, on the other hand, puts all he makes back into the trade of the locality in which he lives.
>
> It is significant also to note that despite the fact that trade in furs had been carried on in Canada for about three hundred years, it is only within the last thirty years that any real concern has been felt for the preservation of the wild life. While the growing scarcity may be partly due to the expansion of settlement, it must be remembered also that beaver, for which the greatest concern is felt at present, was a much more important article of trade and, consequently, much more sought after, yet it was in

no danger of being killed out. Since there were more Indians trapping in those days than there are now, the inference would seem to be that it is only since the White trapper entered the field so extensively that there has been any danger of this animal being killed out.[44]

The white trapper was usually well equipped. When he started the season he knew his grubstake would last until spring, permitting him to trap continuously through the winter. The Indian could not do this, since he was living on credit from the trading post, and spending a good part of his time hunting for food. By circumstance and intuition the Indian had succeeded in conserving the wild-life he depended on for his existence. Now he was witnessing its destruction in a few short years. Two who saw it happening were Alexandre King and James Balsillie. They remember how the white trappers cleaned their country of fur:

> White trappers spoiled the country. Had too many traps, 600, 500, like that. Us natives, well, my brother had 35 and that the most any had, most had 18, 19, 20, like that.[45]

> Every slough, off the Slave River had a white trapper. They would come in and just clean out the slough of muskrats. They would leave nothing for seed. They would kill every beaver in every lodge they found. Then they would get the hell out of the country. The Indians weren't like that; they weren't getting rich, they were living off the land and knew that they had to be a little bit careful anyway.[46]

> The old man L——— and his two sons trapped 730 minks in one winter in the Fort Resolution area. They had 500 traps together.[47]

White trappers denied that they were responsible for the depletion of game and fur. In turn they hurled accusations of their own at the Indians. The bitterness of one attack dramatizes the intense feeling which prevailed at the time:

> The northern Indian is a wanton slaughterer, anything but a conservationist.
> Twenty-odd years ago, on my first trip north, men from Chippewyan told how Indians from that picturesque fur post went eastward to hunt Barren Land caribou – and returned with dog trains of solid caribou tongues, having left the rest of the carcasses to rot or be devoured by wolves and foxes. At Fort Providence I heard Indians boast of killing up to forty moose each in a single winter. A half-breed bragged about how he and his companion one spring killed forty-two geese in two hours, less than half a mile from where our home cabin stood. One Indian told me he killed twelve moose and thirty-six woodland caribou during one winter; he didn't say how many he had killed during the summer. Another reported that he and two companions killed forty moose in less than six weeks. By contrast, Mary and I have killed a total of exactly nineteen moose in the years since 1927, and no deer or caribou at all. Yet the Indi-

ans, and certain whites with bread to butter, wail that it is the white trappers who are responsible for the dwindling game and fur supply.

It is not the white trappers! There are only a few hundred of us in the entire million and a quarter square miles of the Northwest Territories, and it isn't we who are responsible. On the contrary, the blame lies squarely with the Indian. It is he who boasts of wiping out a whole brood of young ducks with a single blast from his shotgun. It is he who cannot resist the temptation to shoot whatever animal or bird crosses his path so long as he has a round of ammunition. It is he who leaves traps and snares set during the closed season. It is he who wipes out the last beaver on a creek and last marten in the foothills. I know what I am talking about, for I have seen him do it.[48]

This was written by Chick Ferguson, a trapper in the Fort Providence area. His reason for coming North and his interest in trapping had nothing to do with conservation, as he himself explained:

That is what our plans called for: three or four years in the Far North, during which time we might get enough saved to make a new start back in the world we'd left behind. Just one or two good fur years, and we'd be set.[49]

He came into the North in 1927 from the United States. His wife joined him in 1928, and except for the period between 1936-1939, they trapped until 1945. The Fergusons owned 800 traps and built eight cabins along their traplines. This kind of an investment proved profitable. In the spring of 1930, Ferguson's fur catch was worth $2000. At the end of the season in 1933, Chick had "the only 100 pelts catch in the Providence district". Another year he trapped "200 pelts, including 58 minks". He closed out 1935 with a total of 448 pelts: 166 foxes, 161 minks, 115 lynx, 4 beavers, and 2 otters. In 1939-1940, his fur catch was again "the best in the district". The winter of 1942-1943 was "the best fur season". In 1945 Ferguson's catch amounted to only 10 lynx, 25 minks, 10 beavers, 75 foxes, a few wolves." He had to face the fact that "the fur cycle was over." He left the North to start a new life as a writer and a photographer. In his autobiography, Ferguson expressed surprise that the Indians did not appreciate his presence in their country. He recalled one occasion when he and his wife were paddling up the Horn River and they "passed a clan of Indians . . . [who] watched us in stolid sullen silence, making it plain that they did not welcome our presence, we waved but they did not respond". He felt no responsibility to them nor to the country. He had only himself and his wife to feed. An individual Indian, on the other hand, would be responsible for feeding many mouths. What he brought back to camp or to the post was shared by all.

The solution of these problems of conservation and protection of wild-life, and of protection for Indians to hunt and trap in their own country, was not to be found along the traplines of the Mackenzie.

Governments: Federal and Territorial

Ottawa was well aware of the situation. On one occasion the Minister of the Interior, Charles Stewart, brought the problem before the House of Commons:

> We are receiving constant complaints from the Indians that they are being driven off their hunting grounds. It is generally conceded that the White man is a much more zealous hunter, covers a greater extent of territory, and takes more fur than the Indian, and is denuding the hunting grounds of the red man to such an extent that it is becoming a serious problem.[50]

But it was a problem of the Government's own making. As the Government of the Northwest Territories emerged and gradually assumed more administrative power in the North, the Department of Indian Affairs seemed less inclined to define its primary responsibility for the Indian population. In this respect, the Territorial Government was never compelled to respect the Treaty promises made to the Indians by the Federal Government. In 1922 the administration of the Northwest Territories Game Act and Regulations was transferred from the Parks Branch to the newly formed territorial administration, first called the Northwest Territories and Yukon Branch of the Department of the Interior. The inexperience and inability of the legislators and law enforcement officers in the Territorial Administration defeated the purpose of the game laws. One inspector admitted that there was trouble in administering the Game Act:

> Upon my return from my first trip in 1922, I reported why this was so. From my personal enquiries I learned that almost every RCMP post or detachment had a different interpretation . . . Found proof that nearly all detachments favoured their friends . . . Frank Conibear [a Fort Smith trapper and trader] frankly and openly admitted that he trapped beaver out of season. I knew of this case from Corp. Walters, RCMP who asked permission from his inspector to visit Conibear's trap line – and get him! This request was refused . . . .
>
> Nearly everyone knew Conibear was trapping illegally but no attempt to catch him – at the same time RCMP went after many others . . . The RCMP go after the poor trapper. When there is wood to be cut, repairs made, or fishing to be done, the Constables in small settlements arrest half-breeds for alleged offences to do this work. I know of many cases . . . .
>
> The big trouble in my days was that the young RCMP were not trained in any kind of administration of game laws, fishing, handling dogs etc., etc.[51]

In 1922 hunting and trapping licences were issued by the Territorial Administration to 197 non-Indian residents, to 115 non-resident British subjects, and to 26 non-resident non-British subjects.[52] The fees were nominal[53] and could easily be offset by the price of a few pelts. In July, 1923, an Order-in-Council established new game regulations for the Northwest Territories. The first clause increased the fees for licences, to "discourage the growing influx of foreign trappers . . . rapidly depleting the wild life resources of the Northwest Territories". A bona fide resident of the Northwest Territories would now pay only $2. instead of $5. But non-resident British subjects would pay $75 instead of $25, and a non-resident non-British subject $150 instead of $50. A non-resident was defined as "any person who has not lived in the Northwest Territories for four consecutive winters."[54] The new regulations had the effect of encouraging immigrants to apply for citizenship[55], but did not discourage them from becoming trappers.

The attraction was high fur prices. A silver fox pelt averaged $164: cross fox, $53; red fox, $16; marten, $24; lynx, $26.[56] Over the years revenue from the fur catch in the NWT improved:

1919-1920:	$1,121,026.
1920-1921:	$1,153,840.
1921-1922:	$1,834,015.
1922-1923:	$2,171,424.[57]

The value of the furs caught by the Mackenzie District Indians averaged about 25 per cent of the total amount. White fox trapped outside of Indian territory made up 50 per cent of the total. One example of the imbalance which existed was at Fort Resolution. In the early twenties, the native population was approximately 727. The white trappers operating in the vicinity numbered 37. In 1923, the muskrat catch in the delta of the Slave River was estimated at 60,000. The Indians accounted for half of these. The other half were brought in by the 37 white trappers.[58] Muskrats could not survive many such seasons, as the N.W.T. District Agent McDougal recognized:

> I expect, now that a reserve will be established at the Delta of Slave River, they will multiply rapidly as the Indian does not kill all the rats. He hunts with a view to conservation as he is a permanent resident while the White trapper hunts to exterminate as he keeps on the move. This applies to all kinds of fur as far as the White and Indian methods of trapping is carried on . . . [59]

The Federal Government maintained a posture of responsibility for the Indians, while taking only half measures to protect them. In 1925, Superintendent General Scott advised the Northwest Territories· Branch:

> . . . it is my view both official and personal that the vital interests of the Indians should be paramount and should have precedence even over the protection of wild life."[60]

The Territorial Administration did not agree. Indian Agents would continue to be in conflict with territorial officials if they supported Scott's policy. Finnie received this memorandum from one of his men:

It would appear that the Indian Agents . . . are not fully co-operating with us in regard to matters pertaining to the administration of the game laws inasmuch as they make mis-statements to the Indians regarding same.

One Indian was tried . . . on the charge of trapping beaver . . . out of season. Mr. Card [Indian Agent] told the Court that he had told the Indians that they could, when hungry, disregard the game laws of the country and kill anything they required to eat . . . .

Regarding the Indian Agent, Mr. Card, giving the Indians permission to kill game in and out of season when hungry, he has consistently done this for the past few years and adopts a very antagonistic attitude towards the Police in general whenever we [N.W.T. Branch] are concerned with any Indian. It is utterly impossible to enforce our Game Regulations under such conditions.[61]

Finnie did not expect much assistance from the Indian Agents in administering the game law, and in the case of Flynn Harris he was right. Harris had been named Justice of the Peace in addition to his duties as Indian Agent at Fort Simpson. Many Indians accused of infractions against the Game Act appeared before him for sentencing. Harris based his decision not only on the letter of the Game Act, but also on the promises made to the Indians by the Treaty Commissioner, which he had witnessed. In 1927, Finnie received this complaint about Harris:

[Three] Treaty Indians admitted the killing of no less than 30 beavers during the closed season. Mr. Harris took the view that no offense has been committed as these Indians required the animals for food purposes and they are permitted to take them during the closed season for this purpose . . . one Pascal (Indian) . . . was tried . . . on the charge of killing two moose out of season. After the evidence being submitted to the Magistrate [Harris], he took a lenient view of the case and gave the accused a lecture and a warning and dismissed the case.[62]

The District Agent also protested: "Harris held two trials as Indian Agent and J.P.: an Indian was fined $25 for making a brew and another Indian was dismissed for shooting a moose calf and bull out of season."[63] This prompted Finnie to take matters into his own hands on October 7, 1927:

The leniency with which Mr. Harris, J.P., of Simpson, has dealt with Indians and Half-breeds coming before him for contraventions of the Game Act, has led us to the conclusion that where Indians and Half-breeds are involved it would be better if they appeared before another Justice of the Peace who is not an Indian Agent. Wherever possible Mr. Harris has dismissed the cases against them. Where there was no alternative he imposed a minimum fine . . . If any other J.P. is available he (Harris) should not be allowed to act in any case where an Indian is involved.[64]

During an inspection tour of the Mackenzie District in 1928, Moran advised Finnie that a new J.P. should be appointed at Fort Simpson:

244

Harris will not convict an Indian, and if he does, it is always a minimum fine. Would advise that Moorhead be instructed, instead of leaving practically all cases to Harris, to try them himself.[65]

This in-fighting among government officials compounded the confusion growing out of new boundaries, new jurisdiction, and new laws. Could the Indian comprehend the contradictions between what government said and what it did? Could he understand the conflicting policies of different levels of government? Where the Federal Government had promised him freedom, the Territorial Government now enforced laws. Where the Federal Government had sought his goodwill, the Territorial Government now ignored him. As successive territorial inspectors made their annual trips down the Mackenzie, their time was taken up with the business of the few hundred white people who lived in the settlements. Information on land, mining, timber, wild life, transportation, and development filled pages of official reports.[66] The best the territorial inspectors did for the 4000 original inhabitants was to count them.[67]

Game Preserves

The idea of game preserves first came from Northwest Territories District Agent McDougal in October, 1922, after he had seen the muskrat being depleted in the Slave River delta. RCMP Inspector Fletcher supported him and suggested that "the country west of Slave River and Hay River be reserved for the Indians. In this connection, I would say that by Indians I mean Treaty Indians and also half-breeds who are natives of the Territories."[68] Breynat promoted the idea in a letter to Ottawa in March, 1923, stressing the urgency of the situation.

> The matter is quite a complicated one, the more so as, in Ottawa, they do not seem to well understand the peculiar conditions of our Far North . . . All the Indians I have met during my continuous traveling, this winter, are afraid they will soon be flooded, in their hunting grounds, with undesirable trappers. And it is the general opinion, among the old timers, traders or Missionaries, that there is no time to be lost if the Indians are to be effectively protected, as they really need to be, if the Government does not want to have to feed and clothe them, in a near future . . . Mr. Harris' view in the matter is that the whole district of Mackenzie should be exclusively reserved for the Indians of Treaty No. 8 and No. 11. I think that such view is the one of all those who are thoroughly acquainted with the conditions of the District. And I would personally recommend it to the Government.[69]

He was asking no more than had been promised when the two treaties were signed; i.e., that the Indian people would have the exclusive right to hunt and trap over the entire area of the Treaties. His reply came from the Director of the Northwest Territories Branch. Finnie agreed in principle, but was explicit in establishing his own priority. If the Indians benefited indirectly, it was fortunate:

> It would appear that the Indians and Whites are not on very friendly terms . . . It has been reported that many undesirable hunters and trappers entered that country last year and in many cases drove the native from his ancestral hunting ground. We have under contemplation regulations amending the Game Laws which will have for its object not only the conservation of the wild life of the great Northland but also the conservation of the Indian himself. We hope to establish a number of reserves primarily for the conservation of wild life, but in these reserves the Indian will be allowed to hunt and trap with the same freedom as he always did.[70]

Breynat was on a pastoral trip through the Mackenzie District when this message came. His secretary, Jean-Louis Coudert, OMI, informed Finnie on June 24, 1923:

> If it is certain, on the one hand, that reserves strictly so called will never be accepted by the natives, it is, on the other hand, not to be doubted that the Indians will greatly appreciate game reserves, where nobody but themselves would be allowed to hunt and trap. They have, in fact, already expressed the wish that white trappers be excluded from the Delta of Slave River, which has been one of their traditional hunting grounds, and where they feel their rights to have been violated of late by the presence of an excessive number of undesirable hunters and trappers.
>
> The Indians of the North Eastern part of Great Slave Lake would also be anxious to reserve for themselves the right of hunting and trapping on that part of the Territories comprised between Fort Rae and the North Eastern end of Great Slave Lake.[71]

When the Territorial Administration acted on September 22, 1923, to establish game preserves, it did so unilaterally. There is no record that the Indians were asked about the size of location. The Treaty rights of Indians were offset by the interests of white trappers, resulting in these land allocations:

The Yellowknife Preserve	Area: 70,000 Sq. miles
The Slave River Preserve	Area: 2,152 Sq. miles
The Peel River Preserve	Area: 3,300 Sq. miles[72]

The benefit to the Indians protected by the Yellowknife and Slave River Preserves was soon apparent. White trappers moved out and trapping and hunting were restricted to Treaty Indians only. As time went on this caused problems for Metis and White residents of Fort Rae and Fort Resolution, both located within the boundaries of a preserve: Yellowknife and Slave River, respectively. They were not only excluded from big game hunting and trapping on the preserve, they could no longer hunt ptarmigan, duck, or small game near their homes. There were never any objections to the first restriction, but many appeals were made to modify the second. One year after the establishment of the preserves, the territorial inspector recommended in his report that the non-Indian residents of Fort Resolution and Fort Rae be permitted to hunt within a radius of five miles of these settlements. Those at Fort Resolution also asked to hunt wild fowl within the Slave River Preserve itself. In 1925, another territorial officer suggested that sixty square miles immediately surrounding Fort Resolution be withdrawn from the Slave River Preserve, and exempted from all hunting restrictions. In 1928, Breynat approved the "legitimate wishes of the white population at Resolution to get relief in intolerable conditions which prevent even killing a partridge or a rabbit on private property . . . and asked that Fort Resolution be excluded from Preserve."[73] Although Finnie agreed that the non-Indian residents were justified in their request,[74] there was no consensus on the size of the area to be excluded, and the matter rested there in 1928.[75]

The Peel River Preserve proved inadequate for the needs of the Indians of the Peel River and Mackenzie Delta area. In August, 1924, they asked McDougal, Fort Smith District Agent, for a larger preserve.[76] That same year, Indian Agent Harris reported that "some explanation as to the hunting reserve were asked . . . which I was glad to be able to give", both at Arctic Red River and at Fort McPherson.[77] In 1926 the situation in the Lower Mackenzie had deteriorated to the extent that RCMP Superintendent Ritchie recommended the establishment of a detachment at Arctic Red River, "to patrol to the Anderson River . . . which (is) being invaded by white trappers.[78]

In other areas of the Mackenzie District the Indians had no protection against the competition of the white trappers. The Indians at Fort Smith, Hay River, Fort Providence, Fort Simpson, Fort Liard, Fort Wrigley, Fort Norman, Fort Franklin, and Fort Good Hope, asked for game preserves. They wanted "to continue to live as they had done in the past . . . in the same old way."[79] A proposal was made to establish a game preserve covering a fifty mile radius around each trading post, but it was dismissed by Finnie.[80] Some of the white trappers complained bitterly that they were kept out of the game preserves. They referred to the North, as "the country with a fence around it."[81] There were some who understood the Indians' dilemma. One Woofter expressed strong feelings on the subject:

In the matter of the large Indian preserves set aside for the natives no real trapper begrudges the native this privilege. The Government had either to do this or feed the Indians, and any one who had witnessed the terrible poverty and want amongst the native inhabitants does not grudge them this land. People living on the "outside" have no conception of the suffering borne by the old people and the children of the Indian tribes. We whites have gone into the country, taken their hunting grounds, used their hunting trails and they do not grumble and still are as honest as ever they were. In the North my cabin is never locked – that is in the Indian country.

The Indian has no chance to compete with the white man. The native with twenty-five traps will be in competition with the white who may own any number, up to a thousand; the white man feeds his dogs on cornmeal and tallow and can travel while the Indian has nothing but a few fish and cannot cover a third of the distance. If I had any say, I would make Indian hunting preserve for a hundred miles on each bank of the Mackenzie River in addition to the preserves already created, and even then the Indian would not be getting justice.

Another line of bunk which is given out is that the fur companies such as Hudson's Bay and the Northern Trading Company are trying to keep the whites out of the country. If they are, how is it that they supply accommodation on their steamers for all comers? They carry in the trappers' goods and go to no end of trouble to get his business . . . .

The Mounted Police are working no hardships on anyone. They are efficient and from them everyone gets a fair and equal treatment. One of their principal duties is to protect the Indians and if the police were not on the job the natives would soon be starved out by some of these chaps who kick about the North and who never do anything but follow the trails blazed by the Slaveys and the Chipewyans.[82]

In January, 1925, the chief at Fort Liard complained to Harris about the increasing number of white trappers coming to Trout Lake every year. Expressing his fears that there would be no hunting grounds left for the original inhabitants, he requested that Trout Lake and vicinity be constituted an Indian Reserve.[83] Harris visited Fort Liard in the summer of 1926 and reported:

Headman Charley Tetcho, who asked for a hunting reserve at Trout Lake, was here and as this is the first time I have seen him since you instructed me to have him give the bounds of the lands he wishes reserved, I put the question to him, but was unable to get a definite reply. I will write you further on this subject.[84]

Harris found a similar situation at Fort Simpson, where the Indians asked for a game preserve of 8,300 square miles:

I was waited on by a large number of the Indians of Slave Band No. 2, headed by their chief and both headmen, and was by them requested to ask you that a Hunting Preserve be granted them . . . The country is being overrun with white trappers, and the fur-bearing animals are being practically exterminated in this vicinity.

I have the honour to strongly recommend that their request be granted, and that the country asked for be preserved for the Indians.

The Indians also ask that if their petition for a Preserve is granted, the bona fide Half-breeds, born in the North-West Territories, and residing here or in the vicinity, be granted permission to hunt on the said Preserve, and have all the rights and privileges enjoyed by the Indians thereon.

There have been forty trapping licences issued to White men by the RCMP detachment here, besides about twelve more who had licences before they arrived in this neighbourhood, for the year from July 1, 1926 to June 30, 1927. Some of these men use as many as three hundred traps, and a large number of them kill far more fur than any of the Indians.

In certain areas, the fur is already practically extinct, and if some steps are not taken, the only source of the Indians' revenue in this country will soon be entirely cut off.

If you decide to grant the request contained in this letter I would respectfully suggest that the Preserve asked for herein be accorded as promptly as possible, as each year the fur-bearing animals are getting more scarce.[85]

Harris' letter was passed from Indian Affairs to the Northwest Territories Branch. At the territorial district level, the agent at Fort Smith, Jerry D. Murphy, was openly hostile:

The White men that I talked to are sympathetic towards the Indians, but all agree that preserves should be created large enough to contain all of them in the hunting and trapping efforts and that they should not be allowed to hunt and trap elsewhere. At present they all complain that although many preserves have been created for them few actually trap there but the majority of them encroach on the territory inhabited by white men . . . .

It appears to me that to cover up any shortages in the fur catch by Indians, their sponsors immediately shout white trappers. The Indian is a natural born killer and destroyer . . . Being improvident they have no thought of tomorrow and rarely is it ever heard that they leave seed in a trapping area. They are not always to blame as I find that resident fur interests encourage them in this method of slaughter. Apparently the slogan throughout the whole fur industry is to get the fur no matter how. It has been reported to me recently that in the vicinity of Simpson and Providence, the fur interests told the Indians that a close season on Beaver was coming into effect this year and encouraged them to make a clean-up. This party reports that young and old went to the massacre. Indians who never have been known to hunt beaver before participating . . . .

I have heard the White trapper maligned so much lately that I am forced to come to his assistance . . . .

In conclusion I would therefore recommend that at present no more reserves be set aside.[86]

The Anglican minister at Hay River, Alf. J. Vale, advised Finnie in January, 1926, that the Indians were beginning "to feel the pressure of the White trappers who are gradually drawing nearer and crowding them out" of their trapping grounds.[87] A recommendation for the creation of a game preserve in the Hay River area was included in the territorial report of 1926.[88] RCMP Inspector Fletcher supported Rev. Vale and the Hay River Indians:

A preserve would be a good thing for these Indians and also for the fur-bearing animals. The Buffalo River and Buffalo Lake are especially good fur countries, particularly for beaver, but if white trappers are allowed to go in, they will quickly clean this district of fur, and they are commencing to do so.[89]

Fletcher predicted problems in the area of Great Slave Lake, near Fort Reliance:

White trappers are getting more numerous every year; numbers of them are now going to the east end of Great Slave Lake. . . . There are three trading posts now operating near Fort Reliance; this is about 225 miles east of Resolution, so you will see that all that can be done from that detachment is one patrol a winter. It may be found necessary in the future to establish a small detachment near Fort Reliance, to keep whites from encroaching on the Yellowknife game preserve, and for the protection of Indians and game. The attraction to this part of the country is the presence of the caribou herds, which always pass this way in their annual migration. I am rather of the opinion that now that this Fort Reliance district is being invaded by white trappers a detachment would be a good thing to prevent the wasteful slaughter of these animals. I do not say that wasteful slaughter is going on, but it may, and by it the caribou migration may be deflected still further to the east.[90]

A police detachment was established at Fort Reliance in August, 1927.

At Fort Good Hope the white trappers were threatening an already scarce fur and game supply. The Indians there asked for two small game preserves, one on each side of the Mackenzie River, close to their settlement. Their petition was signed also by Antoine Binamé, OMI, and four other non-Indian residents, on February 7, 1928.[91] Four years later Harris "told the Indians of the preserve for which I had asked for them, and they were enthusiastic in hoping that it would be granted".[92] It never was.

This request, and the many preceding it from other Indians in the North, went unheeded and unanswered by the two Governments. The representations made by Breynat, Cornwall and others, were equally unsuccessful. Breynat's efforts culminated in a meeting with Finnie in 1928. The need for more and larger preserves, and for better protection for the hunting and trapping rights of Treaty Indians were the issues. In spite of countless letters, meetings and discussions, Finnie would not budge from his position: no more land for game preserves. Breynat suggested that some of the area of the Yellowknife Preserve could be withdrawn, and that land equal to it could be designated as preserve land for other bands.[93] The matter was on the agenda for the 8th Session of the Northwest Territories Council on March 8, 1929. There was no change in the Administration's policy, and no action was taken by the Territorial Government.

Provincial Game Laws, 1922-1929

In 1899, the Indians at Fort Chipewyan and Fond du Lac signed Treaty 8, assured that their freedom to hunt, trap, and fish would be protected by the Federal Government. This jurisdiction was soon replaced by that of provincial governments in 1905, and Treaty promises were conveniently disregarded. Ottawa had no control over the game laws enacted by Alberta and Saskatchewan, and took no steps to establish the reserves promised by the Treaty, and requested by the Indians. Both in northern Alberta and northern Saskatchewan the Indians were left vulnerable to the competition of white trappers much earlier than was the case in the Northwest Territories. They protested game laws and unfair competition annually on Treaty days, but by 1922 they were no better off than the Indians who had just signed Treaty 11.

At the eastern end of Lake Athabasca, the Indians of Fond du Lac, Saskatchewan, were harassed by game laws and the activity of white trappers. Successive reports of Indian Agents paying Treaty each year, indicate the growing aggravation. In 1922, the complaint was "against the Saskatchewan Provincial Police, whom they claimed interfered with them in their trapping. As many of the bands trap in the Northwest Territories, they claimed an independent jurisdiction."[94] In 1923, the same Indians were concerned about the number of well equipped white trappers arriving in the country.[95] In 1924, they complained again that the Saskatchewan Game Laws were enforced against them, but that outside trappers were allowed to break the law.[96] The Indians were willing to obey the law, according to Constable Chapuis, of the Saskatchewan Provincial Police, and gave him no trouble: it was the white trappers getting more numerous every year, who made law enforcement more difficult.[97]

The railway from Edmonton to Fort McMurray was the target for resentment in Fort Chipewyan in 1922. It brought more white trappers into the country who were trespassing on Indian hunting and trapping grounds. Indian Agent Card received an urgent request to designate land for the sole use of the Indians:

> All were very indignant at the way White trappers were crowding them out of their hunting and trapping grounds. They asked that application should be made to the government for the land about Lake Claire and Maima should be set aside as a reserve. That they had always made their living in this district, and claimed that they had a prior right to the district . . . .
>
> There has been trouble for several years among both the Cree and Chipewyan Bands, [in] Fort Chipewyan, about the game restrictions imposed by the provincial government, and by the ever-increasing number of White trappers who have come into the country. In one case a white trapper named Bjarson is claimed to have threatened a number of Indians, and practically, for the time being, driven a number of families from their trapping and hunting grounds and from their homes. Owing to the number of unemployed who come into the country the situation has become acute, and unless action is taken the fur supply will soon be wiped out and the Indians will be direct charges on the government, as other than hunting and trapping there is no work for them. To protect their interests, as guaranteed by treaty, both bands asked for a reserve, not for farming, as they had no wish to farm, nor is the land suited for that purpose, but for

hunting and trapping. To make the matter definite I requested both bands to apply for a reservation, naming the area selected. This application has been received, and is herewith attached. The area is much larger than that which they are entitled by treaty, but the bulk of the land is water and marsh ground useless for any other purpose than that for which they wish it to be set apart . . . Payment was finally made and bad feeling was, for the time being, allayed. The Chiefs of both bands were preparing a joint letter for me to take to Ottawa . . . They asked that I should not only write but if possible should go to Ottawa and voice their interests.[98]

Card returned in 1923 without any word from Ottawa. The best he could do was gather testimonies on the seriousness of the situation:

The Chipewyan and Cree Bands, Fort Chipewyan, are still insistent in their desire for a hunting and trapping reserve in the delta of the Athabasca. The old-time residents of the district support them in their agitation and seem to think that this is the only way to conserve a future supply of game and fur-bearing animals for their maintenance. A very large number of white trappers and Half-breeds, from Lac la Biche and Lac St. Ann were permitted to come into this district last fall. And the Indians claim they trap out of season and use poison. On this latter point I was unable to get proof. In order to have some idea as to the number of these people, as they are nearly all Roman Catholics, I interviewed the resident priest, Father Jaslier, and he estimated that, including women and children, 1000 souls lived on the territory, in addition to the former native population. Chief Jonas, of the Chipewyan Band stated, in council, that unless a reserve was set apart and these newcomers kept out, in two years the fur supply would be completely depleted.[99]

Again in 1924, Card could do nothing but listen to the pitiful stories.

The Chief and headmen were anxious to know what action the government had taken for the setting apart of a hunting and trapping preserve, claiming that their condition was getting more pitiable every year. They asked for the matter to be again placed before the government . . . .

The Chief, headmen and members of the band held a long council, regarding the much discussed Hunting and Trapping Preserve . . .

The Cree and Chipewyan Bands again brought up the urgency of having a Hunting and Trapping Preserve set aside. Apart from interested White trappers, their unanimous wish has the support of local public opinion. They, the Indians, claim that their condition is becoming more pitiable every year, and that unless prompt action is taken, it will be too late.[100]

In the summer of 1925, the Indians inquired "whether any action had been taken with regard to giving them a Hunting and Trapping Reserve"[101] Neither that summer nor the next brought any answer. By the winter of 1926-1927, Chief Jonas Laviolette of Fort Chipewyan made an appeal to Cornwall:

For a long time now I try to get a reserve for me and my people . . . The White men and half-breeds come down here and ruin my country with poison and early trapping . . . Every winter it gets worse and worse and we are all miserable now, and lots of times nearly starving. Mr. Card [Indian Agent] residing at McMurray supposed to be our Boss, but we never see him, only when he pays Treaty – he is here for about four hours in a year, so how can he know we suffer . . . .

Plenty men look after the Buffalo, not one seems to care about us, we can starve and nobody cares . . . . Jackfish Lake has been my people's home for 200 years and more. If this country is given us for a reserve, and we get some help, the fur will come back again and me and my people will be happy again. We are so poor and miserable now that we are ashamed. Won't you, please, help us get our Reserve?[102]

In 1927 there were more discussions on the reserve matter with as little promise of success:

The setting aside, by the Government, of Hunting and Trapping Preserves, for Treaty Indians only, was discussed at length at Fort Chipewyan, and an area, much smaller than that originally asked for, was agreed upon. Some of the Chipewyan Indians, under the leadership of Chief Jonas Laviolette, wished for the immediate survey of the lands promised at Treaty. He claimed that every year more White men come into the country, build houses among them and soon they will have no homes if the land promised them is not surveyed and trespassers kept off. Both the setting aside of Hunting and Trapping Reserves guaranteed by Treaty, are considered very vital matters by the Indians who belong to the Chipewyan Band at Fort Chipewyan. The Crees are not similarly interested, as their hunting and trapping grounds are included in the enlarged Wood Buffalo park, from which White trappers are already excluded.

The lack of uniformity in the Game Laws of the North West Territories, the Province of Alberta and the Province of Saskatchewan, is a source of confusion to the native mind. The Indian tribes, in this Agency have a respect for the law, and wish to keep it, but they have no apparent knowledge of a divided jurisdiction.[103]

Chief Laviolette wrote to Jim Cornwall in February, 1928, finally admitting that the long wait had been in vain:

I have been waiting and waiting for that help you promised me but it has never come. I suppose the Big Boss fooled you too, just the same as he has been fooling me all these years . . . . We are all getting crowded out from our rat grounds . . . Now if we were left alone we would always have enough rats in the spring . . . but with so many outside people around us, they are very soon going to kill off all our rats and leave nothing to breed upon again. After this spring hunt, there will be nothing left and it won't be the Jackfish Lake Indians that have done the damage . . . They pay men to hold a piece of our old country so that the buffalo can feed without anyone bothering him, but the Indians must starve. Do you think it right that the white man should go back on his word like this – why, that Treaty that he made with us was nothing but a lot of lies, he has not done what he promised us at all . . . I would be thankful if you would send my letter down to the Big Boss at Ottawa. . . . And I would like my brother

Indian on the outside to know how the Treaty is being cheated with us. . . .

I want everybody to know the White man has gone back on us, with his bargain with us . . . .

We are getting so tired of asking all the time and no one takes a bit of notice of us . . . I treat my dogs better than we are being treated . . . .[104]

Cornwall forwarded Chief Laviolette's letter to the Deputy Minister of Indian Affairs, to the Minister of the Interior and to the Prime Minister. He had something of his own to add:

I am of the opinion that you would be very well advised in giving these communications something other than the usual answer of – "Received and noted, and will be given consideration."

I am in a position to know that these people are practically starving; it is very largely due to the fact that your Department has never given any personal attention to these people. As you are aware you entered into a solemn Treaty with these people to at least pay some attention to them – "So long as the grass grew and the waters run".[105]

Cornwall would have read the answer he received on March 13, 1928 with disbelief: "The points you bring out have been given specific consideration."[106]

Rumours were being spread among the Indians that they would be forced to stay within the boundaries of a preserve when it would be established. These stories were started by white trappers who had nothing to gain if preserves were set up, and who knew how to play on the Indians' fears of confinement. Chief Laviolette again asked Bishop Breynat for help:

The said information being that if the Indians at Jackfish Lake were given a reserve they would be compelled to live within the boundaries of the reserve, and would also be forced to make a livelihood by following an agricultural pursuit . . . It is not the wish of any of the tribe to become farmers, chiefly because they have no arable land to farm . . . but they are quite willing and anxious to become muskrat farmers . . . Each family of Indians belonging to the Jackfish Lake band should be allotted from three to four hundred acres of muskrat sloughs . . . these individual muskrat ranches should be included within the boundaries of the Indian reserve that has been promised them by the Department. This would insure greater protection for them, as it would then be impossible for the white trappers to trespass on the ratting grounds as they are doing today . . . [107]

In the summer of 1928, the Indian Agent duly recorded that the Indians "brought forward a demand for a Hunting and Trapping Preserve . . . [they were] again insistent . . . and wanted to know the cause of the long delay."[108] In 1929, "the matter and urgency of a Hunting and Trapping Reserve was again stressed and immediate action demanded."[109]

Wood Buffalo Park 1922-1928

The Indians requested game preserves in order that portions of their traditional hunting grounds be protected for their use alone. They depended on the stability of wild-life for their livelihood, and the extinction of any species was a threat to their existence. During the years in which their requests for the protection of fur and game resources were being disregarded, a wood buffalo sanctuary was created in the Northwest Territories to protect that vanishing species.

The buffalo had been protected by law since January 1, 1896. By 1914, the buffalo population had increased to approximately 500 heads, and by 1922, there were between 1500 and 2000 in the Athabasca and Mackenzie districts. When the Northwest Territories Branch took over in 1921, the staff stationed at Fort Smith began planning for the creation of a buffalo park. When news of this reached the Indians, it caused them great concern. The future buffalo park would be carved out of their own hunting and trapping grounds. On Treaty day in 1922, the Indians of Fort Smith-Fort Fitzgerald Band, voiced their feelings to Indian Agent Card:

> Chief Squirrel asked if I had any information of the intention of the government to make a reserve for the wood buffalo, with a consequent exclusion of the band from their ancient hunting and trapping grounds. He was told that I had no information on the subject, that should the matter come up, their interests would be protected. The payments were made to band, a considerable number waiting for the Fitzgerald payments, as they had more to say on the wood buffalo reserve subject.
>
> A long talk took place [at Fort Fitzgerald], regarding the report of their exclusion from a proposed Buffalo Park, the headmen and Indians were greatly agitated, but assured them that I had no information on the matter and that the report was not founded on any facts, as yet revealed . . .
>
> The report of the possible creation of a large reserve west of Smith, as reserve for the wood buffalo, caused a long and hostile discussion. The purpose of which was that from time immemorial they had made their living from this district, and that when they made treaty they were solemnly assured, in the preamble to the treaty, that their former mode of life would not be interfered with except insofar as it would be in their interest, and would be necessary for the preservation of game. It was pointed out to them that there was no official foundation for the report.[110]

The justice of the Indians' claim was evident. To exclude them from the park would be a violation of the Treaty. This was emphasized by Breynat and Card in their efforts to have the Indians' rights recognized.

> When the matter of creating the Wood Buffalo Park was under consideration, representations were made by Bishop Breynat and Mr. Card, the Indian agent at Fort Smith, on behalf of certain Indians who had hunted and trapped over that area in former years. It was claimed that those Indians enjoyed perpetual right to hunt and trap in that area, but that there

would be not more than 30 or 40 of them. (As it subsequently turned out there were three times that number).

In order that the matter of creating the Park be no longer delayed, the Department acceded to this request granting to those Treaty Indians who had hunted and trapped in the area to the north of the Peace River prior to the passing of Order in Council P.C. 2498 of the 18th December 1922, a continuation of the right to hunt and trap therein during the time hunting etc., was lawful in the Province of Alberta.[111]

The Wood Buffalo Park was established on December 18, 1922, and covered 10,500 square miles. Shooting buffalo was strictly forbidden. Treaty Indians were allowed to hunt other game and to trap fur-bearing animals. Very soon, the question was raised of permitting the Metis the same rights. Breynat broached the matter to McDougal, District Agent at Fort Smith:

[Some] half-breeds natives . . . have to live an Indian life, although they may have houses at the fort. Most of them should have been accepted in the Treaty instead of being refused the privilege, as it has been the case. However they are not very many and quite often, they have to meet so many difficulties to secure their living that to forbid to them access to the Reserve [Wood Buffalo Park] for hunting purposes would seem to be imposing upon them too much hardship.[112]

Finnie, of the Territorial Government, and MacLean of Indian Affairs, were brought into the picture. Breynat's efforts were fruitless. In 1924, the Metis were refused the privilege of hunting and trapping in Wood Buffalo Park. Breynat took another approach. He suggested that "the half-breeds be accorded the privilege of taking treaty if they so desire". This idea appealed to Finnie, since it would put "all the aborigines of that district on the same basis."[113] But the Department of Indian Affairs would have no part of it: "it is not desirable to re-open the half-breed question in the Northwest Territories."[114] Breynat continued his appeals for the Metis of Fort Smith and Fort Resolution, but in vain.[115]

Between 1925 and 1928, a total of 6,673 yearlings, two, and three year old bisons were transported by rail and barge from Wainwright Buffalo Park, Alberta, to release points along the Slave River, between the Peace River and Fort Fitzgerald.[116] It was soon evident that the park was not large enough, and an additional 6,800 square miles were added, south of the original area, in 1926.[117] The Indians at Fort Smith and Fort Chipewyan were fearful that their rights were again threatened. At Fort Smith in 1926, the Indian Agent heard complaints about the extension of the Buffalo Preserve.[118] At Fort Chipewyan, the Indians wrote to the Superintendent General of Indian Affairs, on May 6, 1926, expressing their worst fears:

It is felt very strongly here by all classes of residents that . . . restrictions and prohibitions will be enforced little by little, even under the most favorable circumstances, to such an extent, that in the very near future the Indians will be compelled to vacate the country which has been their home for time immemorial.[119]

The answer they received on June 25, 1926, reassured them that the extension of the park would not work any hardship on them.[120] This was repeated by Finnie, in an ambiguous statement which proved to promise nothing:

> It is not the intention or desire of the Department to prohibit any persons, whether Whites, Indians or Half-breeds, who formerly legally hunted and trapped in this area, from continuing to do so . . . So that while the Department wishes to protect the buffalo which may feed over that area, it also wishes to protect the Indians and others who hunted and trapped there in the past.[121]

He had in fact, disclosed quite different plans to the Deputy Superintendent General of Indian Affairs, two months earlier, on April 30, 1926:

> In the time to come I hope we may be able to make the Park a sanctuary and that no person will be permitted to hunt or trap therein. It is a wonderful game country and if given an adequate amount of protection will stock the adjacent country with all kinds of game. Unquestionably it would benefit the Indians, as well as all others living in the vicinity. This, however, can only be done by creating a large reserve for the Indians, perhaps north of Great Slave Lake – one of the conditions being that they should not hunt and trap in the Wood Buffalo Park.[122]

The buffalo were well protected and well cared for. Regulations were strictly enforced. The Public Archives of Canada retain voluminous files on the convictions imposed on native people trying to infringe on the buffalo's rights.[123] One John Gladu, an Indian from Fort Chipewyan, was sentenced to three months in the Fort Saskatchewan penitentiary for having shot a buffalo. If that was not severe enough, he was expelled forever from the Buffalo Park, the country where he was born and raised, and where his family and relatives still lived.[124] Ironically, at the time when the buffalo was so well protected from the Indian and Metis hunters in need of meat, the territorial agent at Fort Smith, proposed that permits be given to "big game hunters with wealth [who] will possibly pay a thousand dollars for the privilege of shooting a buffalo in order to secure a good head".[125]

1. IBNWTA, Transcript of William Squirrel's interview by Joachim Bonnetrouge, 29 February 1972.
2. PAC, RG10, file 1853.
3. PAC, RG10, BS, Vol. 3812, file 55,340, G.M. Matheson, 20 March 1930.
4. IANDO, file 191/28-3, Vol. 1, Report on Annuity Payments in Simpson Agency, 1922.
5. *Ibid.*
6. *Ibid.*, file 191/30-2-1, A.F. MacKenzie Acting Assistant Deputy & Secretary to Harris, 4 May 1922.
7. PAC, RG10, BS. file 336,877, Inspector Fletcher to Officer Commanding, RCMP, Edmonton, 4 September 1922, and to Deputy Superintendent General of Indian Affairs, 4 September 1922.
8. OMIAFS, 091-CH, FR, Vol. 2.
9. F. Waldo, *Down the Mackenzie,* New York, Macmillan, 1923, pp. 94-95.
10. H. Ingstad, *The Land of Feast and Famine,* New York, Alfred A. Knopf, 1933, p. 29.
11. L. Rourke, *The Land of the Frozen Tide,* London, Hutchinson, 1928, pp. 254-259.
12. Chick Ferguson, *Mink, Mary and Me,* New York, M.S. Mill Co. 1946, pp. 108-109.
13. IANDO, file 191/28-3, Vol. 1, McLean to the Commissioner of the RCMP, 20 April 1923, and to C. Bourget, 4 May 1923.
14. *Ibid.*, file 779/28-3, Vol. 2, Agent's Diary, Annuity Payments, 13 August 1924.
15. *Ibid.*, file 191/28-3, Vol. 1, Bourget to Assistant Deputy & Secretary of Indian Affairs, 6 August 1923.
16. *Ibid.*, 5 August 1924.
17. Clermont Bourget, *Douze Ans chez les Sauvages,* Sainte Anne de Beaupré, P.Q., 1938, p. 79.
18. IANDO, file 191/28-3, Vol. 1, Bourget to Assistant Deputy & Secretary of Indian Affairs, 6 August 1924.

19. *Ibid.,* and Report of Corporal Hall to Officer Commanding RCMP, Mackenzie Sub-district, 23 July 1924.
20. IANDO, file 191/28-3, Vol. 1, 6 August 1925.
21. *Ibid.*
22. *Ibid.*, 11 August 1927.
23. *Ibid.*
24. PAC, RG85, Vol. 340, file 991, Diary of a Trip to Aklavik and Return, kept by P.E. Trudel, 7 July 1926.
25. IANDO, file 191/28-3, Vol. 1, Report of Harris on Annuity Payments, 1923.
26. *Ibid.*
27. *Ibid.*, Harris to Secretary of Indian Affairs, 12 August 1924.
28. *Ibid.*, 15 August 1925.
29. *Ibid.*
30. *Ibid.*
31. *Ibid.*, 30 July 1926.
32. PAC, RG85, Vol. 340, file 991, Cornwall to McDougal, 29 January 1925.
33. IANDO, file 1003-2-5, Vol. 1, McDougal to Finnie, 10 October 1922.
34. P.H. Godsell, *The Vanishing Frontier,* Toronto, Ryerson Press, 1939, p. 204.
35. *Edmonton Bulletin,* 2 August 1924.
36. *Ibid.*, 14 November 1922.
37. *Montreal Star,* 9 December 1922.
38. IANDO, file 1003-2-5, Vol. 1, Breynat to Cornwall and to Finnie, 27 January 1923.
39. RCMAFS, file: Conditions des Indiens, Breynat to Scott, 15 November 1922. Scott to Breynat, 15 December 1922.
40. IANDO, file 1003-2-5, Vol. 1, D.N. Murdoff to Finnie, 26 January 1923.
41. RCMAFS, file: Cornwall, Cornwall to Charles Stewart, Minister of the Interior and to Scott, 20 February 1923.
42. PAC, RG85, Vol. 340, file 991, Fletcher to McDougal, 25 July

1923.

43. *Ibid.,* Vol. 581, file 507, Inspector Wood to Finnie, 26 March 1923.

44. RCMAFS, file: Mackenzie, Ralph Parsons, 22 November 1937.

45. IBNWTA, Transcript of Alexandre King's interview by David Smith of the University of Minnesota, 21 July 1972.

46. *Ibid.,* Transcript of James Balsillie's interview by David Smith, 22 July 1972.

47. Author's files, Yellowknife, Transcript of James Balsillie's interview by Louis Menez OMI, of Fort Resolution, 1972.

48. Chick Ferguson, *Mink, Mary and Me,* pp. 112-113.

49. *Ibid.,* p. 8.

50. Canada, Commons, *Debates,* 24 April 1924, p. 2146.

51. RCMAFS, J.F. Moran, *Confidential Notes,* Vol. I, pp. 33-35, Vol. II, p. 38.

52. NWT, Territorial Council, *Minutes of the Sessions,* 3rd. Session, Appendix 18, Maxwell Graham, Report of the Wild Life Division of the NWT and Yukon Branch.

53. Canada, *Privy Council,* OC No. 1053, 1 May 1918.

54. *Ibid.,* OC No. 1234, 10 July 1923.

55. PAC, RG85, Vol. 340, file 991, McDougal, Report on Trip down the Mackenzie River, 9 August 1924.

56. Information Canada, Kind, Number, Total Value and Average Value of Pelts of Fur bearing animals taken in Canada, by Provinces. Northwest Territories, Season 1920-1921.

57. *Ibid.,* Seasons 1919-1920 to 1922-1923.

58. PAC, RG85, Vol. 340, file 991, McDougal to the Director NWT & Yukon Branch, 20 July 1923.

59. *Ibid.*

60. PAC, RG85, Accession 64/128, file 6276, Richards to Finnie, 8 November, 1928.

61. *Ibid.,* Richards to Finnie, 8 November 1928.

62. PAC, RG85, Accession 64/128, Vol. 467, file 5809, Richards to Fin-

nie, 22 September 1927.

63. PAC, RG85, Vol. 340, file 991, McDougal to Finnie, 11 July 1927.

64. PAC, RG85, Accession 64/128, file 5809, Finnie to Richards, 7 October 1927.

65. *Ibid.,* file 5979, Moran to Finnie, 7 July 1928.

66. *Ibid.,* Vol. 351, Vol. 340, series 800-16.

J.F. Moran, *Local Conditions in the Mackenzie District, 1922,* Department of the Interior, NWT. & Yukon Branch; Ottawa, F.A. Acland, Printer to the King's Most Excellent Majesty, 1923.

67. *Ibid.*

68. IANDO, file 1003-2-5, Vol. 1, memorandum, 26 June 1928.

69. RCMAFS, file: Conditions des Indiens, Breynat to Scott, 13 April 1923.

70. IANDO, file 1003-2-5, Vol. 1, Finnie to Breynat, 18 April 1923.

71. *Ibid.,* J. Coudert OMI, to Finnie, 24 June 1923.

72. Canada, *Privy Council,* OC No. 1862, 22 September 1923.

73. RCMAFS, file: Conditions des Indiens, telegram, Breynat to Stewart, Minister of the Interior, 19 June 1928.

74. IANDO, file 1003-2-5, Vol. 1, Finnie to Cory and to Moran, 27 June 1928.

75. *Ibid.,* Richards to Finnie, 26 June 1928.

76. PAC, RG85, Vol. 340, file 991, McDougal, Report on a trip down the Mackenzie River, 9 August 1924.

77. IANDO, file 191/28-3, Vol. 1, Harris to Secretary of Indian Affairs, 12 August 1924.

78. PAC, RG18, F1, file G-1316-1926, Superintendent Jas. Ritchie, 29 September 1926.

79. IANDO, file 779/28-3, Vol. 2, Agent's Diary, Annuity Payments, 1925; Card to McLean, August 1925.

80. *Ibid.,* file 1003-2-5, Vol. 1, Jujiro Wada to Finnie, 20 April 1923.

81. PAC, RG85, Vol. 340, file 991, McDougal to Director NWT

Branch, 4 September 1924.

82. *Edmonton Bulletin,* 2 August 1924.

83. IANDO, file 191/30-1, Vol. 1, Harris to Secretary of Indian Affairs, 1 January 1925.

84. *Ibid.,* file 191/28-3, Vol. 1, Report of Harris on Annuity Payments, 30 July 1926.

85. PAC, RG85, Accession 64/128, Vol. 462, file 5643, Harris to Scott, 20 April 1927.

86. *Ibid.,* G.D. Murphy Actg. District Agent to Director, NWT & Yukon Branch, 12 July 1927.

87. PAC, RG85, file 5075, A. Vale to Finnie, 12 January 1926.

88. PAC, RG85, Vol. 340, file 991, P.E. Trudel to McDougal, 13 July 1926.

89. *Ibid.,* Vol. 452, file 5075, Fletcher to Officer Commanding 'G' Division, 11 March 1926.

90. RCMP, Report of the Commissioner, 1926, p. 80.

91. RCMAFS, file: Conditions des Indiens, Petition to the Director, The Northwest Territories, 7 February 1928.

92. IANDO, file 191/28-3, Report of Annuity Payments, 1932.

93. PAC, RG85, file 1010-7, Vol. la, Memorandum of Finnie, 1 October 1928.

94. IANDO, file 779/28-3, Vol. 2, Report of Annuity Payments, 17 July 1922.

95. *Ibid.,* 11 August 1923.

96. *Ibid.,* 13 August 1924.

97. *Ibid.,* 1925.

98. *Ibid.,* 17 July 1922; Indian Agent to Assistant Deputy Secretary of Indian Affairs, 15 August 1922; Agent's Diary Annuity Payments, 1922.

99. *Ibid.,* Report of Annuity Payments, 11 August 1923.

100. *Ibid.,* 13 August 1924; Indian Agent to McLean, 19 August 1924.

101. *Ibid.,* Report of Annuity Payments, 1925.

102. RCMAFS, file: Cornwall, Laviolette to Cornwall, 10 February 1927.

103. IANDO, file 779/28-3, Vol. 2, Report of Annuity Payments, 1 August 1927.

104. RCMAFS, file: Cornwall, Laviolette to Cornwall, February 1928.

105. *Ibid.,* Cornwall to Scott, 2 March 1928.

106. *Ibid.,* Harry Baldwin, Secretary to the Prime Minister to Cornwall, 13 March 1928.

107. *Ibid.,* file: Fort Chipewyan, Mission Histoire, Laviolette to Breynat, 15 July 1928.

108. IANDO, File 779/28-3, Vol. 2, Report of Annuity Payments, 16 July 1928; Indian Agent to Indian Affairs, 28 August 1928.

109. *Ibid.,* Report of Annuity Payments, 16 July 1929.

110. *Ibid.,* 17 July 1922; Card to Assistant Deputy and Secretary of Indian Affairs, 15 August 1922.

111. *Ibid.,* file 1003-2-5, Vol. 1, Richards to Finnie, 15 April 1929.

112. RCMAFS, file: Metis Rapports, Breynat to McDougal, 3 September 1923.

113. IANDO, file 1003-2-5, Vol. 1, Finnie to Scott, 3 November 1923.

114. *Ibid.,* McLean to Finnie, 8 November 1923.

115. RCMAFS, file: Conditions des Indiens, Breynat to Finnie, 10 October 1928.

116. A.W.F. Banfield and N.S. Novakowski, *The Survival of the Wood Bison (Bison Bison Athabascae Rhoads) in the Northwest Territories,* Natural History Papers, National Museum of Canada, No. 8, 30 August 1960, p. 3.

117. Canada, *Privy Council,* OC No. 1444, 24 September 1926.

118. IANDO, file 779/28-3, Vol. 2, Constable W.J. Garland to Officer, Commanding RCMP Edmonton, 16 July 1926.

119. RCMAFS, file: Conditions des Indiens, Breynat to Stewart, 6 May 1926.

120. *Ibid.,* Stewart to P.G. Mercredi, 25 June 1926.

121. *Ibid.,* Finnie to Mercredi, 30 June 1926.

122. IANDO, file 1003-2-5, Vol. 1,
Richards to Finnie, 15 April 1929.
123. PAC, RG85, Accession 64/128,
Vol. 456, files 5222.
124. RCMAFS, file: Welfare, John
Gladu to McDougal, 10 June 1932.
125. PAC, RG85, file 991, McDougal to Director Northwest Territories & Yukon Branch, 20 July 1923.

Chapter VI

A Decade of Desperation, 1928-1939

It does not seem unjust to admit that the pre-1939 Canadian policy regarding Indians consisted of kindly isolating them within a structure of forgetfulness.

> – J. W. Pickersgill, Superintendant
> of Indian Affairs, 1956

Introduction

A turning point was reached in 1928 when influenza epidemics decimated the Indian population. Loss of life had been heavy in previous epidemics and from tuberculosis, but nothing to compare with the misery experienced throughout the Mackenzie District in the summer of 1928. Indian leaders were lost within the span of a few weeks. Children who did not perish were weakened in body and scarred in mind for years to come. Despite recommendations from every side for a government policy to cope with the conflict between the interests of native people and Northern development, the Federal and Territorial Governments continued to fumble. The Territorial Government was geared to the promotion of transportation, mining, commerce, and the welfare of white residents. A policy of developing natural resources independently of the native people was early espoused by the Northwest Territories Branch. The Federal Government could not totally ignore the potential source of wealth in the Mackenzie District; neither could it ignore the Indian population. The consequent strain on Ottawa resulted in a federal policy of expediency, thinly disguised as a benefit to the Indian people. Reports filed by officials of both Governments gave two views of the North, each with differing goals and priorities. The focus sharpened somewhat in 1936, when the Department of Indian Affairs was reduced to the status of Branch and a Department of Mines and Resources was created. The Deputy Minister of this new Department, Charles Camsell, was named Commissioner of the Northwest Territories.

The growth and expansion of prospecting and mining was largely due to improved transportation and communications services. Airplanes took prospectors to areas hitherto inaccessible by foot or by boat. A total of 640 mineral claims were staked at Pine Point on the south shore of Great Slave Lake in 1929-1930. In the fall of 1930 Punch Dickens piloted Gilbert Labine to the eastern shore of Great Bear Lake, Hunter Bay, Cameron Bay, and Labine Point, where pitch-blende was discovered in 1931. On this site, now known as Port Radium, the richest uranium mine in the world began operation in 1932. The prediction of 100,000 people for Bear Lake did not materialize however, when the mine faltered. Gold was discovered at Yellowknife in 1933. Prospectors and miners from Port Radium rushed to the Yellowknife district. Oil from Norman Wells found a market with the opening of these mines. The refinery produced 4,605 barrels of fuel oil in 1933, and by 1938 was producing 22,855 barrels. In 1935, the Department of Mines carried out a geological survey of an area of 10,000 square miles, north of Great Slave Lake. There followed an increase in mining and prospecting activity, with 400 prospectors searching for minerals in the Mackenzie District in 1937. One company, Consolidated Mining and Smelting, used eleven planes in its prospecting program. For the first time, the mineral production of the Northwest Territories surpassed the fur production in value. Yet by 1939, not one native person was employed in mining or prospecting.

The census of 1931 showed a total population of 9,723 Northerners. Of these 4,670 were Eskimos, 4,046 Indians, and 1,007 whites and Metis. There was little interchange between the whites and natives. For the most part, Indians were not welcome in the mining camps. They could only retreat further from the centres of white civilization. Royal Canadian Mounted Police detachments were established at Fort Liard in 1929, at Fort Wrigley in 1930, and at Cameron Bay (Port Radium) in 1933. By 1928, the Police had constructed a miniature nine-hole golf course at Fort Smith. Not to be outdone, the staff of the Territorial Branch had its own tennis court. Communications between settlements and with the south were improved. At Fort Norman a radio station started operation in 1930. The only telephone wire in the Northwest Territories extended through 97 miles of the Wood Buffalo Park. Mail delivery increased from a few hundred pounds during a winter season to 50,000 lbs. flown to the Mackenzie District in the winter of 1931-1932. The Northern Transportation Company Ltd. recorded increasing amounts of freight in 1934, and launched steel barges on the Mackenzie River in 1937. The Yellowknife Transportation Co. was established in 1938. A total of 4,000 tons of freight was shipped from the south in 1939. Airplanes soon rivaled the boats.

Five weekly flights linked Edmonton and Yellowknife. There were bimonthly flights to Fort Resolution and Fort Simpson by 1939. Airplanes were also used by some trappers to penetrate remote areas and to harvest furs more rapidly. Laws regulating airplane trapping proved ineffectual. Countless game laws became necessary to offset the damage that had been done to the fur industry by two decades of over-trapping. The price had plunged with the depression of 1929, and fur was at its lowest value between 1931 and 1933. Only muskrat trapping was profitable. The tiny village of Aklavik became the muskrat capital of Canada. The Hudson's Bay Company bought out the Northern Traders Co. in 1930, and itinerant traders almost disappeared from the scene. By 1935 southern fur farms produced 30 per cent of all Canadian furs.

Breynat agonized over the miserable condition of the Indians. After hearing the promises that had been made at Treaty time, after witnessing the signing of Treaties 8 and 11, he could not accept that the Indians should be so badly treated in their own country. As his fifty-one years in the North drew to an end, Breynat renewed his pressure on the Government. He collected affidavits from witnesses to the signing of the Treaties, in order to force the Government to honour its Treaty commitments. He wrote to officials of the Federal and Territorial Governments to focus attention on the plight of the Indians. He used the Canadian Press to arouse public awareness to the injustice of broken Treaty promises.

Finally, in 1938, the Government took long over-due action: trapping and hunting licences were issued only to those white people who held such licences previously. The move was anti-climatic. The fur population was so depleted, and fur prices were so low, that many white trappers had already abandonned trapping for the more lucrative pursuits of prospecting and mining.

The Flu Epidemic of 1928

An article printed in the *Edmonton Journal* of June 29, 1927, quoted the Commissioner of the Northwest Territories:

> sustained efforts to maintain in numbers and in vigourous health the Native population are being put forth both for humanitarian reasons and because development must depend upon Native workers.[1]

This statement was either a display of ignorance or a serious misrepresentation of facts. Deaths from tuberculosis alone outnumbered births in most places.[2] Many infants died a few months after birth. Most families lost parents and children alike. Periodic outbursts of smallpox, measles, and Spanish flu took a heavy toll over the years. Far from maintaining their "numbers and vigourous health", the Indians of the Mackenzie District were about to endure an ordeal unprecedented in their history.

The tragedy and horror surrounding the outbreak of the flu among the Indians, is described by the Inspector of the Hudson's Bay Company, Philip H. Godsell, who lived through it himself (See also Appendix XI):

> Late in June, at Fort Chipewyan, just as the *Distributor* was loading up for her first trip to the Arctic, two of the Lafferty boys arrived back from Edmonton where they had gone to sell their furs. A few days later they became quite sick; just a cold thought everybody and let it go at that. Hardly, however, had the steamer commenced to work her way down river ere David McPherson, the veteran pilot, was taken very ill and by the time I stepped ashore at Hay River there were quite a number sick on board. Then as the traveling plague spot, which the *Distributor* had unknowingly become, went cruising on her way she left behind at every post the germs of the disease. Twenty-four hours after her departure, the entire population of each settlement became prostrated with malignant "flu," and ere it spent its force in the Delta nearly six hundred of the natives had gone to the Great Beyond.
>
> Daily the doleful tolling of the mission bells the full length of that vast river proclaimed the passing of another, and still another, soul. Soon it became impossible to dig graves for all the dead, so they were wrapped in their blankets and buried in a common grave.
>
> Daily the broadcasting stations received fresh news of the ravages of the dread disease. Forty deaths at Fort Simpson, thirty-nine at Fort Providence, thirty more at Fort Norman, forty-four at Good Hope, and still the toll came rolling in.
>
> Across Great Slave Lake I drifted for twelve days on board my disabled schooner, short of food, sick myself, with a crew too ill and helpless to work, two of whom died, while a Mounted Police patrol boat vainly searched the shores for a sign of our missing craft.[3]

Godsell's wife, Jean, wrote these details about conditions at Fort Rae and Fort Smith.

> Whilst all the afflicted Whites finally recovered, the swift and savage scourge claimed a terrible rate of mortality amongst the poor natives. It gave little or no warning . . . .
>
> Corporal Halliday and Constable Jack Emerson found a Yellowknife village deserted, with thirty starving dogs left behind. When they made a patrol to Goulet's camp at the Gros Cap they discovered twenty-six Indians had died of the plague, the seven survivors having fled in panic . . . .[4]

When Dr. Bourget visited the Indians to make Treaty payments, he found that many of the Indian chiefs and headmen had died: among them Susie Baptiste, Susie Daniel, Old Marlow, Lamalice, Susie Drygeese, François Drygeese, François Sabourin, Harry Francis, and Zimba.[5] He saw a "race attempting to survive but slowly dying from this White man's sickness", and his medicine was powerless to prevent it.

The influenza killed two hundred people in my agency, and as many along the Mackenzie River. All in three weeks. It left us all . . . weak without resistance, more predisposed than ever to pneumonia and other lung diseases.[6]

When the Inspector of Indian Agencies, Charles Parker, filed his report in 1928, he expressed personal emotion over the tragedy he had witnessed while carrying out his official duties:

One cannot but recall, however, the gruesomeness of the journey from Ft. Norman on. As we progressed down stream the disease became more serious owing possibly to delayed attention. Whole settlements with but two or three able to move about; a chorus of hacking, racking coughs with no other sign of life but hungry dogs howling to be fed. Death started to take its toll and finally at Aklavik we even ran short of material to make rough boxes for burial and had to improvise means.

Pathetic almost to the point of tragedy was the helpless native under the grip of this disease. At Norman on a sunny day, following the payment of Treaty, I was fascinated with the frenzied, almost maniacal gambler's song on the lower level where the Indians were encamped. Someone had commenced the blanket game early in the afternoon and as the day progressed the song was taken up by one after the other, gradually increasing in force of passion to the evening and then gradually dying out with exhaustion and the oncoming grip of influenza. It was like a swan song followed by sullen sickness and ugly death. Then on to Aklavik where a few warm Arctic nights soon gave way to a setting sun and damp penetrating winds, with, still the chorus of agonizing coughs, the only substitute for the elated song of the gambler.

The epidemic was under control by the time I left the country after having taken a known toll of 300 natives with many small bands yet to hear from. Our schools at Resolution, Hay River, Ft. Providence, and Aklavik were all affected and we have reason to be gratified that we lost only one pupil. Too great credit cannot be given to the services performed by sisters and nurses at these institutions. Few of them escaped the disease themselves and at times there would be only one left on her feet to carry on.[7]

Every band asked for a resident doctor, and they were told "that the appointment rested with the Government, but the Agent would favourably recommend it",[8] Bourget's prediction that tuberculosis would become more active as a result of the Indians' weakened physical resistance was realized a few years after the great flu. In an attempt to awaken the Canadian conscience, Jim Cornwall recalled his own experience in an article printed in the *Edmonton Journal:*

. . . Never was I so appalled by their pitiful lot than . . . when I brought 12 of them – men, women and children, representing three families from Rae to Resolution. Everyone of them was verminous and in advanced stage of consumption. This was merely one instance of the condition prevailing everywhere in the Mackenzie District . . . The way we have treated our Indians is a national crime. There is no doubt about that . , . A doctor . . . told me that since coming north a month ago, during which time he has done nothing but study the Indians, he has not found a single physically sound individual . . . There are about 4,000 of them in the Northwest Territories. I can see no hope for them. They seem doomed to extinction.[9]

In the years following the epidemic, Ottawa became increasingly reluctant to expend money on medical care for Indians. Between the years 1931 and 1934, the total budget for Health Service for all of the Indians in Canada, (110,000) dropped from $1,050,000 to $793,000. These figures included salaries for doctors and nurses, and transportation. In 1934, sixty-four cents was spent on drugs for each Canadian Indian. By 1936, the Government was paying medical care expenses of $45,566 for 3,854 Indians in the Northwest Territories.[10] Inspector Parker had cautioned the Department in 1928 against a parsimonious approach to health care for the Indians of the Mackenzie District:

> Our expenditures, in recent years, on medical attention and care for aged and destitute have undoubtedly increased to such an extent as to give some concern to the Department. I can only say that careful inspection and inquiry revealed no unnecessary expenditure nor any carelessness in handling cases or admission of patients and destitutes. If an increased expenditure is regrettable we can only regret that it is necessary and assure ourselves that what is being done now should have been done in the past and must be done in the future.[11]

The Director of Indian Affairs advised all Indian agents on January 14, 1937:

> The Depart. will expect a reduction in drug expenditures and demands of about 50 per cent . . . There will be no funds for tuberculosis surveys, treatment in sanatoria or hospital of chronic tuberculosis; or other chronic conditions . . . nor in fact, for any treatment except for acute sickness.[12]

Two years later, in 1939, the Department issued these directives to Indian agents across Canada:

> A reduction of one day in the average length of stay of sick Indians in hospital would save about $15,000. It should not be difficult to save $10,-000 in drug costs by limiting the amounts of cough mixtures, liniments, tablets, etc. . . . given to Indians . . . The Department never contemplated the operation of a system of free drug stores.[13]

Dr. Bourget resigned in 1935. He recalled that during his last two years as Indian Agent at Fort Resolution, "the Indians were really pitiful, in extremely unhealthy conditions, poor as never before".[14] Doctor M.J. Thompson, in charge of medical services at Port Radium, advised the Director of the Northwest Territories Branch, that "the white population continues to retain its excellent condition". This was not the case for the Indians, but Government intervention could make a difference:

. . . at the present rate there will be very few Indians left at the end of fifteen years. It appears to me that the only solution to the situation is a complete medical check-up on all the Indians, with segregation of those found to be suffering from tuberculosis . . . The number of Indians left in the Territory is not so large that they would make this check-up more than a difficult task.[15]

The *Edmonton Journal* of August 30, 1939, described a desperate picture:

There are a hundred people rotting on the ore-rich rocks of Great Bear Lake.

They are Indians, so sodden with tuberculosis that they can hardly support themselves . . . .

Nine out of ten of them will die of tuberculosis unless something is done – and nothing seems to be possible.[16]

Problems for Both Governments

Information on conditions in the Mackenzie District was supplied to both the Department of Indian Affairs and the Northwest Territories and Yukon Branch of the Department of the Interior by their officers in the field. Charles Parker was Inspector for the Indian Agencies in the late 1920's, while John F. Moran made investigations for the territorial administration. These two inspectors usually travelled on the same steamboats and held meetings on the same day wherever they visited, but rarely exchanged information. Their relationship reflected that of their two Departments. In most cases their views differed greatly; if they were not actively contradicting each other, they were likely uninformed about what the other was doing. Examination of reports and other documents indicate that Parker advocated policies which would better promote the welfare of the Indian population. Moran, on the other hand, showed little consideration or sympathy for the Indians.

In the summer of 1928 Moran visited the Mackenzie District, as a "one man commission". He was to investigate and report on conditions as he found them throughout the District, "with the object of relating the requests of residents . . . and to furnish certain recommendations thought to be in the best interest of the people". He directed his attention to the functioning of government, the fur export tax, the Game Act and Regulations, liquor, native game preserves, Wood Buffalo Park, education, hospitals, fire protection, dog ordinances, and similar matters. Moran distributed an eleven page questionnaire to Mackenzie District residents.[17] One hundred and twenty persons were surveyed between Fort Smith and Aklavik. Russian traders, American fishermen, Canadian trappers, Syrian traders, French Canadian carpenters, Welsh mechanics were all asked to respond; not one Indian was included.[18] Moran's report to the Territorial Government made reference to the existence of the Indian people in the Mackenzie

District in a short section on "Native Preserves". Based on information from the questionnaires, he could recommend "that there should be regulations to prohibit Natives from hunting anywhere but on their preserves," due to the fact that there were complaints that the preserves were too large and that Indians were not confining their operations solely to their own preserves. Moran also reported that:

> Bishop Breynat recommends that all Half-breeds of Fort Smith and Resolution, living the lives of Indians be allowed equal privileges with Indians regarding hunting and trapping in the Wood Buffalo Park, as is the case in the southern part of the park.

Moran opposed this, and reminded the Government, "the gradual elimination of the treaty Indians from the Park . . . is our objective".[19]

Parker also made an inspection tour in 1928. His report[20] is in sharp contrast to that of Moran. He gave the Department of Indian Affairs a thorough analysis of conditions affecting the lives of Indian people. He blamed the game laws and closed season regulations for imposing more hardship than benefit on Indian trappers and hunters.

His own recommendation was that natural resources should be conserved first for the native, who depended on them for his livelihood. Several prevalent abuses came under attack: the transportation of live beavers from the Territories for fur farming; the use of poison in trapping; and the handling of Indians' accounts by white traders. The export tax on all furs received criticism. It meant that the Indians would pay taxes for the benefit of the whites. Parker recommended that "some part of the revenue derived from this source should be expended for the benefit of the Indians". Parker's complete report (see Appendix XII) provided Ottawa with a clear statement of problems and issues during those crucial months on 1928. It deserved careful study.

Two years later, Parker presented a similar report to the twenty-first session of the Northwest Territories Council, held on December 10, 1930.[21] Again he hit hard at white trappers, this time for the benefit of those who issued the licences and made the game laws. The Territorial Government had a responsibility to consider the effects of the closed seasons for various game and fur bearing animals on the economy and health of the Indian people. With such a report before them, the members of the Council could not plead ignorance of the facts.

In 1936, a new federal department was established. The Department of Mines and Resources replaced and combined under one operation the Department of the Interior (which included Indian Affairs), the Department of Colonization and Immigration, and the Department of Mines. In this shuffle, the Department of Indian Affairs lost its separate status and became a branch of the new Department. The Northwest Territories and Yukon Branch became the

Bureau of Northwest Territories and Yukon Affairs, part of a new branch including Lands, Parks and Forests. Charles A. Camsell was appointed the Deputy Minister of Mines and Resources, as well as Commissioner of the Northwest Territories. He had his own idea of government, which was quoted by the press:

> We are the ideal type of Government . . . Six men in Ottawa, of whom I am one, govern the Northwest Territories. We are kindly autocrats. We do what we think best for the people and we don't have to bother with re-election every four years.[22]

The following year there were signs that the Territorial Government might be awakening to reality. This memo passed between high ranking officials:

> I have given considerable thought to the suggestions advanced by His Lordship Bishop Breynat . . . These suggestions include the enactment of further legislation to preserve the fur resources for the exclusive benefit of the native population . . . increase and preserve the natives' means of livelihood and restore them to the semi self-supporting respectable position which they formerly enjoyed . . . .
>
> The Indian and half-breed population of the Territories find themselves in what is freely referred to as an "unenviable" position.[23]

At the same time, the Minister of the Interior, the Commissioner and the Deputy Commissioner of the Northwest Territories, Camsell and Gibson, two representatives from the Hudson's Bay Company, Parsons and Bonnycastle, and Jim Cornwall and Breynat, met in Ottawa to discuss several matters relating to the welfare of the Northern Indians. The issues discussed at the meeting were summarized by Deputy Commissioner Gibson:

> From the standpoint of the Northwest Territories Council we are asked to consider what action should be taken up to prevent white trappers from depleting the game resources of the Northwest Territories . . . It is claimed that further steps are needed, otherwise more Indians will be on relief. We suggested:
>
> a – extending the native game reserves
> b – further restricting the issue of hunting and trapping licences . . . .
> c – placing a limit on the cash value of fur that can be taken during any one season
> d – having the Police check up carefully on the activities of certain white trappers who are said to be conducting their operations in such a way as to absolutely deplete certain areas of fur-bearing animals.
> Mr. Parsons very strongly maintained that the regulations recently enacted to discourage the use of aeroplanes in trapping operations do not go far enough.[24]

That Breynat's arguments influenced the proceedings was confirmed later by Parsons, who congratulated the Bishop:

On the very able manner in which you handled the Indians' case during our meeting with the Minister, in Ottawa. I do not think the Indians ever had a better champion than yourself, and I really feel we are going to get some action at last . . . You can count on our full cooperation in urging and assisting the Hon. Mr. Crerar to implement his assurances that early action will be taken . . . .[25]

Breynat followed the meeting with a letter on March 4, 1937, reminding the Minister that the matter was not to be taken lightly:

It seems to me that our Indians are the more entitled to share in the Government assistance:
a. as they have been the first inhabitants of the country.
b. as according to the Treaty, they are wards of the Government with nobody to voice their claims in Parliament.
c. as they are quiet and abiding people, and never caused any trouble to the Government.
d. while a good many of the White population who are going to receive generous relief are not even Canadian subjects . . . .[26]

Jim Cornwall was not convinced that this meeting would make a difference. He wrote to Breynat:

For the time being, our unfortunate Indian friends are forgotten, as we know politics with Ottawa is a game. Our only hope is to keep after them. If they do not do something within reason, we will treat them to some adverse publicity, and they cannot stand very much of that. They like to work under cover. I am very skeptical of the Indian Department . . . .[27]

Mr. Ralph Parsons . . . passed through here . . . He feels that a check-up at Ottawa is necessary . . . I am personally of the opinion that if Ottawa will not move, and continues to procrastinate, the general public will have to be appealed to through the press in order to get action and wake them up . . . .[28]

Parsons, in fact, did appeal to the public. Through the Canadian Press he urged prompt action by all levels of government:

After carefully reviewing conditions through Canada, it would seem that the action taken by the Province of Quebec is the most efficient from the viewpoint of conservation and the most practical and economical in operation from the viewpoint of the Province.
    The unsettled areas of the Province have been closed to all trapping, except that done by the Indians and Eskimo residents . . . It assures the Indians and Eskimos of the only means they have of making a livelihood and, after all . . . the preservation of these races should be just as much the concern of every Canadian citizen as the conservation of the animal life.
    The same action can be taken by all the other provinces . . . now is the time to take action . . . .[29]

The problems for the Government cannot be separated from hunting and trapping in the Mackenzie District. These were many and complex between 1928 and 1939. They will be examined more closely in a subsequent section.

Metis and Eskimos

The condition of the Metis people presented a continuing difficulty for the authorities in the Mackenzie District. Parker examined this problem with considerable insight in 1928, recommending government action to remedy a serious injustice:

> We should concern ourselves with the "halfbreed living the life of an Indian". These poor outcasts, victims of one of the most iniquitous schemes ever fostered and maliciously operated are deserving of sympathetic consideration. I must confess lack of familiarity with the Half-breed scrip law, and what is said in this report is influenced entirely by what was observed while in the Territories.
>
> When one sees Indians, whole families of them, who speak little or no English or French, who live the lives of Indians, and are quite incapable of supporting themselves otherwise, discriminated against because at some time in the past at their own option or the urge of some interested party they accepted scrip and thus sold their miserable mess of potage, a sense of injustice rises up in indignation and the crying need of re-adjustment will not down.
>
> There are people in the Territories today who should have the full privileges of the Treaty Indian; who never should have been anything else and who today are virtual outcasts eking out a more miserable existence than the Treaty Indian.
>
> It may be granted that there are half-breeds who should be so classed and are not deserving nor in need of paternal protection. A great many of them are creditable citizens and tradesmen. I speak of a class called "half-breeds" who are more Indian than a great proportion of the so called Indians I have on the reserves within my own inspectorate. I could wish I had a few on some of my reserves for prize exhibits of pure blooded descendants of Canada's aboriginal inhabitants.
>
> I would strongly urge the advisability of an independant "half-breed commission" to re-open the whole question and by personal interview and inquiry make a readjustment of the status of these people. There are many cases where these people should be taken into Treaty and allowed to enjoy the same privileges which are now and will be allowed to Treaty Indians. An injustice has been done which the Government of Canada must and can rectify. If returned to the status of an Indian and placed on our Treaty pay lists, payment of annuities could be withheld until such time as the Government was re-imbursed for the amount they drew as half-breeds. I trust that this is a matter which will receive sympathetic support and consider it one of the most important suggestions that is my privilege to make.
>
> It is worthy of note that at the meeting of Indians I was able to hold before the epidemic laid everyone low, the Indians invariably spoke on behalf of the half-breed and asked that they be accorded the same hunting and other privileges enjoyed by themselves.[30]

Parker's recommendation for a Half-breed commission received only partial support in Ottawa. Dealing with individual requests as they were received was still the favoured procedure.[31] And these requests were being received with greater insistency.[32] From the Fort Resolution Agency, Bourget sent a "list of Half-breeds . . . living the lives of Indians, and deserving to be taken on treaty". There were thirty-four families or individuals in Fort Resolution, and four each in Hay River, Fort Rae, and Fort Providence. Bourget added his approval: "The majority will be pleased to be able to have the Department's protection if it can be arranged. For ourself, we believe it is the best act of justice that could be advocated and pressed."[33] Forty-two Metis from Fort Resolution joined the Treaty in 1930. Bourget was confident that they did so of their own free will.[34] The following year these Metis asked to have "one good old man, Jean-Marie Beaulieu as a head man".[35] In later years, Beaulieu explained the treaty with quiet pragmatism:

> A ——— took treaty; he was too poor . . . The guys that wanted to take treaty did so because there were hard times in the summer, no jobs. But if you took treaty, you could get relief in the form of shells, shot, powder, so you could go out and hunt . . . The Treaties got lots more help in relief, houses, than the Non-Treaties got. The Non-Treaties didn't get any.*

When Breynat learned that some Metis at Fort Resolution were taken into Treaty, he suggested that the same "privileges" be extended to those in the Fort Smith and Fort Simpson agencies.[36] The Department did not respond so readily in this instance, however, and many requests went unanswered.[37] Indian Agent Head advised Ottawa that the status of some Metis at Fort Good Hope, Fort McPherson and Aklavik was uncertain:

> From what I can find out a number of Half Breeds applied for Script but never received same. They are now asking for this Script or to be taken into treaty. At the present time there is a situation in several families where one member is a treaty Half-breed and the others non-treaty. This not only works at a disadvantage to these people regarding hunting and trapping rights but is always a source of contention every time treaty is paid.[38]

In 1938 some Metis from Fort McPherson were admitted into Treaty.[39] When the Inspector of Indian Agencies made his report in 1936, he confirmed Head's information:

> They are really much worse off than the Indians . . . I believe our Department should take into treaty all Half-breeds or three-quarter-breeds who are living with Indians, and following their mode of life . . . I did not seem to be able to ascertain which Half-breeds had taken Script, and at some places I was told they had waited either for this or to be taken into Treaty,

*Interviews with David Smith, July 6, and 25, 1968; February 29, 1972.

for some time, but nothing had been done about it . . . There are a number of Half-breeds living in the Northwest Territories who are anxious to be taken into treaty.[40]

A total of one hundred and sixty-four Metis were admitted to Indian Band lists in the Northwest Territories between the years 1930 and 1943. The practice was never well received by the Indian Affairs Branch, however, where the view was expressed that "the admission of this class of persons to band membership was a backward step and should be avoided except where special circumstances existed".[41]

By an amendment to the Indian Act, the Parliament of 1923 brought 6,538 Eskimos under the charge of the Superintendent General of Indian Affairs. Before that time these people had not been under the supervision of any Government department,[42] although their hunting grounds were protected by law. In 1920 an Order-in-Council had directed that "no licence shall confer the right to hunt or trap on Victoria Island (80,450 square miles) or Banks Island (26,335 square miles), Northwest Territories".[43] These preserves were extended in 1926 to include the entire territory of the Arctic Islands (332,320 square miles).[44] In 1927, responsibility for Eskimo Affairs was transferred to the Commissioner of the Northwest Territories.[45] Lord Byng, Governor General of Canada, and Finnie, Director of the Northwest Territories Branch, travelled down the Mackenzie River in 1929. Finnie's report recorded few details on their meetings with the Eskimos.[46] Bob Cockney, an Eskimo of the Mackenzie Delta, played a leading role during this visit and described it in his autobiography:

In summer 1929, we went to Aklavik by boat, my wife and children . . . When we were there, at Aklavik, a representative of the Government came in, O. S. Finnie his name, and he held meetings, proposing a treaty as the Government did to the Indians. As he addressed me, therefore I answered him, asking first how much money each person will receive for 12 months, a year, and he answered me $5.00. I told this to my fellowmen Eskimos, and asked them what they thought about it. They answered "no", they didn't want it, so I told them that I'll tell him that $5.00 is not enough, and I told so to the representative of the Government. We feel that this is not enough, and we don't accept it. Keep your money, but when the Eskimos have tough times give them some food (rations); this will be right, rations to the blind, widows, sick, such action will be of help to us . . . O. S. Finnie told me that I spoke well, there will be no treaty with the Eskimos. We'll act according to your wishes.*

The party did not linger in the Arctic. Having docked in Aklavik on July 31, the *Distributor* was ready to weigh anchor and begin the southbound trip on August 3rd. The message Finnie brought back

*Bob Cockney, Memories on the Non-Treaty with the Government, 1955. Tuktoyaktuk, N.W.T. Original Eskimo written and translated by Father Robert Lemeur, OMI.

was quickly translated into policy. At the twelfth Session of the Northwest Territories Council, December 11, 1929, the Commissioner stated: "Eskimos should not be classed with Indians, who were wards of the nation, and . . . [the Eskimos] really had the status of white men resident in the Territories"[47] Few white trappers reached the Arctic Coast and the Mackenzie Delta before the thirties. The creation of the Arctic Preserves permitted the Eskimo people to maintain their economic independence and to continue their traditional way of life. The total exclusion of white trappers from the Arctic Islands proved to be of more benefit to the Eskimo people than any treaty could have been.

Pressure on Ottawa

Breynat continued his perennial campaign to pressure the Government into honouring its Treaty promises to the Indians of the North. In October, 1936, he appealed through the *Edmonton Journal* for a trapping monopoly for the Indians. Exploration and mining were developing rapidly in the Northwest Territories, providing employment for many white people. If the Indians could protect their trapping economy they would survive and make a good living.[48] In November, he brought to Ottawa a carefully prepared memorandum which described the actual conditions of the Indians and their urgent needs[49] * He presented a logical, dispassionate case. After describing the poor physical condition of the people, Breynat related it to broken Treaty promises, for which the Government alone was responsible. He emphasized that the Indian, if treated justly, would contribute immeasurably to the economy of the North. This could be achieved by serious improvement of health care. More doctors and nurses, hospitals and medicines were required immediately. Education needed Government support, if more Indians were to benefit from the facilities already operating. In the area of social and economic welfare, Bishop Breynat advised that the Indian Agent should consult with the chiefs before sending recommendations to Ottawa. He suggested the development of economic ventures which would be compatible with the life style of the Northern Indians.Trapping licences should not be issued to white men in the Northwest Territories. If this could be regulated most of the other economic problems would solve themselves. Regulations were needed to protect Indian land and possessions from the interests of mining speculators. New housing was urgently needed to remedy

* On November 18, 1936, this document was sent to the Minister of the Interior; Harold W. McGill, Deputy Superintendent of Indian Affairs; T.A. Crerar, Minister of Mines and Resources; J.W. Campbell, President and General Manager of the Northern Traders Co. Ltd.; Ralph Parsons, the Fur Trade Commissioner of the Hudson's Bay Company; J.A. Hutchison, Game Commissioner in the Department of Lands and Mines of the Province of Alberta.

See Appendix XIV

unsanitary and unhygienic conditions. Breynat had a very specific recommendation to insure that the Treaty promises would be honoured in the future:

> After having been a witness to the Treaty and seeing the way the Indians' interests have been handled since, I often wonder how many officials, in the various spheres of the Government, who have dealt or may have to deal with the Indians, may have ever read the text of the Treaty.
>
> Would it not be more advisable to have a copy of the Treaty handed over with every new appointment, with a strong recommendation to fully comply with the spirit of the Treaty?

He analyzed the functioning of Government departments and concluded that it was not to the benefit of the Indians. Indian Affairs could not protect the Indians against the regulations of other departments and Governments which imposed unnecessary restrictions on their old way of life. The practice of appointing a medical doctor as Indian Agent was leading to abuses; again, detrimental to the welfare of the Indians. Their economic and social problems were being neglected, while the white population received medical service at the expense of the Department of Indian Affairs. Breynat urged the Government to assume leadership in protecting and helping the Indians, "without ever losing sight of the Northern conditions nor of the privileges and rights of the Indian, under Treaty." The memorandum pricked the conscience of many people with interests in the North.[50] The Hudson's Bay Company endorsed Breynat's memorandum, and urged the Minister of Mines to implement without delay the recommendation for restrictions on trapping licences:

> There are plenty of Indians and Eskimos in the north to absorb all the wealth the fur resources of the country can annually afford, so there is every reason to restrict trapping activities to them alone and exclude white trappers entirely.
>
> The situation is worse, of course, in the provinces where white trappers have been responsible for serious depletion of the fur resources, leaving the Indians in a very unenviable position and the Government with a high relief bill to pay. Foresight in excluding white trappers (most of them foreigners) in the first place would surely have left a more prosperous Indian today – and a happier, healthier one . . . .
>
> In the North West Territories . . . white trappers must gradually be excluded entirely . . . .
>
> There is every argument in favour of restricting the right to trap in the North West Territories to Indians, Eskimos and Half-breeds alone. This will have the dual effect of conserving fur resources and contributing to native welfare – two very much desired considerations."[51]

In Ottawa the memorandum was read "with a great amount of interest". Government officials "appreciated the suggestions", they promised that "the various matters dealt with would be very carefully considered." One month later, December 1936, the Minister responsible, the Honourable T. A. Crerar, announced to Ottawa newspapers that the Government was launching a new program to assist the Indians in gaining their livelihood:

> The primary aim of the scheme, said Mr. Crerar, would be to see each Indian was helped along in the livelihood for which he was best fitted by location and otherwise . . . . The Department would aim to improve the Indians' skill as trappers, he said. It would instruct them in the care of furs before disposing of them. It would advise them what trade goods to buy . . . . It would endeavour to keep the Indians posted, through the Indian agents, on current fur prices, to prevent exploitation by irresponsible traders – of whom a few still exist .[52]

In January, 1937, the Superintendent General of Indian Affairs was still examining Bishop Breynat's memorandum, and preparing an analysis of it.[53] Cornwall wrote from Ottawa:

> The whole Indian Department is in a state of indecision. They do not appear to have any plan of action worked out . . . It would take them some time to come to any decision, if they ever do . . . . The Indian Department is so thoroughly confused and without a policy.[54]

The Territorial Administration prepared an answer to the memorandum,[55] which was presented to the Sixty-fourth Session of the Northwest Territories Council.[56] A hastily assembled data sheet, it was a clumsy effort to divert criticism and refute implications of negligence. In some cases the list included responsibilities outside the jurisdiction of the Territorial Government, all properly ambiguous and vague.[57] Another version of the situation was printed in the *Edmonton Journal* on January 25, 1937.

> "I earnestly invite an awakening of public opinion to the harm that is now being done," the Bishop [Breynat] pleaded, "so that pressure might be brought upon all responsible officials to see that a great wrong should be righted as soon as possible. A month ago a commission was appointed at Ottawa to investigate the best means of preserving wild life in the North. Why are there never any commissions appointed to investigate the best means of preserving and protecting our Indians, to whom we have definite and sacred pledges of honor, in order that they might be allowed to live their own lives in their own way?"[58]

In the fall of 1937, Breynat used yet another tactic to move the Government. He collected forty-nine affidavits from witnesses to Treaty 8 and Treaty 11, who could swear to the authenticity of Treaty promises. The Minister of Mines and Resources, Mr. Crerar, received this notice from James Angus MacKinnon, Member of Parliament for Edmonton West, on September 19, 1937:

> [Breynat] had expected that more would be done for the Indians in the North as a result of his arrangements with your Department last spring.

He is very put out about this, and is preparing data, I believe, to press the needs of the Indians and the necessity for immediate action, on your Department. I am attaching hereto a memorandum with affidavit, which he is having signed.[59]

Shortly thereafter, the affidavits were delivered.[60] Breynat had signed his personal affidavit in Ottawa on November 26, 1937. He described in detail what he remembered of the signing of both Treaties. The important testimony of Jim Cornwall was included with the other affidavits. It had been signed in Edmonton, on November 1, 1937.

At the same time that Breynat was presenting his affidavits, a group of Catholic missionary bishops and priests were in Ottawa to organize the Oblate Indian and Eskimo Commission. Their purpose was to help find solutions for the social, educational, and religious problems prevalent in Indian communities. Breynat defined the policy of the new organization:

> We should refer to the principle of the aboriginal rights of the Indians in all circumstances, in educational matters, in the area of hospitalization of the sick, and in the safeguard of the Indians' rights to fish and hunt. etc.. . . . Respect for these rights was not inscribed in the texts of the treaties, but it was promised in the name of the Crown by the Royal Commissions responsible for having the Indians sign the treaties . . . .
>
> Unfortunately the text of the Treaties was too vague and did not contain all of the promises that were made verbally by the representatives of the Crown. Nevertheless, these promises were made, and without them the Indians would never had consented to sign the treaties. It was on the faith of these promises, guaranteed by the bishops and missionaries, that it was possible to persuade the Indians to affix their signature . . . These promises were never kept by the Federal Government. Furthermore, when the different provinces were given authority over their natural resources no mention was made of the promises made to the Indians. The provinces exploited their resources without the least concern for the Indians. The whites took the principal, and in some cases their only, means of survival – hunting and fishing.
>
> The whites, by their number and their modern inventions, annihilated the game and fur-bearing animals, so much so that the Indians are unable to compete with them and therefore reduced to the most abject poverty and threatened to disappear in a few years . . . .
>
> The question is whether or not the government desires to keep the Indians as a distinct race, and whether or not the government agrees to take the necessary measure to reach this goal. Only by so doing would it honor the signature of the Crown on the Indian treaties.[61]

The Commission met with Prime Minister Mackenzie King, and plans were made for "the rehabilitation of the Indians in their own customs".[62] In 1939 a resolution was passed by the Oblate Commission, "that the Canadian Government be asked to give back to the Indians their exclusive rights to fish and to hunt in the territories inhabited by them so that they might have means to survive".[63] Breynat resigned as president of the Oblate Indian and Eskimo Commision in 1939, but pursued the goal motivating his declining years:

> I have the intention of going to Ottawa . . . to try to fight once again on behalf of our N.W.T. Indians. I am committed to see that their rights are respected and that the protective measures I have obtained for them be maintained.[64]

A year earlier, Breynat had written an article entitled "Canada's Blackest Blot". (See Appendix XV.) It had been given good advance publicity, and was printed in the weekend supplement, the *Toronto Star Weekly*, on Saturday, May 28, 1938. Breynat's message was directed to the Canadian public:

> Canadians should know all the facts of our Northwest because, unless they act at once, they will some day bear the scorn of all peoples for having blindly allowed a noble race to be destroyed.

He expressed his shame that people of his own race had caused this physical and moral misery: "I have seen my own people claiming Christianity bring sorrow and unhappiness to these poor people of the North."

Breynat presented a factual report on conditions in the North, budget breakdown for the Department of Indian Affairs, statistics on education and medical care. He described the welfare picture in terms everyone would understand:

> The Indians of the Northwest are the most wretched people in Canada. Taking carefully compiled figures for 12 months during 1935-1936 (an exceptionally good year), it is estimated that the per capita income of these Indians was $110. This sum includes money earned as a result of trapping and hunting. Compared with them the most miserable relief recipient elsewhere in Canada lives like a king. In all cities families on relief receive food, clothing, shelter, medical, ambulance and hospital services, full educational facilities and the use of all public utilities.
>
> Bear in mind that these Indians are the original owners of the land that denies them a living.

The sorry plight of the Half-breeds, and the threat to the Eskimo population, were explained at length. He returned to his theme of protection for trapping and hunting. "Trapping and hunting regulations that will fit the natives' scheme of things, rather than the whites', are equally necessary".

Dr. Camsell, Commissioner of the Northwest Territories, received a letter from Breynat, shortly after the article appeared in Toronto. It contained "supplementary comments" which developed the idea of government as an extension of the Canadian people. He held the people responsible and called on them to bring pressure to bear on their political representatives to that the Indians could have the protection guaranteed to them by Treaties. Breynat stressed the fact that the Indians had fulfilled their Treaty obligations, but that the Government had not.

> The main obligation imposed upon the Indians was that they should abandon their right to Natural Resources and promise to respect the rights of the government as acquired from them; to obey the laws and to be peaceful with the whites who would not be long in coming to exploit the Natural Resources of the country. It is a fact that the Indians, generally speaking, have faithfully fulfilled all their obligations but can we say as much about the various governments sent to Ottawa by the white population to take in hand the direction of its own interests?[65]

Here were ideas to provoke serious reflection among lawmakers and citizens alike.

Hunting and Trapping: The Critical Years, 1928-1939

The crisis in hunting and trapping had its roots in the unregulated activity of white trappers. Although ostensibly designed to protect wildlife, and eventually to benefit the Indian trapper and hunter, a series of restrictions seriously threatened the whole structure of Indian life. Laws were made without regard for the Indians' guaranteed rights and were applied without scruple.

Closed Seasons

Regulations designating closed seasons on fur and game animals caused great confusion and hardship for the Indians. Some of their indignation was voiced by Jim Cornwall when he learned that the Governor General had authorized the Minister of the Interior, "to declare a close season on beaver in the Mackenzie District, Northwest Territories, for a period of three years, commencing the first day of October, 1928, and to extend such close season for an additional period of two years, if deemed expedient so to do."[66] Cornwall could not contain his scorn for the improvidence of government:

> I have heard this discussed for years at Ottawa; the necessity of conserving beaver; I never heard one word uttered to connect up the effect of all these ideas and the welfare of the Natives. When this Order-in-Council was decided upon, I wrote to Dr. Scott. I told him future generations would hold him responsible for the privation and suffering that would insure from this restriction. . . . There are so many poor, benighted, half starved, lousy natives who are considered as pawns in the game at Ottawa, that I am convinced, if the general public, in the country at large, were made aware of the situation, something would happen that would be heard from the 49th parallel of latitude to the Arctic, and from the Atlantic to the Pacific. When a Government proves itself to be so badly informed, and so lacking in those qualities that we all expect our Cabinet Ministers to be possessed of, at least a human feeling and understanding of the natives, who by Treaty gave to Canada, for a mess of pottage, one of the richest sections of the British Empire, to allow a group of Civil

280

Servants, whose principal interest in the Territories consists of maintaining their prestige and positions in a Department, and annually digging up some pretext to penalize the people by enacting Orders-in-Council to conserve this and that, in the way of fur and meat, for God only knows what for, and for whom, that makes at best a precarious living only harder . . . .[67]

In preparing this legislation, "all segments of the population" had been consulted between 1926-1928. There is no record, however, that any of the 4000 most concerned and most knowledgeable among the population were ever asked to express their views. Objections were raised by the Department of Indian Affairs, on the grounds that additional relief would be needed.[68] Breynat pointed out that "the beaver would be sufficiently protected if beaver trapping was allowed only for the Indians, and Metis living the same life as the Indians".[69] The final decision was made to maintain uniformity of law throughout the North. Saskatchewan and Alberta had already established a closed season on beaver, and there was risk that a black-market in beaver skins would spring up, if the Northwest Territories did not make its move.[70]

The regulation came at the worst possible time for the Indians. The Indian population was seriously weakened by the many deaths and debilitating effects of the flu epidemic.[71] Furthermore, other fur bearing animals were also scarce, so that without beaver, the Indians would be short of meat. Joining Breynat in recommending special consideration for the Indian people, were Police officials and Indian Agent Card.[72] During the summer of 1928 many Indians voiced their dissatisfaction. Chief Pierre Squirrel of Fort Smith was alarmed and fearful that the next winter would bring great hardship for his people. At Fort Rae, the Indians refused to accept Treaty payment until they had been assured that they could kill beaver. Bourget must have told them that the law would be changed, only to be contradicted by the Police corporal:

I am endeavoring to explain matters to the Chiefs and Headmen of the Indian camps, before they get out of the fort for their hunting grounds in order that this matter will be fixed to some extent, as the word of the Indian Agent is taken as law in this District and on this account the Chiefs only refer to what the Indian Agent has told them, and leaves a confused idea as to what is right.[73]

In most places the Indians were told that it was a matter over which the Agent had no jurisdiction.[74] Breynat and the RCMP were suggesting that "each Indian, being the head of a family, be allowed to kill ten beavers during the two next winters".[75] He sent a telegram to the Minister of the Interior which read:

I respectfully beg to strongly insist that a proviso be added to the Beaver close season Order-in-Council to allow Indians and half-breeds killing beavers this year while land fur still scarce. Such measure would prevent unnecessary hardships especially after the severe epidemic of last summer. Population of the North could not understand that no relieving action be taken after investigation made by Moran and Parker.[76]

The Government's affirmative response came in November, 1928, but not without its own conditions:

Treaty Indians, who are the heads of families, and Half-breeds leading the lives of Indians, who are the heads of families, to trap, in the Mackenzie District, but not in the Wood Buffalo Park, not more than ten beavers each, during the season 1928-1929, but not later than the 15th of May 1929, provided the pelts of the beaver so taken are surrendered to an officer of the Royal Canadian Mounted Police in the Mackenzie District .... The said police, when satisfied that the beaver were taken as above provided, be authorized to issue a supply order on a local trading establishment for the amount of $25 for each pelt so surrendered.[77]

In the middle of the trapping season, the amount to be paid for beaver pelts was changed. The Police could now pay $25 for large pelts only, $17 for medium and $12 for small. Both Cornwall and Breynat advised the Minister of the Interior that "repeated changes in rulings will further provoke residents and Indians". Cornwall could not restrain his exasperation:

[This is] the great weakness of the Northwest Territories Branch. I know of no Regulation that has not been changed at various times; that in itself is bad enough, but the interpretations that have been requested from the Department as to what their Regulations and rulings really mean are an interesting example of the inability of the Ottawa Officials in not being able not only to make a wise regulation, it also proves that they are unable to interpret them after they are enacted. Ninety per cent of the uneasiness has been caused by the various Orders-in-Council enacted to govern the Northwest Territories, and has caused a loss of confidence by the people that have been subjected to these rulings. They rarely, if ever, consult the people whom they are governing.. . . It is only when a crisis comes up that the Minister or his Deputy become interested, and then only long enough to tide-over the present difficulty.[78]

The Indians knew that a large beaver pelt was worth $40 on the market, but they would have been satisfied with an average price of $25. The Government's arbitrary ruling was unacceptable. There followed two years of agitation by Chief Squirrel, Headman Baptiste Beaulieu, Breynat and others, before the Department reverted to the previous regulation, and allowed beaver pelts to be "sold to a trader who is licensed to trade ... in the Northwest Territories".[79]

Northwest Territories Game Act, 1929

New regulations for the protection of game in the Northwest Territories became effective on July 1, 1929.[80] The new Game Act regulated the use of caribou and moose meat, the dates for closed seasons and muskrat shooting. The Thelon Game Sanctuary was established to protect musk-oxen. All of these regulations created unnecessary hardships for the Indians. Breynat sent three telegrams to Ottawa:

> TO D.C. SCOTT, DEPUTY SUPERINTENDENT
> OF INDIAN AFFAIRS,
>
> After carefully reading new Game Act I cannot but fully concur with Inspectors Parker's criticism of same and for humanity's sake you must insist that steps be immediately taken to bring necessary relief to our Indians whose preservation should appeal to the Government as much as the preservation of wild animals.

> TO O.S. FINNIE, DIRECTOR, N.W.T. BRANCH
> DEPARTMENT OF THE INTERIOR,
>
> Received copies of new Game Act and will have them distributed as requested down the river, but failing to understand why so many unnecessary new hardships are imposed upon Natives. I cannot see my way to recommend to them strictly complying with new regulations.

> TO THE HONORABLE C. STEWART
> MINISTER OF THE INTERIOR,
>
> Am sorry to have to inform you that instead of bringing relief anticipated after last year investigation, new Game Act causing great disappointment by provoking untolerable new hardships to Natives . . . I feel it is my duty to quiet our Natives and tell them that no human law can prevent them from honestly securing life necessities for themselves and families in their own country.[81]

During Treaty days in 1929, talks centred around trapping, hunting and Game Laws. Bourget reported on other trouble areas in his agency:

> The population [is] already suffocated with restrictions on ducks and geese, beavers, shorter seasons of trapping, impossibility to hunt rats at their own way, impossibility to use the shotguns when hundreds of them have nothing else . . . The closing of beavers, when the rest of the fur is so scarce, and food so hard to get during certain periods, and when according to all Indians beaver is increasing, were points of discussions for hours . . . .

> We had treaty [at Fort Rae] in good peaceful atmosphere, well disposed Indians, and if serious talks were made on restrictions it was understood that we would do our best efforts with the cooperation of our Department to have readjusted all that could be done. The same questions as at Resolution were treated, beavers, and rats forbidden to be shot with shotguns . . . Fur catch had been poor like it was all over, but a few rats in the Spring had saved their lives in purchasing power . . . .

> [At Hay River] complaints about beavers lasted for hours, even the duck shooting in the spring, and the season of ducks opening too late for the North was well treated . . . the new regulations about rats were also

the theme of long discussion. We explained that we had already taken this question with the Department and that they would be informed as soon as we heard any information.[82]

At Fort Providence the request was for some protection of their hunting and trapping rights:

> A fur preserve was asked by the Indians of that band, claiming that the White trappers may come in larger numbers in the near future if mining developments take place. They would like from Slave point on the lake extending along the north shore of the river McKenzie as far as point half way to Simpson called Head of the line, and extending half way to Rae inland. It may be worth considering. They are such a poor lot in this band that any help which can be given may have a great value.[83]

Bourget could be excused for the pessimism with which he concluded his report:

> The whole of the treaty at all posts left a spirit of lack of confidence from the Indians and the same motto was repeated to the Department agent viz: that the Government had promised to the Indians that they would hunt and trap forever, as long as the sun would shine and many more rhetoric flowers, but that in spite of all that, every year there was new regulations and restrictions, so much so that they were always anxious to know what would be the next one. At some posts it made it difficult for us to explain all these points to their satisfaction.[84]

Officials gave consideration to the grievances enumerated in this report and in Breynat's telegrams. Some amendments were made to the Game Act, but these did not correct all of the difficulties. In subsequent annual reports from Fort Good Hope, Fort Norman, Fort Resolution, and Fort Simpson, the Agents described the continuing dissatisfaction of the Indians with the multitude of regulations still restricting their freedom to hunt and trap.[85] Throughout the Fort Resolution Agency in 1930, the Indians showed great dissatisfaction with the way they were being treated by the Government: not only the closed season on beavers, but many other grievances were laid before the Indian Agent, Dr. Bourget. They complained that since 1923, more and more restrictions were announced each year at Treaty time. They listed the exclusion of many Indians and Half-breeds from the fur preserves, the buffalo park and the musk-ox sanctuary; the shortening of the trapping season; the closing of beavers and ducks; and the provincial fur taxes. Bourget could do little for them, except admit that they were right.[86](See Appendix XVI.)

Beaver Permits

The effect of the closed season on beaver was shown in figures submitted to the Territorial Council in 1930. In the year before the closed season, a total of 7,287 beavers had been taken in the Northwest Territories: 2,289 by non-Indians and 4,998 by Indians. During the first year of restricted trapping, only 3,091 beavers were taken, and these by Indians.[87] But concessions to the Indians were given grudgingly by the Territorial Government. Sentiments expressed at a Council meeting in December 1930, revealed the hard lines that were forming:

> Mr. Moran [Chief Inspector of N.W.T. Branch] pointed out that the Indian does not want to work and because of his laziness preferred setting his trap line down close to the white man's. Dr. Scott [Superintendent General of the Department of Indian Affairs] said that Indians had always been the same and the situation must be faced on that basis. Mr. Cory [Commissioner of N.W.T.] expressed the opinion that, Indians being wards of the nation, it would only be proper that the Government should accept the obligation of seeing that they were properly maintained in a manner that would not interfere with the livelihood of the white trappers. Mr. Parker [Inspector of Indian Agencies] said that the Indian Affairs Department could not see the natives starve, that they did issue rations but that in the opinion of the Indians themselves the rations were a miserable substitute for their natural food. He said that the Department wanted the Indians to live the life of Indians and that because of their nature they could not compete with the white trappers. He thought that a limit might be placed on the number of beaver which an Indian might be permitted to take, the limit being based on the fur resources of the territory. Mr. Cory [Commissioner of the N.W.T.] observed that if the policy recommended by Mr. Parker had been employed by the Government at the time the Western Provinces formed part of the Northwest Territories the white population of that area would be very small at the present time. He said that it would be difficult to justify setting aside one-third of Canadian territory for the exclusive benefit of the natives; also that the country seemed to be quite large enough for both Indians and whites provided proper close seasons were observed from time to time, particularly during low fur cycles.[88]

In 1931, the Government ordered that the closed season on beaver be extended to December 31, 1933. Indians and Metis would continue to have trapping permits, authorizing fifteen beavers per family.[89] This consideration shown to Indians was not popular with white trappers. Years later, Chick Ferguson still harboured strong feelings of resentment:

> If only the white trapper enjoyed equal privileges with the Indian and the half-breed. When we had left Providence in the fall, the beaver season was closed tight to everybody for a three-year period. But by midwinter certain groups had convinced Ottawa that the natives were in danger of starvation unless permitted to kill beaver. So a bizarre and discriminatory new ruling was made . . . This was the first step in what appears to have become a discriminatory campaign designed to eliminate white trappers from the Northwest Territories.[90]

When the Indians' permits were renewed, two traders from Fort Smith tried to organize a protest against the relief measures allowed Indians and Metis. F—— C———, trader-cum-trapper, called a meeting of white trappers, which did not have the results he expected:

> Mr. C——— was arranging matters for his own protection. Some of them accused him of having usurped a large area of country formerly occupied by natives and made the statement that he had tied up a district for his own use that would support ten Indian trappers. The number of traps set by Indian trappers will average about 60 to each trapper. Mr. F——— C——— has about 600 traps set in his District and employs a man under wages to assist him in trapping.
>
> Chief Abraham of the local band of Indians . . . complained of Mr. F——— C——— taking over some trap lines of Indians in his District and stated Mr. C——— had taken over a very large district by surrounding it with trap lines and claiming the sole right to trap not only the land fur but the beaver within the District surrounded by his trap lines.[91]

W. F. Cooke, fur trader and general merchant, organized the "Citizens of the Mackenzie River District" during the summer of 1931. Numbering approximately 100, they sent a petition to the Minister of the Interior, requesting that white trappers as well as Indians be allowed to trap beavers.[92] Harris, Indian Agent at Fort Good Hope, notified Ottawa that an affirmative response to the petition would be a mistake:

> If the beaver are opened for the whites in the country, they will soon be exterminated, as the other fur is being exterminated. . . . If the beaver season is closed for whites *sine die* these animals will furnish a source of revenue for the Indians for many years to come.[93]

Bishop Breynat attended the thirtieth session of the Northwest Territories Council on February 3, 1932. Among other issues which he discussed, the matter of beaver permits was brought to the attention of the members:

> Bishop Breynat expressed the opinion that the Regulations providing for the issue of permits to needy Indians and Half-breeds leading the lives of Indians were being administered too strictly by the Police Officers. He pointed out that an Indian family might not be in need today but would probably be next week and that if they were not permitted to take game when the opportunity offered they might suffer real hardship by being unable to secure beaver when they were in need and thereby in a position to qualify for a beaver permit.
>
> In answer to an enquiry Bishop Breynat said that there was no criticism as to the number of beaver that might be taken (15), simply that the Police officers refused to issue permits in all cases where he considered permits might reasonably be granted.
>
> Bishop Breynat pointed out that Indian territory had been gradually reduced and they had little left that they might now call their own. He said that under the present system an Indian was not encouraged to follow proper conservation methods in connection with his trapping because he knew that if he did not take all the game White trappers would and White trappers were better equipped than the Indians. White men trapped out an area and left, the Indian had to remain. Bishop Breynat suggested that

the beaver be left to the Indians exclusively and that this decision be gradually made known both to the White trappers and to the Indians themselves. Once the Indians knew they only would be permitted to take beaver then they would govern themselves accordingly in connection with their trapping.[94]

Game Preserve

One solution for the economic destitution of the Northern Indians was that the "whole of the North West Territories be set aside as a game preserve for the natives . . . ".[95] Indian Agent Harris supported this idea, and refuted possible arguments against this plan:

> The question of making a game preserve for natives, of the whole North-West Territories, was, so far as I know, first mooted by Hon. Frank Oliver, when Minister of the Interior, in conjunction with the late Inspector H. A. Conroy, and my opinion thereon was asked by the last named gentleman. I was then, as now, in favour of the plan. The principal argument used against this scheme was, as I remember, that it would therefore retard the mineral development of the country. I do not think this contention is of any value, as the real prospectors do not depend on the country for their food, but bring in their own supplies, and those who are prospecting on a shoe string, soon become trappers, and leave all other interests for the purpose of devoting all their energies to the taking of fur; this was particularly true when all fur was high priced.
>
> This proposal has my hearty approval, and I would respectfully further suggest that when a holder of a [Trapping] licence leaves the Territories, and allows his licence to expire for more than a year, that he be placed on the same footing as newcomers.[96]

Breynat paid a personal visit to the Commissioner of the Northwest Territories, urging him to restrict trapping to Indians, Half-breeds, and those whites holding permits.[97] Similar advice was given by Ralph Parsons of the Hudson's Bay Company[98] and by Duncan Scott, of Indian Affairs.[99] Both of these referred to the action taken by the Province of Quebec in 1932, designating the whole northern region of the Province as a game reserve. They recommended a similar action by the Government of the Northwest Territories. The Advisory Board on Wildlife Protection met on February 29, 1932,[100] and was told by an official of the Department of Indian Affairs that hunting and trapping "should be reserved for the natives". Breynat advised the Board not to license any more white trappers, citing their use of airplanes for trapping in remote areas as a serious abuse. By 1932 it was already too late to cancel the licences of those trappers who were well established in the North. Hudson's Bay Company reports indicate that five hundred and fifty-one licences had been issued that season to Non-Indians.[101]

In the fall of 1932, the Territorial Government surveyed the white population regarding the designation of the entire Northwest Territories as a game preserve.[102] The survey, along with endless discussions in sessions of the Territorial Council, proved to be no more than political posturing.

Provincial Game Laws: 1928-1939

When the Federal Government agreed to the "Transfer of the Natural Resources to the Provinces of Manitoba, Saskatchewan and Alberta" in 1929, specific conditions protecting the Indian population were stated:

> In order to secure to the Indians of the province the continuance of the supply of game and fish for their support and subsistence, Canada agrees that the laws respecting game in force in the province from time to time shall apply to the Indians within the boundaries thereof, provided, however, that the said Indians shall have the right, which the province hereby assures to them of hunting, trapping and fishing game and fish for food at all seasons of the year on all unoccupied Crown Lands and on any other lands to which the said Indians may have a right of access.[103]

The Indians at Fort Chipewyan, Alberta, and Fond du Lac, Saskatchewan, had already been subjected to regulations restricting beaver hunting in the Provinces.[104] In a telegram sent on November 15, 1928, Breynat urged the Superintendent General of Indian Affairs "to immediately obtain from Alberta Government a proviso in Beaver close season Ordinance, to allow Indians killing beavers this year in Northern Alberta, especially around Chipewyan".[105] He contacted the Minister of Agriculture of Alberta to inform him of the miserable conditions of the Indians in northern Alberta. He proposed that each Indian family be allowed to kill ten or twelve beavers during the closed season.[106] He argued that needy Indians of Alberta should have the same rights as the Indians in the Northwest Territories.[107] The Minister did not agree. He could not "discriminate" between Treaty Indians, Half-breeds, and white trappers. He suggested that "the Dominion Government . . . accept responsibility respecting rationing of the Indians who are in need".[108] Indian Agent Card reported to Ottawa in 1930 that there was great destitution in northern Alberta. The Indians were asking for limited rights to hunt and trap beaver during closed seasons.[109] At the request of the bands at Fort Chipewyan, Card went to Edmonton to ask the Alberta Game Commissioner to open a portion of the Buffalo Park for Indians to kill a limited number of beaver. He went to Regina with a similar request for the Saskatchewan Government from the Maurice Band of Fond du Lac.[110] Breynat made another appeal to the Minister of Agriculture, [111] and his notes inspired an article of the *Edmonton Journal* of February 11, 1931:

> At Fort Chipewyan, there exists the greatest hardships, no fur, no fish, caribou are far to the West . . . Muskrats are fairly abundant and these poor unfortunates would be happy if they could have them for food, but it is forbidden to kill rats before a given date (March 1st). It is true that the representative of the Mounted Police interpreting the law, at least this has

been said, has given to the Chief of the Crees the authorization to kill a sufficient number of rats to prevent his people from starving to death . . . . The Government of the N.W.T.. . . authorized the chief of each family to kill fifteen beaver . . . . The Government of Saskatchewan . . . has permitted a band of Caribou Eaters . . . to kill 800 beaver. Would it not appear as though the Government of Alberta in the spirit of humanity should show the same generosity?. . .

It is difficult to understand in effect how these Indians are permitted to suffer from hunger in the midst of thousands of buffalo.[112]

Although the Minister remained opposed to granting "privileges" to Indians and not to white men, who were suffering as much,[113] Alberta joined Saskatchewan in amending regulations to permit residents to take ten beavers in the spring of 1932.[114]

The Indians of Fort Chipewyan, through their Chief, Jonas Laviolette, had repeatedly asked for land to be reserved for hunting and trapping. In 1935, land was designated for their use, extending north to the boundary of the Northwest Territories, east to Saskatchewan, south to the 27th Base line and west to the Athabasca River and Wood Buffalo Park.[115] However, non-resident white trappers could still obtain licences[116] with the inevitable consequences of encroachment on Indian land. Jonas Laviolette appealed to Breynat on July 7, 1936:

We cannot do anything. White trappers steal our trapping grounds. They remove our traps. There is nobody to protect us, and we cannot protect ourselves on our own land against these invaders who become masters of our country. James Eylmer, a Lake Brochet trapper, went to Edmonton last spring, he stole my name and showed himself as the chief of this district. He attacked the Treaty Indians. Although the Indian Agent and Police know him, they let him do it . . . Also Raymond Shank attacked Frank Ladouceur and nearly drowned him . . . These foreign White trappers treat us badly, but we can in no way do anything to stop them . . . We desire to have a Game Preserve but we cannot obtain it . . . On our traplines, even very close to our houses, there are foreign White trappers. We cannot be our own boss even right close to our houses."[117]

Chrysostome Ogakiye, Councillor of the Chipewyan Band, echoed his Chief's words: "We would like to lead a peaceful life, but we just cannot have any peace".[118] The two leaders wrote again at Christmas:

Very Reverend and Beloved Bishop.
We wish to give you a few details of our troubles, in this place, and beg your Lordship to see if you could do something for our welfare with the Indian Department, because we see the hard times coming fast; I mean that people from outside, both whites and half-breeds from other places are not leaving us in peace to trap; even our trapping lines are not left alone to ourselves. The trapping lines that we set are not respected, although we worked hard to the trails before those strangers came, and we were on those trapping lines for 30 years and more before those men came

to the country. We are no longer masters of our own trapping lines. We are rather up against it and no one to help us, even the Police and the Indian Agent do not help us on this matter. It seems that we are not Masters of our own Land; Therefore, we would be very thankful to you, dear Bishop, if you could do something for us . . . These half-breeds trappers do not obey the laws of the Province and kill everything they can lay hands on. Let me tell you that they do far more harm than the Indian Department thinks. The white people who come to our hunting grounds are just as bad as the Half Breeds. If the Government does not stop them, we cannot after a certain time, make our own living. We should get a PRESERVE like Resolution, Fort Rae, and Peel River, to keep the strangers out of our own trapping grounds (South of the Lake of Athabasca, the Delta). We spoke about this for many years, and nothing was done.

We are in hope to see opened season for Beaver in Alberta . . . but we see that it is closed still. . . .

We wish also to state that the White people and Half-Breeds of other posts are not paying any attention to the laws of the Country and hunt Beavers during summer. If they are not stopped at once they will kill all the beavers in Alberta . . . .[119]

Breynat sent copies of the letter to the Federal Minister of Mines and Resources, to the Alberta Minister of Agriculture. He reminded them that the rights guaranteed to the Indians by their Treaty with the Crown, were binding on the Provinces as well as the Federal authorities.[120] He received assurance from the Alberta Game Commissioner that some of the difficulties would be eliminated when regulations were framed, which took into account both the protection of Indians and the conservation of game.[121] Breynat solicited assistance from territorial officials in his effort to persuade the Minister of the Interior to exert leadership with the Provinces:

Our Minister should write to the provinces and explain to them that when the Indians surrendered their lands they still counted on being able to hunt and trap for a living and that by the issue of so many Hunting and Trapping Licences the Provinces are depriving the Indians of a major feature of their livelihood.[122]

When Alberta and Saskatchewan imposed new trapping and hunting regulations on the Indians in the spring of 1937, Breynat sent this telegram to Ottawa:

Just returned from Arctic visiting all our missions. Noticing great scarcity of fur. Indian Chief Fond du Lac complaining that they have been asked to pay permit killing beavers. Under all kinds of unnecessary restrictions. Chief has refused to pay with majority of his men. I advised him to continue . . . .

At Chipewyan fourteen Indians have been tried and fined for feeding dogs with cariboo meat, without being given a chance of any assistance not even by the agent, while it is of public notice that white trappers are generally freely doing same without being molested. I again insist upon necessity of making thorough investigation on unnecessary and unfair hardships imposed on Indians by game regulations provincial and federal without consideration for promises made in name of Crown at treaty time . . . .[123]

No Federal intervention resulted.[124] Provinces could continue prosecuting Indians for violations of game laws. Serious abuses, which could not be disregarded, caused Breynat to write again to the Minister of Mines and Resources:

> May I respectfully voice my surprise that the Province of Saskatchewan regards as a privilege for the Indians to be allowed to trap or hunt beaver, on payment of a special fee of one dollar. This may be, and really is a privilege for the whites. But I do not think it could be one for the Indians who have been guaranteed the right of hunting and trapping as they always did, before the Treaty was signed. Indeed, this was one of the conditions under which they accepted to sign it. As I was told by the chief of the Chipewyan Band at Fond du Lac, "If we have to pay this fee for beaver, we may have to pay some other fee next year for some other fur and God knows when we will see the end of this". And the Chief refused to avail himself of this so-called privilege of paying the one dollar fee, and did not trap or hunt beaver last season.
>
> One thing we must always bear in mind. If the Indians have surrendered their right to land etc., they never consented to abandon their right to fish, hunt and trap.
>
> Therefore, I fully hope that there will be some way to have the Provincial regulations amended, and the rights of the Indians fully preserved as solemnly promised when the Treaty was signed.[125]

A transfer of official papers between the governments of Alberta and Canada preceded the establishment of Indian Reserve No. 201 in the delta area of the Athabasca River and Richardson Lake.

> On December 23, 1937, a certificate of title was passed from Alberta Provincial Crown to Federal Crown for the surface rights of the whole of Indian Reserve 201. There was apparently a problem with the respective mineral rights that was not cleared up until October 16, 1947. It was only after that date that the Federal Crown were in a position to declare the area to be a reserve, and . . . they did so by P.C. 1954-817 on June 3, 1954.[126]

This slow procedure had little practical benefit for the Chipewyan Band. On April 4, 1938, Chief Jonas Laviolette wrote to the Alberta Minister of Agriculture with several substantial grievances:

> I am taking the liberty of writing you, in regard to the game Regulations enforced this winter which puts us in an awkward position to make our living at this place [Fort Chipewyan, Alberta], and as Chief of the Chipewyan band, I have to make some complaints to you, and I hope you take steps to remedy the situation, that is to say, that the strangers from outside *(white trappers)* are taking all our best hunting grounds from us, and they do not allow the Indians to hunt near these, and this has been

going on since a good few years. The result is, a good many Chipewyans of my Band cannot find any place to trap rats; and how are we to live, all the place left for Chipewyan belonging to Jack Fish Lake, old Fort and Big Point is the delta, which is barren, no rats there, nothing but sand bars, and we cannot go anywhere also to trap rats.

I wish to mention also, that the present Game Guardian . . . is not fit for a game Guardian, is siding on white trappers only, and Indians never see him to talk to him, I presume that this Game Guardian and a few trappers (his favourites) are the ones that are making laws as they please.

And another thing is, if an Indian sets a few traps before the white trappers, those white trappers take the traps away (Indian traps) and set their own traps there. We cannot call that just, that which happens often; according to our Treaty, we are free to trap and fish and hunt anywhere.

I wish to mention also that the White trappers are taking Big ground and Big Lakes for their own trappings, while a poor old Indian has no chance to kill a few rats, and most of those white trappers are Russians, Germans and Swedes. I want *fair play* for my Band of Chipewyans and I hope the Government comes to our rescue.[127]

Breynat added a personal memo to the Minister:

The Indian people claim (and mind you I cannot say that their claims are without foundation) that they are not sufficiently protected against the competition of the white people as was provided by the Treaty. It seems that Officials of the Government have not the authority and have not the means to foster this protection due to the Indian people.[128]

Chief Laviolette's answer came from the Game Commissioner:

Your letter of April 4th, has been received and contents carefully noted . . . To my knowledge, ineligible [trappers] have been ordered out of the [Fort Chipewyan] area . . . If there has been any slackness in administering the regulations . . . I can assure you it will be rectified.[129]

The Federal Minister of Mines and Resources had received a copy of the letter, and assured the Chipewyans, "We are hoping that . . . additional large areas will be set aside in Northern Alberta exclusively for the Indians and half-breeds".[130] Breynat forwarded a copy of Chief Laviolette's letter to the Inspector of Indian Agencies in Calgary, with a practical suggestion:

This letter doesn't need any comments. It shows how little the Indians are protected against the encroachments of the White people even with the presence of an [Indian] Agent and the Police. It seems to be more and more necessary and urgent that an Indian Superintendent or an Indian Agencies Inspector be appointed to stimulate the Department's employees and to look after the interests of the Indians.[131]

Boycott at Fort Resolution, 1937

The multiplication of restrictions and regulations could only aggravate an already explosive situation. In 1936, the Game Branch of the Territorial Government issued another prohibition, making illegal the use of snares for trapping. Many Indians complained to Breynat that they had not been consulted, nor given any warning. He did not hesitate to convey their message to the Commissioner:

> I have just returned from the North; and it is my duty to call to your attention the new hardships unnecessarily imposed on our Indians by the new regulation prohibiting the use of snares for hunting fur-bearing animals. Such a restriction should apply only to the White trappers. A large number of Indians, poor widows especially, have no means of buying steel traps . . . .
>
> Whenever new demands are made for more restrictions to be imposed on the Indians, I would advise the Government to give to the one making such demands, a gun and nets and let him try and live Indian life on barren land for a few months. On his return, if he ever does return, he will have acquired enough personal experience to discuss the matter . . . .
>
> May I add that on being asked by the Indians for advice on the matter, I would not hesitate in telling them, if they have not enough steel traps, to ignore the regulation and continue trapping with snares as they have always done . . . .
>
> Rather than impose such severe and unnecessary regulations on our Indians who were promised protection by the Government when they signed the Treaty, it seems to me that the Department had better forbid the use of planes for trapping animals, and see to it that White trappers who hold a licence, be given a registered trapping line outside of which they should not be allowed to trap fur-bearing animals. This would be the most effective way, while protecting our Indians, to prevent the extinction of fur-bearing animals.
>
> Kindly consider the above suggestions as further evidence of my desire to co-operate whole heartedly with the Government in the interests of all in the far North and particularly of our Indians who have first rights of living in the country.[132]

Although the Police were instructed to administer the regulations with leniency,[133] there was no fundamental change in the Government's policy of applying game laws to Indians. The injustice of this continued to rankle. In the summer of 1937, the Indians at Fort Resolution refused to accept payment of Treaty money, as a protest against the treatment they were receiving from the Government. The Indian Agent who had replaced Dr. Bourget in 1935, was himself a medical doctor. Confronted by angry chiefs who declared they would not take Treaty until they saw the Governor General, the Agent could only send a telegram to Ottawa:

> Indians at Resolution are today refusing treaty on account of most of rations nor here yet. stop. They are waiting to see His Excellency the Governor General. stop. They pretend also too many restrictions have been brought in the last few years.[134]

The Chiefs, Samuel Simon, Alexis Beaulieu, Pascal Jean, Pierre Smith, and Susie (Joseph) Abel, sent their own telegram on June 26, 1937. "We are not taking treaty until we see a gov't official from Ottawa."[135] News of the confrontation soon reached the press. On June 28-29, headlines across the country announced the Indian boycott. The *Edmonton Bulletin* of June 29, 1937, capsulated the trouble in a few words:

> White Canadians pride themselves on having got along quite peacefully with the Indians. Most of the credit for that belongs to the forbearance of the Indians and the tact and firmness of the Mounted Police; not to the fairness or honesty of the deal we put over the unsuspecting red men. There isn't much in our treatment of the Indians that savors of justice or guarantees welfare and prosperity to the people we dispossessed.

Recognizing that he could do nothing at Fort Resolution, the Agent left for Fort Rae and Yellowknife River Camp. He met resistance at both places, from Indians who complained that the white prospectors and trappers were killing the caribou reserved for them:

> [At Yellowknife] we found the Chiefs in conference. We asked them about Treaty, and the answer was that they would not take it until Resolution had taken it, the Head man, Susie Abel, having been in Resolution at the time of the big conference . . . [After some discussions] they answered that they would take Treaty if [Fort] Rae would take it. We agreed to their suggestion and departed for Fort Rae at 4 P.M. . . . .
>
> [At Fort Rae] several questions were brought as to restrictions of hunting. I told them that the rules were for everyone, but when an Indian is in dire need of food, there was then no restriction, that ptarmigans, rats or ducks could be killed in order to prevent starvation. Another grief was that the Indians were not allowed to feed their dogs on cariboo meat. At this point, I left the floor to Constable Kirkwood who explained that this rule applied only where the fish was available. Finally we started paying [Treaty] . . . when I received a radiogram from Serg. Makinson that he had been appointed by Ottawa to take over treaty work and was waiting at Resolution for my arrival.[136]

Confused and angry, the Indians at Yellowknife accepted Treaty payment, although the chief stated later that "his people were tricked into taking it".[137]

Back at Fort Resolution, Sergeant Makinson was under orders from Ottawa "to make inquiry and report upon the complaints and grievances of the Indians". The Indians welcomed him to act as Indian Agent for the Treaty meeting, stating that "all they wanted was a square deal". They listed their complaints about game regulations: dates of open season for muskrat and fox, the quota on beavers, banning of .410 gauge shotguns for muskrat hunting, prohibition on shooting buffalo and other game even when suffering from starvation. To these they added grievances against the boarding school, medical care and the Agent himself. When the Agent arrived back at Fort Resolution, he found that the chiefs would not take Treaty if he were present. He appealed to Ottawa to send the Agency Inspector from Calgary to settle the dispute, but he was instructed: "Please absent yourself when payments are being made at Resolution and let Sergeant Makinson take full charge of payments". The Indians agreed to accept Treaty payment from Makinson under the condition that Ottawa would consider their complaints.

The Agent did not accompany the party to the other camps around Great Slave Lake. Makinson replaced him as Agent, and Dr. Morrow from Fort Smith performed the medical duties. At Hay River they heard more complaints about hunting regulations, and were asked:

> that the North boundary line [of the Wood Buffalo Park] be moved back towards the Caribou Mountains, to enable them to hunt without a permit in the area . . . The trouble appears to be that Indians who hold a permit to hunt in this area cannot obtain a permit for their sons who are eighteen years of age to hunt beaver in this district. The Indians claim that there are no buffalo in this area but that it is a good beaver country, mostly muskeg and small lakes.[138]

Breynat made his own investigation into the trouble. The priest at Fort Resolution, Father Julien Duchesne, OMI, gave him this account of the boycott:

> Starting by the reasons why such troubles happened, it seems to me that the Indians were quite justified in complaining about the way the Treaty has been interpreted till now. For a long, long time they have been complaining about the restrictions curtailing their freedom to hunt either for fur or for food. Moreover, they believed the assistance to destitute people to be very insufficient. Finally, and this seems to be the main reason of their unsatisfaction, rations and grocery issues, usually distributed at treaty time, have always arrived too late for the past few years. So the Indians cannot get these supplies unless they wait here living in miserable conditions, or they make a special trip from their hunting grounds to the village to fetch these supplies later on . . . It is also apparent that the Indians were indoctrinated and pushed to such actions by some troublemakers . . . Chief Alexis Beaulieu, when told that such ideas of insubordination and of revolt were not from the Indians themselves, but originated with some White people, did not deny it . . . Chief Samuel Simon told me the Indians now wanted for Indian Agent neither a French Canadian, nor a Catholic. They want an Agent who is English and Protestant or a Mason. Their reason for such a choice is that a French Canadian or a Catholic cannot obtain anything from the Government . . . .[139]

Returning from the bush at Christmas time, the Indians were surprised and angry to find that the Agent was still in office:

> There has been a lot of trouble since we had this Agent and we want him out as soon as possible and we would like you to either write or wire for us; we like to hear from you to that effect as we chiefs do not want him

here at all we want another Agent right this winter. We won't have nothing to do with him and will not see him and all we want is a new Agent at once.

Since we left this Agent he has been throwing men in jail even though they didn't have it coming. If he is still here at Treaty time we will not take treaty furthermore.[140]

Appealing to Sergeant Makinson, the Indians wrote:

Last summer when you came down here at treaty you told us you came to fix our troubles between us and our Agent you told us also that he was fired or going soon this was never so as he is still here. Now we also didn't get no reply from Ottawa as you told us we would, now you also told us you were sending out what we said and you would send us the reply and that was never so as far as we could see. We Chiefs have quit that man last year and he could stay for Centurys but we'll never see him. We are writing you now cause you told us if there was anything we wanted to write or know to notify you. We would like you to give us a reply to this effect.[141]

The water transportation season being over, Ottawa did not take action on the Indians' request for a new agent, until the summer of 1938, when Dr. Riopel was sent to replace the Agent.

Too Little, Too Late

It is a matter of record that the Territorial Council was preoccupied over the years with the formulation and enforcement of game laws and regulations. Indian Agents had difficulty in explaining these to the Indians, who did not understand why laws should apply when people were hungry:

The question of killing game for food came up as there were two Indians accused of killing a few rats out of season, and the RCMP claimed that the Indians should have killed other animals, if in dire need of food, as rats are protected under Section 2 of the N.W.T. Game Regulations. The Chiefs claim that when Treaty was signed there were no laws against killing anything at any time for food, and they asked that this Section 2 of the Game Regulations be revised, because they never kill unless they are in need of food, and never for nothing, as they are always short of ammunitions.[142]

Mining activity in the gold fields of Yellowknife created additional problems for the Indians of Fort Rae and Yellowknife. Prospectors were overrunning the Indian Game Preserve, trapping and shooting game. The mining itself did not seem to bother the Indians, but it was the abuse of their game preserve that they protested. They saw white prospectors, trappers and traders getting rich on their land, and when they complained about not being able to obtain employment at the mines, they were told they were "better away from the mining centres, as only skilled men are employed".[143]

The single greatest threat to the survival of the Indian people was the nearly unregulated activity of white trappers. The Governor General of Canada, Lord Tweedsmuir, visited the Mackenzie District in 1937, and returned with this warning:

It is extremely important both for the sake of the native population and of the future prosperity of Canada that the fur bearing animals should be wisely protected. This means that the white trappers should be strictly limited in number . . . .[144]

Neither their numbers nor their activity were seriously limited in the years between 1929 and 1938. In fact, some white trappers increased their devastating efficiency by using airplanes on their traplines. The Northern Traders Co. recognized the danger in this practice:

It is considered that a trapper who uses an aeroplane visiting his trap lines, is at a decided advantage over an Indian, and is against the best interests of the Indians . . . A trapper using an aeroplane is enabled to clean out very large areas of fur in one season, and is also able to confine his trapping only to the areas where fur is most plentiful, for the time being.

The Northern fur country is primarily a Natives' country, and the Indians can never be expected to compete against an aeroplane trapper. The continued use of aeroplanes for visiting trap lines will result in the Indian population soon being thrown upon the Government for their livelihood.[145]

Breynat, who became known as the "flying Bishop", brought the matter to the attention of the Territorial and Federal Governments, but without apparent success:

A number of white trappers fly into the Northwest Territories from Fond du Lac, Goldfields and Chipewyan . . . they trap the source of supply for the Indians who are trapping south and west of them and who are not sufficiently well off to use a plane. In this way the source of supply is being depleted and the trapping south of this area is getting poorer and poorer. When this area is once trapped out the Indians will be unable to obtain a living and will become charges of the government. The only suggestion to protect these trapping grounds would be to make the area south of the Thelon Game Sanctuary a game preserve.[146]

Honorable T.A. Crerar assured us at the meeting which we had in his office . . . "Bishop, you may rest assured that . . . with regard to the protection of the Indians themselves, we are going to take action immediately" . . . Trusting that I could take the promise of the Honorable Minister as definite, I thought it my duty, in order to quieten the Indians I would meet, to tell them about the action the Government was going to take immediately in their favour according to the treaty stipulations.

Now, if in contradiction with the promise made by the Hon. Minister, . . . the final decision of the Department is not to take immediate action, not even contemplate any change, I would appreciate it very much if you would kindly advise me about the proper way to safeguard the prestige of the Hon. Minister and of the Government and my own when, meeting again the Indians, I will have to tell them they cannot any more expect to see any change made in the regulations.[147]

Breynat was protesting legislation which had been passed in February, 1937. It was a half measure which made a farce of restricting the "aeroplane trapper":

> Whereas . . . trappers are using aeroplanes for the purpose of extending their trapping operations and, as a consequence, the game supply upon which the natives depend for their livelihood is in danger of being depleted . . . .
>
> Therefore . . . aircraft shall not be used in trapping operations except as means of transportation between the settlement where a trapper is outfitted and his principal base camp . . . .[148]

Philip Godsell and Ralph Parsons brought their experience and knowledge into the fight against airplane trapping. In their years with the Hudson's Bay Company they had learned the effects of trapping competition on the conservation of wild-life. Godsell blamed the airplane as a factor in the collapse of the fur trade:

> Many trappers now use aeroplanes to penetrate into the very heart of what were once the great natural fur preserves of the Dominion where they are free to pursue their activities unhindered and unseen . . . In . . . large areas as far north as the Mackenzie River region which once supported considerable numbers of Indians, the fur-bearing animals have become almost non-existent and the Natives whom I once knew as propserous trappers have become spineless indigents dependent upon Government relief."[149]

The Territorial Council had difficulty coming to grips with the problem.[150] Financial and commercial considerations would have to be weighed before more rigid control of airplane trapping could be enforced. It was just such a consideration which proved to be the decisive factor in hastening legislation. When it was learned that some trappers were bringing out furs as personnal baggage, "and not paying fur export tax," the Territorial Administration was disturbed.[151] On May 3, 1938, the Mackenzie Mountain Preserve was established, covering 69,440 square miles between the Mackenzie River and the Rocky Mountains.[152] Legislation, applicable to this one preserve only, was explained by an Order-in-Council:

> The use of aeroplanes by trappers has contributed to the rapid depletion of the wild-life . . . and it is necessary in the interests of conservation of the wild-life to restrict the use of aircraft . . . when used in connection with hunting and trapping operations . . . The holder of a licence issued under Section 39 (1) shall not use aircraft as a means of transportation to or from or within the Mackenzie Mountain Preserve in connection with hunting and trapping operations.[153]

It was apparent to the Indian people that this limited protection was not enough to save a ruined economy. At Aklavik they asked that the Peel River Preserve be enlarged to include part of the delta south of Aklavik where muskrat trapping was thriving. The Indians were not given the benefit of such an advantage.[154] Neither could the Indians at Hay River expect much consideration in their efforts to have the Department oppose the large fishing industries planned for Great Slave Lake. Indian Agent Riopel reported to Ottawa in August, 1939:

> If the white man keeps on fishing, hunting, trapping in the Northwest Territories there will be nothing left for the Indians to live on. On these points I tried to reassure them that the Department would not permit anything detrimental to the Indians, being careful not to promise anything.[155]

Godsell, Parsons, and Breynat kept up a vigorous press campaign during these years of 1937-1939. Godsell wrote for the *Winnipeg Free Press* and the *Port Arthur News*, making the point that the Government had broken faith with the Indian. He catalogued the injustices that had been done to the Indian, describing vividly for his readers the abject state in which the Indian found himself.[156] Parsons published a plan by which the Hudson's Bay Company would relieve the economic difficulty of the Indians.[157] Breynat contacted newspapermen in Montreal, Toronto, and Edmonton, hoping "to create in the whole country such a favourable opinion of the Indians as to compel the government to vote the necessary subsidies to start the reforms". While eastern Canadians were reading "Canada's Blackest Blot", the *Edmonton Bulletin* featured a series of seven articles on Northern natives, written by Harper Prowse from Breynat's documents. The thrust of this series was to publicize the unwritten clauses of the Treaty which had been relegated to oblivion by the Government.[158] Godsell wrote to Breynat in February 1938, expressing hope and encouragement in their common endeavour:

> The Government is awakening at last to the plight of the Indians. . . I've been pounding away since 1930 through various magazines and newspapers, etc. with a view of forcing some action which might eventually lead to the betterment of conditions surrounding the half-breed and Indian population of the North.
>
> As far back as 1930 I sounded a warning, pointing out that if some drastic action was not quickly taken by the Government it would not be long ere a large number of self-supporting and self-respecting natives would be transformed into impoverished and dispirited recipients of Government support . . . A situation which as you know, has largely come to pass . . . To my mind the Indian is a far more important factor in the scheme of things than is the beaver . . . .
>
> Unorganized as they are, the Indians, at this critical period, need, it seems to me, a spokesman prepared to present their problems in an intelligent, sympathetic manner to those sources from which help would have to come.[159]

In March, Breynat learned that the Indian Affairs Branch was "engaged in an intensive study of the problems confronting the hunting and trapping Indians throughout the Dominion".[160] In April, the Territorial Council took a hard look at some disturbing economic facts:

> Returns show a marked decrease in the number of fur bearing animals taken in the Northwest Territories and . . . suggestions had been received from departmental officials, missionaries and others, that further limitations be placed upon the issue of trapping licences to white men . . . .
>
> Owing to the fact that the native population was dependent upon the fur resources for their livelihood, the time had arrived when definite action would require to be taken to further safeguard these resources . . . Government expenditures under such headings as Hospitalization and Destitution, had increased substantially in the last few years. This was attributable mainly to reduction of wild life upon which the natives are dependent . . . .[161]

Finally, on May 3, 1938, legislation was passed which would somehow regulate the activity of white trappers in the Northwest Territories:

> On account of the shortage of wild life for the sustenance of the Native population, ...
>
> Now, therefore, . . . hunting and trapping licences under the Northwest Game Regulations shall be issued only to the following: –
>
> 1. Residents of the Northwest Territories as defined by these regulations who at the present time hold hunting and trapping licences and who continue to reside in the Northwest Territories.
> 2. The children of those who have had their domicile in the Northwest Territories for the past four years provided such children continue to reside in the Northwest Territories.[162]

Records show that 366 white, Metis, and Non-Treaty Indians were eligible for licences under the new law.[163] The majority of these were Metis, since most white trappers had already turned from the fading fur trade to the booming mining industry. In 1938-1939, the value of gold mined in the Northwest Territories exceeded for the first time the total value of raw furs traded. Left as they were to suffer the consequences of others' mistakes, the Indians benefited very little from the new legislation. In 1939, the total income for the 3,724 Indians of the Northwest Territories was $301,488. Of this amount, $248,260, was derived from trapping and hunting, while $53,228 came from other sources, including annuities, wages, fishing, and farming.[164] Their privileged position, so bitterly contested and grudgingly granted, proved to be a hollow triumph. Their empty hunting grounds were no longer attractive. Governments and business could now shift to the rapidly growing mining industry, knowing they had successfully exploited the fur industry while it lasted. Whatever profit was left, they could afford to leave for the Indian.

Summary

The years between 1928-1939 saw no more advance in the well-being of the Indians of the Northwest Territories than had the two previous decades. Problems whose origins were in the first contacts between primitive and civilized men, became aggravated with time, developing into complicated political, economic, and social issues. In 1937 the Indians focused attention on the issue which was of greatest concern to them: their hunting, trapping, and fishing rights. The Boycott of 1937, futile as it seems in retrospect, was not without serious political, economic, and sociological significance. The Government was forced to acquiesce to the immediate demands of the Indians at Fort Resolution, while being sufficiently shaken to review the abuses to the game resources which prevailed throughout the Territories. The consciousness of power, albeit fragile and evanescent, was experienced collectively, serving to awaken the pride of race which many had believed to be dead. By 1939 irreparable damage had been done to the native people. It had been shown that legislation aggravated rather than alleviated their misery. The Boycott showed that the future depended on the collective will and determination of the Indian people to find solutions and to bring about change. To which extent present day events have been influenced by those of the 1930's is a matter for speculation.

Notes to Chapter VI

1. *Edmonton Journal,* 29 June 1927.
2. RCMAFS, file: Tuberculose 1910-1946.
3. P.H. Godsell, *Arctic Trader,* New York, G.P. Putnam's Sons, 1934, pp. 304-305.
4. Jean W. Godsell, *I was no Lady,* Toronto, Ryerson Press, 1959, pp. 189-190.
5. IANDO, file 191/28-3, Vol. 1, Bourget to the Assistant Deputy and Secretary of Indian Affairs, 24 September 1928.
6. C. Bourget, *Douze Ans chez les Sauvages,* Sainte Anne de Beaupré, P.Q., 1938, pp. 98-99.
7. PAC, RG85, Accession 64/128, file 6327.
8. IANDO, file 779/28-3, Vol. 2, Report of Annuity Payments, 16 July 1928.
9. *Edmonton Journal,* 7 August 1934.
10. Canada, Indian Affairs, Report 1932-33, p. 14; 1933-34, p. 11; 1935-36, pp. 9, 63.
11. PAC, RG85, Accession 64/128, file 6327, Report of Parker to Scott, 1928.
12. RCMAFS, file: Tuberculose 1910-1946, Harold McGill to all Indian Agents, 14 January 1937.
13. *Ibid.,* Circular No. 706-826 of E.L. Stone to the Indian Agent, 20 January 1939.
14. Author's file, Yellowknife, Bourget to the author, 23 May 1972.
15. PAC, RG85, Vol. 267, file 1003-2-1, M.J. Thomson to J. Lorne Turner, Director NWT. & Yukon Branch, 15 November 1936.
16. *Edmonton Journal,* 30 August 1939.
17. PAC, RG85, Accession 64/128,

file 470.

18. PAC, RG85, Vol. 792, file 6281.

19. PAC, RG85, Accession 64/128, file 6281, Report of J.F. Moran regarding an investigation of conditions in the Mackenzie District of the NWT, 1928.

20. *Ibid.,* file 6327, Report of Parker to Scott, 1928.

21. NWT, Territorial Council, *Minutes of sessions,* 21st. session, 10 December 1930, pp. 141-145.

22. *Winnipeg Tribune,* 14 March 1936; *Ottawa Journal,* 14 March 1936.

23. PAC, RG85, file 1003-2-1, McKeand to Gibson, Deputy Commissioner, 26 February 1937.

24. *Ibid.,* Gibson to McKeand, 1 March 1937.

25. RCMAFS, file: Conditions des Indiens, Parsons to Breynat, 3 March 1937.

26. *Ibid.,* Breynat to Crerar, Minister of Mines & Resources; to Lapointe, Minister of Justice; to McKinnon, MP. for Edmonton West, 4 March 1937.

27. *Ibid.,* file: Cornwall, Cornwall to Breynat, 30 April 1937.

28. *Ibid.,* file: Conditions des Indiens, Cornwall to Breynat, 31 May 1937.

29. *Ibid.,* Parsons to Canadian Press, 22 November 1937.

30. PAC, RG85, Accession 64/128, file 6327, Report of Parker to Scott, 1928.

31. PAC, RG10, BS, file 600,264, Scott to Stewart, 26 January 1929.

32. IANDO, 191/28-3, Vol. 1, Reports of Indian Agents, 1928, 1929, 1930. PAC, RG10, BS, file 600,264.

33. PAC, RG10, BS, file 600,264, Bourget to Assistant Deputy and Secretary of Indian Affairs, 18 February 1929.

34. IANDO, file 191/28-3, Vol. 1, Report of Annuity Payments, 23 September 1930.

35. *Ibid.,* 23 July 1931.

36. RCMAFS, file: Metis, Breynat to Scott, 4 March 1929.

37. IANDO, file 779/28-3, Vol. 2, Report of Annuity Payments, 15 July 1930.

39. PAC, RG10, BS, file 567,205, P.W. Head to A.F. MacKenzie, Secretary of Indian Affairs, 10 July 1936.

39. IANDO, file 191/28-3, Report of Annuity Payments, 28 July 1938.

40. PAC, RG10, BS, file 567,205, Christianson to McGill, 18 August 1936; A.F. MacKenzie to Amyot, Truesdell, and Head, 15 September 1936.

41. *Ibid.,* C.W. Jackson to R.A. Hoey, 12 August 1943.

42. Canada, *Sessional Papers,* 1925, No. 14, p. 9.

43. Canada, *Privy Council,* OC No. 533, 12 March 1920.

44. *Ibid.,* OC No. 1146, 19 July 1926.

45. *Ibid.,* OC No. 709, 31 August 1927.

46. PAC, RG85, Accession 64/128, file 6417, Report of Finnie.

47. NWT, Territorial Council, *Minutes of Sessions,* 11 December 1929, p. 71.

48. *Edmonton Journal,* 24 October 1936.

49. PAC, RG85, file 1003-2-1, Memo of Breynat re the Physical & Economic Conditions of the North West Territory Indians, November 1936.

50. RCMAFS, file: Conditions des Indiens.

51. PAC, RG85, file 1003-2-1, Parsons to Crerar, 7 January 1937.

52. *Ottawa Journal,* 22 December 1936.

53. RCMAFS, file: Conditions des Indiens, Cornwall to Breynat, 22 January 1937.

54. *Ibid.*

55. PAC, RG85, file 1003-2-1, Gibson to Turner, 27 November 1936.

56. *Ibid.,* Gibson to McKeand, 19 January 1937.

57. *Ibid.,* Precis for the NWT Council, 29 December 1936.

58. *Edmonton Bulletin,* 25 January 1937.

59. RCMAFS, file: Indiens-Traités, MacKinnon to Crerar, 17 Septem-

ber 1937.

60. Duplicates of these Affidavits are kept at RCMAFS, file: Indiens-Traités.

61. RCMAFS, file: Indianescom, Minutes of the meeting held on 24 & 25 November 1937.

62. *Toronto Star,* 25 November 1937; *Ottawa Citizen,* 24 November 1937; *Ottawa Journal,* 27 November 1937.

63. RCMAFS, file: Indianescom, Minutes of meeting, 12 October 1939.

64. *Ibid.,* Breynat to Bishop J. Guy, 1 May 1940.

65. NWT, Territorial Council, *Minutes of Sessions,* pp. 1362-1363.

66. Canada, *Privy Council,* OC No. 277, 20 February 1928.

67. RCMAFS, file: Cornwall, memo of Cornwall re mail & Beavers, 5 January 1929.

68. PAC, RG85, Accession 64/128, file 7208, Finnie to Cory, 23 January 1928.

69. RCMAFS, file: Milton Martin 1927, Breynat to Martin, 14 May 1927.

70. Canada, Commons, *Debates,* 12 June 1929, p. 3640.

71. PAC, RG85, file 1010-7, Vol. la, Memorandum of Finnie, 1 October 1928.

72. RCMAFS, file: Chasse-Pêche 1928-1947, Breynat to Card, 2 May 1928; Card to Breynat, 1 June 1928.

73. PAC, RG85, Accession 64/128, file 6276, Memo of Richards to Finnie, 8 November 1928.

74. IANDO, file 779/28-3, Vol. 2, Report of Annuity Payments, 16 July 1928.

75. RCMAFS, file: Chasse-Pêche 1928-1947; Breynat to Card, 2 May 1928.

76. *Ibid.,* telegram Breynat to Stewart, 15 November 1928.

77. Canada, *Privy Council,* OC No. 2146, 28 November 1928.

78. RCMAFS, file: Cornwall, Cornwall to Breynat, 1 February 1929.

79. Canada, *Privy Council,* OC No. 1461, 24 June 1931.

80. *Ibid.,* OC No. 807, 15 May 1929.

81. RCMAFS, file: Chasse-Pêche 1928-1947, Telegrams of Breynat to Scott, to Finnie, and to Stewart, 3 July 1929.

82. IANDO, file 191/28-3, Vol. 1, Report of Annuity Payments, 9 September 1929.

83. *Ibid.*

84. *Ibid.*

85. *Ibid.* Reports of Annuity Payments.

86. *Ibid.* Report of Annuity Payments, 23 September 1930.

87. NWT, Territorial Council, *Minutes of Sessions,* 21st. Session, 10 December 1930, p. 149.

88. *Ibid.*

89. Canada, *Privy Council,* OC No. 1461, 24 June 1931.

90. C. Ferguson, *Mink, Mary and Me,* New York, M.S. Mill Co., 1946, p. 70.

91. PAC, RG85, Accession 64/128, file 7333, McDougal to Finnie, 13 February 1931.

92. *Ibid.,* file 7208, Finnie to Rowatt, 31 August 1931.

93. *Ibid.,* Harris to Scott, 3 October 1931.

94. NWT, Territorial Council, *Minutes of Sessions,* 3 February 1932, pp. 237-238.

95. *Ibid.,* 14 March 1932, p. 247.

96. PAC, RG85, Accession 64/128, file 7332, Harris to Williams, Acting Deputy Superintendent of Indian Affairs, 6 June 1932.

97. *Ibid.,* Rowatt to Hume, 10 February 1932.

98. *Ibid.,* Parsons to Rowatt, 25 February 1932.

99. *Ibid.,* Scott to Rowatt, 16 February 1932.

100. *Ibid.,* file 7333, Extract from the minutes of the meeting of the Advisory Board on Wild Life Protection held on 29th. February 1932.

101. RCMAFS, file: Conditions des Indiens, Parsons to Breynat, 10 March 1937.

102. PAC, RG85, Accession 64/128, file 7332, Richards to Hume, 22 September 1932.

103. *Revised Statutes of Canada 1970.*

Schedule No. 25, para. 12, Ottawa, Queen's Printer, 1970, pp. 380, 381.

104. IANDO, file 779/28-3, Vol. 2, Report of Annuity Payments, 16 July 1928.

105. RCMAFS, file: Chasse-Pêche 1928-1947, telegram of Breynat to Scott, 15 November 1928.

106. *Ibid.,* file: Milton Martin 1928, Breynat to Martin 18 November 1928; Martin to Hoadley 22 December 1928.

107. *Ibid.,* file: Chasse-Pêche 1928-1947, telegram Breynat to Hoadley, 13 December 1928.

108. *Ibid.,* file: Game, Ben J. Lawton to Breynat, 28 December 1928.

109. IANDO, file 779/28-3, Vol. 2, Card to Secretary of Indian Affairs, 26 August 1930; Report of Annuity Payments, 15 July 1930.

110. *Ibid.,* Report of Agent Card, 31 December 1930.

111. RCMAFS, file: Milton Martin, Martin to Hoadley, 9 February 1931.

112. *Ibid.,* file: Milton Martin 1927, Breynat to Martin, February 1931; *Edmonton Journal,* 11 February 1931.

113. *Ibid.,* file: Milton Martin, Martin to Breynat, 10 February 1931.

114. PAC, RG85, Vol. 832, file 7333, Chairman of Dominion Lands Board to Rowatt, 10 March 1932.

115. Alberta, Executive Council, OC No. 298, 6 March 1935.

116. NWT, Department of Industry & Development, Game Branch Archives, *Hunting, Trapping, and Trading Posts Licences 1924-1954.*

117. RCMAFS, file: Conditions des Indiens, Laviolette to Breynat, 17 July 1936.

118. *Ibid.*

119. *Ibid.,* Laviolette and Chrysostome Ogakiye to Breynat, 25 December 1936.

120. *Ibid.,* Breynat to Crerar, 1 January 1937; to Minister of Agriculture of Alberta, 11 January 1937.

121. PAC, RG85, file 1003-2-1, J.A. Hutchison to Breynat, 29 January 1937.

122. *Ibid.,* Gibson to McKeand, 11 February 1937.

123. *Ibid.,* telegram Breynat to Crerar, 5 April 1937.

124. *Ibid.,* Gibson to McGill, 8 April 1937.

125. RCMAFS, file: Chasse-Pêche 1928-1947, Breynat to Crerar, 28 September 1937.

126. IANDEd. file 701/1-21-10, W.H. Thrall to the author, 28 November 1972.

127. RCMAFS, file: Mission de Chipewyan-Histoire, Laviolette to Minister of Agriculture of Alberta, 4 April 1938.

128. *Ibid.,* Breynat to Minister of Agriculture of Alberta, 13 April 1938.

129. *Ibid.,* W.H. Wallace to Laviolette, 26 April 1938.

130. *Ibid.,* file: Fort Chipewyan Mission-Historique, C.W. Jackson to Breynat, 14 May 1938.

131. *Ibid.,* Breynat to P. Schmidt, 13 April 1938.

132. *Ibid.,* file: Chasse-Pêche 1928-1947, Breynat to Commissioner of NWT, 4 November 1936.

133. *Ibid.,* Gibson to Breynat, 23 November 1936.

134. IANDO, file 191/28-3, Vol. 3, telegram Indian Agent to McGill, 25 June 1937.

135. *Ibid.,* Chiefs Samuel Simon, Alex Beaulieu, Pascal Petit Jean, Pierre Smith, and Susi Abel to Department of Indian Affairs, 26 June 1937.

136. *Ibid.,* Indian Agent to Secretary of Indian Affairs Branch, 20 July 1937.

137. *Ibid.,* Report of Sergeant Makinson, 9 July 1937.

138. *Ibid.,* 11 August 1937.

139. RCMA, Fort Resolution, J. Duchesne OMI. to Breynat, 9 September 1937.

140. IANDO, file 191/28-3, Vol. 3, Chiefs Pierre Freeze, Alexis Jean Marie, Pascal Petit Jean, and Samuel Simon to Meikle, 26 December 1937.

141. *Ibid.,* Report of Makinson, 7

January 1938.

142. IANDO, file 191/28-3, Report of Annuity Payments, 8 August 1939.

143. *Ibid.,* Report of Annuity Payments, 23 August 1938.

144. *Edmonton Bulletin,* 31 December 1937, quoted by Parsons.

145. RCMAFS, file: Chasse-Pêche 1928-1947, Memorandum of Sawle, no date.

146. PAC, RG85, file 1010-7, Vol. la, Notes on interview of Breynat with Gibson, 12 February 1937.

147. RCMAFS, file: Chasse-Pêche 1928-1947, Breynat to Gibson, 18 April 1937.

148. Canada, *Privy Council,* OC No. 304, 15 February 1937.

149. *Saturday Night,* 12 December 1936.

150. NWT, Territorial Council, *Minutes,* 71st., 72nd., 73rd. sessions.

151. *Ibid.,* 8 November 1937, p. 988.

152. Canada, *Privy Council,* OC No. 976, 3 May 1938.

153. *Ibid.,* OC No. 2470, 4 October 1938.

154. IANDO, file 191/28-3, Report of Annuity Payments, 28 July 1938.

155. *Ibid.,* 8 August 1939.

156. *Port Arthur News,* 28 December 1937, *Winnipeg Free Press,* 29 December 1937.

157. RCMAFS, file: Conditions des Indiens, Parsons to Breynat, 31 December 1937; undated newspaper clippings.

158. *Ibid.,* Breynat to Parsons, 24 March 1938.

159. *Ibid.,* Godsell to Breynat, 16 February 1938.

160. *Ibid.,* Camsell to Breynat, 15 March 1938.

161. NWT, Territorial Council, *Minutes of Sessions,* 8 April 1938, p. 1321.

162. Canada, *Privy Council,* OC No. 977, 3 May 1938.

163. NWT, Department of Industry & Development, Game Branch, List of persons who held hunting & trapping licences under the Northwest Game regulations on the 3rd. May 1938.

164. Canada, Indian Affairs, *Report,* 1940-1941, p. 184.

Conclusion

Stepping out of the past for the brief duration of this history, men associated personally with the Treaties have told their stories. Jonas Laviolette, Susie Joseph Abel, Monfwi, and Yendo may not become household words, but future generations of Indians in the Northwest Territories and in Northern Alberta will know from their testimonies what happened in the Athabasca-Mackenzie District during those few months in 1899, 1900, and 1921. By listening to them and to others who were there, contemporary Indians and non-Indians, far removed, either by time or space, will have the essential information needed to form their personal opinions of the Treaties.

Throughout the narration, certain themes reoccur, embodying the fundamental significance of the two Treaties. These have been well explained in the text, and a brief glance back will suffice to identify them.

First, it was discovery and development which prompted the Government to make Treaty. In one instance it was gold; in the other oil. After news of potential wealth was spread abroad, rapid growth of transportation and communication systems followed, bringing settlers and exploiters into Indian territory.

Second, the Government, rooted in British legalism, was prompted to recognize the original occupants of the land, by entering into agreements with them, to insure that they would not impede progress, and to compensate them for their inconvenience.

Third, whatever the Government intended to do, cession of land, extinguishing of title or monetary settlement of aboriginal rights, was not explained to the chiefs who signed the Treaty. The Indians accepted the Treaty without understanding all of its terms and implications.

Fourth, the Indians were primarily concerned about preserving their traditional way of life, and protecting their freedom to hunt, trap and fish. They agreed to the Treaty only when they were satisfied that these would remain unchanged.

The prosperity and prestige of Canada in the North was gained at

306

the expense of the Indian people. Their chiefs were summoned from anonymity for a brief moment of political involvement and importance, only to be relegated to oblivion after their usefulness was over. They were used, as were others, to give the semblance of substance to a symbolic gesture. On March 12, 1875, in the House of Commons, Sir John A. Macdonald said, "The Dominion had purchased the whole of the North-West, and it belonged to Canada . . . ." Treaties and those who signed them, were not changing the reality of Canada's dominion over all its territory; they were simply submitting to the inevitable. The subtleties of sovereignty traditionally based on settlement, exploration, or conquest, were lost on a Government which claimed the land by right of purchase from the Hudson's Bay Company.

This mentality contrasted sharply with the concept of land prevailing in the Indian culture. The Indian did not see himself as owner of land, nor as empowered to bestow ownership on another. He considered that the land and its animals, the water and its fishes, were for his use. He would never refuse to share them, compelled by conviction to do so. Nor did he consider that the act of sharing deprived him of his own right to freely use the land as he had previously done. This attitude was rooted in experience and culture, his only basis for understanding the Treaty.

The restrictions imposed on him by game laws were incomprehensible to the Indian. He understood that some were necessary for the protection of wild-life, but he believed that they should be strictly applied to the ones wasting the resources, not to the Indian who depended on hunting for his existence. Instead of protecting the Indian's freedom to hunt, trap and fish, the Government first allowed it to be eroded, and then restricted. This was the cause of immeasurable physical suffering, and a rapid deterioration of the Indian's economic structure. Failure to honour this Treaty obligation was a serious breach of trust on the part of the Canadian Government.

The problems arising from Treaties 8 and 11 were not resolved by 1939, nor have they been to date. Basic differences still separate the thinking of the two parties and always will unless the Indians are induced to substitute other values for their traditional ones. As long as they remain faithful to their culture, there is little common ground with Government for settlement of the basic issues at stake in the Treaty dispute. Priorities for one do not coincide with the priorities of the other. But these two widely divergent world views must find some manner of compromise and coexistence to insure protection for the traditional rights of Indian people.

The threat of physical extinction no longer hangs over the race as it did in the years following the Treaties. Today, Indian leaders must oppose cultural extinction, using all the information and support available to them. The future of Indian participation in the North will depend on knowledge of past commitments made to the Indians, and on success in exacting present fulfillments. This history was undertaken in the hope that it would serve these two purposes to some small degree. The author makes no pretense at a scholarly or definitive study of the Treaties and the times. This is a sincere effort to make available the basic information required to understand the Indian position in filing a caveat against the land of the Northwest Territories . Documents and testimonies were widely used, without undue personal commentary by the author. They should be judged on their own merits, as they have an intrinsic value, irrespective of the one presenting them.

The success of the Indians' efforts to obtain recognition in the North of the future will depend on many factors. Not least among these is the support of the Canadian public. Without this, a satisfactory and lasting solution seems improbable. There should no longer be the attitude of superiority and condescension of past generations in dealing with the Indian. Today a humble recognition of this Government's limitations and this culture's shortcomings should be coupled with a collective determination for justice. "We can't in one year undo the injustices or misunderstandings of a hundred or two hundred years of history. Certainly we can't do it alone." – Pierre Elliott Trudeau, 1970.

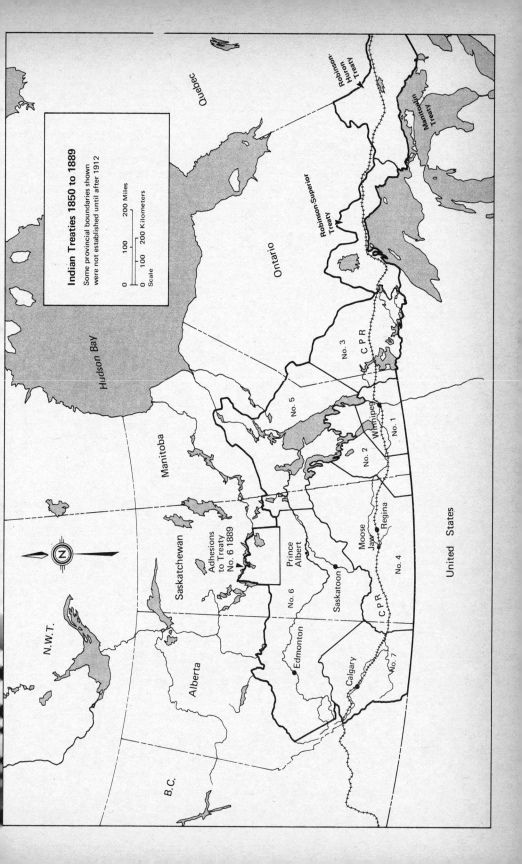

Indian Treaties 1850 to 1889

Some provincial boundaries shown
were not established until after 1912

200 Miles
100

0   100   200 Kilometers
Scale

Hudson Bay

Quebec

Ontario

Robinson-
Huron
Treaty

Manitoulin
Treaty

Robinson-Superior
Treaty

No. 3

C P R

No. 5

Manitoba

No. 2

Winnipeg

No. 1

Saskatchewan

Adhesions
to Treaty
No. 6 1889

Prince
Albert

Moose
Jaw

Regina

No. 4

No. 6

Saskatoon

N.W.T.

Edmonton

C P R

Alberta

Calgary

No. 7

B.C.

United States

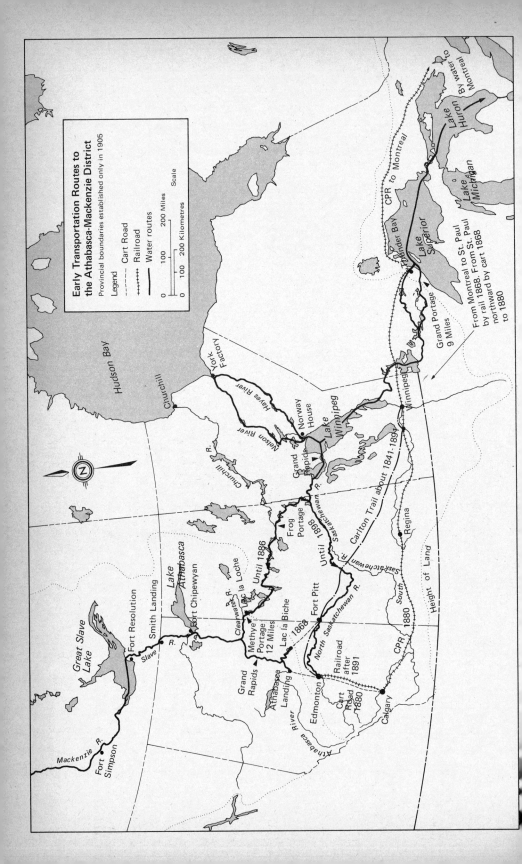

Early Transportation Routes to the Athabasca-Mackenzie District

Provincial boundaries established only in 1905

Legend

- – – – Cart Road
- +++++ Railroad
- ——— Water routes

Scale

0   100   200 Miles
0   100   200 Kilometres

Great Slave Lake

Fort Simpson

Mackenzie R.

Fort Resolution

Smith Landing

Slave R.

Lake Athabasca

Fort Chipewyan

Clearwater R.

Lac la Loche

Methye Portage 12 Miles

Grand Rapids

Athabasca Landing

Athabasca River

Lac la Biche

1868

Edmonton

Cart Road 1880

Railroad after 1880 1891

North Saskatchewan R.

Fort Pitt

Until 1898

Frog Portage

Saskatchewan R.

Calgary

CPR 1880

Height of Land

South Saskatchewan R.

Regina

Carlton Trail about 1841-1885

Churchill R.

Nelson River

Hayes River

York Factory

Grand Rapids

Norway House

Lake Winnipeg

Winnipeg

Hudson Bay

Churchill

N

Lake Superior

Thunder Bay

Grand Portage 9 Miles

CPR to Montreal

Lake Huron

to Montreal

By water to Montreal

From Montreal to St. Paul by rail 1868. From St. Paul northward by cart 1868 to 1880

Until 1886

Lake Michigan

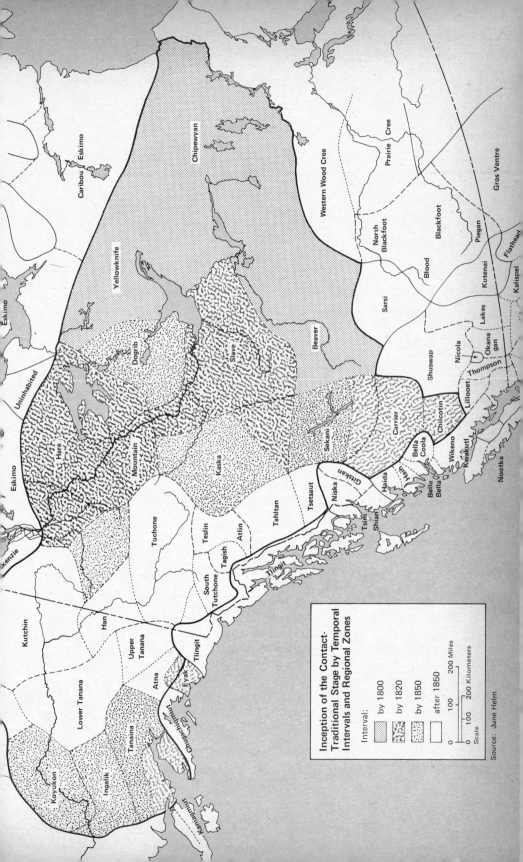

Caribou Eskimo

Eskimo

Eskimo

Uninhabited

Mackenzie

Chipewyan

Yellowknife

Dogrib

Hare

Mountain

Kutchin

Han

Lower Tanana

Upper Tanana

Koyukon

Tanaina

Ingalik

Atna

Eyak

Chugachmiut

Kaniagmiut

Tuchone

Teslin

Tagish

South Tutchone

Atlin

Tlingit

Kaska

Tahltan

Tsetsaut

Niska

Gitskan

Tsim Shian

Haida

Slave

Beaver

Sekani

Carrier

Chilcotin

Bella Coola

Haisla

Wikeno

Kwakiutl

Bella Bella

Nootka

Western Wood Cree

Prairie Cree

Gros Ventre

North Blackfoot

Blackfoot

Piegan

Blood

Sarsi

Flathead

Kutenai

Kalispel

Lakes

Nicola

Okanagan

Shuswap

Thompson

Lillooet

Inception of the Contact-
Traditional Stage by Temporal
Intervals and Regional Zones

Interval:

by 1800

by 1820

by 1850

after 1850

200 Miles

200 Kilometers

100

100

0

Scale

Source: June Helm

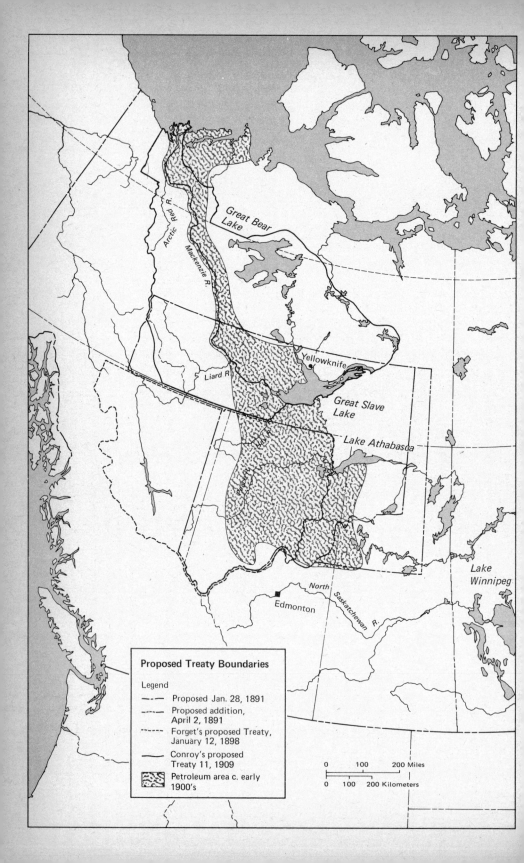

Proposed Treaty Boundaries

Legend

—··— Proposed Jan. 28, 1891

········· Proposed addition,
April 2, 1891

------ Forget's proposed Treaty,
January 12, 1898

——— Conroy's proposed
Treaty 11, 1909

[stippled] Petroleum area c. early
1900's

Great Bear
Lake

Arctic Red R.

Mackenzie R.

Liard R.

Yellowknife

Great Slave
Lake

Lake Athabasca

Lake
Winnipeg

Edmonton

North Saskatchewan R.

| 0 | 100 | 200 Miles |
| 0 | 100 | 200 Kilometers |

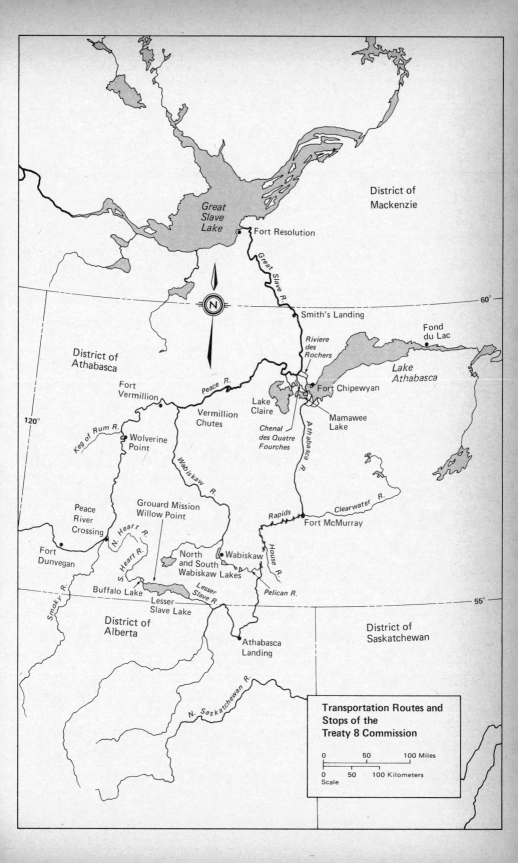

Great
Slave
Lake

District of
Mackenzie

Fort Resolution

60°

Smith's Landing

Fond
du Lac

*Riviere
des
Rochers*

District of
Athabasca

Peace R.

Lake
Athabasca

Fort
Vermillion

Fort Chipewyan

Keg of Rum R.

Vermillion
Chutes

Lake
Claire

Mamawee
Lake

120°

Wolverine
Point

*Chenal
des Quatre
Fourches*

Athabasca R.

Wabiskaw R.

Clearwater R.

Peace
River
Crossing

Grouard Mission
Willow Point

Rapids

Fort McMurray

N. Heart R.

Fort
Dunvegan

S. Heart R.

North
and South
Wabiskaw Lakes

Wabiskaw

House R.

Buffalo Lake

*Lesser
Slave R.*

Pelican R.

55°

Smoky R.

Lesser
Slave Lake

District of
Alberta

District of
Saskatchewan

Athabasca
Landing

N. Saskatchewan R.

**Transportation Routes and
Stops of the
Treaty 8 Commission**

0   50   100 Miles

0   50   100 Kilometers
Scale

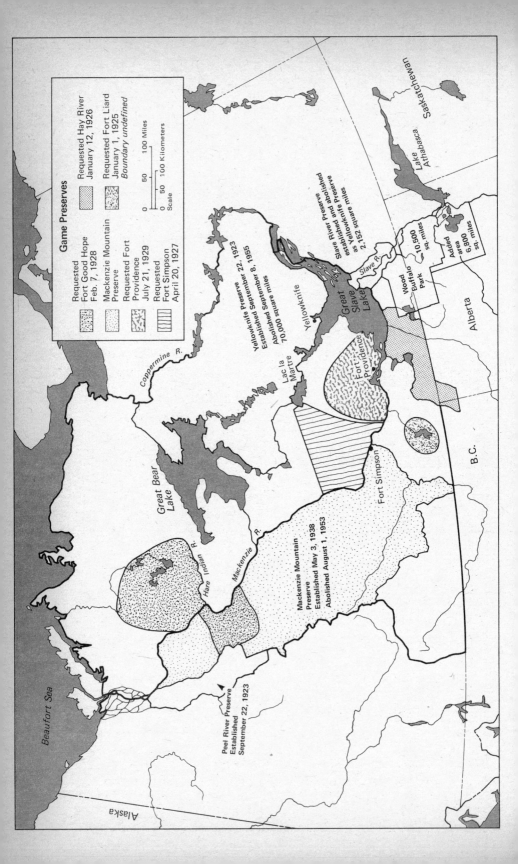

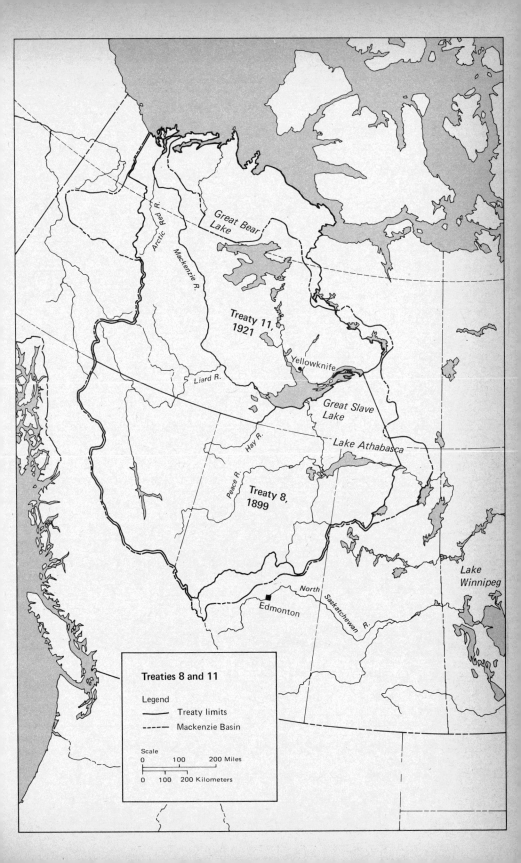

Arctic Red R.

Mackenzie R.

Great Bear Lake

Treaty 11, 1921

Liard R.

Yellowknife

Great Slave Lake

Lake Athabasca

Hay R.

Peace R.

Treaty 8, 1899

Lake Winnipeg

North Saskatchewan R.

Edmonton

Treaties 8 and 11

Legend

—— Treaty limits

--- Mackenzie Basin

Scale

0   100   200 Miles

0   100   200 Kilometers

Appendices

Appendix I

A few dates have been collected here on the history of the Athabasca-Mackenzie Indians. Their contacts with the white men, traders, missionaries, and government officials are also recorded as they greatly influenced the Indians' history. Some events noted here are of a more general nature but also reflected, at least indirectly, on the Northern Indians' lives.

40,000-10,000 B.C.	Man came from Asia to North America.
1492	Columbus reached America.
May 2, 1670	The Governor and Company of Adventurers of England trading into Hudson's Bay (commonly known as Hudson's Bay Co.), was granted a charter by King Charles II.
Early 1700's	Chipewyan Indians acted as middlemen, trading between the HBC York Factory post on the west coast of Hudson Bay and the western tribes. Between the Hudson Bay and the Rockies: "the first contacted tribes – Cree, Chipewyan, then Beaver and Yellowknives – obtained firearms and turned to fur raiding and general bullying of their defenseless Athapaskan neighbours, and when possible, of each other. The "Slave Indians", as a notable example, emerge in the literature as a contemptuous designation by the armed Cree of defenseless groups in the land abutting the southwest side of Great Slave Lake and along the Upper Mackenzie. . . Groups of Sekani and Dogribs were also harried and forced to flee customary territories by Beaver and Yellowknives, respectively."*
1763	Cession of French holdings in Canada to Great Britain.
1771	Samuel Hearne was the first white man to see Great Slave Lake, on his return trip from the mouth of the Coppermine River on the Arctic Ocean to the Hudson Bay. Although employed by the Hudson's Bay Company, primarily interested in fur trading, he was returning from a long journey in search of copper.
1778	Peter Pond, fur trader and the first white man to cross the Methye Portage, founded the "Old Establishment"

*Dr. June Helm et al. "The Contact History of the Subarctic Athapaskans: An Overview". Paper presented at the Athapaskan Conference, National Museum of Man, Ottawa (March 1971). Forthcoming in a Bulletin of the Museum; typed manuscript pp. 14-15.

trading post 40 miles south of Lake Athabasca. He stayed for only one winter.

1779   A group of Montreal based traders formed the "North West Company", which was restructured three times until it acquired its permanent organization in 1787 – Pond joined it in 1784 and Mackenzie in 1787.

1781   First "Treaty" signed by Canadian Indians with the British Crown. The island of Michilimakinak in the strait between Lakes Huron and Michigan surrendered in return for £5,000.

1781-1784   Smallpox epidemics decimated the Western Crees of the Plains and the Chipewyans – an estimated 9/10 of the Chipewyan population died. The depopulation of this rich fur trading area forced the traders to look further North for furs.

1783   The North West Company rebuilt a trading post at the site of Pond's "Old Establishment".

1783   Cree Indians at war against Beaver Indians.

1786   North West Company trading post at the mouth of the Slave River on the South shore of Great Slave Lake. (close to Fort Resolution)

1788   Alexander Mackenzie built Fort Chipewyan at the west end of lake Athabasca, and closed "Old Establishment" post.

1789   Alexander Mackenzie down "the Grand River" to the Arctic Sea. The river subsequently named after him.

1789   North West Company established a trading post at Lac la Martre, about fifty miles northwest of Fort Rae, N.W.T.

1790-1792   Philip Turner explored Athabasca Lake, Athabasca River, and South Great Slave Lake.

1790   Old Fort Providence established about 40 miles east of the present site of Yellowknife. It remained in operation until 1823.

1792   Alexander Mackenzie went up the Peace River.

1793   Alexander Mackenzie from Fort Chipewyan overland reached the Pacific Ocean.

1795   Fort Edmonton established by William Tomison, the "Inland Chief" of the HBC.

1795   North West Company trading post at the confluence of the Mackenzie and Trout Rivers, eighty miles North of the Great Slave Lake outlet. This post was replaced in 1800 by Rocky Mountain House, at the confluence of the Mackenzie and North Nahanni rivers, and later on by Fort Simpson, N.W.T.

1799	North West Company post at Fort Franklin.
1804-1805	North West Company post in the vicinity of actual Fort Good Hope.
1805	North West Company post close to actual Fort Norman.
1815	The first HBC post of the Athabasca district, opened at Lake Athabasca.
1821	North West Company and Hudson's Bay Company "amalgamated". In fact the Hudson's Bay Company absorbed the North West Company. The HBC now had a monopoly on both the fur trade and on transportation.
1820-1821	British Explorer John Franklin's first Arctic Expedition, and a disastrous one, from Great Slave Lake overland to the Arctic Coast. The expedition built Fort Enterprise.
1823	End of several decades of war between Dogrib and Yellowknife Indians; peace made under the respective leadership of Edzo and Akaitcho. HBC documents indicate that the peace was achieved through the help of two HBC employees, Dease and McVicar.
1825-1826-1827	John Franklin explored the Arctic Coast in the summers, wintering at Fort Franklin.
1833-1834	George Back explored the country northeast of Great Slave Lake. Reported that Akaitcho has lost all his authority and that the Yellowknife Indians are but a "wretched remnant".
1835-1838	Smallpox on the Plains. One third of the Plains Indians wiped out.
1837-1839	P.W. Dease and T. Simpson wintered at Fort Confidence (North East of Great Bear Lake) after exploring Arctic coast.
1840	Trading post established by HBC on Peel's River (Fort McPherson).
1848-1849	John Bell, Richardson, John Rae wintered at Fort Confidence.
1849	Catholic Mission established at Fort Chipewyan.

1850-1856	30,000 marten exported yearly from the Mackenzie District.
1852	Albert Lacombe, OMI, Catholic priest, started ministering to the Indians on the Prairies. (Named by the Indian people "The Man of Good Heart").
1852	Father H. Faraud, OMI, visited Fort Resolution from Fort Chipewyan.
1852	(Old) Fort Rae established.

After the fort was established, the Dogribs brought in to the HBC 8,000 to 10,000 caribou each year. The caribou meat was used as trail provisions for the York boat crews carrying goods to and from the North each summer. The March 19, 1853, Fort Rae HBC trading post inventory showed:

> 1,583 lbs. dry meat
> 10,000 lbs. half-dried meat
> 785 lbs. pounded meat
> 540 lbs. (caribou) grease
> 2,000 caribou tongues
> 600 lbs. fresh meat

1853	Catholic priests visited Fond du Lac, Fort McMurray.
1858	James Anderson of the HBC took a census of the Mackenzie District:

Fort Simpson	
Big Island (Ft. Providence)	745
Fort Rae	657
Fort McPherson	337
Liard River	397
Fort Resolution	469
Fort Good Hope	467
Fort Norman	363

Fort Wrigley, Fort Franklin, Aklavik, and Arctic Red River are not mentioned, because at the time of the census there were no trading posts in these communities. The people living near these areas were no doubt included in the count of the nearest settlement.

1858	Catholic Mission established at Fort Resolution.
1858	Archdeacon Hunter, of the Church Missionary Society, Anglican Church, arrived at Fort Simpson and visited Fort Norman and Fort Good Hope in Spring, 1859.
1859	Henri Grollier, OMI, a Catholic priest, visited Fort Rae

and Fort Norman, and established permanent mission at Fort Good Hope.

1859	"Mal du Fort Rae" killed 400 people (epidemic of undiscovered nature).
1859	CMS Missionary Kirkby (Anglican) established permanent mission at Fort Simpson.
1860-1861	H. Grollier visited Fort McPherson.
1860	Fort Anderson established, opened until 1865. HBC discontinued the trading of "spirits".
1861	Kirkby down the Mackenzie to Fort McPherson, and across the Rocky Mountains to the Yukon.
1861-1865	Civil war in the U.S.A.
1862	Scarlet fever among Hare and Kutchin (Loucheux). Catholic Diocese of Athabasca-Mackenzie was established.
1862	Catholic Mission established at Fort Providence.
1864	Emile Petitot, OMI, a Catholic priest stationed at Fort Good Hope, travelled overland to Fort Franklin in winter, then returned by way of the Bear and Mackenzie Rivers. He made similar trips in 1865, 1866, 1867, 1868, 1869, 1871, 1877, 1878, mapped the country accurately and collected large amounts of information on the Indians' life.
1866	Chief Factor W. Hardisty of Fort Simpson reported that over 1,000 Indians had died from influenza in the area from Fort Simpson to Peel's River the previous year. Brother Alexis Reynard, OMI, mentioned scarlet fever epidemics at Fort Providence and Fort Simpson – Petitot reported a measles epidemic.
August 28, 1867	Sisters of Charity, usually called Grey Nuns, arrived at Fort Providence. "Rapidly sick and infirm people and little children crowded the house which was named Sacred Heart Hospital." The first class opened on October 7, Sister St. Michel-des-Saints teaching eleven children. Two years later it was reported: "Our school is doing well. There are 35 children, of whom 27 are orphans. . . Unfortunately we are obliged to refuse admission to any more because we would not be able to feed them". The existence of so many orphans resulted from the epidemics.
1867	Canadian Confederation.

Gabriel Breynat was born in France.

U.S.A. bought Alaska Territory from Russia for $7,200,000.

William Carpenter Bompas, of the Anglican Church, stationed at Fort Simpson since 1865, visited Fort Rae, Fort Resolution, and Fort Chipewyan.

1868-1869	Archbishop Taché pioneered a new transportation route into Athabasca-Mackenzie District, by the North Saskatchewan River, and through Lac la Biche into the Athabasca River.
1869	Smallpox epidemics in northern U.S. and Canada.
1869	HBC surrendered their monopoly rights to Rupert's Land and the "unorganized territories" back to Great Britain. This entire area was transferred to Canada on June 23, 1870.
1870	Red River "Troubles" under Riel's leadership, led to the creation of the Province of Manitoba, on May 12, 1870. Capital was Winnipeg, population 300. Yellowknife Indians disappeared progressively as a distinct tribe between 1870 and 1900. Great Bear Lake Band (Satudene) started to become a distinct group. By 1870, nine trading posts had been established in the Mackenzie District: Hay River, Fort Rae, Fort Providence, Fort Liard, Fort Norman, Fort Good Hope, Fort McPherson, Fort Simpson, and Fort Resolution.
1870-1873	American whiskey runners brought disorder and lawlessness to the Canadian prairies.
1871	Treaties 1 and 2 between Canadian Indian people and Queen Victoria. U.S.A. ended Treaty-making with Indians. Permanent Catholic Mission established at Fort Liard.
1872	Catholic Mission permanently established at Fort Rae.
1873	Dogribs increased frequency of raids into Yellowknife Indian territory. March 8–first meeting of the Northwest Council at Fort Garry (Winnipeg). Their first Act was to prohibit sale of alcohol in the Northwest Territories. North West Mounted Police established.
1874	Treaty 4. Bompas appointed first Anglican Bishop of the Athabasca Diocese. First trading post established in Fort Smith.

Boarding School at Fort Chipewyan, directed by the Grey Nuns.

1875	N.W.T. Act.
	Fort Chipewyan is main centre of Hudson's Bay Company in the Athabasca-Mackenzie District.
	Catholic Mission permanently established at Fond du Lac.
1876	Treaty 6.
	The Battle of the Little Big Horn in Montana.
	Sitting Bull and his Sioux tribe sought refuge in Canada.
	First Indian Act in Canada.
	At Fort Simpson in the Company's provision store, Mr. Bernie "beheld a pile of caribou tongues five or six feet high, and thirty or forty feet in circumference".
	Catholic mission permanently established at Fort Norman.
	First visit of a Catholic Priest to Fort Smith.
1877	Treaty 7.
1880	"The Northwest", a Government promotional pamphlet was published.
	The railway was completed to Calgary, thence northbound transportation was by wagon road to Edmonton and Athabasca Landing. The wagon road was progressively improved throughout the 1880's. Steamboats travelled on the North Saskatchewan River, between Lake Winnipeg and Edmonton.
	Due to overtrapping, some Indians were starving, in the Lesser Slave Lake and Peace River areas.
	British Government handed over to Canada all the Arctic islands north of Canada.
1880-1900	Edmonton was primarily dependent on the Mackenzie Basin Fur Trade.
1880-1936	Department of Indian Affairs had ministerial status and was headed by the "Superintendent General of Indian Affairs", who usually was also Minister of another Department. The actual Indian affairs were in fact administered by the appointed "Deputy Superintendent of Indian Affairs".
1881-1884	Macfarlane conducted population surveys in the Athabasca-Mackenzie Districts.
1881	First visit of a Catholic Priest to Fort Wrigley. Visits continued annually thereafter.

By 1882	Anglican Missions had been established at Fort Chipewyan, Fort Rae (until 1888), Fort Resolution (until 1895), Fort Simpson, Fort Norman, Fort McPherson. First Geological Surveys were conducted in the Athabasca-Mackenzie Districts.
1883	The *Grahame*, the first steamboat on the Athabasca River, was built at Fort Chipewyan.
1884	Anglican Mackenzie Diocese was separated from Athabasca Diocese. The steamboat *Wrigley* was built at Fort Smith to operate on the Slave River, Great Slave Lake, and the Mackenzie River.
1885	Measles and whooping-cough killed one-fifth of the Indians of the Peace River District. At Fort Providence the Big Island Fishery failed to supply all of the 25,000 fish needed at the settlement. 3,000 rabbits were caught instead, and coupled with the supply of vegetables, the rabbit meat saved the settlement.
1886	Methye Portage route no longer used. End of transportation by York boats.
1887	1,584 tons of freight were ferried across the river at Edmonton. 770 tons were for the Hudson's Bay Company, and 412 tons were forwarded to Mackenzie District. McConnell conducted geological surveys along the Liard, Slave, Salt, and Hay rivers, and west of Great Slave Lake. Hyslop and Nagle established a fur trading company. Independent Free Traders built trading posts in Fort Rae, Fort Providence, Fort Good Hope. First trading post established at Fort Wrigley.
1888	At Grand Rapids, 165 miles north of Athabasca Landing, a tramway consisting of 700 yards of hewn timber track, was operated by the Hudson's Bay Company. Select Committee of the Senate, (headed by Schultz), to investigate the resources of the Mackenzie Basin. The Athabasca-Mackenzie Catholic clergy consisted of two Bishops, twenty-three priests, twenty-six Brothers, and twenty-two Grey Nuns. 100 pounds of flour cost $30.00 at Fort Good Hope. Ogilvie conducted a Geological Survey of the Lower Mackenzie Basin. A permanent Catholic Mission established at Ft. Smith.
1888-1890	The trail from Edmonton to Athabasca Landing was improved into a wagon road.

1889	Indian Affairs Headquarters at Ottawa employed forty persons.
	American whalers first appeared on the Arctic Coast (West of the Mackenzie Delta).
	Catholic Mission was established at Fort McPherson, and withdrawn to Arctic Red River in 1896.
1889-1890	Warburton Pike, an amateur explorer, explored from Great Slave Lake to Coppermine and Bathurst Inlet.
1890	Wounded Knee Massacre, in the U.S.A.
1891	Railways reached Edmonton, population less than 2,000.
	Bishop Reeve succeeded Bompas as Anglican Bishop of the Mackenzie Diocese.
	Ogilvie surveyed the Liard, Nelson, and Sikanie Rivers.
	Sir John A. Macdonald died.
1892	Geological surveys made by J.B. Tyrell and Dowling between Athabasca and Churchill Rivers.
	February 21, Breynat was ordained Priest, and arrived at Fond du Lac (Saskatchewan) in the summer.
1893	McConnell made a geological survey, along Finlay and Peace Rivers.
	J.B. Tyrell explored from Fort Chipewyan to Hudson Bay.
	An Anglican Mission was permanently established in Hay River.
1894	O.I. Stringer, Anglican Minister, went to Herschel Island.
	Hyslop and Nagle established their first post at Fort Resolution, and their second at Fort Rae.
	Two white trappers, Carr and Duncan, trapped in the vicinity of Fort Resolution.
	Catholic Mission was permanently established at Fort Simpson.
	Boarding school opened in Hay River by Thomas J. Marsh, of the Anglican Church.
1896	First Act for the Preservation of Game in the N.W.T. came into force.
	Laurier was elected Prime Minister, and an era of prosperity ensued until about 1910.
	Canadian Government subsidized railway construction, and railroads branched across the prairies. The price for farm produce improved. Many technological problems were mastered. The Department of the Interior, led by Clifford Sifton, advertised the Opportunities of Western Canada. Millions of acres of homesteads were granted or sold.

Gold was discovered on the upper Yukon River, and the "Klondike Gold Rush" ensued.

1897-1908	Many fur buyers and traders ventured North as far as Great Slave Lake, most of them backed by wholesalers John A. McDougall and R. Secord in Edmonton.
1897-1899	The trail from Edmonton to Athabasca Landing became a wagon road with regular stage coach service. NWMP Inspector Jarvis led a pioneer patrol from Fort Saskatchewan to Fort Resolution. A Catholic Mission was permanently established at Fort Wrigley.
1897-1898	NWMP patrol, by dogteam, from Fort Saskatchewan to Fort Simpson (2,172 miles).
1898	Mineral claims were staked at Pine Point, N.W.T. The Yukon Territory established.
1898-1899	NWMP detachment at Fort Smith (reopened July 23, 1921).
1899	Treaty 8.
1899-1900	Dr. Robert Bell and J. Mackintosh Bell investigated the geology of the North shore of Great Slave Lake. J.M. Bell wintered at Fort Resolution, then went in 1900 to Fort Norman, where he was joined by Charles Camsell. Both surveyed around Great Bear Lake and returned to Fort Rae overland. David Hanbury discovered a new route from Hudson Bay to the Mackenzie Valley via the Thelon River. Routledge led an NWMP patrol to Fort Resolution and back to Fort Saskatchewan.
1900	NWMP detachment at Fort Resolution only for summer of 1900 (reopened September 3, 1913).
1900	Population of Edmonton reached 2,622. Twenty-seven trading posts were in operation in the Athabasca-Mackenzie District: fourteen belonged to the Hudson's Bay Company, and thirteen to Hyslop and Nagle. Each company had its own transportation system. A Catholic Mission was permanently established at Hay River. NWMP detachment at Fort Chipewyan opened until 1917, then reopened in 1923.
1901	137 non-natives lived in the Mackenzie District. Official postal service to the Athabasca-Mackenzie Dis-

trict consisted of two mails yearly from Edmonton to Fort McMurray, Fort Smith, and Fort Resolution.

Doctor West, travelling with the Treaty 8 party, vaccinated some northern Alberta Indians against smallpox.

1902   Measles epidemic in the Mackenzie District – sixty died in Fort Rae. Sixty-six Indians died of "an epidemic" in Fort Resolution.

April 6, Breynat was consecrated Bishop, at St. Albert (Edmonton).

Catholic Diocese was divided: Breynat became Bishop of the Mackenzie Diocese (twelve missions, twelve priests, thirteen brothers, twelve Grey Nuns), while Grouard remained Bishop of the Athabasca Diocese.

Six trading posts at Fort Resolution.

Hanbury and some Eskimos crossed by dog team from Baker Lake to Pelly Lake on Back River to Arctic coast.

1903   NWMP detachment at Fort McPherson, 1903-1907 and 1909-1921, reopened 1949.

The Grey Nuns opened a boarding school at Fort Resolution.

1904   NWMP detachment at Herschel Island, opened and closed numerous times, definitely closed in 1964.

"The Mackenzie District, including Great Slave and Athabasca Lakes, will in all probability be nothing but a fur-bearing country as far as we know at present". (NWMP Inspector West).

NWMP became Royal North West Mounted Police (RNMP or RNWMP).

1905   Gold discovered at Yellowknife.

Hyslop and Nagle Company trading posts numbered only seven.

The provinces of Alberta and Saskatchewan were created.

N.W.T. Amendment Act: The Northwest Territories were divided into four districts – Ungava, Franklin, Keewatin, Mackenzie. Fred White was appointed first Commissioner of N.W.T. The Act provided for five councillors, but none were appointed until 1921.

Frank Oliver, of Edmonton, was appointed Minister of the Interior.

1906   Treaty 10.

Elihu Stewart, Dominion Superintendent of Forestry, visited the Mackenzie District.

The Dominion Lands Agent in Edmonton reported that

the country North and West of Edmonton could hold 2,000,000 people.
Pioneering accelerated in the Peace River District.

1907 Extensive investigation was carried out on wood bison (buffalo) between Great Slave Lake and Lake Athabasca by Inspector A.M. Jarvis, Ernest Thompson Seton, naturalist, and E.A. Preble. The largest herd they saw was only 25 head strong. A buffalo reserve was proposed the following year.
A Senate Select Committee was appointed in January to determine the potential value of the Mackenzie Basin. A Government promotional pamphlet based on their report was published the same year, titled "Canada's Fertile Northland."
Conroy wrote his first memo asking for Treaty 11.

1908 Wilhjalmur Steffanson and Rudolph M. Anderson entered the N.W.T.
RNWMP detachment established at Smith Landing, closed on November 5, 1932.
Joseph Keele explored between the Yukon Territory and the Mackenzie River, along the Gravel (Keele) River.
Leases for commercial fishing on Lake Athabasca and Lesser Slave Lake were granted to white people.

1909 The official mail service provided five yearly mails to Fort McMurray, Fort Smith, and Fort Resolution; two yearly mails to McPherson.
RNWMP reported scarcity of fur at Fort Resolution.
Second large staking rush to Pine Point.
Oil discovered in paying quantities close to Fort McMurray.
Bishop Breynat's letter advocating Treaty 11.
Alberta Government promoted railway construction and extended financial assistance for building railroads from Edmonton to Peace River, Athabasca Landing, and Fort McMurray.
Sergeant Mellor patrolled from Vermillion to Fort Liard to investigate the disappearance of the two Macleod brothers.

1910 17,000 acres of tar sands near Fort McMurray were leased for exploitation.
Federal Government published another promotional pamphlet: "The Great Mackenzie Basin".
Frank Oliver, Minister of the Interior, visited the Mackenzie District.
RNWMP Inspector Fitzgerald and the four members of his

patrol became lost and died between Fort McPherson and Dawson City, for lack of a competent guide.

The Hudson's Bay Company operated nineteen trading posts in the Mackenzie District.

At Fort Resolution, caribou wore a trail between the priest's house and the store.

The first doctor, Dr. MacDonald, arrived in Fort Smith and stayed until 1931.

1911   Alberta closed beaver trapping.

George Douglas prospected around Great Bear Lake.

519 non-natives were residents of the Mackenzie District.

Indian agencies were established at Fort Simpson and Fort Smith.

1912   The 60th Parallel was defined as the southern boundary of the N.W.T. Ontario, Manitoba, and Quebec were greatly enlarged by land formerly included in the N.W.T.

The railway was completed from Edmonton to Athabasca Landing.

Red-brown crude oil was bought from Norman Wells to Athabasca Landing and Edmonton.

A school was opened in Fort Smith.

Radford and Street were killed by Eskimos in Schultz Lake district.

The first trading post in Aklavik was established.

1913   Hyslop and Nagle Company was bought out by Northern Trading Company. NTC had twelve posts until 1914, and lasted until 1930.

Father Rouviere, OMI, and Father Leroux, OMI, were killed by Eskimos.

Construction was started on a railway from Edmonton to Fort McMurray.

RNWMP detachments were established at Fort Resolution and Fort Simpson.

Drygeese, the signatory of Treaty 8 for the Dogrib Indians, died.

Land surveys were made of the northern settlements from Fort Smith to Fort Good Hope.

Indian Agent Harris arrived at Fort Simpson, to replace Gerald Card.

1914   Lord Strathcona died – Hudson's Bay Company became gradually more interested in general retail stores than in trading posts. "Made beaver" disappeared as a medium of exchange and was replaced by cash.

331

World War I, 1914-1918.
One RNWMP Inspector commanded each of the three sub-districts: Grouard, Smith's Landing, Herschel Island.
Three oil leases were staked by Dr. Bosworth at Norman Wells, and were acquired by Imperial Oil in 1918.
"The Unexploited West", Government promotional publication, was released.
The Grey Nuns opened Fort Smith hospital.

1915	Snuff, a signatory of Treaty 8, resigned from being chief of the Fort Resolution Indian Band, at the age of 102. Smith Landing was renamed Fort Fitzgerald.
1915-1920	Steady rise in fur prices.
1916	Convention between Canada and the U.S. for the Protection of Migratory Birds. The Hospital at Fort Simpson was opened and operated by the Grey Nuns. First NWMP patrol to reach as far North as Fort Norman.
1917	N.W.T. Game Act.
1918	Imperial Oil Company drilled for oil at the following locations: near Fort McMurray, at the West end of Great Slave Lake, at Peace River, and forty-five miles North of Fort Norman. The boundaries of the Mackenzie, Keewatin, and Franklin districts in the N.W.T. were firmly established. Fred White, Commissioner of the N.W.T., died.
1919	Royal North West Mounted Police was renamed Royal Canadian Mounted Police, RCMP, in November. Anglican Church established a mission at Aklavik. W.W. Cory, then Deputy Minister of the Department of the Interior, became second Commissioner of the N.W.T. Near-starvation was general at Fort Rae. A National conference on Game and Wildlife Conservation was held. Smallpox epidemics broke out in Northern Alberta. Lamson-Hubbard trading company was chartered, and operated the first tractor on the Fort Smith Portage.
1920	Fort Resolution Treaty Boycott.
1919-1920	Highest fur prices ever: a result of the post-war boom. 100 trading posts were in operation in the Athabasca-Mackenzie District.
1920	The fur market collapsed in April. Fifteen Fond du Lac Indians starved to death. Oil was discovered at Norman Wells.

F.M. Kitto was commissioned by the Department of the Interior to investigate the natural resources and economic development of the Mackenzie District.

The Hudson's Bay Company celebrated its 250th Anniversary.

First publication of the HBC magazine "The Beaver".

First gasoline boat on the Mackenzie River: LADY OF THE LAKE.

Trapping and hunting on Victoria and Banks Islands were reserved for the Eskimos.

Last scow travelled down from Athabasca Landing.

Large steamers on the Athabasca and Mackenzie Rivers. The *Distributor* was built in 1920, at Fort Smith.

Until 1920, only 300 tons of freight were handled yearly across the Fort Smith Portage by the Hudson's Bay Company, and 100 tons by the Northern Trading Company.

Lamson-Hubbard Company purchased several new vessels, tractors, and trucks.

The Alberta Provincial Railways Department took over the Alberta and Great Waterways Railways.

1920-1923	Many navigation improvements, Government-sponsored, were implemented in the Mackenzie District; accurate charts, navigation aids, improvements in wharfs and harbours.
1921	Treaty 11.

Establishment of the N.W.T. Territorial Administration (sixteen man staff at Fort Smith).

Three main administrative centres were established for the N.W.T.: Fort Simpson, Fort Smith, and Aklavik.

W.W. Cory was the first Commissioner of the N.W.T. to visit the N.W.T. (Fort Smith only).

A permanent detachment of the RCMP was established in Fort Smith.

The first bank of the N.W.T. was opened by the Union Bank of Canada, in a 16 x 16 tent, at Fort Smith.

The "Edmonton and Mackenzie River Railway Company" was incorporated to build a railway from Fort McMurray to Hay River, but did not realize its project.

The railway from Edmonton reached Clearwater River, near Fort McMurray.

Imperial Oil Limited issued a statement: "A pipeline to take the oil from Norman Wells 1,200 miles to the end of steel at Waterways on the Clearwater would cost $40,-000,000."

An oil-burning vessel in the N.W.T. for the first time.

Marconi Wireless Telegraph Company applied for a licence to establish a wireless system in the Territories, but it was turned down. (The N.W.T. first radio stations were established in 1924 by the RCCS.)

The first airplane to fly in the Northwest Territories left Edmonton on February 27, and arrived at Fort Norman on June 2. A second plane left Edmonton at the same time, but broke down at Fort Simpson, and managed to get only halfway back to Edmonton.

The Hudson's Bay Company handled 700 tons of freight down the Mackenzie River in 1921.

The Liberal Government in Alberta, which had been a great sponsor of northern expansion, was defeated by the United Farmers of Alberta party.

Six Councillors were appointed to the N.W.T. Council for the first time. First meeting of the N.W.T. Council took place – the Commissioner of the N.W.T. enacted his first ordinance.

One hundred and forty white trappers were licensed in the N.W.T.

Influenza epidemics – twenty-two Indians died at Fort Chipewyan, eighty at Fond du Lac.

RCMP established a detachment at Fort Norman (February 26, 1921).

The 1920's were the golden age of the free traders in the Mackenzie District.

1922   January-February: first trip by horses and wagons from Fort McMurray to Fort Smith, by Mickey Ryan, in thirty-two days.

RCMP detachment established in Aklavik.

Miss Connibear, daughter of a Fort Smith trader, is the only white girl in the N.W.T.

One cord of fire wood, cut, split, and piled, is usually sold for $4.

Indian Act was changed to include the administration of Eskimo Affairs.

In Fort Resolution, thirty white trappers have their base camp and twenty-one white persons are employed in six trading posts.

The intoxicants imported into the N.W.T. during the year 1922 amounted to

wines	10 gal.
rum	3½ gal.
whiskey	52 gal.
brandy	49 gal.
unspecified liqueurs	158 gal.
TOTAL	**272½ gal.**

1923	Aklavik became the commercial and administrative centre of the Western Arctic.
	Indian Agency opened in Fort Resolution.
1924	Wireless station established in Fort Simpson (Royal Canadian Corps of Signals) the first in the N.W.T.
	The Hudson's Bay Company buys Lamson Hubbard Company and its subsidiary, Alberta and Arctic Transportation Company.
	The Northern Traders Company buys the Northern Trading Company.
	RCMP detachments at Fort Providence, Fort Good Hope, and Fort Rae.
	A gallon of gasoline is worth $3 at Fort Resolution.
	Average daily wages for Indians are $4.
	The Hudson's Bay Company purchased the vessels of the Northern Trading Company.
1925	The railway from Edmonton reached Waterways (near Fort McMurray).
	Wireless station (RCCS) established in Aklavik and Fort Smith.
	RCMP detachment established in Hay River.
	From 1925 to 1930, over 200 trading posts are in operation in the N.W.T.
	Muskrat trapping started on a large scale in the Mackenzie River Delta area.
1926	Wireless station (RCCS) was established at Herschel Island during the summer.
	Catholic mission established at Aklavik. Anglican and Catholic hospital opened in Aklavik.
	All Arctic Islands are established as a game preserve for the Eskimos.
	RCMP detachment established in Arctic Red River.
1927	Wireless station (RCCS) established at Fort Resolution.
	Twenty-two deaths among the Indians of Fort Providence as a result of tuberculosis.
	RCMP detachment established at Reliance.
	The production of raw fur in the N.W.T. reached nearly $3,000,000, the highest ever until then.
1928	Influenza epidemic through the Mackenzie District killed about 600 Indians, approximately ten per cent to fifteen per cent of the population of each village.
	Beaver trapping was closed for three years, then for a further two years till 1933.
	Airplanes started to play an important role in the Mack-

enzie District in prospecting, trapping, exploration, mapping, and mail transportation.

1929	Punch Dickens was the first flyer to cross the Arctic Circle in the vicinity of the Mackenzie River. He piloted the first plane to reach as far north as Aklavik. Wireless station (RCCS) established at Stony Rapids. The Anglican Mission established in Fort Smith. RCMP detachment established in Fort Liard. End of the itinerant traders in the Mackenzie District.
1930	In the winter of 1929-1930, 309 non-Indian Residents and 242 non-Indian non-Residents were licensed to trap and hunt in the Mackenzie District. Indian agency was opened in Fort Good Hope. The administration of natural resources was transferred from the Federal Government to the provinces of Alberta and Saskatchewan. Wireless station (RCCS) established at Fort Norman. RCMP detachment opened at Fort Wrigley. During the 1930's the worst fur famine occurred.
1931	The total population of the N.W.T. was 9,723 of which there were 4,670 Eskimos, 4,046 Indians, and 1,007 Whites and Métis. Pitchblende discovered at Port Radium by Gilbert Labine. Fort Smith Chief Joe Squirrel resigned; he was the last survivor in office of the 1899-1900 Treaty signatories.
1932	Until 1929, through the whole winter, only 400 pounds of mail reached Aklavik. In the winter of 1931-1932, Canadian Airways flew in 50,000 pounds of mail to the Mackenzie District. Port Radium Mines opened.
1933	Gold discovered in Yellowknife. RCMP detachment established at Cameron Bay (Port Radium).
1934	Port Radium Mine activities slowed down. Gold rush to Yellowknife. The Northern Transportation Company Ltd. (NTCL) was incorporated to handle the increasing amount of freight on the Mackenzie River. The Fort Smith Indian Agency closed.
1935	Two airplane companies operated in the Mackenzie District in 1935.

	express	mail	passengers
Canadian Airways with 9 planes flew	337,261 lbs.	102,192 lbs.	1,533
Mackenzie Air Service with 4 planes flew	233,868 lbs.		903

Government grant per day per patient, to mission hospitals, for destitute whites, Métis and Eskimos was increased from $0.50 to $2.50.

1936   Considerable activities in Mining and Prospecting in the Great Bear Lake and Great Slave Lake areas.
Fort Rae Chief Monfwi died.
The new federal Department of Mines and Resources combined and replaced the Department of Mines, the Department of the Interior, the Department of Indian Affairs and the Department of Immigration. Indian Affairs became a branch of the new department.
Hudson's Bay Company bought Revillon Fur Company's assets in the N.W.T.

1937   Fort Resolution Treaty boycott.
Bishop Breynat collected affidavits from witnesses to Treaties 8 and 11.
Most white trappers have become prospectors and miners.
Per capita cost of Indian relief in the N.W.T. for the fiscal year ending March, 1937, was $5.28.
RCMP detachment established at Yellowknife.
Hay River Residential School, run by the Anglican Church, closed down. Anglican church opened residential school in Aklavik.
Northern Transportation Company Ltd. (NTCL) operated the first all steel ships on the Mackenzie River (*Radium King, Radium Queen*).
Total income for the 3,854 Indians of the N.W.T. amounted to

$ 5,446	Farming
18,085	Wages
17,330	Fishing
173,186	Hunting & Trapping
7,230	Miscellaneous
19,090	Annuities
$240,367	TOTAL

1938   The mineral production of the N.W.T. exceeded in value the fur production for the first time.

The Government established a new trapping licensing system.

Yellowknife Transportation Company (YTC) was established.

Norman Wells refinery produced 22,855 barrels of fuel oil.

The Mackenzie Mountain Game Preserve was established.

Hospital built at Fort Resolution and operated by the Catholic Church.

Hudson's Bay Company took over the Northern Traders Company Ltd., the last of its old rivals in the Mackenzie District.

"Canada's Blackest Blot" published.

1939   Hospital built in Fort Rae and operated by the Catholic Church.

Indian Agency was moved from Fort Good Hope to Fort Norman.

Hospital built in Fort Norman and operated by the Anglican Church.

First liquor store in the N.W.T. opened in Yellowknife.

Five weekly flights from Edmonton to Yellowknife.

Bi-monthly flights from Edmonton to Fort Resolution and Fort Simpson.

None of the native people of the N.W.T. was yet employed in mining and prospecting.

4,000 tons of freight were imported into the Mackenzie District from the South.

World War II started.

Appendix II

Affidavits signed by Witnesses to Treaty 8 and Treaty 11:

On	At	By	Witness to Treaty	Signed at
1937				
August 7	Fort Norman	Joe Keni	No. 11	Fort Norman
October 18	Fort Resolution	Johnny Beaulieu	8	Fort Resolution
October 18	Cold Lake (Alberta)	Thos. W. Harris (Ex. Indian Agent)	11	Fort Simpson
October 18	Fort Resolution	Alphonse Mandeville	8	Fort Resolution
October 18	Fort Resolution	Albert Norn	8	Fort Resolution
August 15	Fort Chipewyan	Wayakis Martin (Ex Chief)	8	Fort Chipewyan
September 27	Fort Smith	Abraham Deneyutchele	8	Smith's Landing
September 27	Fort Smith	Frederic MacDonald	8	Smith's Landing
August 7	Fort Norman	Zole Blondin (headman)	11	Fort Norman
September 27	Fort Smith	Johnny Berens	8	Smith's Landing
August 7	Fort Norman	Samuel Keni	11	Fort Norman
August 7	Fort Norman	Johnny Ekaleya	11	Fort Norman
August 7	Fort Norman	Jean Blondin	11	Fort Norman
September 27	Fort Smith	Maurice Beaulieu	8	Smith's Landing
August 15	Fort Chipewyan	Thomas Gibotte (Councillor)	8	Fort Chipewyan
August 15	Fort Chipewyan	Jonas Laviolette	8	Fort Chipewyan
September 27	Fort Smith	Pierre Squirrel	8	Smith's Landing
September 4	Fort Chipewyan	Colin Fraser	8	Fort Chipewyan
August 25	Fort Providence	Victor Lafferty	11	Fort Providence
September 27	Fort Smith	Joseph Marie	8	Smith's Landing
October 18	Fort Resolution	Louison Beaulieu	8	Fort Resolution
August 9	Fort Simpson	Edouard Gouy OMI (Priest)	11	Fort Simpson
August 24	Arctic Red River	Andre Coyen	11	Arctic Red River
September 20	Fort Providence	Frederick McLeod	8	Fort Nelson
October 18	Fort Resolution	Almire Bezannier (Priest)	11	Fort Rae
October 6	Fort Chipewyan	Severin Tsintchoudhe	8	Fond du Lac
September 27	Fort Smith	Edward Heron	11	Fort Rae
August 15	Fort Chipewyan	Pierre Mercredi (Treaty Interpreter)	8	Fort Chipewyan
August 17	Montreal	Frederick C. Gaudet (Ex HBC Manager)	8	Fort Resolution
August 13	Fort Providence	Charles Gourdon	8	Fort Resolution
August 25	Fort Providence	Joseph Bouvier	11	Fort Providence
September 7	Fort Smith	Pierre Fallaize (Bishop)	11	Fort Norman
August 9	Fort Simpson	Joseph Villeneuve	11	Fort Simpson
August 9	Fort Simpson	Tsetso	11	Fort Simpson
August 9	Fort Simpson	Modeste Corneille	11	Fort Simpson
August 9	Fort Simpson	James Horesay	11	Fort Simpson
September 27	Fort Smith	Andre Deneyutchele	8	Smith's Landing
August 10	Fort Chipewyan	John Wylie	8	Fort Chipewyan
August 9	Fort Simpson	Ali	11	Fort Simpson
August 9	Fort Simpson	Harry McGurran	11	Fort Simpson
October 16	Yellowknife	D'Arcy Arden	11	Fort Norman
August 7	Fort Norman	Francois Ekfwentalle	11	Fort Norman
August 24	Arctic Red River	Pierre KN	11	Arctic Red River
August 24	Arctic Red River	Ernest Kendo	11	Arctic Red River
August 24	Arctic Red River	John Kamey	11	Arctic Red River
August 24	Arctic Red River	Andre Clements	11	Arctic Red River

AFFIDAVIT

I, _J. A. R. Balsillie_, a resident of _Fort Resolution_ in the Province of _____, or in the North West Territories,

DO CERTIFY as follows:

(1). I was present when Treaty was made at _Fort Providence._

(2). As the text of the Treaty which had been brought from Ottawa was not explicit enough to give satisfaction to the Indians, the following promises were made to the Indians by the Royal Commissioner, in the name of the Crown:

a. They were promised that nothing would be done or allowed to interfere with their way of making a living as they were accustomed to and as their antecedents had done.

b. The old and destitute would always be taken care of, their future existence would be carefully studied and provided for, every effort would be made to improve their living conditions.

c. They were guaranteed that they would be protected in their way of living as hunters and trappers from White competition, they would not be prevented from hunting and fishing, as they had always done, so as to enable them to earn their own living and maintain their existence.

(3). It was only after the Royal Commissioner had recognized that the demands of the Indians were legitimate, and had solemnly promised that such demands would be granted by the Crown; and also after the Hudson Bay Company officials, the Free Traders, and the Missionaries with their Bishops, who had the full confidence of the Indians, had given their word that they could fully rely on the promises made in the name of QUEEN VICTORIA, that the Indians accepted and signed the treaty.

THIS AFFIDAVIT made in duplicate at _Fort Resolution_ in the Province of _____ (or N.W.T.) this _18th_ day of _October_ A. D. 1937.

SWORN in the presence of

_____
J.P., or Commissioner for Oaths.

J. A. R. Balsillie
Post Hudson's Bay Company
Manager

340

in the year herein first above written.

Signed by the parties thereto in the presence of the undersigned witnesses after the same had been read and explained to the Indians by Peter Mercredi Chipewyan Interpreter and George Drever Cree Interpreter

D. H. Ross

J. A. J. McKenna

Treaty Commissioners

Alex X Laviolette
his mark
Chipewyan Chief

Julien X Ratfat
his mark

Seph X Boyel
his mark
Chipewyan Headmen

Justin X Martin
his mark
Cree Chief

Ant. X Saccanoo
his mark

Thomas X Tyblet
his mark
Cree Headman

P. Mercredi

L. W. Le Doussal   L. M. Le Doussel

A. de Chambeul   A de Chambresiil

Gabriel Breynat   Gabriel Breynat

Colin Fraser
F. J. Fitzgerald
B. F. Cooper
V. W. McLellan.   Mc Laren

Appendix IV

In Witness whereof the Chairman
of Her Majesty's Treaty Commissioner and
the Chief and Headmen of the Chipewyan
Indians of Fond du Lac (Lake Athabasca)
and the adjacent territory, in behalf
of themselves and the Indians whom
they represent have hereunto set their
hands at the said Fond du Lac
on the twenty-fifth and twenty-seventh days of July
in the year of our Lord one thousand
eight hundred and ninety-nine.

Signed by the parties
hereto in the presence
of the undersigned
witnesses, the same
having been first
explained to the Indians
by Louis the Chamberault
& Father Douceur
and Louis Robillard)

David Laird
Chairman of Indian
Treaty Commissioner

Lament his x mark Dzieddin
Headman

Toussaint his x mark
Headman

Solicitors

G. Breynat

Harrison Young.

Pierre Deschambeault

William Henry Burke

Bathurst F. Cooper

Germain Mercredi

Louis his x mark Robillard

Witness S. Young.

H. S. Anderson Sgt. R.N.W.M.P.

(The number accepting Treaty being larger
than at first expected, a Chief was allowed, who
signed the Treaty on the 27th July before the
same witnesses to signatures of the Commissioners and Headmen of the 25th.)

Maurice x mark Piche
Chief of Band.

342

Appendix V

the Indians inhabiting the South shore of Great Slave Lake, between the mouth of Hay River and old Fort Reliance, near the mouth of Lockhart's Rivers, and territory adjacent thereto on the mainland or on the islands of the said lake, having met at Fort Resolution on this 25th day of July in the present year 1900, Her Majesty's Commissioner .... James Ansdell Macrae, Esquire, and having had explained to them the terms of the treaty unto which the Chief and Headmen of the Indians of Great Slave Lake and adjacent country set their hands on the 21st day of June 1899, So gave in the errors made by the said treaty, and agree to adhere to the terms thereof in consideration of the under- takings made therein.

In witness whereof Her Majesty's said Commissioner and the Chief and Headmen of the said Indians have hereunto set their hands at Fort Resolution on the 25th day of July in the year herein first above written.

Signed by the parties thereto in the presence of the undersigned witnesses after the name had been read over and explained to the Indians by Rev'd Father Dupire & Rev'd Father A. Menoste

Charlie Morin
Richard Spiea

J. W. Martin
Ireneus general
.....
J. C. Macrae
C & R L V for the ...... of Chiefs & Indians
A ... & (No name of Chief Pierre Squirrel)

J. F. Macrae

For the Dog Ribs
Fred X George Chief
his mark
War. Met. at Zinn
his mark
Eng. Wa. Zee Zinn
his mark

for the Yellow Knives
Snuff X tee Chief
his mark
Zin- the Zeal
.....
Lucian X Aa Zinn
his mark
Oliver X Affionanay
his mark

Chipewyans
Lawrence Zinne
Laurier Zee

Slaves of Hay River

Chipewyans

L. Chu

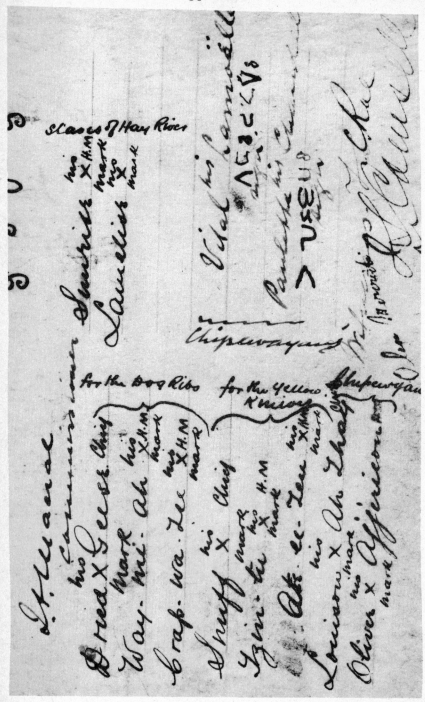

Appendix VII

Memorandum of Lawrence Vankoughnet, January 19, 1887.
(PAC. RG 10 BS, file 241209-1)

The Hudson Bay Company carried on a fur trade with these Indians long prior to the transfer of the country to the Dominion. The Indians of these regions live by trapping fur-bearing animals, the skins of which they sell to the traders. The transfer of the Hudson Bay Company's interest in the country to the Dominion in consideration of value received for the same by the said Company has not practically up to the present time altered in any respect the relations of the Company to the Indians of the portion of the Territories the Indian title to which remains unextinguished. No White settlement has been effected in these regions in consequence of said transfer. Consequently the country still remains as the hunting grounds of the Indians, and the game and fur-bearing animals have not been diminished in number through any action of the Government in settling the country. The Hudson Bay Company have, therefore, insofar as those regions are concerned profited by the payment made to them for their interest therein without any benefit having accrued to the Dominion on account of the transfer by the Hudson Bay Company of this interest in those portions of the Territories.

The Hudson Bay Company before the transfer to the Dominion would in the case of sick, aged, and destitute Indians naturally provide for them when they were unable to provide for themselves; and while in the opinion of the undersigned it is quite proper where White settlement has taken place in the portion of the Territories transferred to the Government, and where such settlement has affected the revenue of the Hudson Bay Company by the diminution in the number of fur-bearing animals consequent from such settlement, that the Government should be at the expense of providing for the sick, aged, and destitute Indians, the undersigned does not, however, see that the Hudson Bay Company can have any equitable claim to be relieved of the care of the sick and aged Indians in those portions of the Territories which they have transferred to the Government but where no white settlement has been effected and no interruption to their trade with the Indians has been caused by Government works or by settlers taking up lands, etc., etc. The Hudson Bay Company, it appears to the undersigned, stands exactly in the same position practically to the Indians of such parts today as it did before the transfer of its interest in the country to the Government.

With regard, however, to the question of making Treaties with the Indians through whose country it is contemplated to construct Railways and other public works, the undersigned is decidedly of opinion that before any such construction takes place, Treaties should be made with the Indians to prevent trouble with them hereafter; and also consistency with the usage adopted in respect to the other portions of the Territories in which public works have been constructed and wherein settlement has taken place, demands that a similar course be followed by in the first place negotiating with the Indians for their title in the soil of the Country wherein it is proposed to construct such works or to effect such settlement.

Appendix VIII

Testimony of Mr. Louis Norwegian, Yellowknife, N.W.T., July 11, 1973.

IN THE MATTER OF: An Application by Chief Francois Paulette, et al., to lodge a certain Caveat with the Registrar of Land Titles for the Northwest Territories.

This transcript is printed here as an example of the Indians' testimonies used in this history.

LOUIS NORWEGIAN, sworn through interpreter.

EXAMINED BY MR. SUTTON:

Q *Mr. Norwegian, where do you live?*
A *Jean Marie River.*
Q *Is that in the Northwest Territories?*
A *Yes, it is in the Northwest Territories.*
Q *Are you a treaty Indian?*
A *Yes, a treaty Indian.*
Q *Which language do you speak?*
A *The Slavey language.*
Q *Are you a member of an Indian band?*
A *I am a member of the Slavey band.*
Q *Of which Slavey band are you a member?*
A *The Fort Simpson Slavey band.*
Q *Are you a councillor in the Fort Simpson band?*
A *We were elected as councillors for many years.*
Q *You answer "Yes".*
A *Yes.*
Q *Where were you born?*
A *I was born in Jean Marie. That is where I have lived up until now.*
Q *When were you born?*
A *I don't know exactly what time when I was born but my years of age is 64 and 2 months. That is how old I am.*
Q *64?*
A *64 and 2 months.*
Q *Was your father a Slavey Indian?*
A *Yes, a Slavey Indian.*
Q *What was his name?*
A *My father, the only way that I know is that his name was Norwegian.*
Q *Norwegian was his name as well?*
A *Yes.*
Q *According to your knowledge and belief, have the Indian people of the Fort Simpson region ever sold or surrendered their land rights to the government of Canada or the Crown?*
A *As far as I know, the government, it never did mention about buying land from the Indians.*

Q   Were you present in Fort Simpson in 1921 at the time the Treaty was first paid to the Indian people of Fort Simpson?

A   Yes, I was there at the time, and my grandfather, the old Norwegian, was the leader at the time of the Fort Simpson band.

Q   Would you describe what happened, to the best of your memory, and would you speak in short sentences so it can be interpreted.

A   My grandfather, the old Norwegian, is the one who tried – the Fort Simpson band tried to make a leader out of him or a chief out of him, and he was the one who was speaking for all the Indians at Fort Simpson. Every time they wanted to give the money, the grandfather who was supposed to be chief, he did not want to take the money for no reason at all.

THE COURT: *I think perhaps we had better get back on to the question.*

MR. SUTTON: *I was asking him to recall what he remembered.*

THE COURT: *I do not think he is talking about what you want. Go ahead.*

MR. SUTTON: *I believe he is.*

Q   Would you continue.

A   I remember that they have meetings to try to pay the treaty, and the Commissioner who paid the treaty tried to make the Indian leader take the treaty first, and they had a meeting for three days, so my grandfather did not want to take the money until he wants to be sure what it is all about, and my grandfather told me, "I am not going to give any money for nothing, and five dollars means a lot, and we want to find out, and why do we take the treaty, so we did not want to take the treaty right away". They mentioned this to my grandfather, that he knows the sun rises in the east and set in the west, and the Mackenzie River flows, and what I will have to promise have been said by the treaty date, and as long as the words exist, whatever the Commissioner told the Indians, the word would never be broken. My grandfather wants to know why they have to take that money from the people, and the Commissioner told him that the treaty that is going to be developed in future years, that there would be lots of white people and if the Indians took the money they may be registered, and if there is enough white people in the country, the government will know wherever the individual Indian is going to be, and that is all the treaty amounts to. . .

Q   Is your grandfather now alive?

A   He died about 30 years ago, my father.

Q   Do you recall what some of the promises that were made by the Commissioner, do you recall what some of those promises were?

A   I know some of them.

Q   Would you state those to the court.

A   If they take the money this would last about a year – a grubstake of any kind.

Q   And it would be there by the fall?

A   Yes, it would be there by the fall.

Q   That the grubstake would be there within a year?

A   He said a load of grubstake if he took the treaty.

Q   Yes?

A   He said if he took the money as the treaty and you want to build a house and maybe 200 miles away from the place, and you want a cook stove and if it is *heavy, the white man has to pack it to where you want it. It is going to be done. That was the promise.*

Q   Do you recall if anything was said about hunting and fishing?

A   My grandfather told me, whatever this country is, whatever will make a living in this country, having a trap is belonging to the country, and belonging to the people in the country, so they have a promise not to interfere with one another. The commissioner promised a letter to the bishop on fishing and trapping in the territory as long as the sun rises in the east and sets in the west and the Mackenzie River flows, and maybe in quite a few years' time they have brought in game regulations –

THE COURT: *I do not want to get into that part.*

Q   Do you recall whether the Indian people agreed in 1921 at Fort Simpson to give up or sell their land to the government of the King?

A   There was a 3-day meeting but, as far as I know, the land and the country never was sold or surrendered to the white man.

Q   Do you recall whether the Indian people agreed to take reserves?

A   They did not mention reserves either, but one thing I hear, that once the Indians took the treaty, the Indians in the various bands in the territory will be in the hands of the government. That is all I know.

Q   You mentioned that your grandfather was the chief, the person chosen as spokesman, is that correct?

A   Yes.

Q   Treaty 11 is Exhibit 4 and –

A   He said he was asked to be the leader but he was not elected a chief. Somebody else took over.

Q   I am reading from page 11 of Exhibit 4, and it indicates that Antoine signed as Chief. Do you have any recollection how that came about?

A   What happened is that they had a 3-day meeting and they have something to eat and when they went home and got supper there was one Indian Antoine was left behind, and they said there was no harm in taking the treaty, so the old man took the treaty. He was not elected. He took the treaty, and that is what happened.

THE COURT: *Perhaps you could ask him if Antoine was recognized as the chief at that time?*

Q   Was Antoine recognized by the people of Fort Simpson as chief of the people?

A   As far as I know my grandfather was a leader at that time, but then this fellow Antoine was not a leader, but he was kind of greedy, and so he took the money while they people was away, and that is why everybody took the treaty, and they made him a chief from then until he died.

EXAMINED BY MR. SLAVEN:

Q   I did not quite follow that. Was Antoine made a chief after he accepted the money and signed the treaty?

A   What is that?

Q   Was Antoine made a chief after he accepted the money and signed the treaty?

A   *They say that once Antoine accepted the treaty the Indians did not make him the chief but the White men made him the chief.*

Q   *All right, thank you. . . .*

Transcript of evidence
pp. 129-132, 135-138.

Appendix IX

The Edmonton Journal, September 26, 1921

The expedition having completed its season's work and made its report thereupon to the Government, it is now announced from Ottawa that the cession of the vast tract in the north has been successfully carried out, with the result that approximately 372,000 square miles of territory have been formally added to the crown possession.

The cession of the territory, as thus effected, is in consideration of the government setting aside certain land reserves that shall be for the Indians' use in perpetuity, on the scale of one square mile to every family of five persons; the payments of annual treaty money to each individual, with a special payment to each band in the territory. It is of interest to note that the latter condition to the treaty provides for the substitution of agricultural implements for the hunting outfit if the natives prefer them. A copy of the treaty has been given to each chief, who is held responsible for his people carrying out their part in the agreement.

While essentially a part of Canada the territory had not been entirely free of its original claims and before it could be fully developed as crown property the Indian rights to it had to be extinguished . . . .

In view of the industrial development of the northland it was found desirable to secure full title to the country, and the only way in which this could be done was to deal with the original owners on terms similar to those previously acted upon in other parts of the west. While the Indians are the wards of the Canadian government, they have still had rights and claims upon their wilderness homeland that had the effect of making them virtually landed owners, and the government had therefore to reckon with them in the process of possession . . . .

While this taking over of the great northland has been fully completed the last great tract of virgin territory in Canada will have passed into the ownership of the crown. It will mark too the last inevitable encroachment of the all-possessing whites upon the one-time realm of the reds.

Appendix X
Bourget's Report, 1923

I was under the impression that the day set for this ceremony was a holiday for all, a godsend for the merchants, a joy for the young folk and the children who, quite often, see money for the first time.

In my ingenuousness, I believed that all I had to do was to stay in my office and have the men march past my wicket. I would call their names and hand over to each of them the handsome sum of five dollars, receiving a thank you in return. But it was not at all like that.

I was informed of the fact that certain Indians received the "treaty" in 1900 and others, living further away, in 1921, and that they had the right to indicate to the official representative their problems with the government, the merchants and the agents, and lodge any other complaints. The chiefs could make endless speeches just like politicians and at the end the agent was often exposed to the rejoinders from others present, similar to the discussions in Parliament when a vote is about to be taken. I was advised to purchase a large tent, install a real office with desks and chairs for the dignitaries, chiefs and councillors, numbering nine, for the bands gathered at Fort Resolution. One police constable, in official dress, would serve as clerk and would assist at each assembly.

I was under the impression, since we were there to distribute the money to all: men, women and children, that they would act like white people and assemble at the tent door from seven in the morning to be the first ones there and the first ones served. No, they believed instead that the last would be paid first.

Up at seven in the morning, we were prepared to receive them in the tent with benches, chairs, desks and flag floating in the breeze. While we were waiting, I was asked to go to the convent where a woman had just brought her baby. It was suffering from diarrhea and seemed at death's door. In fact, it was to die a few hours later. The woman, short and stout, spoke a bit of French, and all that she could explain was that her baby "wasn't well" . . . and that her baby "wasn't like that before"....

The Treaty that the Government passed with the Indians was intended, first in the Western provinces and later in the N.W.T.. to avoid any trouble and wars between the whites and the Indians. Instead of simply taking possesion of arable land and provoking Indian tempers when the white man came to settle, the Government preferred making a "treaty" with the bands who inhabited the parts of the country. It would recognize these as the owners, without legal title, but as first occupants of the lands in these regions.

With this "treaty" the Government asked the Indians to accept the whites as their neighbours without bothering them. Under this agreement the government bought, so to say, the country. Meanwhile, instead of one whole payment, the Indians would be paid every year until their race would die out. The amount paid, five dollars per head, would represent the interest on a relatively high capital. In addition, medical care would be supplied by the Government, along with hospitals whenever possible, schools, money to feed the elderly and orphans, nets, ammunition, tobacco, tea, flour, pork (bacon), clothes for the elderly women, etc., the total in proportion to the population. The Indians would thus be the "children" and the "wards" of the Government.

The Metis had the choice of taking part in the "treaty" and staying like the Indians, or they could accept a larger sum, equivalent to a final payment on their part, but they would no longer be the "wards" of the Government, as it is always true that you cannot have your cake and eat it too. Let's say that it often happened that the Metis, after running through their $240 or losing it to shady brokers, were sorry for staying white which entailed freedom but also responsibilities.

This "treaty" had its good side, but it often missed its humanitarian goal because the distribution of the rations to the elderly and the needy encourages the lazy to get as much of the aid for themselves as they could. With the Indians, the same thing happened as with whites on direct relief; many of the unemployed suffered while the others hoarded.

In Fort Resolution, the "treaty" was signed in 1900 with three bands and, in 1921, for the remainder of the Mackenzie district including Rae and Providence, and the Government took possession of the land situated north of Great Slave Lake up to beyond Great Bear Lake, and even, I think, to the shores of the Arctic Ocean.

My Indians never had a proper agent. There was one in Fort Smith who took care of the Indians in this district and simply came to pay those in Fort Resolution, without having anything to do with them otherwise. In Fort Simpson, however, an agent was there before the "treaty" was signed. Every three years, the chiefs and councillors received clothing decorated with decorations and yellow buttons, military belts, trousers with a gold stripe on the seams, boots which the chiefs did not dare wear for fear of stumbling, and large, semi-military hats similar to those worn by the Mounted Police, with a gold and black badge. The first chief at the time of the signing of the "treaty" received a silver medal the size of a pie plate (silver was then of little value). One side of the medal bore the effigy of the king shaking hands with an Indian, and the other, if I remember correctly, represented a savage in a canoe.

Later on I saw a chief wearing such a medallion on a string around his neck and it resembled a "cowbell." On the days when he wanted to impress me he would run to his tent, if he had forgotten his ornament, and would dash back with it dangling from his neck, threatening to knock him down. It thus became quite a dangerous object and no one could say the opposite.

We were waiting for our Indian gentlemen, hoping that they would soon come and get their money. It was after nine when we sent for the chiefs who were still stretched out asleep, because they had had a dance the night before; others had gone to check their nets on the lake. Not an Indian around our deserted tent, as if we had the pox and were in quarantine. Ten o'clock . . . and nothing but dust, and we continued to wait with thirteen thousand shiny new dollars, fresh off the press.

I would never have thought that possible. Around eleven, two chiefs arrived yawning and stretching, and by this time, I felt like imitating them. They announced that soon the others would be there ready to begin.

Around eleven thirty, the rest arrived and stretched out on the grass. These

351

gentlemen were ready, not to receive their money, but to talk and discuss their living conditions and the new hunting regulations, to make their own new demands, and to ask me what I was doing there. They also wanted to know if I would stay amongst them; if I would give treaty money to the old men and women and to orphans; if I would force the parents to send their children to school; if I would furnish coffins for burials; if I would help them "with a bit of gasoline" during their trips; if I would see to it that the merchants give a higher price when buying furs, if and if . . . and, if I weren't what did I intend to do? The chiefs wanted to show me how they lived so that I would be aware of their suffering. They kept on telling me that they were non-drinkers and that they did not make wine or beer even though I might think they did. Finally they wanted to know why there were not more rations for the poor Indians in the North, who were so badly off . . . .

All of this was not said in the morning, there wasn't enough time! They were simply letting me know that all the chiefs and braves wanted to discuss these subjects when "we'll be ready to begin talking"!

The chiefs felt obliged to talk or they would lose face. The more a chief speaks, the more intelligent he is, even if what he says doesn't mean anything. With Indians as long as they talk and listen to each other, their supporters are satisfied; it is somewhat the same as with the whites.

The mission bell rang for lunch and we had to abandon everything, before even starting. The Indians had just had their breakfast and did not see my point of view, announcing that they were in a hurry since they also had to elect a chief. Yes, they said they were in a hurry and this to me who had been waiting since seven in the morning! If I'm not easy to get along with, or if ever you find me impatient, you can now understand, you who know me, where it came from.

Finally I won my point since I was hungry and dropped everything adjourning until one o'clock sharp. The police went to their lunch and I ran to mine.

At one o'clock, the constable whom I had asked to hurry was at his post standing at attention and I was there too, but . . . nothing doing! They were all gone and we had to start all over again.

We had tons of merchandise to distribute to everyone, besides the money to pay, and I had to prepare for our departure two days later, for a long voyage. Before leaving, I had to try three or four police court cases (I had just been named justice of the peace) and see numerous sick, and none of this (except visiting the sick) could be done before the "treaty" was paid; that had to be done before anything else.

It was a beautiful, warm afternoon and the mosquitoes were being lazy, biting only when necessary, but there was another kind of insect which I had never seen, at least not in such great numbers: a yellow fly which often attacks horses and cattle. It was a sort of horse fly, rather like a wasp but thicker in the waist. These pleasant creatures bit us on the arms, hands and face until we bled. To add even more to our sufferings our money neatly piled on the table threatened to blow away. The yellow flies, called "bulldogs" in the region, made us indifferent to the arrival of the Indians. Any minute now, our dollars, their elastic bands removed, could fly away and we would have a nice deficit which would be hard to explain to our superiors. I had thought it a good idea to place my fortune in sight of everybody, so as to attract our clients to come earlier; I almost regretted it!

With deliberation worthy of a royal court, our chiefs took their place on the benches and the programme began.

All the subjects mentioned above which were to make up our discussion were only a prelude in F minor to the principal movement which was going to follow in F major. An Indian agent who can sit still and let a group like this one talk for hours without getting angry or becoming impatient, and without opening his mouth before his turn came would assuredly make an excellent husband, if I do say so myself.

But everything in this life eventually comes to an end. The speeches, the requests and the complaints ended and it was my turn. I did my best to calm them down and with the help of the sun and the warmth we had what could be called a fine meeting. Nearly six hundred people were there and only a few understood what I was saying.

This comedy ended about five o'clock and we were finally about to pay out five dollars per person as each would give his name, and how many children he had, both girls and boys. We had to assign numbers to the newly weds, sort them out, remove from our lists those who had died and put over to the following year those who had not come.

As we called out the first name, an Indian ran up to tell me that his daughter was bleeding from the nose by the bucketful. I dropped everything, told the constable to watch over the money on the table, and indicated to the fellow to follow me to his teepee where I arrived before him. The little girl was just outside the teepee playing with a little boy but there wasn't a trace of blood on her or anywhere around. She was rather frail looking but quite lively and I asked her father:

"When was she bleeding like you said?"

"Last week where we were staying before we came here."

Poor man! He had probably decided that when he would be at Fort Resolution for the treaty meeting he would speak to the doctor about how his daughter's nose had been bleeding. In his ignorance he had thought the moment well chosen.

I immediately hurried back to my Indians in case they should disappear again and as soon as I had sat down a tribal counsellor, sorry for not having already said enough, motioned to me that he would like to speak again.

"I would really like to know why we Indians are all here and what you are doing here."

"My friend, I wonder myself what I am doing here but please don't ask me for anything more just now."

The previous day, I had given two sacks of flour to the chiefs to help them celebrate the Treaty and to allow the women to prepare bannocks for the festivities. Then in order to have the last word, this same counsellor took up:

"The government's flour isn't good this year."

Cutting him off, I pointed out to him that it was certainly prime quality wheat, the same as mine which was excellent. I sent for what was left of the two sacks to prove this to them by examining the flour right in front of their eyes. The flour as well as the bannocks prepared for the celebration were brought to me. The flour was of high quality and I couldn't keep a straight face:

"My friends, complain as much as you like but anyone here would find that this flour is of the best grade, and I'm going to advise you as if I were your father. Throw these bannocks into the lake because the cook who prepared them will end up killing you with her handiwork."

They were firm but pliable with the texture of rubber and would have made excellent puncture-proof tires.

In my little speech, I had explained to them that I was there to help them, to see to the poor and help the others to live better, to foster trapping, to help get the children into school, to try court cases and to care for the sick. Since I was a government employee, they wouldn't have to pay me anything for my services. In addition, I intended to study their way of life so that I could defend their hunting and fishing rights. I had also been instructed to come down heavily against those who were making intoxicating beverages. When I mentioned this, one particular chief remarked that I shouldn't speak that way, because since I was an outsider my words might encourage the Indians by giving the idea to brew such beverages to those who had previously not been aware of such a possibility. According to information I had already received, this old devil made more home-brew than anyone else in the area.

On the request of their chief, the government had given permission to the Yellowknife Indians to receive their Treaty payments in their own region rather than at Fort Resolution where they had come in the past. As a result, only their leaders had come to the fort and the others waited for us in their home territory. (On our recommendations this was allowed to continue for only a few years.) We had explained to our Department that these Indians, if left on their own far from the missions and forts, became less civilized than ever, that they tended to marry spouses who were too closely related to themselves, and that they all, but especially the young ones, would flee into the bush when they saw us coming.

At Fort Resolution I was so enthusiastic as to invite their chief to travel to his home with me, making it clear to him that he would be my guest. I was far from thinking that, once we had arrived, he would ask to be paid for having been royally dined on chicken.

At the Treaty gathering we had to be constantly on our toes, ready to reply without hesitation to the most ridiculous propositions and to the silliest whims which arose, excellent training for keeping our wits about us. Our customers were often stirred up by Métis who envied them, miniature Riels but without his skill. In the area was one of these Métis, all of whom are despised by honest people, who devoted his life to making trouble surreptitiously.

Ridiculous questions rained down upon us and we were hard put to find answers. An earlier agent had also had the same kind of problem. Some time later a similar adventure happened to me at Hay River. The Indians wanted to know definitely, one way or the other, if they could go duck hunting in the spring. If they weren't allowed to do so, why had they been given complete hunting priveleges? If it were forbidden, then the Government obviously didn't keep its promises.

This question was brought up in the morning and the police were away, having been called out on an urgent case. I explained to our Indians that the Government couldn't give permanent authorization because of an agreement with the United States forbidding spring hunting. However, the Government did not want any Indian to suffer from hunger, and, in addition, I knew that it was a difficult time of the year for them since fishing was also prohibited. Unofficially, I pointed out to them that near the village there were many small rivers and creeks where ducks abounded and that if the police didn't catch them in the act, there was no harm in killing one or two ducks to feed their families. For this I received enthusiastic thanks, or, as the Indians call it, *mercitcho.*

When we met again that afternoon, the police were there including the chief inspector, and my friend the chief asked me with all innocence:

"Will you please tell us where we can hunt on the little rivers as you mentioned this morning, so that the police won't bother us?" At that moment I would have liked to have been quietly smoking my pipe at home rather than listening to such an untimely question.

In 1928 two investigators came from Ottawa, one from the Department of Indian Affairs to study local conditions and the other from the Department of the Interior for his regular biannual (biennial) visit. My Indians were up in arms because they had been forbidden to hunt beaver for two years. After lengthy negotiations where fortunately I was only a spectator, one of the investigators, who wanted to finish up but without giving a definite response, got up and asked the chiefs to gather their followers about, saying:

"We are going to take a nice picture of all of you to send to our great chief in Ottawa and he will be very happy to have it."

"Thank you," said the chief. "These children's games are not urgent. We are going to settle the beaver question, and tomorrow if the weather is good, we'll pose for a picture."

Could *we* have said better?

The same day our investigators discussed the buffalo which were in the nearby national park, not far from Fort Smith, on the 58th parallel, an area as large as a whole province reserved for these beasts. Seven thousand buffalo had been shipped to this park at great expense and when it was noticed that the entire herd had moved south and abandoned the area, it was decided by order-in-council to enlarge the park on the map, which was easier and much cheaper than running after them. As a result the park was made large enough so that the buffalo would never be able to leave it . . . . Isn't education marvellous!

Now these buffalo weren't there to go into the Indians' soup pots but to keep the animals from becoming extinct. Then one of my chiefs, who had sampled this meat and liked it, asked the investigators if he could hunt them if his provisions were low.

"No, it's impossible."

Our Indian then asked quietly and with a long preamble: "Suppose that it's winter and that I find myself with my wife and six children in the buffalo park. I've nothing to feed my family; it's cold in January and hunting is difficult because the moose don't move around much. I'm hungry and my children too and I come upon one of the Government buffalo. One or the other has to die because I don't want myself or my children to starve to death simply because this Government buffalo mustn't disappear from the region. Which of us is to disappear first? I would like an answer, is it me or the buffalo?"

Needless to say the reply was only as vague as Government officials know how. The Government realized with great anxiety and sorrow that it had to help the needy but it also found its good intentions restricted by article 437, rule 739, page 13, adopted in 1913, etc., etc.

On certain days, when it was very hot and humid, it would happen that the new dollar bills for the Treaty payments would stick together and, even though we were very careful, we could give an extra dollar out to one or another Indian. Afterwards it was easy for me to check if I had perhaps been out a dollar because the serial numbers ran consecutively. I didn't have to worry about this because an Indian, when he received his five dollars for himself, his wife, and his children (and double the amount if he had missed the previous year, which could give a total of fifty dollars in some cases) always counted what he had received with his relatives and friends. If there were a dollar extra he would come back to have me check if there was an error. If he were missing a dollar (which I could also check from my serial numbers) he would soon bring back what he had received swearing that he hadn't taken it but that he was short. It wasn't such a bad proof of their honesty. But even better, I once gave thirty-five dollars to an Indian for his family. Ten minutes later, he came back and told me that the boat had just arrived with the news that his daughter had just died in the hospital at Fort Smith, and that as a result he hadn't the right to the five dollars he received for her. As it was impossible for me to confirm this, I told him to keep the money for that year and that his daughter would be listed as deceased the following year. This proves that these Indians would be basically honest if they hadn't been spoiled by the cursed trade.

Appendix XI

Eye-witness accounts of the conditions existing in the Mackenzie District during the summer of 1928, the time of the "Great Flu".

1. Helge Ingstad, a Norwegian, was in the region east of Great Slave Lake between 1927-1929. He landed at Snowdrift at the time of the flu, and describes the experience in *The Land of Feast and Famine*, pp. 150, 151, 152.

I set out for the islands. As I come gliding into a cove where a number of teepees are pitched near the beach, I am met by a singular stillness. No children are playing about the camp, no men come running down to the lake to give me a hand with the canoe. No living thing is in sight, save the dogs, skulking about the teepees.

As I step ashore, I notice some canoes, half-loaded with all kinds of gear, as though their owners were in the act of moving. Up at the edge of the woods I come upon a man sitting on a stump. He rocks from side to side, his face buried in his hands. It is Drybone. "Hello!" I call. "What's up".

He looks up at me with red, streaming eyes and says: "White man's sickness. All Indian sick. Some die, me pretty soon, too." And, with that, he buries his face back in his hands and moans softly.

I go from teepee to teepee, and a most sorrowful spectacle meets my gaze. On the bare earth strewn with spruce twigs lie the huddled forms of the sick – men, women, and children, wrapped up in skins and filthy rags. They are shivering although the air is stifling inside, and they cough up blood and stare at me with strange eyes.

Off in the woods I find three corpses, covered over with aspen leaves.

An old woman is the only one who has escaped the ravages of the diseases. She is sitting in front of one of the teepees and is staring vacantly off into space. The epidemic struck suddenly, she tells me, shortly after several of the hunters returned from a journey south. Of late the people of the camp have been unable to procure food, for no one was strong enough to haul in the nets. She begs me to help her bury the dead before the ravens can get at them. And then the camp must be moved over to the nearest island, for to remain here where the Evil Spirit reigns will mean that death will surely claim them all.

With the aid of a hunting-knife and a crude spade carved from wood, I manage to dig a groove in the earth deep enough, with some crowding, to accomodate the three corpses. Over a covering of moss and turf I plant a cross made from two sticks lashed together, and then, according to ancient Indian custom, I surround the grave with a fence of tall pointed poles.

In the meantime the old woman has made a fire down on the beach and is burning up all the personal possessions belonging to the dead. Then we get busy breaking up the camp. We take down the teepees and roll them up into small compact bundles, and, one by one, I carry the sick down to the canoes. Room is found for the dogs and we shove off, I in one canoe, the Indian woman in another.

Seldom have I experienced such a weirdly melancholy feeling as I did on this particular voyage. In front of me in the bottom of the boat lie the sick, one on top of the other, all of them covered over with a layer of teepees, caribou-skins, and rags. In the bow, a dozen Indian dogs tightly squeezed together. Some of them sit motionless, their heads on the gunwale; others attempt to crowd back on top of the sick. In a twinkling, I must use the paddle to drive them back where they belong.

Abreast of me glides the other canoe. In it sits the old squaw paddling. She is bare-headed, the wind rustling and clawing at her hair. But she pays no heed to this condition, merely keeps on paddling. Her face appears carved in stone, and there is a far-away look in her eyes. Round about us, and bathed in sunshine, lies the heaving expanse of Great Slave Lake; off to the west there is a faint haze through which the dim outlines of islands may be seen. Behind me stretches the mainland with its tiers of forest and bluish hills–the Indians' Country . . . .

When, after a time, we reach the nearest island, I set to work cutting poles and branches of spruce. Then I raise the teepees. It is midnight before I have finished pitching the camp and have comfortably installed the sick. About time to be getting home! Just as I am about to hop into the canoe, the old squaw approaches me with a dog she is holding on leash. It is no more than a mass of shaggy hair and nothing much to look at, save for the eyes. "You take," she says. I explain to her that I want no pay for what I have done. "Kli nezon (Good dog)," she says, pointing to the animal. It had belonged to her husband, whom I had but recently buried, and it would have been an insult to her had I refused, so I stowed the dog away on board and started off.

2. Chick Ferguson, an American, spent many years trapping in the Fort Providence area. In *Mink, Mary and Me*, pp. 13, 14, 15, he recorded his recollections of that summer:

When the steamer pushed its barge ashore at Fort Providence, it was like stopping at a ghost town. There wasn't a soul in sight. Just a few dogs, starved and hopeless-looking, watching from among the rocks. The stillness frightened me . . . . For several weeks Fort Providence had been a jumble of teepees and tents. The Indians from the surrounding country had gathered to have "tea dances", gamble, and get their usual treaty payment. But influenza had struck, and instead of tea dances and merrymaking there had been only suffering and death. Treaty payment had been made several days ago and the Indian Agent had ordered them to leave the fort. Now they were going. Though many were far too sick to travel, most of them did manage somehow to dump tents and blankets and children into canoes and push away from shore.

Some were too sick and weak to paddle, or even to steer. The canoes just drifted like chips with the strong current, idly twisting this way and that in response to the great river's whim. Men, women, and children lay helpless in the bottom of canoes. Some sat with bowed heads, listless, ragged, dirty, beaten. Here and there a man or a squaw steered half-heartedly by dragging a paddle from the stern. One by one they disappeared from sight around the point of Mission Island. It was a disheartening sight, but, sorry though we felt, there wasn't a thing we could do for them.

He recalled what the policeman had told him a few days after the Indians left:

I'm going back down with Father Michel to see those sick Indians. They're in a bad fix. The day they left here one guy died before they got five miles. They just rolled him out on the river bank–they were too sick and weak to bury him. But their starving dogs came along and found him. The guy was half eaten up. He was a mess to bury. And fifteen more died after they got to camp.

3. Father Antoine Binamé, OMI. the resident priest at Fort Good Hope, recounted his experience to Bishop Breynat, who included it in his own book, *Bishop of the Winds*, pp. 180-181.

I was the first to come down with the disease. My Indians were not slow in following my example and in a few days everyone had it. A doctor who was passing through took me around as interpreter, which enabled me to gauge the extent of the epidemic. Everyone was stricken with it. The very night the devoted doctor left us, some began to die. Now I had to be doctor myself, and very soon, there being no one able-bodied left even among the whites, I became gravedigger as well.

Several deaths occured within a few hours. It was all that was needed to drive the Indians to panic. Without losing a moment, most of them, in spite of their fever, dragged themselves to their canoes and just drifted down stream. The more courageous went a little way up the Mackenzie, but they too were soon exhausted and after a struggle contrived to pitch their tents on the bank.

In the general flight from death, one old squaw was left abandoned in the grass between her two dogs. I found her breathing her last. I succeeded in putting up a small tent to shelter her and then prepared her for death. There was no one to feed her. Brother Jean-Marie (Beaudet), though ill himself, found the strength to do some cooking for those left behind, and for a few days we were able to prolong the poor old woman's existence.

In another family, the father and mother were both lying helpless, while their two children waited in vain to be fed. So we had to turn cooks. The mother died a few days later, in appalling agony, but like a saint. Others could get no water to quench their devouring thirst. The infirm were squatting helpless in filth. One old man lay in agony at the door of his hut while another died abandoned by his daughters; I found him surrounded by a circle of greenish spittle. I administered the Sacraments and tried to relieve the sufferings caused by the burning fever. In the morning I counted the dead, rolled up the bodies in blankets, and with the aid of a handcart conveyed them to their last resting place. There I dug a trench, deepening it as required, and with the help of Brother Jean-Marie I lowered the bodies into it as they were, without coffins. After reading the burial prayers, I resumed work with the spade . . . . Often, canoes brought us still more bodies.

Those who had left also needed our help. So with the factor of the Hudson's Bay Company, I set off in a motorboat to find them and amid more scenes of desolation I administered the sacraments freely and distributed the medicine I thought most effective.

Appendix XII

Part of a Report for the year 1928, submitted to the Department of Indian Affairs, by Charles Parker, Inspector of Indian Agencies for the Mackenzie District. The complete text can be found in the Public Archives of Canada, RG85, Accession 64/128, vol. 477, File 6327.

It would be ingratitude on my part not to mention the assistance I received from the Northwest Territories staff in my work at Smith and in making arrangements for the greater part of the trip North. While I was candidly in opposition to their proposed close season on beaver and they were well aware of my attitude in this connection. I received from them nothing but courtesy and any information asked for that they were able to give me was gladly put at my disposal . . . .

Ft. Resolution strikes one as a half breed settlement while Ft. Simpson might better be classed as a white trappers' community. (I speak of course of the summer season) . . . .

The three year close season on beaver appears to be a most unfortunate move in view of actual conditions in the Territories at the present time. The real necessity for such regulation is a debatable point and the arguments in favour of it far from convincing. Careful inquiry failed to find any locality where beaver are almost extinct as stated in the Order-in-Council . . . .

The present time is the lowest period in the well known cycle of fur bearing animals. Co-incident with the low cycle in fur bearers is the almost entire absence of rabbits a staple article of food for both Indian and white. The native must live, or at least has a reasonable expectation that this is his right, in a land he once owned and roamed over without interference by restriction or competition. And during that period of aboriginal domain there never was any serious anxiety as to the extinction of fur bearers or food sources. Cycles came and went and the native met the situation in his own way. The trade prospered and "relief accounts" were an unknown quantity.

I am not one who would wish to recall the days of the "forest primeval" nor would I desire the exclusion of the white who is a useful asset to the country. The advance of civilization has already a strong foothold in the Territories and the future, (even the immediate future), will undoubtedly witness great changes in the country. There undoubtedly are great undiscovered natural resources in the country and the present era of mineral discovery and development has caused curious eyes to turn Northwestward and the urge of the mysterious unknown has taken hold. Lands forlorn and sub-Arctic forests will soon be open pages and development or exploitation is bound to follow.

All this may appear to be a digression looking too far into the future but is meant to be only an acknowledgement that halcyon days of the past are already beyond recall: therefore we must deal fairly and adequately with the present at the same time not being unmindful of the future.

I maintain, and my inquiry during the past summer is my ground for the stand, that beaver are not in any immediate danger of extinction; that a postponement of the close season for a period of two years will not be a menace to the beaver population; that one of two alternatives inevitably face the native if the close season is imposed, i.e., starvation or law breaking. It is reasonable to expect that the latter will be preferred to the former. Can punishment possibly be justified under such conditions? If not of what use is a law which is so unjust that it cannot be conscientiously enforced?

If you will examine the arguments in favor of a close season on beaver as furnished our Department by the Northwest Territories Branch it will be found that repeatedly mention is made of special provision for the native and the low cycle of fur. All these appear to have been ignored and a close season declared at the lowest period of a long low cycle. To say that natives may be assisted by Government relief is both unjustifiable and inadvisable. How is such relief to be issued? Is the Government to ration Indians before leaving the settlements with sufficient food to compensate for the loss of beaver meat? Can any sane person advocate such indiscriminate and unwarranted expenditure? Our expenditures on relief are already greater than they should be and will be augmented this year owing to the recent epidemic. To further increase them for the sake of a close season on beaver does not appear reasonable.

Arguments by white trappers in this connection may reasonably be discounted. The white trapper is in most cases a single man. He takes to his hunting grounds or trap line an almost complete grub stake so that he does not have to depend upon the hunt for food. He is well equipped with every necessity for subsistence and hunting and trapping. On the other hand the Indian obtains in the Forts only sufficient provisions to assist him in moving himself and his family and aged relatives to his hunting ground. He must spend as much, if not more, time in hunting food as in trapping fur.

Argument on argument might be piled up to justify some special consideration for the native but if the fore-going is not sufficient I fear further effort would be useless. I maintain that at the present inopportune time a close season on beaver will be an undue hardship on the native and that any extra expenditure by the Government to meet the distress caused thereby is not justified by actual conditions.

Before leaving the subject of a close season on beaver it would appear reasonable to draw your attention to one other phase which came to my notice while at Ft. Smith. Despite the fact that, according to P.C. 277, which says:

"because of intensive hunting and trapping the Beaver have been seriously depleted and in some areas are almost extinct.",
a permit was granted last year to a white trapper to take ten live beaver and as many live musquash from the Territories for propagation purposes outside the Territories. This permit was granted to a man who, if public opinion is any criterion, is at least not a desirable acquisition to the district. The permit apparently did not specify that these animals should be taken during the open season nor did it specify how they were to be taken. The permit holder turned up at Fort Smith long after the open season had ended with some live beaver in crates. It was evident that one animal had died. It was also evident that the animals could not be blamed for having done so. The crates were in a filthy state and the stench of them was quite marked. It must be noted that the beaver is a cleanly animal.

At any rate two things impress me in this connection:

1. If the permit holder was sincere in his intention to start a fur farm he should have applied to the provincial authorities for a permit to take live animals for breeding purposes and not to the Territories.

2. How many animals, at ordinary rate of increase, are represented by ten live animals over a period of three years?

Is not this inconsistency personified? Is it hard to understand why the natives at Fort Smith having already been advised of a close season, were so infuriated on a certain night in June that, had it not been for sane advice, these live animals would not have left under permit and possibly more might have happened? If one has any small understanding of the situation from the standpoint of the native, the foregoing is not only a pathetically anomalous situation but a circumstance which might easily have had a more unfortunate ending. Possibly the end is not yet.

The ravages of the recent influenza epidemic have created a situation which alone would warrant the lifting of a close season for a year at least as an emergency provision. The natives are now in very low physical condition and sadly in need of native food. To arbitrarily withhold it at this time is unreasonable and inhumane.

Closely allied to this subject is the question of game laws and that of white trappers. Certain changes are patently necessary in the game laws and since my return to Ottawa I am informed by Mr. Finnie that this matter is already under advisement and final action only deferred pending the return of their own officer, Mr. Moran, who accompanied me during the summer. Mr. Moran gathered considerable information in the Territories which will, no doubt, be of great assistance in dealing intelligently with this and other matters. Apart from the suggestion that there should be no open season earlier than November 1st, and that musquash within the Arctic Circle should be protected except from March 1st to June 15th. I do not feel that I am called upon to deal with this question in extenso.

Nor do white trappers come under our Department but in some measure we are interested in the number of them and their methods, inasmuch as they are in competition with Indian trappers. I am not aware how many white trappers are in the country but this would not be difficult to ascertain as they are all licensed. Some are residents of the Territories; some are citizens of Canada from outside the Territories and others are aliens who for a license fee are allowed to trap the furs of the country and after making a satisfactory stake leave with everything they have gained. I learned of one at least who has been in the Territories for six years paying an alien license. It is evident he does not intend to become a Canadian citizen and that so soon as he can make a sufficiently large stake he will return to his native country to the south of us.

I have already said that the country is sufficiently large and its natural resources extensive enough to provide ample living for the native and prosperous business for the legitimate trader. I will go further and say that these natural resources should be conserved first for the native who must depend upon them for his livelihood. It is futile to expect the bush native, such as I saw in the north, to compete with the white man in labor and industry for his living. They are children of nature and able only to live with nature in its element.

The non-resident white trapper is no asset to the country. He is there for personal gain, takes everything and leaves nothing. I fail to see any single justifiable reason for licensing him to strip the country of its fur bearers. These people come in with complete outfits purchased outside the Territories, transport their own supplies down stream on scows and not only trap but trade with natives and then leave the country. Apart from assuring themselves of a large profit they have no interest in conservation and will, before leaving for good, strip their trap lines of every animal they can kill.

I would not give the impression that there are not good and honourable men among these white trappers. There are many and there was ample demonstration of it during the epidemic at Aklavik where whites turned to and helped with the sick and in the burial of the dead. One in particular, Frank Carmichael, gave up everything and travelled fifty miles down stream to assist. He worked night and day at Aklavik and when a call came from someone to go with the Police to bury dead at McPherson and nurse the sick, he was first to volunteer, and went. What I am particularly concerned about is not the individual but the system of licensing an outsider to come in and take out natural resources needed for the native population who are unable to live except by these resources. Whites are quite capable of earning their living by other means and in more useful capacities.

A gradual elimination of the white trapper will go a long ways toward improving conditions and conservation of game and fur bearing animals.

In this connection I would suggest that serious consideration be given to licensed trap lines.

Physically, the Northwest Territories is suffering from two great poisons, home brew and the white trappers' poison used on the trap line.

I was told repeatedly and by reputable people that 95 per cent of the white trappers use poison. Not one such accusation was made against Indians.

Close observers of the fur cycle have noted that the period is lengthening and that no longer can seven years be counted on in the Territories. There would seem to be a lowering in the recuperative powers of the fur bearers equivalent to the low resistance of the natives mentioned elsewhere in this report. It is not unreasonable to attribute this, to some extent at least, to the devastation caused by the use of poison on white trappers' hunting grounds.

When white "trappers" bring out from 40 to 50 wolf pelts in a season any person who has even elementary knowledge of these animals will concede that such a number was not obtained by trapping or use of fire arms. Bounty is paid for these pelts through N.W.T. Offices so that ignorance is no excuse and yet I could learn of no single conviction for the use of poison in the Territories. Of course, they have no game wardens, outside the Buffalo Park, and this may be one reason, although not a justification.

It must be recognized that poison spread for wolves creates havoc with other fur bearers and therein lies its evil effect. The use of poison in any manner whatever for the killing of wild animals cannot be justified and should be stamped out. The present lack of control in this connection can only mean ultimate ruination of the fur industry in the Northwest Territories.

The white trapper, generally speaking, is not a settler but rather a stripper and is no asset to the country. It is hard to understand wherein lies the justification of licensing an outsider to enter the Territories and strip it of fur by fair means and foul for a paltry license fee.

They pay this fee with the intention of making a "stake". They usurp Indian hunting grounds temporarily abandoned by the native to allow the stock to breed and increase. They provide themselves with complete outfits and undertake the slaughter of fur bearers in a manner calculated to make them the most money possible in the shortest time. White trappers' hunts of $3000 to $5000 were reported frequently. Catches of beaver of from 40-70 by one trapper alone and over 100 by two partners were reported. Careful unbiased inquiry failed to learn of one Indian trapper turning in 25 beaver pelts and 10-15 is the common average.

Closely allied to this subject is the Migratory Bird Protection Act, an International Treaty. It would appear that this treaty was entered into without due consideration and accurate knowledge of the North. The intent of the treaty is undoubtedly commendable. Provision does not appear to have been made, however, for Northern latitudes and the open season commences at a time when the ducks and geese are already on their way South, i.e., when it is legal to kill there is nothing to shoot. When one is informed that in one large hotel in Florida 10,000 ducks were served in one season, more than could possibly be killed in the whole territories, the only conclusion is that Canada is preserving these birds for Southern game hogs and asking its aboriginal natives to starve for their profit. I understand this treaty expires in the not distant future and before a renewal is entered into some more accurate knowledge of the situation should be sought from people actually acquainted with Northern conditions. At present it is little less than revolting to think that this God given food is denied to a primitive people in order to provide sport for whites.

There is great need for a change in the open season on muskrat within the Arctic Circle. The present season opens on October 1st and closes on May 15th. From specimen skins examined at Arctic Red River, Fort McPherson and Aklavik, it is evident that these animals are neither full grown nor prime for fall and winter hunting. This is probably due to their late birth. The delta country is a great rat country but is being rapidly depleted by indiscriminate fall shooting and trapping by whites. I know of one white trapper's wife who took 500 rats last season. The slaughter of these immature rats is a great loss in revenue and should be stopped. This can only be done by confining the open season to from March 1st to June 15th, the rest of the year remaining closed. This was discussed with the Indians at the points referred to and I am able to assure you that they are prepared to abide by such a close season and are quite alive to its necessity. There should be no delay in making this change as each fall hunt is doing untold damage to the main fur resource of the delta . . . .

As a Department we are virtually executors of an estate. In many cases we must deal with local commercial concerns as also do our wards, the Indians. But we have not the authority to control their operations. We do not license them to conduct their business nor have we a right to demand from them an accounting of their doings under a license we do not issue. There is nothing in our Indian Act which empowers us to regulate trade or prices charged in trade. All traders in the Territories, however, are licensed by the Northwest Territories Branch and if any regulation seems warranted it would seem that the onus is on the license . . . .

It can safely be said the economic conditions in the Territories are in an unhealthy condition. With all its known and unknown natural resources it is economically sick, due to the lack of vision of the white inhabitants. Up until the present they are depending on a *portion* of the fur catch for the carrying on of business. I say "a portion of the fur catch" advisedly as a large proportion taken by white trappers is not traded within the Territories nor are his supplies bought there.

Single track minds seem to have centered on the fur pelt and its possession at all costs so that competitors may be worsted. The native while being exploited has been spoiled by short sighted traders who can hear no music equal to the ring of a cash register and do not stop to think that even its iron heart will eventually give out . . . .

The country is large and its natural resources sufficient to provide for the native and make room for more than one trader to the profit of all if the trade would only get down to business in a sane and above board manner. The fur trade as carried on at present is a sort of commercial cut throat carried on in a secretive manner with little or no honor as between competitors and in many cases dishonesty in dealing with natives. I realize these are strong statements and hard to prove by actual circumstances but I am satisfied that there are good grounds for all I have said.

Many have suggested that the Government should take over the fur trade of the Territories but it would appear preferable to give the traders a chance first to put their house in order. If, however, conditions do not improve it might be advisable to give serious consideration to the suggestion and in that case an intensive study should be made of the system in vogue in Greenland where I think the Government controls all the fur industry to the benefit of the people and the country.

In the meantime I can see no just reason why native hunters should not have detailed statements of their accounts. Counter slips are used for the whites and should also be used for the native. This would obviate the possibility of manipulation of accounts and the native could always have his Agent or the police check over debits and credits. As it is at present this cannot be done and the native is sometimes the loser. As primary education becomes more disseminated throughout the country the native himself will be able to keep accurate track of his own accounts if given the benefit of detailed statements. I would suggest providing, instead of treaty tickets, a canvas envelope with identification printed thereon, in which the hunter can keep the counter slips for reference when settling accounts. An even better scheme but more expensive would be a small form of pass book with durable covering in which entries could be made.

The trading companies will probably object to this on the ground that an opposition trader would be able to see what they charged for goods and paid for furs. I fail to see why there should be such secrecy if business is being carried on in an honorable manner. If it is not honestly conducted then why should the native be continually exploited for the benefit of dishonest business.

We have in the Territories certain preserves set aside for Indians to hunt upon. One of these includes the whole settlement of Ft. Resolution which means that a resident there could not kill a partridge in his own back yard in open season. There was evidently some oversight in this and it is to be hoped that it will be remedied. One of the preserves is unreasonably large and parts of it so inaccessible that it cannot be hunted. It would appear advisable to consider a reduction in the size of the Yellowknife preserve and the allotment of small preserves for each band along the river but not at, or so close to, settlement as to hinder residents from killing birds, etc., during the open season when such are available near their homes.

The people of the Territories were being advised during the past summer that an export tax was to be placed on all furs in the near future. This of course will be an added hardship to the Indian. It will mean that the Indian will pay taxes for the benefit of the whites. It would appear reasonable to expect that some part of the revenue derived from this source should be expended for the benefit of the Indian.

Strategy of Conflict
    T.C. Schelling Harvard U. 1960

Devolution of Estates Act

Dependents Relief Act

Wills Act

Law of Wills   S.J. Bailey
                Pitman 1973

Canadian Association for the Mentally Retarded
National Institute on Mental Retardation
Kinsmen NIMR Building, York University Campus
4700 Keele Street
Downsview, Ontario M3J 1P3

TO ——————————————————————————— Date ———

FROM ———————————————————————————————————

CIRCULATE 1 ——————————————————————————————

2 ———————————————— 3 ————————————————

☐ For your information   ☐ For your approval

☐ For your opinion   ☐ Discuss with me

☐ For you to handle   ☐ Return to me

☐ For your signature   ☐ Keep or destroy

☐ Prepare reply for me   ☐ Returned with thanks

———————————— REMARKS ————————————

L & T. Act

RSO 1970 C236

- ~~RSO~~ 1972 C123

Change of Name Act

RSO 1970 C60   + amdts

Ontario Guide to Small Claims Ct.

(Pete Kilchrist)

Small C.C. Handbook

(Carswell)

Sm.C.C. Procedures — TCLS

Sm Cl Ct Act   RSO 1970 C 439

Read - Civ Pro Text *

**Canadian Association for the Mentally Retarded
National Institute on Mental Retardation**
Kinsmen NIMR Building, York University Campus
4700 Keele Street
Downsview, Ontario M3J 1P3

TO _____ Date_____

FROM _____

CIRCULATE 1 _____

2 _____ 3 _____

☐ For your information   ☐ For your approval

☐ For your opinion   ☐ Discuss with me

☐ For you to handle   ☐ Return to me

☐ For your signature   ☐ Keep or destroy

☐ Prepare reply for me   ☐ Returned with thanks

———————————— REMARKS ————————————

Appendix XIII

Part of a report prepared by Charles Parker, following his inspection tour of the Mackenzie District in 1930, and presented to the members of the Northwest Territories Council. The complete text can be found in the Minutes of the Northwest Territories Council, 21st Session, December 10, 1930, pp. 141-145.

The general economic situation of our Indians in the Territories is of such paramount importance that I desire to place this matter fairly before you at a time when definite action is imperative, if we are to save the native, and at the same time, leave him some measure of independence and self-respect.

The hunting Indian of the North has gradually been forced to the wall by the competition of White trappers and their illegal methods of trapping. This was dealt with to some extent in report for 1928, but I propose to state the case in extenso once more in the hope that some definite results may be achieved. Unless something can be accomplished along these lines there is little use of an Inspector from this Department making a long and extensive annual or bi-annual (biennial) visit. I think, in any case, that bi-annually (biennially) is quite frequent enough for general purposes.

At the risk of repeating much that is already known to yourself and officials in the department, may I outline the hunting life of the Indian trapper. He is, in most cases, a married man, with a family to support. The children are of little assistance until they reach the age of twelve to fourteen years and are usually married within a very few years of this age. The Indian is traditionally improvident and this inherent characteristic has been fostered, rather than broken down, by the fur trader.

For generations the Indian has depended upon "debt" for his fall and winter outfit. Content to hunt only enough to pay his "debt" in the spring and have, perhaps, a small surplus for summer needs, he has never gotten ahead of the game. In such rare instances as an Indian having a large surplus, the traders have, in the past, encouraged him to spend it. The result is now everywhere abundantly evident. Content at one time with food, clothing, ammunition, etc., Mr. Indian now owns sewing machines, gramophones and out-board motors. The traders found new goods to take away the Indians' surplus. So, the debt system as manipulated by traders has not only held the Indian down but has also encouraged dishonesty and now the two stronger companies in the Territories have decided to eliminate all debt. Instead of doing so gradually, they are rushing into it without warning and many hunters are stranded without means of reaching their hunting grounds with an adequate outfit, but more of this later.

The Indian hunter goes inland with a small outfit of traps and a limited supply of provisions and ammunition. He has to depend upon hunting and fishing for feed for his family and his dogs. This frequently means that he is obliged to follow the food sources which are not always in a section where fur bearers can be trapped. Sustenance must necessarily come first with the result that when spring comes, he may not have had an opportunity to trap fur and his debt remains unpaid.

Indians have each their own particular hunting grounds which are never molested by other Indians. Under ordinary conditions, they conserve their fur bearers, always leaving breeders behind and frequently abandoning one section for one to two years in order to allow animals to propagate. Such, briefly, is the Indian hunter, without going into trapping and hunting methods.

Let us now look at the white trapper. While much that I will put down applies to white trappers in general, I have in mind particularly the whites found in the Territories. He is in almost all cases a single man with no other responsibilities. Owing to his knowledge of business he is able to avoid debt to a large extent. He goes to his trap lines in the fall with a complete grub stake for the winter both for himself and his dogs. He is, therefore, able to concentrate all effort on trapping and killing fur bearers. He is in the country, in most instances, to make a stake and get out and there are a number of cases where the trapper is not even a Canadian citizen. He pays a high license fee to trap, it is true, but he sees to it that he gets the fur to make it worth while.

In my report of 1928, I think I referred to Fort Simpson as a white trappers' settlement in summer time.* They live in a community at the north end of the settlement and, during my visit this year, I took occasion to find board and lodging amongst them in order that I might learn more of them, and their methods. I may say, without equivocation, that I do not think I would find more red, bolshevik sentiment had I gone to Soviet Russia. If such is the type of citizen who is being encouraged to populate the Territories, the Government is going to have a nice problem on its hands before long.

But let me cite the case of only one, and he is not exceptional, to show the contrast as between the white trapper and the Indian. I will not name him, although I have his name in my notes. This particular trapper, with his son, will have this winter, 209 miles of trap line, using 1500 steel traps besides snares and has cabins on the entire trap line for each night, cabins stocked with provisions. To anyone who knows the Indian hunter as I do, having travelled and lived with him the comparison is ridiculous. And yet there be some who think that, given equal rights, the Indian should be able to compete with the white!

The general attitude of the white trapper is that the Territories is a fur country in process of depletion and they are out after their share; a trapper who is a stripper. He takes all he can and leaves nothing behind. He is not a settler in the commonly accepted sense of the term. He is only a transient ready to pull stakes and leave as soon as he has made his stake or finds that it does not pay him to stay. He is altogether an undesirable character who could and should earn his livelihood in other pursuits not open to Indians.

*In the early 1930s, about 200 white trappers gathered at Fort Simpson, every summer, coming from Fort Norman, Fort Liard, and thereabouts. (Léonide Gosselin, OMI, interview with the author, Fort Rae, May 12, 1972).

It is my contention that the elimination of the white trapper from the Territories will materially improve the economic condition of the Indian and insure a continual source of supply of fur bearing animals. At the same time I realize that such a radical change cannot be undertaken without due consideration of those already on the ground. I would, however, strongly urge the advisability of stopping the issue of further hunting and trapping licenses to whites and non-renewal of present licenses in event of the holder leaving the Territories for a season. If this was done, time would gradually eliminate the white trapper.

The beaver question came up again this year and there is much to be said in favour of some special consideration for the Indian. From information I was able to obtain and personal observation, I am satisfied that beaver can safely be killed by Indians without endangering their numbers. I am very much in favour of opening the beaver season to Indians in the spring of 1931 on a limitation basis, i.e., say fifteen to each hunter. Insofar as killing beaver by white trappers is concerned, I am compelled to oppose it by every possible means.

I have no doubt that there are many who are just awaiting the open season on beaver to make a clean-up. Some are even gathering aerial maps to this end and the slaughter, if the season is thrown open, will necessitate a further close season.

If, however, the privilege is extended to Indians, as aforementioned, I have no fear that any further close season will be necessary. I may say that I have used every effort to impress upon the Indians the advisability of observing the game laws, and carefully guarding any special privileges allowed them. . . .

The influenza epidemic of 1928 left its mark on the Indians and the ill effects are still very noticeable. Recurrent bad colds and other ailments find physiques with less resistance than formerly and the result has been a considerable loss of life. . . .

The sudden cessation of "debt" by the traders will work a considerable hardship on the Indians, especially at the start. I am of the opinion that eventually it will be for the better. It may mean, however, that extra relief will have to be issued during the coming winter. Opening the beaver season to Indians in the spring of 1931 would help the situation considerably but should not be done as a measure of relief as expressed in the Order-in-Council of 1928. The hunting and trapping Indian of the Territories should be allowed to earn his living by these means and not asked to subsist miserably on government dole of food rations not suited to his mode of life and physical system.

At Fort Chipewyan the same situation pertains as to hunting and trapping. The Indians are being trapped out by whites. Once a rich fur company, it is now only a musquash country and in process of rapid depletion. The Indians have approached me on the question so forcibly and there have been no results from our representations made to the Alberta Government. This is of vital importance to Indians and if the matter cannot even be put in process of consideration as a result of ministerial representations, then I think it is a matter for Prime Ministers to deal with. . . .

The crying need of the Indians in the Territories, apart from justice in hunting rights, is the building up of their health. To a layman this is startlingly evident and I think some special attention should be given by our Medical Branch to this important situation. If we cannot give the Indian his full freedom to live the life of an Indian at least we should make a serious effort to preserve his health. This is a matter for professional inquiry and action and I suggest some movement along this line.

Appendix XIV

Memorandum prepared by Bishop Breynat, and presented to the Government in November, 1936. Complete text can be found in the Public Archives of Canada, RG85, Vol. 267, file 1003-2-1.

Re the physical and economic conditions of the North West Territory Indians.

Having lived among the Natives of the North as a Missionary for well over 40 years, I feel that I am reasonably well qualified to give an opinion as to their physical state and their means of support of life.

Convinced as I am that their conditions are so serious, I would be remiss in my duty towards them and the Government of Canada if I did not make an effort to bring it to your attention. It is a long story if told in its entirety, which I will not attempt to do in this Memo, but will merely try to cover the situation in a general way and hope to be able to make the picture clear enough so that it can be easily understood. If I succeed in doing that, I will be satisfied and will hope that some attention will be given to the situation, so that relief and improvement of the Natives' condition will follow.

During the period since Treaty was made with the Territory Indians, a matter of 30 years and over, their physical condition has gradually deteriorated, until, at the present time, it is quite alarming – whole families die off, bands containing many families have been wiped out, infant mortality is so high that it is difficult to believe. One often meets old people who have had from ten to fifteen children, of which none is surviving.

When I was at Fort Rae, last September, the Priest in charge of our Mission there told me he had already registered 60 deaths for the year and at Yellow Knife River they had six deaths in one month, out of a population of a little over one hundred. At Fort Rae, the population must be somewhere around seven hundred.

In every camp widows may be found, more or less derelicted, and often the conditions of orphans, if made known in the Press, would bring nothing but discredit to the Government. Tuberculosis and scrofula are very prevalent, and a fever, peculiar to Northern Natives breaks out at times and a great number die – the resistance of the people to any kind of sickness is gradually becoming less.

The low physical condition of the people is quite noticeable to strangers passing through the country and is a subject of public comment in the Press on their return to the outside. Only this summer, a Member of Parliament, Mr. James A. MacKinnon, M.P. for West Edmonton, passed through the North as far as the Arctic. When interviewed by the Press, he especially mentioned the poor physical condition of the Indians that he had observed throughout the North.

The foregoing facts, as stated, should give sufficient information for the purpose of this Memo.

As the economic conditions are effected by the physical, especially for hunters and trappers, as their work is strenuous and out of door during the winter season, sickness of any kind that prevents a trapper or hunter from following his vocation during the proper season directly affects his living – a great part of the lives of these people is spent hunting for meat and when they do not kill, they do not eat.

Their health is of vital importance; if the head of the family is unable to secure any food, they are all hungry together. When bush people are in distress, due to sickness or hunger, they cling together, they contract any disease that may be around and the whole camp or village becomes contaminated.

Many factors have contributed to the present health state of the Indians. Prior to Treaty, he was more or less of a nomad in summer, going to his hunting and trapping ground in the fall, coming to the trading post in the spring. They were a loosely banded people, divided up into several bands – Treaty brought them into union under a Chief, annuity kept them at the posts longer than formerly and they contracted many white habits and ways – they could buy anything their childish fancy craved or that the keen traders suggested to them, so long as they had the fur. Their only curb was a poor fur year.

In time they became physically susceptible to illnesses that were all strange to them. The white trappers (not all) were a big factor in many ways that helped to bring them down. Many things they were allowed to purchase have helped to undermine their physical resistance. They also learnt to brew and this evil is one of the biggest factors that has brought them to their present state, yet practically nothing has been done in order to check such an abuse.

With the opening up of the Territories to mining, white men will over run the trapping and hunting ground of the Natives. There is already intensive prospecting being carried on in the Yellow Knife preserve.

I believe it is imperative that the Government take steps at the earliest possible moment to control the Indian population and to protect them. The time has arrived when they should be subject to regulations and restrictions, they should be kept separated from the whites as much as possible.

This can be done through intelligent governing regulations and supervision and it should be done as soon as possible in order to protect his future existence. He is a hunter and trapper by instinct and heredity, it is the only life he or his ancestors ever knew and there is no other way in which he can make a living. He cannot, like his more southern kin, become a horse, cattle or land man; his is a rock and bush country.

If left in possession of the hunting and trapping privileges and if his health and living conditions are given some sensible attention by the Government, the situation that now exists can be rectified and improved.

He can be reclaimed and with guidance he can get back to his natural state and preserve his ability to hunt and trap and become more or less self sustaining.

Even now he is not without his financial place in the business life of Canada, as a fur trapper his importance is vital to the future of the fur trade. The North West Territory is the largest extent of virgin fur country left in North America.

We found him in possession of the country, he received us peacefully and by Treaty he gave the Crown legal possession. He became a Ward of the Crown and Canada is his Guardian.

As stated in the beginning, this was to be a brief Memo. I feel that I have but barely sketched the story, but hope however that the situation can be realized and that it will receive the serious attention I most earnestly believe it warrants.

The following suggestions will, I hope, be of some help in an effort to formulate a plan to permanently improve the conditions, of the Treaty Indians, as outlined in my Memo.

First it must be emphasized that the Northern country is not and never will be, with the exception of some small areas, an agricultural country. As it has been mentioned, for the Indians, the only means of making his living is fishing, hunting and trapping. It has been the way of living of his forefathers; it was his only way of living when the Government stepped in to acquire his heretofore undisputed rights to the land of that immense territory.

In order to induce him to sign the Treaty, through which he was asked to abandon all his rights to the Queen Victoria, he was promised that the Queen and her Successors would take care of them as would a Mother and, that, as long as the sun would shine, they would keep their right to live their own way of living by fishing, hunting and trapping and that they would be protected.

Personally having had the honor to act as an Interpreter when the Treaty No. 8 was solemnly discussed and, at the special request of the Indian Department, to accompany and help the Royal Commissioner in the MacKenzie District, I perfectly well remember the alluring promises of all kinds which were made, in the name of the Queen, in order to bring the Indians to agree to the Queen's demand. A great many of these promises, not all, (as not a single word has been altered in the text submitted for discussion), are now contained in the official text of the Treaty.

Consequently the least that might be expected by an Indian would seem to be that such promises be always kept in sight whenever a new regulation is proposed which may add new and unnecessary hardships to his old way of living.

In view of such an achievement to be obtained and which would be of such credit to the Government of Canada, the North being the only place where Indians, while being gradually civilized, could be kept living their old way of living, even with the arrival of white miners,

Owing to the special conditions of our Indians in the North, who would soon become a heavy burden to the Government, if they are not given a chance of continuing to live on fishing, hunting and trapping, as they always did,

Owing also to the immensity of the country and the difficulties of communications:

There should be, with headquarters at Fort Smith, and in charge of all Indians of Treaty No. 8 and No. 11, a Government Official, a man of thorough experience of the North, a man with a real heart for the Indian and not afraid to occasionally remain in their camps and live their lives when necessary. He should be invested with enough authority so as to allow him to take immediate action in emergency cases, especially while he would be visiting camps, such action to be taken according to a general policy and general instructions issued by Ottawa.

He would be the man to gather and forward to Ottawa as much information as possible in order to help frame the most reasonable and most appropriate regulations to promote hygiene, education and economic and special welfare among the Indians, with the strict exclusion of any unnecessary interference with their aboriginal way of living. He should always have in mind that his very office is to help and protect the Indians, as Government Wards, and to see that their rights are respected by the white man, also seeing that the latter is not molested by the Indians.

HYGIENE

1. – As all the Doctors have to attend not only to the Indians but also to the White men, whose number is increasing every year, it appears that better results and better co-operation would be obtained if they were all under the same jurisdiction, with one of them as Health Superintendent for the whole North.

2. – They should be young enough and of enough activity to be able to visit Indian camps, summer and winter, and to endure any hardship such a devoted life may entail.

3. – As soon as possible a general survey of the actual conditions of the Indians should be made, at least by a summary examen of as many as possible, when Treaty is paid or on the occasion of a camp visit. Reports to be kept on file for further reference.

4. – One of the first steps to be taken would be to arrange for a meeting, in some central point, of all the Doctors operating in the North, and have them to discuss the actual conditions of the Indians. They would bring in all their personal observations and make their respective suggestions about the best means of checking the spread of tuberculosis, scrofula and the Indian typhoid fever. They should also make a special study of the advisability of making a larger use, as a preventative, of those Serums which are giving such wonderful results all over the world.

With the Schooners actually in the North for the use of the Agents, the meeting of the Doctors could be arranged without entailing any extraordinarily big expense. They could meet every two or three years.

5. – In their meeting the Doctors should investigate the advisability and the possibility of establishing one or two Sanatoriums to take care of such cases of tuberculosis, especially among the children, which may afford good hope of complete cure or serious relief. Any experiment should be started with a few well defined cases, more development to follow according to the results obtained and also according to the line which would prove the most adapted to the prevailing conditions in the North.

6. – Within the limit permitted by the Northern conditions, as much relief and comfort as possible should be afforded to desperate cases of tuberculosis, especially when the patients have no one to look after them and are a too heavy burden, as well as a danger, to the community.

7. – Try and have some registered nurses, of some experience, at one or two places, and, if the results are satisfactory, have one in each important place. They would attend to emergency cases, teach hygiene and would be responsible for calling a doctor when necessary, or sending patients to Hospitals.

8. – In any case prompt action should be taken to dispel the impression given by some heartless white people, who are always objecting to spending money for the protection of the Indians, claiming that it is just as well to let them die out.

EDUCATION

1. – The schools in the North West Territories, notwithstanding special and great difficulties, have achieved quite satisfactory results. The children who have spent some time in schools are stronger. They, especially the girls, have brought home principles and habits of cleanliness, hygiene and housekeeping to such an extent as to cause a real surprise to the whites and to be a credit to the Government and to the Churches.

Boys, when they have not been kept too long in school, generally are better trappers and better hunters and are pretty hard to cheat in business and quite a few of them occasionally prove to be intelligent interpreters.

2. – Yet, owing to the nomadic character of the life our Indians have to live and to the difficulties of communication, it is not an easy job to induce the parents to send their children to school, although they gradually realize the advantages of a good school training.

Better results would be obtained if all the Agents would give a little more of their time and of their heart to recruiting, or at least to help the recruiters.

374

3. – Until lately, the Department of Indian Affairs has been rather slow in helping for better equipment of the schools. It is to be hoped that in the future the Northern schools will receive a more fair share in the funds of the Department disposed for that end.

It should not be any more objected that the schools are owned by the Churches and that the Department cannot spend money on improvement of schools which are not its property. On the very contrary, the Department should be the more generous, as the Churches have done, for many years, at their own cost, what should have been done by the Government, as promised at Treaty Time.

4. – Day schools would be of no satisfactory avail in the North West Territories. Indians do not stay long enough at the trading posts. When they do ask for such a school, it is generally on the suggestion of some white men who have some children of school age. Another Department should attend to the needs of the increasing white population.

Whenever some Indian family is resident at the Fort the children could attend the school, the Indian Department paying for the attendance, as it is done in other places under the same conditions.

5. – There are enough residential boarding schools in the districts, which this Memo is covering, to reasonably meet all the actual needs. The upkeep of small boarding schools is too great on account of the general expenses, and experience shows that should the Indians have a boarding school near to every trading post, they would still feel slow in sending their children, especially when they have plenty of Caribou around their camps. There always will be the difficulty of transporting the children on account of the great distances where the parents live and the difficulty for the latter to visit them as often as they would wish–one or two hundred miles, more or less, would not make a great difference. No school is actually filled to capacity.

Unless the Government is ready to enforce compulsory education, a system which I would not recommend, before opening new schools it would seem wise to wait until such time when our Indians show a better appreciation of education.

6. – A good system of encouraging parents to send their children to schools would be to give some post scholar assistance to those who have been giving satisfaction and have stayed five years in the school. The boys would be given a rifle or a gun, with some traps, the girls a hand sewing machine, etc. As a rule the children should not be kept in school, the boys when they are over 13 or 14 years of age, the girls when they are over 16, unless when they are orphans and they ask to be kept until they are married.

7. – When the children are sent home for holidays, the Agents should adopt the practice, which is generally followed in the southern districts, to see that the children are sent back in time to their school, unless their parents are in a real need of their assistance.

8. – Too often poor orphans are kept in the camps as servants to greedy Indians, they are half clothed, even in winter time. They are also the last to be fed and they never are given any chance to enjoy any sympathy around them. They do not even draw one cent out of the Treaty annuity they are entitled to and which is fully claimed by their guardian.

In order to remedy such a pitiful condition, education should be made compulsory for all the orphans of school age and the Treaty annuity should be directly given to them as pocket money for little fancies.

When they leave school, the Agent or the Church should see that they are placed with some reliable and good people who would train them to make their living by fishing, trapping and hunting.

A few years ago, on my recommendation, the Department of Indian Affairs sent a circular to that effect to his Agents in the North. The circular has been a dead letter so far.

SOCIAL AND ECONOMIC WELFARE

It would be the main work of the Government Official I have suggested to have at Fort Smith, and who should be appointed without any delay, to personally see to the very much needed development of economic and social welfare among our Indians of the North.

In the meantime, I would respectfully take the liberty of making the following suggestions:

1. – A Treaty has been agreed upon by the Indians with the Crown. If the Indians must be ready to submit themselves to such regulations as it may seem advisable to the Crown to issue, for their own protection and for the good of all, it must not be forgotten that with the Crown remains the solemn obligation to see that the promises made to the Indians are faithfully kept. The more so as the Indians have nothing to say and no way to protect themselves when new restrictions, which they could not foresee when the Treaty was signed, are imposed on them.

Would it not be a good thing, in order to put an end to often heard complaints that too much money is spent for the benefit of the Indians, to occasionally and publicly remind the newly arrived, whatever country they may come from to avail themselves of the wonderful richness of this land of Canada, that the Indians of this very Canada have, as first inhabitants of this country and also as Wards of the Crown, the first and imprescriptible right to be protected in every possible way in full accordance with the stipulations contained in this Treaty. The Crown and with the Crown all the newly arrived population must be ready to pay the cost – it is a debt of honor.

2. – After having been a witness to the Treaty and seeing the way the Indians' interests have been handled since, I often wonder how many officials, in the various spheres of the Government, who have dealt or may have to deal with the Indians, may have ever read the text of the Treaty.

Would it not be more advisable to have a copy of the Treaty handed over with every new appointment, with a strong recommendation to fully comply with the spirit of the Treaty, which is a spirit of a motherly attendance to the moral, physical and economic needs of the Crown Wards, which the Indians are, as they have been accepted forever in the name of Queen Victoria.

376

3. – Conscious of the responsibility imposed on the Federal Government, the latter has organized a special Department in order to properly take care of the Indians, to help them in full accordance with the Treaty stipulations and to see that their rights are not encroached upon by anybody.

Unfortunately, other Departments completely absorbed by other responsibilities, of which the responsibility of preserving the wild life animals, have stepped in and dictated regulations which would not fit in the conditions of the Northern Indians and would impose on the latter unnecessary restrictions in their old way of living.

And how could they have been protected when the Head of the Indian Department could not find time to go to the North and get acquainted with the special conditions of the district, until last year when Dr. H. W. McGill made a flying trip to Aklavik.

4. – It should be understood, once for all, that every new regulation caused to be necessary by the increasing influx of white men, prospectors, miners, etc., will generally not fit the conditions of the Indians and would rather prove to be a new encroachment on their legitimate rights. Consequently, provision should carefully be made so as not to impose any new unnecessary restriction on them.

In any case, one should ask for the advice and recommendation of the Government Official, who would reside at Fort Smith, to look after the Indians and their interests and to forward all useful information to Ottawa. He himself, before forwarding any advice on matters of greater importance, would be wise, and it would be but fair to the Indians to have a friendly talk with the Chiefs, hear what they have to say, explain to them the mind of the Government and secure their hearty co-operation.

5. – It would be adopted as a definite policy of the Government not to grant any more trapping licenses to white men in the North West Territories. The trappers who actually own a license would be allowed to keep it with such a restriction as they could make use of it only on a well determined and registered line, said line to be respected by the Indians as well as by the Whites. This would be the best means of stopping trapping by plane, with all its disastrous consequences.

6. – On account of the mining development in the North, it would be wise to protect the interest of the Indians:

(a) By having a small plot of land reserved and surveyed around every actual Indian village on which no white man could put up a building or stake a claim, without the agreement of the Chief and the approval of the Indian Agent.

(b) By issuing regulations providing that no deed entered upon with an Indian concerning discovery of minerals, staking claim and disposing of same will be valid unless signed before the Indian Agent or some other Government Official.

(c) By having the mining act section, which reserves all timber on a claim to the owner of the claim, to read as follows: provided that any Indian may be allowed to cut any wood or timber he may need for personal use.

7. – Indian Agents should be directed to have every infected Indian house put down as soon as possible, to supply floor and roof lumber for erecting new more sanitary building and, on their visit, to see that elementary rules of cleanliness and hygiene be strictly followed.

8. – There might be some possibility of grouping a certain number of Indians, at least among the poor and the derelicted, in one or two villages somewhere, in or near the Buffalo Park, where they could be trained to support themselves with Buffalo meat and fish. Gradually might be developed some kind of industry to prepare dry meat for the Police of the North, the schools and the destitutes all over the North. There may be found some way to tan the Buffalo hides improved from the old way of tanning, as it has been in practice among the Indians for many generations.

It would be one of the duties, and an important one, of the Superintendent residing at Fort Smith, to make a full investigation to start some experiment with one or two families, good willing families may be found for the experiment, and to report to the Government for further improvement.

9. – Something should be done to encourage fur farming among the Indians. It will be slow work because they will have to be induced to settle down a little more, but the very moment one or two have been induced to try, they will soon have followers when success crown their efforts.

But there again, there must be somebody, with experience and patience, to show them how to do it. The above suggested Indian villages might be good places where to make the first experiments.

However, some efforts have to be made, before it is too late, to organize some kind of trade which would fit in with the way of living of our Indians and would help them to support themselves whatever may happen in the future.

10. – Time may have come when the policy of having only Doctors as Agents be gradually abandoned. The policy has proved a good one so far, but the conditions are changing so rapidly in the last three years.

With so many white men rushing into the North, a Doctor Agent has and will have more and more to give a good share of his time to the care of the white men and the economic side of the Indian problem is more or less bound to be lost sight of.

At Fort Chipewyan, by instance, the great majority of the population is white and should not be attended to at the Indian Department cost, while Indian interests are necessarily neglected. It is, or it will soon be more or less the same everywhere, the more so as social duties are now imposed on the Doctors of which there was no thought of a few years ago.

On the other hand, an Indian Agent, if he fully realizes the seriousness of his vocation, will have ample work to keep him busy to promote, among the Indians, hygienic, educational and economic welfare in the full measure they are entitled to, as Government Wards, from the Federal Government.

11. – All half breeds, living an Indian life, at least the children, should be included in the Treaty and have the same rights as the Indians.

Having spent nearly half a century in the North and, more and more, having at heart the interest of our Indians, I have thought it my duty to respectfully submit the above remarks and suggestions to the most serious and favourable consideration of the Government.

On quite a few unsolicited occasions, I have been told by Government Officials in Ottawa, how much they appreciated my interest and hearty co-operation in their hard task to meet, as generously as possible, the ever increasing needs of such an immense territory. Nothing but the same desire of a hearty and interested co-operation has prompted me to prepare this Memorandum.

Whatever may be my long experience, I am not foolish enough to pretend to an exclusive knowledge of the Northern conditions, nor of the most appropriate means to improve such conditions, but I am trying to be second to none in my hearty and perseverant efforts to assist in the immense task which is falling upon the Government.

Whatever is undertaken to help correct the present conditions of the Indians must be adapted to their actual moral and mental state, as well as to their physical and economic welfare. There is nothing theoretical about the problem. The fact is that the Indians must be protected and helped and immediately, while it is still time. It is a case of correcting and trying to eliminate the known causes of their present conditions and leading them into channels where their ability can be used to help themselves – they have a natural ability of a high order. They can sustain and develop themselves by following their vocation as bush men, trappers and hunters. All they need is protection, advice and reasonable help; it is not necessary to go to great expense to get a start. First, a general and well defined policy must be adopted, without ever losing sight of the Northern conditions nor of the privileges and rights of the Indian, under Treaty. Then the work should be started on at once on a small scale and gradually carried out by men of a thorough experience, with firmness, human understanding and common sense. What is necessary and urgently desired to do for these poor people can and will be done.

Appendix XV

Article written by Bishop Breynat and printed in the *Toronto Star Weekly*, May 28, 1938. Under the title, "La Tache La Plus Noire du Canada", it appeared in a newspaper in Quebec City, *Le Soleil*, on July 3, 1938. Copies of it are retained by the Public Archives of Canada, RG85, vol. 310, also vol. 267, file 1003-2-1, and in the Minutes of the Northwest Territories Council, pp. 1363-1360.

"CANADA'S BLACKEST BLOT"

by Bishop Breynat

The story of the white man's invasion of the Canadian Northwest may be named by future historians as one of the blackest blots on the pages of Canadian history. It is an ugly story. A story of greed, of ruthlessness and broken promises. It is the story of the degradation of our Northwest Indians.

Never before has the whole story been told. Canadians have heard only of the fortunes in furs and the gold and silver and radium ores of this stern country. Occasionally they have seen newspaper reports of starvation and suffering among the Indians.

But Canadians should know all the facts of our Northwest. Because, unless they act at once they will some day bear the scorn of all peoples for having blindly allowed a noble race to be destroyed.

For 46 years I have lived and labored among the Indians of the Northwest. Their troubles have been mine; their misfortunes my burdens. Teaching them the Christian philosophy of unselfishness and trying to better their conditions has been my life work. As a priest and bishop I have lived very close to them.

I have seen during those years the coming of the white man – my race. I am not proud of the things I have observed. When I first went into the north I found a proud race of healthy, virile tribesmen. Unspoiled by the white civilization, they lived their natural lives as people of another age. In the remote parts of the north they still hunted with bow and arrow.

Most of them lived in skin teepees. They wore skins and furs. They were honest without the white man's laws. Men respected other men's property. I have seen the day, even as late as 1900, when an Indian who had received treaty money for himself and his family at Fond du Lac, placed more than $100 under a rock in full sight of a whole tribe. That was his cache. He and his family went away. When they returned, although dozens of persons had seen the money buried, it was still there.

In the early days we never dreamed of locking our cabins. We could go away for weeks or months. The Indians would come and go as they chose. They would hold services in the mission chapels. But never did they remove anything that did not belong to them. To-day the story is changed. The white man taught dishonesty by example. To-day we would never leave anything of value even in a locked cabin.

The Indians I found hunted only for food and the trade goods they needed. By the white man's standard they were lazy. He taught them to take all there was of everything. They became apt pupils.

A BLACK PICTURE

In those early days 80 miles of dangerous rapids on the Athabasca river barred the gateway to the country. There were practically no white trappers. But when the railroad was built to Fort McMurray the country was opened to men from all parts of the world. Drawn by the lure of the easy money, the northland swarmed with white trappers and traders.

In fairness, some of these whites made excellent citizens. But too many of them were unscrupulous men whose one idea was to make money. How they made it went unconsidered. They brought whiskey and taught the Indians how to brew. Some of them turned trapping "wholesalers". They spread poisoned bait to kill the fur-bearing animals. They trapped the country "clean" of game.

If the picture seems black to you, imagine how black it has been to me. I

380

have watched my own race come into a country that was once a rugged paradise. I have seen my own people claiming Christianity bring sorrow and unhappiness to these poor people of the north. You Canadians of the south have your own problems. But let me remind you that these Indians are wards of yours. By treaty you promised them protection and a livelihood in return for the land that was once their heritage.

I was present at nearly all places in the north when the treaties were signed. In many places it was my influence which resulted in the Indians signing these documents. I assured them repeatedly that whatever the government commissioners promised in the name of the Great White Mother and the Great White Father would be done. The Indians believed me. It has been a great personal disappointment to see my word broken by the thoughtlessness of a nation.

In 1899 and 1900 the government made treaties with the Indians living south of Great Slave Lake. Everywhere the commissioners went they found unwilling signatories among the tribesmen. At Fond du Lac they failed utterly. Finally Hon. David Laird, treaty commissioner, came to me with tears in his eyes. He told me he had decided to pack up and leave, regretting that his best arguments had been unable to sway the Indians. I then offered to act as interpreter. My offer was accepted.

The treaty which the commissioners presented had been drawn up at Ottawa by men who had no knowledge of conditions in the north. Terms were too vague to satisfy the Indians who were afraid they would be placed on small reserves as the prairie Indians had been. They were bush Indians. They faced different problems.

PROMISES NOT KEPT

They made special demands, which although not included in the treaty, the commissioners promised would be granted. These demands the commissioners mentioned in their reports, but they failed to state that the demands had actually been granted. Promises in the name of the Crown were the following: 1. That nothing would be allowed that would interfere with the Indians' way of living. 2. That old and destitute Indians would always be taken care of, their future existence would be carefully studied, every effort would be made to improve their living conditions. 3. That they would be protected, especially in their way of living as hunters and trappers, from white competition.

In order to prove that these promises had been made, and to give the government ground for action, in the summer of 1937 I visited more than 50 old time residents of the northwest and received sworn statements from them. They were all men who had been present when the treaties were signed and the promises made. These affidavits to the number of 46 have been handed to the federal authorities that they may know the promises were authentic and to give the government grounds for action.

The average Canadian believes that Canada has been generous in her treatment of native peoples. It is true the plains Indians in many districts are economically secure with prosperous ranches and farms. It is equally true that the Indians of the northwest are dying of starvation and disease.

The government has made an attempt to keep the definite terms of the treaty which set out regular annual payments and gifts. There are Indian agencies, there is the annual five-dollar treaty payment. But the indefinite clauses of the treaties and the promises have not been kept.

Some money is spent for medical services and education. Largely at the suggestion of myself preserves have been set aside where only Indians may hunt. Trapping and hunting regulations have been established to conserve game. Restrictions have been placed upon the activities of white trappers and the number of licences issued to them.

In the year 1935-36, latest period for which figures are available, the department of Indian Affairs spent $137,085 on the Indians in the Northwest Territories. In that year the number of treaty Indians was estimated at 3,-854. These figures represent about $35 apportioned for each treaty Indian, or about $175 for each family of five, the average family among these people.

Of this total, administration charges were $27,812, education claimed $37,694, medical services took $45,566, and direct aid to destitute Indians amounted to $26,011.

By treaty the government agreed to educate the Indians. They do this by giving grants to the churches to aid them to maintain schools. But the churches have had to build schools at their own expense, while elsewhere in the Dominion palatial structures are built out of government funds.

FEW DOCTORS AND HOSPITALS

There are 11 schools in the Territories. Five of these are day schools. Six are residential schools. The Anglican church operates five of these, the Roman Catholic church has six. And despite much criticism levelled at residential schools by persons making short visits to the north, they are the only way in which satisfactory work can be done with these children. Much of the agitation for day schools originates with white men who want educational facilities for their own children. These facilities should be provided by the Northwest Territories department which receives all revenues from hunting and trapping licenses, and royalties from furs and minerals.

For those who still criticize at long range I suggest a year's residence in the north. Let them visit the camps. Let them travel the 100 miles that usually separate villages. Let them make these journeys behind a dog team when the temperature ranges between 40 and 60 below zero. Then their opinions will be of some value.

Children from the residential schools are usually healthier than the average Indian child. They have received proper food, medical attention and lessons in hygiene and cleanliness. The boys have learned how to use tools. They are equipped to do business with white men on their own footing. The girls learn to cook, sew and look after a home. Most of these boys and girls grow into successful men and women. As in any other case, some of them do not.

More important than education, however, is health. Good health is the Indian's fundamental requirement. A sick man cannot run a trapline, hunt or stand for hours fishing through a hole in the ice. Yet in 1935-36 the Dominion government spent only $45,566 in bringing medical aid to nearly 4,-000 of the unhealthiest people in Canada, living in an area covering more than 1,000,000 square miles.

In the district of MacKenzie, which together with the Chipewyan agency, covers about 600,000 square miles there are only three Indian department doctors. These men fill the dual role of physician and Indian agent. They have far too much work if they attend their duties as they should be done. Besides these men, the Northwest Territories department has three doctors who act as health officers for all residents of this vast district. Two further medical men are stationed farther north at Chesterfield on the shore of Hudson Bay and at Pangnirtung, Baffin Island. Group these six and wonder how they can attend patients spread over at least 1,000,000 square miles.

In the same area are five hospitals, four of them maintained by the Roman Catholic church, the fifth operated by the Anglican church. Even under ideal conditions it would be impossible for so few doctors with these hospitalization facilities to properly handle sickness.

When Indians become sick they huddle together in their little huts. Communicable diseases – measles, typhoid, whooping cough, influenza and worse – assume epidemic proportions whenever they appear.

COAL $120 A TON

Let me tell you of the Caribou Eaters at Stony Rapids, at the east end of Lake Athabasca. Measles broke out in their camp last December. There was no way to take the news to medical authorities. Those who were well were hard pressed to feed and care for the sick.

Measles may be a minor disease in your community. Among the Indians it is serious. When one of our priests arrived at the village, 12 had died, six of whom were mothers. Nine more Indians died within a few days. There were only three mothers left in the camp. The priest had to cut fuel, fish through the ice for food, and nurse these poor people. The settlement had no meat or flour. Except for a few half-rotten fish caught the previous fall and intended for dog food, there were no supplies but those provided by the priest.

A messenger was finally sent for aid, and for five days the priest travelled among the camps. When the doctor arrived from Chipewyan, 200 miles away, the worst was over and 26 had died. Now there is the problem of providing for the orphans left by those six mothers. But the government will not give us money for rebuilding or enlarging our schools. The result is that these orphans are adopted by other tribesmen whose only interest is to collect additional treaty money for these children.

The Indians of the Northwest are the most wretched people in Canada. Taking carefully compiled figures for 12 months during 1935-36 (an exceptionally good year), it is estimated that the per capita income of these Indians was $110. This sum includes money earned as a result of trapping and hunting. Compared with them the most miserable relief recipient elsewhere in Canada lives like a king. In all cities families on relief receive food, clothing, shelter, medical, ambulance and hospital services, full educational facilities and the use of all public utilities.

Bear in mind that these Indians are the original owners of the land that denies them a living. Bear in mind, too, that the purchasing power of the dollar in the northwest is often only a fifth of the dollar's purchasing power in the south. On the Arctic coast we pay $120 a ton for coal for our missions. Canadians in cities and towns buy this same grade of coal for from four dollars to $10 a ton. Freight rates to Aklavik are $110 a ton. From Edmonton to Fort McMurray, 300 miles, freight rates average about $1.50 per 100 pounds.

Coal might be emeralds as far as the Indians are concerned – they never have it. But they need flour, sugar, rice, lard, oatmeal, tea, tobacco and ammunition. It costs four dollars to ship 100 pounds of flour from Fort McMurray to Fort Simpson: five dollars to Fort Norman: $8.50 to Cameron Bay. Add to that the rate from Edmonton and you have a pound of flour worth as much as 25 cents. Traders and transportation companies have been criticized. But most of them operate on a slim margin. Remember that a trader extends credit for a whole year to his Indian customers. If anything happens to an Indian before he has discharged his obligations, the trader has no means of collecting the debt.

The past winter has been one of the worst in the history of the north. The Indians have actually been starving. One unfortunate was an old man from Liard country. Found near to death, he was rushed by an aeroplane pilot to hospital at Simpson. But he was too far gone. He died shortly after being admitted to the hospital.

Last February an Eskimo died on the trail in the Barren Lands near Coppermine on the Arctic coast. He was travelling to the Coppermine mission to obtain food. His companions were too weak to help him. They barely dragged themselves through to the rescue post. Behind them they left a once strong hunter to perish in the snow. He was found frozen to death by police sent from the post on a rescue party.

At one trading post only one fox skin had been traded up until Christmas. In another part of the country a trapper covered 150 miles of traplines and brought home only one wolf skin. Near Chipewyan, once a rich fur country, the Indians lived on gray squirrels last year. This year even the squirrels were gone.

Fur is scarce and getting scarcer. And the Indian cannot turn to agriculture because the land is unsuited to it. He cannot work in the mines because he is not fitted to any kind of labour where sustained effort is required. He must depend on fishing, trapping and hunting for his living. There are no soup kitchens, no relief camps, no bread lines, "work-with-wages" plans or old age pensions for Indians.

Picture what happens to an Indian family 100 miles away from an agency, police post or mission when the fish supply fails – when there are no foxes, caribou or moose. You have a picture of death by starvation – stark, unpleasant.

How many Canadians distinguish between Indians and halfbreeds? Halfbreeds are the children of two races. Bullied and cheated, they occupy a cruel position. They are not classed as Indians; they are not white men. All too often they rank as nonentities.

When the treaty commissioners went north they were accompanied by a "scrip commissioner" who was to deal with the halfbreeds. He offered these unfortunates a choice between "cash script" or "land script" in return for their signing away forever their heritage in the north. The cash script, valued at $240, could only be used to pay dues to the government. It was not a straight cash payment. The land script gave any halfbreed the right to choose 240 acres of land and secure registered title to his choice.

Most halfbreeds chose the land. They were flattered by the offer that acceptance of scrip gave them the status of white men. They could vote at elections. They could buy all the whiskey they wanted. Like children they traded their northland resources for a handful of acres that were soon taken away from them by white sharpers.

Few of these natives had ever seen a dollar bill. One of my missionaries told me of a halfbreed who traded a large catch of fish for one of those colorful tags sewn on a pair of overalls. Men like him sold their land to business sharks for from $35 to $50. I have no certain knowledge of it, but it is related that some halfbreeds traded their script for a single bottle of cheap whiskey. And in many cases these white sharks ended the trading with a poker game. Nearly always the cash went back into the white man's pocket. The land scrip was later sold at rates from $1,000 to $3,000.

Our halfbreeds frequently take offence at being classed as Indians. They are proud of their white antecedents. But most of them should be regarded as non-treaty Indians. They should be protected under treaty regulations. Happily, arrangements between Alberta and the Dominion government are near completion for the resettlement of many of these people . . . .

Canada has a just debt to pay her northern natives. It is well to remember that the most solemn promises were made to the Northwest Indians. "So long as the grass grows and the waters run and the sun shines" ran the treaty terms, the Indians were to have undisturbed rights, to earn their livings by hunting, trapping and fishing. They were to be protected from white competition.

And from a purely materialistic side, if white trappers are not controlled it will be only a short time until there is no wild life for either white or native trapper . . . .

The administration of Indian and Eskimo affairs in the north should be remodelled to suit existing conditions. It should be under a highly competent district superintendent who should have wide powers and a free hand, guided only by general policies outlined at Ottawa. Increased medical services are a vital necessity. Trapping and hunting regulations that will fit the natives' scheme of things rather than the whites' are equally necessary. Education and relief facilities are important.

I do not suggest that the Indian and Eskimo should be civilized. Only yesterday, figuratively speaking, they were in the stone age. It will require decades before they are ready for the white man's civilization.

They should be encouraged to retain their old customs and dialects. They should be taught pride of race and history. Gently they should be encouraged to become self-supporting. If these things are done, then Canada will point with pride to her natives in the north. The debt of honor will have been paid.

At the 81st session of the N.W.T. Council, on June 21, 1938, Dr. Camsell, Commissioner of the N.W.T., reported he had received another letter from Breynat, making "supplementary comments" to the *Star Weekly* article. It read:

Having regard to an article which appeared in the "Star Weekly" of Toronto under the headline of "Canada's Blackest Blot", I think it advisable to add supplementary comments which did not find their way into the condensed article which appeared in the "Star" but which additional notes are of great importance in order to give the previous article its full value.

I retain full responsibility for the article published in the "Star Weekly" but I desire stating that the article, far from being intended to complicate the task of government, had on the contrary no object other than to assist it in an effort to awaken the public opinion of Canada and to place before our good Canadian people the grave responsibilities, contracted in its name, towards our Indians who were the first inhabitants of the country; responsibilities the thoughts of which tend to disappear as we get farther and farther away from the events which were the cause of its judicial base....

The different governments in power obtained legal possession and the right of free disposition of these natural resources through regular treaties made with the Indians.

Like all treaties, these successive treaties, stipulated the respective rights and obligations for the two contracting parties. The main obligation imposed upon the Indians was that they should abandon their right to the Natural Resources and promise to respect the rights of the government as acquired from them; to obey the laws and to be peaceful with the Whites who would not be long in coming to exploit the Natural Resources of the country. It is a fact that the Indians, generally speaking, have faithfully fulfilled all their obligations but can we say as much about the various governments sent to Ottawa by the white population to take in hand the direction of its own interests? ...

Those Indians find themselves in conditions totally different from those of the south. With the exception of a few districts in the Peace River area, there is no land fit for cultivation on a large scale and, even though there were, the long distances from transportation would present a formidable obstacle to successful operation. Our Indians of the North, up to now, have lived by hunting and fishing – the former includes both food and fur-bearing animals.

When the Royal Commission arrived from Ottawa to negotiate with them the terms of a treaty – which terms were prepared in advance to be imposed upon them rather than freely discussed in a spirit of reconciliation and mutual concessions as often happens in the negotiation of treaties, the Indians placed as their first formal condition that they would retain intact all their rights to fishing and hunting and that the government would protect them in their mode of life, which they insisted upon continuing, and against competition of the Whites. They feared the arrival of the latter which they expected would soon invade their country.

That condition was fundamental with them. Without doubt they appreciated the promises which the government was making them to assure the education of their children, to furnish medical services and to take care of their old and destitute people, but the liberty to continue, without unfair competition on the part of the Whites, their hunters' and fishermen's life took first place in their thoughts, and the recognition of that liberty for themselves and their children was to be the primary condition of their abandoning their right to the lands and the Natural Resources of their country to the government.

I was, personally, present at the treaty of Fort Chipewyan, which I signed as a witness. As interpreter, I took part in the discussion of the treaty with Caribou Eaters at Fond du Lac, Athabasca. I was begged by the Superintendent of Indian Affairs himself, as bishop having under his jurisdiction the greatest number of Indians, to join myself to the Royal Commission charged with *negotiating* – that was the expression employed in the Letters Patent – the treaty with the Indians who lived along the banks of the Mackenzie River to the Sea. The report of the Royal Commission makes mention of the services which I was able to render. I know whereof I speak and I weigh the value of my words when I affirm and declare publicly as bishop, just as though under oath, that our Indians would never – no never – have consented to sign any treaty *if they had not received the solemn guarantee, given in the name of the Crown, not to be molested in their habits of life as woodsmen, living through hunting and fishing, and that they would be protected against competition by the Whites and their methods of exterminating fish and game.*

Forty-six affidavits given by Indians and by friends of Indians serve in support of the foregoing statement.

Unfortunately for the Indians, when the natural resources were transferred by the federal government to the provincial governments no express reserve was made to protect the rights of the Indians. It is true that the provinces in accepting the transfer of the Natural Resources could not avoid assuming at the same time the Indians' mortgage insofar as it concerned their right to continue their mode of life through hunting and fishing.

But the Indians had no right to vote and the voters, newly arrived, would not agree that it was the provinces' duty to guarantee the life of the Indians. "The Indians are the charge of the Federal government", it was cried aloud. On the other hand the goodwill of the federal government has been made more and more difficult through the objections of politicians who ever protest against the "too high" figure of the Budget of the Department of Indian Affairs, even though they never cease to ask for millions upon millions to assist their electors and to rehabilitate colonists who no doubt are worthy of interest and pity but of which a good number are not even Canadian subjects and work more or less under cover against the constitution of our country.

I must, in all fairness, say that in those unorganized territories of the Canadian Northwest our Indians are far better protected. Large reserves have been created for them and serious restrictions have been enacted in the granting of permits for hunting, to new comers.

According to official records of trappers and hunters which I have before me for the year 1934-35 the comparative status of trappers and hunters was as follows:

	Whites	Indians	Indians & Eskimos
Northwest Territories:	507		9,000
Manitoba:	3,755	12,900	
Saskatchewan:	10,245	11,800	
Alberta:	3,792	10,900	
British Columbia	2,597	23,500	

It is to be noted, however:

1. That the greater number of Indians in the Provinces live in the southern parts and consequently those do not get their living through hunting.

2. That the permits granted by the provinces are individual and personal and represent as many persons as there are hunters for fur.

3. That the number of Indians given above represents, on the contrary, the total population of the Indian men, women and children, which means for the purpose of comparison that it would be necessary in order to have correct figures to deduct from the total number of Indians those who were established in the large reserves of the south, then again reduce the number by two-thirds if not three-quarters, in order to find the number of Indian trappers and hunters who are operating in opposition to white trappers and hunters.

4. It is to be noted finally that in certain districts situated in the Northern parts of the provinces it often happens that there are two, three, four or five white trappers in competition with a single Indian and those white trappers have very superior equipment to make the competition more severe.

In order that the comparison may be made with the minimum amount of fairness one must take into account particularly the desire and greed of the white trapper; his modern methods – including poison much too often – in addition to the aeroplane, which is being used more and more by the latter. The Indian has the additional disadvantage of having to spend the best part of his time in the woods, on the lakes and rivers, in order to assure his family's daily food, whilst, generally speaking, the white trapper has no family with him and has taken the precautions of obtaining, at a much lower price than an Indian would pay, his full winter's provisions. Why be surprised if, in spite of the restrictive laws, very hard indeed on the Indians, the fur-bearing animals tend to disappear? The necessity for those laws never would have existed if the solemn promise of protection given to the Indians had been kept. One may go further and say that it is doubtful if those laws have a sound basis when they are made to apply to Indians, in view of the promises which were solemnly made to them in the name of the Crown.

I leave to the readers of this article the conclusions to be drawn therefrom. May I express the hope that our good population, our truly good Canadian population, will feel moved and will hereafter bring pressure to bear upon its representatives at Ottawa and upon the members of the various provincial governments so that at an early date means will be taken to assure to our Indians the full measure of protection guaranteed to them by treaties, in the name of the Crown, and also that there may be voted as large sums as possible by way of necessary subsidies to take care of the needful and destitute Indians who are to be found in all northern tribes, particularly the victims of the tuberculosis plague.

It is well that it should be known that it is with the full approbation of the Rt. Honble. Mackenzie King, Prime Minister of Canada, that I have undertaken this campaign to awaken public opinion and to solicit the necessary sympathy with the object of assuring for our northern Indians the maintenance and improvement of their peaceful life as hunters and trappers living side by side with the Whites who are exploiting the Mineral Resources of our country.

Appendix XVI

Excerpts from the Treaty payments in the Fort Resolution Agency for the year 1930, prepared by Dr. Bourget, Indian Agent. The complete text can be found in IANDO, File 191/28-3, Vol. 1. Report 23-9-1930.

The meeting [at Fort Resolution] was long and tedious; the Indians having many complaints to make. . . The main question discussed at Fort Resolution, and for hours, was the beavers. The claim, legitimate as far as we know, was that the wrong time had been chosen to close the beavers, first because they were rather on the increase at present, and second they were closed at a time when all other fur was practically out of the North, thus creating a serious condition for the Indians in making their living. This, combined with the very poor price received for what fur they had procurred last winter, and the abolition of debts by the traders, specially since the fall of 1928, made the claims of the Indians stronger, in favor of obtaining the reopening of beavers for next spring. or at least permission to procure a certain number. In this we promised to do our very best, realizing the necessity of the reopening for a few years. So during the visit of Mr. C.C. Parker, our inspector, this question was taken, and we belived Mr. Parker is also in favor of this movement.

The whole treaty procedures, this summer at all posts, could be resumed [summed up] in a feeling of general dissatisfaction, for which we were not to blame, but we could understand the point of these Indians, who claimed that since 1923, every year at treaty we had to announce [to] them more restrictions. First the fur preserves which were not to their liking at first, believing they would be put on reserves, later the buffalo park excluding their relatives the half-breeds and Indians who had not previously used it as their hunting ground; later the shortening of trapping season, the closing of beavers, the closing of ducks shooting in spring, (this of course was previous to 1923), the musk-ox sanctuary, excluding the Indians from their own hunting ground, and even in the west section where there are no muskoxen. So these restrictions were all reviewed this summer, and the Indians asked us why all these restrictions were brought, against their possibility of making a living when cost of life was so exhorbitant, with no restrictions on the trade, debts curtailed, season either shorter or closed. At some posts the fur taxes collected this last year brought severe complaints and some bands were near refusing their treaty altogether, claiming that the Traders were openly collecting taxes from them, for the Government, advertising it in the stores, refusing also to purchase shot rats, when many poor Indians did not have a 22 rifle and had nothing but shot guns. The claim was made that the treaty brought them five dollars in the summer, and more was taken away from them in the winter, in fur taxes. Even that new regulation forcing them to declare their fur received a great deal of criticism. This is against the mentality of the Indian to broadcast the amount of fur caught. These legitimate points were treated for hours specially at Rae; where the half breeds, some on treaty, working for traders had made a campaign to the Indians, specially since the debts were curtailed, by instructions of headquarters, that the debts were a thing of the past, and that the Indians being wards of the Government, it was up to the Government to look after them, and instead of that, the five dollars given in summer was taken back in winter to pay for it.

We had to face the music, and really admit in our consciences, that many points were right; and this created an ill feeling during the whole meetings, and the Indians, having reviewed between themselves all the disadvantages to them, were organized in a strong campaign and ready to express their dissatisfaction, in severe terms. The whole of their mentality has been changing during the last few years. Hard times, and the epidemic of flu, ravaging their country, the debts curtailed immediately after the epidemic has rendered the whole population weaker, more liable to disease and deaths, the statistics show it also, they even believe things are worse now that they receive medicines and care, not knowing what to blame for the decrease, and they had to be helped more also since that epidemic, and they have lost their initiative to a great deal. More so they have become more and more arrogant, wanting more; even some chiefs have come to that stage, where being a chief or subchief has brought so much pride to them that they had to be put at their place. This change of mentality has been noticed also by some fathers who know them for years. An example may be brought to show the point. A school has been asked many times for Rae. This we explained the difficulties in having, to their satisfaction. On the same point this summer I was told that if the school was not given they would not send any more children to Resolution, and would apply to some protestant Mission to have one. They would not, as catholics, have thought of this, two or three years ago. The mendicity and begging also have increased to a proportion hard to believe, naturally, since the help had to be given more and more due to sickness, deaths, epidemics, hard times, but now they are getting to a stage where it is absurd. Many of the Chiefs seem to believe that they should administer the country as well as their small groups of men, are becoming bold and arrogant in their transactions at the agency, so much that a headman of Resolution, in his belief that he is a God sent to his band, was telling at treaty that he himself nearly decided to give permission to his Indians to kill beaver, in spite of regulation. This head man had to be calmed down during the summer in his pride and nonsense, and brought to realize he was the second chief only of a small group, not the Governor-in-Council. . .

The treaty at Hay River and Providence was not more pleasant, the Indians, feeling they had reasons to criticize, were even talking of refusing treaty, and one Chief remarked that at no time did we bring them a good announcement of a season open sooner or a new permission, but every year we explained new restrictions in their way of living. The fur taxes at Providence was the cause of talks for hours, and we were told that one store had it advertised that the taxes would be deducted on every pelt. . .

It seems now the general opinion of the traders that as times are serious and hard, the Indians are wards of the Department, but the debts that were so free in good years are finished, and the Indians have only to face their condition without much help from the traders. . .

The Indians of Trout Lake were also present at Providence but their band, miserable, is getting smaller every year. Tuberculosis ravaging whole families. . .

The conditions of children was the poorest of all years . . . At Rae, it was nothing but a mass of scrofular troubles, and T.B. in various forms . . . The statistics for the bands are also a sad state of affairs . . . it is the worst year since 1923, and no doubt for many years previous. . .

Lumber was asked by the Indians, for all the posts, at least enough to build coffins when needed. . . .

Bibliography

Published Material

Abbot, Frederick H., *The Administration of Indian Affairs in Canada.* Washington, U.S. Government, 1915.

Alberta, Executive Council, OC No. 298, 6 March 1935.

————, Revised Statutes, 1942.

Alcock, Frederick J., "Past and Present Trade Routes to the Canadian Northwest." *The Geographical Review,* Vol. X, No. 2 (August, 1920), pp. 57-83.

Anderson, W.E., "How H.B.C. Earned Its Rights in 'The Great Lone Land'", *The Beaver,* March, 1921, pp. 17-18.

Anglican Church, *Letter Leaflets of the Women's Auxiliary to the Board of Domestic and Foreign Missions of the Church of England in Canada.* 1898, 1899, 1900.

————, *Reports of the Missionary Society of the Church of England.* 1899,1900, 1901, 1907 to 1917.

Banfield, A.W.F., and Novakowski, N.S., *The Survival of the Wood Bison (Bison Bison Athabascae Rhoads) in the Northwest Territories.* Natural History Papers, National Museum of Canada, No. 8, 30 August 1960.

Barbeau, Marius, "Our IndiansTheir Disappearance." *Queen's Quarterly,* Vol. 38, No. 4 (1931), pp. 691-707.

Barker, Bertram, *North of '53.* London, Methuen Co., 1934.

Bell, Robert, *Report on Part of the Basin of the Athabasca River, N.W.T.* Geological Natural History Survey of Canada, Published by authority of Parliament, Montreal, Dawson Brothers, 1884.

Benoit, Dom, *Vie de Monseigneur Taché.* Montreal, Beauchemin, 1904.

Bethune, W.C., ed., *Canada's Western Northland.* Ottawa, Department of Mines and Resources, 1937.

Black, N.F., *History of Saskatchewan and the Old Northwest.* Regina, North West Historical Co., 1913.

Blundell, E.T., and Dexter Grant, "The Forbidden Land is Ruled by Tyrants.", "The Forbidden Land is Governed Wisely.", *Maclean's* Magazine, 15 March, 1933.

Boon, T.C.B., *The Anglican Church from the Bay to the Rockies.* Toronto, Ryerson Press, 1962.

Bourget, Clermont, *Douze Ans chez les Sauvages.* Sainte Anne de Beaupré, P.Q., 1938.

Breton, Paul Emile, OMI. *Le Grand Chef des Prairies.* Edmonton, Editions de l'Ermitage, 1954.

————, *The Big Chief of the Prairies.* Montreal, Palm Publishers, 1955.

Breynat, Gabriel, OMI. *Bishop of the Winds.* New York, P.J. Kennedy Sons, 1955.

————, *Cinquante Ans au Pays des Neiges.* Montreal, Fides, Vol. I, 1945; Vol. II, 1947; Vol. III, 1948.

————, *L'Evêque Volant.* Paris, Amiot Dumont, 1953.

————, *The Flying Bishop*, London, Burns & Oates, 1955.

British North America Act. R.S.C. 1970.

Cameron, Agnes Deans, *The New North*. New York & London, D. Appleton & Co., 1910.

Cameron, Wm. Bleasdell, "Peaceful Invasion." *The Beaver,* March, 1948, p. 36.

Campbell, Marjorie Wilkins, *The North West Company*. Toronto, University of Toronto Press, 1957.

Camsell, A.F., "What Happened at Fort Simpson, N.W.T. During Winter 1921?" *The Beaver,* July, 1921, p. 19.

Camsell, Charles, *Son of the North*. Toronto, Ryerson Press, 1954.

Camsell, Charles, & Malcolm, Wyatt, *The Mackenzie River Basin*. rev.ed. Canada, Department of Mines, Memoir 108, Ottawa, King's Printer, 1921.

Canada Indian Treaties and Surrenders from 1680 to 1890. Ottawa, Queen's Printer, 1891. Reprint, Toronto, Coles Publishing Co., 1971.

Canada Indian Treaties and Surrenders from No. 281 to No. 483. Ottawa, King's Printer, 1912. Reprint, Toronto, Coles Publishing Co., 1971.

Canada, Department of Indian Affairs, *Sessional Papers*. 1890-1922.

————, *Annual Reports*. 1910-1936.

————, Department of Mines & Resources, Indian Affairs Branch, *Annual Reports*. 1936-1949.

————, Department of the Secretary of State, *Sessional Papers*. 1870.

————, House of Commons, *Debates*. 1898-1940.

————, North West Mounted Police, Royal North West Mounted Police, Royal Canadian Mounted Police, *Sessional Papers*. 1896-1926.

————, North West Mounted Police, Royal Canadian Mounted Police, *Annual Reports of the Commissioner*. 1897, 1898, 1899, 1926.

————, Privy Council, *Orders in Council*.

————, Senate, *Journals*. 1888.

————, *Statutes*. 1894, 1917, 1923.

Chambers, Ernest, ed., *Canada's Fertile Northland*. Ottawa, Government Printing Bureau, 1908.

————, *The Great Mackenzie Basin*. Ottawa, Department of the Interior, 1910.

————, *The Unexploited West*. Ottawa, King's Printer, 1914.

Chalmers, J.W., "Inland Journey." *The Beaver,* Autumn, 1972, pp. 52-59.

Cody, H.A., *An Apostle of the North*. (Memoirs of R.R. William Carpenter Bompas). Toronto, Musson Book Co., 1908.

Copy of Treaty and Supplementary Treaty No. 7. Reprint, Ottawa, Queen's Printer, 1966.

Cumming, Peter A., and Mickenberg, Neil H., eds., *Native Rights in Canada*. 2nd. ed. Toronto, Indian Eskimo Association of Canada, 1972.

Davies, Raymond Arthur, *Arctic Eldorado*.

Dawson, C.A., ed. *The New North West*. Toronto, University of Toronto Press, 1947.

Dixon, Joseph Kossuth, *The Vanishing Race*. Toronto, Musson Book Co., 1913.

Douglas, George M. *Lands Forlorn.* New York, G.P. Putnam's Sons, 1914.

Duchaussois, Pierre, OMI. *Hidden Apostles.* Dublin, Rome, Buffalo, Ottawa, Oblates of Mary Immaculate, 1937.

—————, *Mid Snow and Ice.* London, Burns Oates & Washbourne, 1923.

—————, *The Grey Nuns in the Far North (1867-1917).* Toronto, McClelland & Stewart, 1919.

Emmett, J.A., "The Trapper's Life in the North." *Canada's Weekly,* 15 January 1937, pp. 541-542.

Ferguson, Chick, *Mink, Mary and Me.* New York, M.S. Mill Co., 1946.

Finnie, Richard, *Canada Moves North.* Toronto, MacMillan Co., 1943.

Fleming, Archibald Lang, *Archibald the Arctic.* New York, Appleton-Century-Crofts, 1956.

Freeman, Lewis R., *The Nearing North.* New York, Dodd, Mead and Co., 1928.

Garrioch, A.C. (Rev.), *The Far and Furry North.* Winnipeg, Douglas-McIntyre Co., 1925.

Giraud, Marcel, *Le Métis Canadien, son rôle dans l'histoire des Provinces de l'Ouest.* Paris, Institut d'Ethnologie, 1945.

Godsell, Jean W., *I was No Lady.* Toronto, Ryerson Press, 1959.

Godsell, Philip H., *Arctic Trader.* New York, G.P. Putnam's Sons, 1932.

—————, *Red Hunters of the Snows.* Toronto, Ryerson Press, 1938.

—————, *The Vanishing Frontier.* Toronto, Ryerson Press, 1939.

—————, "Should the N.W.T. Shut the Door?" *Maclean's* Magazine, 15 May 1934, pp. 26, 51, 52.

Grouard, Emile, OMI, Mgr., *Souvenirs de mes Soixante Ans d'Apostolat dans l'Athabasca Mackenzie.* Lyon, Oeuvre Apostolique de Marie Immaculée, 1923.

Hanbury, David T., *Sport and Travel in the Northland of Canada.* New York, Macmillan Co., 1904.

Hardy, W.G., *From Sea Unto Sea.* New York, Popular Library Edition, 1959.

Harper, Allan G., "Canada's Indian Administration: Basic Concepts and Objectives." *America Indigena,* Vol. V, No. 2 (April, 1945), pp. 119-132.

Hawthorn, H.B., ed., *A Survey of the Contemporary Indians of Canada.* Ottawa, Indian Affairs Branch, 1966.

Hearne, Samuel, *A Journey from Prince of Wales Fort on Hudson's Bay to the Northern Ocean, Undertaken by Order of the Hudson's Bay Company, for the Discovery of Copper Mines, & North West Passage, &c., in the years 1769, 1770, 1771 & 1772.* Reprint, Toronto, Champlain Society, 1911.

Helm, June, "The Dynamics of a Northern Athapaskan Band." National Museum of Canada, *Bulletin,* No. 176, 1961, pp. 166-176.

—————, "Leadership among Northeastern Athabascans." *Anthropologica,* No. 2, 1956.

Helm, June, and Lurie, Nancy O., *The Subsistence Economy of the Dogrib Indians of Lac La Martre in the Mackenzie District of the N.W.T.* Department of Northern Affairs & National Resources, Northern Co-ordination and Research Centre, NCRC 61-3, 1961.

Higinbotham, John D., *When the West Was Young.* Toronto, Ryerson Press, 1933.

Hill, Douglas, *The Opening of the Canadian West*. New York, John Day Co., 1967.

Howard, Joseph Kinsey, *Strange Empire*. New York, William Morrow & Co., 1952.

Hudson's Bay Company, *The Beaver*. Quarterly, 1921-1939.

Hughes, Katherine, *Father Lacombe, The Black Robe Voyageur*. Toronto, Wm. Briggs, 1911.

Indian Eskimo Association of Canada, *Native Rights in Canada*. Toronto, 1970.

Ingstad, Helge, *The Land of Feast and Famine*. New York, Alfred A. Knopf, 1933.

Inman, Henry, *Buffalo Jones' Forty Years of Adventure*. Topeka (Kansas), Crane & Co., 1899.

Innis, Harold Adams, *Peter Pond, Fur Trader and Adventurer*. Toronto, Irwin & Gordon, 1930.

————, *The Fur Trade in Canada*. Toronto, University of Toronto Press, 1970.

Jackson, F.C., "First Trip of 1921 Season of H.B. SS. Mackenzie River," *The Beaver*, August-September, 1921, pp. 13-14.

Jenness, Diamond, *The Indians of Canada*. Ottawa, Queen's Printer, 1932.

Jonquet, Emile, OMI. *Monseigneur Grandin, Oblat de Marie Immaculée, Premier Evêque de Saint Albert*. Montreal, 1903.

Kemp, H.S.M., *Northern Trader*. Toronto, Ryerson Press, 1956.

Kindle, E.M., and Basworth, T.O., *Oil Bearing Rocks of Lower Mackenzie River Valley*. Ottawa, Department of Mines, Geological Survey, Summary Report, 1920, Part B, pp. 37-63.

Kitto, Franklin Hugo, *New Oil Fields of Northern Canada*. Ottawa, Department of the Interior, 1921.

————, *The North West Territories 1930*. Ottawa, Department of the Interior, 1930.

Laytha, Edgar, *North Again for Gold*. New York, Frederick A. Stokes Co., 1939.

Leacock, Eleanor Burke, and Lurie, Nancy Oestreich, eds., *North American Indians in Historical Perspective*. New York, Random House, 1971.

Lefroy, John Henry, *In Search of the Magnetic North*. George F.G. Stanley, ed. Toronto, Macmillan Co., 1955.

Le Père Lacombe, l'Homme au Bon Coeur. D'après ses Mémoires et Souvenirs recueillis par une Soeur de la Providence. Montreal, *Le Devoir*, 1916.

Lewis, Harrison F., "Indians, Treaties and Game." *Hunting and Fishing in Canada*, February, 1953, pp. 10, 11, 24.

Lodge, Tom, *Beyond the Great Slave Lake*. New York, E.P. Dutton & Co., 1959.

MacBeth, R.G., "The Jubilee of the Mounted." *The Beaver*, August, 1924.

MacGregor, James G., *Edmonton Trader*. Toronto, McClelland & Stewart, 1963.

————, *The Klondike Rush Through Edmonton*. Toronto, McClelland & Stewart, 1970.

MacInnes, T.R.L., "History of Indian Administration in Canada." *The Canadian Journal of Economics and Political Science,* Vol. 12 (1946), pp. 387-394.

MacKay, Douglas, *The Honourable Company.* Toronto, McClelland & Stewart, 1936.

Mair, Charles, *Through the Mackenzie Basin.* Toronto, William Briggs, 1908.

Mason, J.A., *Notes on the Indians of the Great Slave Lake Area.* New Haven, Yale University Publications in Anthropology, 1946.

Maturie, Pierre, *Athabasca, Terre de ma Jeunesse.* Paris, La Pensée Universelle, 1972.

McConnell, R.G., *Report on an Exploration in the Yukon and the Mackenzie Basins, N.W.T.* Geological & Natural History Survey of Canada. Annual Report 1888-1889, Published by authority of Parliament, Montreal, William Foster Brown & Co., 1890.

————, *Report on a Portion of the District of Athabasca Comprising the Country between Peace River and the Athabasca River North of Lesser Slave Lake.* Ottawa, Queen's Printer, 1893.

McTavish, George Simpson, *Behind the Palisades.* Sidney, B.C., Gray's Publishing, 1963.

Moberley, Henri John, *When Fur Was King.* London & Toronto, J.M. Dent & Sons, 1929.

Moran, J.F., *Local Conditions in the Mackenzie District 1922.* Ottawa, Department of the Interior, 1923.

Morgan, Henry James, ed., *Canadian Men and Women of the Time.* Toronto, Wm. Briggs, 1912.

Morice, Adrien G., OMI, *Histoire de l'Eglise Catholique dans l'Ouest Canadien.* Montreal, Granger Frères, 1928.

Morris, Alexander (Hon.), *The Treaties of Canada with the Indians of Manitoba and the North-West Territories.* Toronto, Belfords Clarke and Co., 1880. Reprint, Toronto, Coles Publishing Co. 1971.

Myles, Eugenie Louise, *Airborne from Edmonton.* Toronto, Ryerson Press, 1959.

Myles, Eugenie Louise, *The Emperor of Peace River 1886-1952.* Edmonton, Institute of Applied Arts, 1965.

Oblates of Mary Immaculate (OMI), *Missions de la Congrégation des Missionaires Oblats de Marie Immaculée.* 1895-1925.

Office Consolidation of the Indian Act. Ottawa, Queen's Printer, 1969.

Oliver, Edmund Henry, ed., *The Canadian North-West; its Early Development and Legislative Records.* 2 Vols. Ottawa, Government Printing Bureau, 1914-1915.

Onraet, Anthony, *Down North.* London, Jonathan Cape, 1944.

Osgood, Cornelius, *Winter.* New York, W.W. Norton & Co., 1953.

Owen, Roger C., James, J.F., and Fisher, Anthony D., eds., *The North American Indians.* New York, Macmillan; London, Collier Macmillan, 1967.

Patterson, E. Palmer, II, *The Canadian Indian: A History since 1500.* Don Mills, Collier-Macmillan Canada, 1972.

Petitot, Emile, OMI, *Autour du Grand Lac des Esclaves.* Paris, A. Savine, 1891.

Philippot, A. OMI.*Le Frère Alexis Reynard* OMI. *1828-1875.* Lablachère

(Ardéche, France), Notre Dame de Bon Secours, 1931.

Philips, R.A.J., *Canada's North.* Toronto, Macmillan, 1967.

Pike, Warburton, *The Barren Ground of Northern Canada.* London, Macmillan, 1892.

Price, Ray, *Yellowknife.* Toronto, Peter Martin Associates, 1967.

Rae, George Ramsay, *The Settlement of the Great Slave Lake Frontier, Northwest Territories, Canada; from the Eighteenth to the Twentieth Century.* University of Michigan Ph.D. Thesis, 1963, Published on demand by University Microfilm, A Xerox Co., Ann Harbour, Michigan, 1971.

Rasky, Frank, *The Taming of the Canadian West.* Toronto, McClelland & Stewart, 1967.

Robinson, M.J. and J.L., "Exploration and Settlement of Mackenzie District, N.W.T." *Canadian Geographical Journal,* Vol. 32, No. 6 (June, 1946), pp. 246:255; Vol. 33, No. 1 (July, 1946), pp. 43-49.

Rourke, Louise, *The Land of the Frozen Tide.* London, Hutchinson, 1928.

Russell, Frank, *Explorations in the Far North.* Iowa City, University of Iowa, 1898.

Seton, Ernest Thompson, *The Arctic Prairies.* New York, International University Press, 1911.

Shortt, A., and Doughty, A.G., eds., *Canada and Its Provinces.* Vols. 4, 7, 11, 23, Toronto, Glasgow Brook & Co., 1914.

Special Joint Committee of the Senate and the House of Commons appointed to examine and consider the Indian Act, *Minutes of Proceeding and Evidence.* Ottawa, Queen's Printer, 1946-1947.

Stager, J.K., "Fur Trading Posts in the Mackenzie Region up to 1850." Canadian Association of Geographers, B.C. Division, *Occasional Papers in Geography,* No. 3 (June, 1962), pp. 37-45.

Stanley, George F.G., *The Birth of Western Canada.* Toronto, University of Toronto Press, 1960.

Steele, Harwood, *Policing the Arctic.* Toronto, Ryerson Press, 1936.

Stewart, Elihu, *Down the Mackenzie and Up the Yukon in 1906.* London & New York, John Lane; Toronto, Bell & Cockburn, 1913.

Stock, Eugene, *The History of the Church Missionary Society, Its Environment, Its Men, and Its Work.* London, Church Missionary Society, Vols. I, II, III, 1899; Vol. IV, 1916.

Symington, Fraser, *The Canadian Indian.* Toronto, McClelland & Stewart, 1969.

The Civil Service List of Canada, 1903. Ottawa, S.E. Dawson, Printer to the King's Most Excellent Majesty, 1904.

The Way of the Indian. Toronto, CBC Publications, 1963.

Thomas, Lewis H., "The North-West Territories 1870-1905." *The Canadian Historical Association Booklets,* No. 26, Ottawa, 1970.

Tranter, G.J., *Link to the North.* London, Hodder & Stoughton, 1946.

Treaty No. 8. Ottawa, Queen's Printer, Reprint 1969.

Treaty No. 11. Ottawa, Queen's Printer, Reprint 1957.

Turner, John Peter, *The North West Mounted Police 1873-1893.* Ottawa, King's Printer, 1950.

Tyrrell, James Williams, *Across the Sub Arctic of Canada*. Toronto, Wm. Briggs, 1908.

Underhill, F.H., ed., *The Canadian Northwest: Its Potentialities*. Toronto, University of Toronto Press, 1959.

Usher, Peter, *Fur Trade Posts of the Northwest Territories 1870-1970*. Ottawa, Department of Indian Affairs & Northern Development, NSRG 71-4, 1971.

Waite, P.B., *Arduous Destiny: Canada 1874-1896*. Toronto, McClelland & Stewart, 1971.

Waldo, Fullerton, *Down the Mackenzie*. New York, Macmillan, 1923.

Whalley, George, *The Legend of John Hornby*. Toronto, Macmillan, 1962.

Wheeler, David E., "The Dogrib Indian and His Home." *Bulletin of the Geographical Society of Philadelphia*, Vol. XII, No. 2, 1914.

Whitney, Caspar, *On Snowshoes to the Barren Grounds*. New York, Harper & Brothers, 1896.

Wolforth, John, *The Evolution and Economy of the Delta Community*. Ottawa, Department of Indian Affairs Northern Development, MDRP 11, 1971.

Zaslow, Morris, *The Opening of the Canadian North 1870-1914*. Toronto, McClelland and Stewart, 1971.

Newspapers

Calgary Gazette.

Calgary Herald.

Calgary Tribune.

Edmonton Bulletin.

Edmonton Journal.

Manitoba Free Press.

Montreal Star.

Morning Bulletin.

Ottawa Citizen.

Ottawa Journal.

Port Arthur News.

Saturday Night.

Sydney Post.

Toronto Mail.

Toronto Star.

Toronto Star Weekly.

Vancouver Province.

Winnipeg Free Press.

Winnipeg Tribune.

Unpublished Material

Interviews were recorded with the following people.

Transcripts of these interviews are kept at the Archives of the Indian Brotherhood of the Northwest Territories.

Aklavik, N.W.T.
  Stewart, Andrew
Arctic Red River, N.W.T.
  Andrew, Julienne
  Niditche, Amos
Fort Franklin, N.W.T.
  Kenny, Joseph
  Menacho, Albert
Fort Good Hope, N.W.T.
  Boucane, Louis
  Caesar, Louis
  Kakfwi, Gabriel
  Shae, Gregory
Fort Liard, N.W.T.
  Bertrand, Vital
  Dontra, Jean Baptiste
Fort McPherson, N.W.T.
  Firth, William
  Kay (Kikovitch), Johnny
  Thompson, Jimmy
Fort Norman, N.W.T.
  Blondin, John
  Yakaleya, Johnny
Fort Providence, N.W.T.
  Farcy, John Sr.
  Lafferty, Victor
  Landry, Angelique
  Landry, Michel Sr.
  Minoza, Joseph
  Sabourin, Jean Marie
  Squirrel, William
Fort Rae, N.W.T.
  Black, Harry
  Bruneau, Jimmy
  Charlo, Alexis
  Eronchi, Alphonse
  Football, Adele
  Football, Sammy
  Gaudet, Bruno
  Heron, Ned
  Kotchia, Noel
  Lafferty, Adele

Lafferty, Henri
Lafferty, Jonas
Murphy, Elise
Thomas, Vital
Wedzin, Pierre
Zoe, Harry
Zoe, Lazare
Fort Resolution, N.W.T.
  Balsillie, Jim
  Beaulieu, Angus
  Beaulieu, Antoine
  Beaulieu, Johnny
  Beaulieu, Johnny Jean Marie
  Edjericon, Isadore
  King, Alexandre
  Lafferty, Jim
  Norn, William
Fort Simpson, N.W.T.
  Antoine, Julian
  Cholo, Jimmy
  Lafferty, James
  Nadeya, Margaret
  Norwegian, Baptiste
  Norwegian, Louis
  Tanche, Francis
  Trindell, Ted
Fort Wrigley, N.W.T.
  Moses, Paul
  Moses, Philip
  Yendo, Julien
Halifax, N.S.
  Parsons, John A.
Hay River, N.W.T.
  Norn, Frank
Snowdrift, N.W.T.
  Cassaway, Zepp
  Frise, Pierre
  Michel, Pierre
  Nataway, Bruno
  Tassie, Johnny
Sidney, B.C.
  Bruce, W.V.

Yellowknife, N.W.T.
 Abel, Susie
 Drygeese, Henri (Honore)
 Drygeese, (Smallnose) Pierre
 Liske, Antoine
 Sangris, David

Other Unpublished Material

Bourget, Clermont, Letter to the author, 23 May 1972.

Bovey, J.A., *The Attitudes and Policies of the Federal Government toward Canada's Northern Territories 1870-1930*. M.A. Thesis, University of British Columbia, 1967.

Bury, H.J., *Report of the Territory covered by Treaty No. 8 and the District North of Fort Simpson along the Valley of the Mackenzie R. 1913*. PAC, RG10, BS, file 336, 877.

Canada, Department of Indian Affairs Northern Development. Edmonton, file 701/1-21-10.

————. Ottawa, files: 1/1-11-20, 1/1-11-22, 191/28-3, 191/30-1, 191/30-2-1, 191/30-3, 191/30-4, 191/30-11-1, 777/28-3, 779/28-3, 871/3-8, 1003-2-5.

————, Ottawa, Indian Annuities, 1899, 1900, 1921, 1922, 1923.

Carney, Robert J., *Relations in Education between the Federal and Territorial Governments and the Roman Catholic Church in the Mackenzie District, N.W.T., 1867-1961*. M.A. Thesis, University of Alberta, 1971.

Census of Indians in Canada. (N.W.T.) 1900-1924. Ottawa, Department of Indian Affairs cnd Northern Development. Statistical Information Centre, No. 5000-20.

Chroniques de Fort Chipewyan. 1899. ASGM.

Chroniques de Fort Providence. 1921. ASGM.

Chroniques de Fort Resolution. 1920. ASGM.

Chroniques de Fort Simpson. 1921. ASGM.

Crawley, G.A., *History of the Mission of Fort Chipewyan*. (Anglican Church), Provincial Archives of Alberta.

Cueff, François, OMI, Letter to the author, 11 October 1971.

Dewdney Papers, Glenbow-Alberta Institute.

Diaries of the Roman Catholic Missions (Codex Historicus) at the OMIAFS, section 091-CH.:
 Arctic Red River, N.W.T.
 Fond du Lac, Saskatchewan
 Fort Chipewyan, Alberta
 Fort Good Hope, N.W.T.
 Fort Liard, N.W.T.
 Fort Norman, N.W.T.
 Fort Rae, N.W.T.
 Fort Resolution, N.W.T.

Fort Simpson, N.W.T.

Fort Smith, N.W.T.

Hay River, N.W.T.

Duchesne, J. OMI. to Breynat, Letter, 9 September 1937. RCM Archives, Fort Resolution, N.W.T.

Fort Chipewyan Journal. 1899. HBC Archives, B 39/a/60.

Godsell, Philip H. *Chronicles of a Fur Trader.* Glenbow-Alberta Institute.

Grandin, Vital, OMI. Mgr., *Mémoire de l'Evêque de Saint Albert sur ses difficultés avec le Département Indien.* OMIAEd. B-VIII-100d.

Grouard, Emile, OMI. Mgr., Correspondence, OMIAEd. B-II-801.

─────, Correspondence, ASGM, Chipewyan-Historique, Documents 53, 55.

─────, Correspondence, OMIAFS. 091-C12.

Hay River Saint Peter's Mission Diary (Anglican Church) Provincial Archives of Alberta, ACC 70-387-MR 4/3.

Helm June, and others, *The Contact History of the Subarctic Athapaskans: An Overview.* Proceedings of the Athapaskan Conference, National Museum of Man, Ottawa, March 1971, Forthcoming in a bulletin of the Museum.

Historical Sketch of the Origin and work of Hay River Mission, Great Slave Lake, N.W.T. 1893-1956. (Anglican Church) ACAT, MM 52-13, H 39.11.

History of the Force in the Athabasca and Great Slave Lake Area. Ottawa, RCMP Archives.

Hudson's Bay Company Archives, Letters to the author, 2 December 1971, 1 June 1972.

Hunting, Trapping, and Trading Posts Licences 1924-1954. N.W.T. Department of Industry and Development, Game Branch Archives.

Journal of Events, Anglican Mission, Hay River, N.W.T. Provincial Archives of Alberta, Accession, 70.387 MR 415.

Kind, Number, Total Value and Average Value of Pelts of Fur Bearing Animals Taken in Canada, by Provinces. Information Canada, Northwest Territories, seasons 1919-1920 to 1922-1923.

Kitto, F.H., *Report of a Preliminary Investigation of the Natural Resources of Mackenzie District and their Economic Development, made during the summer of 1920.* Ottawa, Department of the Interior, Natural Resources Intelligence Branch, 1920.

Lacombe, Albert, OMI. Correspondence. 1880-1912, OMIAEd. B VII-22.

─────, *En Route pour le Nord avec une Commission Royale.* OMIAEd. D-1-105.

List of Persons who held hunting and trapping licences under the Northwest Game regulations on the 3rd. May 1938. N.W.T. Department of Industry Development, Game Branch.

Moran, John F., *Confidential Notes.* RCMAFS.

N.W.T. Territorial Council, *Minutes of Sessions.* 1921-1940.

Papers and Correspondence of the Church Missionary Society 1897-1901. PAC, CMS microfilms A-120, A-121.

Peace River Diocese Archives. (Anglican Church). Microfilms, Provincial Archives of Alberta.

Public Archives of Canada:
Manuscript Groups 19, 27, 29, 30.
Public Records Section, Record groups 2, 6, 10, 15, 18, 32, 85.
Macfarlane Papers
Halfbreed Commission, Accession 556, 321.

Report of the Commissioner appointed to investigate the unfulfilled provisions of Treaties 8 and 11 as they apply to the Indians of the Mackenzie District. (Nelson Commission), 1959.

Robin, Alexis, OMI. Transcript of interview with the author, 12 October 1971.

Roman Catholic Mission Archives, Fort Resolution, Vital Statistics Records, 1913.

Roman Catholic Mission Archives, Fort Smith, (RCMAFS), files:
Chasse-Pêche 1928-1947
Conditions des Indiens
Cornwall
Fort Chipewyan
Fort Chipewyan-Mission-Historique
Game
Indianescom
Indiens-Traité avec eux
Mackenzie
Metis
Milton Martin
Milton Martin 1927
Milton Martin 1928
Mission de Chipewyan-Histoire
Statistiques Diverses
Tuberculose 1910-1946
Vicariat du Mackenzie, Faits Divers sur les Missions
Welfare
13-7

Stewart, E.G., *Fort McPherson and the Peel River Area.* M.A. Thesis, Queen's University, 1955.

Supreme Court of Canada. On Appeal from the Supreme Court of Alberta Appelate Division, between Michael Sikyea, Appelant and Her Majesty the Queen, Respondent. *Appelant's Factum.*

Supreme Court of the N.W.T. In the matter of an Application by Chief François Paulette *et al.* to lodge a certain Caveat with the Registrar of Titles of the Land Titles Office for the Northwest Territories. 1973. *Reasons for Judgement of the Honourable Mr. Justice W.G. Morrow* and *Transcript of Evidence.*

Usher, Peter, *The Growth and Decline of the Trading and Trapping Frontiers in the Western Canadian Arctic.* Paper presented at the Annual Meeting of the Canadian Association of Geographers, St. John's, Newfoundland, August 21, 1969.

West, W. J., *Papers 1915-1923*. Glenbow-Alberta Institute, BN (9) W 522.

Zaslow, Morris, *A History of Transportation and Development of the Mackenzie Basin from 1871 to 1921*. M.A. Thesis, University of Toronto, 1948.

————— , *The Development of the Mackenzie Basin, 1920-1940*. Ph.D. Thesis, University of Toronto, 1957.

Index

407